Race

A Theological Account

J. KAMERON CARTER

UNIVERSITY PRESS

2008

OXFORD
UNIVERSITY PRESS

Oxford University Press, Inc., publishes works that further
Oxford University's objective of excellence
in research, scholarship, and education.

Oxford   New York
Auckland   Cape Town   Dar es Salaam   Hong Kong   Karachi
Kuala Lumpur   Madrid   Melbourne   Mexico City   Nairobi
New Delhi   Shanghai   Taipei   Toronto

With offices in
Argentina   Austria   Brazil   Chile   Czech   Republic   France   Greece
Guatemala   Hungary   Italy   Japan   Poland   Portugal   Singapore
South Korea   Switzerland   Thailand   Turkey   Ukraine   Vietnam

Published by Oxford University Press, Inc.
198 Madison Avenue, New York, New York 10016

www.oup.com

Oxford is a registered trademark of Oxford University Press

Library of Congress Cataloging-in-Publication Data
Carter, J. Kameron, 1967–
Race : a theological account / J. Kameron Carter.
   p. cm.
Includes index.
ISBN 978-0-19-515279-1
1. Race—Religious aspects—Christianity.
2. Racism—Religious aspects—Christianity.
3. Race relations—Religious aspects
Christianity.   4. Foucault, Michel, 1926–1984.
I. Title.
BT734.C37 2008
270.089—dc22   2007036919

thinking more deeply into the themes of my dissertation and their ultimate transformation to yield this book. Convened by Srinivas Aravamudan (Duke; English) and Charlie Piot (Duke; anthropology), "Race, Justice, and the Politics of Memory"—the title of the year-long seminar—took me to a new level of conversation on the modern problem of race. Particularly illuminating were conversations with Fellows Grant Farrad (Duke; literature), Ian Baucom (Duke; English), and Evelyn Brooks Higginbotham (Harvard; African American studies, history).

Fellowships through the Association of Theological Schools' Lilly Theological Research Fellowships Program and the Woodrow Wilson–Mellon Foundation's Career Enhancement Program during the 2004–2005 academic year afforded me time off from teaching and administrative duties at Duke Divinity School to rethink and begin to rewrite the work. But it was a fellowship from the National Humanities Center in the 2006–2007 academic year that helped me to the finish line (to say nothing of beginning preliminary research and writing on two other projects). It would have taken far longer were it not for the gracious support of these agencies, and of Dean L. Gregory Jones of Duke Divinity School, who allowed me the time off to complete this work. Gratitude is also certainly due to the several research assistants I have had in the process of writing this book.

I have already mentioned a number of my Duke colleagues whose conversations with me around my work have been critical, supportive, and helpful. I must call attention to three of them who have offered guidance and been uniquely keen interlocutors: Mel Peters in religion, Ken Surin in literature, and Romand Coles in political science. Each of them read chunks of my work and offered constructive criticism. My debt to them, and especially to Ken who has been an intellectual mentor, is great. In the Divinity School, Stanley Hauerwas has engaged my work and, in ways both direct and indirect, has helped me crystallize what I was going after in this book. Amy Laura Hall has been incredibly supportive of this work and me. Lauren Winner, a friend from graduate school and now a colleague, has provided an ear for my ideas and taken time to read various chapters of this book. Her powerful pen came to my literary rescue on more than one occasion. There are traces in this book of our conversations on how to theologically conceive the relationship between Judaism and Christianity and on the significance of this relationship for Christian spirituality. I would certainly be remiss not to mention the stellar cast of black faculty at Duke Divinity School. They have spiritually, intellectually, and sometimes even personally sustained me through the process of getting to the end of this work, helping it to be the best work it could possibly be. They are Tammy Williams, William C. Turner Jr., Esther Acolatse, Emmanuel Katongole, Richard Payne, and again Willie James Jennings. I must also say that this book is better as a result of the intellectually stimulating and deeply enriching conversations I have had with Willie during the writing.

Acknowledgments

I am happy to thank a number of friends and colleagues who have offered advice, criticism, and support over the long evolution of this book, which first began as a dissertation at the University of Virginia and since then has been literally rewritten, as they say, from the ground up.

I begin with a word of thanks to my dissertation committee in the religious studies department at Virginia under whose guidance I wrote the first version of what is now this book: Eugene F. Rogers Jr. (now at University of North Carolina–Greensboro), Peter V. Ochs, John Milbank (now at the University of Nottingham), and my external committee member and now colleague, Willie James Jennings (Duke Divinity School). Rather than press me into the mold of their questions, they helped me begin thinking about what was theological about my questions. I have come to appreciate how rare a practice this is and so have come to appreciate Gene, Peter, John, and Willie all the more. Others at Virginia who have been particularly supportive of me in the writing of this work are Charles Marsh, Chuck Mathewes, and the Fellows at Virginia's Institute for Advanced Studies in Culture. Of special mention are the director of the institute, James Davison Hunter, and Jennifer Geddes, now the editor of its journal, *The Hedgehog Review*. I owe the members of the Duodecim Theological Society a debt of gratitude for their supportive and critical engagements with parts of the book.

My time as a Fellow at the John Hope Franklin Center for Interdisciplinary and International Studies at Duke University during the 2002–2003 academic year was especially important for my

Contents

Abbreviations

Adversus haeresus

AH   *Adversus haeresus*

AH-A   *The Ante-Nicene Fathers*, vol. 1: *The Apostolic Fathers, Justin Martyr, and Irenaeus*, ed. Alexander Roberts and James Donaldson (New York: Eerdmans, 1960); complete translation

AH-G   *Irenaeus of Lyons*, ed. Robert M. Grant (New York: Routledge, 1996); selective translation

Dem.   *On the Apostolic Preaching* (Crestwood, NY: St. Vladimir's Seminary Press, 1997). A translation of *Epideixis tou apostolikou kērygmatos*.

SC   *Sources chrétiennes*, ed. Benoit Pruche (Paris: Editions du Cerf, 1947); Latin-Greek-French critical edition, in five multipart volumes under the title *Irenaeus: Contre les hérésies*, corresponding to the five books of *Adversus haeresus*

Abbreviations are followed by volume number, part number, and page number: for example, *AH-A* I.6.35.

Gregory of Nyssa

AR   *De Anima et Resurrectione* (*On the Soul and the Resurrection*)

Robert Louis Wilken (Crestwood, N.Y.: St. Vladimir's
Seminary Press, 2003).

CTE   *Capita theologiae et oeconomiae* (*Chapters on Theology and the Divine Economy*)

Ep. 2   *Epistle 2*, Maximus the Confessor's letter to John the Cubicularius, written circa 626 CE

LMC   *Maximus the Confessor*, ed. Andrew Louth (New York: Routledge, 1996)

MCSW   *Maximus Confessor: Selected Writings*, ed. George C. Berthold (Mahwah, N.J.: Paulist, 1985); includes *Commentary on the Our Father*

PG   *Patrologiae cursus completus: Series Graeca*, 162 vols.; volumes 90 and 91 collect Maximus's works

I follow the standard way of documenting references to *PG*: volume number, page number, and then quadrant of the page. For example, 91.705A. I have modified English translations from *LMC* and *MCSW* as needed.

Race

Prologue

The Argument at a Glance

Why is there a need for yet another book on race, and why is it needed now? Let me answer the first part of the question this way. One can readily enough find useful and informative engagements with the modern problem of race from a number of disciplinary perspectives. One can find them from such socioscientific disciplines as sociology, political science, and economics and such hard-science disciplines as biology and genetics, to say nothing of the engagements with race from within the varied disciplines of the humanities: philosophy and history, as well as literary, religious, feminist, cultural, and (post)colonial studies. Yet one is hard-pressed to find an adequate *theological* account of the modern problem of race. This is all the more surprising given that modern racial discourse and practice have their genesis inside Christian theological discourse and missiological practice, which themselves were tied to the practice of empire in the advance of Western civilization. But it is precisely an account of this problem that is sorely lacking.

Race: A Theological Account is an initial installment in filling this significant lacuna in modern knowledge about how the discourse of theology aided and abetted the processes by which "man" came to be viewed as a modern, racial being. Moreover (and this is the flip side of what I have just noted), this book is an inquiry into the subtle, inner transformation that theology itself underwent in giving itself over to the discursive enterprise of helping to racially constitute the modern world as we have come to know it. In what way is modern racial discourse theological in character? What happened to theology as a discourse that allowed it to become a

racial discourse? And, finally, is there another way of imagining the discursive enterprise of theology, given its complicity in constructing the racialized world and everything that has followed in its wake? This book is driven by—indeed, haunted by—these questions, and I seek to begin to answer them.

My fundamental contention is that modernity's racial imagination has its genesis in the theological problem of Christianity's quest to sever itself from its Jewish roots. This severance was carried out in two distinct but integrated steps. First, Jews were cast as a race group in contrast to Western Christians, who with the important assistance of the discourses of Christian theology and philosophy, were also subtly and simultaneously cast as a race group. The Jews were the mirror in which the European and eventually the Euro-American Occident could religiously and thus racially conceive itself through the difference of Orientalism. In this way, Western culture began to articulate itself as Christian culture (and vice versa), but now—and this is the new moment—through the medium of a racial imagination. Second, having racialized Jews as a people of the Orient and thus Judaism as a "religion" of the East, Jews were then deemed inferior to Christians of the Occident or the West. Hence, the racial imagination (the first step) proved as well to be a racist imagination of white supremacy (the second step). Within the gulf enacted between Christianity and the Jews, the *racial*, which proves to be a *racist*, imagination was forged.

In an intellectual and post–civil rights moment in which it is now acceptable and expected (and rightly so) that one be against the second racist step, in this book I theologically argue against both steps, which I summarize under the shorthand phrase "the theological problem of whiteness." Having identified this problem as its first objective, which I carry out principally in part I, my second objective is executing a new theological imagination for the twenty-first century, one that sutures the gap between Christianity and its Jewish roots and thereby reimagines Christian (intellectual) identity. This latter task I carry out principally in parts II and III and in the surrounding apparatus of the prelude, interlude, and postlude. In the remainder of this prologue, I provide a little more detail in how this book unfolds.

In part I ("Dramatizing Race"), I take the initial steps in developing a critical theological methodology to theorize the modern problem of race. More specifically, positioned between the work of Cornel West and Michel Foucault, chapter 1 represents a theological engagement with contemporary critical race studies. Foucault's work proves particularly useful to my argument, inasmuch as his interest in the question of the invention of "homo sexualis" led him to the question of how it came to pass that the human being was viewed as the bearer of race and then to the question of what was religious or quasi-theological about the invention of modern "man" as a racial being. Foucault brings me to the threshold of an answer to this question, but to actually answer it, I need to go beyond him. In chapter 2's analysis of Immanuel Kant's racial theory, I establish how theology came to aid and abet—indeed, how as a

discourse it came to provide—the inner architecture of modern racial reasoning. I point to how whiteness came to function as a substitute for the Christian doctrine of creation, thus producing a reality into which all else must enter. How theology came to underwrite this racial work has everything to do with the modern quest to sever Christianity from its Jewish roots.

In part I, perhaps more than anywhere else in this book, I am acutely aware of my argument's limitations, recognizing where in subsequent research, which I am already hard at work on, it will need further development. In chapter 1, I engage the work of Cornel West and Michel Foucault as part of my effort to show that modernity's racial imagination is religious in nature. Foucault takes me the farthest here, for he espied the connection between modernity's racial imagination and the transformation of Jews into "semites."[1] If there is a limitation in Foucault's thought on this point it is that he knew not what theological sense to make of the semites' moment of arising. That is to say, he inadequately theorized the Jews' modern-semitic birth. And because this problem was insufficiently defined as a problem, it remained insufficiently addressed in his work.

Having come, then, only to the vestibule in chapter 1, in chapter 2 I dare to enter into the edifice of the problem. It is here that I focus on modern racial reasoning's initial maturation into something of a coherent outlook or its congealing into what can be called a racial-anthropological theory that is at the same time a *Weltanschauung*. This moment of initial, discursive maturity is realized in the Kantian racial vision, which, as I show in chapter 2, is part and parcel of Kant's general, philosophical vision of the social process or political economy of Enlightenment (*Aufklärung*). My claim is that this vision of modernity as the social process of Enlightenment is both a racial vision and a particular kind of theological vision. Indeed, Enlightenment as Kant envisions it is the mutual encoding of the racial and the theological so as to yield the cosmopolitical.

It is worth reiterating that what I engage here is a moment within initial maturing of modernity's racial-theological vision of the human. I do not discuss the early colonialist vision that took hold just about three centuries prior to the Kantian, essentially Protestant, Enlightenment–racial vision in the late eighteenth century. This earlier moment had a Roman Catholic, essentially Southern European, infancy. Constituting a "dark Atlantic" triangulated between Europe, the west coast of Africa, and the Americas, this colonialist vision is symbolically positioned and historically datable between 1442, the year the Portuguese first loaded their vessels with the human cargo of African slaves to be exported back to Europe, and 1492, the year Christopher Columbus came upon "the Indies" and commenced his "India" and "Jerusalem" mission and the conquest of the Americas (with other European competitors soon to follow).[2] The Kantian racial-cosmopolitical vision, which was also a theological vision predicated on the extirpation of Jewish flesh, is unintelligible apart from these

prior events. Stated differently, the Kantian outlook is only the discursive maturing of the racial colonialism inaugurated in the mid-to-late fifteenth century. And again it must be said that in the middle of it all was theological discourse, mainly of a Thomist–Aristotelian sort, coupled with the discourse of canon and civil law, which also functioned in relationship to theology. I was unable to engage these important pre-Enlightenment matters here without ballooning even further an already big book. Their theological consideration must therefore await another, not too far off, day.

In parts II and III of this book—"Engaging Race" and "Redirecting Race," respectively—I take on the question of what it would mean to think within a different theological imagination so as to disrupt the racial logic of the modern body politic. More specifically, chapters 3–5 read the black religious academy in the dawning moments of its wider acceptance in the modern religious studies and theological guild in the late 1960s and 1970s as trying to diagnose and intellectually disrupt the very problem I am going after in part I. This is the theological problem of race generally and more specifically the problem of whiteness itself as the core theological problem of our times. In effect, these chapters consider the black religious academy's early attempts to religiously theorize the modern problem of race. But they also consider why the black religious academy has yet to really plumb the theological depths of modernity's racial problematic, the problematic of whiteness as a *theological* phenomenon and how theology came to function differently in becoming a racial discourse.

It is the task on the one hand of part III and on the other of the prelude–interlude–postlude to do just this. Part III does it by providing a theological reading of four texts that literarily witness to the theological sensibility embodied in New World Afro-Christian faith in antebellum North America: Briton Hammon's 1760 *Narrative* of his life (chapter 6), Frederick Douglass's canonical 1845 *Narrative* (chapter 7), and Jarena Lee's 1836 and 1849 spiritual *Narrative* and *Journal* (chapter 8). My reading of these texts surfaces the intuitive grasp these writers had into what was theological about the modern problem of race generally and the theological constitution of whiteness in particular. Against this false or what at times I call pseudotheological imagination, these texts struggle to inaugurate a different theological imagination. The chapters making up part III foreground this theological sensibility and examine how it was deployed to write the black body out of its modern racial quandary.

Individually and collectively, these texts reengage the way in which Christology, that area within the theological curriculum that investigates the person and work of Jesus the Christ, was problematically deployed to found the modern racial imagination. For at the genealogical taproot of modern racial reasoning is the process by which Christ was abstracted from Jesus, and thus from his Jewish body, thereby severing Christianity from its Jewish roots. Jewish flesh in this moment underwent a religious conversion: it was con-

verted into racial flesh, positioned within a hierarchy of racial-anthropological essences, and lodged within a now racialized chain of being. In making Christ non-Jewish in this moment, he was made a figure of the Occident. He became white, even if Jesus as a historical figure remained Jewish or racially a figure of the Orient. Theology's participation in this process is what makes it modern. Indeed, theology assisted in bringing about modernity precisely in aiding and abetting this process.

Though not speaking in the register of theology, Hammon's, Douglass's, and Lee's narratives are animated by a deep theological imagination, one that—precisely in moving in the direction of envisioning Jesus as the Christ and Christ's flesh as Jewish covenantal flesh and not racial-colonial flesh— moved to theologically overcome the modern problem of race. In short, the Christological sensibility at work in the texts I discuss in part III points in the direction of overcoming the Christian supersessionism that grounds the modern intellectual and theological imagination. Moreover, insofar as they witness to currents within New World Afro-Christian faith, these texts point the way toward reconstituting theology itself as a discourse, a point I strongly press in the epilogue.

The prelude, interlude, and postlude then point out the degree to which this early Afro-Christian theological imagination, as discussed in part III, is in keeping with Christian theological sensibilities that actually predate it and that predate, one might say, the medieval theological mistake that set in motion the intellectual and social processes of the racial production of the human. The prelude explores what was at stake in the second-century struggle by theologian Irenaeus of Lyons against ancient Valentinian Gnosticism's denigration of Christ's flesh—indeed, its denigration of the material order of creation and embodiment. His struggle against ancient Gnosticism, I argue, is analogous to the antebellum Afro-Christian effort, as I isolate it in the aforementioned texts, to reckon with race generally and with whiteness particularly as theological problems. Irenaeus's struggle against the Gnostics' protoracial outlook pressed him to reclaim Christ's humanity as made concrete in his Jewish flesh as a central feature of both Christian identity and the theological imagination. That is to say, Irenaeus's reclamation of Jesus' Jewish flesh caused him to reimagine how theology functions as a discourse or as an intellectual enterprise. Herein lies his significance as an anti-Gnostic intellectual: his theological sensibilities foreshadow those of the nascent Afro-Christian faith.

I make a similar argument in the interlude in which I consider the fourth-century theologian Gregory of Nyssa as abolitionist intellectual. His vociferous and unqualified stance against slavery in any form, a stance that no one else in antiquity espoused, foreshadows the account of freedom that one finds in the early Afro-Christian faith and that I delineate in part III of this book. Uniting the ancient theological abolitionist Gregory of Nyssa and his modern counterparts in New World Afro-Christianity—both in its antebellum variants and,

arguably, in the civil rights struggle for freedom that one finds in a figure such as Martin Luther King Jr.—is the Christological sensibility animating them. Apart from this sensibility, neither Gregory, nor antebellum Afro-Christian faith, nor arguably King himself is ultimately intelligible. This Christological sensibility emphasizes the particularity of Christ's flesh—which is Jewish covenantal flesh and not Jewish racial flesh (this distinction, which is quite important, is clarified in the course of what follows)—as the material horizon within which creation is ordered toward the God of Abraham. Christ's flesh, which is Jewish covenantal flesh, is a *taxis*, a material arrangement of freedom that discloses the historical transcendence of God.

Finally, the postlude's consideration of the seventh-century monk and Christian intellectual Maximus the Confessor proceeds in a way similar to the prelude and interlude. Its reading of the Confessor as anticolonialist intellectual shows how his arguments in defense of a Chalcedonian Christological vision foreshadow the theological critique of race generally and of whiteness in particular that is embedded in the way in which persons of African descent in North America embodied the Christian faith. Indeed, by the end of the book I will have made an argument as to how the theological imagination at work in the outlook of such early church theologians as Irenaeus, the Nyssan, and the Confessor and the imagination at work in "theologians" like Hammon, Douglass, and Lee—yes, my claim is that they were theological subjects every bit as much as they were literary subjects—are not antithetical imaginations. Rather, their theological imaginations converge so as to loosen the white grip on theology as a discourse. (It should already be clear by now, but it is nevertheless worth saying explicitly, that "white" and "race" and even "black" are in this text not merely signifiers of pigmentation. In other words, their referent is perhaps only secondarily to color. Rather, they signify a political economy, an *ordo* or a social arrangement, what Irenaeus calls an *oikonomia*. More on this later.)

This brings me to the other question raised at the beginning of this prologue: Why now? Why is this book on race needed now? It is needed now because the path that theology entered on to discursively constitute and legitimate the modern racial imaginary has now brought it to a crisis, and that crisis is this: it is no longer clear that theology is a compelling discourse—compelling, that is, not for those on its lighter side and thus compelling for its benefactors, but compelling for those, as one theorist has said, on "the darker side of the renaissance" and on the "underside of modernity."[3] This book is one theologian's effort, a denizen himself of the darker underside, to reckon with theology's complicity in forging a modern racial imagination and in that reckoning enact a different kind of theological imagination. The epilogue to this book, as already noted, presses the question of the future of theology as a discourse in the twenty-first century. While the issue of how theology as a discourse functions may upon first consideration be deemed an issue far afield

from the immediate subject of this book, I contend that, in fact, it isn't. In probing how the modern racial imagination and the modern theological imagination mutually articulate each other (and what to do about this), in this book I raise and attempt to answer a more fundamental question: What kind of discourse should Christian theology be?

Prelude on Christology and Race

Irenaeus as Anti-Gnostic Intellectual

> Gnostic writing, when strong, is strong because it is supermimetic, because it confronts and seeks to overthrow the very strongest of all texts, the Jewish Bible. That supermimesis is an intolerable burden, whether for literature or for the fallen poetry of theology.
>
> —Harold Bloom, "Lying against Time: Gnosis, Poetry, Criticism"

> [The Gnostic] imagines there to be three classes of human beings: the spiritual, the psychic, and the material, after the fashion of Cain, Abel, and Seth. It is from these three that the three natures come, no longer in an individual but in the human race as such.
>
> —Irenaeus of Lyons, *Adversus haeresus* I.7.5

In this prelude, I revisit the intellectual struggle that Irenaeus (c. 125–200), bishop of Lyons, waged against ancient Gnosticism in his treatise *Against Heresies* (*Adversus haeresus*).[1] A reading of this text reveals that Irenaeus's struggle with ancient Gnosticism was no mere intellectual disagreement. It was a struggle tied to the claims that Christianity and Gnosticism wanted to make about material existence. Irenaeus understood his struggle against the ancient Gnostic movement, particularly in its Valentinian–Ptolemaeic variant, as a struggle over the meaning of the body both individually and as a sociopolitical arrangement—that is, as tied to or indicative of the body politic. The Gnostic struggle pushed him to distinguish Christianity's way of imagining the body (politic) as tied to Christ's flesh from Gnosticism's vision of the body (politic). Key to Irenaeus's

negotiation of this difference was how he envisioned the person and work of Jesus Christ, or his Christology. It is just this issue—Christology as the discursive site of negotiating the meaning of material existence—that is central to what immediately follows in this prelude and to the argument in this book as a whole.

I should quickly say, however, that I do not intend to detail every aspect of Irenaeus's critique of Valentinianism, a task that exceeds what can be accomplished here without making this a very different book. My inquiry, instead, is guided by the assistance Irenaeus gives me in coming to theological terms with a contemporary problem, a problem that was partly within but ultimately far beyond his own purview. This is the modern problem of imagining the human being in racial terms, and within these terms positioning whiteness as supreme. As a central ideological component in constructing the modern world as we have come to know it, the racial imagination arose inside of, nurtured itself on, and even camouflaged itself within the discourse of theology. That is, it articulated itself in a Christian theological idiom.

While Irenaeus knew neither of the modern problem of race nor of its deeper animating problem—the modern theological problem of white cultural supremacy—he did know of another similar problem. Historian of early Christianity Denise Buell has called this the problem and polemic of "ethnic reasoning in early Christianity." By this she refers to

> the modes of persuasion [employed by early Christians] that may or may not include the use of specific vocabulary of peoplehood. Early Christians used ethnic reasoning to legitimize various forms of Christianness as the universal, most authentic manifestation of humanity, and it offered Christians both a way to define themselves relative to "outsiders" and to compete with other "insiders" to assert the superiority of their varying visions of Christianness.[2]

This passage beautifully captures Irenaeus's critique of the Gnostics as "[imagining] there to be three classes of human beings: the spiritual, the psychic, and the material, after the fashion of Cain, Abel, and Seth." He tells us that "it is from these three that [the Gnostics understand] the three natures [to] come [ek toutôn tas treis phuseis], no longer [merely] in an individual [hena] but in the human race as such [kata genos]" (AH-G I.7.5; SC I.2.110). In Buell's terms, Irenaeus is criticizing a form of "ethnic reasoning" that had come to function inside Christian discourse and identity to construct both outsiders to Christianity (i.e., the hylics, or materialists) and outsiders who are yet inside Christianity (i.e., the psychics, who were lesser Christians—if Christian at all— because they still thought of their identity in relationship to Israel).

Buell's analysis is quite helpful to the argument I formulate here, for she grasps that there is a connection between the racial–ethnic and the religious imagination. She sees, in other words, that they articulate each other. But be-

yond Buell, I seek to provide an account of what was at stake for a person such as Irenaeus in theologically breaking this connection so as to reimagine what kind of people Christians (in continuity with the covenantal people of Israel) are and what remains at stake on this side of modernity in all of this. It will thus be necessary to surface the ongoing theological and nonsupersessionist connection between Christianity and its Jewish roots that is the precondition of Irenaeus's Christological response to ancient Gnosticism. The lifeblood of ancient Gnosis, insofar as it was a movement within Christianity, was its supersessionism. As Harold Bloom has said, in being "supermimetic" the Gnostics sought "to overthrow the very strongest of all texts, the Jewish Bible."[3] This prelude engages Irenaeus's critique of and response to Valentinianism in such a way as to show how his diagnosis of the Valentinian approach to knowing reality (Gnosis)—indeed, to knowing the human in multiple natures—provides a way of similarly diagnosing how modern racial discourse generally and whiteness in particular (as the point from which to organize and "know" the world) was born within and subsequently functioned inside the discourse of theology, thus making theology in the modern setting, certainly from the perspective of the subaltern of the colonized and enslaved, a discourse of racial–colonial death.

In this respect, the argument presented here sets up the arguments developed in parts I and II of this book. Of equal importance is Irenaeus's theological response to Valentinianism, a response in which he articulates one of the most important pre-Nicene accounts of the person and work of Christ, an account that stressed the ongoing significance of Christ's flesh in the work of redemption and in constituting Christian identity. This response is nothing less than Irenaeus's attempt to reclaim theology as a life-giving discourse by distinguishing and separating it from the Gnosticism that had come to infect it. But even more, Irenaeus's theological claim goes far in making theological, and not merely historical and cultural, sense of the emergence of New World Afro-Christian faith. This becomes evident in part III, where I show how the reception of Christianity by New World persons of African descent and the particular way they embodied or performed the Christian faith had embedded in it a theological response to the modern problem of race generally and the problem of whiteness in particular. I argue that, indeed, their reception and embodiment of Christianity constitutes a redirecting and restorative moment for modern Christian theology.

I first take up Irenaeus's analysis of ancient Gnosis, providing an overview of his account of Gnostic cosmology, anthropology, and exegesis, and arguing that they function together with a view to oust all things Jewish from the Christian imagination. My claim is that this concerted effort to overcome Judaism is what binds the racial imagination at work in the forms and systems of thought marking modernity and the anthropological imagination at work in the forms and systems of thought marking the ancient Gnostic movements. I then turn to the Christology Irenaeus works out in response to the Gnostic

problem, a Christology that makes the Jewish, covenantal flesh of the redeemer Jesus of Nazareth the locus from which to understand all created reality in relationship to YHWH, its Triune Creator. His flesh discloses the invisible Father and is that to which the Holy Spirit points and unites creation. The many as constituted across space and time and that is constitutive of the created order are "recapitulated" in Christ, Irenaeus declares, who in his flesh is one with the invisible God. This term "recapitulation" will prove quite important, and so I give it due attention.

While the reader's patience is required early on as I outline Irenaeus's account of the Ptolemaeic–Valentinian system with its seemingly endless proliferation of deities, its winding narrative of their interactions, and, importantly, the fallout of those interactions—the chief one being the creation of the material order—my aim throughout is clear. It is first to present Irenaeus's account of ancient Gnosticism with a view to the insight it provides in diagnosing the modern racial imagination. And on this score, what is crucial about ancient Gnosticism is the anthropology embedded in it. But second, my aim is to critically take up Irenaeus's theological vision of human existence as bound to Christ's covenantal flesh, a vision he formulates in response to ancient Gnosticism. Again, my interest here is guided by my contemporary concern: namely, the extent to which his intellectual vision can assist me in reimagining Christian theological discourse as disrupting strong narratives of identity such as the proto-"racial" one the "Christian" Gnostics of old proposed, as well as the neo-Gnostic one of modern racial practice and discourse. With these two objectives in view, this prelude seeks ultimately to be prolegomena to the larger arguments to follow in the rest of the book.

Irenaeus's Account of Ancient Gnosticism

After a brief but important preface that announces the overall purpose of *Adversus haeresus*, Irenaeus immediately launches into an analysis of the version of Gnosticism advanced by Ptolemaeus, the version of Gnosticism he had the most intimate knowledge of. It was Ptolemaeus's doctrine and that of his followers that had in some sense systematized Valentinianism. Thus Irenaeus calls it "the flower of the school of Valentinus" (*AH-G*, Preface, 2). He might have ignored the rapid growth of this "flower" were it not for the fact that its spread was not just among Christians and others in Rome. But spreading further west, the Gnostics were winning significant converts within the Christian community of Lyons, the community that Irenaeus as bishop and pastor was ordained to care for. It was this pastoral problem of the Gnostics' distortion of Christian identity and their dependence on Christian forms of thought and theological ideas to do so that catalyzed Irenaeus to outline and refute the Ptolemaeic–Valentinian system of "knowledge."

Irenaeus's analysis of the system takes place primarily in *AH* I.1–8 and may be divided into three aspects. First, there is his account of the dramatic struggle within the "Pleroma"—that is, inside the heavenly world (*AH* I.1–3). This drama, which is internal to the heavenly world or, one might say, internal to the divine life itself, leads to a fall of some of the deities into a lesser realm outside the Pleroma. These gods struggle (some successfully, some not so successfully) to make their way back to the higher realm and thus to be saved. The second aspect of the Gnostic–Ptolemaeic system, described in *AH* I.4–5, accounts for life in the lesser domain outside the Pleroma. This lesser but still quasi-divine realm is the "Kenoma," or Void. Finally, *AH* I.6–8 details the Gnostic account of salvation. It is in this third aspect of the Gnostic system that Irenaeus outlines the Ptolemaeic narrative of return to the Pleroma from the Kenoma as a narrative of salvation. It is also in this section that Irenaeus takes up the Gnostic account of the "Cosmos," that material domain below the Kenoma. What I hope to make clear is how the prototypical drama, the ur-drama, of redemption that takes place between the Gnostic Pleroma—populated as it is with numerous deities, some unfallen and others fallen and thus seeking "salvation"—and the Kenoma interfaces with a material drama staged in the Cosmos. This latter, material world is also well populated, but with people who have all hitched themselves to certain gods, some of whom represent paths to salvation or return to the Pleroma, others of whom do not.

As I flesh out these three interlocking dimensions of the Gnostic mythology, keep in mind the following points, for they are the concerns guiding my analysis. My ultimate interests are (1) the anthropology embedded in the Gnostic drama of redemption, (2) the bifurcation of the Christ of (Gnostic) faith (or the heavenly Christ of the Pleroma) from the Jesus of history in the Gnostic system and thus the "Christology" at work in Gnosticism, and (3) the function of scriptural exegesis to sustain the Gnostic outlook. It will turn out that the problems I isolate here with respect to ancient Gnosticism have an analogue in how the modern neo-Gnosticism of racial discourse and practice work. I start with Irenaeus's analysis of Gnostic cosmology as a kind of ur-drama of human identity.[4]

Gnostic Cosmology and the Urdrama of Human Identity

In the invisible and unnameable heights there was a perfect Aeon, prior to all. This Aeon is called Pre-Beginning and Pre-Father and Abyss. Since he was incomprehensible and invisible, eternal and unbegotten, he was in silence and in rest for unlimited ages. With him was Thought, also called Grace and Silence. When this Abyss wanted to emit a Beginning of all, he set it like a seed in the womb of his companion Silence. When she received the seed she became pregnant and generated Mind, similar and equal to the one who

emitted him, alone comprehending the greatness of the Father. This
Mind they call Only-Begotten and Father and Beginning of all; with
him was emitted Truth, to compose the first and primary, indeed
Pythagorean Tetrad: Abyss and Silence, the Mind and Truth.
(AH-G I.I.I)

So begins Irenaeus's analysis of Gnostic cosmology, which purports to have
transcended the Jewish-Christian scriptural story of creation by having uncovered its deeper meaning. Thus, if the Genesis stories start with the words
"In the beginning God created the heavens and the earth," then the Gnostic
myth wants to locate the true beginning to which the scriptural words point.

This true beginning is the archaic moment of the Pre-Beginning, from
which all subsequent beginnings spring, even the beginning of the book of
Genesis. Pre-Beginning–Pre-Father–Abyss implanted a beginning of all things
in his partner, Thought–Grace–Silence, the firstborn of which was Mind–Only-
Begotten–Beginning of all. (That this is refracted through gender and sexuality
is undeniable.) But he was not born alone. With Mind was born Truth. Thus,
there was the first "Tetrad," as Irenaeus calls it, of Pre-Father (male)–Silence
(female) on the one hand and their offspring Mind (male)–Truth (female) on
the other. But like Pre-Father, Mind (Only-Begotten), "sensing the purpose for
which he was emitted," was himself also productive, emitting a seed within
Truth. This union between Mind and Truth brought forth "Logos and Life,
Father of all later than himself, and the Beginning and Formation of the
Pleroma" (AH-G I.I.I). In turn, Logos and Life produced another pair, "Man
and Church." These are the first eight emanations, the "Ogdoad," that emerged
from Pre-Beginning and Silence. But the productions continue. Logos and Life,
according to the Gnostic myth, produce ten more Aeons or Ages, bringing the
number to eighteen, while Man and Church emit twelve Ages of their own.
With the thirty Ages in place, life within the heavenly realm of the Pleroma was
complete, though in fact it was only the completion of Act I, one might say, of
the story. The drama was only just beginning, for in many respects this is all
background to introduce what every good story must have: tension and plot
twist. Centered on the character Sophia (or Wisdom), Act II as I call it of
Irenaeus's telling of the Gnostic saga introduces this tension.

As the last of the emissions, she—yes, Sophia is female in the myth—is
farthest and most tragically removed from the Abyss or Pre-Beginning. In this
part of Irenaeus's telling of the story, we learn that Sophia's tragic distance
from the ground of her being, that is, from the Pre-Beginning, which really is
very much a gendered distance between male and female, leads to her fall, a fall
with the heavenly realm. But because Ages have offspring, this is no less the
case for Sophia. It is just that now her production is what can be called a
"wayward reproduction."[5] She will produce or "create" the material, worldly
realm that human beings—further products of this fall—populate. As "weak

and female," since they result from the uncontrollable passions of the woman Sophia, creation in general and human existence in particular are the products of Sophia's wayward passion, her fall (*AH-G* I.2.4).

If Sophia was to undergo conversion and be redeemed from her fallen condition, her wayward, inner Desire, which is personified as "Achamoth," would need to be restored or healed (*AH* I.4.1). Not only would this be Sophia's salvation, it would also reestablish the integrity of the Pleroma itself. It is just at this point that Gnostic saga, taking place on the heavenly plane of the Pleroma, begins to approximate the Christian story. It shows itself to be parasitic on it. Indeed, it is this dimension of the story—we can call it Act III or the Gnostic story of redemption—that will play itself out again on the plane of material existence and will become the ground in the Gnostic story for explaining the different "classes" or the three different "natures" of human being.

The central characters in Act III are "Limit" (also called Cross), the Christ of the Pleroma (or the heavenly Christ), whose partner is the Holy Spirit of the Pleroma (or the heavenly Holy Spirit), and the offspring of the heavenly Christ and Holy Spirit, the heavenly Jesus. These are the characters central to Sophia's redemption and the redemption or realignment of her Desire (Achamoth). As far as Sophia is concerned, her redemption comes about because her wayward Desire is banished to another realm, the Kenoma (Void). Her Desire is crucified by Limit, that is to say, by the Cross. Thus Wisdom or part of the feminine is restored. But what about the other part of the feminine, Desire itself or what the Gnostics personified as Achamoth? How is she healed and therefore redeemed?

Here is where the story of material existence and within this story that of the three "classes" or natures of human beings formally begins, the part that everything that I have said so far has been leading to. For it is here that Irenaeus outlines how the heavenly Christ and Holy Spirit work to redeem Desire. And yet, it is just at this point as well that one sees how, according to Irenaeus's theological analysis, the Gnostic drama of the redemption of the Pleroma through the redemption of Sophia–Desire is in fact an urdrama that all along has been encoding another drama, the drama of human identity, which entails the policing of materiality (or, more specifically, the policing of bodies) in the interest of the liberation or salvation of Desire. In short, it is at this point that Irenaeus wants to show how the urdrama of the Gnostic gods encodes a drama of human redemption. The hinge between the two dramas is the liberation of Desire from its bondage to the body or to matter. Moreover, the entire drama in both its heavenly and earthly dimensions is an interpretation of Scripture. Indeed, it is a deployment of scripture in the production of human identity. The identity generating this hermeneutical exercise is an explanation and, further, a justification of what the Gnostics took to be the various "natures" and classes of human being. I now move to how Irenaeus interpreted the Ptolemaeic Gnostics on these matters.

The Three Substances and Three Species of Humanity:
The Gnostic Drama of Redemption

Irenaeus provides much detail regarding the Gnostic story of the redemption of Desire. For my purposes, what is important is this: Desire's salvation requires separating out those passions embedded in her that are either wholly unredeemable or, with effort, are partially redeemable from those passions that reflect Desire's true spiritual essence and thus, properly speaking, are of the Pleroma. The Gnostics represented these three aspects of Desire's passions as three distinct substances. The passions that are bad and thus utterly unredeemable were banished from Desire altogether to form the material, or hylic, substance. The passions that with some work could be converted formed the second substance, which is passible, or psychic, in nature. And last, the passions that reflect Desire's true origin in the Pleroma constitute the final, superior substance, which is spiritual in nature.

But how, more specifically, did the creation of a Cosmos occur from all of this? Desire partnered with a "Demiurge," who it turns out is the God of the Old Testament, the God of Israel. Israel's God is the one who actually crafted the material world of the Cosmos from the hylic substance. This is how those wayward and utterly unredeemable passions were banished from Desire. Moreover, it was the Demiurge, or Israel's God, who also formed the earthly man from the cosmic (hylic) substance. Upon forming him, he breathed into him a psychic element. But the psychic element does not take hold in everyone. Those in whom it takes hold are the psychics. Thus, on the one hand there is the *psychic* man, who can turn either downward toward matter or upward toward spirit and who is capable of education. And on the other hand there is the *hylic* man, who being wholly from the earth remains corruptible, uneducable, and thus thoroughly constrained by the body, weighed down by the baseness of the flesh and of material existence.

But there is something else to bear in mind: when the Demiurge breathed out the psychic element, unbeknownst to him he secretly breathed out and implanted in a select few a *pneumatic*, or spiritual, element. This element is the spark from the Pleroma, the possession of which constitutes this other class as the true elect or illuminati. As another class or species of human being altogether, these special, pneumatic persons are of the spiritual substance of the Pleroma itself. This is the ground of their existence, not the Demiurge. As far as their existence is concerned, the Creator God of Israel is bypassed altogether, and so the pneumatic are untainted or constrained by the material reality below.

Hence, the three substances of Desire—the pneumatic element, which is consubstantial with Desire herself; the psychic element from Desire's educated and converted passions; and the hylic element from her uneducable and thus

unredeemable passions, Achamoth's "sublime waste," so to speak—are tied to the three species of humankind, two of whom are under the control of the God of Israel, the Creator Demiurge, and the other under the pneumatic superintendence of Achamoth, or Desire, in her purity and thus under the guidance of the Pleroma itself.[6] This latter class or race, who have a pneumatic nature, make up the true church of the elect (the Gnostics), of which the Christian church and the people of Israel are but vague, distant, and inferior representations. Irenaeus summarizes the Gnostics' claim this way:

> Thus it came to pass, then, according to them, that, without any knowledge on the part of the Demiurge, the man formed by his inspiration was at the same time, through an unspeakable providence, rendered a spiritual man by the simultaneous inspiration received from his Sophia. For, as he was ignorant of his mother, so neither did he recognize her offspring. This (offspring) they also declare to be the Ecclesia, an emblem of the Ecclesia which is above. This, then, is the kind of man whom they conceive of: he has his animal [or psychic] soul from the Demiurge, his body from the earth, his fleshly part from matter, and his spiritual man (ton . . . pneumatikon anthrôpon) from the mother Achamoth. (AH-A I.5.6; SC I.2.89–90)

Herein is displayed the convergence of Gnostic anthropogony (their doctrine of the heavenly "man") and anthropology (their doctrine of the earthly "man"). Herein also lies the significance of the Christ of the Gospels, for it is particularly with respect to him, understood within the terms of Gnostic religious and theological principles, that one sees the mirroring between anthropogony and anthropology.

The point at which the mirroring happens is salvation. The salvation of Sophia or her subjugation to the Limit of the Cross and her taking on of a pneumatic, rather than a merely psychic or material, form in this moment is the more fundamental story, according to the Gnostics, being narrated in the story of the Christ of the Gospels and the saga of the Cross. One might say that the four elements composing the earthly Christ—none of which, it must be noted, is actual flesh since the hylic substance (or materiality) as such cannot be redeemed in the Gnostic system—also reveal the heavenly Cross and its power to banish unredeemable, material passions. One could go as far as to say that, for the Gnostics, untoward passion is matter or body, and it is just this that is subjected to the Limit of the Cross. Thus, the first element composing the earthly Christ is directly from Desire in her fallen state. This element ties the earthly Christ to that middle, quasi-divine realm of the Void. The second element is psychic and comes from the Demiurge. The third comes from the divine plan, the "economy." And the fourth, which doesn't quite get a name, is

from the heavenly Savior himself. This element ties the earthly Christ to the heavenly Christ and thus directly to the Pleroma. Christ's sufferings take place with respect only to the second and third elements or the psychic and material aspects of his existence (*AH* I.7.2), for this is where the psychics struggle against the passions of material existence in order to obtain salvation. In struggling against the passions, the psychics are in fact struggling against the Demiurge (or Israel's God), who mired them in material existence in the first place.

As for Achamoth (or Desire herself), who is of a pneumatic constitution, and for the pneumatic race of humans, they will enter the Pleroma. Desire will be restored to Wisdom (Sophia), and the pneumatics will also enter the pleromatic heavens. Such is their eschatological destiny. And finally, those psychics (who give in to their passions, thus remaining trapped in material existence and weighed down by the body) and the hylics (who have no hope of transcending themselves and aspiring toward supramaterial existence) will go the way of all matter: they will undergo the fires of apocalyptic destruction (*AH* I.7.5). The material Cosmos will perish, and they along with it. Such is Irenaeus's account of the Gnostic myth, which when all is said and done is deeply concerned as he interprets their mythology with anthropology and the justification of a superior "race" inside the discourse of Christian theology. A version of this problem will resurge in modern racial discourse and practice, as I show in part I of this volume.

Beyond the God of Israel: Gnostic Exegesis

Having outlined in the first seven chapters of *AH* the Gnostic mythology and the deeper, problematic anthropology embedded in it—what can be called an anthropology of hierarchical essences—Irenaeus then forcefully argues against it, claiming that at its root is an exegetical practice that must be countered. The problem of Gnosticism is the problem of its scriptural exegesis.[7] Irenaeus therefore embarks on a counterexegetical practice of human existence, a different deployment of scriptural interpretation. While in what immediately follows I detail the Irenaean counterexegetical practice, more important, I am ultimately gesturing toward the constructive theological claims I make in the rest of this book: namely, that a problematic exegetical practice is also at the heart of modern racial discourse (as it was in ancient Gnosticism). Early Afro-Christian practice, in which for some writers autobiography functioned as scriptural exegesis, proved in fact to be a quite appropriate response to the scripturalizing practice undergirding modernity and its slave economy. This early Afro-Christian exegetical practice countered the particular kind of practice of theological interpretation—for all theological interpretation is not alike—at the heart of modern racial reasoning. This particular kind of practice of theological interpretation is what sustained whiteness at the level of its inner architecture and the racial identities (including blackness) that whiteness

generated. Thus, the theological imagination at work in early Afro-Christian existence (as witnessed in the texts I consider in part III) strove to disrupt the problematic way scriptural exegesis has come to function in constructing and regulating the body (politic).

But to return to Irenaeus: he signals as early as the preface to book I of *Adversus haeresus* that his qualm with the ancient Gnostics turned on the relationship between scriptural exegesis and Gnostic, pseudo-Christian belief. "Some persons reject the truth," he says,

> and introduce false statements and "endless genealogies, which provide questions," as the Apostle says, "rather than the divine training that is in faith" (1 Tim. 1:4). They combine plausibility with fraud and lead the mind of the inexperienced astray and force them into captivity. They falsify the words of the Lord and make themselves bad interpreters of what was well said. (*AH*-G Preface, 1)

The problem of Gnostic scriptural exegesis surfaces again near the end of his analysis of their system of belief:

> Such is their doctrine, which the prophets did not proclaim, the Lord did not teach, and the apostles did not transmit. They boast that they have known it more abundantly than anyone else. While citing texts from unwritten sources and venturing to weave the proverbial ropes out of sand, they try to adjust, in agreement with their statements, sometimes parables of the Lord, sometimes prophetic sayings, and sometimes apostolic words, so that their fiction may not seem without witness. They contradict the order and continuity of the scriptures and, as best they can, dissolve the members of the truth. They transfer and transform, making one thing out of another, and thus lead many astray by the badly constructed phantom that they make out of the Lord's words they adjust. (*AH*-G I.8.1)

Thus, the problem of scriptural exegesis bookends Irenaeus's analysis of ancient Gnosis.

After analyzing their system, Irenaeus spends the next four sections of the chapter providing examples of how Gnostic exegesis works: how, as he says, they "patch together old wives' fables, and then endeavor, by violently drawing away from their proper connection, words, expressions, and parables whenever found, to adapt the oracles of God to their baseless fictions" (*AH*-G I.8.1). I need not recount his examples. It is the point of the examples that bears highlighting, inasmuch as they illustrate a problem that is deeply connected to modern racial practice and discourse as it emerged inside the discourse of Christian theology in the formation of the modern world. That point is this: Gnostic exegesis did not function to reconstitute the identity of scriptural readers. It neither drew them *into* the scriptural witness to Jesus nor drew

them *out of* the Gnostic "racial" narrative of the supposed superiority of pneumatic over psychic and hylic peoples. (Part of Irenaeus's own constructive task was to establish the fictiveness of these very anthropological distinctions, as well to undo the class sensibilities at work in them.[8]) Rather, Gnostic exegesis functioned in justification of these religious-"racial" distinctions that were made to function almost imperceptibly inside theological discourse. It did not transform identity; it affirmed them in it.

Gnostic exegesis did two things so as to function theologically in this way. First, it situated an interpretation of any given scriptural text on one of three possible levels of mythic history, which correspond to one of the three classes of human being. A given interpretation would be situated either at the highest level of the Pleroma and then linked to the pneumatics, or at the middle level of the Kenoma and allocated to the psychics, or at the lowest level of the material Cosmos and tied to the fleshly hylics.[9] But second, Gnostic exegesis operated by a deeper hermeneutic principle: the severing of Christianity from its Jewish roots. In decoupling Christianity from YHWH the Abrahamic God, the Gnostics were able to reimagine Christian identity in protoracial terms, terms that supported the supremacy of the pneumatics (or Gnostics) over the other species of humankind. Indeed, if Elaine Pagels is correct, the Gnostics seized on the Pauline doctrine of election in order to rewrite it in Gnostic terms. So construed, Paul's concern was not with YHWH's irrevocable promises to Israel as the people of his covenant and, in this way, for creation as a whole and in all of it particularities. Instead, his concern, the Gnostics contended, was over the election of the true, pneumatic Christians—that is, the Gnostics.[10] They are a "new" Israel—the true church beyond Israel, the gathering of pneumatics who are an image of the nonmaterial "Ecclesia" (one of the many Ages that I did not examine in detail earlier) of the Pleroma.

It is just this dual problem—that of exegesis functioning to support rather than disrupt the logic of Gnostic "racial" reasoning and the problem of a vision of Christianity as severed from Judaism and thus from the God of Israel whom Jesus of Nazareth reveals—that Irenaeus, having diagnosed, sought to theologically move beyond. His crucial move against it is to insist, on the one hand, on the actual fleshly, material existence of Christ for disclosing God in his unified identity as Creator–Redeemer and, on the other, on the unique modality of Christ's covenantal flesh in the unified divine economy (*oikonomia*) of creation–redemption. Irenaeus insisted that Christ's flesh disrupts an anthropological hierarchy of essences precisely in being tied to the history of Israel and thus to the history of God's dealings with this people. In other words, Irenaeus sees Jewish covenantal flesh functioning unlike flesh interpreted in terms of ontological or even cultural essences. The flesh of the covenant is not situated within, nor does it inaugurate, an anthropological chain of being.

This is what makes Irenaeus a figure worthy of contemporary engagement and not one of mere antiquarian interest. He thinks within a theological

imagination suited to diagnosing how modern racial discourse generally and how whiteness in particular functions. It is suited to diagnosing how in the dawning moments of the modern world and in its initial moments of philosophical maturity, particularly in late-eighteenth-century Kantian thought—I explore this in chapter 2—racial discourse came to function inside Christian theological discourse to constitute the modern world as we have come to know it. Irenaeus imagines Christ's covenantal flesh as disrupting the substantialist hierarchy of cosmological and anthropological essences that marked Ptolemaeic–Gnostic thought. Irenaeus's goal was not simply to defeat the Gnostic argument. His larger goal was to rescue theological discourse from what in Gnostic hands it was becoming: a discourse of death, the death of embodied life. While bearing on all, this vision of the death of materiality bore out in the most deleterious ways on nonpneumatic bodies. I am trying to do something similar to what Irenaeus is doing, albeit from this side of modernity—and with all that is entailed in this. But for now, I tarry a little longer with Irenaeus, for there is more that I want to highlight about what he was doing as I move closer to a direct engagement of the modern problem of race as a theological problem. His effort to redirect Christian theology beyond the Gnostic sensibilities that had come to operate within it falls within the purview of his Christology. To this I now give brief attention.

Irenaeus's Response to Ancient Gnosticism: Christ's Covenantal Flesh and the Notion of Recapitulation

Irenaeus gives a condensed, initial response to Gnosticism in *AH* I.9, a response that he unpacks at various points throughout the five books making up the treatise. I have already noted that of central importance for him is Christ's flesh in the economy of redemption. Christ did not assume a "psychic body" but a material one (*AH-A* I.9.3). Moreover, Irenaeus's insistence on the centrality of Christ's flesh is tied to his effort to engage in a different kind of exegetical practice, one that responds to the way in which, as Cyril O'Regan has said, "Valentinian narratives encompass the biblical narrative and completely disfigure and refigure it."[11] Irenaeus wants to expose this. Thus he says,

> According to them the Word did not originally become flesh. For they maintain the Savior assumed a psychic body, formed in accordance with a special dispensation by an unspeakable providence, so as to become visible and palpable. But *flesh* is that which was of old formed for Adam by God out of the dust, and it is this that John [the gospel writer] has declared the Word of God became. (*AH* I.93)

What he wants to do is offer a counterexegesis of the very scriptural texts the Gnostics drew on to make their claims regarding the hierarchy of

anthropological essences and the supremacy of those of a pneumatic nature within the hierarchy. Thus, Irenaean counterexegesis seeks both to refigure the Gnostics' prior disfiguring and refiguring of biblical narrative and to provide a different narrative, a counterexegesis, of the self. Inasmuch as this is the case, Irenaeus's theological and exegetical imagination prefigures the theological imagination and exegetical practice at work in the dawning moments of New World Afro-Christian faith in responding to modern racial practice and discourse. (This I take up in part III, paying attention especially to Afro-Christian faith in antebellum North America.)

Irenaeus made two claims regarding Christ's flesh in theologically responding to ancient Gnosticism, claims that are important for the argument I develop throughout this book. Both are at work in the following passage in which Irenaeus once again marks a line between the claims of Gnosticism and those of Christian theology. The Gnostics, he says,

> wander from the truth, because their teaching departs from Him who is truly God. They do not know that His only begotten Logos, who is always present with the human race, united to and mingled with His own creation, according to the Father's pleasure, and who became flesh, is Himself Jesus Christ our Lord, who did also suffer for us, and rose again on our behalf, and who will come again in the glory of His Father, to raise up all flesh, and for the manifestation of salvation . . . . There is therefore, as I have pointed out, one God the Father, and one Christ Jesus, who is coming throughout the whole economy [*ho elthôn kath holên tên oikonimian*], recapitulating all things in Himself [*kai ta panta eis heauton anakephalaiôsamenos*]. But in every respect too He is man, the formation of God; and thus He took up man into Himself, the invisible becoming visible, the incomprehensible becoming comprehensible, the impassible becoming capable of suffering, and the Word becoming man, thus recapitulating all things in Himself. This was so that just as in super-celestial, spiritual, and invisible things, the Word of God is supreme, so also in things visible and corporeal [the Word of God] might possess the supremacy, and, taking to Himself the preeminence, as well as constituting Himself Head of the Church, He might draw all things to Himself at the proper time. (*AH*-A III.16.6 [trans. slightly modified]; SC III.2.313)

The first thing Irenaeus argues against the Gnostics is the unity between Christ as God and the flesh of the man Jesus that is assumed. In arguing this way, he distinguishes his claims from "these blasphemous systems" that "divide the Lord, so far as they are able to do, saying that he was formed of two different substances [the pneumatic and the psychic], but not the hylic [or material]" (*AH*-A III.16.5). It is in his flesh that the invisible and the visible

come together, for with respect to God, there is no opposition between the divine or the invisible and the material or the visible, between the uncreated and the created. Indeed, Irenaeus argues God's difference from creation must be understood in light of the distinction already at work in the way in which God is God. God's positive relationship to creation occurs inside God's positive relationship to himself as God. It is this positive relationship that is on display in the invisible Father's electing love for the eternal Son as the one who renders visible the invisible Father. Thus the dynamism between the visible and the invisible constitutes God's way of being God, the divine aesthetic.

Moreover, the visibility by which the Son renders visible the invisible Father extends to the act of creation itself, which takes place through the Son. Therefore, creation itself and the many making it up exist through the visibility by which the Son of the Trinity discloses the invisible God. Creation participates in the Son's work of making the Father visible. In the Son, they are icons, or images, of God and thus are marked with an invisible depth that exceeds what appears, though that invisible depth articulates itself precisely in what appears. In this strict sense, then, creation—contrary to the claims of the Gnostics—does not exist "outside" of God in a region beyond the Pleroma. In fact, the notion of a Pleroma set over against a Kenoma and a Cosmos is insufficient to account for the relationship between God and creation, for creation exists in the deepest intimacy with, even as it remains distinct from, God. Moreover, this very intimacy is an intimacy—and this is Irenaeus's point—that occurs inside the Father's love for the eternal Son who makes the Father visible even in the Son's materiality: that is, in his flesh in the economy of creation–redemption.

Thus, though the Father's love is uniquely directed toward the Son in the Holy Spirit and therefore in this regard is exclusive, the Father's love is not exclusionary. It entails within it the capacity to love and create—the two finally are synonymous for Irenaeus—and to love what is created. But loving what is created entails the capacity on God's part to "mingle" himself, as Irenaeus puts it, with creation, all the while as Creator maintaining his distinction—inasmuch as love presumes distinction—from the creation. The site from which God as Creator mingles with creation yet maintains his distinction from creation is Christ's flesh. It is with creation and the flesh of material existence that the invisible Father communes in loving the visible Son in the economy of creation and redemption. In arguing thus, Irenaeus comes up against the too simplistic Gnostic notion that there is an opposition for God between the immaterial and the material, between the divinity and humanity. By contrast, he argues for their unity-in-distinction, which enables the human, and thus fleshly, material existence to reveal God's divine or supramaterial existence. The important point here is that there is no accessing the divine or the supramaterial apart from its revelation, and thus mediation, in the materiality of creation and the flesh. It is just this point that will be affirmed in the heat of the

Christological controversies leading to Chalecedon in 451 CE and that will be championed by no less a Christologian than Maximus the Confessor (see the postlude of this book): the one and the same Jesus Christ is the singular embodiment of what it means to be divine and human.

But there is a crucial second move Irenaeus makes and that for the most part the Christian theological traditions after Irenaeus do not develop. It concerns the unique modality of Christ's flesh in how it discloses God. To account for this, Irenaeus turns to the Pauline notion of "recapitulation," a notion that, in fact, is not limited to Paul but that Irenaeus finds throughout Scripture (specifically in Paul though; e.g., Rom. 13:9; Eph. 1:10). "There is," Irenaeus says, "one God . . . and . . . one Christ Jesus our Lord, who is coming throughout the whole economy, recapitulating all things in himself. . . . The Word [became] man the Word, thus recapitulating all things in himself" (AH-A III.16.6). John Behr observes that "recapitulation" (anakephalaiôsis) describes for Irenaeus the relationship between the Scriptures of the Old Testament and the Gospels of the New, as both are held together through the events of Christ's flesh as those events culminate with the cross: "Recapitulation summarizes the whole [of a] case, presenting [a restatement of it] in epitome, bringing together the whole argument in one conspectus, so that, while the particular details made little impact [alone], the picture as a whole might be more forceful. Recapitulation provides a résumé which, because shorter, is clearer and therefore more effective."[12]

With this notion, Irenaeus is able in effect to explain the ongoing link between the Old Testament Mosaic Law, which the prophetic writings uphold, and the fourfold Gospel, which the Epistles elaborate. In so doing, he moves to overturn a key pillar of Gnostic theology and exegesis: namely, the inferiority of the God of Israel and the Old Testament Scriptures in which the story of this God in relationship to the people of Israel is told. Moreover, he is able to theologically reverse the Gnostic move to transcend YHWH and overthrow the Jewish Bible that is tied to YHWH. The Old Testament Law, he says, is recapitulated in Christ's flesh. His body (politic) is a conspectus, a rhetorically potent and compacted reiteration, of the Law, that ratifies YHWH's covenant with Israel and analogically with creation as a whole. Irenaeus makes this point perhaps most forcefully not in Adversus haeresus but in the only other text that we have of his, the Epideixis, or The Demonstration of the Apostolic Preaching:

> And that, not by the prolixity of the Law, but according to the brevity of faith and love, men were going to be saved. Isaiah, in this fashion, says, "He will complete and cut short [his] Word in righteousness; for God will make a concise Word in all the world" [Isa. 10:22–23; Rom. 9:28]. And therefore the Apostle Paul says, "Love is the fulfillment of the Law" [Rom. 13:10], for he who loves God has

fulfilled the Law. Moreover, the Lord also, when he was asked, which is the first commandment, said, "You shall love the Lord your God with [your] whole heart and [your] whole strength; and the second like it, you shall love your neighbor as yourself. On these two commandments," he says, "depend all the Law and the Prophets" [Matt. 22:37–40]. So he has increased, by means of our faith in him, our love towards God and towards the neighbor, rendering us godly, righteous and good. And therefore he made "a concise word" ... in the world.[13]

The winding, elongated story of YHWH's dealings with his people as centered in his covenantal Law, Irenaeus says, was "cut short" and "fulfilled" in another Law, the Law of love that was enfleshed in the "Word of righteousness." It must be quickly said, however, that this cutting short and fulfilling of the Law in another Law should not be read as an early instance of Christian supersessionism, the notion that Christians replace Israel as God's people, that God discards the Jews in favor of Christians.[14] Rather than this, the cutting short of the Law is the production of a ""concise word," which as an epitome or résumé [of the Law] is clearer and therefore more effective, increasing our faith in God, our love for him and our neighbor, and so providing salvation. Yet, while being "cut short," the Word of God remains identical."[15]

That is, there is a deep unity between the Old and New Testaments, a unity tied to the unity that I spoke of above, the unity between God and creation as secured by and revealed in Christ's crucified flesh. "The Gospel, as the recapitulation of Scripture, is its fulfillment."[16] And thus, though a concentrated expression of the Old Testament Law and of the Prophets, the fourfold Gospel, Irenaeus argues, is continuous with the Law and the Prophets through Christ's flesh. His flesh is continuous with the flesh of Adam and Israel insofar as his body and history derive from theirs. And yet, his flesh is discontinuous with what went before inasmuch as it inaugurates a redeemed pattern of life that brings to a crescendo the pattern of life witnessed to in the Law of the Old Testament. Therefore, discontinuity (insofar as he is a summary of a new pattern of existence)-in-continuity (insofar as the new pattern of existence he summarizes and newly inaugurates was in some sense yet embedded in what went before) is concentrated in Christ's flesh.

This basic framework allows Irenaeus to say, for example, that the birth of Christ, whose condition of possibility is the fiat of Mary of Nazareth, recapitulates the birth of Adam, just as Mary's action recapitulates Eve's. However, they do so in such a way as to inaugurate a new pattern of existence and of generation, a new arrangement or economy of birth. "Recapitulating this [Adam]," he says, "the Lord ... received the same arrangement [oikonomia] of embodiment [sarkôsis] as [him], being born from the Virgin by the will and wisdom of God, that He might also demonstrate the likeness of embodiment

[sarkôsis] to Adam, and might become the man, written in the beginning, 'according to the image and likeness of God'" (Dem. 32). As was the case with the first Adam, Christ's birth—and Mary's fiat, which in the order of redemption authorized that birth—recapitulates the creation of humankind in such a way as to imprint a new modality of existence on it, a modality of the cross, the ascetical mode of life that refuses to tyrannically possess the world (AH V.18.3; Dem. 34).

Moreover, as he passes through all of the stages of life, from infancy through adolescence to adulthood and finally death itself, Christ recapitulates all of the generations of human existence across space and time, from Adam to himself and into the future. In a particularly vivid way, Irenaeus states the following to capture the breadth of creation's concentration in Christ's flesh:

> This is why Luke presents a genealogy of seventy-two generations from the birth of our Lord back to Adam (Luke 3:23–28), linking the end to the beginning and indicating that he is the one who recapitulated in him, with Adam, *all the nations and languages and generations of men* dispersed after Adam. Therefore Paul calls Adam the "figure of the one to come" (Rom 5:14) because the Word, Fashioner of all, preformed in Adam the future divine plan for humanity around the Son of God, since God first predestined the psychic man, obviously, to be saved by the spiritual. Since he who would save preexisted, what would be saved had to come into existence so that the saving one would not be in vain. (AH-G III.22.3; italics mine)

Irenaeus's claim has profound ramifications for the diagnosis of modern racial discourse I develop here and for the constructive theological agenda I sketch in response to it. Most interesting for my purposes is his turn to the issue of language, nationhood, and generation or birth. These three areas function crucially in the formation of the modern world as we know it through the protocols of race, for modern racial discourse emerges in relationship to language, the formation of modern nations within Western civilization as "imagined communities," and the problem of biology or *bios* in which birth played a key role.[17]

I will refrain from commenting on the issue of nationhood and biology since I have something to say about these matters in chapters 1 and 2. As far as the modern problem of language is concerned, Tzvetan Todorov shows in a compelling way how language functioned in relationship to the modern practice of colonial conquest, which is deeply tied to the problem of racial discourse and economic practice. In the context of an analysis of the Spanish conqueror Hernán Cortés's conquest, with fewer than 600 men supported by twenty horses and ten small cannons, of the Aztec civilization or what is now Mexico, Todorov observes that

the Spaniards . . . establish Nahuatl as the national native language in Mexico, before effecting Hispanization; the Franciscan and Dominican priests will undertake the study of native languages as they later assume the teaching of Spanish. The preparation for this conduct has begun much earlier, and the year 1492, which had already seen the remarkable coincidence of the victory over the Arabs, of the exile imposed on the Jews, and of the discovery of America, this year is also the one that sees the publication of the first grammar of a modern European language—the Spanish grammar of Antonio de Nebrija. The knowledge, here theoretical, of language testifies to a new attitude, no longer of veneration but of analysis and of a new consciousness of its practical utility; Nebrija writes in his Introduction these decisive words: "Language has always been the companion of empire."[18]

Todorov points to how language itself becomes the vehicle of conquest. In many ways, Columbus himself was clear about this. Again as Todorov says, commenting on remarks Columbus makes in journals he kept during his first voyage: "When Columbus finally acknowledges the foreignness of [the] languages [of one of the groups of people he comes across], he insists . . . that it be also the foreignness of all the others; on the one side, then, there are the Latin languages, and on the other all foreign tongues."[19] What one sees here is Columbus arranging language within a hierarchy that situates the Latin languages, especially Spanish (Latin itself being the language of theological discourse), over all other languages. But precisely in doing this, Columbus enacts colonial conquest on the linguistic level. He enacts empire. Moreover—and this is the part that neither Todorov nor an otherwise deeply insightful contemporary critical theorist such as Walter Mignolo begins to do justice to— Columbus and other conquistadors after him engage in colonial conquest, both linguistically and otherwise, inside Latin as the language of theological discourse.[20] Theology starts to function in a new way precisely in this moment.

But herein lies Irenaeus's significance, for he says that human language across time and space gets recapitulated in Christ. Now given how Irenaeus has been arguing, this cannot be a theological expression of colonial linguistic conquest on his part, for we have seen that he argues that in being recapitulated in the Gospels and in Christ's flesh, the Old Testament is not tyrannically overcome. Rather, it is re-presented as in conspectus, and in that concentrated form its freedom to signify the Creator acquires a new, iconic depth. It is made even more potent to witness to YHWH or to be YHWH's creaturely discourse (*logos*). It follows, then, that languages are not subdued any more than is the Old Testament to become God's "colonial" possessions. The words of creation (the *logoi*) are not lost in the Word of God (the *Logos*). Rather, they pentecostally or interlinguistically articulate each other. Given this, one must speak not

merely of Christ's humanity. One must speak of his humanity as an *interhu-manity* that constitutes a new, *intra*humanity. That is, Christ's humanity is the historical display of an intradivine communion between Father and Son in the Holy Spirit that itself opens up, by the same motion of the Holy Spirit in Christ's flesh, a new communion internal to human existence. In short, Christ's flesh as Jewish, covenantal flesh is a social-political reality displayed across time and space into which the Gentiles are received in praise of the God of Israel. Given this, we must say that Christ's flesh in its Jewish constitution is "mulatto" flesh. That is to say, in being Jewish flesh it is always already *in-ter*sected by the covenant with YHWH and in being *inter*sected it is always already *intra*racial (and not merely multiracial). Its purity is its "impurity," which is the "impurity" of its being covenantally *inter*sected by YHWH as its life-giving limit.[21] Israel is the people that exists by virtue of being upheld in being by YHWH, and in so being upheld Israel witnesses to what it means to be a creature before the Creator. Therefore, the line of supposed "purity" between God and this people is already *inter*sected, rendered "impure," or "contaminated." If the covenantal (not contractual) existence of this people means anything, it surely means this. This people is an analogy of creation itself, for its existence testifies to the "contaminated" relationship between God and what God has created. The covenantal people of Israel witnesses to crea-tion its own fruitful "contamination" before YHWH as its life-giving limit. And hence, this people cannot be superseded, for to supersede it represents the effort to establish fictive lines of purity within creation (is this not what whiteness, and its production of racialized bodies, sought to do?) and thus supersede the Creator. In his interhumanity, which is an intrahumanity, Jesus as the Israel of God *is* the livinig reality of the covenantal promises of the God of Israel. He therefore is the discourse (*Logos*) of creation, the one in whom all of the words of creation (*logoi*)—its differences, one might say—inhere. In the specificity of his Jewish, covenantal flesh, he is creation's life-giving limit. He is the living reality of YHWH's promises to Israel and thereby for the world. Jesus' existence, which is covenantally Jewish, is therefore Pentecostal.

In Christ, then, language is liberated from the fiction of purity and thus from every structure of dominance and slavery (this is how Irenaeus interprets sin and the fall of the first Adam [e.g., *AH-A* V.21.1–3]). Freed from the control of a master or mastering language—this is what Todorov describes when Nahuatl is established as the national native language so that it can be made subject to the colonial language of Spanish and ultimately Latin—language itself (that is, creation) is restored to its original freedom to signify its Creator. Christ enacts this linguistic liberation, the release of language and thus hu-mankind from the slavery of conquest and tyrannical possession. Yet it was precisely this vision of language and human existence that ancient Gnosticism on the one hand and the neo-Gnosticism of racial discourse that is the inner architecture of the modern/colonial world on the other hand sought to fore-

close. For both, being parasitic on a Christian theological vision of identity, refuse to reckon with what it means for Christian identity to function inside Israel's relationship with YHWH as YHWH's covenantal, not racial, people.

This leads to the other important aspect of Irenaeus's way of imagining how in Christ's flesh the recapitulation and so the liberation occur of all languages, nations, and generations from structures of tyranny. He is clear that it occurs in relationship to Christ's flesh specifically as a recapitulation of Israel's story. In short, Christ's fleshly recapitulation of all nations and languages—indeed, his recapitulation of creation as such—is concentrated in his recapitulation of Israel as the people of YHWH's covenant. This comes out in two important passages, AH-G III.22.2 and III.22.4.

In the first passage, Irenaeus has just answered the question of why Christ proceeds from the woman Mary when the first Adam does not proceed from the woman Eve. His answer is that there is really no contradiction, for as "the first Adam was taken from the [virgin] earth and fashioned by the Word of God, [so also] it was necessary that the Word himself, working in himself the recapitulation of Adam, possessed a like origin" (AH-G III.21.10). In the next section Irenaeus asks a rhetorical follow-up question: "Why would Christ have come down into [Mary] if he was to receive nothing from her?" He answers in effect that beginning with her fiat Christ receives everything from her, for "if he had received nothing from Mary he would never have taken foods derived from the earth" (AH-G III.22.2). At this point, Irenaeus signals how through Mary, Christ is tied to all humanity and so recapitulates the order of creation, insofar as he, like all human beings, required "food derived from the earth." But then he says the following:

> [And if he had received nothing from Mary] . . . after fasting forty days like Moses and Elijah he would not have felt hunger because his body needed food; John his disciple would not have written of him: "Jesus sat, wearied from the journey" (John 4:6); nor would David have proclaimed, "They have added to the pain of my wounds" (Ps. 69:26); he would not have wept over Lazarus (John 11:35); he would not have sweated drops of blood (Luke 22:44); he would not have said, "My soul grieves" (Matt. 26:38), nor would blood and water have come forth from his pierced side (John 19:34). All these are signs of the flesh taken from the earth, which he recapitulated in himself, saving what he had formed. (AH-G III.22.2)

It is evident here that Irenaeus imagines the *simultaneous* recapitulation of the stories of creation and of Israel as centered in the narrative witness to Jesus. There is for him only one conclusion: these are not two different stories. Their relationship is one in which Israel concentrates the story of creation in itself. YHWH's story with Israel is the hermeneutic of creation. Irenaeus wants to establish how the discourse of creation and the discourse of Israel constitute a

singular discourse bound together in Jesus' body. They are a theological preface to Christology, a preface that, in fact, carries Christological content. But the story of Israel, which Mary concentrates in herself and that she passes on to Jesus as his mother, necessarily mediates that content.

Irenaeus makes the point about the triangulated relationship between creation, Israel–Mary, and Christ as held together through the notion of recapitulation in another text. He is engaged in theological exegesis of Luke 1:38, which speaks of Mary's fiat, in relationship to Gen. 2 and the story of Eve:

> Like the Lord, the Virgin Mary is also found obedient when she says, "Behold your servant, Lord, may it be for me according to your word" (Luke 1:38), but Eve, disobedient, for she disobeyed while still a virgin. For just as Eve had Adam for a husband but was still a virgin . . . and by disobeying became the cause of death for herself and the whole human race, so also Mary, with a husband predestined for her but yet a virgin, was obedient and became the cause of salvation for herself and the whole human race. (AH-G III.22.4)

Irenaeus to this point has been speaking of how Christ recapitulates creation, that is, the first Adam, but does so by means of Mary's fiat. However, the fiat in fact recapitulates Eve, too. Irenaeus then almost imperceptibly shifts into a new register, that of how the recapitulation of creation in Christ's flesh under the aspect of Mary's fiat is at the same time a recapitulation of Israel, the Law, and the Prophets in Christ's flesh. Making this point, the above passage continues:

> For this reason the Law calls the one betrothed to a man the wife of the one betrothing her, even though she is still a virgin, signifying the recycling that Mary effected for Eve. For what has been tied cannot be loosed unless one reverses the ties of the knot so that the first ties are undone by the second, and the second free the first: thus it happens that the first tie is unknotted by the second and the second has the place of a tie for the first. This is why the Lord said that the first would be the last and the last first (Matt. 19:30, 20:16); and the prophet indicates the same thing saying, "In place of the fathers that they were, they became your sons" (Ps. 45:16). For the Lord becoming the First-born from the dead (Col. 1:18) and receiving the ancient fathers into his bosom, regenerated them into the life of God [anegennêsen autous eis zôên Theou], himself becoming the first of the living because Adam had become the first of the dead. (AH-G III.22.4; SC III.2.443)

Having progressed from the recapitulation of creation to that of Israel, the passage reaches its theological centerpoint in Christ, who recapitulates the "ancient fathers" in his flesh. Irenaeus says that this enacts a reversal of

the order of birth. Christ gives birth—his term is "regenerate" (*anagennaô*)—to Israel's patriarchs: paradoxically, the son gives birth to the parents.

But Irenaeus does not stop here. The recapitulating cycle then loops back, so to speak, for in regenerating the patriarchs of Israel, he says, Christ in effect became Adam again. Having passed through the theology of Israel, Christological discourse expands back out to creation. This reading is confirmed by the way Irenaeus concludes his reflections here. He turns to a reflection on the Lucan account of Christ's birth, showing that it expands back to creation: "This is why Luke (3:23–38) began his genealogy with the Lord to trace it back from him to Adam, thus indicating that the fathers did not give life to the Lord but he regenerated them in the Gospel of life." But this is because the woman Mary, through her fiat, is the mediating cause of salvation: "So too the knot of Eve's disobedience was loosed by Mary's obedience, for what the virgin Eve had bound by her unfaith, the virgin Mary loosed by her faith."

In arguing this way, it is as if Irenaeus is saying that the recapitulation of all things in Christ occurs in a concentric feedback loop. Creation itself is a concentrated expression of the love the Father has for the eternal Son through the Holy Spirit. That is, it is a condensed narrative that captures without diluting the rhetorical plotline of the depths of God's love for the Son, a love that embraces within itself even that which is not God (i.e., creation). In this sense, creation in its own way recapitulates the divine life as the "structure of supreme love."[22] But then as if even this condensed story were still too prolix, YHWH presents the story of Israel, beginning with the call of Abram-become-Abraham to create ex nihilo a people who before did not exist, as a compendium of the story of creation, which too came into being. And so to grasp the story of Israel is to grasp the story of creation. And finally again, in an effort to contain what yet appears to be too elongated a narrative filled with plot twists, reversals, and surprises, Christ himself "cuts short" the story of Israel into the résumé of his own material body and historical life, only then to have this loop back to the story of creation, but now under the aspect of the second Eve. He is the biography of this people and as such is the biography of creation. But in so being, he proves to be God's own autobiography, God's writing of Godself.

Arguably there are three ways to understand these concentric relationships and their feedback loop, all of which are necessary for the integrity of theology as a discourse.[23] The first way to understand them is linearly, or diachronically. Here the plotline of the story of YHWH's love begins with creation, moves to the story of Israel, and culminates in the story of Christ and the *Triduum mortis*. In diachrony, the narrative of God's love follows the linear progression of the scriptural narrative as we canonically have it, beginning with the creation stories. Concentrating in itself the entire narrative of YHWH's love, creation becomes the optic through which to see the subsequent moments of the narrative. Creation concentrates in itself the story of Israel and the gospel of

Christ's cross even as it diachronically points ahead to these episodes of the drama.

But there are two additional ways of understanding the narrative of YHWH's love, both of which are synchronic as opposed to diachronic. In the first form of synchrony, creation as proton and Christ as eschaton are read through the mediating term of Israel and the story of this covenantal people with YHWH. Coming in the middle of time, Israel "cuts short" the story of creation. Its existence concentrates creation. And yet as the middle term between creation and Christ, Israel is a condition of possibility of the final movement in the narrative, just as Mary is a condition of the final movement. Hence, Israel–Mary is the condition of possibility, the mediating causality in the order of redemption, of the coming of Christ. In this way, beginning and end, proton and eschaton, are read in media res—and must be so read.

The second form of synchrony—and the final way of understanding the concentric relationship between creation, Israel, and Christ and their feedback—like the first form of synchrony also disrupts a purely linear ordering of time. It disrupts diachrony insofar as it concentrates the beginning that is creation and the middle that is Israel in the eschatological end of Christ's flesh. In this regard, the eschaton is not merely last (as in diachrony). It is first. It is proton also. Here the eschaton is first. Irenaeus grants theological priority to this dimension of the concentric relationships, for from his perspective it was Christ as the Word of God who was always at work from the beginning of creation. Christ is the concrete form of the mystery of YHWH's love in its progression toward ever-increasing visibility in the order of creation–redemption. Indeed, it is precisely this love that brings creation–Israel, the first and second terms in the economy (*oikonomia*), into being. And yet, though he prioritizes the eschatological aspect of synchrony, the emphasis on the person and work of Christ does not mean the supersession of either creation or Israel. The second aspect of synchrony replaces neither the first aspect of synchrony nor the diachronic aspect of YHWH's love. Each aspect of YHWH's love as read through Scripture and as constitutive of human identity must work simultaneously to give an adequate account of what it means to enter into Christ's flesh.

Irenaeus's grand theological point is that if any one of the aspects of the concentric relationships between creation, Israel, and Christ is lost, theology as discourse becomes distorted into a Gnostic or Gnostic-like discourse of death.

In the specific case of ancient Gnosticism, an emphasis on the second aspect of synchrony (i.e., Christology) apart from the diachrony (i.e., creation) and the first aspect of synchrony (i.e., Israel) skewed the discourse of theology toward a discourse of death, the death of material existence. The Gnostics refused the concentric relationship of diachrony, which highlights the materiality of creation, and they refused the first aspect of synchrony, which highlights Israel as the people of YHWH's law and covenantal promises. The ancient Gnostics thus ended up with a nonmaterial Christ (one situated be-

tween pneumatic and psychic mankind), one lacking interhuman and inter-linguistic Jewish flesh, flesh that was not embedded in the history of Israel. Moreover, in lacking such flesh and history, there was a disconnect between Christ and the history of non-Jewish peoples and their languages. Lacking all of this, in the hands of the Gnostics, theology as a discourse lacked internal buffers against the protoracial development of an anthropological hierarchy of essences that could function inside Christian theology itself.

Conclusion: Toward a Theological Account of Race

But what of the discourse of modern theology, particularly as it relates to the modern practice and discourse of race? In part I (chapters 1 and 2) of this book, to which this account of Irenaeus's engagement with ancient Gnosticism is a prelude, I tell the story of how the loss of the first aspect of synchrony—the aspect pertaining to Israel—as a meaningful feature of Christian identity in modernity made possible the emergence of a racial imagination. More specifically, I tell the story of how the loss of a Jewish-inflected account—and thus a covenantal, nonracial account—of Christian identity cleared the way for whiteness to function as a replacement doctrine of creation. Hence, the world was re-created from the colonial conquests from the late fifteenth century forward in the image of white dominance, where "white" signifies not merely pigmentation but a regime of political and economic power for arranging (*oikonomia*) the world. To use the language of critical theorist Walter Mignolo and sociologist Immanuel Wallerstein, "white" is a locution for the "modern/colonial" (Mignolo) "world-system" (Wallerstein).[24] Chapter 2 reads Immanuel Kant's theorizing of race as in effect theorizing whiteness as the moment of (racial) creation linked to the overcoming of Jewish flesh. In this way I seek to outline the neo-Gnosticism of modern racial discourse generally and of whiteness particularly and isolate its theological moment of arising. Part I presses toward a theological account of the modern problem of race.

Part II (chapters 3–5) tells of the African American religious academy's effort to in some sense diagnose this situation, as Irenaeus had to diagnose the ancient Gnostic situation. The constructive theological argument of part III shows how aspects of Afro-Christianity, particularly in its dawning moments in North America, are Irenaean insofar as Christian identity is thought of in theologically diachronic *and* synchronic terms. Hence, the time of black folks is situated inside the time of Israel, where in the economy of redemption, both creation and Jesus himself are situated, and thus inside the historical transcendence of YHWH or the "time" of God.[25] This positions Afro-Christian faith to offer a narration of racialized existence that transcends the narrative of racial oppression constitutive of the New World drama. It positions Afro-Christian faith, precisely by virtue of being Christian in the non-

supersessionist sense outlined here, to offer a different account of the meaning of those "raced" into the "purity" of blackness and more broadly those "raced" into the various "purities" of nonwhiteness in the New World. Christ's life recapitulates racialized existence, in this case black racialized existence, in such a way as to inaugurate a new narrative of freedom. So understood, Afro-Christian faith, as was the case with Irenaeus's account of Christian identity forged in the kiln of his engagement with Ptolemaeic Gnosticism, embodies an effort to rescue the discourse of theology from being a discourse of death. But this is to get ahead of the story. For now, I turn to parts I and II, "Dramatizing Race" and "Engaging Race."

PART I

Dramatizing Race

A Theological Account of Modernity

I

The Drama of Race

Toward a Theological Account of Modernity

For my own part, I think the specific articulation of racism is within nationalism . . . . The fundamental problem therefore [has been] to produce the people. More exactly, it [has been] to make the people produce itself as a national community.
—Étienne Balibar, preface, *Race, Nation, Class: Ambiguous Identities*

The war that is going on beneath order and peace, the war that undermines our society and divides it in a binary mode is, basically, a race war . . . [one in which the] social body is articulated around two races.
—Michel Foucault, *"Society Must Be Defended": Lectures at the Collège de France, 1975–1976*

Over the course of this and the next chapter I provide an account of the problem of race that differs from what is typically given. Indeed, I attempt to position this problem inside what may appear to be an altogether unrelated issue—namely, the question of what is religious or "pseudotheological"[1] about our modern forms of sociopolitical life generally and about the modern state, or what the political philosopher Étienne Balibar has termed the "nation form," in particular.[2] More specifically, I make a case for how matters of race, religion, and the modern state as the organizing form of civil society and public culture are far from unrelated. In considering the question of race within this constellation of concerns, I analyze how, in fact, race functions to support the coming-to-be and the

sustaining of modern society at an inarticulate level. This inarticulate level is the level of what Fredric Jameson has called "the political unconscious."[3]

To give voice to the politically unconscious level of modern social and political life is to give attention to the modern problem of race. But it is not only this; for to render articulate the modern political unconscious is to give attention to the problem of race under the aspect of the modern problem of religion. It is to account for the modern problem of race in relationship to the *Judenfrage*, the so-called Jewish question, inasmuch as the *Judenfrage* is at the core of the modern problem of race, religion, and the politics of the modern state. In asking the Jewish question, modern intellectuals—from philosophers and statesmen to legal, orientalist, and biblical scholars—struggled to reckon with the theological and political significance of Jewish existence in light of a newly emerging, enlightened social arrangement within the Occident, an arrangement that they themselves promoted. It is this social arrangement that I refer to when I speak of modernity. Over the course of chapters 1 and 2, I query the connections between the question of race (or the *Rassenfrage*) and the *Judenfrage* in grounding the modern world. In querying the connections, I seek to establish that the modern problem of race is ill understood, if not misunderstood, if how the theological (or more precisely the quasi-theological or pseudotheological) functions politically is not accounted for, indeed, if what is theopolitical about the modern world in its colonial unfolding is not accounted for.[4]

I say theological *and* political (or theopolitical) to signal that my claim calls for analyses of the problem of race (and, relatedly, of the Jewish question) that explore the senses in which such a discourse is bound to the nature and practice of modern politics and thereby indelibly tied to what is religious about modernity and the way it parodies theology at the same time that it cloaks this fact. The discourse of race is critical to the cloaking process and thus functions as a vital cog within modernity's own religious and quasi-theological machinery, a machinery intent, as the quotation by Étienne Balibar that opens this chapter alerts us, on producing bodies and people, but bodies and people of a particular sort. It produces bodies and people that can populate an enlightened, global, and cosmopolitan social order, the domain of civil society.[5] The people produced is the modern citizenry; the body, that of the modern citizen; and the social order enacted and perpetuated, that of the modern (nation-)state. Given this, the politics of race and the politics of the modern state are of a piece, for both are religious or pseudotheological in character. Failing to reckon with this fact not only leaves the problem of modern racial reasoning inadequately understood but also can yield responses that risk—unwittingly, no doubt—reinhabiting, at the politically unconscious, theopolitical level, the very problem that needs overcoming.

In chapter 2, I scrutinize this inarticulate, theopolitical level of the problem by exploring the linkages that emerge around race, religion, and the discourse on the modern state in the cultural exchange of ideas that took place as late-

eighteenth-century German intellectuals—who were inspired by the Enlightenment (*Aufklärung*) and who were the vanguard of an emerging, nonaristocratic German middle class (*Bildungsbürgertum*)—sought to respond to the sociopolitical crisis that confronted them. The crisis confronting these intellectuals (*Aufklärer*, as I may call them) was their increasing disillusionment regarding the viability of an enlightened state founded on the principles of "enlightened despotism or absolutism" and over the reactionary turn on the part of some in Prussia and across the German territories away from Enlightenment proposals for the rational organization of society. The political moment that best represented the Prussian culture's reaction against *Aufklärung* was the ascendancy of Frederick William II to the Prussian throne after the death of Frederick the Great in 1786. The two rulers represented divergent intellectual and political sensibilities: Frederick was sympathetic to and, indeed, a promoter of the Enlightenment cause;[6] Frederick William, by contrast, was the *Aufklärung*'s avowed enemy, seeing in it the source of what he took to be Prussian cultural decay. In this feeling, Frederick William represented the sentiments of many Prussians.

How did Enlightenment thinkers, whose political influence had now come to a breaking point and whose social positions as the arbiters of public culture were now threatened, respond to this situation? Well, beginning in the 1770s and throughout the 1780s, they began reexamining the nature of politics in general, and the nature of civil society and the politics attending public culture—that zone between the private (or the domestic) and the political (or the arena of statecraft)—in particular. Their goal was to reconstitute this zone, the domain of public culture, in light of the changing cultural and political situation and thereby reconstitute the social order as such. Aesthetics—understood more as the study of sensibility or sense phenomena apart from its subjection to the deterministic laws of nature, and less, as more recent understandings would tend to have it, as the study of "art for art's sake"—would prove crucial to the ambitions of the *Aufklärer* to reconstitute the body politic through a reconstitution of public culture.[7] Aesthetics was a way of talking about the autonomy of the reasoning subject. My objective is to probe how race and religion figured in the *Aufklärer*'s efforts to reimagine the meaning of public culture vis-à-vis an aesthetics and politics of autonomy and thereby to solve their crisis.

To illuminate these matters, I focus attention on the theorist who has the distinction of having bequeathed to the modern world not just one of the most influential accounts of the meaning of Enlightenment, politics, and civil society but also its first rigorously scientific and philosophically sophisticated and, hence, its first fully developed theory of race. That thinker is Immanuel Kant.[8] Mediating between Kant's vision of politics and his vision of public culture, and thus what is at the heart of his vision of a reconstituted body politic, is his account of the human being as autonomous or as abstracted from

the body, from materiality, and therefore from all worldly goods. The grand presumption that enabled the Kantian anthropological vision, however, was his ceding of ownership of the body and the goods of this world to the state. With the state's ownership of the body as an unarguable issue for him, he could then imagine the individual as the palette on which the state publicly displayed its power, especially by calling bodies to wage war in the name of the body politic. The challenge confronting *Aufklärer* like Kant was how to form (*bilden*) autonomous people and thus citizen or cosmopolitan subjects in the face of a racial-oriental alien within the Prussian-occidental body politic: an alien whose "national character" was given to heteronomy, and thus toward the body, rather than autonomy. This racial alien, who was a potential contagion to the body politic, was the Jew. The challenge of both public and political culture was how to overcome this racially heteronymous element.

Thus, a large part of my task is to establish that the trajectories of race on the one hand and politics and public culture on the other were not independent. Indeed, it is to show how they hold together. More specifically, it is to establish that a two-sided issue binds together the Kantian vision and, by extension, the ongoing "project" of modernity. That two-sided issue concerns the theopolitical question of the meaning of Jewish existence for a world coming of age as modern on the one hand and the question of the political and pseudotheological significance ascribed to whiteness as the basis of Western civilization on the other.[9]

This foreshadows features of the argument in chapter 2, however. Here, as a prolegomenon to chapter 2, I consider two important, contemporary accounts of the problem of race: two attempts to narrate the story of the modern invention of race that starts gesturing in some of the directions just suggested. These accounts are important not because of their success in telling this story—in fact, I judge their telling of the story helpful but, in the end, inadequate—but because they identify key components of the story, components that in the next chapter I reassemble into a different narrative of race, religion, and the formation of modernity.

The first account of race has been influential both within and outside the black religious academy. It is the genealogy of race offered by philosopher of religion Cornel West, as detailed in his early work, *Prophesy Deliverance! An Afro-American Revolutionary Christianity.*[10] The endgame of my engagement with West's account of race is not simply its refutation. By investigating his account of the problem and calling attention to its most prominent limitations, I seek to begin building a rationale for approaching the problem of race differently: a rationale that puts theology at the center of an interrogation of the modern problem of race. It is just this that one is unable to do inside of West's framework but that must be done in order to disclose the inner workings of modernity's racial dilemma. In this respect, then, I am interested in what is inadequate about West's account of race and in viewing this inadequacy as

emblematic of what is inadequate in a number of recent analyses of the problem. The inadequacy concerns the fact that there is little to no engagement with what is religious, theological, and political—all at the same time—about the problem; that is, there is little to no engagement with the convergence of the theological and the political in modernity's construction of race. In short, then, in the first part of this chapter I query why a theopolitical account of the problem of race, one that isolates the ways in which this discourse arises as a parody of theology, has not been forthcoming.

In the second part of the chapter, I look at another recent, also genea-logical, account of race, that formulated by the French philosopher Michel Foucault in his 1975–1976 Collège de France lectures, *Society Must Be Defended*.[11] Though Foucault's genealogy of race chronologically precedes West's, it is only now beginning to garner serious attention in the English-speaking world. One reason for this inattention has been the general inaccessibility of Foucault's lectures to a wider readership.[12] But though Foucault dealt most extensively with the problem of race in the lectures—to the point of offering a genealogy both of it and of the modern state—he also offered an important account of modern racial discourse in the last chapter of the introductory volume of his *La Volente de savoir* (or *The History of Sexuality*, as the title has been translated into English).[13] Apart from the fact that West's notion of genealogy is of Foucauldian pedigree and therefore a consideration of Foucault can shed some light on West's own agenda, my interest in Foucault is larger than filling out West's intellectual background. I address Foucault's account of race because of the assistance it gives me in establishing a rationale for ap-proaching the problem of race differently. It does this in two respects.

First, apart from the fact that his account of race holds significant promise for critical theorizing about race, as the work of such scholars as Ann Laura Stoler, Étienne Balibar, Giorgio Agamben, and others makes clear, Foucault's work on race is important for my argument because his analysis of the problem takes into account what West's does not: Foucault's analysis of the problem of race is bound to an analysis of the problem of the modern nation form—to the problem, that is, of how the modern state gives form, shape, and substance to the political. In saying this, I do not mean to insinuate that only Foucault's account of race makes this move. One need but look to the work of David Theo Goldberg or Paul Gilroy or Charles W. Mills for other examples. Each of these theorists engages the problem of race and makes connections between modern racial discourse and the discourse of modernity and its politics. Thus each of them in his own way offers an important correction to the silence hovering over West's account of the problem.

Second, Foucault's genealogy goes further. His engagement with the prob-lem of race is not content to simply mandate an engagement with the problem of modern politics; his genealogy of race, which he positions within a gene-alogy of the state, makes important moves in opening onto a genealogy of

religion, one that would identify how the *Judenfrage* functions as the constantly ramifying inner mechanism that propels modernity and moves its discourse of race. In other words, Foucault's account of the problem points to the need to answer the question, What is religious and pseudotheological about modern racial discourse and the discourse of modernity? I argue that Foucault's work, including his work on race, provides the rudiments of an answer. His work on race and the links he suggests between it, religion, and politics must, therefore, be reckoned with. Indeed, through the links he sees between these supposedly separate regions of knowledge, Foucault brings us into the vestibule of the modern problem of race. And yet, because it is unable to make the full turn toward an analysis of what is *theo*political and pseudo*theological* about the problem of race, it, too, I argue, is finally inadequate. Hence, the task of chapter 2: to provide a theological account or a theological theorizing of the problem of race. But first, to West's genealogy of the problem.

Cornel West's Genealogy of Race

How have recent accounts of the modern problem of race answered the following questions: What are the factors that made possible the invention of "homo racialis" and out of this "homo ethnicus," the human being conceived of as a race-bearing and then an ethnicity-bearing animal?[14] And what are the mechanisms by which those factors interacted so as to make thinking of persons in racial terms not just a possibility but, indeed, an inevitability? To begin to answer these questions, I consider Cornel West's genealogy of modern racism as he elaborated it in *Prophesy Deliverance*. His genealogy is important because in probing the factors that made possible "the emergence . . . of the idea of white supremacy . . . within the epistemological field of modern discourse [in the West]," he offers an answer to these questions.[15] But I am interested not only in the answers he gives; I am just as interested in the method he employs for arriving at those answers. That method is the method of genealogy.

It is important to understand what this method is *not* designed to do. In employing genealogy West shows that he is less concerned with making strictly historical claims about white supremacy. He is less concerned, as a purely historical matter, with the variegated expressions of white supremacy as, for instance, in the American Jim Crow South or any other site of the "black Atlantic." This is not to imply that West opposes historical interrogations of the problem of race and racism; indeed, to an important degree his work presupposes historical inquiry into the problem. But West is out to isolate what is quite often difficult to isolate on strictly historical terms, namely, what it is about "the very structure of modern discourse *at its inception*" that allowed and even mandated it to "[produce] forms of rationality, scientificity and objectivity

as well as aesthetic and cultural ideals" that "require[d] the constitution of the idea of white supremacy."[16]

Moreover, he wants to get at "the evolving"—and, by implication, the ongoing and metamorphosing—"internal dynamics of the structure of modern discourse in the late seventeenth and eighteenth centuries in western Europe—or during the Enlightenment." He is interested in what it is about this structure that would allow it to produce a modernist discourse in politics, economics, law, and so forth *along with* a discourse on race. Investigating the problem in this way allows West, in some sense, to explain how modernity's internal dynamics and factors operate "discursive[ly to exclude]...the idea...of black equality in beauty, culture, and intellectual capacity." In short, he wants to explore the micrologics of modernity, to deconstruct or conjugate its history so as to explore how the "idea [of black equality]" came to be banished and finally "silence[d]."[17]

Naming the factors that have contributed to the silencing of black aesthetic, cultural, and intellectual equality and how it is that those factors conspired to "require the constitution of white supremacy" demands a procedure for analyzing them other than, but not to the exclusion of, history—at least, history as it typically functions as a way of making truth claims by simply delimiting the facts of what happened in the past. That something other for West is the genealogical method, for genealogy is that mode of inquiry suited to probing how power operates and reinvents itself under new, constantly evolving circumstances. West is careful to distinguish his inquiry into power in relationship to race from what he calls the historiography of the "revisionists and vulgar Marxist(s)," who focus more or less on power as it operates through concrete historical actors, be they individuals (such as sovereigns or any other potentate) or collectives (such as parliaments or mobs). West tells us that his mode of genealogical inquiry focuses instead on the "subjectless" powers driving modern Western discourse. Modern racism and its embedded notion of race, according to West, arises indirectly from these subjectless powers that are always at work in "the praxis of human subjects."[18]

Before looking more closely at what West takes the elements of modern discourse to be, it is worth considering what West means by power, how exactly it can be subjectless, and why this matters for coming to terms with the racial dimensions of modern discourse and ways of being in the world. To do this, it is important to come to terms with what he means by speaking of a *structure* to modern discourse. Having reckoned with what West means in speaking this way, we can reckon with how he understands modern racial discourse in terms of modernity's structure.

West's objective is to put an end to any understanding of race that would see it as a static, nonmutating category, a category that corresponds, so to speak, with a purportedly real racial *something*—actual races, one might say—out there in the world. Viewing matters in this way is an example of the philosophical

problem of representationalism about which philosophers such as Richard Rorty have much to criticize.[19] As regards the problem of race, a representationalist outlook supposes that there are stable and immutable ideas about race or the races that correspond to and thus represent the empirical phenomena of the various races. West rejects this idealist way of thinking about race and, indeed, sees it as part of the problem. He rejects it because even the idea of race is historically situated and constituted. This, therefore, means that the idea of race, bounded by the flux of time and history, is under constant change and negotiation. Under a representationalist gaze, to talk about race is to talk about the idea or the *thought* of race. According to West, this is wrongheaded. For him, to interrogate race is to interrogate not so much *thought* about race, which expresses itself as a kind of metaphysical idealism that more or less essentializes race by having the idea of race or racial essences float above a racialized reality. Rather, to interrogate race is to interrogate our *thinking* about it, which is always already linked to embodied structures within which race, or what is often meant by it, is known only in the realities of life itself.

To interrogate modernity's *thinking* about race is to interpret it within the arc of time and to see its emergence as reflexive of political and cultural, or more simply historical, change. Hence, a nonrepresentationalist approach to race commits us not just to coming to terms with how the idea of race evolves; it commits us to reckoning with both the changing cultures and historical sites within which ideas about race traffic and with the structure or rule-governed grammar, the micrologics, according to which racial ideas and practices shift and mutate. One might say that the historian, strictly speaking, takes up the former inquiry, while genealogists such as West, take up the latter. As a genealogist, West is interested in the structure or the grammar by which race is a cultural production that in constantly reproducing itself has a reflexive and thus circular effect on culture. A schema of representational correspondence in which the pure, metaphysical idea of race is parallel to the empirical reality of race is inadequate to the actual state of things. Indeed, it is a ruse that papers over the actual state of things. West is convinced that the more appropriate way to get at the problem of modern racism, then, is by reckoning with "the life and logic" of the structure of power that flows through the subjects and institutional apparatuses of culture, subjects and institutional apparatuses that themselves are logically distinct from and therefore relatively independent of culture itself.[20]

But a quick caveat lest West be misunderstood. The independence of subjects and apparatuses does not mean a reversion to the idealism and philosophical representationalism that he follows Rorty in criticizing. West is simply trying to account for the fact that ideas about race can and do affect culture, leading to effects that go beyond the subjects and institutional apparatuses through whom and in which the so-called ideas of race are enacted. It is for this reason that West wants to engage the "subjectless" quality of power as

regards race and modern racism. This is what he means when he says that power has a "life and logic of [its] own, [but] not in a transhistorical realm." Its life and logic unfold "alongside [of, though it is] not reducible to[, the] demands of an economic system, interests of a class, or needs of a group."[21] In saying this, West reflects the influence of Foucault's conception of power, which of course is linked to Foucault's genealogical method.[22]

To clarify this point, it might be worthwhile to briefly turn to Foucault himself. Power, Foucault tells us, is not reducible to a "general system of dominance exerted by one group over another, a system whose effects, through successive derivations, pervade the entire social body."[23] He further contends that "the analysis made in terms of power must not assume that the sovereignty of the state, the form of the law, or the over-all unity of a domination are given at the outset; rather, these are only the terminal forms power takes."[24] If not in these terminal forms, in what then does power consist? Foucault's answer to this is crucial for West's own conception of power and how it can be understood as subjectless while not being a metaphysical idea. Foucault says:

> It seems to me that power must be understood in the first instance as
> the multiplicity of force relations immanent in the sphere in which
> they operate and which constitute their own organization; as the
> process which, through ceaseless struggles and confrontations,
> transforms, strengthens, or reverses [those relations]; as the support
> which these force relations find in one another, thus forming a chain
> or a system; ... and lastly, as the strategies in which they take effect,
> whose general design or institutional crystallization is embodied
> in the state apparatus, in the formulation of the law, in the various
> social hegemonies.[25]

West's effort to probe the structure of modern discourse and the coming-to-be of modern racism in terms of subjectless power must be understood against this Foucauldian understanding of power.

West, like Foucault, is not only interested in "the terminal forms of power"—that is, in its final and various "institutional crystallization(s)." He wants to access the ubiquitous "substrate of force relations" that makes modern discourse what it is, for this substrate is the matrix out of which white supremacy arises and ramifies.[26] To use a Foucauldian idiom, West wants to analyze modern racism in terms of modern discourse and thus in terms of that "permanent, repetitious, inert, and self-reproducing ... [power] effect" that always already envelops and subtends everything.[27] In this way, modern racism will be analyzed not in terms of a given historical moment; rather, it will be analyzed in terms of its historicity: that is, in terms of history's own inner logic or mechanisms that are always present with and within any given moment. It is fair to say, though West does not put it this way, that to account for these mechanisms of modern discourse is to account for the mechanisms of modern

racism, and to account for the mechanisms of modern racism is to account for the mechanisms of history as a mode of knowledge and truth in the West. It is to offer a philosophy of history. Thus West's effort to explicate modern racism in terms of the structure of modern discourse (and in accordance with the ubiquity of power as the "intentional and nonsubjective"[28]—understood in Foucauldian terms, as the "grid of intelligibility of the social order"[29]) is an effort to explicate it in terms of a philosophy of modern racism and thus, as just intimated, in terms of a philosophy that accounts for history's immanent dynamism.

A twofold point, then, can be made that captures Foucault's significance for West's genealogical project. First (and to continue to employ Foucault's framework, which West draws on), power must be understood in terms of its varying "local centers"[30] and through the nodes on the "dense web...[of] apparatuses and institutions ... [through which it] passes ... [but] without being exactly localized in them."[31] But one cannot stop here, for to do so is to follow the path of vulgar Marxism, the path on which power is understood reductively in terms of its most palpable manifestations in a given time and place and according to the dictates of "a specific state structure,...[an] over-all domination,...[or in] law."[32] West, like Foucault, is not content to rest with such a notion of power, one that understands power as exhausted in and thus wholly intelligible in terms of its subjective manifestations.

Hence, the second way in which power must be understood: in terms of its inertness, its permanency, and its subjectlessness. Understood from this vantage, power is not limited to some local concentration or manifestation. It is inert, but not in the sense that it is static. Rather, it is inert in the sense that the system of constantly circulating and ramifying relations that constitute power, the relations that make it what it is, is never supervened by power's local manifestations. Instead, local manifestations of power exhibit, as Foucault says, "pattern[s]"[33] intrinsic both to the changing dynamics of relationships of force and to the modes of knowing that attend those processes. Foucault's genealogy of modern racism, as I argue more fully below, pays careful attention to the former (what it is that makes relationships of force what they are) in order to better probe the latter (the knowledge that arises out of and accompanies such relationships). Indeed, for Foucault, genealogy cannot separate the two since it is genealogy's task to probe their interconnection. West's genealogy, by contrast, gives little to no attention to the former and instead moves straightaway to the latter. This has problematic repercussions for his overall account of race.

However, before addressing these repercussions directly, I first need to briefly consider what accrues to West in approaching the matter in the way he has—that is, in homing in on the features of Enlightenment knowledge that are conducive to the idea of white supremacy. The chief benefit is that it allows him to focus critical attention on the "discursive structure" or power grid within

which changing relationships of force, such as that of white supremacy, operate in the modern world. On inspection, West discerns a tripartite structure to the "metaphors, notions, categories, and norms"[34] that circumscribe how people of African descent come to be situated in the modern imagination. The first historical process or structural dimension to modern discourse that makes the circumscription of black life possible is the scientific revolution, the second is the Cartesian transformation of philosophy, and the last is the classical revival.[35] The first of these processes is important because it marked a shift in the ground of authority for affirmations of truth. The locus of authority is no longer in the domain of the church. It is now lodged in science and in science's procedures of verification through observation and the collection of evidence. Through observation and evidence scientific laws can be advanced and discoveries made.

Closely linked to this shift in the locus of authority from the church to science is the shift that occurred in philosophy. To justify this claim, West refers to the philosophies of Francis Bacon and René Descartes. The ideas of these two philosophers reveal how philosophy came to be marked by a new aim: namely—and this is said with specific reference to Bacon—"to give humankind mastery over nature by means of scientific discoveries and inventions."[36] But for West, Descartes is the defining figure because he articulates a philosophy that supports the general mission of human mastery over nature precisely by marking out a path from "the subject to objects, from the veil of ideas to the external world, from immediate awareness to extended substances, from self-consciousness to things in space, and ultimately from doubt to certainty."[37] That path is the path of representation. Indeed, it is the image or representation that links the subject in its interiority to the world in its exteriority.

But this is already to point toward the third historical process (and the one that is most crucial in West's analysis of the structure of modern discourse), the revival of classical aesthetics. Classical ideas of beauty fill the gap between the subject's picture or copy of reality and the actual things of the world. Thus aesthetic ideals are what provide ultimate authority in the modern world. They provide the means of authenticating the truth. As West points out, however, the problem with the way modern aesthetics works is that it establishes a "normative gaze"[38] by which it is determined that blacks do not adequately measure up to the standards of truth (in science), the good and morality (in philosophy), and beauty (in the aesthetics of culture). West is clear that the normalizing gaze does not emerge overnight. It unfolds in stages. First, there is the rise of natural histories with their grand classificatory schemes rooted in scientific observation. Following the claims of natural history is the biologizing of those claims through the rise of new "scientific" disciplines such as phrenology (the reading of skulls) and physiognomy (the reading of faces). But guiding all of this, West argues, are European values based in a retrieval of classical aesthetics and

cultural values.[39] With the discursive processes of the new science, the new philosophy, and the new aesthetics in place, modern discourse has embedded within itself the conditions for the coming-to-be of modern racism.

It is precisely at this point that the chief limitation of West's analysis presents itself. One senses that West himself is somewhat aware of the limitation and attempts to hedge, for having delineated his genealogy he moves to answer a question that might be raised against it: Was it *inevitable* that the idea of white supremacy, and thus the phenomenon of modern racism, would arise, given the structure of modern discourse and the forms of rationality, scientificity, and objectivity it spawned, or was the emergence of white supremacy and modern racism the result of a purely random confluence of certain conditions? West answers the question somewhat equivocally, for on the one hand, "there is an accidental character," he says, "to the discursive emergence of modern racism." And again, it emerges as the result of "a kind of free play of discursive powers which produce and prohibit, develop and delimit the legitimacy and intelligibility of certain ideas within a discursive space circumscribed by the attractiveness of classical antiquity."[40] In this respect, there is a contingency to the emergence of the idea of white supremacy and modern racism. Yet on the other hand, West is suspicious, even if the grounds of his suspicion are somewhat vague, of claims for what amounts to the utter contingency of the emergence of modern racism. He falls back and reiterates what his genealogy is meant to do and what it is not meant to do. He reminds us that it "does not purport to be an explanation of the rise of modern racism" as such; instead, it is "a theoretical inquiry into a particular neglected variable, i.e., the discursive factor" within reigning models that seek to explain the phenomenon of modern racism.[41]

Fair enough. But the question as to the inevitability or contingency of the discursive emergence of modern racism remains, particularly because his genealogy was billed as giving an account at the discursive level, which West problematically reduces to matters of epistemology, of why "the very structure of modern discourse at its inception . . . require[d] the constitution of the idea of white supremacy" as an expression of modern racism.[42] This is precisely what has not been shown, however. West's genealogy powerfully shows the epistemological, or what he calls the discursive, conditions that made possible the idea of white supremacy as an expression of modern racism, but it does not provide insight into the mechanisms by which those discursive factors interacted so that modern racism and the idea of white supremacy moved beyond epistemic possibility and into discursive actuality. West does not explain how the discursive factors that derive from the new science, the new philosophy, and the new aesthetics interact so as to constitute modern racism and to become what philosopher David Theo Goldberg has called an "ideological conception."[43] This is precisely what one is left wondering about in West's genea-

logical analysis, and it leaves unanswered the question of whether modern racism and the idea of white supremacy emerged contingently or of necessity.

To overcome this limitation, a method is needed that does more than simply hold constant certain so-called nondiscursive variables for the sake of analyzing the discursive ones alone. Rather, the two must be approached in their codeterminancy. Goldberg, in framing his own critique of West on similar matters, puts his finger on the problem: "The concept of 'racialized discourse' [must] show how, methodologically, socioeconomic materiality [West's non-discursive factors] and ideological conception [something closer to West's discursive factors] are mutually interactive and codetermining."[44] Goldberg further argues that to penetrate to the level of how socioeconomic materiality and ideological conception (the purportedly nondiscursive and discursive factors) interact is, among other things, to uncover the "grammar," or the deep structure, of modern racial discourse. It is to reckon with the "preconceptual plane" and the "primitive terms" on which and by which modern racial reasoning is what it is precisely in and through its varied regionalized expressions across space and despite the changes it undergoes through time.[45] It is this cultural grammar and inner lexicon, a grammar and lexicon that mediate the meanings of race, that West's genealogy leaves undeveloped.

The genius of Goldberg's insight is that, building on thinkers like Foucault and Balibar, he sees a deep link between racial knowledge and social science on the one hand and what Foucauldian political philosophers Michael Hardt and Antonio Negri have more recently called the "modern sovereign or absolutist state" on the other.[46] As Goldberg says,

> [There is a] relation between formally produced racialized knowledge, especially at the hands of social science, and the State. Étienne Balibar insists that the relationship to the Other at the heart of modern racism is necessarily mediated by State intervention. One of the basic modes this intervention assumes is concern over production of racialized knowledge. State conceptual mediation is as old as the category of *race* itself.[47]

Hence, it is in probing the connections between modern discourse and the discourse of the state (which then mutates into a discourse on the nation) that genealogy might begin to seize on the *Entstehung*, the moment of arising, of modern racism at the level of its inner cultural grammar and syntax. The risk of not probing this connection is that the discourse of the modern state, which is really a discourse on a particular form of political constitution and community, might itself be assumed (even if under the banner of democracy) at its most problematic moments, rather than critically interrogated. This section is an attempt to show that just such a problem—the problem of assuming rather than critically interrogating the forms of modern statecraft and the work

religion is called on to do in founding and maintaining those forms—may be going on in West's genealogy of modern racism and in the broader argument of *Prophesy Deliverance.*[48]

At fault in all of this is the problematic bracketing of the nondiscursive factors surrounding the formation of a racial and even colonial imagination in the modern world. It is problematic for at least two reasons. First, attention is not given to the specifically theological and religious dimensions of the emergence of such a modern racial/colonial imagination as they embed themselves in the discourse of the state. This omission comes about because the theological and the religious fall within the domain of nondiscursivity. Second, the failure to give attention to what may be deemed the nondiscursive theological aspects of modern discourse as they relate to the racial imagination has the effect of obscuring the specifically religious/theological dimensions of even the so-called discursive, epistemological aspects of modern discourse and its embedded racial/colonial imagination. How do the new science (of the true), the new philosophy (of the good), and the new aesthetics (of the beautiful)—the discursive elements of modern discourse, according to West—represent a disassembling and then a reassembling for its own purposes of Christian theology's understanding of the true, the good, and the beautiful? And how do they do this at the juncture of the Jewish question, and how does a discourse of race emerge out of this? Lastly, how is the discourse of modern state sovereignty (which mutates into a discourse on the nation) constituted so that it reinvents itself at the same time that it masks the way it operates parasitically on theology as simulacra of a Christian soteriological vision of redemption, though the agent of redemption is different, namely, "Leviathan" (Hobbes)? That is, how does the discourse of modern state sovereignty conceive of the state as democratic "redeemer" inasmuch as it is the "creator" of a new mode of political existence and thus a new way of imagining community?

All of these questions remain open in West's genealogy and throughout the rest of the argument of *Prophesy Deliverance.* Nor are they taken up in West's otherwise impressive post-*Prophesy* oeuvre. Granting that there is some merit to this line of inquiry, it goes some way in explaining why the various forms of black Christianity, which is West's object of concern in *Prophesy Deliverance,* are not within the horizon of this text read theologically. That is, they are not read as attempts at a lived or performed theology that seeks to resist modernity's pseudotheological pretensions through its instantiation or embodiment of a mode of sociopolitical existence that orients itself chiefly from within what I would like to term the Christ form rather than taking its cue solely from the modern nation form. There is no denying that there have been and are forms of black Christianity that are prophetic in West's sense of the term. My inquiry, however, concerns how their propheticism at the same time exceeds the prophetic in West's sense and thus is what makes prophesy possible. It is to ask, in other words, how they are prophetic, but in a theo-

logically richer sense. I more fully describe this theologically richer sense of the prophetic beginnings of Afro-Christian faith in part III.

Michel Foucault's Genealogy of Race

Foucault, the Modern State, and Religion

In advancing this analysis of the problem of race in the modern world, I now more closely address the work of Michel Foucault, especially his genealogy of modern racism, which he anticipates in the last chapter of volume 1 of *History of Sexuality* and gives a more robust account of in his 1975–1976 public lectures at the Collège de France entitled *Society Must Be Defended (Il faut défendre la société).*[49]

The task here is not to give a thoroughgoing analysis of Foucault's gene-alogy of modern racism.[50] To do that, much more would need to be said than the boundaries of the current inquiry permit. My ambitions here are more limited. First, I want to establish why reckoning with, instead of bracketing, the discourse of the modern state is not ancillary to coming to terms with the problem of modern racial reasoning but, rather, is central to it. Foucault's genealogy of modern racism is important for just this reason: it, unlike West's genealogy, does not bracket the (nondiscursive) problem of the state and thus the problem of the political. Rather, it sees it as both internal and integral to the problem of modern discourse.

Foucault's genealogy suggests an important relationship at the micro-logical level between the modern problem of race and the nature and forms of the political in modernity. More specifically, Foucault's analysis entails an ac-count of the mechanisms by which modern political sovereignty shifts from being constituted predominantly through the absolutist state, then to being constituted secondarily through imperial nations or nation-states, and finally to having its latest incarnation in what he calls the order of biopower or biopolitics. Foucault sees race, and ultimately the problem of racism, as a crucial thread holding together this entire fabric. Moreover, he sees race and racism as yoked to the problem of and even the anxiety over religion in modernity's ongoing constitution and reconstitution of itself. This, as I read Foucault's analysis of race, is his signal achievement. In effect, Foucault argues that this anxiety produces a veritable dialectic at the heart of modernity, a dialectic that has everything to do with race and racism. Foucault helps us see, in part at least, what this anxiety entails, though he himself, I argue, in the end does not escape its gravitational pull. He remains its hostage.

Before proceeding further to indicate the nature of this anxiety and from there to map the direction of the remainder of this chapter, it is worthwhile to take a step back to render a little more concrete Foucault's taxonomy of the forms

that modern political power or sovereignty have taken. I begin with what he calls the "absolutist" state. This form of governance, according to Foucault, is most like the form of political governance that marked premodern feudal or medieval Europe. Autocratic rule was the sine qua non of premodern sovereignty, which continued in the absolutist state of early modernity. Yet between the premodern, medieval, and early modern expressions of autocracy there was an important difference: premodern autocratic rule was consolidated in the potentate or king, whereas early modern autocracy was consolidated in the state and its bureaucracies and apparatuses. The primacy of autocratic rule in the absolutist state meant that it evinced a structure similar to that of medieval political sovereignty. What made it modern was that political power no longer rooted itself finally in the king's body, despite the fact that the king, the prince, or the like often still represented the unity of the territory and of the people. The locus of unity came to be reimagined as located in the state and in its bureaucracies. The state, so understood, represented a way of imagining community both beyond the king or potentate and beyond the subjects of a given territory.

This is not to claim that either the king or the subjects of a territory disappeared, for, in fact, the king remained as the residue of premodern forms of sovereignty. What actually occurred was that under that form of governance inaugurated in early modernity and known as the state, both king and subject would each become subject to the state. The state itself, therefore, came to have a kind of all-embracing life of its own. In due course, even the political significance of the king waned in light of the rising significance of the state. The two poles between which sovereignty would eventually come to operate were the state and the subjects of a given territory. In the earliest stages of modern political sovereignty, however, power remained for the most part embodied in the absolutist, autocratic state, with the king or potentate as its representative, so to speak. One thinks of pre-nineteenth-century Prussia as but one example of an early modern, absolutist state in the sense sketched here.

Following the early modern form of the absolutist state, according to Foucault, came the nation form and the closely related entity, the nation-state. In this form of political governance the state bureaucracy that marked early modernity remains in place; however, it comes to be bound up quite intimately with the subjects of a given territory—that is, with "the people." Indeed, a symbiotic unity emerges at this stage of the unfolding of modern statecraft between government and the people. Governance is done in the name of the people and, in fact, becomes the action of the people to constitute and even to reconstitute, to produce and even reproduce, themselves (as Balibar would say). Thus, the shift that the nation-state represents in the unfolding of modern sovereignty is this: rule or governance becomes the rule of the people on behalf of and, therefore, for themselves, albeit through the medium of the nation-state in which as "the people" they vest themselves. The pendulum has shifted

to the second of the poles between which modern sovereignty, as Foucault theorized, operates.

But a further caveat is needed here. Yes, the people operate to produce and define, to reproduce and redefine, themselves; and, yes, they do this by vesting themselves in and as the nation and thus jurisprudentially in and as the nation-state, with the result that an identity in principle arises between the people and the state, an identity that is itself productive of "peoplehood," of nation. But the constitution or production of the people as nation happens over and against other external people, over and against other nations or nation-states. This "over and against," Foucault tells us, is the over and against of war. Stated differently, the people of the nation-state, the population, is produced in a re-lationship of bellicosity to "the other" that is external to the people. Foucault sees intricate mechanisms, mechanisms of pugnacity, at work in this process, mechanisms not just intent on producing the people but also interested in managing the population and the problems that arise as a result of producing bodies, subjects, and citizens for the nation.

There will be occasion to revisit this quite important dimension of Fou-cault's thought. The point here is that the problem of population is negotiated through an analytic of war, an analytic through which one people is related to and distinguished from another external people or population, and that in relating and distinguishing populations in this way it also became necessary to employ the same bellicose mechanisms to address the problems, deviancies, and so-called abnormalities of the population. In this way society came to be disciplined precisely by disciplining or "normalizing" the body so that it could be used in the work of defending society against its principally external ene-mies. Bodies must be disciplined on the micrological level, the level of everyday life, so that the body politic on the macrological level can be strengthened. Foucault's work on sexuality, like his work on madness, incarceration, and so on, must be situated here, for in taking up this question—the question of when humans started thinking of themselves as sexual beings ("homo sexualis")— he is, in fact, probing the politics, technologies, and ethics of modern sub-jectivity. He is asking the question of how bodies came to be articulated within modern grids or nexuses of power in the interests of forging "the people" and in this way disciplining them, one might say, into being or, more accurately, into becoming. Such, according to Foucault, is the problem of governance or "governmentality" in modern disciplinary society.[51]

Now, if one buys the insightful and provocative argument of Adrian Hastings about the construction of modern nationhood, one must say that England would be the chief example of the modern nation in which sover-eignty comes to be vested in the people so as to produce and constitute them. Contrary to Eric Hobsbawn, Benedict Anderson, and other historians, Hast-ings contends that it is England that begins the modern trajectory of the form

of the nation-state, which eventually gets taken up by other Western states.[52] A number of claims Foucault makes in his lectures on the defense of society seem to support Hastings on this point.[53] But beyond even this, one could say that it is the United States of America and what Michael Hardt and Antonio Negri have called "the U.S. constitutional project" that, arguably, culminate the trajectory of the modern nation form.[54]

Finally, the latest incarnation of political sovereignty, according to Foucault, occurs as power becomes "biopower" and thus takes the form of biopolitics. I find what Foucault means by biopower difficult to completely pin down and not always cogently expressed.[55] This, I think, has to do with the fact that his notion of biopower represents the very frontier of his thought. It represents his effort to articulate the new conditions under which the territorialized state now operates. He somewhat elusively named this condition biopower or life (bios) itself. Its elusiveness notwithstanding, I nevertheless take his central contention with regard to it to be direct enough: biopower, it can be said, represents the synthesis of the central currents animating the previous two phases of power.

Foucault theorized that the first phase of modern sovereignty, whose autocratic sensibilities were in many ways continuous with the exercise of sovereignty in the Middle Ages, was engaged in a project of the political management of society, a project that centralized power in the state and that sought to produce and integrate citizens into the state, making them political and legal subjects. The state accomplished this by means of its administrative, bureaucratic, and jurisprudential capabilities. Thus, the first phase of sovereignty centralized power and sought to increase the strength of the state.[56] But there was an inverse process at work *at the same time*: the process of decentralization, of individuating. These processes of centralization and decentralization produced what I termed earlier a veritable dialectic at the heart of modernity.

In the second phase of modern sovereignty, the individuating process is heightened, with the result that the problem of the individual, or more specifically, the problem of state intervention on the individual-cultural level of social existence, becomes acute. Its acuteness notwithstanding, it yet remains the case though that at this stage of the unfolding of the political in modernity, individual life and culture itself are policed in the interests of making a stronger state. That is, the decentralizing impulse remains within the arc of power's centralizing imperative. The state as a delimited territory remains the horizon of governance. Foucault elucidates this point through analyses of an array of sixteenth-century and seventeenth-century texts, in which he concludes the following about the "police State," which in his taxonomy is but an aspect of the nation-state. "The police," Foucault says, "is the term covering the whole new field in which centralized political and administrative power can intervene."[57] Moreover, as the all-embracing internal arm of government,

the police deals with religion, not, of course, from the viewpoint of
dogmatic truth but from that of the moral quality of life. In seeing
to health and supplies, it deals with the preservation of life; concerning trade, factories, workers, the poor, and public order—it deals
with the conveniences of life .... In short, life is the object of the
police: the indispensable, the useful, and the superfluous. That
people survive, live, and even do better than just that: this is what the
police has to ensure.[58]

And they do so with a view to maximizing the state's power. And so, the
question is, what is new in power's biopolitical phase? Answer: Biopolitics. As
Foucault's biographer James Miller has said, biopolitics represented for Foucault the coming together in practice of "these two ways of thinking." Biopower brings together centralization and decentralization, discipline and
control, territorialized and deterritorialized power. Miller continues, "The result was a hybrid new art of government, concerned as never before with
regulating and monitoring the outward *and* the inward life of each and every
citizen."[59] Political power, as Foucault said in a 1979 interview, "now reaches
the very grain of the individual, touches his body, intrudes into his gestures,
his attitudes, his discourse, his apprenticeship, his daily life."[60] We have
moved from the society of discipline to one of control.

But if this is the case, Miller's interpretation of Foucault's thesis must be
revised. It is not so much a mere coming together of the prior two phases of
modern sovereignty that one sees in biopower as it is an inversion of the central
pole through which modernity is constituted. Power as decentralized in culture
and life itself becomes the arc within which all governance is articulated. Thus,
in the biopolitical situation, control becomes "ever more 'democratic,' ever
more immanent to the social field .... The behaviors of social integration and
exclusion proper to rule are thus increasingly interiorized within the subjects
themselves." Control now "extends well outside the structured sites of social
institutions through flexible and fluctuating networks."[61] In the situation of
biopower, as Hardt and Negri would say following Foucault's lead, power has
become universal, exercising itself through the "omniversality of subjects."[62]
Its entire field is *bios* itself. "Biopower," therefore, "refers to a situation in
which what is directly at stake in power is the production and reproduction of
life itself."[63] The biopolitical correlate of biopower is the problem of globalism
or what Hardt and Negri have called "empire."

Foucault's analysis of the mutations of modern political sovereignty is
interesting because of its perspective on the centrality of racial discourses, a
perspective that represents Foucault's intervention into the anxiety that lies at
the heart of modernity. As stated earlier, it is this anxiety that drives modernity's dialectic, and Foucault's intervention hinges on the link he sees between

race, religion, and the structure of modernity. This religio-mythological in-frastructure, the inner religious grammar, is what Foucault locates at the heart of the discourses of race and modern statecraft. He reads the Janus-faced problem of race and the politics of modernity in terms of what amounts to a politics of the Old Testament or, more specifically, a political hermeneutics of ancient, biblical Israel. In my view, this move is crucial to his analysis of race and to other claims he makes about modernity. Modernity's inner anxiety is a racial anxiety, and this racial anxiety is an anxiety over the Jew, what the Jew religiously and theopolitically symbolizes. With this claim, Foucault breaks important ground for probing what racial discourses do in the ongoing work of constituting modernity. But it is here, as well, that one sees that Foucault remains trapped within the very history and anxiety he is attempting to narrate himself and the rest of us moderns out of. He remains trapped insofar as his genealogical narrative not so much discloses modernity's inner mechanisms as reinscribes it. Though the remainder of this chapter is an exposition of this claim, allow me to briefly describe the conundrum in which Foucault remains embroiled, the anxiety that lies at the heart of modernity.

Foucault sees ancient Israel as the prototype of what he calls a counter-history. Israel identifies itself as a people and sets itself as a people against foreign sovereigns such as Pharaoh; thus Israel creates for itself a historical narrative counter to the hegemonic narrative told by the oppressor. Foucault understands this counterhistory as the prototype of modern historical dis-course, in which the histories of various peoples come to be seen as the struggle against the hegemon or external sovereign forces, and he conceives these mod-ern counterhistories in terms of race—specifically, the struggle between races as dominated peoples seek liberation from the dominating hegemonic sover-eignty. Thus, the political hermeneutic of ancient Israel functions in a positive way—namely, in the creation of the *enlightened* modern state. Ancient biblical Israel, within this hermeneutic gaze, is symbol of modernity.

Yet, though in an important respect Foucault breaks significant ground in seeing a theopolitics of Jewish existence as the link between the state and modern racial reasoning, he also misconstrues the relationship by seeing a negative res-idue attached to ancient—and by implication, it would seem, to contemporary—Jewish religion. Foucault fears that the distinction between Jew and Gentile, which is crucial in Israel's prototypical self-identification as a counterhistorical people, contains a dangerous seed of hegemony itself; such a distinction con-ceived in modern racial terms can lead to an internalization of the counterhistory *within* the people themselves, so that instead of a liberating struggle between races, resulting in freedom from tyrannical sovereignty, one ends up with a struggle within "the race" to overcome disparate (racial) elements, resulting in late modernity's "biological, statist racism"[64] and ultimately in biopolitics. In this misinterpretation of the relationship between a political hermeneutic of Israel and modern racial reasoning, Foucault reenacts, rather than overcomes, mo-

dernity's pseudotheological anxiety over what Jewish existence signifies for the modern world. Having established this claim, I will be positioned in the next chapter to clarify the nature of modernity's anxiety over Jewish existence, how it spawns a discourse on race, and what all of this has to do with theology.

The Prospects of Foucault's Analysis: Linking
Race, Religion, and Modern Sovereignty

If Foucault's genealogy of sexuality as laid out in History of Sexuality seeks to answer the question of when people began to think of themselves as sexual beings and what instigated this new mode of human self-knowledge, his genealogy of modern racism seeks to answer a similar, interrelated set of questions: When did people begin thinking of themselves as principally racial beings, and what factors instigated such thinking? Answering these questions is part of Foucault's project of describing how the body is disciplined and controlled, how it is governed, in modern and late-modern society. Foucault makes clear in the concluding chapter of volume 1 of History of Sexuality ("Right of Death and Power over Life," a chapter that he took to be "the fundamental part of the book"[65]) that the questions of sexuality and race are not parallel. Rather, they are intersecting inquiries. What links them, he tells us, is the advent in late modernity, particularly beginning in the nineteenth century, of power's new modus operandi, its "new procedures."[66] The new procedures of power are the procedures of "biopower"; its new historical analytic is that of "biohistory."[67] The problem of modern racism—along with the problem of sexuality, Foucault believes—is to be located here.

But what does Foucault mean by biopower and biohistory, and how do such notions cast new light on our understanding of modern racial reasoning generally and on the problem of modern racism in particular? Key to answering this question is reckoning with the political theory and genealogy of modern governmentality that Foucault explains in the last, important chapter in History of Sexuality. It is there that he outlines what he means by biopower and, importantly for this inquiry, how a modern racial imagination emerges as the infrastructure of what will eventuate in a biopolitical order.

The term biopower, as just suggested, represents for Foucault the new way in which power functions in late modernity. Its newness represents a radicalization of the ways in which power operated in and structured the early modern world, namely, around modernity's greatest discursive invention, "man." According to Foucault, the philosopher Immanuel Kant was a key figure in this discursive invention with his central question, "Was ist der Mensch?" ("What is man?"), a question that oriented his entire philosophical and cultural outlook. This question (which Kant parses out into the further questions, What can I know? What ought I do? And for what may I hope?) makes up a philosophical anthropology[68] intent on giving a cartography of the

"order of things," or so Foucault argues in his book bearing this title.[69] Indeed, *The Order of Things* had its genesis in Foucault's unpublished *thèse complémentaire* on Kant's 1798 *Anthropology from a Pragmatic Point of View*, which Foucault rendered into French for the first time. Foucault, given his research into Kant and his other reflections on the nature of the modern world, claims that it is through the invention of "man" that the modern subject is made and constantly remade as part of an ongoing project.

The nineteenth-century emergence of biopower, of power as refracted through certain "scientific" conceptions of human biological processes, is a continuation of power's old procedures, centering on an anthropology of man. These procedures go back to the very dawning and constitution of the modern world. The task of the final, crowning part of *History of Sexuality* is to locate the problem of sexuality, as a vantage from which there can be knowledge of man, within the broader framework of power's transition from being instantiated through nations (the manifestation of power in the second phase of modernity's political evolution under the nation form) to its instantiation through *bios* or bare life itself (the manifestation of power particularly from the nineteenth century forward).

To state it differently, Foucault is interested in the continuity-in-discontinuity, in the constants, so to speak, that holds together how "the people" are constituted within the latest two moments in the unfolding of the modern world. The first is the moment in which "the people," or the modern subject as a sociopolitical unit, is constituted through individuals' handing themselves over to the sovereignty of states. This is the basic logic by which "the nation" as a territorialized people comes to be. The second moment is biopolitical and concerns how peoplehood comes to exceed any particular national territory. In becoming transnational, the territory of the power becomes omniversal. Fulfilling the Enlightenment's quest for cosmopolitan universality, the territory of power becomes *bios* or life itself and in its totality. As stated in the previous section, this is not to say that the nation vanishes. Rather, it is to say that the horizon within which it operates has shifted. It has become borderless.

Now, while sensitive to the differences between these moments in the constitution of modern peoplehood and subjectivity, Foucault, as already mentioned, is more interested, I think, in what holds them together. Sexuality, insofar as it is an important index of biology, of borderless and unmediated *bios*, is a vector from which to probe this bond. But there is a deeper dimension to the problem of sexuality in the constitution of territorialized and deterritorialized, modern and postmodern (or hypermodern), subjectivity. The deep structure of the problem of sexuality as a vector onto life itself in the production of modern subjects, of modern man, is race, and it is race that links the different forms of peoplehood in early and late modernity, respectively. Foucault begins to spell this out in the concluding section of *History of Sexuality*. There one of his chief concerns is to assert that racial thinking does new work in the nineteenth cen-

tury and into the twentieth century even as it remains in some sense continuous with the work it once did in prior phases of modernity's unfolding; biopower is the term under which he names this new work. That is, race comes to work in a decentralized and deterritorialized way. It begins to work biopolitically, and it begins to articulate itself within the global flows, communications, and currencies of power—flows and currencies that exceed any one nation's borders.

Foucault effectively moved toward an analysis of the emerging global order, of how culture or everyday life was becoming the terrain on which power transactions occurred. Foucault, therefore, began to see that a biopolitical context called for a politics of culture that seeks for ways to inhabit the radically democratizing possibilities of the global situation, but only by decoupling these possibilities from the new form of sovereignty (i.e., biopower) that seeks to own this terrain, the terrain of *bios* itself and in its totality, outright. Part of Foucault's task in drawing out the democratic possibilities latent in the late-modern moment of biopower was to name how a discourse of race becomes a discourse of racism. Moreover, on my reading, in the course of delimiting this new, biopolitical work that race does, Foucault also gives insight into what is continuous in how the discourse of race functions across the transition from early modernity's territorialized constitution of subjectivity and peoplehood to late modernity's deterritorialized constitution of them.

Before pressing these matters further, it is worth asking simply from what has already been said, can *History of Sexuality* bear the weight of this reading? After all, Foucault in this work—especially in that all-important last chapter—argues that biological, statist racism is of recent, late-nineteenth-century vintage. It would seem, then, that the problem of race does not mark modernity at the level of its primary constitution, at its core. This line of reasoning is in part true, but only in part; for such a verdict holds only when accounting for the problem of race "in its [late] modern, 'biologizing,' [and] statist form."[70] Foucault recognizes, however, that narrowing the problem in this way is short-sighted, and here is where the 1975–1976 lectures, which were given during the same year that *History of Sexuality* was in press, assume such great importance; for the lectures significantly expand the analytic and explanatory reach of the problem of race.

Stuart Elden's explanation of what Foucault's lectures sought to accomplish captures just this point. The lectures, Elden observes, want to account for "the war of races that precedes modern racism, and, in particular, how the war [of races] can be seen as part of the constitution of the state."[71] Hence, if in *History of Sexuality* Foucault interprets racism as the crowning effect of biopower's historical evolution in the nineteenth and twentieth centuries, in the lectures he sees racism as the inner grammar of a discourse of conquest, the principle analytic of the constitution of the modern state and of a "political theory of war."[72] Moreover, he understands racism as a basis from which to appreciate "historiography as a political force, . . . history writing as a political

act, . . . and historical narration as a tool of the state and as a subversive weapon against it."[73] But history is a political force, a political act, and a tool of the state or a subversive weapon against it, so Foucault wants to demonstrate, just to the extent that it is drawn into projects of justifying the so-called legitimacy or right of one given race to rule another. In this respect, history becomes a mode of knowledge that justifies power.

Even more than these points, however, the lecture series is important, given my purposes, because even as the lectures chart these lines of inquiry, they also indicate, if in the end inadequately, the theological and religious[74] nature of the problem of race and thus the quasi-theological and religious nature of the constitution of the modern state and presumably its ongoing pseudotheological constitution across the field of biopower. Foucault, in short, points to what West's discourse was finally unable to get at: the convergence of the plotlines of race, religion, and the modern state. Shortly I show how Foucault conceives of this convergence as taking place around the meaning of the life of ancient, biblical Israel and what that life signifies for the modern world. Yet I argue that despite this insight, he does not probe it deeply enough. This is because the method of genealogy blinds him precisely at this juncture from seeing how modernity's anxiety has to do with its obfuscation of the *theological* meaning of Israel's understanding of themselves as a people. Rather than reckoning with this and its rippling effects throughout modernity, Foucault reenacts a nontheological, racialized interpretation of this people. In so doing, he repeats modernity's supersessionism. This problem reached its first crystalline expression in the thought of Immanuel Kant. Allow me to trace the route to this conclusion by looking more closely at Foucault's 1975–1976 lecture series, especially the third and fourth lectures.

Foucault begins his third lecture by briefly summarizing the accomplishment of the previous two. In those lectures, he says, "We said a sort of farewell to the theory of sovereignty . . . as a method for analyzing power relations."[75] Such a theory and method are inadequate chiefly because they presuppose something like the statist unity of sovereignty; that is, they reduce power to the unity of a sovereign, be it the sovereignty "of one individual over others, of one group over others, of one class over others."[76] In this conception of power, sovereignty never has to account for itself, though it accounts for and grounds all else. It is that "from which powers spring."[77] Foucault's problem with this conception is that it does not take account of the fact that "power . . . circulates" as a "chain," a "network," or a web.[78] As discussed, Foucault in *History of Sexuality* asserts that the concentration of power in the unity of the sovereign is but the terminal form that power takes; power itself

> must be understood . . . as the multiplicity of force relations . . . ; as
> the process which, through ceaseless struggles and confrontations,

transforms, strengthens, or reverses [those relations]; as the support which these force relations find in one another; . . . and lastly . . . the strategies in which they take effect . . . embodied in the state apparatuses, in the formulation of the law, in the various social hegemonies.[79]

In addition and most important, an understanding of power in terms of the unity of a sovereign remains oblivious to power's modern modes of operation. With the advent of modernity, power functions no longer in feudal fashion, in which a potentate rules "over the land and over the produce of the land," and in which the political collective, the people, is constituted as the corporal body of the king.[80] Rather, in the modern modes of power, "bodies and what they do"[81] are the field over which power operates. Power in its new modes constitutes the political collective, not as the corporal body of the king, but as the social body of the nation—that is, as the people itself, without the mediation of a sovereign. This constitution of the people as the social body of the nation occurs through what Foucault calls the "normalization" of bodies.[82] Insofar as power's constitution of the modern political collective eschews sovereignty, it presents an antihegemonic aspect.

Foucault uses the problem of war to analyze this antihegemonic aspect and thus to account for the power relations at work in the constitution of the people in modernity. He observes that over the course of time from the Middle Ages to the dawning of the modern era, the nature of warfare was transformed: war ceased being a private affair. "Day-to-day" or "private warfare," as it was actually called, "was eradicated from the social body, and from relations among men and relations among groups," and "gradually, the entire social body was cleansed of the bellicose relations that had permeated it through and through during the Middle Ages."[83] The state thus came to have the sole prerogative of waging war, and with this distinguishing prerogative in hand, the state banished warfare to the margins of society. The business of warfare became the responsibility of a carefully "defined and controlled military apparatus," left to a class of "technical and professional" practitioners, namely, soldiers.[84] This is the story of the birth of the army as a modern institution.

But there is another side to the story. Might it be the case, Foucault asks, that "if we look beneath peace, order, wealth, and authority, beneath the calm order of subordinations, beneath the State and State apparatuses, beneath the laws, and so on, [that we will] hear and discover a sort of primitive and permanent war," that we will discover that war is being waged "just beneath the surface of peace," and that it will prove true that bellicosity is "the principle that allows us to understand order, the State, its institutions, and its history"?[85] Foucault's rhetorical answer to this battery of questions is "Yes"; but in so answering, he recognizes that he must explore the principle that lies behind his

affirmation. The principle he isolates is this: "Politics is the continuation of war by other means."[86]

This principle, Foucault tells us, represents the inversion of the principle enunciated by political philosopher Karl von Clausewitz in his 1827 work, *Vom Kriege* (*On War*), in which he states that "[war] is a continuation of policy by other means.... War is not merely a political act, but a truly political instrument, a continuation of political commerce, a carrying out of the same by other means."[87] Understood in this way, politics as the instrument of peace— the means, that is, by which peace is maintained—is the norm. War, therefore, represents a state of political exception, the unusual condition resorted to from time to time to reach the objective of peace. Foucault notes, however, that with this principle Clausewitz was himself inverting a prior axiom: namely, that war, the condition of bellicosity, is in fact the norm and that politics is simply the continuation of the norm of war, but by other means.

Thus, with his inversion of Clausewitz's axiom that "politics is the continuation of war by other means," Foucault sought to make two claims—one explicit, the other more implicit but no less important for his work. On the one hand, he was claiming to return to a principle that "existed long before Clausewitz" and to take it with deft seriousness.[88] Yet he was also more implicitly claiming that Clausewitz's principle renders thematic the fact that modernity functions under a perpetual state of exception or emergency, the uninterrupted condition of the crisis of politics. Indeed, the state of exception or emergency—namely, the condition of war—is modernity's inner analytic, its syntax and grammar.[89]

Foucault unpacks this principle by analyzing the emergence in modernity of a "new . . . strange discourse," a "historico-politico" one about how society came to be the way it is.[90] This new historical discourse, the discourse of "counterhistory,"[91] was committed to disclosing how "war" in fact "is the uninterrupted frame of history."[92] While in one respect war in modernity is relegated to the periphery of the social body, the discourse of counterhistory gives rise to the view that war in a different form occupies the center of the social body and, in fact, constitutes the social body.[93] Hence, this new discourse of and about history stands against the way in which history as a discourse had functioned to this point. Foucault tells us in the fourth lecture that through the late Middle Ages, history functioned on the model of the Roman annalists,[94] who, like Livy for example, were bent on providing a "politico-legendary history of the Romans" or, more specifically, a "Jupiterian" history of the sovereignty of the Caesars.[95] A central objective of this form of historical discourse was implicitly to "[identify] . . . people with monarch, and nation with sovereign."[96] Its goal was to subsume "the entire social body" under the dazzling light, glory, and power effects of sovereignty,[97] which was bent on "[binding] everything together into a unity—which is of course the unity of the city, the nation, or the State" as that unity was embodied in the sovereign.[98]

What distinguishes the new history from the old is that it is anti-Roman and thus historical precisely by being counterhistorical. It does not proceed on the model of the Roman annalists. Instead, it

> breaks [up] the continuity of glory .... It reveals that the light—the famous dazzling effect of power—is not something that petrifies, solidifies, and immobilizes the entire social body, and thus keeps it in order; [rather, that dazzling light of sovereign power] is in fact a divisive light that illuminates one side of the social body but leaves the other side in shadow or casts it into the darkness. And the history or counterhistory that is born of the story that is born of the race struggle will of course speak from the side that is in darkness, from within the shadows. It will be the discourse of those who have no glory, or of those who have lost it and who now find themselves perhaps for a time—but probably for a long time—in darkness and silence. Which means that this discourse ... will be disruptive speech, an appeal.[99]

All of this is to say that the new (counter)historical discourse reveals history as the story of the struggle between races, between those held up in the light by sovereign power and those left in the darkness by it. It is the story of taking sides, and as such a story, counterhistory discloses what side sovereignty is finally on. It no longer occludes the fact that there are winners and losers. That is, historical discourse is no longer the discourse that explains how the Romans became Romans, or the Gauls Gauls, or the French French, or what have you. It is discovered that "[the] history of some is not the history of others" and that "the history of the Saxons," for example, "after their defeat at the Battle of Hastings is not the same as the history of the Normans who were the victors in that same battle. It will be learned that one man's victory is another man's defeat."[100]

What Foucault points out here is how modern historical discourse shows that war is the analytic of the identity of people groups or nations, and no longer simply that by which glory accrues to potentates—how war is an analytic of the identity not just of the victors as a people group, and not just of the vanquished as a people group, but of victors and vanquished in their *continued* group opposition to one another even under the conditions of so-called peace, and how this peaceful opposition comes to be expressed in politics and codified in law and finally enforced by government, by the state, as the means through which to produce itself as a people. It is in this way that the nation—the "We" in "We the People," so to speak—is forged[101] and legally and politically organized as "the State" in order to secure itself as "the People." Counterhistory, therefore, is an act of memory—to speak theologically, of *anamnesis*—of remembering in a certain way: counterhistory remembers how the unifying light of the present order of things presupposes and is sustained by group

opposition. What all of this means is that a fundamental and ineradicable rift runs through the fabric of society, and this rift produces and founds the state. It means that "[we] are . . . at war with one another; [and that] a battlefront runs through the whole of society, continuously and permanently. . . . [It] is this battlefront that puts us all on one side or the other. There is no such thing as a neutral subject. We are all inevitably someone's adversary. A binary structure runs through society."[102]

But it means something else as well. Foucault spends the better part of the lectures telling us that the continued bellicosity simmering just beneath the surface of peace, law, and government, a bellicosity that both produces and reproduces subjects and peoples in binary opposition to one another, is, in fact, racial. Bellicosity produces the people, the nations, and the state by producing and reproducing the social body along the axis of race. Indeed, war produces and reproduces racial subjects even as it produces and reproduces "the racial state."[103] "The war that is going on beneath order and peace, the war," Foucault says, "that undermines our society and divides it in a binary mode is, basically, a race war . . . [one in which the] social body is articulated around two races."[104]

Now, it is important that Foucault not be read as conflating race war with racism, for he, in fact, carefully distinguishes the two. He praises race war for its emancipatory possibilities, for the fact that, as he sees it, it inaugurates a history that counters the history of sovereignty. Being counterhegemonic, race struggle offers counterhistories of the social body, histories by which it becomes evident that the social body is no longer the king's corporal body but, rather, is a heterogeneous body.[105] By contrast, "the expression 'racism' or 'racist discourse,'" Foucault insists, should be reserved "for something that was basically no more than a particular and localized episode in the great discourse of race war or race struggle . . . . It was a reworking of that old discourse, which at that point was already hundreds of years old, in sociobiological terms, and it was reworked for purposes of social conservatism and, at least in a certain number of cases, colonial domination."[106] Unfortunately, Foucault does not expound on the colonial aspects of the problem of modern racial reasoning, which my analysis of Kant in the next chapter shows were central to the issues being addressed. Nevertheless, it is clear why Foucault finds racism to be the menace that it is. Racism reflects how the otherwise praiseworthy "race-ing" of the social body bears within itself the seeds of its own destruction—indeed, the destruction of the very social body that it constitutes; for in late modernity the principle of race struggle is employed in the reinvention of the logic of sovereignty.

The return of sovereignty into the constitution of the modern political collective does not imply a return of the feudal, sovereign-to-subject model of power; rather, the social body itself becomes the locus of sovereignty. It is important to note that Foucault in no way suggests that one theoretically begins with an already constituted modern collective social entity and that power

ripples out from there. This would simply reinvent the model of feudal sovereignty that sees power as unified in a potentate and then moving outward from that center. Instead, Foucault says that it is in the very manner by which power produces and reproduces the social body that sovereignty makes its return. The struggle *between* the races that counterhistorical discourse brings to the fore as the primary constituting force of the modern state begins in the nineteenth century to transmute into a struggle *within* "the race." It becomes an internal matter of the people against the people, and so a matter of the people, of *bios*, against itself. When this happens, the in-itself emancipatory notion of *races* gets redeployed biologically to secure the collective, the *race*. Security takes the form of protecting the collective, the race, from contamination and degeneracy. It takes the form of defending society from itself. Race struggle as a struggle against sovereignty thus devolves, as Foucault tells the story, into statist, biological racism as the means of unifying and defending the sovereign social body.

The various disciplines of modern scientific knowledge act both as medium and justification of this form of racial sovereignty. It is the "tight grid of disciplinary coercions that actually guarantees the cohesion of [the] social body," the cohesion, that is, of the sovereign collective.[107] These disciplines, which "create apparatuses of knowledge...and multiple fields of expertise" and which "refer to [the] theoretical horizon...[of] the field of the human sciences..., constitute the silent basement of the great mechanics of power" in its quest for norms or rules through which to secure the social body.[108] Stated differently, fields of knowledge such as the disciplinary practices of medicine, the biological sciences, the social sciences, and especially the discourse of history emerge to greatly expand knowledge, but with a view to assist in protecting "the integrity, the superiority, and the purity of the race": that is, of the collective conceived racially.[109]

The task of Foucault's lectures, then, was to persuade his auditors—and now his readers—of the veracity of his social theory, and in the course of doing this to simultaneously praise the shift in how power now operates in modernity to resist sovereignty, while also taking seriously its limits, limits that account for the eventual rise of modern racism in the nineteenth century. It can be said that, for Foucault, modernity is a *pharmakon*—both a medicinal potion and a poison. Foucault points out the limits of the modern social order in the interests of overcoming them, and thus, one might say, in the interests of salvaging the best of modernity and its counterhistorical, counterhegemonic possibilities. Thus in properly reckoning with the limits inherent in how modernity is constituted, one is better positioned to "[look] for a new right," a right that is neither of the old feudal, premodern sort nor of the modern variety rooted as it is in collective biopower and thus in a recuperated notion of sovereignty. This new right—the right of justice—must be one "that is both antidisciplinary and emancipated from [the disciplinary] principle" altogether.[110]

Given this terse summary of Foucault's suggestive lectures, a summary that admittedly puts aside a number of critical questions and that leaves other matters wholly unpursued, I nevertheless am now in a position to ask how the discourse of race ultimately functions for Foucault in the constitution of modernity. The question can be answered as follows: the discourse of race or, more specifically, of race struggle, functions mythically, religiously, and in the end quasi-theologically. Indeed, it is a mythical discourse according to which the social order that is modernity moves in a cyclical logic of fall and redemption. The people that paradigmatically express this logic of race struggle and counterhistory, and hence the logic of modernity at its best in resisting sovereignty, is the Jewish people, the people of ancient, biblical Israel. A careful reading of Foucault's fourth lecture justifies this claim insofar as it points to how both the real (or lived) and the mythological (or "imagined") dimensions of race in the modern world converge on the religious and theological significations of Jewish existence.

Here is where I want to begin finalizing the justification of my claim that Foucault taps into the deep structure of the problem of modern racial reasoning by raising the question of race, religion, and the mythical, even as he reinscribes the structural logic of the problem at the point where these lines intersect on the theological meaning of Jewish existence for the modern world. It is also where I want to start pointing toward my engagement with Kant's thought in light of the Dohm-Michealis debate, which centered on the question of whether Jews could be "civilly improved," which is to say, made German citizens or full citizens of any other European land.

The Problems with Foucault's Analysis: Reinscribing Christian Supersessionism

That modernity is born of counterhistory; that at its best, it *is* counterhistory (and at its worst, it reiterates sovereignty); and that it has inaugurated a mode of historical consciousness by which identity is seen as liberated through the struggle of races: these are all themes mentioned above as central to the argument of Foucault's 1975–1976 lectures. What is yet to be more fully expounded is the mythical, religious, and even quasi-theological nature of Foucault's narrative. He mentions both in the lectures and in the last chapter of *History of Sexuality* that myth, particularly myths about blood purity, was a crucial component of nineteenth-century and twentieth-century racism, especially the racism of Nazi Germany. More than just an ad hominem remark, Foucault's comments about myth open an important perspective on his argument. In *History of Sexuality* he observes that what came to mediate the shift from the administration of power through "a symbolics of blood" to its administration through "an analytics of sexuality" was race.[111]

In the former state of affairs, "blood was a reality with a symbolic function" that worked in the interests of upholding that zone of power that was imagined as above the social field of everyday life. Functioning symbolically, "power spoke *through* blood" and thus was a sign of such so-called superior realities as "the honor of war, the fear of famine, the triumph of death, the sovereign with his sword, executioners, and tortures."[112] So understood, blood spoke beyond itself, beyond its reference to bodies as such. One could very well say, to recall language I used earlier, that blood functioned symbolically to uphold power's centralizing capacities—its capacity, that is, to draw everything together around the territorialized state and within the limits of society, insofar as those limits follow the territorial limits of the state.

Things change with the transition from a "symbolics of blood" to "an analytics of sexuality." "In a society of 'sex,'" Foucault tells us, "the mechanisms of power are addressed to the body, to life, to what causes it to proliferate, to what reinforces the species, its stamina, its ability to dominate, or its capacity for being used."[113] Functioning now in a decentralized way, power came to work in the interests of "the blood of the caste . . . [indeed, in the interests of] the blood of the people" so as to bring about a perfect, "eugenic ordering of society."[114] This was the new way in which nation and peoplehood were conceived. Besides making use of a number of new modes of knowledge (such as statistics, census studies, and medicine, to name a few) to justify itself, and besides making use of themes such as "health, progeny, race, the future of the species, [and] the vitality of the social body,"[115] late-modern sovereignty also drew on myth to justify itself.[116] This general logic is at work in the following passage from *History of Sexuality*:

> Beginning in the second half of the nineteenth century, the thematics
> of blood was sometimes called on to lend its entire historical weight
> toward revitalizing the type of political power that was exercised
> through the devices of sexuality. Racism took shape at this point
> (racism in its modern, "biologizing," statist form): it was then that a
> whole politics of settlement (*peuplement*), family, marriage, education,
> social heirarchization, and property, accompanied by a long series
> of permanent interventions at the level of the body, conduct, health,
> and everyday life, received their color and their justification from the
> mythical concern with protecting the purity of the blood and ensuring the triumph of the race. Nazism was doubtless the most cunning and the most naïve (and the former because of the latter)
> combination of the fantasies of blood and the paroxysms of a disciplinary power. A eugenic ordering of society with all that implied in
> the way of extension and intensification of micro-powers, in the
> guise of an unrestricted state control (*étatisation*), was accompanied

by the oneiric exaltation of a superior blood; the latter implied both the systematic genocide of others and the risk of exposing oneself to a total sacrifice. It is an irony of history that the Hitlerite politics of sex remained an insignificant practice while the blood myth was transformed into the greatest blood bath in recent memory.[117]

In this passage we can read Foucault as offering a condensed answer to an implied question: How could a symbolics of blood continue to have cachet under conditions of an "analytics," or a science, of sexuality? His answer is that it could because the critical issue is neither primarily the symbolics of blood nor the analytics, or the science, of sexuality in their own right; rather, the crucial issue is the mythology underlying both. This mythology is two-edged: on the one hand, it inspires liberation from or resistance to Roman-style history and sovereignty; on the other hand, it can be made to invest the logic of sovereignty with new energy and in the process, as mentioned above, convert the discourse of the struggle of *races* against sovereignty and tyranny into a discourse of *race* and thereby give birth to racism.[118]

The question, then, is, How is this transformation possible? What is it about the mythology undergirding modernity that enables this possibility? It can be said that in seeking an answer to this question, Foucault is in fact seeking a genealogical explanation of the phenomenon, an account of how the discourse of *races* could metastasize into a discourse of *race*, and in this sense he is seeking a genealogy of modern racism(s). For racism represents a falling back into sovereignty, albeit the tyrannical sovereignty of the collective, of the group, now figured racially. The fourth lecture suggests that religious myth provides Foucault with his genealogical explanation of how this fall could occur; for within the religious myth that Foucault sees as upholding modernity, he sees as well the mechanism by which the collective itself can become the new site of sovereignty. That is, he sees how the mythology that upholds modernity in its rise from sovereignty simultaneously entails the possibility of its fall—its religious and mythological fall—back into sovereignty. Thus in some sense, religious myth—at least as presently configured and functioning to ground modernity—never fully overcomes sovereignty but is part of its dialectic. Indeed, it can be said that in a fundamental but unspoken way the mythological orientation of modernity harbors the attitude of sovereignty, allowing it to endlessly ramify or reproduce itself in ever-new permutations.

Another way to express this is to say, employing language from Foucault's essay "What Is Enlightenment?" that the mythical orientation that both is modernity and grounds modernity is at once "modern" (in its sense of undermining sovereignty) and antimodern or "countermodern." The ultimate implication of this assertion is that the religious myth underwriting modernity harbors both its redemption and its fall; indeed, it is always already a fallen or

compromised redemption. Enlightenment will always be in need of enlightenment. What emerges, then, between the lines and in the interstices between "the said and the unsaid"[119] of Foucault's explanation of the place of religious myth in modernity's apparatuses of power is that modernity is a religious performance of mythic proportions, one that is ever poised, with respect to sovereignty, between redemptive liberation and a sinful fall back into the oppression of sovereignty, now at the site of the collective. We learn from other places in Foucault's oeuvre and also from James Miller, Foucault's biographer, that as Foucault saw it, the answer to this problem is to be liberated—or, perhaps better, to be disentangled—from the collective. This entails seeing neither the sovereign nor the collective as life's precondition but, rather, seeing the body as such—albeit, as subject to a different "ascetic" script, a different way of caring or being "[concerned] for the self as the practice of freedom"—as life's ultimate precondition and as the place where the ultimate agon against sovereignty is to be waged.[120]

What is worth paying particular attention to for my purposes is how Foucault positions Jewish faith in his narrative, how it becomes the means through which to reflect the modern world at its "counterhistorical" best—and also at its "historical" worst—back to itself. I am interested, in other words, in how Foucault's reading of the myth that founds and that *is* modernity positions the Jew—more specifically, the people of ancient, biblical Israel—in relationship to his genealogy of race. I am also interested in how as a result of his mythical reading of modernity, Jews provide modernity with a hermeneutic of itself: that is, they provide modernity with an interpretive grid of "the said and the unsaid" that constitutes its apparatuses of power and the systems of relation linking those apparatuses together. And last, I am interested in how it is that Foucault's way of imagining all of this unwittingly reenacts modernity's anxiety-filled relationship to the theopolitical significance of Jewish existence.

Allow me now to textually substantiate my worry over how Foucault seems unwittingly to harbor modernity's anti-Jewish anxiety. Having given an account of what he means by counterhistory, Foucault then elaborates on it by imputing religious qualities to counterhistory. In so doing he can be read as also expounding on claims made in *History of Sexuality* to link myth to the rise of the state racism of Nazi Germany. Understood against the backdrop of the lectures, Foucault's claim is that in the case of Nazi Germany, myth was deployed in a religiously problematic way. Through the lectures, Foucault also lets us know that there can nevertheless be a positive use of religious myth, and this is evident from his claim that the counterhistory of the struggle of races "prophetic[ally] rupture[s]" the static, unifying aura of sovereignty. This rupturing should be understood in the Old Testament scriptural sense. Hence "[the] new discourse," he informs us, "is similar to a certain number of epic, religious, or mythical forms which, rather than telling of the untarnished and

uneclipsed glory of the sovereign, endeavor to formulate the misfortune of ancestors, exiles, and servitude...[while waiting] for the promised land and the fulfillment of the old promises." Moreover,

> [with] this new discourse of race struggle, we see the emergence of something that, basically, is much closer to the mythico-religious discourse of the Jews than to the politico-legendary history of the Romans. We are much closer to the Bible than to Livy, in a Hebraic-biblical form much more than in the form of the annalist who records, day by day, the history of the uninterrupted glory of power....
> At least from the second half of the Middle Ages onward, the Bible was the great form for the articulation of religious, moral, and political protests against the power of kings and the despotism of the church. Like the references to biblical texts itself, this form functioned, in most cases, as a protest, a critique, and an oppositional discourse....To that extent, it is not surprising that we see, at the end of the Middle Ages, in the sixteenth century, in the period of the Reformation, and at the time of the English Revolution, the appearance of a form of history that is a direct challenge to the history of sovereignty and kings—to Roman history—and that we see a new history that is articulated around the great biblical form of prophecy and promise.[121]

I quote this passage at length because in it—and throughout the rest of the fourth lecture—Foucault exposes the mythico-religious and even quasi-theological undercurrent of his account of modernity, an account that views modernity as an agon of history and counterhistory and the notion of race as that which fuels the antagonism.[122]

One discovers that the story being told in the lectures about the confrontation of counterhistory and history is actually another way of genealogically peering behind the Protestant Reformation and the principle of revolution it inaugurates so as to view the Reformation not simply as a discrete historical event but, instead, as a religious disposition, a mythical posture, or (as he says in the essay "What Is Enlightenment?") an "attitude," the "attitude of modernity [itself]...[in its struggle] with attitudes of 'countermodernity.'"[123] It is important to observe that for Foucault, the Protestant Reformation, both as historical event and as exemplifying the principle of modernity, operates in this schema according to the analytic of the war of races in its resistance to "the power of kings and the despotism of the church [read: Roman Catholic Church]."[124] The Reformation, in short, displays the attitude of modernity; the attitude of *dandysme*, of experimentation for the sake of self-realization and artistic self-elaboration; and lastly of "heroic," rather than merely tragic, existence on the boundary of death so as to finally plunge the stake into the heart of sovereignty.[125]

But modernity, exemplified at its counterhistorical best in this way under the aspect of the Protestant Reformation, plays the role of type to another, one might say "proto-counterhistorical" race: namely, the Jews. The fourth lecture seems to imply an analogy between the principle or attitude of modernity as exemplified in the Protestant Reformation in its challenge to the despotism of the church and the tyranny of kings on the one hand and "the mythico-religious discourse of the Jews" on the other. Jews, in the guise of ancient, biblical Israel, are either the prototype or the antitype of modernity. As a people of prophetic resistance to the tyranny and oppression meted out to them at the hands of sovereigns such as the ancient Egyptian pharaohs and Babylonian rulers, ancient Israel is the sociocollective embodiment of the principle or attitude of counterhistory. They embody it not through recourse to the logic of sovereignty; rather, it could be said that in the history of Western political thought and practice, ancient Israel is the fountainhead of a different political ordo, a counterhistorical one in which Israel's existence as a people is founded on seeing the struggle of races as the inner, redemptive mechanism of history. Israel, in its ancient and in its modern embodiment, does this by defining itself as a collective, a distinct people—that is, as Jews—in contrast to its oppressors, who down through history have defined themselves through the unifying glory of the sovereign, be he the Egyptian pharaoh, the Babylonian king, the German Führer, or any other tyrannical figure.

Thus to sum up this particular point: counterhistory or the inner attitude of modernity has a twofold mythological and religious signification. First, there is the implication that the principle of counterhistory, which functions according to a logic of race struggle, in fact enacts the Protestant principle of reformation, which for Foucault is about revolution, the principle of counterhegemonic resistance to sovereignty. Second, there is the further implication from this that the inner basis of the principle of Protestantism, and thus the inner basis of the principle of race (struggle), lies in the mythological and religious discourse of the Jews. This means that Foucault, at least on this score, reads Jewish existence in positive terms, as that which must be embraced. Jews are the vantage from which to understand the counterhegemonic. This is because they deliver to Western civilization and political thought a mode of life figured through a discourse of the races that tends toward freedom (at least an Enlightenment notion of freedom). In so doing, they provide a mythological and religious basis for the counterhistorical "attitude of modernity," rooted as it is in a discourse of *races*, of race struggle. To invoke language employed at the beginning of this chapter, Foucault has tapped into the fact that the question of race arises inside the question of Israel, inside the question of the theopolitical meaning of Jewish existence.

And yet there is a troubling downside to reading the life of Israel in this way—as the index or interpretive grid or religious symbol of the modern world. Such a reading also makes Israel the index of modernity's discontents insofar

as those discontents cluster around the way (racial) collectivity can also spawn a new form of hegemonic sovereignty, the sovereignty of the collective conceived of as the *race*. It is the sovereignty of the collective, particularly when its meanings are interpolated through the knowledges that the biological and health sciences yield, that generates a discourse of *race* and so of racism. All of this means that Israel occupies an odd mythopoetic position in the Foucauldian scheme of things. On the one hand, Israel must be embraced to the extent that it is the fountainhead of the attitude of counterhistory and thus prototypically of the attitude that is modernity. Simultaneously, Jewish existence must be overcome to the extent that its racializing of existence (through the war of races figured through the Jew-Gentile distinction) can lead to racism, to a notion of blood purity or racial group superiority, and thus to preventing modernity from fully elaborating itself and living into its *dandysme* or counterhistorical attitude. In other words, Israel's prototypical racializing of existence can lead to a problematic performance of the nation and constitution of the state.

Foucault's tenth lecture can be read as addressing just this problem in nineteenth-century historical discourse. That is, Foucault is trying to account for the shift in how counterhistory itself came to no longer be so much a (counter)narrative that exposes sovereignty's source in past acts of invasion and thus leads to the struggle *between races* but, rather, came to be internalized as a struggle *within* the present state, a struggle over the defense of society and so of "the *race*." He wants to account for how it transpired that "the fundamental moment is no longer the origin, and intelligibility's starting point is no longer the archaic element; it is, on the contrary, the present."[126]

Foucault calls attention here to a shift in late modernity in how historical discourse conceived the nation and its future. This shift manifested itself in the fact that counterhistory ceased to speak of a current coded race struggle arising out of past events and started to cast it in terms of an ongoing war with occupying forces. In his account of the way in which historical discourse functioned among the English Levellers and Diggers in their explanation of who the Normans and William the Conqueror really were, Foucault intends to show how this shift began.[127] Historical discourse functioned less and less to suggest that the current state of things reflects the effects of an invasion and occupation; instead, the purveyors of history began to view the present as being in a sense ahistorical and replete in itself. Thus "the present becomes the fullest moment, the moment of greatest intensity," despite the many (racial) rifts and cleavages that mark it. Indeed, it is from these aberrant rifts that the present must be saved for the sake of its future; the present must be purged so that the "virtual" and "functional totality of the nation" can become the "actual" and "real universality of the State."[128]

The critical implication that Foucault calls attention to is the way in which the privileged moment for historical discourse shifts from a supposedly pristine past in need of counterhistorical resistance to the nation's present en-

deavor to produce and reproduce and realize itself as the perfect state. Under these circumstances, historical discourse comes to function under a "principle of national universality."[129] To be sure, this universality is not a sanguine state of affairs, for in every productive and reproductive effort the social rift, the binary opposition, continues to be produced and reproduced. But it is produced and reproduced now *within* the race, not *between* the races. The task of society, which has become a civilian rather than a militaristic one, is the still bellicose task of achieving victory,but now by eliminating its internal rifts. Its task, in short, is to defend itself against itself. It is now a war for purity within the race, a war for racial purity, one might say. According to Foucault, this shift in social dynamics, which follows the shift in the nature of historical discourse, lays the groundwork for racism, particularly statist, biological racism. Such racism is actualized when the effort to produce and reproduce the nation is coupled with the biological and medical sciences.

None of what has been said commits us to a reading of Foucault that suggests that he somehow intends to implicate Jews as complicit in the nine-teenth- and twentieth-century racism meted out against them. Indeed, he un-equivocally opposes racism (and especially anti-Semitism[130]) and understood his work as an intellectual labor to expose its causes and to change its reality. My point, however, is that consideration of Foucault's claims regarding the mythical basis of race, religion, and the modern state suggests an unwitting reenactment of modernity's anxiety about the theopolitical meaning of Jewish existence. That anxiety shows itself here around this question of the meaning of the people, of the collective, of the nation, of the state. It centers on an insuf-ficient theological grasp of the covenantal status of this people and its election.

Hence, what the lectures have no way of interrogating are the ways in which Israel embodies and is called to a performance of what it means to be a people, more specifically, YHWH's people, beyond the modern nation-state as an "imagined community," even if in late modernity the nation-state is in many ways borderless.[131] That is to say, Foucault's lectures cannot imagine Israel as a covenantal people and therefore as a people constituted (however, imperfectly) beyond modernity's hegemonic and counterhegemonic alter-natives. He fails to query how modernity represents a deformation of Israel's covenantal status into a racial status. Indeed, by not acknowledging the *theo-logical* significance of Israel's existence or interrogating how modernity re-presents an attempt to triumph over what Israel theologically signifies, Fou-cault's discourse remains trapped within the story of the modern racializing— we can even say, orientalizing—of the Jew. My claim, stated differently then, is this: Foucault's genealogical inquiry did not—and perhaps, due to its pre-suppositions, could not—go far enough. In the end, he, as Cornel West did, brackets the theological from his genealogy of modernity and thus from his analysis of modern racial discourse. Foucault, in fact, admits as much in the introductory remarks to the fifth of his 1975–1976 Collège de France lectures:

The divide, the perception of the war between races predates the notions of social struggle or class struggle, but it certainly cannot be identified with a racism of, if you like, the religious type. It is true that I haven't talked [so far in these lectures] about anti-Semitism. I intended to say a bit about it last time, . . . but I did not have time. What I think we can say . . . is this: Insofar as it is a religious and racial attitude, anti-Semitism had so little influence on the history I was trying to trace for you that it does not have to be taken into account until we reach the nineteenth century.[132]

He continues by claiming that anti-Semitism as a distinctively religious or theological problem is of recent vintage:

The old religious-type anti-Semitism was reutilized by State racism only in the nineteenth century, or at the point when the State had to look like, function, and present itself as the guarantor of the integrity and purity of the race, and had to defend itself against the race or races that were infiltrating it, introducing harmful elements into its body, and which therefore had to be driven out for both political and biological reasons. It is at this point that anti-Semitism develops, picking up, using, and taking from the old form of anti-Semitism all the energy—and a whole mythology—which had until then been devoted solely to the political analysis of the internal war, or the social war. At this point the Jews came to be seen as—and were described as—a race that was present within all races, and whose biologically dangerous character necessitated a certain number of mechanisms of rejection and exclusion on the part of the State. It is therefore, I think, the reutilization within State racism of an anti-Semitism which had developed for other reasons that generated the nineteenth-century phenomena of superimposing the old mechanisms of anti-Semitism on this critical and political analysis of the struggle between races within a single society.[133]

In the next chapter I challenge Foucault's claim that "[insofar] as [the Jewish question] is a religious and racial attitude, [it] had so little influence on the [story of modernity or more specifically on the story of the rise of the modern State and of the political in the modern world] . . . that it does not have to be taken into account until we reach the nineteenth century." By taking a closer look particularly at the late-eighteenth-century *Aufklärung*, I show, contra Foucault, that the story of the modern invention of race had everything to do with the story of the modern invention of religion; that both of these stories were of a piece with the story of the rise of the modern nation-state as a new form of political economy or sociopolitical governance; and that the so-called Jewish problem was a key subtext in all of this.[134]

This new form of governance was soteriological in character but was able to be so only by absorbing key features of Christian thought, with the result that the modern state, through its pretensions toward (especially European) nationalism, gets figured as the new agent of redemption. In this sense, modernity from the first harbors quasi-theological or pseudotheological pretensions, pretensions that were at work in the formation of modern racial discourse as one of its supporting discourses for the "total revolution" of society.[135] It is worth stating again that a key subtext of this revolutionary saga is the *Judenfrage*.[136] The negotiation of this question in the struggle to constitute the modern (nation) state, to use Immanuel Kant's language, was nothing short of a grand religious drama. Thus, it is to the Jewish question and "the great drama of religion"[137] surrounding it, to the shifts that occurred in Christian theology in the working out of answers to it, and finally to the emergence of a discourse of race that arose in significant part under its provocation that we must now turn.

2

The Great Drama of Religion

Modernity, the Jews, and the Theopolitics of Race

God has not cast away his people which he foreknew.... Therefore even at this present time there is a remnant according to the election of grace.

—St. Paul, Romans 11:2, 5

[One must] distinguish the way in which Jesus spoke as a Jew to Jews from the way he spoke as a moral teacher to human beings in general.—The euthanasia of Judaism is pure moral religion, freed from all the ancient statutory teachings, some of which were bound to be retained in Christianity (as a messianic faith). But this division ..., too, must disappear in time, leading ... to what we call the conclusion of the great drama of [religion] ... when there will be only one shepherd and one flock.

—Immanuel Kant, *Religion and Rational Theology*

How different might have been the story of the last two thousand years on this planet grown old from suffering if the link between Jesus and Israel had never been severed.... [For] the Christian Church has tended to overlook its Judaic origins, ... the fact that Jesus of Nazareth was a Jew of Palestine.

—Howard Thurman, *Jesus and the Disinherited*

Allow me to review briefly where we've been as a precursor to where we're going. I concluded the previous chapter with the claim that the story of the modern invention of race could not be adequately told apart from the story of how Christianity came to be mythologized,

reimagined as the paradigmatic modern "religion," and that the story of Christianity's transformation into a mythic "religion" and ground of Western civilization could not be adequately told apart from the story of the politics of that transformation. That politics is one whereby "the people" marks out its identity by articulating itself no longer within the consciousness of and as an appendage to the will of the sovereign king but in binary relationship to some other people that it is not. This shift in how states and in how citizens within a state came to identify themselves signals that a new kind of consciousness has arisen: the consciousness of modern nationalism, and more specifically, the consciousness of the modern nation-state.[1] Moreover, within the dictates of this new mode of consciousness, a new kind of political agency arose, one in which the sovereign's will came to be viewed as representative of the collective will of "the people." The sovereign's body and the people's body became coeval. The modern body politic arose. Eventually, this newly emergent mode of political agency came into its own with the rise of modern republicanism or representative, liberal democracy.

This newly emergent political moment, when the modern state refounded itself as the modern *nation*-state, predicated itself on a new type of anthropology. This anthropology, or account of the human being, had at its core a discourse of race (replete with a logic of racism) that was itself tied to how Christianity came to be "rationally" repositioned within the framework of modernity's political economy and, in the process of this repositioning, was decoupled from its Jewish roots.[2] It is this severance of the link between Christianity and its Jewish roots and between Jesus and Israel (to use Howard Thurman's language) that goes to the heart of the modern theological-political *Judenfrage* and, at the same time, to the heart of the modern problem of identity and race (or what I call the *Rassenfrage*), especially as it articulates itself in (and distorts) theology. In analyzing this problem, I offer in this chapter an account of modernity and demonstrate how it is that in functioning according to and harboring a logic of race, modernity functions according to and harbors with devastating consequences an anxiety over Jewish existence and over what Jewish existence theopolitically signifies for a modern world struggling to come of age.

I explore these matters through an engagement with the thought of philosopher Immanuel Kant (1724–1804). My attention centers on his account of the question that on his own admission was at the core of his philosophical research: *Was ist der Mensch?*—What is man?[3] As Kant's late work *Conflict of the Faculties* (1798) made clear, this question of philosophical anthropology and, indeed, of thought itself was nothing less than an account of the "great drama of religion." According to Kant, the religious drama of human existence hopes for a cosmopolis, an ideal time, place, and sociopolitical order, an ethical community, in which "there will be only one shepherd," that is, one ideal "religious" figure, who is a representation of the species as a whole and thus is a cultural reflex, a symbol of its moral development.[4] The symbol of the per-

fection of the species, this ideal religious figure, is able by his moral example to guide the species to full self-actualization. Retaining his pietistic Lutheranism, Kant identifies this ideal religious figure as Jesus Christ. Moreover, in alluding to the New Testament, he observes that the Christ he has in view is the figure who, as moral symbol, guides the species to realize itself as "one flock" or as a unified people (cf. John 10:16). Kant's language reveals that the modernity he envisioned is not areligious. Nor is it inimical to Christian thought forms. Rather, it redeploys Christian thought forms inside of, indeed, as a cultural reflex of Western civilization.

While an entire monograph could be written on just this phenomenon and its consequences, my interest here is more limited. I am interested in the convergence of the *Rassenfrage* and the *Judenfrage* in the hoped-for modern cosmopolis, the perfect world order in which the ideal of the unity of the human species actualizes itself in the perfection of a race type, the white race. Kant refers to this perfected race type, in allusion to the Pauline language of Romans 9–11, as a "remnant race," a kind of new or different Israel or people of chosenness. This is the basis for Kant's emergent political-cultural nationalism of whiteness. In this chapter, I outline how Kant's new configuration of man as homo racialis and his new, "enlightened" configuration of homo politicus are based on a new conception of homo religiosus as it is articulated within his vision of modernity as a great drama of religion. Specifically, I am interested in how whiteness became a theological problem that camouflages itself as just such a problem, how this theological problem continues to mark modernity, and how Kant's thought can help me articulate the problem.

To this end, I begin with an analysis of Kant's 1770s reflections on race, his effort to make sense of the alien who is external to Prussia and Europe. It is here that Kant bequeaths to the modern world its first scientific theory or philosophical account of race.[5] Functioning also as a teleologically structured philosophy of history, Kant's theory of race articulates an account of the destiny of the species as coinciding with the global perfection and spread of whiteness. I take this up under a section titled "Kant and the Drama of Race." I then consider how Kant's anthropological mapping of the nonwhite external world was less about coming to terms with the "other" and part of a more primary project: mapping and politically organizing the internal world of Europe and especially Prussia, the internal world of the Occident, and, in the end, the internal world of whiteness itself. *Aufklärung*, or Enlightenment, names the sociopolitical process of the internal organization and perfection of the species, a process that had as a central component isolating the other who was internal to the body politic of whiteness. It is here that I show this internal other to be the Jews, which Kant reads as a race group, one inferior to the European or to the race of whites.

What becomes evident, then, is this: race is the discourse to constitute whiteness in relationship to a non-Jewish alien without and a Jewish alien within the body politic. I take up this second set of sociopolitical matters in a

section titled "Kant and the Drama of Politics." And finally, in a section on "Kant and the Great Drama of Religion," I consider how this process is part and parcel of the reconstitution of Christianity as modernity's supreme, rational religion. The result of the process is that Christianity is made the cultural property of Western civilization. It is here that it becomes clear how whiteness, as the "biological" underpinning of modernity, proves itself to be a new expression of an older theological problem, the problem of Christian supersessionism. What is new is that Christian supersessionism now expresses itself as the racial ground of modernity.

Kant and the Drama of Race

Theorizing Race

Kant's 1775/1777 essay, "Of the Different Human Races,"[6] presents a significant challenge to the interpreter of Kant on race. This challenge consists of bringing together his philosophical interest in the hard, empirical sciences with his interest in the conditions of knowledge (epistemology), the imperatives of morality (moral philosophy), and the politics and overall trajectory of the unfolding of Western culture and civilization (political philosophy and the philosophy of history). How do the philosophy of science and the science of philosophy relate in Kant? The contention here is that both together mark Kant's interest in anthropology. But it will be shown that a particular conceptualization of race lay behind even this. I begin on the side of the hard sciences with Kant's engagement with the discourse of the "organism," or the science of living form, as it was called in the mid-eighteenth century.

Kant's understanding of the organism, of what makes a living thing what it is, was hammered out in conversation with the scientific community of his day about the nature of "living form" and in conversation with this same community on the closely allied topic of "teleology." In her effort to explicate the organism's peculiar modernity, philosopher and political theorist Susan Meld Shell has observed the following:

> [An] organ (Latin: *organum*; Greek: *organikos*) is a tool or instrument; Aristotle uses "organikos" to refer to tools and also to bodily parts or members that (in contrast to "kinetikos") are not actively in motion. During the middle ages, "organum" meant, primarily, a mechanical contrivance (such as the well-known musical instrument), but also, albeit less frequently, "bodily part" in roughly the Aristotelian sense. "Organism" as a specifically modern term combines both meanings in the single notion of a living system: an organism is a whole made up of interdependent, tool-like parts that function as tools or instruments of one another.[7]

Shell then makes an additional observation, one that lies at the heart of Kant's own frustration with how several of his contemporaries had come to talk about the nature of living form. She observes that

> the "organic" in this [emerging] modern sense, says nothing specific about the end toward which the system is ordered other than that of its own preservation. It says nothing about the soul (in its increasingly discredited scholastic meaning), and is thus neutral in the increasingly contentious metaphysical dispute between mechanism and Aristotelian teleology.[8]

The problem of the lack of teleological explanation beyond mere self-preservation, then, is what is at stake for Kant.

The problem becomes all the more acute for him once one asks why there are different races of humankind, why the human species has self-organized into distinct "races" at all. In other words, how does the racialization of the species contribute to its self-preservation and thus make sense of it as a *living form*? Does racialization serve a purpose beyond self-preservation? Indeed, what does self-preservation even mean when speaking of the human species? Natural description, which according to Kant is all that the scientific community of his day (from Carl von Linnaeus's work forward) was engaged in, can't begin, as he saw it, to adequately address these important, interrelated questions. All it could do was *describe* the so-called racial distinctions of the species at a particular historical moment; it could not *explain* those distinctions. It could neither situate those distinctions within a longer-range historical narrative of the species' development nor discern purpose or intention with regard to racial distinctions. In short, it could not render racial distinctions intelligible to the understanding (*Verstand*).

At a fundamental level, Kant could not stomach such an intellectual outcome, and thus he mocks the previous scientific accounts as "useful entertainment." In the opening paragraph of his advertisement for the 1775 lecture course on race, Kant says:

> The lecture course which I am announcing is to be more a useful entertainment [*Unterhaltung*] than a tiresome activity. For this reason, the research that accompanies this course announcement will certainly include something for the understanding [*Verstand*], but it will be more of a game [*Spiel*] for it than a deep investigation.[9]

The talk about it being a "game" is made tongue in cheek, for Kant does believe that there is real and important knowledge, "something" as he says, to be had regarding knowledge of the races. Such knowledge can perhaps illuminate broader questions about the species as a whole. But acquiring such knowledge will require that the *how*-question (i.e., *How* has it happened that there are different human races making up the one human species?) and the

why-question (i.e., *Why* has human nature subdivided itself thus, or what end does human racial difference serve?) be asked and answered in light of what Kant calls "a natural system for the understanding." It will require, in other words, that the fact of human racial diversity "[be brought] . . . under laws" for proper understanding of the human being as a living form. It is only as the understanding proceeds in light of a natural system that human racial diversity can be rendered as rationally intelligible, that it can yield "something" for the understanding. But it becomes clear in Kant's 1775/1777 race essay that human nature has chosen for itself the path of internal pluralization according to racial distinctions because it serves the interests of the full flowering and flourishing of the human species and the realization of its ends. But how is this the case?

After making his somewhat tongue-in-cheek announcement (by many accounts, Kant did have a sense of humor[10]) about the playful inquiry he is about to conduct into human racial diversity, Kant then moves, as he says, to retrieve "something" as regards this topic for the understanding. His argument revolves around what appear to be two contradictory points, which the essay is meant to reconcile. I'll begin with the second: the conclusion that Kant wants to draw from his empirical observation that there are differences of phenotype or skin color. Once the anthropologist has made this "objective" observation and, of course, "rightly" analyzed it, the conclusion to be drawn is clear-cut: differences of phenotype are pegged to racial distinction within the species. "[We] only need to assume four [of them] . . . : (1) the white race; (2) the Negro race; (3) the Hun race (Mongol or Kalmuck); and (4) the Hindu or Hindustani race." Indeed, "all of the other characters of peoples" (i.e., peoples or races that do not fall clearly within one of the four race groups) and their "enduring distinctions" "derive . . . [either] from these four races or as races that originate from them. The first of these two alternatives," Kant says, "occurs when different races (among the standard races) interbreed; the second occurs when a people has not yet lived long enough in a specific climate to take on fully the character of that race peculiar to that climate." As this passage would have it, there are four races from which all race traits and even subsequent race groups derive. But Kant immediately reduces even this fourfold distinction of the races to a binary one: "Negroes and whites are the base races." What is the argument in support of this reductive claim? Well, as Kant sees it, none is needed, for as he says, it is so clear that "Negroes and whites are the base races" that the "reason for assuming [it] is self-evident."[11] In the end then, all racial distinctions exist on a continuum between the two base races of Negroes and whites.

But why would nature bid the species to racially proliferate itself between this polarity, especially when one takes into account the very real, and for Kant troublesome, possibility of "wayward reproductions" within the species (i.e., the mixed race or "blended" person; the mulatto) and the fact of the moral deficiencies of some of the fully formed races? The example supplied in the

1775/1777 essay of the fully formed race that gave Kant pause in this regard is the Negro. As a race, he says, they are "lazy, indolent, and dawdling." What, then, is nature's objective, its endgame, so to speak, given what can go naturally wrong in the "evolutionary" unfolding of the human species?

Kant informs us that, in effect, nature has done with respect to the human species just what it has done with respect to all organic life. It has equipped the species to exist and flourish by supplying each with the requisite adaptive capacities for self-organization across space or geographical location and across the long march of history. These adaptive capacities Kant calls "seeds" (*Keime*) and "natural predispositions" (*natürliche Anlage*); as such, they are hardwired into the organism *as a whole*. Kant's account of natural predispositions embedded in organic life points to how the development of an organism, on his interpretation, is not random, but speaking of natural predisposition does not imply that organic life organizes itself according to natural laws that mechanistically restrict it or otherwise passively determine it. The species has agency; as a whole, it is an agent. What is unique about an organism, Kant seems to be groping toward saying, is that the freedom of an organism, particularly, the human species as a whole, and its predispositional laws (*Keime und natürliche Anlage*), in fact, cohere. Kant will refine just this point about the unity of freedom and law as the core of humanity's self-legislative capacities in the moral philosophy he will develop in the 1780s and 1790s. But as one can see, the seeds of it all—pardon the pun—were sown at least as early as the 1770s.

Kant's 1770s explanation of the coherence of freedom and law is as follows: "The causes lying in the nature of an organic body (plant or animal) that account for a specific development are called seeds . . . , [which] equip . . . [the organism] through hidden inner measures for all possible future circumstances." So equipped, the species can maintain itself; despite whatever condition in which it finds itself, the species can flourish. Kant then ties these claims about "seeds" and "natural predispositions" back to the language of race:

> Such migration and transplantation may even lead us to believe that
> new species of animals and plants have arisen, but these apparent
> new species are really nothing other than deviations and races of the
> same genus [*Abartungen und Rassen von derselben Gattung*] whose
> seeds and natural predispositions have only occasionally developed in
> different ways in the long course of time.[12]

Now while it is true that the link Kant makes here between deviations and races on the one hand and seeds on the other occurs within the context of examples about animals and plants, it yet has to be recognized that he is setting up an explanation for how this business about seeds and natural predispositions can clarify the question of human racial diversity. The scientific framework of biological or organic life is the framework within which he wants to situate the

question of human racial diversity. By situating the *Rassenfrage* in the biological sciences, Kant naturalizes the very notion of race—"race has always been with us"—thus granting scientific legitimacy to the category of race.

But just before applying this basic framework to the situation of the human species and to the question of racial diversity, Kant brings in a notion that will occupy him, in many respects, to the end of his career. This is the notion of teleology, though the term itself is not explicitly invoked in "Of the Different Human Races." The notion of a teleological orientation of the species is the touchstone of Kant's account of the implantation of natural predispositions or seeds within a given species or genus that makes possible the emergence of "deviations and races . . . in the long course of time." It is clear to him at least that neither chance nor the mechanistic laws of causality can explain why a species diversifies itself or "occasionally [develops]" in this way and not that, in one way and not another. The inadequacy of mechanism to explain the phenomenon of racial diversification within a species becomes clearer, particularly when (to revert to his own specific examples) the original external stimulus for the development of an additional layer of feathers, say, or a thicker hull around a species of wheat grain are no longer present, yet these "racial" traits are nevertheless passed on to subsequent generations within the species. How is this possible? Kant resolves the conundrum of the reproduction of traits even when the external stimulus for its original appearance is gone by saying that the reproductive transmission of these traits points to inner "purposive causes,"[13] a purposiveness that lies within the species itself, and is not attributable merely to external factors. It is this inner purposiveness linked as it is to "seeds" that allows the species to develop in a way "appropriate to the circumstances," to new and changing circumstances, and that makes those changes fixed and permanent. Kant's use, then, of examples from the animal kingdom and plant life are illustrations meant to establish a claim to the fixity or permanence of race.

With this organicist framework established, Kant is now prepared to read the situation of the human species in light of it and thus bring the weight of this framework to bear on the question of human racial difference. The human species has been outfitted with "numerous seeds and natural predispositions," he says, some of which "[have] developed and others held back" so that "we might [be] fitted to [any] particular place in the world."[14] Thus, it is for the species' need to occupy the entire globe and to be able to survive anywhere on the planet that "solicitous nature"[15] has equipped the species with the seeds of its flourishing. Under the right regional conditions, the various seeds would germinate to yield various races. Kant homes in on air quality and sunlight as the two most important external factors that can stimulate "the generative power" to activate certain seeds to affect the process of raciation. After a considerable period of time, certain seeds "become deeply rooted and [stifle] the other seeds." The result is that a race emerges. Given the deep rootedness of

certain seeds and the stifling of others in the formation of a given race, once a race actually forms, that race will "[resist] further transformation, because the character of the race has become predominate in the reproductive powers."[16] Hence, Kant says (choosing his words carefully), the external factors of air quality and sunlight *could* be responsible for establishing a race."[17]

It is important that Kant only claims that climate and sunlight *could be* responsible for raciation. For Kant, the climate is a mediate cause, but the immediate cause of raciation lies elsewhere. As Mark Larrimore has put it in his fine analysis of Kant's theory of race and understanding of the races, for Kant "every race was already prefigured *in potentia* in the first human beings,"[18] who are "the lineal root genus"[19] of the species. In 1786, Kant published an essay that makes explicit the claim that Adam and Eve of the Genesis stories of creation are this lineal root genus, those in whom every race was figured *in potentia*.[20] What must be attended to is Kant's understanding of this lineal root genus, in whom the four natural races were *in potentia* prefigured, as the actual or the immediate agent or cause of raciation. This stem genus is "the original human form" that has given rise to the other races.[21]

Since, however, "we cannot hope to find anywhere in the world an unchanged example of the original human form," the stem genus, what kinds of judgments then can be made about this now-lost prototype who is "the immediate cause of the origin of [the] different races"? The 1775 version of the race essay, which was the advertisement for a summer course at the University of Königsberg, offers the following answer:

> If we ask with which of the present races [*Rassen*] the first human stock [*Menschenstamm*] might well have had the greatest similarity [*die meiste Ähnlichkeit*], we will presumably—although *without any prejudice* because of the presumptuously *greater perfection of its color* when compared with that of the others [emphasis added]—pronounce favor on whites. For human beings, whose offspring should be acclimated in all climatic zones, would be most adept for this if they were originally fitted for the temperate climate, because this climate lies within the middle of the most extreme boundaries of the conditions within which human beings should be advised to live. And this is also the region where we—from the most ancient time to the present—find the races of whites [*die Rasse der Weißen*].[22]

Science can gain knowledge of the prototype only by reading back from its closest present-day approximation, the present-day inhabitants of the most climatically moderate zone of the globe. These people will most resemble the prototype. They will exhibit the least deviation from the original stem genus. This is because they have maintained a global position closest, as the preceding quotation indicates, to "the middle of the most extreme boundaries of the conditions within which human beings should be advised to live."

By the time of the 1777 essay ("Of the Different Human Races"), Kant is explicit about the global position that lay in media res: it is the zone "between the 31st and 52nd degrees latitude in the old world (which also seems to deserve the name old world because of the peoples that inhabit it). The greatest riches of the earth's creation are found in this region and this is also where human beings must diverge least from their original form."[23] Indeed, already in the 1775 course announcement, Kant's claim is that the inhabitants of this region have a "greater perfection of skin color," and this is precisely why they tell us the most about the original stem genus. Which race group occupies this geographical position? According to the course announcement of 1775, it is "the races of whites [*die Rasse der Weißen*]."

But in the short interim between the 1775 course advertisement and its modification into the 1777 essay, Kant modulated his language in an important way. It is not "*die* Rasse *der Weißen*" that occupy the geographical zone of climatic and therefore racial balance. Rather, "we . . . find [there]," Kant simply says, "white, indeed, brunette inhabitants [*weiße, doch brunette Einwohner*]. We want, therefore, to assume that this form [*Gestalt*] is that of the lineal root genus [*Stammgattung*]." What is important for my argument is that the specific term "race" (*Rasse*), which Kant consistently applied to the Negroes, Huns, and Hindustanis to explain their origins, has for whites now dropped out. It is not "the *races* of whites" that occupy this region; they now are only white, brunette inhabitants. Kant completes his argument by suggesting the following scheme of the races in relationship to the lineal root genus:

LINEAL ROOT GENUS:
White of brownish color
First race: Noble blond (northern Europe)
    from humid cold
Second race: Copper red (America)
    from dry cold
Third race: Black (Senegambia)
    from humid heat
Fourth race: Olive-yellow (Asian-Indians)
    from dry heat[24]

In contrast to his lengthy account of the origins of Negroes, Huns, and Hindustanis in which he is clear that they are races, Kant refers to whites with terms ranging from *Gestalt* (form) to *Abartung* (deviation) to *Schlag* (kind). As he sees it, whites are a group apart. They are a "race" that is not quite a race, the race that transcends race precisely because of its "developmental progress" (*Fortgang*) toward perfection. That Kant's chart refers to the "noble blond" of northern Europe as the first race (*Erste Rasse*) must not confuse this basic point, for we have already seen that, properly speaking, this group is really an *Abar-*

tung from the stem genus (*Stammgattung*). At best they are a special kind of "race." And even this stem genus of white brunettes, which itself is not a race, is properly speaking only the remnant, we might say, of the stem genus. They are a remnant moving toward raciation, progressing toward becoming a race.

Thus, whiteness is both "now and not yet." It is a present reality, and yet it is also still moving toward and awaiting its perfection. The teleological end, which is the consummation of all things within the economic, political, and aesthetic—in short, within the structural—reality called "whiteness," is on the one hand made present and available now in white people and in white "culture." And on the other hand, it is through these white people and culture that the full reality of whiteness will globally expand to "eschatologically" encompass all things and so bring the world to perfection. As I show below, Christianity as rational religion and Christ as the "personified idea of the good principle"[25] are the guarantee that whiteness, understood not merely and banally as pigment but as a structural–aesthetic order and as a sociopolitical arrangement, can and will be instantiated in the people who continue Christ's work, the work of Western civilization. Rendering race invisible in all of this, Kant calls this not the work of whiteness but the task of the species as such.

Perfecting Whiteness: The Progress of Western Civilization

As so far narrated, this account of Kant on whiteness might suggest that for him the significance of "the races of whites" is that they are not quite a race. They avoided the whole messiness of race by virtue of having stunted the process of racialization. Consequently, they are not a race in the same way that the other human races have become races. The other races have become races in such a way as to be held hostage to their own particularity. Their particularity as race groups is excessive or out of balance inasmuch as it aims at only its own particularity. Indeed, they suffer under the entropy of their own particularity: they can't get over themselves. Thus, the racialization process has occurred for the darker races in such a way that their racial existence is an impediment to their human existence, where "human" here stands for the universal. It would seem, therefore, that it is a boon that whites are not a race. It is a boon that, having not completed the racialization process, they are supraracial and therefore exist beyond race, right?

Well, not quite. Kant actually seems to suggest something else: namely, that it is of the nature of the human organism in its racial unfolding across the *longue durée* of time and the great geopolitical and geoeconomic expanse by which Europe (and Euro-America) gazes out on the rest of the world, not just to instantiate itself in the particularity of the races. Its objective, more precisely, is to instantiate itself in the particularity of a *perfect* race group. Perfection here is to be understood in terms of an aesthetic (and thus an ethics) of balance over imbalance, of completeness over incompleteness. It is this perfection that was

the destiny of whites as they made developmental progress toward becoming a race, and it is this perfection that was lost by the other races, particularly by the black race. I say "particularly by the black race" because it is in contrast to the Negro race that Kant is able to establish the uniqueness of white flesh. Here we see the work performed by the "self-evident" claim Kant makes earlier in the essay that "Negroes and whites are the base races."[26] If the white race exemplifies humanity on its way to perfection, the black race embodies the departure and failure to attain this perfection. In the Negro race, white flesh observes a race so mired in its particularity as never to be able to speak with universal force and, therefore, as never positioned to be an analogy or index of the universal. Black flesh lacks universal gravitas. It is trapped in its particularity in such a way that it always needs to justify its existence before universal white flesh. In short, the particularity of black flesh reflects an aesthetics, which for Kant is an ethics and a politics, of excess and imbalance—the excess of bodily particularity over rational universality: the imbalance between law and freedom.

For Kant, the teleological movement toward the perfect race—carried out by white flesh and contrasted to the limitations of the black race—is not yet complete. Indeed, his project, I claim, from the great critical and moral philosophy, with its account of aesthetics and its teleology of culture, to his political and religious outlook, is an attempt to work out how *Aufklärung* as humankind's stepping out (*Ausgang*) of immaturity into maturity is the sociopolitical process by which the project of whiteness is to be completed as the project of reason. The reconstituted and enlightened body politic completes the task of the (perfect) "race-ing" of the body.

Before turning to a fuller development of this reading of Kant, race, and the politics of whiteness, I call attention to one of his unpublished reflections on anthropological themes (*Reflexionen zur Anthropologie*) that deals with race groups, no. 1520 in the collection. *Reflexionen 1520* is of particular interest due to its strong parallels with the *Menschenkunde* that are believed to have been taken in 1781 or 1782. While the *Menschenkunde* are notes students recorded on hearing Kant's anthropology lectures, the *Reflexionen* are the personal notes, the jottings, and fragments of thought Kant himself kept on various ideas and topics throughout much of his intellectual career.[27] The *Reflexionen 1520* fragment is believed to have been penned in the decade of either the 1770s or 1780s, the period during which Kant was not only still thinking about and writing on race but was also working out the details of (in the 1770s) and publishing (in the 1780s) the critical project and the outlines of his political philosophy. It is reasonable to believe, therefore, that *Reflexionen 1520* and the *Menschenkunde* are contemporaneous. Moreover, they "show strong parallels" regarding the claims they make about the races, though "the most extreme claims in the fragment have no parallels in *Menschenkunde*."[28] Together *Reflexionen 1520* and the 1781–1782 *Menschenkunde* affirm my basic claim that

Kant saw the project of white raciation as still very much alive. But, it is in the extreme claims of *Reflexionen* 1520 that I am ultimately interested, because those claims afford us a way to understand how Kant imagined *Aufklärung* as an intricate series of sociocultural and sociopolitical processes that, in realizing the species' destiny, would complete white racialization both on the global or cosmopolitical level and on the national or metropolitan level, the level of the politics internal to whiteness.[29] The *Menschenkunde* offers the following breakdown of the races:

There are Four Races on the Earth; these are . . .

1. The American[-Indian] people cannot be formed; they are not able to receive education [*Bildung*]. They have no driving or motivating force [*Triebfeder*]; for, they lack affect and passion. They are not given to romance, and thus don't have many children. They hardly ever speak; they don't cuddle one another; they also care for nothing; and they are lazy.

2. The Negro Race, one could say, is the complete opposite of the American[-Indians]. They are full of affect and passion, quite vivacious, talkative and vain. They can be educated [*Sie nehmen Bildung an*], but only to be a servant; that is to say, they can be trained. They have many motivating forces, are also sensitive, are afraid of lashings, and also do much out of honor.

3. The Hindus surely have drive, but they have a strong degree of calm, and all of them look like philosophers. That said, they are yet given to intense anger and to love. They can be trained to the highest degree, but only to the arts, not the sciences. They never raise their reflection to the level of abstract concepts. A greater Hindu person is one who uses law but largely towards fraudulence and has a lot of money. The Hindus always remain the same way; they will never make progress, even if they had gotten an earlier start in educating themselves.[30]

4. The Race of Whites contains within itself all motivations and talents. Therefore, one must consider it with special care. To the race of whites belongs the entirety of Europe, the Turks, and the Kalmucks. If ever revolutions occurred, they were always realized by whites. The Hindus, Americans, Negroes have never had a part in them. Beneath Whites, one could establish the scale of oriental and western groups [*die Eintheilung des orientalischen und occidentalischen Schlages*]. Also thirdly, one could here account for the Finnish nation.[31]

This breakdown and characterization of the races agrees, more or less, with what Kant says about them both in the 1775/1777 essay and in his private

fragment, *Reflexionen* 1520. The private fragment, however, includes a claim made in neither of these. It is reasonable to infer from this that Kant chose to air this view neither in his public writings nor in his public lecturing. "All of the races," he says in his private note,

> will be stamped out [*Alle racen werden ausgerottet werden* . . . ; they will undergo an inner rotting or decay leading to their utter eradication] (Americans and Negroes can't rule themselves. They serve therefore only as slaves), but never that of whites. The stubbornness of the Indians in how they use things is at the root of their problem. This is the reason why they do not melt together with whites.
>
> It isn't good that they are interbreeding [*sich vermischen*]. The Spaniards in Mexico.[32]

The startling claim appears in the first sentence, with its graphic choice of words and complex sentence structure. The key verb in the sentence is the transitive verb *ausrotten*, which generally means to annihilate, destroy, eliminate, or eradicate. Kant uses it in the future tense and, importantly, the passive voice (*werden ausgerottet werden*). In writing the verb *ausrotten* in the passive voice Kant is able to leave grammatically unclear the causal agent of the verbal action, the subject that does the stamping out of all races.

Yet, while the causal agent of the action may be grammatically unclear, the trajectory of Kant's argument itself seems to clarify who this agent is. All races will be stamped out, he suggests, because of limitations that arise from within those races themselves, limitations that cannot be overcome. These limitations have stunted their racial development, leaving them in a state of imbalance, which is tantamount to leaving them immature. The imbalance centers on a lack of equilibrium between the necessary *Triebfedern,* or bodily passions and driving forces of life, on the one hand, and the mental or intellectual talents for education, for *Bildung,* on the other. Both are needed and must be properly balanced for the species to realize its destiny. And so, Kant's judgment against the Amerindians is that they lack the *Triebfedern* needed for sexual reproduction. Furthermore, they cannot receive education, he says. By contrast, Negroes have an excess of bodily, sexual passion and, rather than not being able to receive education, they simply cannot be educated at all. Thus, Kant concludes, neither "Americans [nor] Negroes [can] rule themselves. They [can] serve therefore only as slaves." As regards the Indians of Southeast Asia, or the "Hindus," Kant says in effect that they are slaves in another sense: they are slaves to money. Indeed, they are "[stubborn] in their use of things." All of this bespeaks their improper relationship to law, which itself is indicative of their inability to make progress in education. Thus, while the limitations of the Amerindians and Negroes are essentially bodily, the limitations of the Indians of Southeast Asia are basically educative and intellectual—and, crucially, religious.

Although each race suffers from a different kind of imbalance, the core problem for all of them is their inability to be self-governing or autonomous. The limitations, in other words, are expressions of moral heteronomy as inscribed in the very fabric of their racial makeup, in what is permanent about them. These limitations lead to the inner decay that destroys the nonwhite races. In other words, the agents implied by the passive sentence, "All races will be stamped out," are actually those races themselves. It is as if Kant is saying that all races will be destroyed as a result of their own internal rotting or decaying, a rotting or decaying whose catalyst is the racialization process itself.

None of this, however, applies to whites. For, "All races will be stamped out...but never that of whites." Mark Larrimore has observed that "the odd sentence structure of this note ('all...except') shows the thought process of someone for whom 'all races' does not automatically include the whites."[33] They are the exceptional race whose drives and talents are thoroughly balanced and thus are not subject to racial implosion or annihilation. Indeed, they are the race in which this balance of bodily drives and intellectual talents are progressing toward full maturation. It is here that we see the "now and not yet" structure of white racial perfection in the modern imagination. This now and not yet structure speaks to the fact that, in the white race, the perfection of the human race is historically present, though it is incomplete (because the white race has not yet fully instantiated itself in the white brunettes). They must yet work out their salvation with fear and trembling, as it were. What, in the end, are we left with? Kant deracializes the white race so that it can be the perfect bearer of perfect racial identity.[34]

But Larrimore's claim about Kant's sentence structure can be refined and pushed even further. For, the odd sentence structure of this note ("all...except whites" or, in my translation, "all...but never that of whites") reveals the thought process of one for whom the destruction of "all races" is occurring through the same sociocultural and political mechanisms that are establishing and bringing to maturity another, not-yet-fully-raced group. This is the race of whites. The destruction of all races on the one hand and the nondestruction of whites on the other are imagined as a singular, intertwined sociocultural and political process of the advance of Western civilization. This is evident in that, as Kant's parenthetic claim regarding the fitness of Amerindians and persons of African descent for slavery strongly implies, white enslavement of the Negro race and the colonialist expansion of western Europe into the hemispheric south and west are vehicles by which the racial development, the maturing of whites, is in fact furthered.

Indeed, the stamping out of the nonwhite races, from Kant's perspective, coincides with their being brought into the global advance and cosmopolitical maturing of whiteness as the revolutionary social-political process and arrangement of Enlightenment in the 1784 essay bearing this title. Thus,

following his fourfold schematic breakdown of the races, Kant says in the same unpublished reflection:

> All revolutions of the world have been produced by the race of whites. Nomads have only power and on their own have not produced enduring or lasting revolutions. The three other races [have produced] none at all . . . . Our ancient history of mankind certainly goes forward by the race of whites.[35]

To clarify who the subjects of "ancient history" are, Kant adds a parenthetical note that says, "not Indians, blacks." Immediately following this, the unpublished reflection makes brief, summarizing claims regarding the two groupings that lie behind the fourfold grouping of the races: "The Oriental and Occidental Groups" (*Der orientalische und occidentalische Schlag*).[36] The fourfold racial breakdown collapses into a binary one.

Given this, what white folks must most fear, because of the close racial and cultural contact their racial development entails, according to Kant, is the potential for and deleterious effects of miscegenation, or racial intermixing. Racial or cultural intimacy—this is what is to be most feared insofar as it could lead to what one theorist has recently called "wayward reproductions" within the species or, more specifically, the derailing of "the race of whites" from its destiny.[37] Promiscuous relationships, therefore, must be policed and avoided at all costs. The possibility of the mulatto, of "impure" interracial existence, is the fear of all fears.

Kant had introduced this very worry over wayward reproductions already in his 1775–1777 essay on the races. Now, however, we see that it is also something that he obsessed about privately and, indeed, into the critical phase of his thought. But there is a difference between his public and his private obsessions over the matter. Kant's public worries over wayward reproductions were worries over the presence of the alien who came into the land to contaminate the racial bloodlines of a whiteness that was yet in silent development in the northernmost regions of the German lands. The alien, as Kant tells us, came into the land and began to short-circuit the developmental processes by which whiteness was moving toward perfect racial instantiation. Thus, the worry of this essay is with the other in our midst, the alien within.

The worry of the private *Reflexionen* 1520 is of a different sort. It is a colonialist worry over the exportation of whiteness into non-European places. It worries over the physical geographies or bodies of the alien. For Kant, the premier instance of this worry over what can go wrong as whites pursue nature's mandate for humanity to cover the entire globe, and in so doing come into contact with the alien without, is that of his fellow Europeans, the Spanish. The problem here is with how to export whiteness in such a way that it does not become tainted with inferior blood and thus become susceptible to an imbalanced mix of driving and motivating forces. What is important in all of this is

that, whether he is speaking of the problem of the alien within (i.e., with the production and reproduction of whiteness within its own, European borders) or the problem of the alien without (i.e., with the production and reproduction of whiteness beyond Europe), Kant's ultimate concern is with the success of the universalist project of modernity, the project of whiteness as the advance of cultured civilization (which is the advance toward the perfect race of humans).[38]

Thus, it is between these two poles that the question of white progress must be negotiated: the pole of the cosmopolitical (the alien without) and the pole of the domestically political (the alien within). It is no surprise then that Kant's first public attempts to unfold his political philosophy as a reflection on the meaning of *Aufklärung* is articulated between these poles, the poles of the universalism of cosmopolitan society (*weltbürgerliche Gesellschaft*) and domestic civil society (*bürgerliche Gesellschaft*). Moreover, it is no surprise that he would release the essays that take up these respective poles in the same journal, the *Berlinische Monatsschrift*, the premier journal of Prussian Enlightenment ideas, and, indeed, in back-to-back issues of the journal in 1784.

The first essay, "The Idea of Universal History with Cosmopolitan Intent," constructs the "idea"—in the sense laid out in *Critique of Pure Reason*[39]—that there is a logic of the historical progress of civilization at work in nature, a teleology shall we say. Such an "idea of universal history" is necessary in order to posit "the goal of the understanding's [or reason's] actions."[40] In this teleological framework, nature operates according to a peculiar, subtle, but finally violent cunning to complete the development of humanity's species-capacity for reason. By means of the violent cunning of reason, and the teleology of history that is its inner analytic, enlightenment arises on a global scale as the means of moving the human species beyond its "unsociable sociability." But the unsociable sociability that Kant has in view is the intraracial antagonisms between the European nations, the nations populated by whites, as they became increasingly prone to fighting one another over the colonized lands in the non-European parts of the world.[41]

For my purposes, the important thing to be clear about is that Kant's racial anthropology, which was an incipient political anthropology, while primarily concerned with the problem of the alien without, with the dawning of the critical philosophy in the 1780s quickly turned to a problem that weighed heavily both on him and on many of his contemporaries: the problem of the alien within. It remains to be seen who this alien within is. Suspending that question for now, it can yet be said that intimations of a concern with the alien within is already present in Kant's racial anthropology as he developed it in the 1770s essay, which foregrounds the problem of the alien without, the other at the periphery of the Occident. My claim is that with his 1780s turn to the formal structure of a rational or "enlightened" vision of the body politic, Kant has turned neither from the question of white perfection, the problem of the alien, nor from his concern for the advance of Western civilization and the

establishment of Christian culture. Thus, to reflect on the problem of the alien body, whether without (which has been the concern of this chapter so far) or within (which I take up next), is to attend all along to the perfection of the white, occidental body.

Kant's 1780s thought represents—and this is the fundamental argument of the next section—a shift toward exploring the *political* contours of that perfection as it organizes itself on an axis whose coordinates are occidental center–oriental periphery. It is to this shift in emphasis from the 1770s work that brought race to the foreground and pushed politics to the background to the 1780s work that brought politics to the foreground and pushed race to a camouflaged but yet determinative background that I now turn. Bear in mind, however, that in considering this shift in accent in Kant's thought, my concern is to isolate moments—and certainly not all of them—that suggest that his earlier arguments regarding the races generally and white perfection particularly have not receded. They now only function under the banner of the universal, political advance of Western civilization. Thus, the argument that I sketch in the next section is this: race controls Kant's ostensibly egalitarian politics of global civil society and a domestic civil society in its functioning under the auspices of modern democracy. Moreover, it controls it in such a way as to require the subjugation of the racial alien outside the West as well as the racial alien who has been displaced *within* the Western political order.

Kant and the Drama of Politics

In sketching this argument I focus mainly on Kant's *Anthropology from a Pragmatic Point of View* (1798), which develops what I would like to call a racial pragmatics. This racial pragmatism is the (mostly) unseen engine driving Kant's pragmatic anthropology in its aspiration to become a political anthropology in which whiteness—of course, never having to name itself as such because it functions under the universal nomenclature of the "human species"—realizes itself in a reconstituted sociopolitical order, a moral and autonomous order rooted in the conceptual world of reason rather than a heteronomous order driven by the intuitions of the world of the senses. *Aufklärung* names the process that will bring about this reconstituted social order in which the latter order is transformed into the former.

The Prepolitical Pragmatics of Race: The Anthropology Text

If earlier I engaged Kant's 1775 course announcement and the subsequent 1777 revision and publication of this announcement as his first essay on race ("Of the Different Human Races"), I now seek to locate Kant's theorizing

about race within the wider framework in which he explored the issue. That wider framework is his anthropology lecture course. For some time, Kant offered a private course in anthropology, but beginning in the winter semester of the 1772–1773 academic year, he incorporated this private course into his public lecturing at the University of Königsberg, teaching the course annually for the remainder of his career as a university professor, to 1796. The last text he had a direct hand in seeing through to publication, *Anthropology from a Pragmatic Point of View*, documents Kant's anthropology course. My concern with this text and with the course that it documents is with the light it casts on his account of race and, vice versa, on what his understanding of race contributes to a deeper understanding of the broader philosophical anthropology he articulated from the 1780s critical phase of his thought to its 1790s postcritical phase in which religion became an explicit subject of theorization with the publication particularly of *Religion within the Limits of Reason Alone* (1793).

Kant clarifies what he sought to accomplish in the anthropology lecture course in his 1773 letter to the Prussian enlightenment intellectual Marcus Herz.[42] A Jewish physician who had been Kant's one-time pupil and who sought to style himself a "philosophical doctor" along lines articulated by the philosopher-physician Ernst Platner, Herz wrote a celebratory review of Platner's 1772 *Anthropology for Physicians and Philosophers*. In this text, Platner sought to give an account of anthropology that would establish it as a true science (*Wissenschaft*), which meant establishing it as the discipline that brings together anatomy (or disciplines that consider the body apart from the impulses it receives from the soul) with the philosophical disciplines (i.e., aesthetics, ethics, psychology, and logic), or the disciplines that consider the soul or nonbodily matters apart from the body. For Platner, anthropology is the third and true science in that it is the discipline that synthesizes these disciplines. Bringing together philosophy and anatomical medicine, anthropology seeks to conceptualize the "entire human being" in the comprehensiveness of its mind-body unity. For this reason, anthropology, as Platner viewed it, is the loftiest and most practical of the modern sciences.[43]

Kant's letter to Herz provides an occasion for Kant to respond to Platner's general anthropological vision with a vision of his own. Kant believed that his approach to the human being would establish him, and not Platner, as the one to make anthropology a "proper academic discipline." Kant says to his one-time student in this letter that he will be the one to make this intellectual breakthrough because, in contrast to Platner's anthropological vision, his vision of pragmatic anthropology is not motivated by the need to resolve the metaphysical tangle of the dualism between mind and body. Rather, grounding itself in an "entirely new conceptual science," a science of "transcendental philosophy," Kant's anthropology will get new mileage out of this very dualism. Kant puts it this way in his letter:

This winter I am giving, for the second time, a lecture course on anthropology, a subject that I now intend to make into a proper academic discipline. But my plan is quite different. I intend to disclose the sources of all the practical sciences, the science of morality, of skill, of human intercourse, of the method of molding and governing human beings [*der Methode Menschen zu bilden und zu regieren*], and thus of everything that pertains to the practical. I shall seek to discuss phenomena and their laws rather than the possibility of modifying human nature per se. Hence I omit entirely the subtle and, to my mind, eternally futile inquiries as to the manner in which bodily organs are connected with thought. I include so many observations of ordinary life that my listeners have constant occasion to compare their ordinary experience with my remarks and thus, from beginning to end, find the lectures entertaining and never dry.[44]

As already noted, Kant marks off his approach to anthropology from Platner's, Herz's, and others of their ilk by his refusal to get bogged down in arcane speculation and "subtle and . . . futile inquiries as to the manner in which bodily organs are connected with thought." Instead, Kant's anthropology grounds itself, as is the case as we have already seen with his 1775–1777 race essay, in Kant's own powers of observation: that is, in his ability to survey, and thereby surveil, "ordinary life" and extract from it the laws according to which one's life is to be molded and governed so as to make one's way through the world. But it is just this descriptive notion of "observation" on the one hand and this prescriptive one of "molding and governing human beings" on the other, as the poles between which pragmatic anthropology functions, that need further interrogation. And for this one must turn to *Anthropology* itself.

Anthropology's introduction is arguably where Kant unpacks his terse, epistolary claim to Herz that pragmatic anthropology is charged with the task of discerning the "laws" for "molding and governing human beings." "All cultural progress [*Alle Fortschritte in der Kultur*]," Kant says,

by means of which the human being advances his education, has the goal of applying this acquired knowledge and skill for the world's use. But the most important object of culture [*Kultur*] to which he can apply them is the human being: because the human being is his own final end.—Therefore to know the human being according to his species as an earthly being endowed with reason especially deserves to be called *knowledge of the world* [*Weltkenntnis*], even though he only constitutes one part of the peoples of the earth.

A doctrine of knowledge of the human being, systematically formulated (anthropology), can exist either in a physiological or in a pragmatic point of view.—Physiological knowledge of the human being concerns the investigation of what *nature* makes of the human

being; pragmatic, what *he* as a free-acting being makes of himself, or can and should make of himself.... [This latter task] is precisely what concerns us here.[45]

For Kant, anthropology's chief concern is with the human being's empowerment to act freely in the world. Indeed, its concern is with the formation of the character necessary to act freely and in accordance with "what [the human being] . . . makes of himself, or can and should make of himself." Thus, contrary to physiological anthropology's whim for "theoretical speculation" and its penchant for searching out "for example . . . the traces of impressions remaining in the brain," speculation that "is a pure waste of time," Kantian anthropology's object of concern is the prescriptive activity of human self-empowerment.[46] Pragmatic anthropology aspires to transform the human being from a simple creature endowed with reason (*Vernunft*) to one who grasps what the gift of reason is for and who employs reason properly—that is, who employs it to its proper end. Pragmatically understood, the human being has been endowed by "Nature" with reason so that it can act in freedom. Reason, therefore, is not a speculative (*vernünfteln*) tool; its interest is in assisting the human being to enact a particular kind of agency, the agency of freedom, an agency that leads to "knowledge of the world." Pragmatic anthropology, then, is the science that aids the human being to cultivate itself toward this end, the ends of culture (*Kultur* and, ultimately, *Bildung*),[47] which are the ends of freedom.

As if to bring a final note of clarity to what he means in saying that human reason is for purposes of cultural self-knowledge, which is practical "knowledge of the world," Kant gets explicit about where this process of pragmatic self-empowerment into a freely acting creature leads:

> Such an anthropology, considered as *knowledge of the world*, which
> must come after our *schooling*, is not yet actually called *pragmatic*
> when it contains an extensive knowledge of *things* in the world,
> for example, animals, plants, and minerals from various lands and
> climates, but only when it contains knowledge of the human being as
> a *citizen of the world* [*Weltbürger*].[48]

Thus, far from being a merely descriptive activity, pragmatic anthropology is prescriptive. It seeks to transform the human being from a merely *rational* creature to a *political* actor in the world, a *Weltbürger*, who transforms the external, material world. The pragmatic process of self-cultivation leads to the formation of the human as a political actor. But it only leads there, paradoxically, by suspending one's relationship to the external world, by having a relationship of "disinterest" to it, as Kant comes to say in the third *Critique*, the *Critique of Judgment*, or as he says in the *Groundwork for the Metaphysics of Morals*, by being autonomously, and not heteronymously, related to it.[49]

It is only from within a strictly nonpolitical comportment toward the material world (that is, from within the nonmaterial "culture" of inwardness) that one shapes, molds, and governs the material, political "culture" of outwardness. Through a mode of intellectuality that has a relationship of disinterest to material culture and that seeks to shape human agency within such a relationship in order to form cosmopolitan citizens, pragmatic anthropology already envisions the move from the nonpolitical domain of self-cultivation to a fully politicized mode of human agency. It aims at conceiving the human being's proper political agency as the agency of autonomy, an agency that comes into its own in a cosmopolitical or internationalist vision of the collective political freedom of nations in a future republican world order and in a vision of domestic civil society whose political form is that of a democratic republic.

This becomes abundantly clear in the last section of *Anthropology*. In sketching the kind of political order toward which pragmatic anthropology aspires, Kant says that the human being must be "educated" into a pragmatic vision of "the good" society.[50] The kind of education Kant has in view is an education "that must come after [formal] schooling."[51] It is an aesthetic or inner education, a form of "self-cultivation," "self-civilization," and "self-moralization," in which the human being transcends the material world and "the impulses of comfort and good living, which he calls happiness . . . [in order] to make himself worthy of humanity by *actively* struggling with the obstacles that cling to him because of the crudity of his nature."[52] This aesthetic education, which the "arts and the sciences" assist in bringing about, leads to the "progressive organization of citizens of the earth into and toward the species as a system that is cosmopolitically united."[53]

In driving home the force of what this higher education to the good accomplishes in setting the conditions that make possible the formation of a cosmopolitical world order of nations, Kant turns to the rhetoric of "revolution" and "enlightenment," indeed, to the rhetoric of the species' "emergence from self-incurred immaturity," the very rhetoric that he uses in his 1784 essay "What Is Enlightenment?" At issue here is not first and foremost a political revolution: it is an internal one, a revolution within the subject itself by which the subject does not merely employ "book-learning [to increase] knowledge" through "rationalizing [*vernünfteln*], playing with mere experiments in the use of reason without a law of reason."[54] Rather, this is a revolution in which one subjects oneself to laws or maxims of reason. As self-imposed laws, laws that arise from and for the subject itself and that therefore express a unique kind of agency, these "unalterable commands" express the unity of freedom and law.[55] They express the autonomy and freedom of the subject in itself and for itself, an autonomy and freedom that enact themselves precisely in the suspension of the subject's relationship to the external, material world of bodily life.

This is the subject's agency. The laws by which the agency of autonomy and freedom are enacted are "1) To think *for oneself*; 2) To think oneself (in communication with human beings) into the place of every *other person*;" and "3) Always to think *consistently* with *oneself*."[56] Having stated these "unalterable commands," Kant says that "[anthropology] can furnish examples of each of these principles, but it can furnish even more examples of their opposite."[57] Kant conceives of these examples as, in effect, observable case studies of the successful and unsuccessful enactment of the laws of reason. They demonstrate that "[the] most important revolution from within the human being is 'his exit from [*Ausgang*] his self-incurred immaturity [*selbstverschuldete Unmündigkeit*].'[58] Before this revolution he let others think for him and merely imitated others or allowed them to guide him by leading-strings. Now he ventures to advance, though still shakily, with his own feet on the ground of experience."[59] Positive and negative examples function in pragmatic anthropology to "schematize" or concretize Kant's "categorical" claim that it is the species' destiny to walk out of immaturity, out of its inability to speak or use language (*Mund*) properly, and into maturity. Yet, there is a need for more negative examples. Functioning as inverse, illustrative guides, negative examples also mediate the mature emergence of the species, but they do so by casting the gaze on those who have been unable to ascend into maturity.

Perfecting Whiteness—Redux: Positive and Negative
Examples and the Anxiety over the Jews

Kant claims anthropology's ability to provide examples of those within the species who either successfully or unsuccessfully enact the unalterable commands of reason is in book I of *Anthropology*. To understand the function of the negative examples, it is first necessary to clarify how, for Kant, the German nation embodies the ideal. In his section on "The Character of the Peoples," which immediately precedes the penultimate section on "The Character of the Races" and the final section on "The Character of the Species," the principle nations Kant considers are the French, English, Spanish, Italian, and German.[60]

His interest in these *Volk* is not in terms of their "characteristics as nations," characteristics that are, as he says, "acquired and *artificial*."[61] Nor is his interest in them tied to "climate and soil," an argument he fully develops in "Of the Different Human Races," as we have already seen. Kant's interest in these peoples is in terms of their "innate, natural character, which so to speak lies in the blood mixture of the human being."[62] Considering these peoples from this vantage explains why "the two *most civilized* peoples on earth, England and France," he says, "are in a constant feud with each other."[63] These nations feud because they "[have] contrasting characters."[64] The French are "courteous" and on the whole "lovable." Moreover, an "infectious spirit of

freedom" marks them indelibly.[65] This is their character. The English, in contrast, who are descended from the ancient "Britons," have developed into aggressors. This is because their geographical situation as an island people has insulated them from attackers at the same time that it has encouraged them to be attackers. The English disposition, therefore, in contrast to the French, is nonamiable.

In framing the matter in this way, Kant establishes English and French character as the binary poles between which he situates the character of the other western European nations. But it is the Germans who balance the character of the European peoples, for "[of] all civilized peoples" they exhibit the proper balance of "good character," a balance able to bring whiteness to perfection.[66] The Germans are already, Kant basically says, the quintessential cosmopolitan people, for "[in] his dealing with others, the German's character is modesty. More than any other people, he learns foreign languages, he is . . . a wholesale dealer in learning, and in the field of the sciences he is the first to get to the bottom of many things that are later utilized by others with much ado; he has no national pride, and is too cosmopolitan to be deeply attached to his homeland."[67] The German spirit of cosmopolitanism allows them to do what the English and the French have been unable to do in their relationship with one another: namely, cease waging war and thus destroying the progress of the species, which is the progress of the nations of whites.

Kant is not making an argument against "war" as such. What he wants to put an end to is war among the civilized, white nations as they fight over who will control which parts of the nonwhite world. Kant can commend the German people because, at the time of his writings, they had no colonial holdings. Their interest in colonialism, contrary to the French and the English, was disinterested independence from the empirical conditions of colonialism, which made them (theoretically at least) better colonial masters of the world. This is what historian Suzanne Zantop has called precolonial Germany's "colonial fantasy."[68] It is this disinterestedness or autonomy that positioned the Germans, as Kant saw it, to direct the other European nations in how to lead the species in its mission to cover the globe. They are the most free. Autonomy must lead the way.

But this same quality of autonomous disinterest made the Germans a positive example in another respect: namely, in establishing the kind of domestic civil society or nation that makes possible the realization of a cosmopolitan society. For, just as a relationship of disinterested autonomy is to mark the cosmopolitan order, so, too, is such a relationship to mark the structure of domestic politics, the political structure of the nation. The German, therefore, Kant says, "neither rationalizes [*vernünfteln*] about the already established order nor thinks one up himself."[69] Indeed, "he would rather submit to despotism than get mixed up in innovations (especially unauthorized reforms in government)."[70] The German, in short, has a relationship of autonomy to the

external, material world of politics. How does one make sense of this seeming incongruency, or perhaps even paradox, between Kant's pragmatic and moral anthropology of autonomy and freedom, on the one hand, in which the human being is free to think for oneself or be self-legislating, and on the other hand, his political philosophy, which extols submission to the state and its laws even if those laws are despotic? How does one reconcile an anthropology that envisions the human being as free with respect to itself but bound with regard to the state?

One way to interpret Kant at this point is as the fountainhead of German conservatism, which as an interpretation surely has something to commend it.[71] However, I seek not to get lost in, or sidetracked by, the two-dimensional question of Kant's conservatism or liberalism, for there is something else that is more pressing about his thought: namely, his vision of how the German reconciled the human being as a rational entity able to "order the chaos of experience and legislate it in an autonomous manner" and the human being as an entity subject to the "laws of civil society that regulate the way we act in the world as intuitive beings, that is, as human beings who may be swayed by desires aroused by our perception or intuition of the empirical world."[72] It is in reconciling these seemingly paradoxical moments in his anthropology that Kant imagines the species realizing itself. Michael Mack captures how Kant reconciles them:

> We are free and can establish rules legislating the natural world in an autonomous manner. In order to do so, we have to subscribe to the rules of civil society. Here we happily abrogate our right to intuitive happiness, as aimed at in a heteronomously legislated society. We willingly follow restrictions imposed on our empirical and material desires by obeying a strict 'Mine-and-Yours' ownership and property distinction.[73]

This means that "the autonomy of the individual paradoxically presupposes a political system that enforces the idea of holding objects 'intelligibly' rather than being determined by their sensible conditions."[74]

This autonomy presupposes a political system in which the material order, the order of the worldly goods of the body, is ultimately owned by the state, whereas the immaterial order of freedom, the order of mind, which is the realm of the intellectuals, intellectuals such as Kant, is owned by public culture. Indeed, this latter realm is "culture." Culture, therefore, is the domain of autonomy or true subjectivity and is marked by the "abstract movement away from the worldly, in radical polarity to heteronomy as the movement toward empirical objects" or toward the body and the goods of materiality.[75] Pragmatic anthropology guides the human being into detachment from worldly goods in order to be a world citizen (*Weltbürger*) or one suited to occupy and thus own the entire world. In this regard, pragmatic anthropology seeks to assist the

human being to make itself into an autonomous agent, one who, in detaching itself from "happiness" and thus from all worldly goods, cedes the body and all that is material to the state. Such is the precondition of autonomy: Kant envisions a situation, not unlike the Prussian sociopolitical order, in which "the state . . . transforms the individual [indeed, the body itself] into an instrument for the public display of state power."[76] It is in this way that the body articulates the body politic and its aspirations.

But here is where negative examples come in. As discussed earlier in this chapter, a significant objective of Kant's account of race is interpreting the nonwhite, racial alien, those who reside outside of Europe, as those who are unable to have an autonomous relationship to materiality and thus to worldly goods. They cannot abstract themselves from their own bodies and enter into an autonomous way of existence. In short, they do not know how *to be* in the world for the sake of *being* itself. Kant does not rehash the arguments in support of his racial contentions in the pragmatic anthropology since he addresses these negative racial examples in the separate course on race and in his separate writings on race. He does, however, in *Anthropology* and thus in the anthropology course, call attention to a different kind of negative, racial example. This is the example of the Jews, whom he interprets as displaced racial aliens, aliens displaced within the Prussian body politic and thus displaced within the white nations of Europe. These Jews, Kant says, are Orientals or "Palestinians living among us."[77]

In focusing attention on the Jews as the sole negative racial other in *Anthropology*, Kant makes them stand in for all nonwhite flesh. Put differently, all nonwhite peoples become positioned within, or an articulation of, the *Judentum* (a broad catch-all term to encompass the Jewish people and all things Jewish, including Jewish religion or Judaism); the *Rassenfrage* becomes a moment within the *Judenfrage*. And hence, what was a fourfold schema of the races in the 1775–1777 race essay—the white, Negro, Hun (Mongol and Kalmuck), and Hindu or Hindustani—reduces to a binary opposition between white and nonwhite flesh qua white and Jewish flesh, between occidental whiteness and oriental (Palestinian) Jewishness.[78]

His central concern is not to theorize how the Jews are the basis of all degeneracy; he basically assumes as much.[79] Rather, his central concern is to find a way to reconceive civil society in such a way as to police oriental contagion residing within the Occident, a contagion poised to derail a vision of the autonomy of life, which he argues is to be realized in and sustained by democratic, civil society. These oriental Jews, "[having] earned the not unfounded reputation of being cheaters, on account of the spirit of usury," and being a heteronymous people, are a "nation of cheaters."[80] They are a people whose character is such that they ignore the property, monetary, and legal regulations that proscribe how one is to relate to material gain. Consumed with the in-

terests of material life, the Jews are a "nation" (within the European nations) whose consuming interest in material life has led them to refuse submission to the rules governing modern civil society. They are a heteronymous people.

Kant does not stop here, though. He does not want merely to "[moralize] to this people in regard to the matter of cheating and honesty." Instead, he says, "I prefer . . . to give my conjecture on the origin of this peculiar condition (that is, of a people consisting of merchants)." The upshot of Kant's explanation of the "origin of [the] peculiar condition" of the Jews is this: their heteronymous and sensuous nature arises from their religion, which after their dispersion throughout the world they have carried with them. In fact, they find comfort in their condition from the Scriptures themselves (albeit, from a nonrational, nonmoral reading of them, according to Kant): "[The Jewish] constitution, which is sanctioned by *ancient statutes* [italics mine] and even by us under whom they live (who have certain holy books in common with them), cannot be repealed without inconsistency, even though they have made the saying 'Buyer beware' into the highest principle of their morality in dealing with us."[81] Thus, instead of returning thanks to the nations that have offered them refuge, the Jews, bound by their "ancient superstition," have chosen to make up the difficulty they have found in making their way in foreign lands by "outwitting the people under whom they find protection, and even one another."[82] In short, the religion of the Jews enslaves them to the material, empirical world. What sets the Jews apart, however, from the other alien, nonwhite races, the alien beyond Europe, is that this racial alien, Kant in effect says, is living among us. And thus, their oriental-racial contagion is poised to infect the occidental body (politic). The occident risks mulattic contamination. This is the ultimate source of Kant's anxiety over the Jews. They are the proverbial neighbor next door, whose son has an interest in your daughter. They are that neighbor who we fear will send the entire neighborhood to pot (and of course, send "autonomous" equity values plummeting).

This is the place to briefly restate the point made at the beginning of chapter 1 of this book, where I highlight that Kant's thought reflects the degree to which he was a cultural thinker, an intellectual whose thought represented an intervention into the broad, late-eighteenth-century crisis of public culture.[83] At the heart of the crisis was the place of religion generally and Christianity particularly in modern society and, more specifically, the question of whether the *Judentum* was at the heart of the crisis of Prussian "Christian" culture and, indeed, of modern western civilization. The debate took the form of whether the Jews could be assimilated into Prussian culture (or the other cultures of Western Europe) and, if thoroughly assimilated, have citizenship rights extended to them.

Kant's argument resembled that of another Aufklärer, Christian Wilhelm von Dohm (1751–1830). In his celebrated 1781 tract *Über die bürgerliche*

Verbesserung der Juden (*On the Civil Improvement of the Jews*), Dohm offered a conditional "yes" to the question of whether or civil rights should be extended to the Jews of Prussia. Interestingly, his argument proceeded on the basis of a logic that yoked race and religion. Kant's thought was in many respects like his fellow Aufklärer, for he too offered a conditional "yes" to the question of whether the Jews could be civilly improved and thus have qualified civil rights extended to them. Moreover, he along with Dohm employed a racial-religious logic that called for reconstituting the body politic on the basis of a vision of autonomy, or freedom, as the destiny of the species as a signal feature of his proposal.

Thus, these *Aufklärer* shared a similar vision of the autonomy of a public culture of enlightened intellectuals schooled in the aesthetics of transcending the empirical sphere of worldly goods. Moreover, they understood that their work was to influence the sphere of political culture, transforming or reconstituting it by injecting freedom into it. And yet, they both advanced arguments that at root were religious in relationship to the aforementioned political and cultural arguments. The religious and the political-cultural were two-sides of a singular reality. Therefore, they both called for Prussians (and, implicitly, the Western European powers) to rationally reconstitute Christianity, transforming it into a religion on whose basis a vision of Western civilization and culture rooted in the precepts of reason could be established. In short, both were interested in the nationalist project of reconstituting the German lands on the basis of Enlightenment principles.

While Dohm advanced this vision as a political operative or civil servant in Frederick II's Prussian administration—he began his career as archivist and councillor of war in Frederick's department of foreign affairs in 1779—Kant took a more "detached" posture as critical metaphysician, but yet as civil philosopher and social theorist.[84] From this posture he would be the one to offer a full-orbed theory of this moment, indeed, of the social processes making up this moment of *Aufklärung*. However, what finally sustains his social vision, which he codifies in various of his writings, from the critical and moral philosophy to the philosophy of law to the pragmatic anthropology, is the "dejudaization" of Christianity itself, which, put positively, means its "rationalization." Such a rational religion would serve as the basis of modernity itself, as the basis for the religious expression of whiteness, and as that through which the species will realize itself in and as an ethical, human community.

Kant's objective, therefore, was never the overcoming of religion. The point he sought to make was that only a particular kind of religious orientation was detrimental to the species' self-realization: namely, the kind of religion that binds the creature to the material order rather than disciplining the body into being the property of the state on the one hand, so that at the level of the aesthetic sphere of public culture the human being could be free to "make something of himself" on the other. In making something of itself in the aesthetic domain of free intellectuals, the human being could autonomously

craft itself as a mature subject by exiting the immaturity of a heteronymous relationship to worldly goods. Religion is not optional; it is necessary to the species' self-making out of heteronomy into autonomy. Thus, Kant says (on the last page of the *Anthropology* no less):

> It also belongs to the character of our species that, in striving to-
> ward our civil constitution, *it also needs a discipline of religion* [italics
> mine], so that what cannot be achieved by *external* constraint can
> be brought about by internal constraint (the constraint of conscience).
> For the moral predisposition of the human being is used politically by
> legislators, a tendency that belongs to the character of the species.
> However, if morals do not precede religion in this discipline of the
> people [which, as Kant sees it, is the case with Jewish religion],
> then religion makes itself lord over morals, and statutory religion
> becomes an instrument of state authority (politics) under religious
> despots: an evil that inevitably upsets and misguides character by
> governing it with deception.[85]

With this claim in place, Kant turns in his religious writings, formulated in the overlapping postcritical period of his career and last phase of his life, to a reinterpretation of Christianity as a nonstatutory religion set off against all statutory, which is to say non-Christian, religions and most especially Jewish religion.

Yet, Kant's nonstatutory and rational reinterpretation of Christianity functions at an unreflective or politically unconscious level to pseudotheologically legitimate or "sanctify" whiteness and the strivings of Western civilization. What we see in Kant is the ideological use of Christianity. This, I contend, is the genealogical moment—and here I mean "genealogy" in a way broadly analogous to Foucault's use of the term as a "moment of arising"—in which whiteness reveals itself as a "Christian" theological articulation of modern civil society as tied to "bios" or life ethnographically or racially conceived.[86] In this articulation, Christianity is reimagined as "racially" severed from and ethnographically triumphant over its oriental Jewish roots. Functioning in the modern world as a revitalized Gnosticism, or more specifically as a kind of neo-Marcionism (see this book's prologue), Christianity, reconstituted as the moral religion par excellence of reason, extols a Jesus who, rather than disclosing YHWH or the God of Israel as the ground of redemption for Jews and Gentiles alike, instead affirms what the human species "can or should make of itself." The rational Christ affirms that the species can, and therefore should, make itself into a moral creature and not simply rest content as a creature with powers of speculation or rationality (*Vernünfteln*). In short, rational Christianity and its central figure, the rational Christ, give reason for the human species to hope that the ideal toward which it strives is possible. The final section of this chapter examines this Christology to show how it functions

to pseudotheologically "sanctify" whiteness and legitimate the strivings of Western civilization.

Kant and the Great Drama of Religion

Coming to terms with Kant's Christology requires an understanding of how he figures the relationship between the identity of Jesus and the establishment of justice, right, and, as he says in one of his late essays, "perpetual peace" among nations in a cosmopolitan society.[87] *Religion within the Boundaries of Mere Reason* (1793) is where he details this relationship, formulating an account of law that is to be the basis of a cosmopolitical order, as he calls it in *Anthropology* and in other nonexplicitly religious writings, or what he calls an "ethico-civil" community in his religious work. My interest in Kant's account of law and the Christology sustaining it is in how the racial and the political converge on and are held together by a religious vision of the species, indeed, a religious vision of whiteness. My argument is that Kant accomplishes this convergence through a reading of Paul and Jesus that sunders the Old Testament, as sensuous, heteronymous, and bound to the empirical, from the New, as nonsensuous, autonomous, and transcendental. In short, I am interested in Kant's project of severing Christianity from its Jewish roots. The severance is accomplished through a rational interpretation of the meaning of law.

In making this argument, I begin with Kant's reading of Paul and the law, and from there consider the Christological and even the soteriological grounding he provides. If Kant's reading of Paul and the law discloses the theopolitics ensconced within his account of religion, then his reading of Jesus and the law, or his Christology, is the vanishing point or elusive tangent at which his accounts of race and politics meet. His Christology discloses how a deep-seated anxiety over the Jews, an anxiety that fears them as a potential contagion of whiteness, operates below the radar—but not so deep that it cannot be detected—of his thought. How does Kant seek to overcome the specter of racial contamination, the fear that the species—read: white folks (*Volk*) as the bearers of Western civilization—will not realize its destiny? Kant's answer is to interpret Jesus as the representation of the species' victory over "radical evil," as he calls it in book I of *Religion*, as the principle of heteronymous slavery to sensuality and bondage to the empirical world. It is to interpret him no longer as a figure of Israel's heteronymous covenant, which metes out rewards and punishments as tied to this empirical world. Instead, it is to interpret him rationally or as a racial-moral figure of the Occident, who has overcome the Orient. With this move in place, whiteness comes of age as modernity's perennial theological problem, a problem tied to "the euthanasia of Judaism" as the basis on which to police all nonwhite flesh in the realization of the strivings of Western civilization.

Paul and the Law (of Modern Civil Society): Theopolitics of Religion

For Kant, there is a fundamental asymmetry in how to establish a just constitution within states and how to establish a just relationship between states. In the former case, coercion or force can be combined with freedom and law to establish and maintain a sociopolitical arrangement intent on managing the species' tendency toward unsociable sociability, or "radical evil." Such a solution, however, is not available for managing the unsociable sociability that manifests itself between states, because the use of force at this level can and often does lead to war between nations, and such war can destroy the species. On what basis, then, can the political progress of the species toward peace between states be founded? Kant's answer is that it must be founded on the species' moral progress. The species' political progress (its progress in managing the external relations between individuals through the development of legal systems) and the species' moral progress (its progress internally and at the intellectual level of ethics and self-legislation) meet at the same place. Book III of *Religion* identifies this meeting place as the formation of an ethical commonwealth, a community in which politics and morality are fused, but in such a way that the former is based in the latter. Kant puts it this way:

> A *juridico-civil* (political) *state* is the relation of human beings to each other inasmuch as they stand jointly under *public juridical laws* (which are all coercive laws). An *ethico-civil* state is one in which they are united under laws without being coerced, i.e., under *laws of virtue* alone.[88]

Thus, an "ethico-civil" community, founded on nonstatutory "laws of virtue," is the ideal toward which the species strives. It is the moral world that the species seeks to construct out of the sensible world but on the basis of pure reason.[89]

The account Kant gives of law is key to bringing the modern political state to perfection by transforming it into a hoped for ethical state, which beyond the political state is intent on establishing "a union which has for its end the prevention of . . . evil and . . . [the establishment of] the dominion of the good principle."[90] In a purely political state, one whose laws are not yet rational or established on the a priori basis of the autonomy of reason, legislation does not occur with a view to the species as a whole. Rather, law's province in such a situation is narrow and parochial; it concerns itself only with those within the borders of a given state and, moreover, is meant to manage the property relations between individuals within that state. The chief concern of law is ensuring that property is fairly and equally distributed and that when infractions regarding property ownership occur, there are remedies. Thus, legislation in the nonrational, purely political state does not occur with a view to humanity abstracted from its empirical relationship to property or worldly

goods. Or, put in more Kantian terms, legislation does not occur with a view to humanity as an end in itself or as a kingdom of ends. Rather, law is rooted in the "natural" order of happiness insofar as happiness is linked to corporeal well-being.

Kant believes, however, that things have changed for the better with the advent of modern, enlightened civil society in which politics becomes rational even as citizens order their lives, as *Anthropology* exhorted, on the pragmatic basis of reason. The modern state, and particularly for Kant, the modern Prussian state and the German "nation," represents a categorical advance beyond the primitive state or political order. Its advance lies in its different conceptualization of law. Michael Mack has ably and persuasively captured what is at stake in Kant's thought on this point.[91] He notes that "Kant maintained that the modern state acts according to the rationale of ethical autonomy," which means that it enacts a model of society based on the separation of concepts from intuitions.[92]

Concepts for Kant are transcendental or nonempirical and thus are grounded in reason.[93] Because the integrity is independent of the senses and all empirical objects, the conceptual world of reason is a world of autonomy. The laws by which the conceptual world of reason functions are for Kant, therefore, laws that are to be adhered to not for the sake of rewards or punishments. Having a sublimity all their own, the laws of the conceptual world of reason are to be adhered to for their own sake. Indifferent to the worldly goods of the body, the laws of the conceptual world of reason command obedience, pure and simple, to the body politic. The body politic thoroughly absorbs, owns, and inscribes itself onto the body. Indeed, having been handed over to the body politic so that the true self can be intellectually free or autonomous, the body becomes the aesthetic palette on which the state can paint its intentions by calling for absolute obedience in corporeal matters.

Kant's essay "An Answer to the Question: What Is Enlightenment?" (1784), with its affirmation of unconditioned obedience to Frederick the Great, theorizes just how Prussian society was an exemplar of a society of autonomy, a society in which the autonomy and freedom of individuals to reason as much as they liked was grounded "paradoxically . . . in a political system that enforces the idea of holding objects 'intelligibly' rather than being determined by their sensible conditions."[94] In other words, the laws of Prussian society fulfill Kant's definition of what, according to the *Groundwork for the Metaphysics of Morals* (1785), makes a law moral: namely, that it be purged of anything empirical or, in the words of *Religion*, that it be virtuous. To quote from the *Groundwork*: "If a law is to be morally valid, i.e., if it is to be valid as grounds for compulsion, then it must carry with it absolute necessity; . . . the grounds for such compulsion must therefore not be sought in the nature of humanity nor in the conditions of the world in which the human being is placed, but in an a priori manner solely in the concepts of pure reason."[95]

The intuitive world of the senses contrasts with all of this. It is a world in which all relations are structured as relations to particular empirical objects. Thus, in an intuitively and heteronymously structured world, the point of the law is not simply to manage relations between persons. It is to manage all relations in accordance with what Kant calls in *Metaphysics of Morals* "Mine-and-Yours" property relations. Societies structured through autonomy, which Kant understood to be the case in such early capitalist societies as his own, abstract from and have a relationship of disinterest to "Mine-and-Yours" property relations and, indeed, to the empirical world as such. Therefore, the chief concern in such societies is not with production with a view to the *ownership* of the goods of production, which in themselves are goods of this empirical world. Rather, the concern is with production that has no other end but production. Its concern is production for production's sake (economically speaking) and obedience for obedience's sake (legally speaking). Money in such a society, then, is not tied to any empirical object per se, for rationally understood "money...abstracts away from the material of economic traffic and [considers] only the form."[96]

This is not the case in societies modeled on the intuitively heteronymous world in which "a direct, intuitive response to particular empirical objects and likewise an intuition of received divine commandments shape the mental outlook of the people concerned."[97] Law in such societies is always tied to inclination, to concern over rewards and punishments. And because money is a commodity instrument, in strictly heteronymous economic and political societies, there can be cheating. Indeed, such societies can come to be constituted at the level of national character as merchant societies, and its people can in character become essentialized as merchant people, people so oriented to the goods of this world that they would cheat to uphold that world. This, according to *Anthropology*, is the case with the "Jewish nation," for they are a "nation of cheaters." Moreover, according to the *Metaphysics of Morals*, their law is "pharisaical" inasmuch as it codifies a "doctrine of happiness" that seeks "something that...frees from punishment." The "pharisaical watchword" of the Jewish law, Kant says, is this: "It is better that one man dies than that the whole people perish."[98]

And because the law of this people is pharisaically oriented toward betterment in this world and makes absolutely no claims on human conscience, their religion is really, as he says in *Religion*, "not a religion at all" (*Das leztere ist eigentlich gar keine Religion*). As a purely heteronomous religion of force and coercion, Judaism is "a collection of mere statutory laws supporting a political state," which itself is nothing more than "the union of a number of individuals who, since they belonged to a particular stock [*sie zu einem besondern Stamm gehörten*], established themselves into a community under purely political laws [*bloß politischen Gesetzen*]." Thus, Judaism "was intended to be merely an earthly state [*sollte es ein bloß weltlicher Staat sein*]" with "theocracy as its basis

[*diese Staatsverfassung Theokratie zur Grundlage hat*]." The god of this theocracy, the God of Israel, is not the God of reason or, more specifically, of the people of reason. Rather, the God of Israel is "an earthly regent making absolutely no claims upon, and no appeals to, conscience."[99] What all of this reveals about the Jewish people is that the character of this people, which is tied to their stock, is a racial character. But this racial character is at the same time religious. Their character arises from a racial-religious mind-set. This mind-set, Kant says with essentialist overtones, is the mind-set of the slave (*Sklavensinn*), the mind-set of a people bound to the empirical world rather than the transcendental world of reason.[100]

The rational religion of Christianity, which Kant unconsciously ties to the stock of the races of whites in whom the species will realize its destiny in an ethical commonwealth, stands in stark contrast to this characterization of Judaism. Interestingly, however, Kant articulates the contrast through a reading of Paul in which the law that Paul advocates as the basis of the ethical community is not Torah, the law of Israel. Indeed, Paul's concern for humanity stems from his understanding of the law in terms of its inner "Spirit" (*Geist*) instead of the merely outer, corporeal, and therefore empirical "letter." As Kant says,

> So far as the agreement of actions with the law goes, however, there
> is no difference (or at least there ought to be none) between a hu-
> man being of good morals (*bene moratus*) and a morally good human
> being (*moraliter bonus*), except that the actions of the former do
> not always have, perhaps never have, the law as their sole and su-
> preme incentive, whereas those of the latter *always* do. We can say
> of the first that he complies with the law according to the *letter*
> (i.e., as regards the action commanded by the law); but of the second,
> that he observes it according to the spirit (the spirit of the moral
> law consists in the law being of itself sufficient incentive) [cf. Rom.
> 2:29 and 7:6]. *Whatever is not of this faith is sin* [Rom. 14:23] (in
> attitude). For whenever incentives other than the law itself (e.g.,
> ambition, self-love in general, yes, even a kindly instinct such as
> sympathy) are necessary to determine the power of choice to *lawful*
> actions, it is purely accidental that these actions agree with the
> law, for the incentives might equally well incite its violation. The
> maxim, by the goodness of which all the moral worth of the person
> must be assessed, is therefore still contrary to law, and the human
> being, despite all his good actions, is nevertheless evil.[101]

Alluding to Romans 2:29 and 7:6 and making direct reference to Romans 14:23, Kant reinterprets Paul's letter-spirit distinction such that the letter of the law, the *gramma* of what is "said," gets aligned with heteronomy and the intuitive world of corporeality, while the spirit of the law, the *pneuma* or tran-

scendental substrate of what is "unsaid," gets aligned with the sphere of autonomy, the world of reason.[102]

In placing the *Geist* or *pneuma* of the law beyond the profanity of the law's letter, what Kant, in effect, does is "[disconnect] moral law from both anthropology and the *conditio humana*, the conditions in which man lives as inhabitant of a fallen, . . . imperfect, and dangerous world." This is because "Kant's *Geist* commands the complete separation from material life" and therefore "rejects the body in a radical manner."[103] To sin is to live apart from sufficient motivating incentive of the law itself, apart from any relationship the law may have to empirical or corporeal reality. This is precisely what the Jews, on the basis of their laws of heteronomy, do not—indeed, cannot—do. The law of the Spirit, therefore, is at the heart of Christianity, which (in Kant's view) is the representation of the realization of the cosmopolitan society, a society that moves beyond (by moving in opposition to) the heteronomy represented by and embodied in Jewish people. It is the law conceived in this way—as spiritual, where spiritual does not connote care for the body—that grounds the "religiosity" of whiteness or the "spirituality" of the species as such.

Kant's reading of Paul, therefore, presents a rationally triumphalist account of Christianity as moral religion over the antirational, which is to say, the nonreligious "religion" of the Jews. But by tethering this reading of Paul to his account of the ethical commonwealth or to cosmopolitan society in book III, Kant is able to interpret Christianity as rooted in and as a perfected representation of the autonomy of the moral law and, beyond this, to give his rational interpretation of Christianity a Pauline warrant. In short, with Paul's assistance, Kant put in place the rudiments of a critical-rational theology of modern civil society. In the name of Paul, Kant presents Christianity as the ultimate expression of Western culture and civilization—ultimate because it represents them as teleologically complete. Because of Christianity (rationally construed, of course), the human species has "reason" to hope that its effort to reshape the sensible world into a morally cosmopolitan one will not end in futility. Herein lies the theopolitics of religion, or more specifically, of Christianity converted into modern, rational religion.

The upshot of Kant's rational reading of Paul, then, is this: Paul clearly grasped what was moral, and thus virtuous and of enduring significance, about Christianity. Insofar as Christianity was modernity's quintessential religion of virtue, its religio-cultural reflex, it presaged in representational form the coming ethical community, the cosmopolis. Therefore, Kant's reading makes Paul a figure of the Occident, despite the fact that on Kant's racial terms he is of the Orient. In an odd way, then, in the Kantian imagination, Paul is both of the East and not of it (and of the West, and not of it, too). Paul had a way to transcend—or perhaps, better, to be "transcendental" with respect to—his Jewish, covenantal identity.[104] This moment of transcendence is precisely what imagines Paul within the horizon of racial reasoning.

Jesus and the Law (of Modern Civil Society): Theopolitics of Race

Kant provides a Christological basis for his rational reading of Christianity, Paul, and the law. Indeed, if book I of *Religion* reads Paul as erecting a binary divide between the spirit and the letter in his rationally religious interpretation of Christianity, and if book III offers an account of Christianity's ability to represent the coming ethical community, which is founded on moral law, then in book II Kant offers an account of the identity of Jesus meant to sustain his theopolitical reading of Paul, of moral law (of modern civil society), and of rational Christianity. Rational Christology (book II of *Religion*) is the hinge holding together a rational reading of the law beyond Torah (book I of *Religion*) and Christianity's ability to be a religious representation of the coming rational community (book III of *Religion*).

Central to book II's argument is the claim that Jesus Christ is "the personified idea of the good principle" that has "come down to us" so that human beings, in fulfillment of their "universal . . . duty," may "elevate [themselves] to this ideal of moral perfection." Reason presents this "prototype of moral disposition in its entire purity . . . to us . . . for emulation" and as an example because "[from] the practical point of view this idea has complete reality within itself."[105] In this personification of the good principle, the idea of a will that is thoroughly determined by the moral law and thus the idea of a will that is autonomous and not heteronomous is complete. And because it is complete, it can be a model to us. Thus, in presenting this moral prototype, which "resides in our morally-legislative reason," for our emulation, reason's idea of moral perfection takes on new potency for us: "the very idea" of the perfection of the species now "can give us force," indeed, "the strength of a force like that of a moral disposition . . . [that though] surrounded by obstacles . . . [it] yet—in the midst of the greatest possible temptations—[is] victorious."[106]

Consequently, the prototype of the moral Christ confirms not only that "we *ought* to conform to it": it confirms that "we must also *be able* to";[107] for ought presupposes can. Moreover, the prototype confirms humanity's hope that the duty to transform the sensible world into a moral one can be accomplished, for in him the moral law is an "unconditional and yet sufficient determining ground of our power of choice."[108] Therefore, the significance of Christ is not historical, though his significance is represented historically in the gospel narrative. As the personified idea of the good principle, he discloses an inward disposition and the hope that this inward disposition, the disposition to moral autonomy, will have historical, real-world effect in the formation of a "kingdom" founded on the disposition that is represented as complete in his "divine" person. In him, there is the radical affirmation of the purely spiritual, the moral, and the autonomous. And finally, this is all confirmed in his "atoning" work, which (rationally understood) represents the thoroughgoing dying away

to the material, the empirical, and the heteronymous as the determining ground of human action.

Kant represents Christ's person (his "divinity," rationally understood) and work (of "atonement," again rationally understood) in revolutionary terms. In this he harks back to the language of revolution in the 1784 "Enlightenment" essay and the lectures on pragmatic anthropology with its aspirations toward the political. To be more specific, particularly with respect to his rational soteriology or theology of the atonement, Kant represents Christ overthrowing Judaism and inaugurating a complete rupture between Christianity and its Jewish roots. Salvation consists precisely in this overthrow inasmuch as it makes possible a new form and mode of government. This new form of government exists beyond a purely political "Kingdom of Evil" whose laws are statutorily determined and thus are bound to and determined by the world of empirical goods. Much of this is brought out in an important passage in *Religion* in which Kant provides a reading of the Old Testament that draws attention to the fall into sin in Genesis, the establishment of the people of Israel as a nation, and the emergence of Christianity's figure of "Revolution," Jesus Christ. Because of its significance, I quote it at length:

> The human being was originally appointed the proprietor of all the goods of the earth (Genesis 1:28), though he was to have only their usufruct (*dominium utile*) under his Creator and Lord as the supreme proprietor (*dominius directus*). At the same time an evil being is introduced (we have no cognition of how he became so evil as to betray his master, for originally he was good) who, through his fall, has lost whatever estate he might have had in heaven and now wants to acquire another on earth. But, since earthly and corporeal objects give him no pleasure (he is a being of a higher species—a spirit), he seeks to establish dominion *over minds* by causing our first parents to rebel against their overlord and become dependent on him. And so he succeeds in setting himself up as the supreme proprietor of all the goods on earth, i.e., as the prince of this world.... A Kingdom of Evil was thus set up on earth in defiance of the good principle, and all of Adam's (natural) descendants were subjugated to it—and this with their own free consent, since the false show of this world's goods diverted their gaze from the abyss of perdition in store for them. Because of its rightful claim to dominion over the human being, the good principle did indeed retain a hold through the establishment of a form of government solely directed to the public and exclusive veneration of its name (in the *Jewish* theocracy).[109]

The significance of the establishment of "Jewish theocracy" was not totally "unreligious," for Jewish theocracy did keep the name of the "good principle"

alive. But on its downside, Jewish theocracy, the rest of the passage discloses, aided and abetted the dominion of the evil principle over the good. Therefore, Judaism, as Kant says in another part of *Religion*, is really not a religion at all. It is a form of heteronymous government. It is only a political institution, for "in this [form of] government," he says,

> the subjects remained attuned in their minds to no other incentive except the goods of this world and only wished, therefore, to be ruled through rewards and punishments in this life—nor were they in this respect capable of other laws except such as were in part imposed by burdensome ceremonies and observances, in part indeed ethical but only inasmuch as they gave rise to external compulsion, hence were only civil, and the inferiority of the moral disposition was in no way at issue—so this institutional order did no substantial injury to the realm of darkness but only served to keep ever in remembrance the imprescriptible right of the first proprietor.[110]

Against this backdrop, Kant introduces the rational and revolutionary rupture that is the personified idea of the good principle, or Christ, who is the prototype of the moral disposition:

> Now there suddenly appeared among this very people, at a time when they were feeling the full measure of all the evils of a hierarchical constitution, and were feeling it as well, perhaps, because of the Greek sages' moral doctrines on freedom which, unsettling as they were for the slavish mind [*Sklavensinn*], had gradually gained influence over them and had induced most of them to reflection [*Besinnen*: broadly synonymous with *Vernünfteln* or "speculation"]—they were thus ripe for revolution—a person whose wisdom, even purer than that of the previous philosophers, was as though descended from heaven; and he announced himself indeed as a true human being, so far as his doctrines and example were concerned, yet also as an envoy of heavenly origin who was not implicated, at the time of original innocence, in the bargain with the evil principle into which the rest of the human race had entered through their representative (their first progenitor); "in him, therefore, the prince of this world had no part." The sovereignty of this prince was thereby put in jeopardy.[111]

In the quotation just prior to this one, Kant offers a reading of the Old Testament within which he offers an account of the emergence of Jewish religion and of its deficient response to the establishment of the evil principle. Jewish religion is deficient in Kant's estimation because it only addresses the external matters that pertain to the dominion of the evil principle among human beings. Indeed, in addressing only matters pertaining to "rewards and punishments" and "burdensome ceremonies and observances," Jewish reli-

gion shows itself to be but an expression of Jewish theocracy and, indeed, an inadequate, primitive form of politics to boot. But more than this, in Kant's estimation the deficiency of Judaism is not merely religious: it is also racial insofar as it is tied to the "slavish mind" of this people. Thus, Israel's inadequate form of government and its inadequate form of religion bespeak a racial inadequacy. Indeed, these inadequacies signal Judaism's inability to overturn the evil principle of heteronomy, and as such they actually reinforce the dominion of the evil principle, the principle of heteronomy.

Christ's religious significance is that he is the representation of the sudden overthrow of the evil principle. He is a revolutionary figure, with respect to both the evil principle and the Jewish people. He is the representation of their overthrow. But notice also that the Jewish people were ripe for the appearance of the figure that would overthrow them, not because there was something internal to this people that prepared them for revolution. They only started to feel the full measure of the evils of their hierarchical sociopolitical order because of their encounter with "the Greek sages' moral doctrines on freedom." It was the encounter with another race group that started to awaken the Jews. And even this was only a partial awakening, for the moral doctrines coming from the Greeks in point of fact disoriented the Jews' "slavish mind."

Notice also the flip side of this last point: Kant sees Christ's wisdom as continuous not with the Jewish people, for "[this people] belonged to a particular stock," who "established themselves into a community under purely political laws [and] hence not into a church."[112] Rather, Christ's wisdom is continuous with, though it represents a purer form of, the wisdom of the Greek philosophers. The *Greek* philosophers. Thus, Christ's divinity, by which he is represented "as though descended from heaven," inaugurates a discontinuity, at the level of his humanity or his flesh, with Israel. And yet, at the same time, his divinity inaugurates a moment of continuity with the wise sages of Greece—a continuity that in being racial-religious, insofar as it is a wisdom that operates at the level of *Geist*, brings Greek wisdom to perfection.

In this moment, *Christ ceases to be Jewish*. Or, perhaps better: he is a hybrid, though his hybridity comes at the loss of his covenantal identity as a Jew. The narrative that he enacts is not in continuity with Israel's covenantal history with YHWH. It is not a life that brings to crescendo the song of YHWH's covenant with Israel, a song at whose crescendo the entirety of creation and all the nations "pentecostally" hum the melody and play along.[113] Instead, Kant's figuring of Christ as no longer Jewish at the level of morality and ethics, which for Kant is the level that counts, is the figuring of him as the urmoment in the coming to be of Western civilization. Christ is not a figure who disrupts and draws us out of the reality that whiteness crafts for itself (and for those deemed nonwhite in the white reality). For Kant, Christ represents the wisdom of Europe at the moment of its Greek birth.[114] He cloaked occidental wisdom in oriental garb.

The Euthanasia of Judaism: Whiteness Come of Age
as a Theological Problem

With the rational advent of Christ as a phenomenon of reason, an advent that follows the itinerary of his life from his birth to his death on the cross, there is also the racial advent of whiteness as a form of governance, as a sociopolitical arrangement, and as a regime of power and knowledge. The signifier under which this order of being functions is "morality" qua "autonomy." This is the reality that whiteness has prepared for itself; indeed, it is whiteness. Yet Kant sees this process by which whiteness unfolds as a racial, political, and ultimately religious drama fulfilling itself in a vision in which ecclesiastical sectarianism, by which he means differences both *within* Christianity and *between* various faith traditions, is overcome. Kant lays out this "eschatological" vision—though "teleological" vision is more accurate inasmuch as teleology refers to a process wholly immanent to "civilization"—in an important passage in one of his last works, *Conflict of the Faculties* (1798). The passage again captures, but now from the vantage point of a teleologically refracted Christology, Kant's effort to sever Christianity from its Jewish roots.

The question Kant addresses in this passage is whether it is good that "many kinds of religion (properly speaking, kinds of ecclesiastical faith) . . . exist in a state."[115] He distinguishes two levels on which to respond. As a matter of the purely external affairs of government, Kant's answer is that surely it is good that there is pluralism of faiths in the public square, as it were, of modern society. Such tolerance is to be considered a "sign . . . that the people are allowed freedom of belief."[116] This, however, is only a first level of response to the question, the level of the external shape and legal practice of government. There is for Kant another level to consider. At this deeper, secondary level, the issue is less about the external laws of the state and whether they legally allow pluralism of "ecclesiastical faith" traditions and more about whether "such a public state of affairs in religion" has "the principle . . . [of the] universal agreement on the essential maxims of belief" underlying it.[117]

Kant is happy to report that, in his opinion, in the waning moments of the eighteenth century there is reason to believe such a principle and consensus of universal agreement as to the essential maxims of belief is emerging. In support of this contention he invokes the example of the Jews, declaring that even among them there is a "[purification] of religious concepts" under way and a "[throwing] off [of] the garb of the ancient cult, which now serves no purpose and even suppresses any true religious attitude."[118] Indeed, this newfound attitude among the Jews, an attitude that was not even evident in that recently deceased and most venerated of *Aufklärer* Moses Mendelssohn, is now evident, Kant says, in the proposal of "a highly intelligent Jew," one Ben David, who proposed that the Jews "adopt publicly the religion of *Jesus.*"[119]

Kant's claim was that Ben David's proposal shows the Jews' significant increase in civilization and education, an increase that bespeaks their "[readiness] for all the rights of citizenship," their readiness to become full citizen subjects of the Prussian state.[120] What Kant sees in Ben David's proposal, should the Jews adopt it, is their acceptance of the key tenet of the rational religion of modernity: namely, autonomy. In following Ben David's proposal, then, the Jews would be displaying freedom or the ability "to distinguish the way in which Jesus spoke as a Jew to Jews," which is parochial, "from the way he spoke as a moral teacher to human beings in general," which is universal.[121] They would be opting for the latter over the former: morality over external legality, autonomy over heteronomy.

At this point, Kant lets loose some of the most biting rhetoric to be found in his corpus. He approvingly says that in opting for Jesus as the moral teacher of humanity, Jews such as Ben David would so thoroughly assimilate themselves to the realities of the West that they would become occidental and thus white; that, in effect, they would opt for the "euthanasia of Judaism" (*Euthanasie des Judenthums*). Kant equates the euthanasia of the *Judenthum* with "moral religion" itself:

> The euthanasia of Judaism is pure moral religion, freed from all
> the ancient statutory teachings, some of which were bound to be
> retained in Christianity (as a messianic faith). But this division of
> sects, too, must disappear in time, leading, at least in spirit, to what
> we call the conclusion of the great drama of religious change on
> earth (the restoration of all things), when there will be only one
> shepherd and one flock.[122]

Kant's closing allusion to John 10:16 where Christ is referred to as the "one shepherd," who in a future eschaton will preside over "one flock," does not emerge here as out of place. Indeed, the Christological allusion is thoroughly in keeping with the general outlook of the theology of atonement that sustains Kant's entire vision of the coming ethical community as a religious process and event, for throughout book II, Kant speaks of the death of Christ as a dying away from (*absterben*) bondage to empirical reality. This dying away from or "euthanasia" with respect to empirical reality, however, is represented in Kant's rational theology of the atonement as a dying away to all that Jewish existence signifies politically, racially, and religiously. Kant puts it this way:

> [The] master's very death (the last extreme of a human being's suf-
> fering) was the manifestation of the good principle, that is, of hu-
> manity in its moral perfection, as example for everyone to follow. The
> representation of this death ought to have had, and could have had,
> the greatest influence on human hearts at that time—indeed, so it

can at any time—for it most strikingly displays the contrast between the freedom of the children of heaven and the bondage of a mere son of earth.... And, since the principle appeared in an actual human being as example for all others, this human being "came unto his own, and his own received him not, but as many as received him, to them gave he power to be called the sons of God, even to them that believe on his name" [John 1:11–12]; that is, by exemplifying this principle (in the moral idea) he opened the doors of freedom to all [er eröffnet die Pforte der Freiheit für jedermann] who, like him, choose to die to everything that holds them fettered to earthly life to the detriment of morality; and among these he gather unto himself "a people for his possession, zealous of good works" [Titus 2:14], under his dominion, while he abandons to their fate all those who prefer moral servitude.[123]

Thus, the "euthanasia of Judaism," which Kant figures as coeval with the realization of the coming ethical community, only brings to completion a rational theology of the atonement in which the death of Christ is a dying away from Judaism and from all that makes one a "son of the earth" rather than a son of God. In short, it is a dying away from all that holds one "fettered to earthly life to the detriment of morality."

What the Kantian vision discloses, then, is that the dramas of race and politics in modernity are, in fact, a great drama of religion. Yet, behind the veil of this great religious drama is a less easily detected but controlling story, the story of how whiteness came of age as a theological problem that camouflages itself as just such a problem. When looked at from this vantage point, whiteness as a theological problem is inseparable from the production of the modern citizen on the one hand, who as citizen subject is constructed in such a way that the body articulates the body politic. And on the other hand, it is inseparable from what the Italian philosopher Giorgio Agamben refers to as the modern state's constitution of itself through bios or bare life, life that is bounded by and ever exposed to death.[124] This "death-bound subject" is "homo sacer," or "sacred man," the figure whose life is ever exposed to death or sacrifice for the life of the nation-state.[125] Furthermore, Agamben grasps that the quintessential homo sacer figure of modernity is the Jew.[126]

But what Foucault understood beyond Agamben, and what has been important for the argument developed here in part I of this book, is this: homo sacer's sacrality is simultaneously religious and racial. Indeed, homo sacer's dark body is the body not fully assimilable to the body politic, except by a process of excruciating violence. This violent process of assimilation is a singular process of racialization and "religionization": religion racially dramatizes the body (politic) and vice versa.[127] It is the religio-racial process as an immanent teleological process that functions internal to imperial power. It is this

process that constitutes the Western metropole as white and in relationship to the colony as nonwhite. Such is the two-sided nature of modern Christian supersessionism. That is, homo sacer's sacrality contains within it modernity's *Rassenfrage*, which has as its animating center *Judenfrage* or the theological problem of Gentile Christianity's refusal to think its existence from within the bosom of Abraham, Isaac, and Jacob. The three chapters making up part II of this book offer a reading of the field of African American religious scholarship as an ongoing attempt to diagnose this situation and respond to it. To this I now turn.

PART II

Engaging Race

The Field of African American Religious Studies

3

Historicizing Race

Albert J. Raboteau, Religious History,
and the Ambiguities of Blackness

The movement from *vaudou* to hoodoo [is paradigmatic] of the larger
history of African religion in the United States . . . . [The] African
theological background has disappeared and what remains is a folk
custom.

       —Albert J. Raboteau, *Slave Religion:*
The "Invisible Institution" in the Antebellum South

There are analogies between African traditional religions and Orthodox Christianity . . . [which are grounded in] God's natural revelation.

       —Albert J. Raboteau, "Afterword," in *An Unbroken*
Circle: Linking Ancient African Christianity to the
African-American Experience, ed. Fr. Paisius
Altschul

Since its publication in 1978, Albert J. Raboteau's *Slave Religion: The*
"Invisible Institution" in the Antebellum South has been justly hailed as
an epochal production in Afro-American religious thought. One re-
viewer acclaimed it "necessary reading. It surpasses," he says, "pio-
neering work by W. E. B. DuBois, Carter G. Woodson, and E. Franklin
Frazier to be the most significant study of slave religion yet."[1] Its
significance lies in its attempt to give an account of the complex
historical unfolding of New World black faith. In this chapter, I interrogate this still important and, I submit, unsurpassed work
from the vantage of this study's preoccupation with the theological
structuring of modern racial reasoning. I am interested to see how

Raboteau as historian, beginning with *Slave Religion* and continuing in some of his more recent work, makes a signal contribution in showing how black religion generally and Afro-Christianity particularly disrupt the logic of modern racial reasoning, which I outlined as a theological problem in part I of this book.

From this vantage, *Slave Religion*'s contribution is in how it indirectly provokes the question of the relationship between religious and theological claims on the one hand and the nature of history as a modern science and its practice of historical narration on the other. In short, *Slave Religion* insinuates the question of the philosophy and, indeed, the theology of history, which as Karl Löwith once put it, asks about *"meaning in history."*[2] The question of meaning becomes all the more acute when raised by the sufferers of modernity's historically "sweet violence."[3] For this reason, *Slave Religion* exceeds its disciplinary confines, holding out the promise of a philosophical but ultimately theological revaluation of the meaning of race by way of its valuation of the meaning of slave religion and black faith as historical realities. My task in this chapter is to explicate this promise, even as I point out what I take to be a deep ambiguity in the thought of the early Raboteau of *Slave Religion*.

Let it be quickly said, however, that determining *Slave Religion*'s ambiguous moment with respect to the meaning of black faith is but one, albeit an important, part of the task. My argument cannot rest here because Raboteau himself does not. Indeed, by pointing toward a *theology* of history—toward an account of history suited to the phenomenon of black faith generally and Afro-Christianity particularly—the later Raboteau effectively rereads and in a crucial way clarifies himself.

Before saying more on this subject, I want to make clear what is at stake in what I characterize as *Slave Religion*'s ambiguity as it pertains to the issue of meaning in history. This ambiguity has exposed *Slave Religion* to problematic appropriations and readings whereby black religion is interpreted as nothing more than a cultural reflex. Understood in this way, race, culture, and religion, are imagined as hermetically enclosed, sealed within themselves, and "opaque" to any exteriority. Black folks can only speak as "black." In the parlance of critical theory, they become "reified" or made "essential." The ambiguity of *Slave Religion*, therefore, is this: Raboteau's attempt to offer a historical narrative of the coming-to-be and subsequent early development of slave religion and black faith could be read—and, indeed, has been read—to say that at their ground is the citadel of "Africanity," the impervious domain of a cultural "blackness" itself. The "religious" is but a reflex of the racial-cultural ground of being. And "religion" is but the institutional or material matrix of the religious reflex. Read in this way, we do not move beyond the modern "transcendentalizing" of race and the ethnographic analytics of religion. Indeed, we stay entangled within it. Accordingly, central to the ambiguity surrounding *Slave Religion* such that it can be read in this potentially hazardous way is an insufficiently developed philosophy and ultimately theology of history, one sui-

ted to uncovering how modernity's pseudotheology of race, as outlined in part I of this book, is theologically unsettled in the performance of New World Afro-Christian faith. For the central question is this: Is Christianity but the reflex of an identity or consciousness that is more primal or fundamental than the Christianity taken and performed by those who "made Jesus their choice"? Is it but a religious expression of a pragmatic and democratically pious response to a racialized and enslaving modernity?[4]

It is precisely here, however, that Raboteau's later work (*A Fire in the Bones*, for example, and of some of his lesser-known essays) is of such crucial importance. Raboteau, in his post–*Slave Religion* literature, begins to clear up the ambiguity surrounding the meaning of black faith. He does so by suggesting a theology of history that, in proceeding from what can be characterized as a notion of the beautiful out of which can emerge a theological aesthetics, signals a disruption of the colonizing gaze of race. My concern is to trace the outlines of this aesthetic theory of iconic beauty and then, in part III of this book, to inhabit it.

What follows here is an argument as to how the two epigraphs for this chapter—the first, from *Slave Religion* (1978); the second, from his chapter to *An Unbroken Circle* (1997), then reiterated as recently as early 2003 in his Alexander Schmemann Lectures delivered at St. Vladimir's Theological Seminary[5]—hold together.

History and the Question of Culture(s)

I begin by offering a reading of *Slave Religion* that highlights the ambiguity to which I have referred. Raboteau observes that *Slave Religion* is only a propaedeutic to the study of African American religion. As prolegomenon, it queries the historic coming-to-be and initial unfolding of New World black religion. Excavating that coming-to-be can be a tenuous enterprise, however, for the simple and important reason that it is shrouded in the historic, but by no means wholly inaccessible, darkness of the antebellum South's "invisible institution." Fortunately, this institution has left its traces that, though faded to some extent by the effects of time, nevertheless remain sufficiently clear to follow. These traces, which one could say archaeologically testify, are the artifacts out of which Raboteau wants to provide a history of slave religion and early black faith. The history of slave religion and early black faith, as the conclusion to *Slave Religion* indicates, leads to "Canaan Land."[6] Canaan Land, though often described by slaves and many first-generation freed persons in a futurist and escapist language, was at the same time a religiously and politically subversive language through which black freedom was struggled for and negotiated.

Raboteau's concern in *Slave Religion* is to tell the story of the emergence of multivalent religious languages and practices of New World peoples of African

descent out of the invisible institution of slavery. Thus part II of the book—"The Invisible Institution," which constitutes the bulk of his historical narrative—is concerned with uncovering the inner operations of this "institution." And he proffers that the invisible institution served to incubate what would eventually become an expression of Christianity distinct from the "false Christianity" of white oppressors. This distinct Christianity is Afro-Christianity.

Though deeply appreciated as setting the standard in the field of African American religious history, more recently *Slave Religion* has been criticized for overly defining the "hush harbor" religious practices of the invisible institution as Christian; in fact, some scholars view the evidence, such as we have it, as neither affirming nor denying this claim,[7] and others point to the indomitable presence of the African gods over the God of Christian faith. As far as *Slave Religion* is concerned, answering the question of the hermeneutics of black religion requires an investigation of what is at stake when he considers "The African Heritage"; for it is here that Raboteau engages in a kind of hermeneutics of history in which philosophical presuppositions are ambiguously spelled out. Thus my analysis focuses here.

To appreciate Raboteau's thought, one must engage his reading of the Herskovits-Frazier debate in cultural anthropology, because the argument advanced in *Slave Religion* unfolds in terms of his reading of that debate.[9] A number of twists and turns marked the debate, but the issue came down to this: How do we account for the difference in cultural sensibilities (i.e., religion, music, and art) among peoples of African descent against the dominant and enslaving culture of the New World? With respect to slave religiosity, as Lawrence Levine put it, this is really "a question of origins":[10] Did the cultural and religious distinctiveness of diasporic African peoples reside in the presence or absence of certain African retentions or Africanisms?

Sociologist E. Franklin Frazier answered negatively, claiming that, as Raboteau summarizes him, "African traditions and practices did not take root and survive in the United States. It is Frazier's position," says Raboteau, "that the process of enslavement and the passing of earlier generations born in Africa destroyed the culture of the slaves. The vacuum thus created was filled by Christianity, which became the new bond of social cohesion."[11] The "process of enslavement" was deculturative, claimed Frazier; slavery in North American utterly stripped the slaves of any substantive links (language, familial and religious bonds, etc.) with Africa, and for all practical purposes slavery eradicated "African memories, . . . patterns of behavior and attitudes toward the world." Again summarizing and quoting Frazier, Raboteau says, "Slaves had to develop 'new habits and attitudes' in order 'to meet new situations.'"[12]

Thus, there is no continuity with the African past. There is only an assimilated American present for rendering the African, in effect, nothing but American. And Christianity proved crucial to slave assimilation and the transition from being African to becoming American. Through Christian images

and the stories of the Bible, slaves and their progeny lived in light of a new symbol system and so arrived at a "new world-view," one that, given the new situation, "gave meaning to life."[13] So on the question of origins, of whether the cultural and religious distinctiveness of diasporic African peoples resided in the persistence of certain African retentions, Frazier responded negatively. He argued that the process of enslavement destroyed everything identifiably African about African people.

Frazier's position is diametrically opposed to that of the noted anthropologist Melville J. Herskovits. More specifically, it was in direct opposition to the position of the later Herskovits, the Herskovits of *The Myth of the Negro Past*.[14] Before considering the position of the later Herskovits as it frames Raboteau's argument in *Slave Religion*, it might be helpful to sketch the general thought of the earlier Herskovits. Herskovits had a distinguished career as an anthropologist, training under Franz Boas, often called the father of American anthropology. Boas received his training as an anthropologist in the Berlin school of ethnology, which, it is important to note, applied certain aspects of German Idealism, Romanticism, and rationalist philosophy to the emerging field of ethnology. Two conflicting strands in the Boasian tradition of anthropology become pronounced in Herskovits and are highlighted in his early and later thought, respectively.

According to Adam Kuper, the Boasian tradition "wavered between describing [culture] as an accidental accretion of traits and as 'an integrated spiritual totality,' animated by the 'genius' of 'a people.'"[15] The former strand tends toward an assimilationism on the question of culture and reads culture in terms of universalizing homogeneity. Stressing culture as "an accidental accretion of traits" results in minimizing and relativizing, if not outright denying, the differences constitutive of people groups and begs the question, "An accidental accretion of traits" to what? It is this "what" that is at issue. Thus, in following the first strand of Boasian thought, certain of his students, including the early Herskovits, were inclined to speak more of culture in the singular, and of "a culture," and less so of cultures in the plural. Culture, in the singular, is that under which all cultures are subsumed. All racial groups, in short, converge in culture.

To be sure, there can certainly be a cultural-critical edge to the first strand of Boasian thought. It can be a way to argue for the sociopolitical elevation of a people group in light of a cultural egalitarianism. Culture so understood equalizes and groups all under its arc. In fact, this critical edge is evident in the thought of the early Herskovits. His criticisms of the racist and anti-Semitic tendencies in American life bear this out. He proclaimed, as did Boas, the fundamental similarity of all peoples in the United States of America. In this view, behavioral differences (what are now commonly referred to as "cultural differences") are neither biologically encoded nor psychically enshrined. The earlier Herskovits, as a first-strand Boasian thinker, advanced a theory of

culture that directly opposed racialist hypotheses, be they of the Lamarckian variety or of cultural evolutionists.[14] Culture, as the early Herskovits understood it, names that which makes all humans fundamentally the same. Culture is the great leveler.

In short, Herskovits's early understanding of culture looks a great deal like the universal reason and the racial stem genus of the German philosophic tradition extending back to Kant and his anthropological writings, though it must be said that Boas does attempt to distance the implications of his thought on culture as leveler from the historic racism of this tradition of thought. In the hands of the early Boas and his student Herskovits, culture overcomes or levels racial difference and is thus deployed as a tonic against racism.

In light of this, it is worth noting how close, conceptually at least, the early Herskovits and Frazier actually are. Both the early Herskovits and Frazier can be read as cultural levelers. But there is a difference. Frazier names America itself as the unifying culture; American culture gives culture to the cultureless. But because of this way of deploying the notion of culture as leveler, Frazier lacks the wherewithal to critique the racism embedded in American culture. The early Herskovits's deployment of the notion of culture as leveler functions differently. His claim about culture (in the singular) functioned toward a radical end: namely, to critique racism in America.

Despite this critique, Herskovits found himself, as Walter Jackson observes, "the odd man out."[15] The problem surfaced in the face of the Harlem Renaissance's notion of the "New Negro," a notion to which Herskovits himself was most sympathetic. He, in fact, would contribute an essay to *The New Negro* (1925), the programmatic collection of essays edited by Alain Locke that exemplify the art, literature, and thinking of the Harlem Renaissance.[18] The problem for Herskovits was that Harlem Renaissance thinkers were moving in the direction of the second strand of Boasian thought, while he was still essentially a first-strand thinker. In the second strand of Boas's thought, understandings of "race" and "culture" were transformed by paying closer attention to the distinctive marks of people groups and reveling in them. This distinctiveness was seen now as mediated through *cultures*. In short, adherents of the second strand began to think of culture in the plural as the tide shifted toward a more serious appreciation of what is distinctive in America's polyphonous national life as a whole. A reckoning with cultural pluralism was dawning. This led the New Negro to a self-understanding that required a deep appreciation of what is uniquely African about New World black folks.

The new configuration was not meant as a reverse valorization of a monolithic blackness in place of a static whiteness. As George Hutchinson says,

> Claiming American cultural nationalism ... was not in simple opposition to some monolithic white concept; it was part of a broad

movement of imaginative transformation we have little acknowledged, precipitated in part by the dramatic changes in material relations that brought members of formerly segregated groups together
in liminal spaces of relative speculative freedom, transracial commerce and conflict, and intellectual experimentation.[19]

The literature of this period abundantly witnesses to this phenomenon. The
early Herskovits found himself "the odd man out" because his thought lacked
a way of appreciating the cultural uniquenesses of black folks and their contributions to the broader American cultural life.

As a good Boasian anthropologist, Herskovits embarked on fieldwork to
explore the bases for thinking this way. Herskovits's fieldwork centered on
various diasporic African peoples, and his conclusions led him in the 1930s
in the direction of the second strand of Boasian thought, and thus closer to
Harlem Renaissance thinkers. His efforts culminated in *The Myth of the Negro
Past*, and the new direction of his thought received praise from no less a lu-
minary than W. E. B. DuBois. You will recall that, according to Kuper, the
second strand of Boasian thought, also indebted to certain Germanic associa-
tions, envisions culture as "'an integrated spiritual totality,' animated by the
'genius' of 'a people.'"[20] This way of conceiving culture allows one to speak
more freely of cultures in the plural. Furthermore, conceiving culture as
marked by "the 'genius' of 'a people,'" while at the same time not rooting
genius in biology, causes other factors, such as the social and historical determinations of culture(s), to figure centrally. Capitalizing on the second strand
of Boasian anthropology allows one to see genius in precisely the supposed
grotesquery of blackness and the various ways in which blackness is enacted.
The second strand, in other words, draws on what is unique and specific about a
people to decenter race as the centering category, or index, of humanity.

In Hutchinson's summary, the formation of "racial groups, Boas argued, is
a social rather than a biological phenomenon." This means that "cultures
should be understood on their own terms, as having developed within particular circumstances, with their own specific histories and standards of judgment."[21] To understand a culture on its own terms is to understand it as a
development within its own specific history, a history whose hermeneutic is
embedded within itself. Hutchinson observes that Boas and his students recognized the need for a historical method able to recover and uncover the specific histories of cultural groups. Thus they advanced a new method and
practice of historical inquiry that "carefully [collects] the folklore and material
culture of an area and [arranges] it according to the canons of interpretation
used by the culture itself."[22] This new practice is ethnography, which, through
the analysis of language, aesthetic and literary productions, folk artifacts, and
religion, in many ways does the work of history. It tells the story of the *Volksgeist*. Under the conditions of the second strand of Boasian thought, then, the

analysis of cultures becomes important in a way that it was not under the first strand of Boasian thought.

Is this simply another way to reify culture, albeit now pluralized as the movement of the *Volksgeist*? Theologian Kathryn Tanner indicates how such reification could and often did occur within such a discourse:

> Differences in customs, values, and beliefs [become] . . . one might say, their own principles of interpretation; there [is] no secondary mechanism of biology or universal principle of psychic law working in, through, or behind them. They sustained *themselves*, simply by being repeated and by the force of habit and traditional authority that such repetition generated. They sustained themselves, in other words, mainly through unconscious processes of habitual repetition . . . . The specific historical context of a people's practice was itself therefore the primary explanation of differences among peoples' customs, values, or worldviews. In keeping with the Germanic associations of *Kultur* with the inherited traditions of particular locales, these different historical contexts were termed cultures.[23]

To be sure, the move from Hegel's *Geist* to Herder's *Volksgeist* does not necessarily have to reenact the essentialism of a self-referential Absolute, because *Geist*-become-*Volksgeist* could be understood as "low-flying," as always moving close to the ground, to the *Volk*.[24] Thus, the turn to what is distinctive about a people group does not necessarily, though it could, open onto a black nationalism as a totalizing enclosure built out of the materials whiteness created. Rather, the argument against racism can be understood as migrating into the register of the cultural *hybridity* of American pluralism. Such pluralism would take seriously the amalgam of cultural identities constituting the American project. Culture, in short, in the low-flying register of the second strand of Boas's thought, becomes dislodged from the determinism of biology or even from the determinism of the category of America.

Though this is certainly a way of trying to resuscitate the notion of culture while leaving dead the tendency to erect a monolithic superstructure, a totality, a significant part of the argument of this book generally, and of the chapters making part II particularly, lies in making a theological claim as to why even this is inadequate. For now, I will simply say that, even in inhabiting the discourse of "cultures" rather than simply "culture," it remains somewhat open as to the extent to which the discourse of cultures succeeds in actually decentering race as a strong or founding category of thought and life. The significance of this for reckoning with Raboteau is this: theoretically speaking, Raboteau situates the history told in *Slave Religion* within the framework of "low-flying" culture, within the discourse on cultures, as a way of historically articulating how black faith sought to break out of the constraints of modern racial reasoning. But the fit in doing this is, at the most crucial junctures,

uncomfortable at best. Indeed, as I show in the following section, it introduces a theoretical ambiguity into his historical argument.

Slave Religion and the Ambiguities of Blackness

Raboteau notes that Herskovits divides the "myth of the Negro past" into a constellation of five submyths: (1) black folks are childlike by nature; (2) only the genetically inferior stock of Africans underwent enslavement; (3) there was no uniting ethos for the enslaved Africans who came from all quarters of the continent; (4) the advanced civilization of the European and Euro-American master was so attractive to the enslaved African over their own savage level of existence that they would have gladly traded in their own cultural vestiges and heritage had it persisted; and (5) black folks, given all of this, are a people without a past because slavery thoroughly extirpated that past and in the end reduced it to nonexistence.[25] Where does Raboteau take issue with Herskovits? Well, it turns out that he does not take issue with anything material or substantive with Herskovits's deconstruction of "the Negro myth." His qualms, at least as registered in Slave Religion, are really quibbles.

Consider, for example, Raboteau's critique of Herskovits's claim that Christian baptism as practiced in Afro-Christianity is an Africanism, a specific African retention from water cults in Africa (Nigeria and Dahomey). According to Herskovits, as Raboteau summarizes:

> The Baptists' insistence on immersion was an attractive rite to Africans familiar with water cults because the concept of baptism is one "that any African would find readily understandable." In Africa, Dutch Guiana, and Haiti, possession by water spirits drives the possessed devotee to hurl himself bodily into a stream, pond, or river. Similarly, in the baptismal service of rural black Baptists the spirit occasionally falls upon the new Christian emerging from the water.[26]

Raboteau faults Herskovits because of the insufficiency of the example to make the case that an African survival is at work. In registering his qualm with Herskovits's example, Raboteau observes that the descent of the Holy Spirit at baptism has the warrant of Scripture. This example, therefore, only shows that "culture contact was not in every case culture conflict."[27] There can be congruity in outward expression between features of African ritual life, say, in the water cults, and (European and Euro-American) Christian ritual practice, say, in the descent of the Spirit in baptism.

Raboteau's quibble, in short, is that Herskovits offers an example of mere commonality in outward expression, an example of the ability of external African religious practice to adapt to new circumstances in the acculturative process. He has not shown, and this seems to be where Raboteau wants to lay

the force of his critique, how something distinctively African persists under and behind European forms; for the descent of the Spirit at baptism admits of explanation on purely Christian or scriptural grounds. As Steven Vaughn astutely observes, Raboteau does not "[debate] the validity of Herskovits' search for 'archaic retentions.' . . . Rather than question Herskovits' premise, Raboteau only questions his analogy."[28] In other words, Raboteau accepts the logic of the second Boasian strand of thought as registered by Herskovits. The attempt remains to uncover a stable African self, an African consciousness, that persists under the phenomenon of New World black existence and religious life. What therefore must be shown with respect to Christianity is not, for example in the case of Christian baptism among slaves, that slaves gravitated to Christianity, or more specifically to the Baptist denomination, *because* they saw in it conceptual similarities that triggered a cultural memory of African water cults. According to Raboteau, this, in the end, is susceptible to explanation *within* the terms of Christianity without the need for explanation through the phenomenon of retentions.

Here we approach Raboteau's distinctive way of addressing the question of slave religion. As I show, the distinctiveness surfaces due to the seriousness with which Raboteau takes the Christian element in antebellum slave religion. This presses him to go beyond Herskovits, who because of a more static approach to Africanity and religious consciousness is unable to sufficiently account for this Christian element. To do this, Raboteau attempts a more nuanced ethnographic history. Drawing on an essay by Erika Bourguignon, he distinguishes "two . . . levels of ethnographic 'fact': an observable behavior pattern and a system of cultural beliefs and interpretations. These [together] . . . structstructure expectations and therefore behavior."[29] I now briefly show how Raboteau deploys this two-leveled distinction to get at the complexity of Africanity as a heritage in living interaction with Christianity as itself a heritage or living tradition. Raboteau's distinction as deployed in *Slave Religion* is sufficiently ambiguous as to work counter to the dominant trajectory of his thought, a trajectory that, in terms of the concerns of this study, works to explode the modern analytics of race, understood as a sealed enclosure, and thereby dislodge the religious hegemony of whiteness. This dislodging occurs as Africanity or blackness as self-enclosed cultural consciousness, the blackness that whiteness created, is also exploded or dislodged.

In Raboteau's narrative, faith content, or the system of cultural beliefs and interpretations, forms the primary level of ethnographic history; expressive style forms the secondary level. Raboteau argues for continuity on this secondary level with the African past, a past that is, in fact, present. The vibrancy of the African heritage is due to the fact that it is a living tradition and practice, not a "thing." As such, it can be composite and can even "unite" with other heritages, traditions, and practices. The African religious heritage, at least as far as its various stylistic expressions are concerned, can unite with other faith

traditions. This is why, for example, "patterns of motor behavior preceding and following the ecstatic experience" may reveal a "continuity between African and American forms of spirit possession."[30] This helps Raboteau account for what he considers to be distinctive about blacks' singing of Euro-American Protestant hymns; even in the singing of Protestant hymns, continuity is maintained with African forms of religious expressions. This is true as well for New World black music from the spirituals to the blues: that is, whether the referent of the artistic expression is non-African or African, stylistic continuity with the African heritage remains.

An example of this is Raboteau's analysis of ring shouting: "In the ring shout and allied patterns of ecstatic behavior, the African heritage of dance found expression in the evangelical religion of the American slaves."[31] Regarding stylistic and cultural-linguistic expression, he notes that "similar patterns of response—rhythmic clapping, ring-dancing, styles of singing, all of which result in or from the state-of-possession trance—reveal the slaves' African religious background."[32] This is why "the shout [not baptism] is a [more] convincing example of Herskovits' theory of reinterpretation of African traditions; for the situation of the camp-meeting revival, where enthusiastic and ecstatic religious behavior was encouraged, presented a congenial setting for slaves to merge African patterns of response with Christian interpretations of the experience of spirit possession, an experience shared by both blacks and whites."[33]

This entire scheme works for Raboteau because of a neat dualism between the two levels of ethnographic fact, a dualism designed to separate form or stylistic pattern from content or meaning. While he vigorously asserts a continuity between African styles of religious expression and those practiced in the New World, regarding faith content, he says, "Different theological meanings are expressed and experienced in [the African heritage and evangelical religion]." This is where Raboteau faults Herskovits for confusing the two levels of ethnography. For example, according to Raboteau, Herskovits has insufficiently distinguished the Christian and African forms of spirit possession, seeing continuity where there is in fact discontinuity. (This also is something of the point Raboteau wished to make against Herskovits's interpretation of baptism as practiced in Afro-Christianity.) In the case of spirit possession in African religions, the personality of the god displaces that of the devotee: "Personality traits of the god are expressed in the patterned action of the possessed devotee who makes the god present to the cult community.... The devotee becomes the carrier of the god."[34]

In the phenomenon of Christian ecstasy in the Holy Spirit, however, there is no such displacement of the personality of the worshipper. The difference, claims Raboteau, is of the utmost significance, for it places the experience in differing belief contexts, rendering them susceptible to differing interpretations. But Raboteau's argument is not simply a hermeneutical one; it is ontological

precisely by being hermeneutical. The differing belief contexts yield differing interpretations because they signal a genuinely different experience of being in the world. In light of the faith context, Raboteau concludes that "while there may be similar effects . . . on this level of faith event, there are major differences between spirit possession as it occurs in African and Latin American cults, on the one hand, and the ecstatic shouting experience of United States revivalism, on the other"; thus "there is discontinuity . . . between the African heritage . . . and the black . . . tradition in the United States."[35] The African gods are not present here, particularly with respect to the North American context. Ostensibly, the Trinitarian God of Christian faith, insofar as one speaks concerning Christianity, is present, and cannot be seen through to some more primal ground of Being.

As already noted, a number of scholars have objected to this ostensible privileging of Christianity. Donald H. Matthews, in his *Honoring the Ancestors*, is one such objector. He says, "Raboteau states that the experience of spirit possession in African and African American religion is different on the basis of their differing linguistic referents. This statement leaves readers to wonder how Raboteau is able to verify which deity is possessing the believer."[35] Matthews can raise this question because on Raboteau's own terms the only thing that is historically observable and thus subject to the ethnographic gaze is stylistic expression. Whatever content to be communicated is to be communicated through style, a conclusion Matthews draws from Raboteau's distinction between style and faith content, which together structure behavior. Matthews chides Raboteau for, at best, being ambiguous on this crucial point and, at worst, smuggling in a Christian apologetic. Matthews wants Raboteau to be more consistently a historian qua ethnographer and not qua clandestine theologian.

Even more, Matthews observes that there are moments even in Raboteau's consideration of cultural-linguistic style and expressivity that, to the consternation of his argument, an ethnographic orientation wins the day over a theological one, for "[Raboteau's] evidence . . . actually contradicts his conclusions."[37] Matthews's claim has some merit in that it points to the methodological and philosophical ambiguity by which Raboteau's discourse can be read as a retreat into a discourse of racial and cultural transcendentalism, though in my view the retreat does not signal the real trajectory of Raboteau's thought. For given Raboteau's emphasis on "tradition" as itself dynamic and his insistence on this as the horizon within which to situate slave religion, the methodological and philosophical retreat is in fact at odds with the overall tenor of the history he tells.

Raboteau generally succeeds in explaining the plasticity of African expressivity. Thus, his conclusion is right that the transmission of the African heritage was not by way of "static 'Africanisms' or . . . archaic 'retentions.'"[38] Indeed, he states early on that historical investigation shows that what is African about African diasporic people displays an expressive cultural adaptivity.

The African inheritance bequeathed to New World black folks is better described as so many "living traditions" that have "[put] down new roots in new soil, bearing new fruit [and producing] unique hybrids of American origin."[39] At the root of African cultures as found on New World soil is the vitality of their spiritualities, along with the openness of their religious sensibilities to unite syncretically "with other religious traditions" and yet maintain "the continuity of a distinctively African religious consciousness."[40]

But here again the ambiguity shows up. Is "consciousness" historical as well—that is, is it "traditioned"? And if it is, of what "tradition" is it a part? We know that the discourse of racial consciousness, which emerged in modernity as a religious discourse, is itself a tradition, but not an open-ended one. Indeed, even within *Slave Religion*'s own terms of analysis, can it not also be asked whether in speaking of "*religious* consciousness" one has surreptitiously crossed the dialectical threshold into the domain of the first artifactual level of faith, the level of content? It is precisely such a question that leads Matthews to ponder whether Raboteau is a clandestine theologian.

Herein lies the tension. On the one hand, *Slave Religion* promulgates a nonessentialist understanding of "living tradition" and seeks to understand African consciousness within this horizon. In line with this, it also advances an understanding of religious practices as nonreified. And yet, it speaks of "a distinctively African religious consciousness" concerned with what appears at times to be a static and stable African or racial essence of blackness. Insofar as this is the case, the discourse of *Slave Religion* remains within the gravitational pull of a racialized understanding of identity. The Raboteau of a potentially stable African consciousness seems to be at odds with the Raboteau of a malleable, elastic, and historical Africanity that is no slave to the brute forces of a stable "nature" and that can therefore be read in Christian terms.[41]

The theoretical vacillation between plasticity and essentiality, I contend, follows from the framework of historical dialectic that attempts to hold the two levels of "artifact"—the level of content and the level of style—in dynamic relationship without confusion. (This is a problem that I return to in the next section when I begin examining Raboteau's post–*Slave Religion* work.) Moreover, for all of Raboteau's desire to make sense of what was Christian in and about slave religion, it is precisely the Christian element (Matthew's claim that Raboteau is a clandestine theologian notwithstanding) that gets lost in his early analyses. Indeed, the Christian element gets lost insofar as it becomes the husk within which a more primal, even if "traditioned," African consciousness functions. This consciousness is more or less the cultural core of blackness. And in the end, black Christian folks, insofar as they might be understood as theological subjects, are quarantined within African consciousness.

One further brief example to crystallize these matters concerns Raboteau's handling of the Negro spirituals as a feature of slave religion. It is here as well that he attempts to uncover at the site of the North American diaspora a "deeper

level of reinterpretation" of African consciousness. Raboteau makes the observation that "ring shouts were also called 'running sperichils.'"[42] He then observes that "while the lyrics and themes of the spirituals were drawn from Biblical verses and Christian hymns, and although the music and melodies were strongly influenced by the sacred and secular songs of white Americans, the style in which the slaves sang the spirituals was African."[43] One sees again the positing of stylistic transparency in order to see through to a more fundamental spiritual context than the one in performance at the level of style. As already indicated, Matthews finds this objectionable. He dissents most from Raboteau's parsing of meaning from style, a point on which Raboteau insists. Having distinguished meaning from style, Raboteau then makes the strong claim that the spirituals were "performed in praise of the Christian God." Even still, there is an interesting ambiguity in Raboteau's claim, for he also maintains that in the spirituals "the names and the words of the African gods were replaced by Biblical figures and Christian imagery."[44] One wonders precisely at this point whether it is primordially the African self in praise of the African gods, albeit renamed under biblical figures and Christian imagery, that remains intact and at work.

My claim here is not that Raboteau collapses his distinctions between content and style such that the African gods live on but only by wearing Christian clothes. Yet it is precisely the ambiguity that leaves the argument he advances in *Slave Religion* perilously close to arguments made by others in which the fatal, reifying step about African retentions is actually taken. Such is the case, for example, in Robert Farris Thompson's *Flash of the Spirit: African and Afro-American Art and Philosophy*.[45] This influential text draws heavily on religion for its claims about art, history, and philosophy but does so in such a way as to preclude Christianity from being a tradition that lives alongside African religions. Indeed, African religions themselves lose the sense of being permeable and malleably open. The problem is exemplified in Thompson's comment regarding the practice of Catholicism by Yoruba Americans, which is emblematic of what is the case throughout the New World: "Yoruba-Americans, outwardly abiding by the religious proprieties of the Catholics who surrounded them, covertly practiced a system of thought that was a creative reorganization of their own traditional religion. Luminously intact in the memories of black elders from Africa, the goddesses and gods of the Yoruba entered the modern world of the Americas."[46] New World black religion, therefore, represents so many varied "transatlantic reinstatements [that] extend the attributes of Elegba"[47] or other Yoruba deities of traditional African religions. The artifacts of history are an archaeological testament to the tenacity of a persistent and persevering African subject to which the peculiarities of New World existence must explanatorily submit.

All of this, I maintain, returns us to the shadow that Herskovits methodologically casts, not just over *Slave Religion* but over "the development of both

Afro-American Studies and African Studies in the North American academy."
Indeed, it points to the influence Herskovits and his general approach to things
of exotic racial province continue to exert in "[shaping] current debates about
the African Diaspora."[48] I have already indicated that the early Herskovits was
"the odd man out" with Harlem Renaissance thinkers because of the assimi-
lationist tenor of his thought. This was the Herskovits of the 1920s. I then note
that Herskovits, due to intimate and sustained contact with a number of Harlem Renaissance thinkers such as Alain Locke, started to take more seriously
the presence of something distinctly African about New World black folks. This
among other things drove him to renewed anthropological fieldwork. He
started to document the new movement of his thought with a 1930 essay, which
would eventually become *The Myth of the Negro Past*. Raboteau was keen not to
accept Herskovits's somewhat static and purist approach to race and culture.
This is apparent from his handling in *Slave Religion* of Africanity as *heritage* and
from his use of the language of *tradition*. This is precisely why it is accurate to
say that Raboteau is not, strictly speaking, a Herskovitsean historian. Raboteau's understanding of Africanity as "living tradition" precludes this.

But there is the matter of Raboteau's early difficulty in historically navigating *Christianity* as a living tradition. Doing so would have required engaging
the question of what it means to speak of the hermeneutic encounter of traditions generally and, more specifically, the nature of that encounter when one
of the traditions is Christianity appropriated by those on the underside of modernity. At the general level, it would have been necessary for the early Raboteau to give an account of New World blackness as itself a hermeneutical
encounter. This, in part, is what theoretician and historian of religions Charles
H. Long attempted in his *Significations* (1986), though, as I argue in chapter 5
of this study, he remains in the end beholden to modernity's troublesome
discourse of religion. More on this later.

Another way of handling the hermeneutical encounter of traditions would
have been to give an account of the kind of tradition that Christianity is, such
that it can receive the traditions of Africa (or the traditions of any people, for that
matter) to re-tradition those traditions, and indeed, in the process itself be re-
traditioned. To account for this—or something like this—would have been to
offer a historiographical method more suited to the study of Afro-Christianity
as a Christian reality that arose out of the horrors of slavery, specifically, and
out of the experiences of the sufferers of modernity/coloniality, generally. To
be sure, this would not satisfy the Matthewses of the academic world, but it
would have offered a more cogent account of Afro-Christian life as a *Christian*
emergence.

That is to say, with some such method of historiography in place, the early
Raboteau might have been able to articulate more consistently the history he
sought to tell at the level of the details in accordance with the overall trajectory
of his thought. *Slave Religion*, as we have it, left these crucial theoretical and

hermeneutical questions inadequately addressed. And because of this, the language of "African consciousness" itself remained insufficiently historicized. There is now neither a rigorous enough analysis of "African consciousness" as a *tradition*, nor an analysis of how the emergence of Afro-Christianity from slave religion begins to break down the discourse of whiteness. This is because at its base lay, on the early Rabouteau's reading, the discourse of Africanity or blackness, the very blackness whiteness created. With all of this left under-theorized, Raboteau's early work was ambiguously poised, trying to maintain its balance and not slip into the logic of racial purism or the discourse of a transcendental, cultural blackness, the blackness located within the "tradition" of whiteness.

"Praying the ABCs": Narrative, the Intellectual, and Raboteau's Post–*Slave Religion* Dialectics

In the remaining two sections of this chapter, I trace the post–*Slave Religion* Raboteau as he tries to clarify himself on the question of history and historical method. That effort unfolds in two stages, the first of which I characterize as a (productive) misstep, out of which emerges a significant breakthrough.

My interest in tracking Raboteau's post–*Slave Religion* effort to formulate a method suited to the historical study of black religion generally and Afro-Christianity particularly is at the heart of the overall concerns of this study. This is because what I find interesting in Raboteau's exercises in self-clarification is his attempt to interpret both slave religion and the subsequent emergence of Christianity among peoples of African descent in the New World as, to put matters in my own language, the historical display of a Christianity struggling to understand itself as lodged in YHWH's covenants with Israel. As I show in the next section, Raboteau moves in this direction by moving from a post–*Slave Religion* dialectics of history to an account of (African American) religious history as rooted in a theology of the icon and therefore, by implication, in Christology. This section takes up Raboteau's first step in recasting his dialectical approach to history.

In many respects, we have already confronted Raboteau's dialectical approach to history. It is precisely dialectic that is at the heart of the methodological quandary surrounding *Slave Religion*. This quandary concerns the relationship between faith or religious content on the one hand and style or expressivity on the other. The former is inaccessible to scientific, historical scrutiny; the latter is not. The former is the site of rupture or discontinuity with the African past; the latter, being the site of continuity, is not. The balance in which content and style are tenuously held together displays what can be called a dialectic of history. This is a dialectic, however, in which, strictly speaking, faith and its content are in themselves unhistorical, for faith in *approaching*

history does not deeply inhabit it. Rather, being asymptotic in its approach, faith only vaguely touches history. Thus, within this dialectical framework, faith is transhistorical or suprahistorical. This means that, at root, faith—religion itself, one might say—is beyond history and historical analysis. It is transcendental. Nevertheless, faith and its transhistorical content have real, perduring effects in history, effects that are mediated through style.

This is the basic position of *Slave Religion*. And it is this general intellectual framework that produces ambiguity in interpreting the first side of the dialectic, the side of faith, and thus its vacillation in how to discern the meaning of religion. This wavering shows up in how the early Raboteau interprets the historical effects of religious faith vis-à-vis style. Sometimes the historical effects of religious faith, which registers itself in terms of style, witnesses to the gods of African consciousness (for, after all, style is the side of the dialectic in which there is continuity with the African past), while at other times these stylistic effects bear witness to Christianity's God. In short, the question Raboteau indirectly bumped up against without being able to find an adequate intellectual solution was the question of religious meaning, the question of how to make claims and levy judgments about what is *historical* regarding faith.

Raboteau begins to confront this question head-on in his 1992 essay, "Praying the ABCs: Reflections on Faith in History." The essay, which would be republished as the prologue to *A Fire in the Bones* (1995), is important because in it Raboteau pushes beyond the dialectical approach guiding *Slave Religion*, though he is still beholden to dialectic. The endeavor to put a new spin on it, however, allows Raboteau to work toward a more rigorous historicizing of faith, the very thing that was methodologically difficult for him to accomplish in his early work. This means that the new approach to dialectic in "Praying the ABCs" allows for a blurring of the line dividing faith and history, such that faith can be understood historically, and, importantly, such that history as an intellectual enterprise can be understood as a kind of faith practice. In this way, "Praying the ABCs" struggles toward a new way of imagining the relationship between faith and cultural expression or style—indeed, between "the African Heritage" and "the Invisible Institution."

How is this accomplished? In "Praying the ABCs," Raboteau circles back to a perennial concern of *Slave Religion*: the dialectical relationship between faith and history. As was the case with his earlier work, of utmost concern in his post–*Slave Religion* work is relating the two sides of the dialectic. This is no mere pedantic concern on Raboteau's part, for he recognizes that how one construes this relationship either opens up or forecloses certain narrative, and thus interpretive, possibilities for understanding both slave religion and the practice of historical investigation into African American religious history. How one relates faith and history, then, determines history itself insofar as history, while having the past as the material on which it works, is an activity very much of the present.

But whose present? Here is where the existential dimensions of Raboteau's work proves important to his research, for in a moment of deep transparency Raboteau acknowledges that his inquiry is about "the faith of black
Americans in education as a solution to the intractable racial inequality of our
society." It is about the intersection of "faith and the academic"—indeed, to
speak more broadly, the intellectual "life." Or, as he says in perhaps the most
personal moment in the essay, it is about the "dialectical relationship of affinity
and challenge" between "[my] faith and my historical scholarship" as they
"reinforce and criticize each other in a variety of ways."[49] In short, to raise the
question of the relationship between faith and history is to raise the issue of
how living the life of the mind, in the academy or otherwise, is an act of faith.
The question is, What kind of faith act is it? This question is all the more
pressing when the life of the mind at issue is that of the Christian intellectual
qua black intellectual: the black Christian intellectual.

There is an inchoate recognition on Raboteau's part that modern racial
discourse, which historically arose at the site of religion and has employed the
idioms of the academy, poses a perennial challenge to the black intellectual
who would dare occupy the academy and deploy its idioms and discourses to
do her work. The black intellectual cannot be an intellectual in the way others
have been intellectuals, if for no other reason than that in modernity "black
intellectual" has historically been an oxymoron. The way the intellectual life is
both configured and executed, therefore, must be rethought. In its own way,
"Praying the ABCs" stages just such a rethinking precisely at the location of
the existential condition, the veritable conundrum of the black intellectual in
modernity. What is interesting is that the conundrum of the intellectual—in
Raboteau's case, the historian—in a racialized world proves to be the conundrum of making historical sense of black religion generally and the emergence
of Afro-Christianity in the very formation of the black intellectual. Herein lies
the significance of how Raboteau even opens the essay:

> In 1862, a teacher named Harriet Ware attended a funeral on one of
> the South Carolina sea islands. Ware, a white missionary, was sur-
> prised by the ceremony that her black pupils, all of them recently
> freed slaves, devised to observe the burial. "As we drew near to the
> grave we heard all the children singing their A, B, C, through and
> through again, as they stood waiting round the grave for the rest to
> assemble.... Each child had his school-book or picture-book...in
> his hand,—another proof that they consider their lessons as in some
> sort religious exercises." Like Ware, many missionaries were im-
> pressed by the former slaves' "superstitious" regard for schooling and
> amazed at the sacrifices they were willing to make to obtain book
> learning despite the poverty, uncertainty, and precariousness of their
> lives in the postbellum South.

> ...I would like to use [the image of those former slave children praying their ABCs] as an emblem [and icon?] for the following reflections upon the relationship between faith and the academic life, in particular the relationship between faith and history.[50]

In "Praying the ABCs," dialectic is reimagined through the imagery of the convergence of spirituality and intellectuality in such a way as to navigate the issue of what it means to be a black intellectual and thereby reimagine the convergence of history and faith.

History and faith, Raboteau argues, are two ways of ordering events. History sequentially arranges events, ordering them as a worldly process that reveals their structure, meaning, and consequence or how they hold together. As a science beholden to the particularities and concreteness of events, history "[tells] stories about the ways that people lived in the past."[51] It does so, however, by making no recourse to a transcendent "beyond" to explain and decipher "the signs of the time" and the meaning or rationality of the events it narrates. This must not be taken to mean that there is no element of faith in what the historian does. Quite the contrary, for while history may not be moved by *religious* faith, it is moved by faith—of some kind. This is evident in that "events do not speak for themselves"; they call for historians to speak on their behalf. But who are historians if not agents of faith?

> Historians, as distinct from chroniclers, construct narratives that try to reveal the meaning of past events . . . . In this very fundamental sense, history is based upon an act of faith, the faith that events are susceptible of meanings that can be described in narration. Historical narrative places a mythic structure upon events by the very act of arranging them in a sequence of meaning, with a beginning, a middle, and an end. Instead of viewing time as a random chaos of atomistic experience, history assumes that the past has structure, meaning, and consequence.[52]

History challenges religious faith in its "demonstration to believers of the historicity of their religious doctrines and institutions." In this it serves an important critical and constructive function for religious faith. On the one hand, it does the critical work of being a guardian against "any religion's tendency to present a triumphalist myth of itself as a timeless, universalist institution preserving the unchanging deposit of doctrine transcending time and disparate cultures."[53] But on the other hand, history aids theology in the constructive work of "[reminding] Christian believers of the scandal of the Incarnation, the historical specificity and contingency of Jesus and of the 'Jesus movement' in its origins and subsequent development." In short, in both its critical and constructive roles, "history promotes an appreciation of [the unique]" and the particular, and thus does important faith work, if not theological work.[54]

Religious faith approaches reality differently. Though it, like history, structures the events of human experience into "a coherent pattern," religious, particularly Christian, faith contends that the source of the meaning of life's events "ultimately lies outside history in the will and providence of God." The serious inadequacy of this formulation as a theological statement need not detain us here. The point I am after is the work the claim does in Raboteau's argument. Christian faith, insofar as it "historically" reflects on itself, does so from the "perspective of eternity": from an otherworldly horizon that has as its goal the telling of "salvation history."[55] The unique challenge it poses to history is to own its faith-based perspective, the fact that it, too, is an endeavor rooted in faith. Raboteau formulates the challenge as a series of questions that faith forces the intellectual enterprise of history to confront:

> How can you know what events or what characters are significant?
> How can you find a vantage point within history from which you
> can judge the significance of human events? And without such a
> vantage point, aren't your interpretations arbitrary and all too prone
> to the fallacy of presentism, that is, judging the significance of
> what happened in the past by reference to issues of particular sig-
> nificance in the present?[56]

The rhetorical force of this battery of questions is that historians can give themselves no assurances in answering them.

What then are we left with? The mere dialectical pendulum swing between faith and history? Were this the case, Raboteau would simply be rehashing the problematic theoretical framework of *Slave Religion*. In fact, however, he does not stop here. While he still maintains that the relationship between faith and history is dialectical, he now adds something more. He introduces an important, new notion, the notion of "the narrative construction of reality," or "plot": "History and religious faith coalesce for me in their mutual admission of the necessity of plot."[57] To admit the necessity of plot is to admit that at root both religious faith and history as an intellectual practice in the present attempt to stitch together the pieces of the past to find "the 'hidden wholeness' of life, the connectedness of apparently fragmented and chaotic bits of experience and knowledge."[58]

Raboteau does not uncritically celebrate one mode of emplotment over the other. Indeed, within the two distinct ways of stitching together history's remains—the way of religious faith and the way of the intellectual practice of history—there can and have been problematic ways of telling our stories. This point comes out in Raboteau's assessment of how historians have constructed the story of America. He observes that within the historians' guild there has been the problem, exemplified most starkly by those mired in and quite often oblivious to their whiteness, of putting together the tapestry of history in such a way that

the dominant culture, academic as well as popular, ignored the presence or distorted the role of African-Americans in the nation's history. Black Americans, if historians discussed them at all, figured prominently only in the story of slavery and in the topic of race relations. In both cases, they appeared not as actors in the national drama but as victims or problems. As an oppressed minority, they represented an unfortunate but minor exception to the main plot of American history: the gradual expansion of democracy to include all citizens. A few countervailing voices protested the inaccuracy of this consensus version of our history, but in the main, black people and their culture remained absent from courses in American history down to the 1960s. We were, so to speak, invisible. And the results of invisibility were devastating. In the absence of black history, a myth of the American past developed, a myth that denied black people any past of significance.[59]

Raboteau makes a number of important points here, but what is most significant for my purposes is the attention he calls to history's traditional activity. This is the activity of locating the citizenry within "the nation's history," within "the national drama," and within "the main plot of American history: the gradual expansion of democracy to include all citizens."[60] There is a politics to historical emplotment; indeed, there is a politics of history, for history does the work of identity formation: "History functions as a form of self-definition. In its pages we read ourselves."[61] To this can be added that we read ourselves *dramatically*, as participants in a drama. Building in part on the work of colonial historian Edmund Morgan, Raboteau calls attention to history's inability to weave African Americans into the national drama other than as a problem for the drama. Why has this been so? New histories must be offered that at times supplement and at other times wholly reorient the drama of the nation.

Such are the historical difficulties regarding emplotment with which the academic discipline of history has struggled. Sadly though, religious faith generally and Christian faith particularly have not fared much better. Indeed, religious faith has often aided and abetted history by validating the skewed, exclusionary plotline advanced as the history of America. Faith's difference from history, however, is that it has promulgated the storyline of America in the idioms of religion. Yet, whether one speaks of history as functioning through a national myth of whiteness or through a Christian mythologization of whiteness, what has united both religious faith and history is whiteness. Thus, American Christians, Raboteau rightly points out, often "[turned] Christianity into a clan religion," such that American Christianity more often than not became an expression of "the jingoism of the age." Understood in these mythological terms, the terms of whiteness, American Christianity—and one can surely extend this to Christianity in much of the West—stood condemned

of "worshipping Anglo-Saxonism [or some other mythic expression of white-ness, like Aryanism at its absolute worst, for example] instead of Christ."[62]

The crucial question is this, however: What does "whiteness," whether at work in the intellectual arena of history or in the domain of religious faith, signify here in relationship to the plotline of America and the narrative con-strual of the Western, Euro-American reality? In my terms, terms consistent with the framework of the post–*Slave Religion* Raboteau of "Praying the ABCs," whiteness is the "political unconscious" of false emplotment.[63] Indeed, it is a religious-historical way of mythically construing reality. Or, to employ terms drawn from the social theory of Pierre Bourdieu, whiteness names the acti-vation of a certain set of dispositions.[64] These dispositions cover the full panoply of reality. Thus, the activation of these dispositions creates the scholar (in this case, the historian), and, then once created, these same dispositions name the conditions under which the scholar intellectually labors or plies his craft and into which the scholar is habituated (*habitus*). The traditional con-strual of reality such that historians have been unable or unwilling to renarrate the story of American so as to make sense of black existence—and the exis-tence of others as well—reflects the degree to which historians have activated and lived into the dispositions of the academic. Thus, to be a historian is to activate that set of dispositions that enables a certain form of storytelling while disabling others.

Moreover, a Bourdieuean framework helps us understand something else: namely, that the activation of the dispositions of the scholar, which is the disposition of whiteness refracted through and warranted by the intellectual life, works in concert with the activation of the dispositions of religion, par-ticularly as the category of religion has come to be constituted as a modern category of thought and existence. It is important to note that the activation of the dispositions of religion happens both at the popular level and at the level of its academic or intellectual study. When Christian faith functions nationalis-tically, it functions as a modulation within the dispositions of whiteness.

What the icon of former slave children, who in *praying* their ABCs *pray* the intellectual life and thus search for wholeness among the fragments but under the aspect of faith and prayer—what this icon of intellectuality represents is another way of taking up the fragments of existence that slavery has left in its wake, and "plotting" those scraps into something that despite itself can nour-ish. Lard, fatback, and neckbones become a meal. Slavery's remains could be put together in such a way as to propel the former slave children forward even as they stood at a grave site, at death's ever-present door. In doing this, former slave children engaged in the faith work, which for them was also the historical work of replotting their identity into a story that could more fully make sense of them and their New World existence. How did they do this?

Raboteau suggests an answer in "Praying the ABCs" and begins to fill it out in subsequent chapters of *A Fire in the Bones*. The former slave children were

able to do this because they activated and lived into another set of dispositions, the dispositions of Israel, not as a race group but as a people of YHWH's covenant. They lived into Israel's covenantal dispositions through the liturgical or churchly mediations, such as prayer, of Jesus of Nazareth. It is possible, but in the end unpersuasive I think, to read the slaves and the former slave children as acquiescing before Christianity, the religion of the masters, as an opiate for their plight. I find it more compelling that the slaves and their late-nineteenth-century progeny came to understand the faulty historical foundations on which the plotline of American manifest destiny rested. They came to understand that it rested on the supersessionist claim of "the image of America as a New Israel. This myth of national identity depicts the European migration across the Atlantic from the old world to the new as an escape from Egyptian bondage to the Promised Land of milk and honey."[65]

Raboteau lucidly highlights this significant feature of how the slaves and the former slave children pulled together the fragments of their existence in America into a story of historical wholeness. They dismantled the myth of America as New Israel and out of its fragments forged a new story of their existence, a new religious history of themselves and of America as well. For them, the story of what Paul Gilroy has called the "Black Atlantic"[66] is the story of

> the Middle Passage [as] a voyage from freedom in Africa to perpetual bondage in an America that in biblical terms did not resemble Israel but Egypt. "Go down, Moses," sang these American slaves, appropriating the story of Exodus, "and tell ol' Pharaoh to let my people go." As the historian Vincent Harding has noted, it is an abiding and tragic irony of our national history that white America's claim to be a New Israel has been constantly denied by Old Israel still enslaved in her midst.[67]

Raboteau follows this up with commentary that gestures toward my point about history being tied to a set of dispositions that allows a particular orientation in analyzing events of the past out of which can be woven another *history*. "Clearly these conflicting interpretations of the past," Raboteau says, "are not simply questions of fact, resolvable by more historical research." That is to say, a pure science of history (history as *Wissenschaft*)—whose task it is to accumulate by means of historical research data for analysis and thus access history's core—cannot alone adjudicate these differences of interpretation because the material yielded by such research is always filtered through the consciousness (and unconsciousness) of the specific intellectual.

The question therefore is, What kind of consciousness (and unconsciousness) is at work? These differences of interpretation "result from the fact that history has served in the past and still serves today to establish and legitimate the identities of various communities. The conflicting claims upon history made by the search of different communities for meaning raises the

issue of whose story it is that history tells."[68] The story that America specifically and the West more broadly has taken up as the fragment out of which it sought to constitute itself as a nation, as a body politic, was the story of Israel. It is this story that is being told badly so as to constitute white America to the exclusion of others, but chiefly to the exclusion of those raced as non-white generally and black particularly.

When the slaves and their progeny grasped this, their response was to retell the story of their existence, but to do so as a different way of understanding the story of Israel as a living story. They told Israel's story from the location of Israel's exodus from Egypt. The story of the Exodus culminates in, and indeed is written from the perspective of, the Sinai covenant, which sealed the relationship between YHWH and YHWH's people, Israel. In chapter 2 of *A Fire in the Bones*, Raboteau narrates with particular force and eloquence how African Americans told and lived into Israel's story. He titles that chapter "African-Americans, Exodus, and the American Israel," from which I quote at length:

> By appropriating the story of Exodus as their own story, black
> Christians articulated their own sense of peoplehood. Exodus sym-
> bolized their common history and common destiny. It would be hard
> to exaggerate the intensity of their identification with the children of
> Israel. AME pastor William Paul Quinn demonstrated how literal the
> metaphor of Exodus could become when he exhorted black Chris-
> tians, "Let us comfort and encourage one another, and keep singing
> and shouting, great is the Holy One of Israel in the midst of us.
> Come thou Great Deliverer, once more awake thy almighty arm, and
> set thy African captives free." As Quinn reveals, it was prayer and
> worship services that made the connection so immediate. Sermons,
> prayers, and songs recreated in the imagination of successive gen-
> erations the travail and triumph of Israel.
>   . . . In the ecstasy of worship, time and distance collapsed, and the
> slaves became the children of Israel. With the Hebrews, they traveled
> dry-shod through the Red Sea; they, too, saw Pharaoh's army "get
> drowned"; they stood beside Moses on Mount Pisgah and gazed out
> over the Promised Land; they crossed Jordan under Joshua and
> marched with him round the walls of Jericho. Their prayers for de-
> liverance resonated with the experiential power of these liturgical
> dramas.
>   Identification with Israel, then, gave the slaves a communal
> identity as special, divinely favored people. This identity stood in stark
> contrast with racist propaganda depicting them as inferior to whites,
> destined by nature and providence to the status of slaves.[69]

The identification between persons of African descent in America and the people Israel avoids the modernist problem of supersessionism because that

identity is mediated through the worship of the Jew, Jesus of Nazareth. (I say "modernist problem," because in modernity, as I argue in chapters 1 and 2 of this book, supersessionism articulates itself through race generally and through whiteness more specifically. This is Christian supersessionism's new element. There I offer a theological theory of race that unmasks how whiteness is modernity's perennial theological problem.)

Black flesh comes to inhabit Israel's covenantal story, which is nothing less than the story of creation itself. In this way, African Americans retold history so as to begin dissolving the hegemonic history of whiteness through a new religious orientation toward the fragments of the events of the past. Black flesh, their claim was, must exit—hence, the insistence on the centrality of the Exodus story—the arrangement of whiteness (as must whites themselves), an arrangement in which they are "black," by undergoing a political conversion. This is the conversion by which they entered into the body of Israel and into Israel's covenant with YHWH as non-Jews (or Gentiles) through the Jew Jesus. In this way they imagine and live into a history of Exodus, a history of exiting the ways in which whiteness racializes all flesh. This history is nothing less than the history of YHWH-God.[70]

Raboteau's reading of the Christian faith of many of the former slaves and their progeny raises a challenge: What would it mean to do historical work—or work within any domain of modern intellectual life—from the set of dispositions and the *habitus* that the slaves and their progeny as historical agents activated when they entered into Israel's covenantal liturgy in their Christian worship of YHWH as revealed in Jesus of Nazareth? They understood this liturgy as the objective condition of their subjectivity, and it was in their subjectivity as worshipping agents that the objectivity of Israel's covenantal liturgy as the precondition of life was made available. What kind of intellectual dispositions made possible their holding together of the fragments of the past into a story of wholeness? It was the dispositions that lodged the telling of history in the vantage point opened up by Jesus' Jewish, which is to say, nonracialized, flesh. In many respects, in part III of this book I attempt a fuller articulation of these dispositions, locating them in a nonsupersessionist Christology as a response to modern racial reasoning.

From the Dialectic to the Theology of History

Once again, Raboteau has anticipated aspects of what I want to do. This is evident in his most recent work, including the important 2003 Schmemann lectures.[71] In this post–*Fire in the Bones* work, Raboteau peers with the slaves into what he calls the Bible's picture of "a fully articulated ritual relationship with the Supreme Being." This relationship sets the contours of a "theology of history."[72] At the ground of such a theology is an "analogy between African

and Evangelical styles of worship," an analogy that "enabled the slaves to reinterpret the new religion by reference to the old."[73] I contend that with this notion of "analogy" Raboteau struggles against a dialecticism of faith and history that he nevertheless continues to hold onto. He pursues theoretical reflections that function strictly on the faith side of the dialectic and yet allows them cachet on the history or intellectual side of the dialectic.

"Analogy" assists Raboteau to work toward what might be termed an incarnational understanding of faith and history, of Christian consciousness and African heritage, an understanding that integrates the two sides through the plotline of the person of Jesus in his Jewish humanity. It is clear that humanity here is not a "thing" or a "nature." It is a mode or way of inhabiting the world, what the seventh-century theologian Maximus the Confessor called *tropos hyparxeos*. Jesus of Nazareth activates human existence in a particular way, under a peculiar or unique set of dispositions. These dispositions are the dispositions of a Christian spirituality, that, it should be clear from how I have laid this out, is not opposed to embodied existence and therefore to history. Christian spirituality is an orientation toward history and a way of inhabiting the world. It names how we actualize or enact our creatureliness and live into our contingency.

The spirituality that Raboteau considers is specific to the Roman Catholicism out of which he came and the Eastern Orthodoxy in which he now practices Christianity. Broadly speaking, the spirituality specific to these traditions, but especially to Orthodoxy, acknowledges that creation is "enspirited." It has being and it is uniquely what it is by being animated by a "principle" of existence. In this way creatures have life from "beyond" themselves. But this "beyond" is thoroughly impressed within every creature, making each creature the specific creature that it is and making it, in its difference from every other creature, nevertheless in union with every other creature and thus with creation. What makes the human being distinct among creatures is that the human is conscious of its status as creature and what this status entails. Thus, the human being is not only enspirited but is enspirited by being "ensouled." It can be conscious of its difference from every other creature, recognizing that this difference is grounded in the primal difference between creation and the Creator, who grants it its principle of being, and that this difference is for the sake of its unity or coinherence with those from whom it is different, namely, God and other creatures.

This goes far in explaining why the term that Raboteau now employs for the relationship between African heritage and Christian existence, history and faith, is importantly not "syncretism," as was the case in *Slave Religion* or as Peter Paris (*Spirituality of African Peoples*), Donald Matthews (*Honoring the Ancestors*), or Robert Thompson (*Flash of the Spirit*) might champion; for syncretism smacks of the emergence of a third "something." Rather, "coin-

herence," a personal and thoroughly Trinitarian and Christological term, now names for him the relationship:

> The resonances or points of convergence between Orthodoxy and African-American spirituality... are profound. The first resonance is historical. Ancient Christianity is not, as many think, a European religion. Christian communities were well established in Africa by the third and fourth centuries. In Egypt and Ethiopia, traditions of worship, monasticism, and spirituality have remained authentically African and authentically Christian down to the present day.[74]

The second resonance is spiritual: there are analogies between African traditional religions and Orthodox Christianity.[75]

As this passage witnesses, Raboteau's thought has made a significant advance. The Raboteau of *Slave Religion* united slave religion to African religions geopolitically: that is, by passing through the Caribbean to South America and into North America. The general supposition was that the connection with Africa and African religions terminated geographically *and historically* at the time of the seventeenth-century conquests, plunderings, and deportations. In this quotation, however, we see Raboteau radically historicizing African religions by refusing to freeze African religions in their sixteenth-century and seventeenth-century contact with European and Euro-American modernity.

In resisting such privileging, Raboteau at the same time resists what V. Y. Mudimbe has called a modern "gnosis" or invention of Africa.[76] In effect, Raboteau asks, Why privilege the sixteenth- and seventeenth-century moment of cultural contact with the West, as significant and important as it is, as the urmoment to which slave religion must be connected and through which it must be interpreted? He now recognizes an even fuller dynamism to Africa and its religions, a dynamism that pushes him as historian to note the vibrancy of Christian communities in Africa in the apostolic and patristic epoch of the church, a vibrancy that continues to echo through history. In short, Raboteau reclaims Christianity itself as an African religion, but without losing sight of how this all passes through Israel's covenants with YHWH as enacted in Jesus of Nazareth.

Raboteau's further historicizing of both Christianity and the African heritage is closely connected with his use of analogy. He does not give a full account of how he employs the notion. However, the contexts in which he invokes it display how what he speaks of dialectically in *Slave Religion* and *A Fire in the Bones* could now be regarded as working like beveled gear teeth in the person and dispositions of Jesus Christ. From within such an understanding of reality, the dialectic that was at work in Raboteau's early texts is now, to use the grammar of Chalcedon, held together without confusion in the person (*hypostasis*) of the eternal Word, Jesus the Jew. Analogy, therefore, does

the important theoretical work of grounding the claim that Africanity and Christianity are mutually inhering living traditions. "In classical theological terms," Raboteau says, "these analogies [between African religions and Christianity] constitute a protoevangelion: a preparation for the Gospel based on God's natural revelation to all peoples through nature and conscience."[77] Analogy thus does the work of natural theology.

I return to the problem of natural theology as a racial problem in modernity in chapter 4, where I take up the work of theologian James H. Cone. For now, it can be said that Raboteau deploys analogy as a Christological trope within natural theology. He understands it as determined by the particularity of the Crucified One and by the "scandal of [his] Incarnation."[78] One way to make theological sense of this is to understand Raboteau as historically elucidating a "mystagogy" of New World blackness. Such a mystagogical interpretation of reality is similar to that of Maximus the Confessor. In the postlude of this book, I consider aspects of Maximus's interpretation more closely as it relates to my attempt to undo modernity's pseudotheology of race. For now, I limit my remarks to the observation that for Maximus, existent beings—including the histories in which they are embedded—are unique and irreplaceable inflections of the eternal Logos. This means that the interior "principles" (*logoi*) of black existence, traditional African religions, and the African heritage—"principles" out of which meaning arises and is forged amid the struggles against the nihilistic collapse of meaning and of being—have their *proton* and *eschaton* in the incarnate Logos, Jesus Christ. It is because of such an incarnational and, ultimately, Trinitarian principle that the *factum* of Christian faith can itself be historically spoken of. But even more, it is this theological *factum* that keeps the quest to discern meaning in history from becoming a futile or metaphysically wishful enterprise.

But this is also why Raboteau as historian can say, "African spirituality *foreshadowed* ancient Christianity," and this in seven distinct ways.[79] There is no need to elucidate them all here, but I refer to some salient and recurring themes insofar as they establish Raboteau's movement from historical dialecticism to an "iconic" reading of history, and thus toward the possibility of a theological engagement with history. How Raboteau recasts his engagement with history in iconic rather than dialectical terms can be summarized as follows: Black existence and black faith relate to the eternal Logos as an icon relates to that which it represents. In this way, the invisible becomes visible even as it retains its invisible depth, a depth rooted in a freedom (for God the Creator), which cannot be policed and thus enslaved.

I contend that this general outlook is not at all subject to Richard Rorty's and other similar critiques about epistemological correspondence or the search for conditions of adequate representation. Hence, it is not a species of the phenomenon of "mirroring" in modern philosophy. For the philosophy of the

icon in Christian thought does not simply mime the features of Greek ocularity by which there is a dualism between "contemplation and action, between representing the world and coping with it."[80] Understanding Being in its lived expressions as in varying degrees iconic complicates the Rortian, neopragmatist understanding of "vision" or ocular metaphysics.[81] For though the icon or image (both legitimate renderings of the Greek term *eikon*) as a phenomenon of creation is to be rigorously distinguished from what it "represents," the icon's representing capacity is not reducible to that of a passive or inert mirror. Understanding the representational capacity of the image in this way is precisely what gives rise to the need to theorize the correspondence between type and archetype, between mirror and what is mirrored.

Insofar as it is an index of what it means for a created thing to be just that, something *created*, the icon and thus Being itself is better understood in the following way. The icon, and therefore Being itself, is both translucent and opaque. It is translucent insofar as the historically and existentially constituted image of God or created Being is a reflection of divinity, albeit on the surface of creation. In this sense, to be a creature is to be sheer *impressio* and pure *emphasis*. It is to have one's existence stamped somewhat like the imprint of a seal on a coin, to have one's face or expression (*phasis*) imprinted into Being or drawn into the enduring effect of existing rather than not existing at all. In short, it is to be created, to be brought into the realization of creaturely and therefore contingent identity.

But as Gregory of Nyssa in the fourth century CE rightly saw and Bonaventure would later affirm in the thirteenth-century medieval West, there is a fruitful ambiguity here, because imbedded within creaturely Being's appearing or its having been "passively" created or impressed into existence is its "active" and free participation in bringing itself to appearance or visibility. In other words, Being is not merely *impressio*. It is also *expressio*. As expression, image consciously and intentionally offers itself and in offering or presenting its face it discloses that face as the very surface of the Infinite. Stated differently, in actively and freely (according to a creaturely freedom) showing itself, creaturely Being also discloses the face of Infinite Being (just as conversely, Infinite Being in this instance reveals that its own iconic capacities can be displayed through the medium of finite, creaturely Being). It follows, therefore, that Being—and here I am speaking specifically of creaturely, finite, and therefore contingent Being—properly understood is dynamic (rather than static). It is a static vision of existence that in large part gives rise to the problem of Western ocular metaphysics. Moreover, this dynamism—which is the dynamism of human nature as well, insofar as human *being* is a particular modality of what one must even mean when speaking of "creaturely Being"—is but another way of saying that existence as such is iconic. *Instasy*, or the identity by which a human being *is* itself, is an *ecstasy*, a transcending of the self precisely in being

oneself. *Instasis* or identity is therefore an *ekstasis* or a standing beyond the self. This is the gift of Being, the veritable profundity of existing rather than not existing at all.

I have taken this brief detour down a technical philosophical road not merely to establish why this is not simply an iteration of Western metaphysical thinking. My ultimate point is to establish that something quite important follows from this, both for the theological reading I am advancing of Raboteau's work and for the way in which I read James Cone's and Charles H. Long's work in chapters 4 and 5, and that point is this: creatures present themselves or are visible in such a way that their visibility cannot be captured or enslaved without a massive and violent distortion of their existence as creatures. In this respect, one might say that creaturely existence is opaque, a term that I use in chapter 5. But their opacity and, hence, their visibility as creatures, it must quickly be said, is of a particular sort: What it means "to be" is to be *visible* but precisely as the visible icon of the *invisible*. Creaturely opacity must be understood within the horizon of the icon. That is, creatures in the particular forms in which they appear are opaque (there is something that is uncapturable about creatures without distortion of what it means to be a creature). But their opacity is the opacity of the icon, whose opacity and translucency are not in binary relationship (as is the beautiful to the grotesque, or the rational to the irrational, or the civil is to the savage in Western metaphysics). To say the one—the opaque—is already to have said the other—the translucent. Black existence in bearing witness to the form of Christ displays just this theologically iconic nature of creation.

What this means regarding African traditional religions—the topic Raboteau has engaged in *Slave Religion* and in other work—is that one need not interpret them in strict opposition to Christianity. Nor, for that matter, need one employ some species of the notion of syncretism, a *tertium quid*, with all of its problems to draw them together. Rather, as Raboteau has clearly gestured toward saying especially in his later work, one must make the hermeneutic turn, which is also a kind of linguistic turn, to interpret the plurality the African religious heritage in light of its iconic capacity and Christological destiny. For insofar as African spirituality sees the world as "enlivened with spirit," it anticipates classical Christianity's understanding of the world as theophanic and Christoform. Raboteau points out that African traditional religions tend to see the world as charged with the divine. The same can be said for Christianity, certain forms of Protestantism notwithstanding. This is because the world, according to such forms of Christianity, is the icon of the icon of God, an image in the image of Jesus Christ, the bearer, in the fullness of his divine person and of his Jewish flesh, of the glory, or *kabod* YHWH, the unspeakable Name in which all of the names of creation are uttered.

This means that Jesus Christ in his particularity is a communal person, the ground of a full-orbed body politic. This is thoroughly consonant, says

Raboteau, with African spirituality's understanding of the self as a web of relationships. The analogy between Christian existence and New World black existence reaches its zenith in the experience of suffering. As ancient Christianity proclaimed, so Raboteau seems to affirm: "The blood of the martyrs is the seed of the Church." Nascent Afro-Christianity expresses the reality of the person Jesus Christ and his covenantal, which is not to be construed as a racial, existence as a Jew insofar as "the slave . . . resembled Him more than [did] the [slave]master." The slaves were cruciform, for they inhabited modernity in "follow[ing] His way of the cross."[82]

None of this, for Raboteau, reasserts an arrogant "triumphalism" on the part of Afro-Christianity. As an incarnate, bodily, and concrete faith, it is ever reminded, because of its historicity, "that part of faith is doubt" and that our horizons are marked by finitude.[83] As a result, "this was no easy faith for slaves exposed [as they were] to constant toil and regular violence at the hands of professed fellow Christians. We should not underestimate the difficulty of living such beliefs. The temptations to despair, to reject Christianity as a religion for whites, to abandon belief in a God who permits the innocent to suffer were very real."[84] Yet out of such doubt came a "sense of community [extended] to include the powerless, the poor, the weak, the inarticulate and to make present the invisible, those left out or ignored as pejorative others."[85]

Here is the moment of transformative possibility ensconced within New World Afro-Christian faith. The borders of its Christological and Trinitarian economy of being in the world are made to embrace, engage, and thereby transfigure through struggle the political economy in which it found itself. In so doing, faith began to weaken modernity's discourse and pseudotheology of race. It opened up a new disposition on history. Thus, far from being antihistorical, faith becomes history's *telos*—or, better, a realization, even if not yet a thoroughgoing one, of the eschaton. Faith bears the fullness of history and is shown to be fraught with burden, struggle, and fulfillment in its participation in the fullness of time. Faith, thus, "confirms and completes the experience [of history] by reminding us that there are no aliens, no others, but only sisters and brothers."[86] The journey of history and faith "leads not only to knowledge but to compassion";[87] it is the search for transformed social relations, the anticipation of and yet continued quest for a different way of being in the world.

For Raboteau, that way of being in the world is the way of prayer, which for him holds the key to the enigma of history and of the African heritage as tied to the mystery of the man, Jesus of Nazareth. "Faced with the mystery of discerning God's design in history," he says, "I find myself returning to the company of those former slave children, praying their ABCs":[88] " 'Princes shall come out of Egypt and Ethiopia shall soon stretch forth her hands unto God' (Ps 68:31) was not so much a prophecy as it was a prayer."[89]

The question that remains for Raboteau, his guild of religious historians, and, indeed, for all intellectuals—black, white, and others besides—who care

about these matters, is this: What would it mean to refuse dialectical intellectual arrangements altogether, arrangements that allow us to neatly but in-
sistently sequester the dispositions of faith from the dispositions of the modern academic, and then rewrite history, do literary criticism or philosophy or
sociology or political science or what have you as Christian intellectuals? What
would the intellectual life then look like? How would *Slave Religion* have to be
rewritten? But more to the broader issues of this book, how much more would
the pseudotheological backbone of whiteness be broken for the sake of the redemption of us all, were we to escape the intellectual dispositions of whiteness
and the ambiguities of blackness that it creates?

4

Theologizing Race

*James H. Cone, Liberation, and the Theological
Meaning of Blackness*

What is one to make of these theologies of redness, blackness, or
blueness of deity and being? It is the intent and structure of theology
as a mode of discourse that is at stake.

> —Charles H. Long, *Significations: Signs, Symbols,
> and Images in the Interpretation of Religion*

When Christianity was introduced to slaves, Africans converted
it . . . by refusing to accept any version of the gospel that did
not harmonize with the African spirit of freedom . . . the African
personality.

> —James H. Cone, "Black Worship," in *The Study of
> Spirituality*, ed. Cheslyn Jones, Geoffrey Wain-
> wright, and Edward Yarnold

James H. Cone's theological interrogation of New World Afro-
Christian faith pioneers in the history of American theology. Its
groundbreaking nature lies in its attempt to uncover the theological significance and political promise of black faith and existence given
the racist practices and dispositions of America and, indeed, of
modernity. These practices and dispositions are the practices and
dispositions of whiteness, which, for Cone, is theological in nature. In
short, they are the practices and dispositions of white theology. In
contrast, Cone calls his own intellectual program a "black theology
of liberation." Its task has been to unmask the ideological superstructure of whiteness.

What makes white theology, in fact, *white?* This question centers this chapter's considerations of Cone's formulation of black theology. For how this question is answered reveals the degree to which black theology as a mode of theological reflection adequately identifies what is aberrantly theological about the modern, Euro-American discourse of race and racial character. Additionally, it reveals the degree to which black theology offers a philosophical and theological corrective to the problem of white theology. In this chapter, I assess the degree to which black theology dislodges the *white* in white theology. But I also consider the extent to which black theology remains beholden to the logics of modern racial reasoning. My goal is to bring to the forefront the significant ground that Cone's theological program, particularly in its early phase, breaks in uncovering the heterodox theological structure of modern racial reasoning and to render explicit the Christological themes latent in his analyses. In a critical gesture beyond what Cone himself says, I also point out the Trinitarian implications of his Christology to further highlight the groundbreaking nature of his, as Karl Barth might say, "irregular dogmatics."[1]

But more specifically, I argue that the brilliance of Cone's thought—indeed, its underdeveloped apex—is in its analysis of Being's "concreteness," which is revealed in Jesus of Nazareth. A concrete conceptualization of Being stands over against abstract conceptualizations of Being, along with their attendant racial politics. Central to Cone's analysis is the place he accords, especially in his early thought, to Jesus' Jewishness. Hence, the breakthrough in his thought: the humanity that the God of Israel assumes in Jesus of Nazareth is the location from which God secures and affirms all of creation in its historical unfoldings. Therefore, contra the logic of modern racial reasoning as outlined in part I of this book, Jesus' Jewishness is not racially arrayed against non-Jews but, rather, is the perpetual sign of God's embrace of Jew and non-Jew (or, in scriptural parlance, Gentile) alike.

Thus black theology, understood from this vantage, gestures toward a theology of the nations, one that emanates from and is consonant with a Christian theology of Israel. Indeed, it is a theology of "a nation within a nation," a theology, that is, of black existence in its diasporic wanderings through the strange land of late modernity. In short, I argue that with this perspective as its pinnacle, Cone's black liberation theology comes to the threshold of an intellectual program that theologically disrupts modernity's analytics of race. However, and for reasons that will be explained, the breakthrough in Cone's thought unravels in that his program unwittingly reinscribes the aberrant theology (or pseudotheology) of modern racial reasoning. This occurs insofar as Cone's ontology disallows transcendence and thus recapitulates the inner logic of modern racial reasoning.

This critique, in part, has already been advanced by theological ethicist Victor Anderson, who has characterized Cone's theology, and a number of genetically similar projects, as beholden to "metaphysical" or "ontological

blackness."[2] Ontological blackness, Anderson says, is the tendency toward racial reification by which race is "treated as if it objectively exists independent of historically contingent factors and subjective intentions." As such, it produces a categorical or essential "racial consciousness."[3] Anderson sees in ontological blackness a claim that makes race, though always present, the exhaustive principle of identity, its thoroughgoing index. This, he interestingly says, is a form of "cultural idolatry," a term whose meaning in itself and in relationship to the "radical monotheistic faith" with which Anderson contrasts it needs filling out. Because this remains unthematized in Anderson's otherwise penetrating and often fruitful analyses, he leaves the specifically *theological* contours of this idolatrous "cult of black" or racial "genius" itself insufficiently scrutinized.[4] Thus, in going beyond Anderson, I seek to expose why Cone's theological critique of modern racial reasoning, through its ultimate refusal of theology, is in fact not trenchant enough where it most needs to be: namely, on the subject of what makes whiteness a theological problem—What makes white theology, in fact, white?[5] In so doing, I seek to show how Cone's theology reproduces the aberrant theology of modern racial reasoning.

A disclaimer is in order before moving forward. Assessing black theology through the figure of Cone is not meant to be reductive, rendering moot the importance of the theological and religious endeavors of prior generations of thinkers who expended formidable intellectual energy in probing the sociocultural and political import of black faith. This inquiry proceeds with the acknowledgment that black theology sees beyond its predecessors only by standing on their broad intellectual shoulders. Nor, for that matter, is my focus on Cone's thought meant to minimize the importance of his contemporaries or other forms of theological reflection, such as womanist theology, that are the immediate offshoots of Cone's thought, as if Cone's approach to black theology were the alpha and omega of black religious thought. It is, however, to recognize the unprecedented scale on which Cone's theological project has been enacted and consequently the unmatched influence it has exerted in virtually single-handedly forming a discipline of study and a specific mode of religious reflection.

His influence has been exerted not only within academe but also within the so-called broader public square. Cone's stature as a public intellectual can be seen, for example, in that he was the key drafter of the June 13, 1969, statement on "Black Theology," a statement that represented the growing theological consensus that developed between black clergy and academics at the time on the scope and substance of the fledgling theological enterprise of black theology. As such, the document in many respects culminated a series of public statements—such as the statement on "Black Power," which was published in the *New York Times* on July 31, 1966, and "The Black Manifesto" of April 1969—that sought to declare the meaning of black faith in the tumultuous era of the 1960s. Cone's first book, *Black Theology and Black Power*, would precede

the final draft of the statement on "Black Theology" by only a few weeks and thus can rightly be judged to be an intellectual account of the public and religious mood represented in the "Black Theology" statement.[6] With his intellectual finger so close to the religious pulse of the era, Cone was positioned in many respects to establish the theological terms of engagement with the realities of black faith and life in America, and his stature as a public intellectual has been upheld in the recent PBS documentary *This Far by Faith*.[7]

Theological Concreteness: The Initial Search

Cone is acutely sensitive to the problem of abstraction in theology. He understands it to be the perennial problem of white theology and Euro-American racism as a whole. Indeed, as he sees it, a commitment to thinking and acting abstractly is central to why neither white theology nor the white church authentically expresses the Christian faith. White Christianity does not entail concrete living, though it passes itself off as doing so. As such, white theology is neither a practice of reflecting on God's concrete relationship to humans nor a concrete reflection on how humans relate to one another. Rather, white Christianity is an abstract mode of life, and white theology is an abstract mode of thought. What does Cone mean by this?

Answering this question requires an appreciation of how Cone sought to inhabit the theological thought world of Karl Barth, on whose theological anthropology he completed a doctoral dissertation.[8] Of central importance for Cone's understanding of Barth is the categorical or, in Kierkegaardian terms, the absolute, qualitative difference between God and the creature, the infinite and the finite, eternity and time, and Christ and culture. More than merely an ontological difference, Cone emphasizes that for Barth, again in Kierkegaardian fashion, the difference between God and human beings points to a sickness that plunges humanity into death, a fated sickness unto death.[9] Cone's early imbibing of this form of thinking gives him a vantage from which to deploy black theology as a religious critique of culture. It gives him a way to show how American racism is, in fact, a kind of "natural theology" run amok, a species of the racialized natural theology theorized in part I of this book. Christ's qualitative difference stands over and against the so-called natural order of things, against the racialized theology at work in America. It is the task of Cone's black theology to speak out of and to think within the qualitative difference that is Jesus Christ. This method of theological inquiry is quite Barthian. As a method, it is what allowed Barth to mount his own theological critique of and resistance to the natural theology of German National Socialism.[10] Cone's own imbibing of this form of theological dialecticism by which Christ stands over and against a false reality is apparent in the title of his first

published theological monograph, *Black Theology and Black Power* (1969), and, indeed, it continues to mark his most recent monograph as of this writing, *Risks of Faith* (1999).

Yet as the title of *Black Theology and Black Power* illustrates, Cone modifies in an important way Barth's style of theological dialectic.[11] While in Barthian fashion Cone affirms Christ's qualitative difference from the nation, from culture, and even from race, he presses beyond Barth to affirm that, nevertheless, God can be related to these sites of identity. It is just that the first, more strictly Barthian, affirmation of qualitative difference from these sites holds in check the second, less-Barthian, affirmation. This means that, already early on, Cone's dialectical Christology, which had a pronounced Barthian accent, had latent within it a theology of culture, which was less Barthian. Indeed, dialectic was the way by which culture theologically expressed itself. Black theology's task was to elaborate the conjunction between Christianity in a way that a strictly Barthian approach to the matter could not address.

Or, thought about in terms of Cone's first book, through dialectic, the early Cone sought to establish what he took to be the proper relationship between, on the one hand, black theology as a practice of the black intellectual imagination (which in black theology's case functioned at the site of black faith), and on the other hand, the sociocultural movement known as "black power" (which, too, was a "religious" expression, an expression of black faith). In Barthian fashion, Cone's claim was that "the Christian experience of revelation" in Jesus Christ is what grounds and so binds them together:

> Christianity begins and ends with the man Jesus—his life, death, and resurrection. He is the Revelation, the special disclosure of God to man, revealing who God is and what his purpose for man is. In short, Christ is the essence of Christianity. Schleiermacher was not far wrong when he said that "Christianity is essentially distinguished from other faiths by the fact that everything in it is related to the redemption accomplished by Jesus of Nazareth." In contrast to many religions, Christianity revolves around a Person, without whom its existence ceases to be.For this very reason Christology is made the point of departure in Karl Barth's *Church Dogmatics*. According to Barth, all theological talk about God, man, church, etc. must inevitably proceed from Jesus Christ, who is the sole criterion for every Christian utterance. To talk of God or of man without first talking about Jesus Christ is to engage *in idle, abstract words which have no relation to the Christian experience of revelation.*[12]

Cone also approves of the Christ-centered point of departure in Wolfhart Pannenberg's Christology, which Cone took to be a fundamentally Barthian undertaking and drew on to further his own point:

> All theological statements win their Christian character only through their connection with Jesus.... Theology can clarify its Christian self-understanding only by a thematic and comprehensive involvement with the Christological problems.... As Christians we know God only as he has been revealed in and through Jesus. All other talk about God can have, at most, provisional significance.[13]

Cone's approval of Barth and the Christological Barthianism of Pannenberg is no mere sycophantic gesture to a supposed superiority of German or European over American theology. Rather, Cone sees Barth's theological method as grounded in the New Testament itself. Thus his invocation of these aspects of their theologies indicates his allegiance to Scripture:

> One has only to read the gospel to be convinced of the central importance of Jesus Christ in the Christian faith. According to the New Testament, Jesus is the man for others who views his existence as inextricably tied to other men to the degree that his own Person is inexplicable apart from others. The others, of course, refer to all men, especially the oppressed, the unwanted of society, the "sinners." He is God himself coming into the very depths of human existence for the sole purpose of striking off the chains of slavery, thereby freeing man from ungodly principalities and powers that hinder his relationship with God.... Through an encounter with Jesus, man now knows the full meaning of God's action in history and man's place within it.[14]

Several things become immediately clear as to what Cone means in the claim that all theological language must be concrete language, and, inversely, that the bane of white thought, of white theology, and of the white church is its commitment to abstraction.

First, concrete thinking is thinking in which Jesus Christ is central. For he is the concrete; indeed, he is *concretissimum*. Knowledge of God sought through reason alone leads to abstraction; for God can be known only by and through God. Within the terms of Christianity, this means that the thought of God that would not be merely the idolatrous thinking by the human being must coincide with God's self-disclosure in Jesus Christ: "We know who God is, not because we can move beyond our finiteness but because the transcendent God has become immanent in our history, transforming human events into divine events of liberation."[15] Christology, then, is not just one of many foci of systematic theological reflection. Rather, Christology is the sum and substance, the alpha and omega, the proton and eschaton, the capstone of Christian thought. It is that which keeps Christian thought from veering into the abstraction of natural theologies.

Epistemologically, such theologies attempt to know God on the strength of unaided reason; ontologically and metaphysically, they assume an analogy and thus an equivalence between God and the creature. This necessarily leads to the construction of idols, which emerge when the creature takes itself to be concrete in itself, that is, apart from the *concretissimum*. Herein lies the fallacy at the ground of white theology and its mode of thought. When it comes to the knowledge of God, Cone, following Barth, takes it that enlightened reason proves itself only to be benighted reason, whose misstep is to equate God and the human thought of God. Cone, once again following Barth, finds such an equation intolerable. The centrality of the theme of the "infinite qualitative distinction between God and man"[16] comes into full view precisely at this point. Jesus Christ is the revelation of God to the creature and, as such, reveals what it means to be a creature—indeed, what it means to be a human being. For "[in] faith two things happen: God gives Himself to the believer, and He gives him knowledge of himself; both God's being and man's being are disclosed. Apart from Christ, man has no knowledge of his true being."[17]

Thus second, Christ is not merely the summit of humanity's religious ideals: Jesus Christ is the iconoclastic revelation of God against such religiously human ideals. Because Jesus Christ "is God himself coming into the very depths of human existence," he is also the affirmation both of the radical ontological distinction between God and the creature and of the epistemological distinction between the creature's thoughts about God and about itself, and God's thought about God and about creation, the human being in particular. So to think concretely is to think in and from God's revelation, the locus of which is Jesus Christ. He is the location of the truth about both God and the creature. Accordingly, for the early, Barthian Cone, Christ is the truth of existence and the revelation of the meaning of Being.

Cone, however, does not simply mime Barth. He fairly quickly begins to improvise in light of him. Barth's claim that Jesus Christ as *concretissimum* is the truth about human existence is a crucial point on which Cone innovates. "[Because] God participates in the historical liberation of humanity, we can speak of God only in relationship to human history."[18] Here Cone approaches the theme of human liberation from the vantage of the broader theme of the relationship between God and human history. Indeed, the only way to speak of God is in relationship to human history. Thus human history has some purchase on talk about God. Though Cone, arguably, is still within a fundamentally Barthian theological frame of reference, he at the same time moves beyond that framework. Cone's early Barthianism acknowledged an analogy of relationship (*analogia relationis*) between God and the creature insofar as both exist in an "I–Thou" relationship.

Seizing on Barth's interpretation in *Dogmatics* III/1 of the Genesis stories of creation, Cone says in this regard, "In the being of man, the basic

relationship is between man and woman; in the being of God, it is among the persons of the Trinity. In both cases the personal relationship is stressed." The similarity of the creature's and God's respective modes of existence points to the fact that "man is a being who has his existence as he exists in personal relationship to God."[19] Cone, following Barth, is clear that the relationship between God and the creature does not pass through Being itself.[20] So how should the similarity be understood? Cone, in acknowledging that "we can only speak of God in relationship to human history," seems to press beyond his Barthianism; he seems to leave open the possibility that the connection between human history and speech about God is more than simply formal and therefore potentially empty, whether regarding us or Christ—that is, either in anthropology or in Christology. Form in some way bears within itself and consequently communicates content. Hence, form, as already pointed out, must be more than formal. But it is the nature of this "more than" that determines Cone's "Barthianism beyond Barth." In due course, I give more precise attention to this "Barthianism beyond Barth." But before doing so, I consider further the connection between relationality and concrete thought and the concreteness of existence.

The importance of relationality for Cone should not be understated, for just as human concepts of God always stand in a relationship of epistemological impoverishment to God their referent, so also human concepts about the human being are epistemologically impoverished. Positive or cataphatic anthropology thus requires a negative anthropology. Such an anthropology is meant to indicate that the meaning of the human arises not from itself but out of dialogical and relational encounter with another human being. This other is a "Thou," not an "It." For "according to the New Testament, Jesus is the man for others who views his existence as . . . tied to [others] . . . . He is God himself coming into the very depths of human existence."[21]

Given this, two important points can be made, points that together gesture toward the theological breakthrough in the problematizing of the logic of modern racial discourse that I earlier indicated. The first point is this: for Cone, knowledge of God emerges only through encounter with God, the God who is disclosed as a human being in Jesus Christ. This means that creation itself and human existence in particular are wrapped up in the divine *taxis* or *ordo* by which God encounters and knows God. The divine nature thus expresses itself by impressing itself in creation in general, and in the human being in particular. Out of the dynamic of the divine *expressio* and *impressio* arises the meaning of human existence.

Cone himself does not thematize the Trinitarian presuppositions of his proposal. But one possible way of doing so would be to understand the Trinitarian relations in such a way that the divine nature, in eternally actualizing itself, is always already poised to relate itself to creation: that is, to that which is by nature not God, should God elect to create. This possibility arises out of

the "positive nothingness" marking God as God. Such a nothingness is the "not" constitutive of the persons of the Trinity whereby the God Father is not the Son, and the Father and Son are not the Holy Spirit. This "not" is not a fourth hypostasis of God; rather, it is the positivity of the Father's love for the Son whereby the Father "surrenders" his divinity to the Son without as such ceasing to be the divine Father. This logic pervades the divine life. In the Father's self-surrender to the Son lies the possibility of creation. This is because the Father's self-surrender to the Son is the articulation of himself as Word, indeed, as the Word in whom is contained all other possible words, even the word of creation. Insofar as this is the case, the risky exposure and vulnerability of love lies at the ground of creaturely being. The possibility and ultimate reality of sin is to be located here insofar as sin radically understood is the tyrannical exploitation of the exposure and risk of love, the positive nihil, grounding creaturely existence. Hence the positive nihil as a transcendental quality of being becomes a negative one of evil, suffering, and violence; there is no a priori bulwark of foundational protection against this.

   This brings me to the second point, and it concerns the question of how Cone conceptualizes evil as absurd nothingness. His reason for thinking of evil in this way is of a piece with his insistence on conceiving of God in terms of concreteness and as pure event. In declaring that God is pure (or nonstatic) event and that therefore God is the concrete, living God, it follows that the abstract is that which is static and nonliving—indeed, that which tends toward death. As such, abstraction stands in opposition to God. But what else is static, nonliving, and tending toward death than nothingness or the Nothing? So to the extent that evil can be theorized, this is what it is: nothingness. It follows from all of this for Cone that God's being, divinity as such, can only be a being-in-liberation from what instigates death and nonlife inasmuch as they are abstractions from the life that is God. This brings Cone to the conclusion that the revelation of God by which God knows God in and through God, a revelation that occurs in Jesus of Nazareth, is itself a liberative activity, one that discloses the meaning of the symbol "God."

   Withholding judgment for the moment on what I take to be philosophically and theologically problematic about this understanding of "nothingness" and therefore of "evil," I find it important to note the connection Cone sees between the liberative eventfulness of God's concrete being as such and the various activities of liberation in the world. Its importance lies in addressing the issues of how God's concrete being-in-liberation is revealed in the world and how this revelation relates to the Jewishness of Jesus. Cone says, "The God in black theology is the God of and for the oppressed, the God who comes into view in their liberation."[22] This statement can be further glossed to say that the God of the oppressed comes into view in the struggle of the oppressed for liberation. "God," so understood, is the symbol that "[answers] to the human condition,"[23] a condition already manifest in the life of the historical Jesus,

who in the fullness of his humanity engaged "sinners" and the "the little ones" and worked for their freedom, uplift, and emancipation. By 1975, Cone will be explicit and insistent in *God of the Oppressed* that the fullness of the humanity of the historical Jesus lifts off from the fact that he *is* a Jew. The *is* here is the strong ontological "to be" that constitutes the existence of the Savior, the fact of his *being*. *Is*, in other words, is existential.

I turn to a fuller explication of the Christology at work in *God of the Oppressed* momentarily. The important point for now is this: for Cone, Jesus' Jewishness, which, to speak in ontological terms, is the *being*-ness that the eternal Word takes on in entering history thus becoming a human *being*, is not inconsequential to concrete thought. It might be claimed that Cone's retrieval of the significance of Jesus' humanity and thereby his Jewishness is just another Barthian moment seized on for the theological articulation of black faith. To be sure, Barth's emphasis on Jesus' Jewishness was groundbreaking in its own right. But what Cone does with this Barthian moment moves him, in important ways, beyond Barth. For Cone, the Jewishness of Jesus is tacitly invoked as a means of moving away from imaging others in abstract terms and toward viewing and engaging them concretely. This gesture anticipates more recent directions in contemporary theological research that seek to come to terms with Christian supersessionism.[24] A number of these recent theological developments have also been inspired by Barth's theology. The brilliance of Cone's early insight into the significance of Jesus' Jewishness and, thus, into the problem of Christian supersessionism is the connection he intuits between this problem and racial reasoning in the modern world.

I claim that it is just at this point that we are brought to the acme of Cone's "beyond-Barthian" thought insofar as it aids in thematizing black existence with a view toward a theology beyond the pseudotheology of race in modernity. The suggestion—and let me stress, suggestion—of Cone's thought and thus the direction toward which I would want to push it is this: the dialectical gap between Christ and culture, between time and eternity, viewed in Christological and Trinitarian terms is really no gap at all. This is because the distance between them, the *diastêma*, and difference between God and the creature, as Gregory of Nyssa and the Cappadocians would put it, is always already traversed *within* the very person of the Logos and in the unity he has with the Father through the Holy Spirit. Indeed, the traversal of time by eternity—the idea at the core of a theological understanding of transcendence—is, in fact, what frees creation to be itself. It is how Abram is freed or given an orientation, as he leaves Ur of the Chaldees, to be Abraham (cf. Gen. 12:1–8), and how Jacob, after wrestling with the angel and walking away with a limp, is set on the path by which he is now Israel (cf. Gen. 32:23–32). This orientation is the melody that expresses the divine nature.

Theologians of the later patristic period understood this melody as the will of God and spoke of our attunement to or riffing within it as the transfor-

mation of our mode of existence beyond divisions of self-enclosure and into the ecclesial or churchly harmonics of Israel–Christ.[25] To be attuned to the divine harmonics is to play Israel's covenantal song. It is in the thought of the seventh-century theologian Maximus the Confessor, the subject of the postlude of this book, that many of these connections are clarified. All of this is to say that transcendence thought within the theological framework outlined here, and at least reasonably suggested within Cone's early thought as it built on but stepped beyond Barth, is precisely what allows the thought and, indeed, the performance of difference. But difference here is not the kind of difference articulated in the 1896 Supreme Court decision *Plessy v. Ferguson*, which codified "separate but equal" as the law of the land regarding race relations and which multiculturalism at its worst simply reinforces. Rather, difference theologically understood arises from the positivity of the hypostatic distinctions within which the possibility and, according to the will of God, the actuality or concreteness of creation is located. It is precisely this understanding of difference—difference as witness to and participation within the Trinitarian hypostatic distinctions—that modern logics of race foreclose. Unfortunately, neither Cone nor subsequent proponents of his general approach to black liberation theology sufficiently develop the radical import of this aspect of the early Cone's thought.

This brings me back to the critique I previously withheld against Cone's construal of nothingness, nonbeing, and therefore evil. One can see that there was no need for Cone to mythologize and thus hypostatize the nothing as that which stands against God and as that which God's being "courageously" fights against in God's being-toward-liberation. To do so betrays his philosophical nominalism on the question of evil insofar as evil is imagined as precisely what we know, while God as liberator is known only to the extent that there is evil— or, rather, that we experience evil and develop sociopolitical and cultural ways of coping with it. But if this is the case, does it not follow that God and the religious are but cultural reflexes? Are they not reducible to moments within the unfolding of a cultural *Geist*, which as such is known a priori in itself? And does it not follow as well from this that such an interpretation of blackness and the meaning of black faith actually recapitulates the structures of modern racial reasoning insofar as at the basis of modern racial logic and racist practices is, as Cone himself insightfully declares, the problem of abstraction, the problem whereby creation is engaged and understood (abstractly) within itself and by itself rather than from within and, indeed, by the concrete living God?

Anthropologically, the conclusion to be drawn from this line of reasoning for my purposes is that this experience of nothingness—the "negativity" of the nothing—at the hands of oppressors risks becoming and, as I hope to show, actually does become the ultimate horizon of experience. This effectively seals off the creature from God by confining it to the region of the negative nihil of creaturely being and existence. Theologically, what results is this: the negative

experience of nihilism and the struggle against it is made total, so much so that God and the religious as such are subsumed within it. God and the religious, within this problematic framework, are ontotheologically annexed to a vision of being as univocally reduced to a negatively nihilistic experience of temporality. Such a reduction, as Karl Löwith observes in interpreting the consolidation of Western nihilism in the thought generally of Nietzsche and especially of Heidegger and their metaphysics of being, bodes the death of the gods. For when being and time become convertible terms, it becomes an open question as to whether being is capable of or can manifest a god at all.[26]

This line of reasoning in Cone's thought clashes with his other, under-developed line of reasoning wherein, in my words, evil has no existence of its own. The "negativity" of the nothing and therefore of evil is not and cannot be final, though under the guise of "radical" evil it attempts to pass itself off as final. Within a Christian theological framework, a way to make the case for the nonfinality of evil, even as one deals with it in the utmost seriousness, is to recognize that evil has no being or substance in itself, though its effects are devastatingly real, painful, and death dealing. What is gained in recognizing that evil has no substance in itself is the further recognition that resisting it, fighting its power, is not futile. Liberation is possible. Indeed, the possibility of liberation from evil arises from evil's own insubstantialness: to be sure, it has only *ontic* expression, but has no *ontos*. It "is" no-thing. Augustine's way of making just this point was to say that evil is a parasitic distortion of the good: evil arises from the creature's attempt to reify for itself the insubstantial zone, the nonspace, so to speak, between the Trinitarian persons, the space by which the Father *is not* the Son and the Spirit *is not* either the Father or the Son. Evil is the creature's attempt to seize this positive nonspace of the hypostatic distinctions of the Trinity and transform it into a negative enclosure for itself: "The fool has said in his heart, 'There is no God.' . . . There is no one who does good" (Ps. 14:1).

This theological possibility remains dormant in Cone's early thinking about evil in insubstantial terms. As an outgrowth of his overall and early Christological commitment, Cone could have observed that evil, as a possibility that becomes historically and existentially actual, arises as a perversion of the "positive" nothing by which the creature *is not* God and God *is not* the creature. The "not," within this "positive" horizon of the Trinitarian nothing, is not a "not" that annihilates; rather, the "positivity" of the nothing indicates the orientation of creature and Creator toward each other. Thus, it is the "not" that frees the creature into being. It is the "not" that liberates us into existence. It is creation.

But there is an almost immediate slippage from the profundity of this philosophical and theological possibility. Cone declares that Jesus worked for the oppressed, the outcasts in society, as himself an outcast—that is, as a Jew. With this, Cone makes Christology—more specifically, a kind of Christology

from below—the point of departure for black liberation theology. It is a Christology grounded in the specific way in which Jesus was a human being: as a Jew. Out of the Jewishness of Jesus, God in Christ related to and identified with the oppressed, the humanity of the "sinners" he encountered and for whose liberation he worked. In *God of the Oppressed*, Cone argues this point under the rubric "Jesus Is Who He Was."[27] Probing who Jesus was as a revelation of the concrete allows one to discover how notions of God, as the symbol that answers the question of the human condition, reveal the meaning of humanity. As Cone says, however, it is not enough to retrieve who Jesus *was*. One must also consider who Jesus *is*, and this ostensibly still under conditions of concrete thought. Querying who Jesus is in his present concreteness reveals the answer to the question of the human condition as well.

Cone sees a problem, though. He is critical of any Christology that would unduly sever the relationship between the Jesus of history and the Christ of faith. Because the Christ of faith is only knowable through the Jesus of history, separating the Jesus of history from the Christ of faith is a sure sign that abstraction lurks nearby. Therefore, Cone insists that at no moment is the Christ of faith knowable apart from his concrete historical manifestation as Jesus of Nazareth. Does this mean that there is an easy equivalence between the Jesus of history and the Christ of faith? Cone thinks not. In his view, the continuity between the New Testament historical Jesus and any contemporary historical Jesus is *not* in a shared history as such, though in both moments history mediates the revelation of God. Rather, Cone links the moments existentially given the irremediable fragmentation of history. This raises the question of the "existentiale" (in the generally Heideggerian sense via Bultmann and Tillich) in which these moments are united. We can delay this question for the moment; what is important to observe at this point is that, for Cone, a sign of abstract thought is the cleaving of the Jesus of history from the Christ of faith, such that one values one over the other. Cone will have nothing to do with this as it smacks of Docetism and of a Gnostic pseudo-Christianity in which the Jewishness of Jesus is contemptible.

In putting the problem of the Jesus of history and the Christ of faith in these terms, Cone makes another important breakthrough for modern theology by disclosing the aberrant theological structuring of modern racial reasoning. He reveals what the early church often sought to creedally safeguard about what it means to be human. The reflections of the early church on the meaning of the human were mediated by way of its reflections on the humanity of God incarnate as a Jew, Jesus of Nazareth; and these reflections acted as repudiations of early heresies like those espoused, for example, in Docetism, Apollarianism, Nestorianism, and Eutychism, which all in varying ways called that humanity into question. Embedded in Cone's claim that the humanity that God assumes in Christ is specifically Jewish, which is to say, it is a humanity that performs YHWH's covenant with Israel, is the tacit recognition

that Jewish flesh, covenantally understood, is flesh in the way in which raced flesh is flesh. That is, it is not flesh that can only be itself by being violently arrayed against Gentile flesh. Again covenantally understood, Jewish flesh is flesh that receives those by "nature" not in its family to be in its family, to carry forward its bloodline. It is in this way that Israel is a nation and people unlike any other, a nation without analogy.

Israel's meaning and significance emerge, on the one hand, by its being flanked by and thus related to the God of Israel, who elects the Jews and so creates them ex nihilo to be YHWH's people. Importantly, on the other hand, though, Israel's meaning and significance arise out of its being related to the nations before whom the drama of the Jews' election unfolds. The drama of Israel thus is not insular, for it unfolds in such a way as to enfold the nations into its drama and thereby into the theodramatic constitution of existence or creation as such. With this possible trajectory within black theology, Cone suggests a theological unraveling of modernity's pseudotheology of race.

The implication I draw from Cone at this point, which I characterize as a significant breakthrough for modern theology, is quite Irenaean insofar as Irenaeus also stressed, as indicated in the prelude, the significance of Israel for Christian faith. Indeed, this was the touchstone of his anti-Marcionite and anti-Gnostic polemic. Cone, in the early stages of his thought, intuits what is at stake in theologies of history such as those of Irenaeus or Melito of Sardis, another second-century Christian thinker, in their insistence on the salvific import of the physical dimensions of the incarnation. For instance, Melito's commitment to understanding the God that Christians worship as the God of the Old Testament, that is, as the God of Israel, and his insistence that Jesus, in his Jewishness, is the bodily manifestation of this God foreshadow Cone's theological move against modern racial reasoning in which the black body is an abstracted terrain for mastery by oppressors. Here Melito prefigures the tenor of Cone's thought: "The Lord, when he had put on the human being ... suffered for the sake of (those) who suffered. . . . This one is the Christ. This one is the King. This one is Jesus."[28]

Cone's early theological move has implied within it a recognition that Christ's center of consciousness as a Jew nonidentically repeats itself through the consciousness of the church, through the consciousnesses of the church's members throughout time and cultural location. Such repetition would be impossible apart from the humanity of Jesus, which is inseparable from his Jewishness. All of this begs for a Christology that deals with the humanity of Jesus as a Jew, a Christology that explicates the significance of his existence as a Jew but against the backdrop of our moment that has deeply trained us to think and perform our existence racially. This task must await another day. The point I want to communicate now is that such a theological direction is a very real possibility within the horizon of Cone's early thought.

Theological Concreteness: Its Allusiveness

Yet, it is precisely at this point that we descend to the nadir of Cone's thought, the moment that undoes the original, antisupersessionist promise that suggests itself by thinking about "who Jesus *was*" for a theological account of black faith. How does this undoing occur? I suggest that it is because Cone remains, to the end, a dialectical thinker. This is evident in that he maintains an insuperable hiatus between "who Jesus *was*" in the world of the scriptural witness and "who Jesus *is*" now *pro nobis*. The problem may be raised as a question: What is continuous between the Jesus of Scripture, who *was* manifest in the history—or perhaps better, the histories—that Scripture records, and the contemporary Jesus, who *is* manifest in history's now?

For Barth, *analogia fidei* establishes the connection.[29] Cone, however, who started out following Barth, becomes unpersuaded by him. For Cone, the point of continuity shifts from an analogy of faith situation between Jesus and us to an *analogia existentia*, an analogy of existential situation and condition between Jesus and us. This move is the culmination of a shift in methodological approach and philosophical orientation. The shift is from the sway of Karl Barth to that of Paul Tillich, that other dialectical thinker of neoorthodoxy. It is this specific way of understanding the doctrine of analogy—that is, in terms of *analogia existentia*—that allows Cone to resolve the dialectical relations between "Jesus *is* who he *was*," "Jesus *is* who he *is*," and "Jesus *is* who he *will be*" into "Jesus *is* black."[30]

From this assertion one sees that Christianity is interpreted as the answer to a singular, transhistorically existential and ontological situation: the struggle for being against the threat of nonbeing. Hence, a hermeneutical and fundamental ontology is now in place that makes possible the unity of being and beings as they fend off nonbeing. Witnessing to this nonbeing is the fragmentary nature of being's history, and, indeed, of the histories of existent beings in which occurs the unfolding of the history of being. Oppression results from privileging a given history within being as the dominant or unifying narrative of the history of being as such; the unity striven for in this case, however, is one that vanquishes and renders invisible those histories outside of the history of the conquerors. What is Cone's response to this problematic situation as framed in this way? Against oppressors and their will-to-historical unity, resistance can only be maintained from what itself is a nonhistorical, existential moment.

Vis-à-vis Tillich, this Heideggerian-inspired hermeneutic ontology of the existential condition of being structures and makes possible the unity between the scriptural witness and all moments ancillary to that witness. We get a glimpse of how this works in Cone's interpretation of liberation in Old

Testament Scripture. He observes, "The Exodus is the point of departure of Israel's existence, the foundation of her peoplehood established at Sinai."[31] This event cannot be disentangled from history, and as such is thoroughly political, social, and economic. For what is the Old Testament? It is "the drama of God's mighty acts in history,"[32] acts that show the concern of God for the weak and defenseless. Cone observes a clear pattern in the drama of Hebrew Scripture: "The poor are defended against the rich, the weak against the strong. Yahweh is the God of the oppressed whose revelation is identical with their liberation from bondage."[33] He also observes that ancient Israel often persisted in infidelity to the Exodus event in that the people did not always side with the defenseless as it was their covenant duty to do. Ancient Israel was to be marked by care and hospitality, especially for those who God cares for and those to whom God is hospitable—that is, to those on the underside of history. Infidelity in this respect was infidelity to covenantal existence *tout court*.

In the course of biblical history, Jesus of Nazareth came both to fulfill and to exceed the covenantal faithfulness of ancient Israel. In him is the continuity as well as the discontinuity between the testaments. He is continuous with the historical work of the God of Israel in his being the defenseless one who sides with the defenseless for their liberation. In this way, Jesus is the concrete revelation of God. He is the truth of being, the revelation of the victory of being over nonbeing in the struggle that is the ground of Being. By reading the Old Covenant, as witnessed in Hebrew Scripture, in light of the New Covenant, as witnessed in Jesus Christ—a time-honored way of interpretation that has deep roots in the Christian tradition—Cone extends retroactively the hermeneutical reach of his philosophy of being. This in no way lessens the importance of history in Cone's thought. Indeed, he is innovative precisely in his introduction of history, particularly that of the dispossessed, into the heart of American theology. The problem is that this is accomplished by way of a passage through a Heideggerian-like ontology that would reduce being, if not to time as such, to a certain experience of time. In this experience, time is marked by struggle in the form of the withdrawal of being in nonbeing. Thus history, as important as it is for Cone, is now subservient and answers to a broader narrative of struggle and rivalry between being and its concealment or withdrawal back into nonbeing as the condition that makes history possible and, indeed, moves it as a history of liberation.

This reading of Cone as theological exegete gains further warrant when one considers how he frames the issue of the discontinuity between the covenants. I have already observed that for Cone the revelation of God in Christ is the moment of profound continuity in the self-revelation of God between the covenants. In this, the covenants are one. Thus, "Jesus' life with the poor reveals that the continuity between the Old and New Testaments is found in the divine will to liberate the oppressed from sociopolitical slavery."[34] But the

discontinuity is equally profound for Cone. He asks, "[In] what sense does the New Testament witness take us beyond the Old and fulfill it?" He answers:

> The new element is this: the divine freedom revealed in Jesus, as that
> freedom is disclosed in the cross and resurrection, is more than
> the freedom made possible in history. While God's freedom for the
> poor is not *less than* the liberation of slaves from bondage (Exodus),
> yet it is *more than* that historical freedom. And it is this *more*
> which separates the Exodus from the Incarnation, the Old Testament
> view of the Savior as the Victor in battle and the New Testament view
> of the Savior as the One who "give[s] up his life as a ransom for
> many" (Mark 10:45 NEB). While both stress the historical freedom of
> the unfree, the latter transcends history and affirms a freedom not
> dependent on sociopolitical limitations.[35]

It would be tempting at this point to read Cone as disparaging history altogether, viewing it as the barrier to liberation. However, he stresses that to transcend history is not to disparage it, nor, for that matter, to take leave of it. The transcendence of history is the uncovering of a God who is more thoroughly immanent to history: that is, more immanent to any one, specific, and historically liberating story. It is this fact of greater immanence that conditions any specific story of liberation. This perspective may be called that of transcendental immanence, which as such is the route to being; it is the path to gain sight of ultimate concern *in* history, while yet maintaining the inseparable distinction between being and history. Hence, Cone ascribes a limit to both the Old and New Covenants. Indeed, it is a limit that extends to every instance of particularity, which would include every moment or historical epoch.

The New Covenant, however, though limited by virtue of its historicality, nevertheless overcomes its own limit insofar as it is conditioned by a certain "more than" as well. The limit in this case that is subject to a "more than" is the Jewishness of Jesus. The limit that the Jewishness of Jesus represents is overcome by the "more than" of the cross–resurrection event. This event universalizes the particular so as to broaden its reach beyond the Jews, their history, and their God. The upshot is this: in quite Hegelian fashion, reaching the particular requires its sacrifice in order to retrieve all particularity. The history of being thus becomes the history of its broadening and universalizing in this way; that is, it becomes the history of an eternal and everrecurring sacrifice. The struggle for liberation, which is the struggle for being, expresses this universalizing. As the following quotation shows, the cross–resurrection event effects this universalizing:

> The cross and the resurrection of Jesus stand at the center of the New
> Testament story, without which nothing is revealed that was not

already known in the Old Testament. In the light of Jesus' death and resurrection, his earthly life achieves a radical significance not otherwise possible. The cross–resurrection events mean that we now know that Jesus' ministry with the poor and the wretched was God himself effecting his will to liberate the oppressed. The Jesus story is the poor person's story, because God in Christ becomes poor and weak in order that the oppressed might become liberated from poverty and powerlessness. God becomes the victim in their place and thus transforms the condition of slavery into the battleground for the struggle of freedom.[36]

One way in which this chapter has framed the question at issue here is the relationship between the universal and the particular. Another way of approaching the question is by addressing the problem of the relationship between "history" and historicism or histories.[37] I am suggesting a reading of the early phase of Cone's thought in which he desires—and from my perspective, rightly so—to have both "history" and histories. There were theological impediments, however, as he himself quickly discovered, with getting there. These impediments forced him away from his early Barthianism and eventually toward what may be characterized as an ontology of blackness.

Theological Concreteness: The Problem with Barth

Before commenting on this ontology, it is worth probing a bit further the question of the difficulty that Cone came to have with his early Barthianism, so as to eventually assess the degree of success he had in escaping it. There are at least two reasons for the difficulty as Cone saw it. By his own admission, Cone grew increasingly wary in his use of principally European resources for developing his theological program. Many of his early critics, including his brother Cecil Cone,[38] pressed this point. For my purposes, I need not consider this here. Rather, I want to venture an explanation of his second reason for discontent: the degree of the adequacy of Barth's own theology for articulating a black theology of liberation. Exploring this will position me to consider the alternative for probing the meaning of black faith. It will also position my further assessment of the limits of Cone's program for a theological account of race.

In his first book, *Black Theology and Black Power*, Cone locates the strength of Barthian theology in its tenacious resistance to identify too closely the gospel and culture. The incommensurable difference opens up space for critique insofar as theological transcendence requires that one not elide the distinction between the claims of culture or even of the state and the truth as revealed in Jesus Christ. Creaturely truth is not divine truth. Theological transcendence

can thus function to weaken hegemonic structures by unmasking them as so much ideology. For Cone, that weakening and unmasking occurs through the resistance of the oppressed because resistance serves the interest of truth. Herein lies what Cone calls "the finality of Jesus," a finality that lies "in the totality of his existence in complete freedom as the Oppressed One who reveals through his death and resurrection that God is present in all dimensions of human liberation."[39] Yet virtually in the next breath, Cone exposes what he takes to be the limits of such an understanding of theological transcendence: "No matter how seriously we take the carpenter from Nazareth, there is still the existential necessity to relate his person to black persons."[40] Cone takes it that from such an understanding of theological transcendence it is difficult to understand the relationship between God and creation. The difficulty is only exacerbated when one takes into account that the man Jesus, who as a human being is a creature among creatures, nevertheless reveals the transcendent God to creation. Given this, theological transcendence renders it difficult to speak critically of the relationship between black persons—their history, struggles, and so forth—and the fleshy, yet transcendent, person of Christ. What is difficult to articulate in Barthian terms is how creaturely truth participates in God's truth.

Hans Urs von Balthasar's assessment of Barth's theology parallels Cone's in this respect. Indeed, one could say that Balthasar—to be sure, motivated by a different set of concerns and situated in a different cultural milieu—beat Cone to the punch in criticizing Barth's theology on the matter of taking insufficient account of the recipients or human bearers of revelation. The problem, as Balthasar saw it, was a sign of a malformed doctrine of creation and a truncated assessment of the place and significance of "nature" in relationship to the grace of God. This miscue pushes Barth to resist grounding the continuity between Christ and Christians of various historical epochs in ecclesiology, because it would indicate too close a connection between revelation and the recipients of revelation. More specifically, it would align revelation too closely with the human situation so as to make the former dependent on the latter. Behind National Socialism, in Barth's theological assessment, is the notion of revelation as dependent on and equated with the human situation. A problematic ecclesiology mediates the dependence.

With his "actualism" principle, Barth laid out a different way of understanding the relationship between revelation and the human situation into which it arises.[41] Balthasar, however, saw another impetus behind Barth's principle of actualism. Actualism is a barrier against aberrant ecclesiologies such as that of Roman Catholicism. Much of Barth's invective against the Catholic doctrine of the *analogia entis*,[42] which in the early volumes of the *Church Dogmatics* he regards as the doctrine of the antichrist, has the principle of actualism behind it.[43] Though his ire against this doctrine tempered considerably with time and further theological reflection, his fundamental

suspicion of and resistance to it did not abate. It is worth considering a passage
in which Barth's criticism of the *analogia entis* is particularly sharp:

> [The] presupposition [of the Roman Catholic dogmatics] is that the
> being of the Church, Jesus Christ, is no longer the free Lord of its
> existence, but that He is incorporated into the existence of the
> Church, and is thus ultimately restricted and conditioned by certain
> concrete forms of the human understanding of His revelation and of
> the faith which grasps it .... Our fellowship with this faith is broken
> by the way in which grace here becomes nature, the action of God
> immediately disappears and is taken up into the action of the re-
> cipient of grace, that which is beyond all human possibilities changes
> at once into that which is enclosed within the reality of the Church,
> and the personal act of divine address becomes a constantly avail-
> able relationship. Roman Catholic faith believes this transformation.
> It can recognise itself and God's revelation in this constantly available
> relationship between God and man, and in this revealedness. It af-
> firms an *analogia entis*, the presence of a divine likeness of the
> creature even in the fallen world, and consequently the possibility of
> applying the secular "There is" to God and the things of God as
> the presupposition, again ontological, of that change or transforma-
> tion, of that depriving of revelation and faith of their character as
> decision by evasion and neutralisation.[44]

Given this critique, can there even be a connection between the self-revealing
God and the bearers of God's revealing, and, if so, how is that connection to be
understood? Barth's answer is that Jesus Christ is the connection. Yet, this in
turn raises the question of the connection between Christ and creation, which
includes the recipients of revelation, their social location, and the historical
exigencies marking the reception of revelation. I point to just one instance in
the *Church Dogmatics* where Barth attempted to work out this intricate web of
connections:

> The only possibility of a conception of dogmatic knowledge remain-
> ing to us on the basis of Evangelical faith is to be marked off on the
> one hand by the rejection of an existential ontological possibility of
> the being of the Church and on the other hand by the rejection of
> the presupposition of a constantly available absorption of the being of
> the Church into a creaturely form, into a "There is." On the one
> side we have to say that the being of the Church is *actus purus*, i.e., a
> divine action which is self-originating and which is to be understood
> only in terms of itself and not therefore in terms of a prior anthro-
> pology. And on the other side we have also to say that the being of the
> Church is *actus purus*, but with the accent now on *actus*, i.e., a free

action and not a constantly available connexion, grace being the event of personal address and not a transmitted material connection. On both sides we can only ask how it may be otherwise if the being of the Church is identical with Jesus Christ. If this is true, then the place from which the way of dogmatic knowledge is to be seen and understood can be neither a prior anthropological possibility nor a subsequent ecclesiastical reality, but only the present moment of the speaking and hearing of Jesus Christ Himself, the divine creation of light in our hearts.

λαμπειν εν ταις καρδιας ημων [For God ... has made his light *shine in our hearts* ...] (Cor. 4:6, compare Paul with the "Let there be light" of Gen. 1:3).[45]

Wherein, then, lies the connection between Christ and church? It resides in the *actus purus* of grace as the "event of personal address," which, Barth then tellingly adds, is "not a transmitted material connection." This is but another way of affirming what Barth later says about grace itself:

[Grace] comes upon the creature as absolute miracle, and with absolute power and certainty.... As the fulfillment of that prior divine decision, it redounds *per se* to the praise of the freedom of grace: of its independence both of the majesty and of the misery of our human volition and achievement; of the sovereignty in which it precedes and thus fully over-rules our human volition and achievement. All serious conceptions of the doctrine [of the election of grace] (more or less exactly and successfully, and with more or less consistency in detail) do at least aim at this recognition; at the freedom of the grace of God. We can put it more simply: They aim at an understanding of grace as grace.... All serious conceptions of the doctrine also agree that in this free decision of God we have to do with the mystery of God, i.e., with the divine resolve and decree whose basis is hidden and inscrutable.[46]

So if grace is of God and is that by which God reaches the creature, it cannot have its basis either in anthropology or, finally, in ecclesiology because these are material and historical connections. History, neither in itself, nor even if elevated by God, can in itself bear the divine representation. Given this, then, where ought one to locate the happening of grace as *actus purus*? Barth answers, in Jesus Christ.

But is such a formulation of the answer sufficient? For does it not lead to a curious understanding of Jesus Christ, particularly of his humanity, which is an instrument of the divine self-representation (cf. Heb. 1:3; Col. 2:9)? Yet this is precisely what both Barth's formulations of "grace as grace" in the previous quotation and his understanding of faith will not allow. About faith he says,

"[Faith] is in no way bound up with time's forms of appearance. There is no time in the experience of God."[47] The problem appears as well in his account of God's eternity, which he triangulates between the church on the one hand and Jesus Christ, the head of the church, on the other:

> [The Church] yearns to have a part in [eternity's] perfection. It con-
> forms itself to its perfection. But it lives in time and therefore in the
> distinction between this perfection and what it can itself display here
> and now. It cannot display the totality of life-obedience in which it
> may thank and serve God. It can certainly believe but cannot see that
> it is itself the place where the honour of God is all in all.... It does
> not see the totality in which God is here and now glorified in its
> existence. It can certainly find this glorifying in its Head, Jesus
> Christ, but not in itself as His body. Finding it in Him, it necessarily
> misses it in itself.... [These] limits, this difference between it
> and Him, remain. This does not mean that it is excluded from the
> glory of God, or even from its full reality. But it does mean that the
> form in which it shares in it here is another and special form—a
> temporal and therefore provisional form in contrast to the perfect
> form for which we may here and now wait, and to which the Church
> may move.[48]

Jesus Christ fully bears the glory of the Father as head of the church, but the church as the body of Jesus Christ does not bear that glory precisely be-cause of its passing "temporal and therefore provisional form." Jesus, as head of his body, does not pass away; nor is he in the ultimate sense temporal since he is "the perfect form for which we may here and now wait." The church, as Christ's body, however, is, like creation, in a state of utter passivity with respect to its relation to God. Insofar as this is the case, Barth concludes that the church is a passing form. In such a construal, activity and passivity stand in utter opposition. Consequently, what cannot be entertained is how both the church and creation, as interpreted from the theological standpoint of their having come to be in and through the Word and by the Spirit, might be conceived as truly active in their relationship to the Triune God.

What secures their activeness in the *œconomia*, and what Barth cannot give full weight to, is the fact of their mediation in and through the humanity of Jesus Christ. Nature is perfected in his humanity so as to become the human nature that is graciously divinized as the exalted creaturely *sophia*. As such, that is, under the ever-greater grace of God, creation truly contributes something to its relationship with the Triune God; for its contribution is always already effected under the aspect of the Son's active contribution, as it were, to his eternal generation from the Father. Were Barth's thought to move in this direction, what Cone's thought seeks could be theologically realized. That is, Cone might have had a way of receiving Barth's thought as a way to interpret

the historical manifestations of black religion in general and of Afro-Christian faith in particular, as well as the struggle for freedom exemplified in them, as articulations of the freedom enacted and revealed in Jesus Christ.

In defense of Barth, it might be said that his actualism and the complementary notion of "dialectical inclusion" in fact, though not on these terms, accomplish the same objective, and therefore this reading of Barth, which seeks to theologically account for Cone's misgivings with his theology, betrays a fundamental misunderstanding of Barth. George Hunsinger's interpretation of Barth's notions of actualism and dialectical inclusion may show that they do, indeed, accomplish the above objective:

> The pattern of dialectical inclusion is used . . . to describe (but not explain) how the history of each and every human being is objectively enclosed in that of Jesus. That same pattern is then used in conjunction with the pattern of actualism to describe (but not explain) how the history of Jesus is in turn objectively included in that of each and every human being. The objective moment of salvation is thereby understood as being at once fully actualized once and for all and yet not encapsulated or imprisoned within its central and definitive form of temporal occurrence. Without compromising this central and definitive form, the objective moment as such assumes secondary and derivative form by actualizing itself in relation to the history of each and every human existence. . . . The transition effected by the existential moment of salvation is seen as a transition from the opaque mystery of sin to the luminous mystery of faith. It is therefore a transition from nonacknowledgement . . . to acknowledgement, from a mode of participating in salvation which is virtual and unresponsive to a mode which is active and alive. Faith as such does not create or contribute anything new. It consists solely in the existential actualization of a salvation which cannot be conceived except as already objectively actualized.[49]

Hunsinger interprets Barth as having included the history of each and every individual in the objective and actual moment of the revelation of the Son of God as Jesus Christ. Hence, the historical particularities of the recipients of revelation, on his reading of Barth, are not given short shrift. This contrasts with the reading ventured above, because here revelation's recipients are secondarily—that is, dialectically—included within the objective and, as such, primary reality of Jesus Christ.

But I am not fully convinced by Hunsinger's reading of Barth on this point, nor, I venture to suggest, would Cone be. For the question is not whether our existential moment of faith is dialectically included in the objectivity of Jesus Christ; rather, it is whether the reception of the luminous mystery of faith itself, "the divine creation of light in our hearts," has a history that, though

determined by the subjectivity of creation, is nevertheless grounded in the objectivity of Jesus of Nazareth, without occluding that subjectivity. An affirmation of this would entail a way of affirming how creation even from the vantage of its subjective activeness could yet reveal God. In short, the question that must be posed to interpretations of this sort regarding Barth's actualism is this: Is the moment of creaturely regress in response to God itself active, and that in such a way as not to obstruct the gratuity of God's objective grace? Barth's actualism, which Hunsinger explains in terms of dialectical inclusion, would still, I think, answer negatively.

The problem to which I am pointing has been cogently expressed by Balthasar, Barth's friend and fellow Swiss:

> Protest though he will and despite the "open-ended" use he makes of the transcendental categories, a tendency toward constraint and system is unmistakable in Barth. Indeed, this constraint clings to the whole project of the *Church Dogmatics*, so much so that it affects its articulation at every limb and joint.... In Catholic terms, we may call it...a failure of balance. We are referring to Barth's christological starting point. Such a starting point is quite legitimate—indeed if we want to take the Bible seriously, it is absolutely essential. But it is a big step from there to the *narrowing* of everything to that one point. The priority of Christ over creation and sin in no way requires that the whole work of creation has to be so painfully forced to occupy the Procrustean bed of Barth's christological schema. This straitened schematization becomes evident at that juncture in his argument where we notice that he has not left enough breathing room between creation and covenant. Barth certainly *pre*-supposes creation, but it is still too much merely a presupposition: he does not give it its proper due.[50]

At another point Balthasar observes:

> Obviously, as long as the Christology of the council of Chalcedon does not have the first and the last word, it would be meaningless to talk of a Church with the four [Catholic] notes.... [For] only from Christ will Barth learn that there is room for a genuine and *active* human nature alongside God. And indeed this human nature will be active precisely as *human* nature even though it is grounded wholly on the act of revelation and will depend entirely on it.[51]

Cone in substance, I think, would agree with this critique insofar as it points out that Barth is unable to approach the truth of creation from the side of the creature. Barth can thematize creation as having objective meaning in Christ; however, he cannot Christologically account for the subjectivity of creation.

All of this raises the question, as Balthasar was keen to point out, of the status of the humanity of Christ, which is the question lurking behind Cone's worries. For Barth, Christ's humanity united with the divine nature in such a way that precludes the rest of creation from being brought into that union and leaves creation effectively in a no-man's-land. Creaturely nature becomes a sublime residue that the divine nature refuses to harness. Arguably, this lurks behind the unintended abstraction in Barth's thought, out of which emerges the inadvertent Jewish supersessionism that lies dormant in the deep structure of his Christology.[52] The loss of Israel in Barth's thought may therefore be connected to the questionable status of the humanity of Jesus Christ as a perduring center of activity in relation to his divinity *and* in relation to the subjectively active centers of consciousness of the members of Christ's body.

The Balthasarian critique is thus consonant with Cone's reservations insofar as Balthasar's critique revealed how Barth's Christology can only account for history, as it were, *deductively*. Such a deductive approach alone is inadequate to go to the heart of the concerns of black theology, particularly in its emerging moments, with its concern to examine how black folks in their suffering of and cultural contact with the New World nevertheless theologically harnessed and redirected modernity.[53] The black struggle for freedom—with its tacit acknowledgment that freedom attends being as such, that therefore freedom is an inherent "right" of human beings, and, finally, that the exercise of freedom is primarily a response to having been granted the gift of being and, thus, the gift of existence—exemplifies how, from its underside, New World black folks came to inhabit modernity disruptively. That is, they theologically redirect its energies and insights. Thus freedom, for example, which is a central feature of modern consciousness, has for black faith its ultimate meaning in relationship to God. Because of the inflexible transcendence–immanence, God–world, and Christ–culture dialectic, it is difficult on strictly Barthian terms to theologically interpret and critically clarify the meaning of black faith.

Theological Concreteness: Tillich and the Ontology of Liberation

But how far, finally, does Cone remove himself from this problem? I have shown that in his attempt to give a theological account of race vis-à-vis an account of black faith, there is a loss of Israel in the form of a loss of the concrete humanity of Jesus Christ as well. Thus at the moment of its nadir, as I have been characterizing it, Cone paradoxically reproduces the Barthian problem. This is so in that the problem persists of the inability to reckon with the enduring humanity of Jesus Christ as Jewish. In this, Cone, his protestations notwithstanding, does not stray too far from this troublesome aspect of Barth's thought.

Yet the result of Cone's reception of Paul Tillich's thought as a constructive theological alternative to the Barthian dilemma only exacerbates the problem,

because his appropriation of Tillich prodded him to locate his conception of blackness and, therefore, of race within the tight and well-nigh suffocating space of an ontology that has banished transcendence. This penultimate section of the chapter begins to trace the lines from this philosophical and theological orientation to what Victor Anderson has called "ontological blackness."[54] The task is completed in the final section of the chapter, where I consider how Cone receives Tillich's dialectical Idealism within the parameters of dialogical thinking. I point out how this yet remains a problem and how Tillich's engagement with the question of being might have been received into black theology differently so as to move beyond what remains troublesome in both dialectical and dialogical conceptions of existence.

By 1986, still speaking with a slight Barthian accent, Cone nevertheless makes explicit a shift that began in *A Black Theology of Liberation* (1970), and that was well under way by the time of *God of the Oppressed* (1975). The following statement captures the shift: "There is no 'abstract' revelation" because "theology is *contextual* language . . . defined by the human situation that gives birth to it." Thus, he concludes that "although God is the intended subject of theology, God does not do theology. *Human beings do theology.*"[55] To be sure, Cone's conclusion is correct: theology is a human endeavor. Yet it is nevertheless necessary to consider the new philosophical and theological orientation out of which this conclusion arises, for it gives this otherwise correct conclusion a particular slant that itself must be investigated. That new philosophical and theological orientation is the thought of Paul Tillich. For Tillich, theology provides answers to the fundamental question that philosophy, the pure ontological science, asks. What is this fundamental question? To draw on the language of the philosophical ontology of Martin Heidegger, in which Tillich was quite versed, it is the question that only *Dasein* can raise: the question of its own existence and, indeed, of being itself. As such, the ontological question is the root question of all reflection. The various fields of thought provide but regional or "ontic" answers to the global or "ontological" question that, properly speaking, only philosophy raises. As Tillich puts it, "The ontological question [is] the root question of every philosophy," and as such it "underlies [every] type of philosophy."[56]

But what, specifically, does "being" signify? For Tillich, it signifies the *power* of being or, indeed, the *power* that is being. Being as *power* imbues all that is with life—that is, with existence—though this power itself is distinct from the beings whom it makes alive. Concretely existing beings have the power of being as the ground of their being. Therefore, to truly be or be alive is to exist from within this fundamental ground. In this regard, Tillich says, "In our search for the 'really real' we are driven from one level to another to the point where we cannot speak of level anymore, where we must ask for that which is the ground of all levels, giving them their structure and their power of being.

The search for ultimate reality beyond everything that seems to be real is the search for being-itself, for the power of being in everything that is."[57]

Why, however, is there a need to pursue ultimate reality or concern, given that being itself attends every concretely existing being as the power of its existence? That is, why is there a need to pursue—and, indeed, what is the nature of this pursuit—that which always already attends existence as such? Tillich's answer reveals the dialectical structure of his thought and ontology. The human pursuit of ultimate concern is a search to transcend *the* Finite: the finitude of existence that is but the shadow of the power that is the ground of existence. This means that the power that is being itself must be understood as infinite. Indeed, it is *the* Infinite. But what does it mean then to pursue ultimate reality? For Tillich, it means to transcend that nonbeing that is but the necessary shadow of the power that is infinite being or life itself. The search for ultimate concern, therefore, is the quest to triumphantly exist in being over extinguishing forces of nonbeing. In this triumph, the power of being testifies to itself in beings, for in the pursuit of ultimate concern an identity is established between ultimate concern or the infinite and those who pursue ultimate concern against the tide of the finitude of nonbeing.

Tillich's identification of ultimate concern as infinitude and the power of being is not a theistic claim, let alone a specifically Christian one. Rather, the distinction between infinitude and finitude for him represents a tension within *Dasein* itself. Because of this tension, being can be—and, in fact, is—a question for the human being. The infinite–finite dialectic thus structures concretely existing beings as such. It follows from this that transcendence is a moment within the immanent structure of being such that infinitude is the refusal to rest in nonbeing. Infinitude, so understood, is life; finitude, which has nonbeing as its mode of being, is, as it were, attuned toward the nothingness of death. Consequently, to exist in the power of being is to exist in the affirmation of being over nonbeing. The ontic or contextually regional science of theology may call the infinite "God"; but actually, what theology tends ontotheologically to term the "Divine Being is not a being beside others. *It is the power of being conquering non-being.* It is eternity conquering temporality. It is grace conquering sin. It is ultimate reality conquering doubt. From the point of view of the New Being it is the ground of being, and therefore the creator of the New Being."[58]

Tillich is fond of translating his language regarding being into the ethical, but no less ontological, language of courage, which he reflects on in a sustained way in *The Courage to Be*. "The title of this book, *The Courage to Be*," he says,

> unites both meanings of the concept of courage, the ethical and the ontological. Courage as a human act, as a matter of valuation, is an ethical concept. Courage as the universal and essential self-affirmation

of one's being is an ontological concept. The courage to be is the ethical act in which man affirms his own being in spite of those elements of his existence which conflict with his essential self-affirmation.[59]

And thus in agreement with Stoic philosophy, he says, "The courage to be transcends the polytheistic power of fate . . . [for] the soul of the wise man is similar to God. The God who is indicated here is the divine Logos in unity with whom the courage of wisdom conquers fate and transcends the gods. It is the 'God above god.'"[60] In a similar vein, he says, "It is the function of an onto-logical concept to use some realm of experience to point to characteristics of being-itself which lie above the split between subjectivity and objectivity and which therefore cannot be expressed literally in terms taken from the subjec-tive or the objective side. Ontology speaks analogously. Being as being tran-scends objectivity as well as subjectivity."[61]

To exist in courage, therefore, is to exist beyond the struggle for being, for in this respect courage is being itself. It is the power of being in which ob-jectivity and subjectivity exist in an original unity as the pure eventfulness and dynamism of being. For this reason, though Tillich speaks of being and courage as God, he nevertheless takes it that this formulation is not subject to ontotheological criticism, because embedded in this overall outlook is a re-valuation of the meaning of religious symbols, the meaning of religion, and the meaning of man as homo religiosus. This revaluation is, being situated in the German Idealist philosophical tradition, both Hegelian and, finally, Nietz-schean. On the revaluation of religious symbols, he says:

> The word "God" is filled with the concrete symbols in which man-kind has expressed its ultimate concern—its being grasped by something unconditional. And this "something" is not just a thing, but the power of being in which every being participates.
>
> This power of being is the *prius* of everything that has being. It precedes all special contents logically and ontologically. It precedes every separation and makes every interaction possible, because it is the point of identity without which neither separation nor interaction can be thought. This refers basically to the separation and interac-tion of subject and object, in knowing as well as in acting. The *prius* of subject and object cannot become an object to which man as a subject is theoretically and practically related. God is not object for us as subjects. He is always that which precedes this division.[62]

The symbol "God" points to the unity of the power of being that precedes every opposition or distinction between subject and object. As such, the symbol "God," when understood properly as an indication of the power of being that

attends all being, actually points to the destruction of every transcendentalist or ontotheological approach to God.

Here is the clearly anti-Barthian nature of Tillich's thought. The destruction of transcendence, as it is understood, for example, by Barth, is important for Tillich in that such a destruction overturns understandings of God that would perpetuate an opposition between transcendence and immanence. This philosophy of life has embedded within it a philosophy of "the death of God," at least of the God of utter transcendence. Given what I said earlier, one can see the appeal of this to Cone as a potential response to the Barthian dilemma. Explaining himself on this point, Tillich says:

> Nietzsche is the most impressive and effective representative of what could be called a "philosophy of life." Life in this term is the process in which the power of being actualizes itself. But in actualizing itself it overcomes that in life which, although belonging to life, negates life. One could call it the will which contradicts the will to power . . . . Courage is the power of life to affirm itself in spite of this ambiguity, while the negation of life because of its negativity is an expression of cowardice . . . . Life, willing to surpass itself, is the good life, and the good life is the courageous life . . . . The obedient self . . . is the self which commands itself and "risketh itself thereby." . . . These words [from *Thus Spoke Zarathustra*] reveal the other side of Nietzsche, that in him which makes him an Existentialist, the courage to look into the abyss of nonbeing in the complete loneliness of him who accepts the message that "God is dead."[63]

In an interesting way, this makes "Nietzsche the anti-Christian" nevertheless an important "Christian" thinker. For in refusing "the submissive self" in favor of "the self-affirming self,"[64] a self that would dare "in . . . complete loneliness" to be courageous before "the abyss of nonbeing," Nietzsche indicates a retrieval of the significance of the divinity of Christ and the meaning of human being insofar as Christ's divinity is his courage. In this respect, Christ's divinity reveals the infinite power of being over nonbeing through the totality of his life: "In every moment [of his life], the anxiety of finitude and the existential conflicts are overcome. That is [Christ's] divinity . . . . What he is, is healing power overcoming estrangement because he himself was not estranged."[65]

But it is important to observe that the obverse of this revaluation of the meaning of the religious symbols "God" and "Christ," symbols dear to Western civilization, is a revaluation of the meaning of culture as well and, thereby, of humanity as homo religiosus. In my view, it is at this point that the "ontologizing" effects of Tillich's revaluation of the religious symbols "God" and "Christ" become most palpable for Cone's black theology. Its palpability has to do with its revaluation of the meaning of transcendence itself. I have already

shown how transcendence or the infinite operates in Tillich's thought, but it is necessary to connect this to his understanding of culture.

Tillich observes that the modern West understands religion and culture as opposed to each other, when, in fact, they are not. The church, for example, tends to understand its relationship to the broader culture "heteronomously," while secular culture tends to understand its relationship to religion and the church "autonomously." These, Tillich says, are false dichotomies, for in reality they exist in a "theonomous" unity:

> The words "autonomy," "heteronomy," and "theonomy" answer the question of the *nomos* or the law of life in three different ways: . . . [An] autonomous culture [represents] the attempt to create the forms of personal and social life without any reference to something ultimate and unconditional, following only the demands of theoretical and practical rationality. A heteronomous culture, on the other hand, subjects the forms and laws of thinking and acting to authoritative criteria of an ecclesiastical religion or a political quasi-religion, even at the price of destroying the structures of rationality. A theonomous culture expresses in its creations an ultimate concern and a trans-cending meaning not as something strange but as its own spiritual ground. "Religion is the substance of culture and culture the form of religion." This was the most precise statement of theonomy.[66]

The structure of this, for Tillich, is Christological insofar as Jesus lived a theonomous life. Religion was the substance of his being. Such is the claim of Christianity:

> The God who is manifest in Jesus the Christ is the true God, the true subject of an ultimate and unconditional concern . . . . Christianity can claim this extraordinary character because of the extraordinary character of the events on which it is based, namely, the creation of a new reality within and under the conditions of man's predica-ment. Jesus as the bringer of this new reality is subject to those conditions, to finitude and anxiety, to law and tragedy, to conflicts and death. *But he victoriously keeps the unity with God, sacrificing himself as Jesus to himself as the Christ.* In doing so he creates the new reality of which the Church is the communal and historical em-bodiment.[67]

Tillich describes here the meaning of revelation and how the church and, by extension, culture and history are implicated in revelation. Revelation is the experience of being "grasped . . . [by] the truth concerning the mystery of being and [one's] relation to it,"[68] of being grasped by "an ultimate and unconditional concern." One knows one is in the experience of revelation if and only if what is being revealed is the experience of being's self-negation. As Tillich sees it,

Jesus as the Christ fulfills this condition, because God, as the unity of courage and being, undergoes self-negation as Jesus, who nevertheless "keeps the unity with God, sacrificing himself as Jesus to himself as the Christ."

Contained in this process is an attestation that this particular revelation of being is both final and a new methodology of inquiry into the meaning of being: "A revelation is final if it has the power of negating itself without losing itself.... The question of the final revelation is the question of a medium of revelation which overcomes its own finite conditions by sacrificing them, and itself with them."[69] Here we broach the matter of the new form of theological questioning appropriate to the experience of revelation. Tillich says that it is the method of the "universal" that is able to empty itself of its content. As such, it is a method "suited to any object; and yet [it has] a native soil, the particular branch of knowledge in which [it] originated." In this case, the particular branch of knowledge is theology, for "theological method...is a universal application of theological questioning to all cultural values."[70] According to Tillich, the business of theology, then, is to give "a general religious analysis of all cultural creations" and thereby "[produce] from its own concrete religious standpoint the ideal outline of a culture penetrated by religion."[71] It reflects on

> [the] shattering of form through substance [such that now]...form
> loses its necessary relation to content because the content vanishes
> in the face of the preponderance of the substance. Through this, form
> acquires a quality of detachment, as of something floating freely
> in space; it is directly related to substance; it loses its natural and
> necessary relation to content; and it becomes form in a paradoxi-
> cal sense by allowing its natural quality to be shattered by the sub-
> stance.[72]

But is not the form that is shattered the historical Jesus, the Jewish Nazarene, so that the substance of the universal Christ might, like the phoenix, rise from the ashes? And therefore, is this not an anti-Jewish philosophy of culture?

Theological Concreteness: Culture and the
Question of Jewish Flesh

What, then, did Cone find appealing about Tillich's theological program for the development of a black theology of liberation? As I see it, what was most useful for Cone's theological agenda was Tillich's reconstrual of transcendence. The question of transcendence for Tillich is the question of what it means to transcend the self insofar as it is bound within a subject–object dialectic. Transcendence for Tillich addresses how the self might flourish by remaking itself

beyond the confines that a subject–object binary structure might impose on the self.

In all of this, Tillich is thinking within the German idealist philosophical tradition. This tradition in philosophy posits that a subject–object rift runs through the very fabric of existence. Indeed, this rift occurs because of being's self-objectification and therefore its self-pluralization as a world of concretely existing beings. This is the moment the subject–object divide occurs, the founding moment of inauthenticity. To effect a return to unity, to a state of the self existing in authenticity, beings must transcend themselves. In so doing, they must overcome their inauthentic nonbeing, their finitude, which is the source of evil. What this means in theological terms is that transcendence does not name YHWH, the God of Israel; rather, for Tillich "God" is the symbol under which one speaks of the overcoming of finitude, the deathly shadow of nonbeing that attaches itself to existence. This overcoming is a feat of courage, the "courage to be." This notion of courage, yoked as it is to the revaluation of transcendence, proved quite useful to Cone's formulation of black theology beyond what he saw as its Barthian false start.

Yet a significant question arises with such an outlook: Can there really be relationality in a Tillich-like ontology, given that the relationship between subjects and objects in such an ontology is only a passing moment toward unity, rather than being constitutive in some sense of unity?[73] The question takes on heightened importance because, for Tillich, the *Seinsfrage*, the question of being, is also the *Kulturfrage*, the question of culture, its ontological significance and meaning. Because in the Tillichian outlook all moments of reality must be understood as so many reflexes, albeit necessary ones, of the power of being in its courageous struggle against nonbeing, it follows that cultures, history, and people groups have no lasting value in and of themselves. Like the historical Jesus who is overcome by the universal Christ and in this way realizes infinite unity, so, too, is it the case that cultures, histories, and people groups must be overcome: that is, they must exhibit courage in order to be liberated into the infinitude of their existence. The problem, however, is that it is precisely black culture's enduring, revelatory significance that Cone's black theology seeks to uphold. Consequently, Cone can only incorporate Tillich's insights with modifications.

Cone cannot take up Tillich's "subjectivism," according to which being objectifies itself as world and thus splits itself as subject–object. This is the dialectic within being that comes to be as a result of being's "Gnostic" fall from its original unity. Indeed, the subject–object split, which structures existence, is the dialectic that is now being itself. Less concerned to emphasize this idealist notion of an original unity toward which being aspires to return, Cone employs the Barthian talk of the God–world relationship as one of "wholly otherness" with a view to redirecting Tillich's claims regarding the passing

moment of the subject–object relationship, which must ultimately be sacrificed. Because of the way Tillich has conceived his dialectical ontology, this subject–object relationship does not endure and therefore is not opaque. As Cone sees it, Tillich is right that being's passage through the world is one of struggle, indeed, a liberation struggle, against nonbeing; however, the terminus of that struggle does not reconstruct the original unity. Rather, it brings the relationship between subject and object into a perfection in which the distinction itself remains.

To make his point, Cone turns to dialogical, rather than dialectical, language. This approach was put in place through his engagement with Barth's Christology and theological anthropology and in conversation with Martin Buber's interpretation of reality as an I–Thou relationship. Whereas Tillich is fond of speaking of the subject–object struggle, Cone sees this as the struggle between the I and what the I perceives and thus constructs as an It. Yet this It is, in fact, an I. The struggle within being is a struggle of what is perceived as an It to be perceived in its own I-ness or, more precisely, as a Thou in relation to the I. When this happens the I–It relationship is transformed into an I–Thou one. This is the struggle of the protagonist in Ralph Ellison's landmark text of black letters, *Invisible Man*. Because the I–Thou relationship is constitutive of existence and therefore of what it means to be—this is Cone's ontology, as I have cast it—the I–Thou relationship does not pass away.

Such an ontology helps Cone's theology, at least on the face of things, to accomplish perhaps its central objective: to render critically explicit the enduring meaning of black existence through an analysis of black faith. Insofar as this is the case, Cone makes a significant contribution to revaluing the meaning of race, because blackness from its own vantage within the expansive horizon of being reveals the depths and significance of what it means to be in the world. In other words, Cone sees a connection between the meaning of black existence and an I–Thou ontology: the meaning of black existence and black faith is revealed in the struggle to transform a relationship in which black people are cast as Its into relationships that recognize them as Thous. The struggle for liberation, therefore, ontologically reveals the human condition. This move is possible, as I see it, because Cone "personalized" the Tillichian dialectic of courage by recasting it in dialogical terms. In effect, Cone attempts to merge the personalism of Barthian theology with what he takes to be correct in Tillich's thought: namely, his revaluation of transcendence through his identification of courage or struggle as cultural power (as "black power") and therefore as the ground of being.

To be sure, this went some way in transforming Tillich's thought, given the objectives of black theology. Nevertheless, it is still worth asking whether Cone's transformation of Tillich's idealism was radical enough. Did Cone push his groundbreaking insight into the "personal" constitution of being to

its needed limits so as to ontologically free black existence? I argue that he did not, because the one point that does not change in the struggle to transform I–It structures into I–Thou structures is how I-ness itself functions as the normalizing term of the polarity. Whereas in I–It structures, the I dominates the other, thus making it an It, in I–Thou structures, the I relates to the other but allows it a separate-but-equal status in relationship to itself as I. In this way, the I positions the other as Thou. But something more than this is needed, for on its own, this is really only a settlement with whiteness, not its overcoming. The settlement, however, is alluring because the upside of the settlement with whiteness is a settlement with blackness. Yet here is where Victor Anderson's critique is most powerful, because the settlement with blackness is a settlement with the blackness that whiteness created. And therefore, the settlement with the blackness that whiteness created is a settlement with whiteness, albeit in the idiom of cultural blackness or cultural nationalism.

This line of reasoning, which is internal to black theology, runs up against another line of reasoning internal to it. This second line of reasoning, following from black theology's I–Thou ontology, says the following: if it is the case that black existence reveals the human condition such that whites lose themselves as oppressors by entering into the horizon of black existence and, conversely, blackness itself is transformed by receiving into itself those exiting the status of whiteness, then it follows that the framework of binary separateness in an I–Thou structure is too deeply impoverished to even begin to explain the kind of miscegenation toward which black theology seems to gesture. The very meaning of I in relation to Thou, of Thou in relation to I, is itself something beyond what an I-Thou dialectic is capable of experiencing. It is this problem that was never worked out, for from within a purely dialectical framework it can't be worked out.

This problem dogs black theology because its liberation formulation of I-ness and Thou-ness, where Thou-ness itself is simply I-ness considered from the side of the object, has not broken far enough away either from Tillich's immanent dialecticism or, for that matter, from what is most limiting in Barth's transcendent dialecticism. From Tillich and from Barth, Cone inherits the theological and philosophical problem of how to envisage the I in non-oppositional relationship to the other. In Barth's case, the problem prevents him from being able to conceive of the positivity of the world and therefore of how it can reveal God. It also has the unintended consequence, in his doctrine of election, of leading to a supersession of Israel. This in many respects occurs because Israel, as an index of creation in its opposition to God, stands over and against Christ. In this sense, God in Christ is everything, while creation qua creation (despite that even by grace it comes forth from God) is nothing.

In some sense, Tillich has the same problem, but now on the level of the immanence of being. Being, in its totality as the power of being, is everything. This, however, does *not* lead to the conclusion that being, in its diremption, to use a Hegelian term, as the world of concrete subjects and objects, is likewise everything. Rather, insofar as the world of subjects and objects must courageously sacrifice itself to the power of being, they are nothing as well. In this respect, like Barth's, Tillich's thought (to be sure, for different reasons) has embedded within it a relationship between subjects and objects, between the I and the other, that is zero in sum. Being as the power of being on the one hand and the world of concretely existing beings on the other can only be opposed to each other; one side of the opposition is poised to be the all-encompassing, "ontological" totality against the other. This oppositional struggle for the right to be hegemon registers in the language of courage, which Cone takes up, without sufficiently distancing himself from these specific problems, into black liberation theology's account of black existence. Consequently, Cone does not challenge the way in which I-ness as a structure of identity-in-self-possession—that is, as construed in zero sum terms—repeats the problem, albeit dialogically.

Theological Concreteness: A Christian Theology of Israel

Beyond an ontology of separateness, I propose a theology of participation, the content of which is YHWH's covenantal relationship with the one to whom YHWH has elected YHWH's self. This one is the covenantal and theological—and therefore, to say it again, not the racial—people of Israel. Hebrew Scripture and then the New Testament bear witness to this covenant. It is in light of the reality of the covenant that Chalcedonian Christology itself must be understood so as to decenter dialectic, which is to say, ontologized understandings of the person and work of Jesus. Understood in the light of YHWH's covenant with YHWH's partner Israel and thereby with the world, Chalcedon is to be conceived of as witnessing to a theology of covenantal participation in which the life of YHWH is thoroughly implicated in and suffuses the life of Israel. Indeed, YHWH is known only in this suffusion, for such suffusion is proper to YHWH-God and is constitutive of YHWH's transcendence. This can be called YHWH's identity in historical transcendence with Israel and thereby with the world. It is precisely this participatory transcendence, this ecstasy by which God *is* God for us, that makes creation transcendent within itself in its ecstasy back to its Creator, YHWH. The problem with dialectical thinking and related forms of philosophical thinking is that they begin from closure and then have to negotiate passage through an "ugly broad ditch" between things that are closed.[74]

But in modernity as looked at from its underside, this ditch is the ditch of coloniality, which itself is the ditch of the racial imagination built upon the severance of Jesus from the covenantal people of Israel and thus Christianity from its roots in the reality of YHWH's historical transcendence toward the world through YHWH's covenant with this people. The covenant witnesses to the fact that for God, and only because of God's identity as God for us, there is no ditch to be crossed by us. God has from the first bound Godself to us in God's communion with Israel as a communion for the world. This is the inner logic of the identity of Jesus, the inner logic by which Israel is always already a mulatto people precisely in being YHWH's people, and by which therefore Jesus himself as the Israel of God is Mulatto. At the level of his identity, or *who* he is, Jesus carries forward, and does not supersede, Israel's identity as partner to YHWH for the world. He is miscegenated, and out of that miscegenation discloses the God of Israel as the God of the Gentiles too. What the covenant framework discloses, then, is this: Because YHWH is on both the Creator and creaturely sides of the covenant holding it, a dialectical framework of I-Thou, while useful in some regards in responding to problems in the world, proves ultimately inadequate. Indeed, it is not radical enough.

And this brings me back to the analysis of James Cone's black liberation theology, which is the principle subject of this chapter. The conclusion to be drawn from my analysis is this: black liberation theology's refusal to see the I, and in fact all of creation, in gratuitous terms, that is, as a covenantal reality, leaves the problem of whiteness uncontested, insofar as at root it is a *theological* problem. As a theological problem, whiteness names the refusal to trade against race. It names the refusal to enter into dependent, promiscuous, and, in short, "contaminated" relations that resist an idolatrously false purity. The blackness that whiteness creates names the same refusal, albeit cast as the photo negative that yet retains the problem. What is needed is a vision of Christian identity, then, that calls us to holy "impurity" and "promiscuity," a vision that calls for race trading against the benefits of whiteness so as to enter into the miscegenized or mulattic existence of divinization (*theôsis*).

Tragically, however, for all of its good—and there is much to celebrate about black liberation theology though the project outlined here is an attempt to go beyond it—black liberation theology's attempt philosophically and theologically to salvage the blackness that modernity has constructed by converting it into a site of cultural power (and thus into a site at which to stage the "courage to be") is not radical enough. This is because it ironically leaves whiteness in place. In order to name and assault more radically the problem of whiteness, what is needed is an understanding of Christian existence as ever-grounded in the Jewish, nonracial flesh of Jesus and thus as an articulation of the *covenantal* life of Israel. Lazarus, rather than Dives, ever abides in the bosom of Abraham–Israel (Luke 16:19–31), as the Christ child himself does in

Mary–Israel's arms and, indeed, in her womb. For, as it is only YHWH who creates ex nihilo, so also is it only YHWH who makes those who were once not a people now, ex nihilo, a people, and who "calls things that are not as though they were" (Rom. 4:17). In short, only a Christian theology of Israel establishes the framework within which to overcome the theological problem of whiteness.

5

Signifying Race

Charles H. Long and the Opacity of Blackness

If one is to have a theology, it must arise from religion, something prior to theology.

[The] religious consciousness of... blacks... is the repository of who they are.

Theologies opaque must become deconstructive theologies—that is to say, theologies that undertake the destruction of theology as a powerful mode of discourse.
—Charles H. Long, Significations: Signs, Symbols, and Images in the Interpretation of Religion

The account of the meaning of black faith and thereby of New World blackness considered in this chapter is that of the historian of religion Charles H. Long. Along with Mircea Eliade and others at the University of Chicago, Long was an important figure in the establishment of the history of religions as a field of intellectual inquiry, and his thought in its reach and suggestiveness presses beyond any narrow conception of religious inquiry. Indeed, it is because of the extensiveness of his intellectual program that the considerations of his thought in this chapter cannot be exhaustive. Rather, I consider his thought from the vantage of the room it leaves for a theological interrogation of black faith and existence and for an unmasking of the theological problem of whiteness, given that he conceives of theology in ways reminiscent of Tillich's thought: that is, as an answering discipline. In Long's specific case, it answers to modernity's more general category and phenomenon of religion, though the

modern conception of this category has been tied to the problem of race. This I sought to establish in chapter 2, in my consideration of how Kant deploys the category in league with his construction of race, a construction of which we are heirs. I am interested in how Long construes the relationship between the religious and the theological. The epigraph at the beginning of the chapter encapsulates Long's general view, and this chapter can be read as a critical commentary on it: "If one is to have a theology, it must arise from religion, something prior to theology."

But what is religion, and where is it to be found? I recount Long's answer to the first part of the question—What is "religion"?—and engage its significance in what follows. As regards the second part of the question, it can briefly be said now that religion is to be found in the "religious consciousness," which, as the second epigraph indicates, is "the repository of who [black folks] are."[1] What, if any, kind of inquiry into the theological meaning of New World blackness, whether in its churchly or "extrachurchly" expressions, can there be in Long's outlook? This is the question taken up in this chapter.

Long's work in many respects provides a theoretical infrastructure for the early Raboteau if the early Raboteau is read in congruity with the outlooks of Robert Farris Thompson (*Flash of the Spirit*) and Donald Matthews (*Honoring the Ancestors*), or in congruity with the reading Peter Paris gives of Raboteau's *Slave Religion* (in *The Spirituality of African Peoples*).[2] I show in chapter 3 that Paris reads in Raboteau a religious history of African consciousness. All of this is to say that Long can be read as providing the philosophical orientation on the meaning of history that is ambiguously present in *Slave Religion*. Thus he addresses the methodological slippage in that text by pushing it in the direction of "religion." Long's work can also be read as giving the philosophical infrastructure to James H. Cone's post-Barthian black liberation theology (see chapter 4). He does this by providing a more rigorous method by which to read the later, more Tillichian Cone of black cultural consciousness against the grain of the earlier Cone. In this way, black theology becomes intelligible by converting it into an "opaque" theology. (I engage the notion of the opaque more fully as this chapter develops.)

As one surveys the discipline of African American religious studies, from history to theology to philosophies of religious humanism, it is indisputable that Long's view of religion generally and his view of black religion particularly is more or less the order of the day in the field of African American religious studies.[3] Insofar as this is the case, Long and religious scholars who are heir to his general approach to religious studies would take African American religious thought in a direction counter to the direction I start to sketch at the end of the last chapter and that I develop further in part III. Indeed, it can be said that through his interpretation of black liberation theology as an opaque discourse, Long culminates the intellectual trajectory of black liberation theology as a pure science of religion: as *Wissenschaft*. Reading Long charitably, it can be

said that he does not seek to overturn black liberation theology. His purpose is to complete it, to give it the orientation toward religion that would allow it to meet its objective of interpreting the various sites of existence (i.e., "black power" or what have you) as so many expressions of living in the power of being or, as Long is more prone to say, as so many expressions of the religious as such. My objective in this chapter is to raise a note of serious alarm regarding this direction of the field.

In doing this, however, I also need to explain the appeal of Long's view of religion, after the significant reign of Cone's approach or those generally indebted to his approach to theology and the study of black religion. The appeal, I think, comes from the broader explanatory power of Long's approach to African American religious thought. This can be seen, to consider but one example, in the work of the prolific Anthony Pinn, Agnes Cullen Arnold Professor of Humanities and Professor of Religious Studies, at Rice University. Pinn's indebtedness to Long's theory of religion is explicit. Long provides him a theory of religion expansive enough to interpret cultural phenomena "beyond the confines of theological conformity and strict theistic expression."[4] Drawing critically on Long's notion of opaque theology, Pinn says that "theology is deliberate or self-conscious human construction focused upon uncovering and exploring the meaning and structures of religious experience within the larger body of cultural production. It is, by nature, comparative in a way that does not seek to denounce or destructively handle other traditions."[5] "Conceived in this way," Pinn says, "African American theology's only obligation, then, is the uncovering of meaning and the providing of responses to the questions of life that explain experience, assess existing symbols and categories, and allow for healthy existence."[6]

Having added to Long's approach to *Religionswissenschaft* a broadly pragmatist philosophical orientation on the one hand and aspects of the theology of Gordon Kaufman on the other, Pinn finally observes, "Theology must address religious experience without concentrating on a particular tradition."[7] This is the only way to ensure that "theology . . . has public, not private or parochial foundations."[8] It is the only way to ensure that theology's foundations "[are] not restricted . . . to the language and traditions of a particular esoteric community or to the peculiar experience of unusual individuals."[9] Theology conceived in this way is "public theology." For Pinn, as for a number of other scholars of black religion, Long provides a theory of religion that is able to surmount theological narrowness in general, and, more specifically, a narrowness that can lead to the intellectual, if not sociopolitical, hegemony of any specific faith tradition.[10] Such an intellectual posture is clearly a post-Christendom interpretation of religion, an interpretation in which religion as such is prior to and, in fact, legitimates Christianity or any particular religion for that matter. Religion is the transcendental, the liberating universal. In Long's own words:

> The church is one place one looks for religion.... But...the church was not the only context for the meaning of religion.... The Christian faith provided a language for the meaning of religion, but not all the religious meanings of the black communities were encompassed by the Christian forms of religion. I have been as interested in other forms of religion in the history of black communities— as those forms are contained in their folklore, music, style of life, and so on.... The religion of any people is more than a structure of thought; it is experience, expression, motivations, intentions, behaviors, styles, and rhythms. Its first and fundamental expression is not on the level of thought. It gives rise to thought, but a form of thought that embodies the precision and nuances of its source. This is especially true of Afro-American religion.[11]

Christian theology is interpreted here, and I think rightly so, as a certain "structure of thought" that is a specific "language for the meaning of religion." It is a particular discourse, a specific mode of existence—and I might add, at its best, it speaks as such. Long is surely correct about this. When Christianity acts as a universal, hegemonic discourse, it in fact betrays itself and, as colonialism and slavery (to cite but two examples) attest, wreaks havoc. Long's history of religions project rightly seeks to intellectually rectify this problem and seeks to do so by theorizing the religious performances and lives of persons of African descent in modernity.

Hence, my engagement with his account of religion. I seek to assess the degree to which it can foster an account of race that unmasks and adequately responds to the problem of modern racial reasoning as a problem for both religion and theology. I argue here that, due to his particular construal of theology and religion and the judgments that follow from it, Long's interpretation does not provide an adequate solution to the problem of modern racial reasoning. Indeed, I show how unwittingly his project continues to occupy the very territory that makes whiteness the theological problem that it is. Yet my task is not to dismiss Long's intellectual agenda. His thought is too important for that. It is, rather, to point toward a resolution of its concerns by situating them within a different horizon of religious and theological meaning and ultimately within a different framework for the meaning of existence as such. In this sense, this chapter leads into the constructive aspect of this book's argument in part III.

The chapter proceeds first by investigating Long's approach to the discipline of the history of religions. In light of this, it probes his approach to the study of black religion and, consequently, his approach to theology given his understanding of religion. This task requires that I give an account of his notion of the opacity of religion, theology, and, ultimately, his understanding of what it means "to be" or exist. This leads, finally, to a consideration of what

I take to be the tight space Long's outlook leaves for a theological interpretation of reality in general and of New World black existence in its variegated inflections in particular. This tight space turns out, paradoxically, to be a tight space for any kind of interpretation of reality that would insist on the ultimate *positivity* of the unique, the specific, or the particular. In other words, and again paradoxically, his thought proves in fact a tight space for really engaging difference or the "other," be it the other that is God, to speak theologically, or all of the various "others" within the creation. It is the other who cannot be of infinite or enduring worth in Long's framework, for as I show, the other as with Kant's notion of sublimity is that which triggers the reflexive capacities of the self in the depths of the self's own opacity. The other, in other words, is only a trigger for *self*-knowledge. Insofar as this is the case, Long's project reflects back to modernity its own deep aporia.

Charles H. Long and the Modern Study of Religion

Though protest is a prominent feature of Long's thought, he nevertheless is more than a protest intellectual, for in Long's thought, protest is embedded within a broader attempt to reimagine reality and its meanings or significations. More specifically, Long's attempt to reimagine the nature of human existence is, in fact, his attempt to probe the depths of reality through an analysis of the nature and meaning, not simply of any specific religion but, rather, of religion qua religion.

The problem of modern racial reasoning, against which Long's intellectual program voices dissent, is symptomatic of a larger quandary: the obfuscation of the meaning of religion and thereby the meaning of humanity. The simple study of any given religion can, in fact, limit one's investigation of this greater concern. For this reason, "to say that you are studying or teaching Islam, Buddhism, Hinduism, or primitive religions does not necessarily mean that you are concerned with the specifically religious element in these complex systems of human experience." To be concerned with the "specifically religious element" of these phenomena is to be concerned with the provocation of the various religious expressions themselves. This, in short, is the affirmative task marking Long's thought as that of a scholar of religion, indeed, as a historian of religion. He says, "A self-conscious concern with this problem [i.e., being concerned with the phenomenon of religion as such] has characterized the discipline of the History of Religions from its beginning."[12]

To appreciate Long's concern more fully, it is important to situate both him and his field of inquiry. Long pinpoints the beginning of the history of religions approach to the study of religion qua religion (against the sociological [Durkheim], psychological [James], economic [Marx], or what have you) in the work of the eminent German Sanskritist Max Müller (1823–1900), who taught

at the Taylorian Institute at Oxford University from 1848 to 1900.[13] Müller influenced the founding of a number of chairs in the history of religions on the European continent. According to Long, Müller is important for the history of religions because, drawing on German Romanticism, he saw a strong connection between religion and language. Two significant ramifications followed from this understanding.

First, it located the origin of religions (along with languages) in historical and empirical specificity, as opposed to ideal a priori structures. In this, the history of religions approach to studying religion contrasted with a Kantian epistemological understanding of religion in which religion simply regulates morality from the noumenal domain. Second, in seeing in religions (again, along with languages) a historical trajectory and rooting religions in their empirical specificities, one can discern "a universal intent" in religion, and this "universality may be seen in terms of origins and history or in method."[14] We return to a kind of *sensus communis* idea, but apart from transcendental philosophy. That is, Müller inflects the *sensus communis* of religions and languages historically and empirically. Long makes the following observation: there is "a kind of Romantic *sensus communis* of language and style" that insofar as being closely connected to the religious experience leads to "a *sensus numinous*."[15]

There were far-reaching consequences for theology resulting from this approach to religion. Long states those consequences this way: "Müller's efforts . . . related the study of religion to the study of languages, and in this connection he . . . put forth speculative theories regarding the origins of language and religion."[16] These "speculative theories" were in fact competing with the speculations of theologians, operating as they were from the perspective of Christianity as *Kulturprotestantismus*.[17] Wherein lay the competition? Long takes as emblematic the resistance of Adolf von Harnack, the noted nineteenth-century historian of Christian doctrine, to a chair in history of religions in German universities. Harnack's opposition was rooted in a kind of German cultural nationalism that led him to conclude, in a 1901 speech delivered at the University of Berlin (as summarized by Long), "that such study would lead to dilettantism"; for, as Harnack saw it, the truth of the matter was this: "Those who wished to study others' religions should study them through Christianity."[18] One can certainly understand this claim in such a way as not to be destructive of the traditions of the religions under consideration. But Harnack's warrant for the admonition to study other religions through Christianity seems to follow more from a presumption of German cultural and philosophical superiority than from a rigorous theological engagement with other religions. For this reason, as Long says summarizing Harnack, "Christianity is the absolute religion and anyone who knew one religion knew them all."[19]

Long's analysis rightly understood that Harnack's resistance to the study of other religions on their own terms, which is what the emergent discipline of

the history of religions proposed, concealed a larger problem about which I have already made passing reference. That larger, concealed problem was that Harnack's resistance had for its ground a cultural vision of European superiority that the new discipline potentially called into question. Long's analysis also recognized that the cultural vision of European and, indeed, of German superiority, had, in fact, assumed Christianity, for purposes of religious legitimation, into itself. In short, Christianity became fully identifiable with the meaning and destiny of European and, by extension, American consciousness or, even broader still, with the consciousness, meaning, and destiny of Western civilization. Christian theology, insofar as it was annexed to such an understanding of cultural Christianity, was necessarily implicated in the problems of such a universalizing and problematically totalizing, if not imperial, vision. The importance, consequently, of the rise of *Religionswissenschaft* in contradistinction to the *Wissenschaft* of the reigning *Kulturprotestantismus*, of which Harnack's thought was emblematic, lay in how it sought to unmask the work of intellectual colonization performed by Christian theology. In so doing, *Religionswissenschaft* as an academic pursuit proved to be a politically countercultural enterprise intent on making visible the religious other in its full linguistic density, irreplaceability, and, as Long will say, "opacity."

But something seems to be lacking in his otherwise clear-sighted analysis of what, coming out of the nineteenth century, intellectually ailed theology. For Long, the confrontation between the emerging *Religionswissenschaft* and Harnack's theological outlook illustrates the ailment. Long seems to insufficiently acknowledge that Harnack's understanding of Christianity as "the absolute religion" in many ways brings to culmination a deformation of theological reflection that has been some time in the making. Harnack's exaltation of Christianity as "the absolute religion" follows from a rationalized reinterpretation of Christianity. A signal feature of this reinterpretation involved a schematizing of religions such that religions were conceived as indices of humanity or its lack. Since in chapter 2, I investigate these matters in relation to Immanuel Kant's rational religion, which I argue is an aspect of his philosophical anthropology, there is no need to repeat them again here. It is nonetheless worth reiterating for purposes of the present discussion that Kant's transformation of Christianity into "rational religion" was intent on suppressing, oppressing, and ultimately stripping from Christianity what was Jewish about it. This suppression not only represents a troublesome form of Christian supersessionism against the Jews, it also represents a suppression of the positivity of the eternal Word's relationship to the world's religions as so many expressions of what it means to be human. In other words, there is a link between the supersessionism against the Jews that functioned at the European metropole and its replication with respect to non-Christian religions at the colonial outposts. And thus, supersessionism proves is a global problem generative of the questions of religion (*Religionsfrage*), which homo religiosus asks as

the hermeneutical question of the *meaning* of religion. It is this global problem of religion as asked from the metropole as the question of religion, the *Religionsfrage*—the issue that I want explicitly to unfold in my continued analysis of Long's thought—that *Religionswissenschaft*, the modern science of religion, investigates. My point here is to tie what is at stake here in the issue of religion to modernity's supersessionism problem, and to call attention to how as a critical theological problem it is absent from Long's analysis of what lay behind Harnack's theological-religious outlook.

To put the matter otherwise, the theological outlook conditioning Harnackian theology that, so I am claiming, Long seems not to acknowledge, is an outlook that has at its center the intellectual extirpation of a primal other—the Jew—from the imagination of Western culture. Indeed, the banishment of this first other is the condition of possibility for the expulsion of all others from the idyllic "paradise"—the cosmopolis—that modernity sought to construct as an enlightened Western (Christian) civilization. The result of this extirpation is the creation of a distinctively modern, hierarchicalized notion of religion, which Christianity crowns. It is true that such an understanding of Christianity as the absolute religion makes a problematic equation between Christianity and religion. Therefore the question that Long and the tradition of *Religionwissenschaft* raise as a challenge to the hegemony of (Christian) theology over other religions and, thus, over religion qua religion is rightly posed.

However, Long seems not to recognize that the twofold question (of other religions in relationship to Christianity and of religion in its own right) has been theologically radicalized in Christ, as Nicholas of Cusa argued in his treatise *De Pace Fidei*.[20] This is because the question and, in some sense, the reality of the religions and of religion in its own right are situated within the person of the eternal Word in his concreteness as Jesus of Nazareth, the Jew. This also means that both the reality of the religions of the world and the questions they pose, and the question of religion as such that only *Dasein* as homo religiosus can pose, are perpetually present in the eternal Word, Jesus of Nazareth, and therefore within the social or ecclesial field that he is. This ecclesial unfolding expresses the eternal Word, in his multiplicity and perpetuity, in creation as his mystical, but no less real and therefore true, body politic, which expresses his Jewish body.[21]

In this respect, then, as already stated, Harnack's position against *Religionswissenschaft* represents a deformation, a deradicalization, of Christian thought and self-understanding insofar as Christian theology assumes the question of non-Christian religions and of religion qua religion within itself. Indeed, Christian theology can do this without obfuscating those questions. In the preceding chapters, I intimate what this means both theologically and even philosophically, and I continue to do so at points in this chapter. In part III, I provide a reading of the emergence of black Christian faith as an event in

which the radicalization that I am suggesting is in fact dramatized and performed. The fundamental point I seek to make now, however, is simply this: Long's vision of what ails theology may be overdetermined by the theological assumptions built into Harnack's resistance to *Religionswissenschaft*. The result of this overdetermination is a certain shortsightedness as to the task of theological reflection in connection with reflection on religion in its own right and on non-Christian religions. In other words, because theology's task and meaning have been so determined, in Long's view, by the history of the contact and conflict between theology and *Religionswissenschaft*, the possibility that Christian theology represents a radicalizing of religion's questions is not considered as a real possibility. This problem will come to be inscribed in important ways in Long's own interpretation of such opaque theologies as black theology.

Let me anchor in a specific text the problem to which I am pointing. In assessing the value of Max Müller's research for the beginnings of the history of religions as a domain of inquiry, Long says: "In the case of Indo-European languages, [Müller] thought he had discovered a new primordium for Western culture—a primordium different from that of the Hebraic tradition."[22] But if finding "a primordium different from that of the Hebraic tradition" is at the root of the new discipline and its approach to religious phenomena are we, then, not still within the same rarefied atmosphere that animated Harnack's own vision—indeed, the vision that goes back to Kant himself? This is a vision in which the universal can be attained only by prescinding from the particular. There can be no *concretum universale*, concrete universal. Thus, Christianity's rootedness in the traditions of ancient Israel and, therefore, which inhere in Christ's reality as human must be overcome. Müller and Harnack can be likened to Herder and Kant: they share the same fundamental interest in the universal but want to get there differently. The former celebrates the particular as a route to the universal; the latter rides imperialistically, that is, roughshod, directly to the universal. Long takes up Müller's—and indirectly, W. E. B. Du Bois's and Herder's—standpoint with its problems, for he along with Müller wants to understand the universality of being as, in some sense, not bound to religions themselves in their concreteness. For the "primordium [that is] different from that of the Hebraic tradition" is the "primordium of human consciousness," which expresses itself in "the nature of experience itself."[23]

But what is the status of the "primordium of human consciousness"? In its challenge to early modern theology, *Religionswissenschaft*, Long says, started to speak of the "primordium of human consciousness" as itself universal. And thus there came to be an initial movement away from the emphasis on *sensus communis* within historical time. The importance of historical time and the centrality of language would eventually be retrieved. But until then, there was a move within *Religionswissenschaft* toward the more speculative moment of a

sensus numinous, which served as a point of reference in determining what it meant to declare that the human being is homo religiosus. The "religious" as such is the primordium of human consciousness. Herein lies the possibility of religion and its sundry manifestations in religious experience.

Long's summary of the thought of Rudolph Otto in his *Idea of the Holy* (1917) captures the force of this. Long notes that, for Otto, "the category of the religious [is an] *a priori* in the human consciousness," and that "the *religious* [therefore] . . . achieves ontological status." Being, therefore, is religious; for religion is an irreducible category of the human way of existing, having "[come] into existence with man—the earliest stage of man is the religious stage." Thus, "formally speaking, the religious experience is the same for the earliest man as it is for the mystics in the highly developed religions of Judaism, Christianity or Hinduism."[24] The religious, which structures being as such, then, constitutes the *sensus communis* as *sensus numinous*. This is one of the central claims of the discipline of the history of religions, according to Long.

To be sure, there have been various ways of expressing the religious primordium. Otto conceives of it as encountering the "Holy" (in terms reminiscent of rationalist aesthetics) in its full sublimity; Joachim Wach conceives of it as the "experience of ultimate reality"; G. van der Leeuw says it is the confrontation with "power";[25] Mircea Eliade, one of Long's teachers at the University of Chicago, conceives of the religious as residing in the distinction between the sacred and profane as revealed in religious symbols. In Eliade's case, religious symbols (i.e., a rock, a tree, the sky, or what have you) require both historical and phenomenological analysis. Such an analysis reveals an existential historical situation; it "[shows]," says Long interpreting Eliade, "how man understood his own being in various historical periods."[26]

The trajectory from Müller to Eliade is important for understanding Long's thought, for in the span between them, at least three features of the discipline emerge: history, hermeneutics, and culture. Each is a facet of the religious as the primordium of human consciousness and precedes theology. In this and the next subsections, I address the first two of these, history and hermeneutics. In the next major section of the chapter, I address Long's engagements with the third of these, culture. It is my contention that through each of these—history, hermeneutics, and culture—Long, in effect, suggests a theoretical reorientation for the field of African American religious studies. Through his approach to history he pushes the ambiguity in Raboteau's early work in the direction of a history of religions. The next section shows how Long's approach to culture reads the later Cone against the grain of the earlier Cone, thus pushing African American theology in a different intellectual direction, the direction of the opaque. Long's rather Schleiermacherian account of hermeneutics is really the linchpin. Indeed, hermeneutics is the philosophical core for Long's account of both history and culture. Thus, it is the philosophical heart of his intellectual program.

On History and the Modern Study of Religion

Müller early on recognized the importance of history for an understanding of religion and language. He did not understand history in terms of the "salvation history" of Judaism or Christianity. Rather, for Müller, the historian of religion is to understand any given religion from within its own historical development. *Sensus communis* and *sensus numinous* are historical in orientation, but the history they unfold is more universal. The paradoxical observation Long notes regarding Müller is that he "[abolished] the dogmatic categories which [limited] the meaning of human life to its historicity—through the study of history! He [hoped] to renew the West by seeing it within the context of a universal history as its past and a world culture as its present and future."[27]

Though "the First World War destroyed the optimistic euphoria that surrounded the Müller [generation's]" inebriation with a kind of historical utopianism, and though for a while "the [religious] primordium was no longer sought . . . within historical time,"[28] by the time Eliade makes his contributions to the field, the significance of history is retrieved. According to Long, Eliade's importance for the discipline, among other things, is that he reconceived the religious a priori and the sui generis character from within the various histories that constitute those religions. This is the importance of history and the archaic in the history of religions. The history of religions supposes histories and not the dominance of any one history over another. I return to Long's account of history at subsequent points in the chapter.

On Hermeneutics and the Modern Study of Religion

The second matter of importance follows closely on the question of history: the centrality of hermeneutics as the question of religion and language. On this matter, the history of religions draws on the work of Friedrich Schleiermacher, for whom interpretation is not narrowly confined to the study of sacred texts, particularly the Bible. Schleiermacher lays the groundwork for interpretation theory to be a discipline no longer subordinate to theology. Rather, hermeneutics has to do with the interpretation of human existence and the human sciences as a whole. This means that the religious, understood within the context of the modern hermeneutical situation, encompasses the totality of existence. The distinction between the sacred and the profane in religious symbolism, then, is a distinction, not a dualism. In fact, hermeneutics as a constitutive feature of the history of religions calls into question dichotomies of this sort and as such opens new, more inclusive possibilities for the interpretation of the human.

Clarity on this point comes from Long's exposition of aspects of Otto's and Eliade's thought. Regarding Otto, Long interprets his notion of the "schematization" of the religious constitution of human consciousness in the following way:

> Because Otto had defined the religious experience so narrowly [i.e., as irrational or nonrational] the notion of schematization was necessary if the religious experience was to have a relational character. Otto had to show how the religious experience was related to the moral, aesthetic, and sociological dimensions of culture, etc. Otto's schematization demonstrated how the religious experience took on other dimensions of the human consciousness and thereby expressed itself within the context and under other cultural forms.[29]

Otto's understanding of the religious as encounter with the *numen*, the Holy, however strained and indebted to the epistemology of neo-Kantianism, nevertheless grasped that the religious embraces the totality of human existence without reducing the religious to some more supposedly fundamental explanation. Human existence in its totality is religious, and the discipline of the history of religions is given the hermeneutic task of deciphering the meanings of this totality. The religious is a hermeneutical category understood in the broader Schleiermacherian sense of the interpretation of the entirety of the human mode of being in the world.

Long makes a similar point regarding hermeneutics by expounding Eliade's notion of "the center," as well as his notion of "revalorization." The brilliance of these notions for Long is that they make the same point Otto does about the religious as an all-embracing category of human existence, but without recourse to the somewhat overly rationalized notion of schematization. I only consider Long's engagement with Eliade's ideas about the center and revalorization to draw out their significance for hermeneutics and their consequences for Long's interpretation of the meaning and significance of theology.

First, the hermeneutics of the center. In terms reminiscent of Derridean deconstructionism, Long claims that the new hermeneutical situation driving the discipline of the history of religions destabilizes the Western metaphysical *episteme* of a grounded and grounding center of consciousness.[30] The grounding principle of the centered and centering consciousness is variously signified as *eidos*, *arhe*, or *ousia*—the letter, writing, or God Consciousness. From the grounding principle, human thought gains validity and objectifies empirical others, who lie outside the centering consciousness, as objects to be thought, grasped, and thus known. Imperialism arises out of this general epistemological orientation. Long makes the important and insightful point that the history of religions, by methodologically calling the Western *episteme* into question, reveals that rationality and civilization, for example, are grounding religious symbols for the modern West.

Through these symbols, which are religious in that they suppose an orientation toward the sacred that reveals what it means to be human, the West constitutes the empirical other by means of an opposing religious symbolism of the irrational and primitive, which are to be conquered. The history of

religions as a discipline calls this epistemological structure into question precisely by refusing its logic of center and periphery, coded through the polari-
ties rational–irrational (or nonrational), logical–illogical (or even prelogical),
reality–myth, and civilized–primitive. The history of religions as a discipline
proceeds from the inadequacy of this (religious) symbolism for constituting
modernity.

What religion, as conceived in modernity, is therefore unable to grasp is
this: there are real people at the margins and periphery of Western thought. By
contrast, *Religionswissenschaft* calls for "a new" (indeed, "a hermeneutical")
science that refuses these binarisms.[31] As a result of that refusal, *Religionswissenschaft* can reckon with the reality of humanity in its full breadth. Recognizing that the epistemological center no longer holds (and never really
did), the discipline of the history of religions offers a different, more hopeful,
interpretation of human existence, which, "with its emphasis on the long
event, and seeing the past in varying rhythms, continuities, convergences, and
discontinuities, is able to give prominence to the authenticity of those nonhistorical, nonliterate, nonpowerful—in the modern sense of those terms—
meanings of the human." The meanings uncovered in the history of religions
are religious in that they "[push] beyond all the specific modern modes and
paradigms, whether of language, logic, or writing, to the fullness and poverty
of being which is designated by the term 'sacred.' "[32]

As I see it, Long's insight into the challenge posed by the emergent discipline of the history of religions to modern theological and religious inquiry is
groundbreaking. Indeed, it is here that, arguably, Long unfolds his most radical insight. That insight regards how the religious and the sacred as features of
the quest for self-realization and human fulfillment in fact signify what I call
the fullness and poverty of being. Thus, according to Long, the hermeneutical
insight inhering in the notion of the center as connected to this understanding
of the sacred as expressive of the "the fullness and poverty of being" necessarily
entails a decentering of the metaphysical and epistemological edifice of the
West. Such a decentering is necessary to the extent that the binary center–
periphery logic marking the West is fundamentally areligious, atheistic, and
antihumanist insofar as it is predicated on a binary opposition between the
wealth and poverty of existence; but understood rightly, the "religious" and the
"sacred" as such, *anthropos* or the human being in its diverse expressions and
richness, and finally the *theion* or the "gods"—each are indexed through "the
fullness and poverty of being" in their coinciding unity.

This goes to the heart of Long's critique of modern theology coming out of
the nineteenth century and into the twentieth. Wealth and fullness are aligned,
with recourse to Christianity, as "the absolute religion," with the center that is
the West, while poverty, which is privative and therefore negative, is associated
with the marginalized non-Western and non-Christian other. Long sees theology as heretofore practiced as inextricably enmeshed in the metaphysical and

epistemological entanglements marking the center–periphery, fullness–poverty binaries of the West. Theology is performed from the center-fullness side of the axis. Unfortunately, as stated above, Long's reduction of Christian theology to its Harnackian or Harnack-like performances does not allow him to reckon with other types of Christian theological performances, both within and on the underside of the West, performances that might actually be consonant with and perhaps even radicalize his own brilliant insights into the poverty and wealth of existence. One thinks, for example, of the theological performances of the thirteenth-century theologian Bonaventure and the fourteenth-century theologian Julian of Norwich, who both understand Christ as the revelation of the poverty and wealth of existence.[33] And from the underside of the modern/colonial West, one thinks of Harriet Jacobs, whose pen name in *Incidents in the Life of a Slave Girl* (1861) was Linda Brent.[34]

The new hermeneutical situation brought to the fore by the history of religions is also apparent in Eliade's notion of "revalorization." Long says:

> Eliade's formulation of the structure of religious symbolism moves beyond schematization for the religious symbol takes into itself various layers and types of experience and expression [such that the] religious quality of the symbol is expressed by the "revalorization" of these layers and types of experience. The revalorization is that quality of the symbol which enables it to refer to that which is transcendent. It is the quality of the symbol as religious which enables it to hold together in a unity many and often contradictory aspects of experience.[35]

According to Long, Eliade's notion of revalorization (along with Otto's attempt to express something quite similar, albeit more rationalized, through "schematization") is the expression of modernity's new hermeneutical situation. Revalorization names the fact that the religious symbol accrues to itself multiple historical layers of human and cultural experience to be uncovered by the interpreter. But if the multiple layers of the religious symbol emerge from the archaic, it follows that the interpreter has a fundamentally "archaic" structure and that the present moment arises out of an often fragmented and fractured memory.

Add to this Eliade's contention that religious symbolism is total and inexhaustible, and, according to Long, one now is in a position to understand the wealth of possibilities open for the history of religions as a hermeneutical discipline, the object of which is the human phenomenon in its full disclosure. Eliade's insight means not only that there is an inexhaustible content to the symbol but also that the ways of interpreting and creating the present reality of life are similarly boundless. In this light, understanding the religious ought not be bound to Western religious traditions, philosophical categories, or

theological discourses as formulated to this point. For what Eliade says regarding the religious symbol vis-à-vis the hermeneutics of revalorization, is, according to Long, equally applicable to the pluralism of the human phenomenon: "Eliade believes that religious symbols present to us a spiritual universe. Although these symbols may invite thought, the thought that they invite must not be restricted to the categories of the West. It may be that the symbols by their very nature invite different and varying types of thought."[36]

On Culture and the Modern Study of Religion

This point helps explain why America represents a new and important "hermeneutical situation," the hermeneutical situation of culture. It drives Long to say, echoing John Locke, "In the beginning was America."[37] One of the ways in which the symbol, in its inexhaustibility, gives rise to thought (often not in the categories of the West or, when using those categories, weakening them) is through situations of cultural contact.[38] Contact situations present the possibility of new beginnings and, thus, of renewal in what it means to be human. America represents just such a situation. Hence, "the enigma of America, the dilemma of my culture" is that it is a "hermeneutical situation,"[39] a situation rendered intelligible only upon decoding America as (religious) symbol. In decoding America, one articulates, among others things, the meanings of American religion as the performance and articulation of human renewal. But in this hermeneutical situation, America as symbol cannot be strictly defined from the vantage of the European settlers and their colonizing efforts, for America was before the Mayflower and the slaves were before the New World.

Long points out that a stumbling block to the interpretation of existence as the interpretation of America is that there is a language and mythology in place that resists coming to terms with the new situation. To employ terms of a Derridean vocabulary, one might say that this language and mythos is "monolinguistic," and as such prevents plumbing the depths of the actual hermeneutical situation that is America. The monolinguistic mythos keeps the meaning of America located, as it were, within a mythical cycle that is a kind of nondisruptive eternal return of the same. This cycle is structured through the center–periphery logic of the European and Euro-American West. In this logic "America—or what comes to be called America—[is] an imaginative, cartographical, economic, and phantasy notion of Europe." Furthermore, this logic fosters a discourse about America that "not only served the ideological and religious conquest of the New World but it also formed the cultural parameters of distinctively American cultural languages. This discourse has, more often than not, provided the framework and content for the discussion of anything cultural or religious in the lands across the Atlantic." The problem, however, is that "such a discourse has...obscured other realities of the

American situation" in that "the language and discourse of savagism, Christianity, and civilization have become the normative modes of denying the cultural–historical meaning of cultural contact, the mutual borrowing, the dependence of Europeans on Indians and slaves."[40] Thus the language of America and of the New World, along with the mythic realities that that language has come to signify, has ultimately, as its modus operandi, a form of denial that coincides with terror.

The result of placing "aborigines and slaves within the context of a new time" is that time and, indeed, "history [function] as terror."[41] Long, against such a hermeneutics of terror and terrorism, seeks to articulate a different philosophy of language and a different hermeneutics of existence, both grounded in a notion of revalorization and an attendant hermeneutic ontology. Such a notion helps one see that the New World is something neither totally European nor fully Indian, neither totally American nor fully slave. The New World is not whole and thus should not be understood in terms of a linguistic monolith. Rather, one must approach the hermeneutical situation that is America through "close historical and comparative religious studies" that are "capable of integrating the differing temporal and cultural rhythms" constituting America and, indeed, the Western Hemisphere. The important point as it relates to hermeneutics in the history of religions for Long is this: "The language of one of the participants is no longer the normative structure of discourse."[42]

Thus, we come in Long's thought to the issue of "the relational character of religious expression and experience" in history and the contact and formation of cultures.[43] As Long saw it in his early essays, this—the problem of religion and culture—was still fairly uncharted terrain in the field of the history of religions. As a problem, it was a species of the question of hermeneutics that the history of religions opens up. As Long observes, religion studied from a history of religions perspective inquires into "the relatedness of religion to other dimensions and patterns of culture and history."[44] And as he further explains, this problem "has to do with the correlation of pattern in culture with the structure of religious symbols." The problem is most acute when "the history of a culture must be constructed from religious symbols and artifacts."[45] The question of the relational character of the religious, how it structures and is at the root of culture, insightfully suggests that culture itself is a religious manifestation. Religion in this sense is "a modality of the ordinariness of life."[46]

Perhaps a way to better appreciate Long's important insight is through a consideration of what he sees as the significance of cargo cults for understanding how culture is a religious expression. He says that with cargo cults "some of the fundamental problems of religious–cultural dynamics" emerge.[47] Long quotes Kenelm Burridge's definition of a cargo cult:

> Cargo cults compare most directly with the Ghost-dance cults of
> North America, and the prophetist movements among African peo-

ples. Typically, participants in a Cargo cult engage in a number of strange and exotic rites and ceremonies the purpose of which is apparently to gain possession of European manufactured goods such as axes, knives, aspirins, china plates, razor blades, colored beads, guns, bolts of cloth, hydrogen peroxide, rice, tinned food, and other goods to be found in a general department store. These goods are known as "cargo" or in the Pidgin English rendering Kago.[48]

Cargo cults are the result of an imperial cultural contact and represent the impact of an alien culture on the religious imagination of an indigenous culture. What is important, however, is that cargo cults provide a vantage, one that arises from the contact between modernity's conquerors and vanquished, from which to probe the meaning and significance of that contact itself. Out of the contact between cultures arises a new cultural formation, one that is cultic and thus religious in structure; for the new culture that begins to form out of cultural contact is patterned after the cult. Indeed, for Long, it repeats the religious-cultic form. In this respect, culture itself then is a religious and a hermeneutical situation.

To explain how this works, Long draws on van der Leeuw's interpretation of religion as power wherein religion is the encounter with an extremely impressive "Something Other." The cargo cult emerges out of contact with "the scientific, industrialized Western culture with its religious ideology" as the powerful Something Other.[49] Yet since the imperialist Westerners did not confront a tabula rasa in the native cultures they overtook and since their domination did not completely annihilate the native cultures, one is bound to raise the question of the reciprocity or "the confluence of two respective forms of cultural creativity."[50] Long observes that for a number of the native cultures there existed the expectation of the apocalyptic coming or return of the deity, who would institute cosmic renewal. Such a notion was vaguely comparable to ideas about a bearer of salvation in such religions as Christianity, Judaism, Buddhism, and Zoroastrianism. So "the coming of the Europeans . . . only intensified this original notion of return and renewal."[51]

In viewing the contact situation as a religious experience that structures the encounter itself and that, at the same time, institutes a cultural pattern, there was great continuity and reciprocity between cultures in the imperial situation. Long says, "The indigenous cultures were often receptive to the Westerners and to their teaching of their culture and religion, for the Westerners not only possessed the power to dominate but were at the same time a fulfillment of the general notion of power already present in the indigenous culture."[52] However, there was also discontinuity insofar as Westerners did not fully meet the expectations embodied in the indigenous cultural traditions. The renewal brought by Westerners represented an erosion of religious expectations for native cultures in that the sacred cosmos brought by the imperialists centered on a

money economy, productivity, and the like: "The indigenous cultures have become part of the periphery of the great mercantile Western centers, and through this process they have lost their own centers."[53]

The cargo cult, consequently, must be understood as a cultural production that responds to the exigencies of the contact situation. This production, however, occurs in the mode of religious experience. "The Western impact on the primitive cultures of the world," says Long, "should be seen from the point of view of this mode of apprehension."[54] What is this mode of apprehension and what fundamentally does it suggest about the phenomenon of culture qua religion? It suggests that the cargo cult is not a *purely* indigenous cultural creation, for either the conqueror or the vanquished. The key word here is "purely," for the cargo cult results from the subsumption of "these strange-looking beings who came in large ships from nowhere, bearing strange tools and artifacts and beliefs . . . under the structure of their own mythical apprehension."[55] The cargo cult represents an encounter with the West "under an indigenous structure of apprehension."[56] Again, Long explains:

> Members of the cult undertake the mythicization of history, but this time it is not simply the reduction of the new culture to the old mythic categories; the mythic possibility remains, but the old myth has been ruptured by the new power. The cultists now undertake the creation of a new cultural myth that will enable them to make sense of the mythic past and the historical present in mythic terms.[57]

This passage helps us see that the "indigenous structure of apprehension" under which the West and everything it represents is subsumed is religious in nature. Thus culture itself is a religious act that, in its response to power, can be a liberating act. That is, culture qua religion is enacted as much at the periphery as at the center. This is seen in the case of the cargo cult in that it marks a form of cultural creativity that disrupts Western cultural, cultic, and therefore religious categories. From the periphery emerges a destabilization of the center that does not attempt to refound or reinstate the center. The cargo cult embodies a marginal cultural philosophy whose inherent critique of the West rests in its attempt not to memorialize a center–periphery logic. Rather, the center and periphery are in constant dialectical interaction.

In the end, then, if I understand Long correctly, religion relates to culture in such a way as to free the latter from the need for an absolute subject and absolute center, a subject and center that participate in the discourse of the West's center–periphery structure of being. Despite America's participation in and perpetuation of the center–periphery logic of the West and its way of imaging the order of things, America nevertheless is a potentially tragic, yet potentially comic "enigma." As such, the hermeneutical situation that is America is a situation both of potential problem and of creative possibility. This, as Long says, is "the enigma of America, the dilemma of my culture."

America is an enigma precisely because it is constituted in contact with the periphery, and this contact is in fact religious, but religious in such a way that religion itself precedes the specifically religious discourse of the West, namely, theology. Long's interpretation of liberation theologies as "theologies of the opaque" must be situated here.

America as Religious Phenomenon and the Structure of Black Consciousness

In light of what has been said so far, it could further be said that America, read against the grain of its domination in cultural contact, nevertheless is a sociopolitical representation of the way in which religion as such structures existence. This, for Long, is no reason to valorize America or its civil religion. Indeed, he is critical of the ways in which historians typically tell the story of America. They usually begin with the coming of the Puritans from Europe, proceed to narrate the breakdown of the Puritan theocracy, consider the Great Awakenings, and, finally, recount the movement of religion across the Western regions of the American landscape. There is also another way that the story of American religion is often told. Rather than being told through a certain narrative construal, it is told through religious symbols that get invested with American cultural content. Some of those symbols have been "errant in the wilderness," new land, Israel, and New Israel. Long claims that both of these approaches to American religious history—the narrative and the symbolic approaches—are inadequate inasmuch as each renders the religious reality of non-Europeans invisible or nonreal. To the extent that this is the case, America defies its promise as a sociopolitical representation of religion as such. That is, it defies the "hermeneutical situation" that it is, a situation in which it has laced within itself the existential question both of being and of religion. In this way, America is a not simply a hermeneutical situation; it is a hermeneutical problem.

The hermeneutical problem that is America is this: How is America to be narrated? This is also to ask: How are existence itself and its meanings to be narrated? In chapter 3, I deal with one person's way of addressing this problem, American religious historian Albert J. Raboteau. Long, too, provides an answer, but from his vantage point as a historian of religions. Getting the "story" right is not a matter of simply adding "the invisible ones," as Long says, "as addenda to a European dominated historical method,"[58] which was Raboteau's plea. Neither is a methodological inversion the solution, one in which black ideological values, or the values of whoever the oppressed group may be, dominate. This, as discussed in chapter 4, was Cone's way of addressing of the problem. For Long, the problem is more profound, and thus a solution must be more subtle and nuanced. The problem is only secondarily a matter of historical

narration; primarily it concerns questions like What is *America?* What is *religion?* What *historical method* allows one to elucidate *American religion?*[59] The last of these questions is especially poignant, for in elucidating America and American religion, one must do justice to the facts of American history and, at the same time, "overcome the concealment of peoples and meanings from the majority group in America, and still further, give visibility to those who were rendered invisible through the concealment." This requires for Long a wholly different methodological orientation; as he says, "The problem has to do with the pattern, the network, the nexus onto which the facts of...history are interpreted. I am raising a question that is very close to the problem of myth."[60]

Long, I think, has raised a most crucial question, one that, in fact, raises again issues that surface especially in chapters 1 and 2 of this book. My concern there in large part is uncovering the mythic or pseudotheological structures of modernity. Those structures are tied to modernity's processes of racialization. Long also is pressing up against this problem, the problem of modernity's generally and America's specifically mythic structures. Long resolves the problem of historical methodology—"the problem . . . [of] the pattern, the network, the nexus onto which the facts of . . . history are interpreted"—with a history of religions-inspired philosophy of history.[61] This philosophy of history has its own theological dimension, which Long captures in the notion of opacity. In Long's case, opaque theology and history contrast with the iconic or incarnational theology and history that mark the writings of the later Raboteau. In this regard, Long provides a counterresponse to the later Raboteau's resolution, as it were, of aporias in Raboteau's earlier work.

How do Long's philosophy of history and theology of the opaque proceed as a response to the problem of "story" and religious "narrative" and "narration"? Following Eliade, Long takes "myth" to mean "the *true* story" of the inner life meanings of the concealed and oppressed in their intersection with the inner life meanings of those who conceal and oppress them. By uncovering this constantly moving intersection, Long seeks to tell "the *true story* of the American peoples."[62] In short, a truer mythology is required to get at America's meaning as religious performance. The true story of the American peoples that Long wants to uncover proceeds from a "second naïveté" that calls into question the tradition of a historical *épistème* that normalizes the American historical facts into an epic or "mighty saga of the outward acts."[63] Such a saga has entailed taming the "wilderness," putting the "savages in their places," or otherwise suppressing the reality and voice of the other. Thus the second naïveté theoretically questions the holiness of the American historical *épistème* or regime of knowledge and national self-understanding. Insofar as that *épistème* tames and conquers the other—that is, the wilderness, the "wilderness creatures," and what are deemed wilderness practices—it perpetuates a myth of dehumanization, and thus is a fundamentally areligious and atheistic discourse of the center.[64]

Theology has been a discourse complicit in this hermeneutic normalization through conquest, suppression, and taming. Indeed, Long's assessment of theology, in the context of coming to terms with America under the moment of the first naïveté, mirrors his assessment of theology vis-à-vis Harnack's resistance to the intellectual coming-to-be of *Religionswissenschaft* as a modern academic discipline. Theology is part of the "hermeneutic mask [that] conceals the true experience of Americans from their very eyes."[65] The interpretation of religion in America, an interpretation that can be broadly called American theology, is not unlike its transatlantic counterpart as represented in a Harnackian approach to theology in that American theology tells of "the saga of the outward acts" of America. Thus American theology is part and parcel of an American mythological language of conquest, a language intent on maintaining the invisibility of the other.

If theological discourse is to continue, it must proceed from a second naïveté in which theology is no longer a discourse of a center–periphery logic with theology itself as a normalizing center. It must recognize the religious primordium or a priori of America, which as religious is always an encounter with what van der Leeuw terms a "Somewhat." The human being, as homo religiosus, establishes its meanings through encountering a Somewhat; that is, the meaning of human existence is attained in its encounter with an oppugnant, nontransparent, and opaque Somewhat or other. Thus human existence is constituted through nontransparent, opaque encounters, in the shadows of which there is being, existence, and meaning. Following from this, religious experience, properly so-called, is an experience that also casts a shadow back on the one encountering the Somewhat. The significance of the Somewhat is that, in a way reminiscent of the dynamic sublime in Kant's account of aesthetic judgment, it is the occasion by which the subject comes to know itself as opaque. In this sense, the Somewhat occasions a dark, darkening, and "black" consciousness, and in this sense it inaugurates life as the "blackness" of "enlightened" reality. Indeed, to employ a language that Long himself does not, but that I find nonetheless expositionally useful even if it partially betrays Long's own intentions, the religious conscience is structured through a luminous darkness.

One can now see more clearly why America, for Long, is a sociopolitical situation of hermeneutical significance, a situation that harks back to a religious primordium, and why America as a hermeneutical situation is a liminal place ever poised to become "another reality," "another place."[66] America's meaning suggests the archaic structures of the religious consciousness, a consciousness obfuscated and hidden, intentionally so, from the majority and dominating culture, but lived in and experienced by the subjugated. Black being is fundamentally religious and mediates religion precisely because it is a hard, opaque, and nontransparent reality through which America, in its encounter with black existence, can become "another reality," "another place." But Long wants to claim that black being is religious in another sense as well. It

is religious insofar as black folks, in experiencing the dominant culture as an oppugnant Somewhat, are made to experience themselves opaquely also. Black existence can make of itself "another reality" as well, a reality fraught with new possibilities. This occurs precisely through the various ways in which it bumps up against the dominant culture. Furthermore, it can be said that in making itself "another reality" through its religious experience of itself as opaque with respect to the dominant culture, black being metaphorically positions itself Somewhere-else and thus pushes America itself to be "another place." One might say that this making of "another reality" and movement to "another place" constitute the sociopolitical contours of opaque, black reality.

It is this ontology of opacity that fuels Long's reticence toward black theology. Take, for example, his chiding of Joseph Washington for accusing the black church of being too consumed with civil rights and not concerned enough with theology.[67] Long takes it that Washington misses the point about how the black church's work for civil rights is a signification of the religious. Long claims that Washington (and the interpretation of theology that he represents) fails to recognize that, insofar as the black church speaks theologically, it does so in a different key than modernity's normalizing theology does. It does so in the intonation of religion as such. That is, it does so out of the opacity of black existence in modernity. In the civil rights struggle, the black church sought to express and insist on black visibility in the face of those intent on making black existence transparent and thus contained within the structures of a white, translucent reality. It insisted on the opacity of (the black) reality and thus was a performative theology of the opaque, one that sought to expose the hypocrisy of the American mythological language.

Embedded in Long's reinterpretation, against Washington, of the meaning of theology is a revaluation of theology's intentions and significations. Long seems to be saying that the civil rights struggle with the black church as its locus in no way means that the struggle followed from the black church's distinctly Christian theological commitments. For Long, the church is foremost a cultural, reflexive expression of the religious as such. It is one such response through which black folks experience their own opacity as they constantly bump up against the oppressor. Thus if the black church, like other black cultural expressions as so many encounters with a Somewhat, has in any sense a theological meaning, it is grounded in and is an articulation of the religious in its original silence. The danger facing black theological speech, which for him is a danger facing all theological speech, is that black God-talk will itself devolve into a power play to master the full silence of the religious, and thus of language and being itself. For the fullness of the religious and the fullness of language are parallel.

Entailed in this claim is another that says that the theological languages of black religion are not and, indeed, cannot be dogmatic. Hence Long's interpretation of the civil rights struggle: "The location of this struggle in the church

enabled the civil rights movement to take on the resources of black cultural life in the forms of organization, music, and artistic expression, and in the gathering of the limited economic resources." In taking on these resources, the cultural–religious black freedom struggle challenged America to be another place and to live from another reality. It was able to do this because of its religious performance of encountering a Somewhat. The spirituals spoke of this other reality, this Somewhat, as God. But it was also often spoken of as another place, a Somewhere, "sometimes the islands of the Caribbean, but more often Africa."[68] What is important to grasp is Long's insistence that the Somewhat and Somewhere not be objectified through a theological discourse of the center. Rather, the Somewhat or Somewhere structures "the black religious consciousness." Indeed, it is "an archaic form in the black consciousness."[69]

Of course, Long does not want to retreat into an ahistorical language of "a *sensus numinous.*" This he recognizes as one of the early problems of *Religionswissenschaft.* Thus about the black religious consciousness and its relationship to Africa, he says:

> [The image and reality of Africa] is an archaic form in the black
> consciousness; it is at the same time a reminder of historical origins,
> an eschatological hope, an affirmation of a vague homeland, and a
> gesture of solidarity with those who also "came to know the man."
> This sense of otherness, or the sense of the other which has arisen
> out of the black experience, is equally present when the black thinks
> of America as a free society; for if blacks are to be free persons in
> American society, this society will indeed have to be a radically different society; it will be in *an-other* society.[70]

So if there is to be a theology—one that flows from the archaic religious fundament of being and that is therefore categorically different from the "centering" theologies of the powerful—of what sort must it be?

Opaque theologies flow from religion as the primal fact of existence. They thus affirm human existence as encounter with a Somewhat. Religion affirms the human as real and thus as opaque. Consequently, opaque theologies affirm the hardness of existence and disavow notions of transparency. They "deny the methodological and philosophical meaning of transparency as a metaphor for a theory of knowledge."[71] Long's critique of James H. Cone's black theology, which is the subject of concern in chapter 4, is instructive in illustrating the point. Long lauds Cone's theology insofar as it insists on the hardness, opacity, and oppugnancy of the black reality. The hardness of the black reality, its opacity and thus the fact that it bespeaks the religious, Cone signals with the claim, "God is black"; Long similarly applauds theologian Vine Deloria's claim that *God Is Red.*[72]

Long's laudations specifically hail the recriminatory note that resounds from such theologies. Though they share American civil religion as a common

denominator of sorts with the dominant American theologies, they nevertheless are opaque theologies insofar as they share American civil religion only
long enough to criticize it for its transparency toward the other. In short,
opaque theologies are theologies of accusation and resistance; they are oppositional.[73] The oppositional nature of such theologies is both ontological and
linguistic, and at root, according to Long, is about power. Hence, Long notes
Cone's ontological claims to the blackness of being and the theological significance of black power in the context of American theology and culture. Cone's
theology, then, according to Long's critique, is antitheological or even nontheological in terms of a centering theology of dominance, insofar as the affirmation of the blackness of being and power denies notions of the transparency of existence first to God and then to the other.

In Long's view, notions of iconicity, which embrace a hermeneutic of
transparency, are epistemologically inadmissible for oppositional theologies,
because "iconic" theologies do not see existence as oppositionally structured
through power: who has it, who does not, and how discourses participate in it.
Opaque theologies, on the other hand, draw out these oppositional structures
of power. It is here that Long makes explicit his understanding of the function
of opaque theologies in critiquing dominant theologies as discourses of power:

> Theologies are specific modes of religious discourse that have be-
> come overwhelmingly predominant within the Christian church.
> Theologies are about power, the power of God, but equally about the
> power of specific forms of discourse about power. These discourses
> are about the hegemony of power—the distribution and economy
> of this power in heaven and on earth—whether in the ecclesiastical
> locus of a pope or, more generally since the modern period, the
> center of this power in the modern Western world. It is this kind of
> power which is attacked in the opaque theologies, for this power
> has justified and sanctified the oppression rendering vast numbers
> of persons and several cultures subject to economic-military op-
> pression and transparent to the knowledge of the West.[74]

Understood from a perspective of a history of religions, opaque theologies
proceed from religion and thus oppose discourses of power that trade on
notions of transparency, which is, according to Long, precisely what theology
as a normative discourse does. What this therefore means is that opaque and
liberation theologies can only be deconstructive. They unmask the operations
of power by using a language intent on restoring the religious as a constitutive
feature of human flourishing in its totality. Stated otherwise, opaque and liberation theologies provide a language for the religious, a discourse for being.
The claims "black is beautiful" and "God is red" are deconstructive in that they
point to a mode of existence formed out of the hardness of reality—that is, out
of an ocular that sees and experiences the "world...as a stone";[75] this as

opposed to the transparency with which the conqueror presumes to construct the being of the conquered. Experiences of opacity are the occasion for the experience of ultimate reality and "the ultimacy of reality,"[76] which is but the experience of encounter with a Somewhat.

Thus there is a demarcating line distinguishing opaque theologies from the dominant and dominating theologies they criticize. That line of demarcation is this: opaque theologies have no wish to reinstate or extend the meanings or structures they criticize. In short, they do not seek to reinstate a theologically "strong ontology," one might say, following philosopher Gianni Vattimo,[77] in which theology is a discourse of power. They criticize the Western theological foundations by ferreting out the transcendent meanings in the notion of God, Christ, church, or what have you, transcendent meanings determined by definable human structures. From the vantage of opaque theologies, these definable human structures inhere, as dominant and dominating theologies would figure it, in the absurdity of oppressed bodies. Thus it is the business of deconstructive theologies, flowing as they do from the priority of the religious primordium wherever it shows itself, to uncover these transcendent meanings and to decenter "the primordium of reason and rationality."[78] The deconstructive and transcending enterprise of opaque theologies, then, is to articulate the meaning of humanity by giving language to the religious element of existence as encounter with a Somewhat without making the fatal move of mastering its silence of being, or the religious. Opaque theologies are a species of negative theology.

This returns us to Long's reticence toward black theology, which shows itself to be a reticence toward theology as such. Cone launched his theological enterprise as a challenge to Christian theology from the stance of (black) power. But power itself, as Long sees it, was insufficiently interrogated in black theology. As a result, in drawing on the work of William R. Jones,[79] Long claims that power in black theology, because of its use of a Christian hermeneutic, comes unwittingly to signify the *transparency* and thus necessity of suffering. A strong, rational structure of thought is thus reconstituted: "The precondition for Black liberation as the objective for Black Theology is the prior affirmation of Black suffering as oppressive."[80] With this precondition, claims Long, black theology falls from its deconstructive posture into the very mode of reflection and way of being in the world that it criticizes. This raises, for Long, the question of whether not just black theology but, as such, "the structure of Christian existence is capable of defining or expressing freedom for those who suffer."[81]

Central to black theology's handicap at this point is how it restricts the experiences and modes of blackness to a "transparent" index of meaning: namely, an index of necessary, if not redemptive, suffering. Insofar as this is so, blackness comes to be overdetermined by the hermeneutic of existence posited by the Christian churches in North America, because they refuse to

theologically account for the religious as it expresses itself in the varied "extra-church orientations" of black culture, which "have had great critical and creative power."[82] In short, black theology, because of its presumption of the normativity of Christianity as universal religion, like the Harnackian theological outlook, cannot account for the "new primordium that is universal within the actualities of history."[83] Stated differently, black theology retreats from its deconstructive posture because it lacks a "Black cultural methodology" that can "[extend] the range of . . . soteriological communication" beyond strictly Christian categories.[84] Again, Long seems to ask, Is this not the fundamental problem of theology as such? "Is theology in any of its manifestations capable of sustaining this conversation or will it be sustained at another level that grows out of a more difficult conversation—a conversation that is an attempt to communicate the religious elements of one's cultural experience to another?"[85]

Alas, we arrive at Long's final criticism of theology qua black theology: it remains a "centering" discourse precisely because its Christian commitments will not allow it to theologize in light of the universal primordium in its various historical manifestations. In this, black theology refuses to proceed in light of the "primordial [religious] structure [of] consciousness," from the proper archaic moment of being—the religious Absolute (my term). In other words, as a matter of methodological procedure, black theology, as a distinctly Christian mode of intellectual reflection, does not ascend to the moment of religion, which as a moment "precedes the master–slave dichotomy." This aboriginal moment is the primal structure of the religious consciousness itself, which precedes theology. For Long, it must be this way, for the Absolute, which is the religious, is the first and proper moment of critique, the place from which to launch "a critique of the critique" or a critique of the Enlightenment itself, and so fulfill the ambitions of the Enlightenment. Critique issues from what Eliade calls the "the mythic consciousness," which Long says, "dehistoricizes the [master–slave] relationship for the sake of creating a new form of humanity—a form of humanity that is no longer based on the master–slave dialectic. The utopian and eschatological dimensions of the religions of the oppressed stem from this modality."[86]

Freedom, Language, and Theology: Speaking in Tongues

In this concluding section, I seek to raise more critical questions concerning the philosophical and theological implications of Long's notion of opacity, as far as they impinge on my concerns here, and in light of these questions to begin looking forward to part III, where I move explicitly to give a theological reading of New World Afro-Christianity, particularly in North America, but

with broader implications for Black Atlantic studies and for the direction Christian theology must go in the twenty-first century.

At the heart of my critical engagement with Long's thought is the question, Does Long's in many ways illuminating and fruitful notion of the opaque, proceeding as it does from the a prioricity of the religious as such, fare in the end better than the modes of theological discourse he criticizes? Does the notion of the opaque as an account of the structure of reality assist any further in disclosing the meanings in black religions and in black religion, and, importantly, in how those meanings disrupt the reign of whiteness? I claim that in part it does, while at the same time ultimately Long's notion of opaque is limited because of the way it understands the "concrete," which also goes to the heart of how Long figures the opaque. I argue that the opaque as an account of the structure of reality is limited insofar as it institutes a new reign, albeit according to a different ocular, the ocular of the different modulations of blackness and of transparency. It is somewhat paradoxical that this is the case, for Long seeks to inaugurate a new, "postmodern" aesthetics within which an opaque ocular can function.

Yet, insofar as it remains committed to a vision of the religious that precedes and enables an account of any given religion in its concrete manifestations, Long, in fact, reinscribes a thoroughly modernist, rational aesthetics. It differs from rational aesthetics only in this: rather than being positioned next to the beautiful as the index of the moral capacities of the human being in its universal powers of cognition, it champions a vision of the sublime that is positioned now next to the oppugnant, the opaque, and the grotesque. The benefit of this shift of perspective is that human existence can no longer be interpreted through an aesthetic calculus that would render the meaning of human existence, by virtue of the (universal) powers of cognition, morally transparent and, therefore, manipulable. Rather, because human existence eludes the x-ray vision, as it were, of a universal, aesthetically rational gaze, every gaze or exercise of thought that attempts to make sense of or narrate the world (the second naïveté) only tells one about the subject doing the narrating and, particularly, its religious or antireligious disposition or mode of being in the world. That is, it only tells of the subject's mode of being in the world with respect to the first naïveté.

This way of stating the matter casts Long's notion of the opaque in terms of what might be called a phenomenology of blackness in its "thereness" as *Sein da*; for the second naïveté is a phenomenological reduction, "a bracketing of experience," Long says, in order to get at the heart of experience. That is, the second naïveté attempts to discover through the givenness of the phenomenon—in this case, the phenomenon of blackness as oppugnant reality—"that link which establishes our existence with the world."[87] Opaque theologies are phenomenological in that they see in religion that primal link of existence with

the world. The structure of the religious therefore repeats itself, as we saw in the case of Long's analysis of the cargo cult, in the structure of the hardness and oppugnancy of reality as occasioned by encountering a Somewhat. Long insists that the reduction "is not a 'leap out of our skins.'" Indeed, it is a reckoning with our "skins," with the density of our somatic and embodied existence, a reckoning that "permits a meditation on our own existence—a meditation possible through the appearance of the 'other.'"[88] Thus the encounter with a Somewhat or oppugnant other, like the Kantian sublime, is gnoseological. That is, it occasions a self-knowledge, which through the reflexivity of thought and existence brings to culmination the immanent powers of concretely existing beings—in this case, black being. With the exercise of such powers, a knowledge and reflective love of the self occurs. Black faith, one might then say, is so many "rituals," broadly conceived, of apocalyptic self-disclosure and self-knowledge. This is because at the ground of this faith is religion as such, which bespeaks the "blackness" of all reality.

Given this, I think two important questions should be raised. The first concerns the very status of the Somewhat that occasions an opaque as revelation of the self. I cannot fully develop this concern and respond to it here; thus, my comments are necessarily cursory, though I give more consideration to the implications for Long's interpretation of Afro-Christianity, which is at the center of my second concern. Central to my first concern regarding how Long interprets existence under the rubric of encountering a Somewhat is the question of whether in such an outlook the other qua other really appears in its own phenomenality and, therefore, in its own distinctness. But additionally, I question how the notion of "encounter" itself is being understood. For if the work of encounter is merely to bring the subject to self-realization in its opacity, then encounter, if it may be called this, amounts to a kind of solipsism between the subject as impoverished and the subject in an opaque orientation toward self-realization and thus toward fullness. In such a case, the Somewhat is but a cipher, a mediating moment, through which subjectivity must be passed on the way toward self-realization. This means that there really is not confrontation with the other as such; rather, the notion of the opaque represents a kind of reversal of the transparent gaze that structures modern racial reasoning and the forms of religious and theological thinking attending it. Both outlooks—the logic of the other in modern racial reasoning, and its logic in Long's theology of the opaque—share this problem: the other as other cannot be a positive, perduring, and irreplaceable reality for the I.

This limitation in philosophical orientation is acutely felt in Long's interpretation of Afro-Christianity as theorized now within the intellectual horizon of the opaque. This is my second point of concern: namely, the bearing such an understanding of the opaque has on how one narrates any given manifestation of culture, including religions in their concreteness. In short,

I am concerned that the notion of the opaque strikes at the heart of Afro-Christianity, bleeds out its content, and embalms it with "the religious."

To explain, it will be recalled that reality for Long embraces a plenitude of cultural expressions. These expressions, which are so many expressions of religion, include, among other things, the various religions. That is, religion as such is not to be restricted to its specifically Christian manifestation of religion among New World black folks. Indeed, it is not to be restricted to any one religion. In this, Long is completely right. But as I see it, it does not follow that the specific cultural manifestations of the religious do not have a certain irreducible opacity in their own right.

The problem to which I refer is starkly seen in Long's consideration of how people of African descent received Christianity through their own tragic and peculiar experience, but filtered through the languages of Scripture and the general structures of Christian belief (dogma). Regarding the use of scriptural language and imagery among slaves and former slaves, Long says, "To be sure, the imagery of the Bible plays a large role in the symbolic presentations [of black religion], but to move from this fact to any simplistic notion of blacks as slaves or former slaves converted to Christianity would, I think, miss several important religious meanings. The biblical imagery was used because it was at hand; it was adapted to and invested with the experience of the slave."[89] There is a sense in which Long is right. Christianity among the slaves was received within the horizon, as he says, of the "the experience of the slave." Thus, the slaves held to "the Trinitarian distinction . . . for experiential rather than dogmatic reasons."[90] In this respect, the God of Christian faith is that *extremely impressive* Other"[91] who is the opaque cipher against which the self realizes or becomes itself. This is why, according to Long, as far as the slaves were concerned, "the modalities of experience of the Trinity is what is most important," modalities that themselves are not necessarily or even essentially historical. They are modalities or modulations within the religious consciousness. The task, then, is to relate these modalities of experience as signified in Christian religion to the "experience of God . . . within the context of the other images and experiences of black religion"[92] as being so many modalities of the religious consciousness in confrontation with a Somewhat.[93]

Long draws on the text *God Struck Me Dead*, a collection of autobiographical remarks by ex-slaves, for two examples that make his point about the "inner dynamics of the conversion experience."[94] In both examples, the religious practice of prayer figures centrally. But Long interprets the slaves' experience of prayer as a fundament of their consciousness. What he seeks to derive from the testimonies, as he reads them, is further evidence that for black folks their confrontation or encounter with God is itself not historical: "Though biblical language is used to speak of his historical presence and intervention in history, we have neither a clear Hebraic nor what has become a

Christian interpretation of history. I am not implying that the deity is a *deus otiosus*, for there is an acceptance of historical reality, but in neither its Hebraic nor its traditional Christian mode."[95] Where, then, does the encounter occur? For Long, it occurs in the crisis of consciousness, which is itself historically framed by black folks' "history in America," a history that has always presented itself, he says, as a "situation of crisis." Hence, "God has been more often a transformer of their consciousness" and "the basis for a resource that enabled them to maintain the human image."[96]

But does not this way of interpreting what happens in any given religious experience, practice, or tradition—in the case of Long's own example, it is the practice of Christian prayer—create more problems than it solves? The first problem is what can be called a positivism of history, indeed, of the black experience of history in America. Such a positivist approach to history has the effect of establishing a sociopolitical positivism in which the horizon or upper limit of black existence becomes America itself. The deep structure of this historical positivism is the black religious consciousness as such, which itself has no history. The task of the historian (of religion) is to uncover the structures of black consciousness by archaeologically uncovering their traces in the sands of history. Stated otherwise, history is but the analytic of consciousness, which itself does not dialogically unfold so as to move and grow, not simply *under* the provocation of encountering an other, but rather *in* the provocation itself such that there is no escaping the encounter. History as structured through the positivity of encounter itself is precisely what Long's notion of the opaque refuses: hence, his philosophical positivism. For Long, history does not structure the religious consciousness as such, and because it does not, religious experience and practices and, at the end of the day, culture itself, are only so many aesthetic accoutrements, at best, of a consciousness that always already, in a priori fashion, is intact. The paradoxical result is that there can be no history within this understanding of the opaque.

It is this general framework that ultimately and problematically prejudices Long's interpretation of the slave testimonies that he cites to justify his claims about history and consciousness. From the testimonies Long concludes:

> These two narratives are illustrative of the inner dynamics of the
> conversion experience. The narratives combine and interweave the
> ordinary events with the transformation of the religious conscious-
> ness. It is not merely a case of God acting in history, for the historical
> events are not the locus of the activity but then neither do we
> have a complete . . . mystification of consciousness. It is the combi-
> nation of these two structures that is distinctive in these narratives;
> clues such as these might help us to understand the specific nature
> of the black religious consciousness. . . . This quality of the pres-
> ence of the deity has enabled blacks to affirm the historical mode by

seeing it more in terms of an initiatory structure than in terms of a progressive or evolutionary understanding of temporality.[97]

The questions confronting such an interpretation of the religious consciousness are these: Does individual consciousness itself (as well as a given community's collective similarity in conscience), have a history, can it progress, and, in short, is it marked by time? If history itself is not the locus of activity, but rather consciousness, "where" then is consciousness? Is not consciousness—like mind and, therefore, thought itself—always refracted through, as Long at one point says, the "absurdity" of oppressed bodies? And if so, as the individual body, as well as the social body or body politic, grows and changes, can it not be said, too, that consciousness, as the way in which one experiences and knows oneself, also changes, and that this change is positive? But is it not also the case that even the way in which one is conscious of oneself and, therefore, the way in which one is self-conscious, are themselves mediated through and structured by an other, as Charles Sanders Peirce, among others, saw?[98]

This would mean, then, that there is a positivity of the other and, therefore, a positivity of difference as such. Long's interpretation of Afro-Christianity disavows what I am calling here the positivity and, indeed, the actuality of difference. This is partly, I think, because he has made the decision that the deity understood in Christian terms as Trinitarian does not positively and actually encounter the creature. Rather, the invocation of a Triune God, from his history of religions perspective, is an expression of the religious consciousness. For Long, therefore, black folks pray because they *have to*. They are a "religious" people, and thus they pray because that's what religious people do: it is in their nature—their consciousness—to do so. Stated differently, the aesthetic practice of prayer is but a trace of the religious consciousness, as it were, realizing and so fulfilling itself through its encounter with a Somewhat. This Somewhat is the crisis situation that America presents to the black religious consciousness. But is this not just another way of saying that as a religious people, black folks remain in bondage, that they are not free, being bound by the determinations of the religious consciousness?

Moreover, what goes unasked by Long is this: Is there any significance, as these testimonies would have it, *to whom* black folks, in the examples given, pray? For those who actually are doing the praying, it appears that prayer is significant as a Christian practice not just because it transforms the religious consciousness. Prayer is also significant because, for its practitioners, as Long's own examples attest, the transformation of the religious consciousness, which itself is grounded in the exigencies of history, transforms the drama of historical existence itself, thus opening it up to a new way of unfolding. In short, for them prayer is a modulation or index of freedom; indeed, by virtue of who it is to whom one prays, prayer *is* freedom. Long again is right in his observation that

the struggles of existence in America push the narrators, in their respective ways, to pray. The hardness of existence in America, then, is the Somewhat that instigates a transformation of the religious consciousness. But if history touches the religious consciousness, which can be provoked to pray, and the religious consciousness (because it is historical) can be transformed by history, then history itself, in some sense, is touched by God; not only that, but God, traveling as it were on the wings of history and, indeed, on the wings of being itself, can, from the interior of being, pragmatically restructure history. Hence, being and time are internally calibrated (*instasy*) as structurally open (*ekstasy*) to be more than any "sinful" determination of history—be that determination slavery in America, Auschwitz in Europe, or Apartheid in South Africa.

This is but another way of saying that God, in Christian terms, is not an-other either to history or to historically constituted beings in the way that oil is an-other to water. Long's notion of the opaque as a means of probing the significance of a deity or deities for the religious consciousness wants to fit the Trinitarian God of Israel into this Procrustean bed. But, as the religious experience and practice of prayer seem to suggest from Long's own examples, God relates to the world as its genuine other not because God is an-other to the creature but because God is first and foremost "non-other" (*non aliud*, as Nicholas of Cusa once put it)[99] to the creature. As *non aliud*, the Triune God of Israel disrupts all logics of creaturely other-ing. This is one of the important claims of Trinitarian thinking, a claim driven from within the practices of Christian faith and spirituality, including, and perhaps supremely, the practice of prayer. Trinitarianism, so understood, renders intelligible the phenomenon of prayer as genuine conversation—that is, as the conversation that decenters all tyranny or ontic and epistemic regimes of power as the ground of existence. It is the conversation that creates new possibilities of existence. As such, prayer as the structure of creation is the conversation or encounter that is the backdrop against which all other conversation or encounter occurs. Such an approach to prayer goes far in explaining how the prayers of the slaves had freedom as their content or animating center. (Herein lay the historical and philosophiccal-theological provocation of the later Raboteau's suggestions in his "Praying the ABCs." See chapter 3.)

This theological interpretation of the "religious consciousness" of antebellum, Christian slaves is, finally, at odds with Long's understanding of the opaque. For with the opaque, through its positivism of consciousness and its archaeological analytic of history, there can be no conversation because there can be no genuine encounter. And this is because the Somewhat is the Somewhat of consciousness. The Somewhat is not, in the theological sense of which I speak, other for consciousness. The Somewhat functions, therefore, within the myopia of the I. It follows from this that there really can be no speech, language, or genuine discourse. Instead, in Longian perspective, the fullness of speech that is being itself becomes muted into the insular silence

of an enclosed, which is to say, positivistically constituted, religious consciousness. This is because the religious consciousness is opaque to all others and translucent only to itself. Thus, only it can interpret itself.

Long's understanding of the (black) religious consciousness, therefore, harbors an aesthetic that, in fact, mirrors the aesthetic performance of whiteness. What is common to modernity's pseudotheological aesthetic of whiteness and to Long's aesthetic of the black religious consciousness is that neither aesthetic "speaks in tongues" (Acts 2), neither knows how to inhabit languages not its own, and thus both are, as Jacques Derrida might say, monolinguistic. Neither knows of the intercommunicability of all speech, thought, and existence, grounded as they are in the unity of the wealth (*simplex et completum*) and poverty (*non subsistens*) of being. Neither do those who operate out of the intellectual dispositions of whiteness or out of the dispositions of the blackness that whiteness has created know how to probe the significance, for a world religiously constituted through race and nation and now through the stateless configuration of bodies in social space, of the fact that being (*esse*) is always being-in-act. It is always *actus essendi*, explicating its fullness in the history of concretely existing beings (*ens*), who display in their own concrete existence just this unity of wealth and poverty and thus just this fullness of existence.[100] Nor lastly, do they grasp that modernity's biopolitical organization operates according to a logic that separates wealth and poverty, aligning the former with certain groups and the latter with others, according to discourses of race that hide themselves precisely as racial discourses. Failing to reckon with this, Long's "negative theology" of the religious consciousness figured through the significations of black religion forecloses the possibility of a Pentecostal overcoming of whiteness on the part of New World Afro-Christian faith and a living into a new logic of existence.[101]

The question one is left with is how to make sense of New World Afro-Christian faith as a *theological* phenomenon that, in its reperformance of the master's religion, disrupts modernity's enslaving narrative of civil or cosmopolitical religiosity. This is just the question, however, that is unanswerable, so I argue in this chapter, within the Longian intellectual framework. Yet it is just this question that I take up in the final part of this book, but only after an interlude in which I briefly consider the significance for this study of the fourth-century theologian Gregory of Nyssa whom I read as an abolitionist intellectual.

Interlude on Christology and Race

Gregory of Nyssa as Abolitionist Intellectual

If [the human being] is in the likeness of God, and rules the whole earth, and has been granted authority over everything on earth from God, who [can be] his buyer, tell me? who [can be] his seller? To God alone belongs this power; or rather, not even to God himself. For *his gracious gifts*, it says, *are irrevocable* (Rom. 11:29). God would not therefore reduce the human race to slavery, since he himself, when we had been enslaved to sin, spontaneously recalled us to freedom. But if God does not enslave what is free, who is he that sets his own power above God's?

—Gregory of Nyssa, Homily IV on Ecclesiastes

In part I of this book, I argue that the modern invention of race or the story of its naturalization is a problem that is pseudotheological or religious in character. More specifically, I argue that behind the modern problem of race is the problem of how Christianity and Western civilization came to be thoroughly identified with each other, a problem linked to the severance of Christianity from its Jewish roots. As Christianity came to be severed from its Jewish roots, it was re-made into the cultural property of the West, the religious basis for justifying the colonial conquest that took off in the fifteenth century with the Portuguese and the Spanish, and that reached a zenith both in performance and in intellectual theorization as colonial and intellectual power shifted to France, England, and Germany begin-ning in the sixteenth century and culminating in the nineteenth century. Remade into cultural and political property and converted into an ideological instrument to aid and abet colonial conquest,

Christianity became a vehicle for the religious articulation of whiteness, though increasingly masked to the point of near invisibility.

Thus, with the advent of modernity, the problem is no longer simply Constantinianism or even neo-Constantianism (as John Howard Yoder or others might say).[1] Rather, it is now the problem of what I would like to call the color of Constantinianism. To raise the issue of color or race in the constitution of modernity is to reckon with how modern political power came to articulate itself not merely in religious terms as if abstracted from the body. It is to reckon with how it does so precisely through the protocols of the body (politic), but now conceived as a body (politic) that bears race. That is, it does so through imagining certain bodies as obedient bodies and other bodies as bodies to be obeyed. The frame of obedient bodies in relationship to bodies to be obeyed, a frame which functions through analytics of race is the frame of the modern body politic. To reckon with this problem, as I seek to do in part I with its focus on the late-eighteenth-century maturing of racial discourse, is to reckon with the political economy of whiteness as the perennial, though increasingly invisible, theological problem of our times.

In part II, I offer a reading of the field of African American religious studies as attempting, through its interpretations of black religion, to theorize religion beyond whiteness and theorize black existence beyond the enslaving and otherwise deleterious effects of the "modernity/coloniality" horizon.[2] While the field has made and continues to make important intellectual strides, its efforts in this regard have had mixed—and, indeed, I contend mostly unsuccessful—results, principally because of either inadequate or no engagements at all with the fundamental problem: how white intellectual formation is in fact a religious, cultural, colonializing, and colonizing formation. In other words, whiteness as a theological problem has been insufficiently treated. At its heart is a problematic vision of the human as closed within itself, sealed off from possibilities of cultural intimacy and thus reciprocity. Rather than the site of intimacy, culture becomes the site of closure and containment. Critical in this is how theological discourse itself was deployed in the interests of cultural closure or of European hegemony over the rest of the world. How did theology come to function in this way? A symbiotic discourse of race and of religion, operating under a notion of the universal, became the new inner architecture of theology: the racial-religious discourse of whiteness. Having insufficiently named and treated this problem, black religious intellectuals have unwittingly perpetuated the theological problem of whiteness. That is, in pursuit of liberation (a goal I share) they have tended to submit non-white existence to theological closure precisely through their appreciation of black folks as contained racial-religious objects rather than as theological subjects in relationship to YHWH as God of the covenant.

Naming the Unnameable Problem:
On the Theological Interpretation of Scripture

To set up the arguments of the three chapters making up the final part of this book in which I consider how New World Afro-Christianity redirects modern racial discourse precisely by redirecting modern Christianity, this interlude briefly engages an aspect of the thought of the fourth-century theologian—called at the Seventh Ecumenical Council of 787 "the father of the fathers"—Gregory of Nyssa. What interests me are the defining features of Gregory's vision of the just society: his unequivocal stance against "the peculiar institution" of slavery and his call for the manumission of all slaves. I am interested in reading Gregory as a fourth-century "abolitionist" intellectual. I speak anachronistically but nevertheless accurately. His antislavery outlook surpassed not only St. Paul's more moderate (but to be fair to Paul, in its own moment, revolutionary) stance on the subject but also those of all ancient intellectuals—pagan, Jewish, and Christian—from Aristotle to Cicero and from Augustine in the Christian West to his contemporary, the golden-mouthed preacher himself, John Chrysostom in the Christian East.

Indeed, the world would have to wait another fifteen centuries—until the nineteenth century, late into the modern abolitionist movement—before such an unequivocal stance against slavery would appear again.[3] And in comparison with the late-modern abolitionist arguments of such luminaries as William Lloyd Garrison, Maria Lydia Childs, and Harriet Beecher Stowe, Gregory of Nyssa's antislavery argument still surpasses. How so? Gregory's abolitionism expresses an exegetical imagination that reads against rather than within the social order. I return to this claim near the end of this interlude. The question I seek to raise now is this: What enabled Gregory to do this? How is his hermeneutical practice as a reader—and, more important, as a pastor and preacher—of the Scriptures able to accomplish many of the ends of a hermeneutics of (feminist, postcolonial, or liberationist) suspicion, while at the same time be more, not less, radical than such reading strategies?

In answering this question, I argue that it was the theological imagination fueling Gregory's exegetical and homiletic practices, and ultimately his orientation as an ascetic thinker of the spiritual life, that enabled his radical theological abolitionism. Moreover, I am suggesting a connection between the theological imagination out of which Gregory operates and the theological imagination that was emerging within certain currents of Afro-Christian faith in its New World dawning. But to return to Gregory, this alone—recognizing that Gregory's abolitionism was tied to his ability to read Scripture theologically—and thus interpret reality theologically—is insufficient to explain his historical uniqueness on the issue. I say this because Gregory's Cappodocian

contemporaries and fellow champions of Nicene orthodoxy—I am thinking here of his elder brother Basil of Caesarea and his friend Gregory of Nazianzus, who became known simply as "the Theologian"—were also *theological* readers of Scripture and interpreters of reality, who in contrast to Gregory accepted slavery as a part of the social order.

Gregory of Nazianzus advanced a theological position on slavery that was basically identical to the position Augustine in the Christian West develops in his magnum opus, *City of God:* slavery, Gregory of Nazianzus says, is a sinful distinction.[4] It is a distinction that arises because of sin, and therefore—and here is the problem—it is a distinction to be accepted as part of the present reality.[5] The esteemed Basil says the same thing: "In this world, then, it is thus that men are made slaves, but they who have escaped poverty or war, or do not require the tutelage of others, are free."[6] Slavery, Gregory and Basil are saying, is, simply put, just the way things are. But Basil goes even further, for while affirming that "no one is a slave by nature" as a part of the argument he works out in defense of the divinity of the Holy Spirit against the Pneumatomachians (those who fought against the Spirit's codivinity with the Father and the eternal Son), Basil nevertheless says the following in his *theological* interpretation of Noah's statement in Genesis 9:25 ("Curse be Canaan; a servant of servants shall he be unto his brother"):

> Men are either brought under a yoke of slavery by conquest; . . . or they are enslaved on account of poverty; . . . or, by a wise and mysterious dispensation, the worst children are by their fathers' order condemned to serve the wiser and the better; and this any righteous inquirer into the circumstances would declare to be not a sentence of condemnation but a benefit. For it is more profitable that the man who, through lack of intelligence, has no natural principle of rule within himself, should become the chattel [*ktêma*] of another, to the end that, being guided by the reason of his master, he may be like a chariot with a charioteer, or a boat with a steersman seated at the tiller [an allusion to Plato's *Republic*].[7]

Having said this, Basil then tries to sand down the jagged edges of his statement by enlisting a problematic theology of creation: "Even though one man be called master and another servant," he says, "nevertheless, both in view of our mutual equality of rank and as chattels of our Creator, we are all fellow slaves."[8]

Thus Basil employs a model of mastery and slavery to understand the relationship between the Creator and the creation. Insofar as this is the case, the sociopolitical logic Basil employs, the logic of the body (politic), is, potentially at least, tied to his broader understanding of the identity of the Creator. Basil's vision of the social order, in other words, in which necessarily some are slaves and others are free, functions as a substitute for the doctrine of

creation at the same time that Basil maintains an "orthodox" theology of creation. Indeed, his orthodox theology of creation gives him a grammar to articulate and thus read Scripture theologically but yet within the social order.[9] In short, both Basil and Gregory of Nazianzus, as did Augustine in the West, made their peace with the ancient institution of slavery and with "the sinful distinction," as Gregory of Nazianzus calls it, between some persons who are slaves and some who are free, some to be bodies of obedience and others to be bodies to be obeyed.

Gregory of Nyssa as abolitionist intellectual theologically refuses this settlement, whereas his Cappadocian comrades read Scripture in such a way as to theologically—yes, theologically—accept it. This presents a disturbing situation for those who advocate reading the Scriptures theologically, a situation that can no longer be evaded; namely, that one can read Scripture within the theological grammar of the Christian faith and yet do so in such a way as to read within and indeed theologically sanction, if not sanctify, as Michel Foucault says, "the order of things."[10]

This all begs the question that I ultimately want to get at in what follows: What is the deeper moment within Gregory of Nyssa's theological interpretation of Scripture that causes him to read against rather than within the social order? For all theological interpretations of Scripture are not alike—as the formation of modern biblical scholarship from the eighteenth into the nineteenth century, that moment when the modern theological interpretation of Scripture as linked to cultural and nationalist ambitions intellectually took off, makes abundantly clear.[11] What is it about Gregory's practice of reading Scripture theologically that makes him an abolitionist intellectual? What compels him to argue for the unqualified manumission of all slaves, a stance that distinguishes him not only from nontheological readers but also from other would-be theological readers of Scripture? It is this question that must be answered. And so, let me begin answering it with an exploration of Gregory's exegetical imagination in the locus classicus of his position against slavery: Homily IV on Ecclesiastes. From there I look more closely at the theological imagination fueling Gregory's practice of reading Scripture. Central here will be his complex Christological understanding of the image of God, which admittedly is far from exhaustively though I hope adequately dealt with here.

The Exegetical Imagination: Gregory's
Fourth Homily on Ecclesiastes

Gregory's homilies On Ecclesiastes were a part of the earlier commentaries he wrote on the ascetical and spiritual life of the Christian reader of Scripture.[12] For Gregory, the goal of the ascetical and spiritual life was the same as the goal of the theologico-intellectual life: the contemplation of God's activity in the

impoverished, suffering Christ at the cross. As Gregory argues in his *Anti-rrheticus against Apollinarius* and reaffirmed in his *Catechetical Orations*, it is "the God revealed through the Cross" that is the subject of Christian theology. This God is revealed in the eternal Christ, wounded from the foundation of the world, which includes his temporal wounding, in the economy of redemption.

Mediating the task of theologically contemplating the eternal Christ and the ascetical practice of spiritually contemplating the eternal Christ is the task of exegetically contemplating the eternal Christ. What this means is that through the mediation of exegesis, which is to say, through the scriptural contemplation of Christ—a task, mind you, that comes into full bloom in the work of preaching and the ministry of the sacraments—theological contemplation (or the task of theology) and ascetical contemplation (or the task of sanctification, or living in the Holy Spirit) have, in the end, the same goal: namely, drawing the reader of the Scriptures more deeply into the unfathomable mystery of the eternal Christ. In being drawn into this mystery or in making increasing progress into Christ, the one engaged in theological contemplation and the one engaged in ascetical contemplation—the scholar on the one hand and the layperson on the other; pulpit and pew—are both engaged in the singular task of having their desires shaped and reshaped by the object of their affection. This is accomplished precisely by coming into deeper union with that object, namely, Christ.

In this regard, the believer's existence as a lover of Christ—one's identity, shall we say—is ecstatic (from *ek-stasis*; this theme returns again in the postlude on Maximus the Confessor as "anticolonialist" intellectual). That is, the self is most fully itself only as it exits the self, only as it exits those modes of identity tied to this worldly order of things, tied to its modulations and modes of power, and tied to the ways this worldly order has structured our loves. The self is most fully itself as it exits that worldly reality—the "cosmos," in Johannine terms; the "totality" as postmodern, critical theorists, might say—so as to enter into a new self, into a new order of love, and thus a new way of being in the world. This new order is the Triune order as "the structure of supreme love."[13] One enters this new mode of existence (*tropos tês huparxeos*), and so dons Christian identity, by entering into the person (*hypostasis*) of the eternal Christ, Jesus of Nazareth. This is the goal, Gregory contends, of both theology (that discourse that reflects on these matters) and the ascetical or spiritual disciplines as carried out in *praktikê*, the life of Christian praxis.

Christian identity, in this respect, then, is leaving behind one mode of identity and ecstatically entering into another. Moreover, this movement by which the Christian is the one who enters into Christ is, according to Gregory of Nyssa, an infinite or unending movement. Referring to Paul's participial usage of the Greek verb *epiktaomai* in Philippians 3:13, he calls it *epektêsis*. While a tome could be written simply on Gregory's fascinating understanding of the Triune God as infinite,[14] what I stress here is actually the flip side of Gregory's notion of an infinite, ecstatic progress or journey into the infinite

God; namely, that the infinite movement or ecstasy into the eternal Christ on the part of both the theologian and the ascetic, through the contemplation of the Scriptures, *is* an exiting of the reality of this worldly order of things. It is an exiting of the reality in which love and desire are idolatrously turned back on the creature to become, as Maximus the Confessor says, a structure of tyranny (*turannos*). What the exegetical contemplation of Christ accomplishes, then, is the liberation of the reader of Scripture from tyrannical self-enclosure precisely by reconstituting the reader's identity in Christ. In other words, the exegetical contemplation of Scripture makes readers more than textualists. Contemplative-exegetical reading, as a form of what Paul J. Griffiths calls "religious reading," is in this respect world transforming inasmuch as it reconstitutes the world of the reader by making the reader an inhabitant, as it were, of the world of the religious text.[15] But even here Griffiths must be glossed, for it is all too easy for such "narrative theology" reading strategies to be textualizing strategies and as such fall subject to Gregory's and Maximus's "tyranny" critique. Contemplative-exegetical reading is the reading that is part and parcel of be made *ek-static* to the reigning order of things. Such reading is a feat of asceticism (*askesis*). It is a feat of asceticism with respect to how one has been positioned in social-space and with respect to how it inculcates one into a different "habitus," as Pierre Bourdieu would say.[16] In other words, such reading remakes, rather than reinscribes, identity. Indeed, in Gregory's case— and in the cases of Briton Hammon (chapter 6), Frederick Douglass (chapter 7), and Jarena Lee (chapter 8) in this book—such reading structures Christian identity and one's relationship to the social order.

If Gregory's later work, especially his massive homiletic commentary on the *Songs of Songs* and his treatise on the *Life of Moses*, reflects on what it means to journey into the luminous darkness of the eternal Christ and so, through him, to progress "from glory to glory" *into* the Triune God, then his earlier homiletic commentary *On Ecclesiastes* explores the flip side of this, which is the opening gesture in the journey into Christ. It explores what it means to *exit* our worldly loves so as to inhabit Christ, or as Paul says to be "in Christ" (*en Christô*) as one's locus of identity and seat of existential orientation. It is in this context that one must situate Gregory's reading of Ecclesiastes generally, and certainly his interpretation of the words found in Ecclesiastes 2:7: "I got me slaves and slave-girls, and homebred slaves were born for me, and much property in cattle and sheep became mine, above all who had been before me in Jerusalem."

On Gregory's reading, Ecclesiastes, the Preacher, has been telling the story of his journey toward wisdom. But that journey has required the Preacher to reorder his loves and thus recognize the proper creaturely status of things. This status is one in which objects disclose God (and thus are theological subjects in their own right) and not merely objects to be owned or possessed. It has required his acknowledgment of his false loves to the social order and that he leave behind those false loves and the worldly order that has structured his

loves toward fleeting, creaturely objects. The Preacher's words for doing this, for both acknowledging what he has loved falsely and leaving behind the worldly order of those false loves in pursuit of wisdom, are "All is vanity" (Eccl. 1:2). Gregory interprets the Preacher in Ecclesiastes 2:2–11 as continuing his account of, indeed as confessing, the ways in which he has loved wrongly, how he has loved the creature and ultimately himself over the Creator. Opening the homily, he says, "We still find the occasion for confession controlling [the Preacher's] argument" (HE, 74). What is the Preacher now confessing? He is confessing his participation in a slave-owning society by having slaves among his possessions. The Preacher is making a public acknowledgment of how vain and futile he has been in this regard and that he could no longer participate in a social order predicated on slaveholding and at the same time be a follower of YHWH or make progress in wisdom.

Indeed, Gregory reads the Preacher as announcing the most serious indictment of the life he used to live. The Preacher was arrogant and smugly comfortable in that arrogance, perhaps so much so that he was blind to the depths of his own vain sinfulness. "For what is such a gross example of arrogance," Gregory has the Preacher ask, "in the matters enumerated above [that is, in the prior verses of chapter 1 of Ecclesiastes]—an opulent house, and an abundance of vines, and ripeness in vegetable-plots, and collecting waters in pools and channeling them in gardens—as for a human being to think himself the master of his own kind" (HE, 74)? Slaveholding, the Preacher comes to see, is the attitude and practice of mastery. It is the very expression and "feeling of Pride" inasmuch as it "turns the property of God into his own property and arrogates dominion to his own kind, so as to think himself the owner of men and women" (73). What does this do, asks Gregory, but lead the one who would be master "[to overstep] his own nature through pride, regarding himself as something different from his subordinates" (73)? It is this acknowledgment or public confession on the part of the Preacher of the vanity entailed in his getting for himself "slaves and slave-girls, and [that] homebred slaves were born for [him]" as part of his concerted campaign to accumulate "much property in cattle and sheep" (Eccl. 2:7) beyond what anyone else "who had been before [him] in Jerusalem" (2:9) had accumulated that opens the way for Gregory's fierce and unparalleled denunciation of slaveholding.

His denunciation begins by calling into question the chief supposition of the slaveholding system: the anthropological distinction between superior and inferior that grounds the logic of mastery and slavery. Drawing perhaps on the argument of his elder brother Basil, Gregory invokes a doctrine of creation that levels all relations within the created order. Since only God is Lord and Master, and therefore everything is subject to God, there can be within the created order no such distinction between human beings as master and slave. What this means for Gregory is that with respect to itself or within the many relations constitutive of it, human nature is free. Human nature is not bound by

ownership. This comes out in Gregory's comment on the Preacher's public confession, "'I got me slaves and slave-girls.' What do you mean" in confessing this? Gregory asks (*HE*, 73). Having raised the question, he answers it by beginning his full argument against slavery:

> You condemn man to slavery, when his nature is free and is self-determining [*eleuthera . . . kai autexousios*], and you legislate in competition with God, overturning his law for the human species. The one made on the specific terms that he should be the owner of the earth, and appointed to government by the Creator—him you bring under the yoke of slavery, as though defying and fighting against the divine decree. (*HE*, 73)

Gregory's use of the terms *eleutheros* (free) and *autexousios* (self-determining) to describe the condition of human nature is crucial here. In an essay on Gregory's fourth homily on Ecclesiastes, Maria Mercedès Bergadá has argued that *eleutheros* covers freedom in the civil and political arena as opposed to external constraint in these spheres, while *autexousios* refers to that freedom by which the self is not held in internal constraint or bondage to itself, to its own desires.[17]

In employing these terms, Gregory points to human nature's freedom from tyranny on all levels, both external and internal tyranny. This means that human nature evinces a sovereignty that itself is an image and likeness of the sovereign God, who is bound by no constraints, neither "external" in relationship to creation nor "internal" in relationship either to the Triune persons themselves or to the divine nature that the persons in their relations to each other enact.[18] Thus, in the proper sense, God is free; while in the analogical sense, humans are free—that is, in "analogy" to God.[19] This means that human freedom is an analogue of and as such participates in the divine freedom. This begins to come out and do important work for Gregory's argument in the lines following the preceding quotation in which Gregory invokes one of the Genesis stories of creation—highlighting on the one hand its language of the human being as ruler and on the other its language of the human being existing in the image and likeness of God—to bolster his case against slavery. In other words, Gregory begins to read the Scriptures intertextually—Genesis and Ecclesiastes as informing each other—in order to unearth a scriptural grammar for a theological anthropology that makes the case for him against slavery. Given the importance of the passage, I quote it in full:

> You have forgotten the limits of your authority, and that your rule is confined to control over things without reason. For it says *Let them rule over winged creatures and fishes and four-footed things and creeping things* (Gen. 1, 26). Why do you go beyond what is subject to you and raise yourself up against the very species which is free, counting your

own kind on a level with four-footed things and even footless things?
"You have subjected all things" to man, declares the word through
the prophecy, and in that text it lists the things subject, "cattle" and
"oxen" and "sheep." Surely human beings have not been produced
from your cattle? Surely cows have not conceived human stock? Irrational beasts are the only slaves of humankind. But to you these
things are of small account. "Raising fodder for the cattle, and
green plants for the slaves of men," it says. But by dividing the
human species in two with "slavery" and "ownership" you have
caused it to be enslaved to itself, and to be the owner of itself.
(HE, 73–74)

It is at this point that Gregory unleashes his full invective against, as we
moderns might say, "the peculiar institution":

"I got me slaves and slave-girls." For what price, tell me? What did
you find in existence worth as much as the human nature? What
price did you put on the rationality? How many obols did you reckon
the equivalent of the likeness of God? How many staters did you get
for selling the being shaped by God? "God said, let us make man in
our own image and likeness." If he is in the likeness of God, and
rules the whole earth, and has been granted authority over everything
on earth from God, who is his buyer, tell me? Who is his seller? To
God alone belongs this power. (HE, 74)

At this point in Gregory's argument, one might think that he is simply rehashing his elder brother's theology of creation, the key moment of which was
Basil's claim that only God is Master. Indeed, does not Gregory himself say as
much at the very beginning of his sermon in a reference to Psalm 118:91? "This
kind of language [the language of getting slaves and slave-girls for oneself] is
raised up as a challenge to God. For we hear from prophecy that *all things are
the slaves of the power that transcends all*" (HE, 73; italics in original).

Though Gregory sounds a lot like his elder brother, I contend that, in fact,
his use of his brother's language is a rhetorical ploy to actually undercut such
an interpretation of God as Creator and Lord. By the time Gregory is done, it
becomes clear that mastery and lordship are not simply conceptually different
from the way we think of and experience earthly mastery and lordship in an
unredeemed order. In such an order, mastery and lordship are inflections of
sheer power. Gregory's theological undoing of the discourse of power both
explodes the logic of earthly lordship *and* disrupts, in Christ, the social imaginary itself by which power sociopolitically displays itself as mastery or as
"power/knowledge," again as Foucault might say.[20] In short, YHWH's lordship is of a wholly different order or economic arrangement (*taxis*). Hence,
Gregory continues the passage above:

[To God alone belongs this power;] or rather, *not even to God himself.* For "his gracious gifts," it says, "are irrevocable" [the gift of Israel's election; Rom. 11:29]. God would not therefore reduce the human race to slavery, since he himself, when we had been enslaved to sin, spontaneously recalled us to freedom. But if God does not enslave what is free, who is he that sets his own power above God's? (*HE*, 74; italics mine)

Since the gracious gift of freedom, which for Gregory is the quintessence of human nature, cannot be taken back (as the definition of a gift requires, Jacques Derrida's interpretation of Abraham's binding of Isaac notwithstanding), it follows that human nature cannot be sold.[21] Human nature and its worth are a mirror (*speculum*), and hence "a likeness," of the infinite.[22] "How [then] . . . shall the ruler of the whole earth and all earthly things be put up for sale?" Gregory asks:

For the property of the person sold is bound to be sold with him, too. So how much do we think the whole earth is worth? And how much all the things of the earth? If they are priceless, what price is the one above them worth, tell me? Though you were to say "the whole world," even so you have not found the price he is worth. He who knew the nature of humankind rightly said that the whole world was not worth giving in exchange for a human soul [cf. Matt. 16:26–27]. Whenever a human being is for sale, therefore, nothing less than the owner of the earth is led into the sale-room. Presumably, then, the property belonging to him is up for auction too. That means the earth, the islands, the sea, and all that is in them. What will the buyer pay, and what will the vendor accept, considering how much property is entailed in the deal? (*HE*, 74–75)

It has been pointed out by scholars such as Lionel Wickham that Gregory is wrong in his analysis of ancient slavery, for as Roman law had it, the property of the person sold is not sold with him. But Daniel Stramara is correct in his observation that Wickham and others completely miss Gregory's point, which is that the human being is and remains free even if we construct a world order, a society, divided between those who own and those are owned.[23]

This contract or, more accurately for Gregory, this covenant of creation that brings forth the creation in freedom to be a likeness to God and so a likeness to God's freedom is not superseded by the contractual or legal structure of Roman society and law. God's covenant of creation as a covenant with Israel—note Gregory's reference to Romans 11:29—endures. Indeed, slaveholding society, Gregory's argument strongly implies, is necessarily supersessionist and Gnostic (in the sense spoken of here in the prelude on Irenaeus). For it presumes the overcoming of the Old Testament by the New. Therefore, Gregory's exegetical practice calls into question claims that Niceno–Chalce-

donian Christianity is necessarily supersessionist against Israel.[24] He recognizes that no "scrap of paper [or] written contract or monetary exchange" can abrogate God's contract, or, better, God's covenant with creation, which is his covenant with the people of Israel (HE, 75). It is this covenant that Christ secures and that he draws all of creation into. Thus, though Gregory does not quite put it this way, one can say that to enter into Christ is to journey into YHWH's covenantal guarantee of the freedom of Israel to be YHWH's people and thus into the freedom of creation to belong to YHWH. This path, Gregory notes, is the theological path of equality:

> If you are equal in all these ways, therefore, in what respect have you something extra, tell me, that you who are human think yourself the master of a human being, and say, "I got me slaves and slave-girls," like herds of goats or pigs. For when he said, "I got me slaves and slave-girls," he added that abundance in flocks of sheep and cattle came to him. For he says, "and much property in cattle and sheep became mine," as though both cattle and slaves were subject to his authority to an equal degree. (HE, 75)

With these words, Gregory completes his argument against the institution of slavery, calling all Christians by virtue of their identity as Christians, whose domicile is the territory of YHWH's covenantal relationship with creation through Christ–Israel, to manumit all slaves. This call implies (and this would not have been lost on Gregory's auditors) the need to restructure society, particularly a society that would claim to be "Christian."

The Theological Imagination: Christ, the Image of God

Given how he winds up his argument against slavery, one might ask whether the actual engine driving Gregory's vociferous opposition to the institution of slavery and, indeed, his exegetical practice is his theological vision, or whether his abolitionist outlook is driven by a broader "humanist," and thus not necessarily theological, sensibility. Is his vision humanism or not, and if it is theological, what difference does this make? At this point in this interlude, I argue on the basis of the very structure of his own argument that Gregory's abolitionism is based in his theological understanding: more specifically, in his Christological understanding of the Image of God.[25] It is his vision of Christ himself as the principle Image or Icon of God the Father, the Image in whom human beings have been fashioned to themselves be images of God, that gives him the vantage from which to offer his critique of the ancient practice of slavery. For all of its speculative depth and daring, Gregory tethers his Trinitarian and Christological vision of the Image of God to YHWH's irrevocable promises to Abraham and through him to Israel. That is, this vision arises

from his theological reading of Scripture. Thus, as it turns out, while to be sure it is Christ who is the Image of God, more accurately it is Christ in his full humanity as Christ–Israel who is the Image of God. He is the "Image" in whom human beings as the "image" have been fashioned. He, as Christ–Israel, is the one into whom human beings are to venture in exiting whiteness and the other racial constructions that whiteness produces.

The Chiastic Structure of Gregory's Argument against Slavery

Gregory employs the familiar rhetorical device of chiasm—from the Greek word *chiazô*—to structure his exegetical argument against slaveholding. Arguments employing this device tend to arrange the clauses constitutive of the argument crosswise. At the center of the chi-structured argument ("χ") is a nonduplicated middle term, which, being the argument's hinge, carries its weight and conveys its crux.[26] Thus, as Nils Wilhelm Lund explains, "the center" of a chiastic argument "is always the turning point."[27] It is the point where "there is often a change in the trend of thought, [the point where] an antithetic idea is introduced." Lund calls this "the law of the shift at the center." Moreover, Lund identifies another important feature of chiastic argumentation that is important for Gregory's specific employment of rhetorical chiasm. He summarizes it under what he calls "the law of shift from center to the extremes."[28] Under this law, "identical terms are often distributed in such a fashion that they occur in the extremes and at the center." Drawing on Lund's analysis of chiasm as a rhetorical strategy in texts of the ancient world, Stramara shows how chiasm structures Gregory's argument against slavery in the fourth homily on Ecclesiastes. He says:

> The basic structure is as follows:
>
> *a* a human being to think himself the master of his own kind
> *b* regarding himself as different from his subordinates
> *c* nature is free, possessing self-determination
> *d* property: irrational creatures
> *e* image and likeness of God: rationality and freedom
> *d'* property: inanimate objects
> *c'* impossible to master the image of God which is free
> *b'* no superiority over subordinates due to title
> *a'* who are you to think yourself the master of a human being?[29]

Drawing on Lund's observation regarding "the law of shift from center to the extremes" in chiastically structured arguments, one can see how Gregory's humanism is radically theological and, therefore, that his abolitionism, lodged within his humanism, is itself radically theological. What enables his abolitionist orientation is how he imagines the key term at the chiastic center of his

argument. This is the notion of the "image and likeness" of God, a notion that bears within it a vision of the human as rational and free. Therefore, the conclusion of Gregory's argument is intelligible only from this theological center. Consequently, Stramara is surely correct in concluding that "the main argument for the abolition of slavery occurs not at the conclusion of [the] homily but at [its] center."[30] Indeed, one might go as far as to say simply on rhetorical grounds that the center operates and orients the claims made at the rhetorical periphery.

But because this rhetorical or chiastic center–periphery logic regarding the image of God is also already a logic of theos, a theologic, it must be asked what the theological content of the image of God, which binds the argument together, is. For the notion of the image is what orients Gregory's posture as an abolitionist intellectual: that is, as one who imagines the human being as free, by virtue of one's creation in the likeness of that image (cf. Gen. 1:26).

I reiterate in this context an idea touched on earlier and point to its significance for the argument I am developing in this book and that I press further in part III. That point is this: Gregory's theological abolitionism plays itself out as a vision of Christ's body as killable and indeed as killed flesh that has been resurrected.[31] His abolitionist orientation is internal to his Easter outlook on the "Holy Pasch" as the soteriological work of Christ. It is an abolitionism that relocates bodies inside the social space of Christ's wounded flesh.

Now, while one might accept the claim that Gregory's abolitionism, or his account of freedom, is broadly theological or religious in nature, one might yet balk at the claim that his abolitionism is necessarily Christological or, put differently, that his vision of the person and work of Jesus Christ gives specific content to his language of the image of God. After all, there is no mention of Jesus Christ anywhere in the fourth homily except in its benediction where Gregory, as a more or less standard way of concluding a sermon at the time, says, "the grace of our Lord Jesus Christ, to whom be glory for ever" (HE, 84). In such an absence of reference to Christ in the homily itself, what warrant is there for the claim that a specifically Christological vision is at work in his abolitionist vision of the human?

The Work of Christ: Easter and the Liberation of Slaves

While it is true that Gregory does not mention Christ explicitly, he does in fact refer to him in an important but implicit way in making his argument against slavery. The implicit reference is to Christ's soteriological work. After saying that only God has the power to buy and sell the human being ("To God alone belongs this power"), Gregory then explains why, in truth, "not even God himself" has this power (HE, 74). This power is precluded on the basis of the nature of God's relationship with the human being as the apex of creation. This

relationship is not one of necessity. Since God did not create out of necessity, God's relationship to creation is not held together through a master–slave relationship in which bondage and necessity are the central features. Instead, says Gregory with recourse to Romans 11:29, the creature's existence is a gift. It is the product of the sovereignty or freedom of God. It is just this freedom that the human being images as the mirror of the very Being, which is the very act, of freedom that brought it forth. Indeed, should it happen that the creature's freedom, for whatever reason, is effaced and the creature becomes enslaved or falls under mastery to another, the only remedy would be for the God of freedom to freely enter the condition of the enslaved creature and from there, the location of the slave, restore the slave to the wholeness of freedom.

Gregory says that it is precisely this that has happened. The creature has fallen into bondage to itself and now is enslaved to all manner of death, chief being physical death. Indeed, before the judgment seat of death, all are equal. "Your origin," Gregory says to the one who would dare own another human being, "is from the same ancestors, your life is of the same kind, sufferings of soul and body prevail alike over you.... Are not [slave and owner] one dust after death? Is there not one judgment for them?—a common Kingdom, and a common Gehenna?" (*HE*, 75). Yet, Gregory also recognizes that while physical death equalizes at the end of life, the sufferings of this life, tied as they are to the history of nations and to social, economic, political, and even intellectual forces and structures, are unevenly distributed. Thus, "social death," as the contemporary sociologist Orlando Patterson calls it, is a manifestation of the bondage of physical death awaiting us all.[32]

Gregory is concerned with the ultimate enemy that is death. But apparently God is concerned with death understood both physically and socially inasmuch as both modulations of death mutually articulate the other. What is to be paid, as it were, to buy the human being out of the "death contract," the contract of physical and social death, which together efface the image of God (cf. *HE*, 75)?[33] By virtue of the human as a mirror of the Infinite and thus as a participant in the Infinite, only the Infinite God could make such a payment. And moreover, the only thing such a God could pay with—and here Gregory's logic interestingly starts to look like Anselm's of *Cur Deus Homo*—is himself. Indeed, says Gregory, God has paid just such a price, for "he himself, when we had been enslaved to sin, spontaneously recalled us to freedom" (*HE*, 74).

That Gregory is rhetorically alluding here to Easter is another matter that would not have been lost on his auditors, for Gregory preached these homilies during the Lenten season of 379 to prepare his congregation for Easter. Moreover, in a sermon that he once preached during the Easter season (*On the Holy Pasch* [*In Sanctum Pascha*]), Gregory makes the explicit connection between the Easter work of Christ and the abolition of slavery:

"This day" then "which the Lord made, let us rejoice and be glad in it" (Ps. 117, 24), not with carousing and reveling, not with dancing and drunken mirth, but with divine thoughts. Today the whole world can be seen gathered like one household for the harmony of a single song and neglecting every ordinary business, refashioned as at one signal for earnest prayer.... And truly the present day is well compared with the coming day which it portrays: both are days of human gathering, that one universal, this partial. To tell the absolute truth, as far as gladness and joy are concerned, this day is more delightful than the anticipated one, since then inevitably those in grief will also be seen when their sins are exposed, whereas the present pleasure admits no sorrow. The just man rejoices, and the one whose conscience is not clear awaits the restoration which repentance brings, and every sorrow is put to sleep for the present day, while none is so distressed that relief does not come from the great splendour of the feast. Now is the prisoner freed, the debtor forgiven, the slave is liberated by the good and kindly proclamation of the church, not being rudely struck on the cheek and released from beatings with a beating, nor being exhibited to the mob on a stand as though it were a show, getting insult and indignity as the beginning of his freedom, but released and acknowledged with equal decency. (*HP*, 7–8)

But as if there were doubts still remaining as to his seriousness about liberating slaves on the basis of the church's proclamation, Gregory says the following to assure his auditors that he is not speaking with mere rhetorical flourish or vacuous fulsomeness:

You masters have heard; mark my saying as a sound one; do not slander me to your slaves as praising the day with false rhetoric, take away the pain from oppressed souls as the Lord does the deadness from bodies, transform their disgrace into honour, their oppression into joy, their fear of speaking into openness; bring out the prostrate from their corner as if from their graves, let the beauty of the [Easter] feast blossom like a flower upon everyone. (*HP*, 8)

And then comes the connection of all of this with Easter and, more specifically, with the one who bears the marks of death-bound or enslaved existence but under the aspect of the resurrection. The resurrection means the liberation of slaves:

If a royal birthday or victory celebration opens a prison, shall not Christ's rising relieve those in affliction? Greet, you poor, your provider; you debilitated and physically disabled, the healer of your sufferings. For through the resurrection hope come zeal for virtue and hatred for vice, since with resurrection removed one saying will

prevail with everyone: "Let us eat and drink, for tomorrow we die" (1 Cor. 15, 32). (*HP*, 8)

The Person of Christ: The Deeper Meaning of the Image of God

But there is another dimension to the work that God accomplishes in Christ that drives Gregory's argument against slavery. This is the dimension of the *person* of Christ, which is the identity that the *work* displays or enacts. The person, along with the work of Christ, is also tied to the notion of the image of God. But to grasp the significance of the person of Christ in relationship to Gregory's emphasis on the theological language of the image of God and how it moves him to read Scripture against the social order, one must look to other places in his oeuvre in which he clarifies the connection between the person or identity of Christ, his *hypostasis*, and what he calls the Image of God. The link Gregory makes between the identity or person of Christ and the Image of God helps us see more clearly how his stance against slavery is internal to his theological outlook.

This is displayed most clearly in his minor dogmatic treatise *On the Creation of the Human Being* (*De Hominis Opificio*), which is an extended theological meditation on the Genesis account of creation. It includes a re-flection on the very passage that he puts at the chiastic center of his argument against slavery in the fourth homily on Ecclesiastes: Genesis 1:26—"Let us make human beings in our image, after our likeness." The key passage for my purposes is in chapter 22 of *On the Creation*:

> I take up once more in my argument our first text:—God says, "Let us make man in our image, after our likeness, and God created man, in the image of God created man, in the image of God created He him [Gen. 1:26]. Accordingly, the image of God, which we behold in universal humanity, had its consummation then; but Adam as yet was not; for the thing formed from the earth is called Adam, by etymological nomenclature, as those tell us who are acquainted with the Hebrew tongue.... Man, then, was made in the image of God; that is, the universal nature [*hê katholou phusis*], the God-like thing [*to theoeikelon chrêma*]; not part of the whole, but all the fullness of na-ture together [*ouchi meros tou holou, all' hapan athroôs to tês phuseôs plêrôma*] was made by omnipotent wisdom.[34]

But Gregory has already made a critically important point earlier in the treatise that must be incorporated into the claims he makes here. It helps us under-stand why it would be a mistake to see Gregory's distinction between the fullness (*pleroma*) of humanity and its historical unfolding as simply a Chris-tianized Platonism in which the fullness of human nature functions as a Platonic form, the form of the human species. He says:

We must . . . examine the words carefully: for we find, if we do so, that
that which was made "in the image" is one thing, and that which is
now manifested in wretchedness is another. "God created man," it
says; "in the image of God created He him." There is an end of the
creation of that which was made "in the image": then it makes a
resumption of the account of creation, and says, "male and female
created He them." *I presume that every one knows that this is a departure
from the Prototype; for "in Christ Jesus," as the Apostle says, "there is
neither male nor female."* Yet the phrase declares that man is thus
divided.[35]

Together these passages display something crucial about the image of God as
Gregory understands it. In the strictest sense, the image of God must be
understood on two interrelated levels. It must first be understood on the level
of the image as "prototype," the level of what he calls the "God-like thing." And
then there is the secondary, but no less real and important, level in which the
image of God as prototype is populated, so to speak, or filled out. On this
secondary level, the image of God in its prototypical form is given spatiotemporal or geohistorical depth and content precisely by being filled out by
actual historical persons, beginning, as the Genesis stories of creation would
have it, with male and female. The secondary level of the image of God,
therefore, articulates the prototype in the numerous creaturely inflections and
differences making it up, beginning with male and female.

But Gregory has another point to make, and it is with this point that one
sees how un-Platonic Gregory is, though he clearly draws on thought forms
and modes of rationality indebted to Platonism. Picking up on the Pauline
language of Galatians 3:28 about there being in Christ neither male nor female, Gregory links this passage to the Genesis stories of creation, interpreting
the statement "God created man . . . in the image of God created He him" of
Genesis 1:27 to be, in actuality, a reference to Christ himself in whom, according to the Galatians passage, there is neither male nor female. Galatians
3:28 gives Gregory a Christological way of understanding Genesis 1:27. Christ
himself is the Image of God the Father, the one who is freedom. As prototype,
he images and, indeed, is the Image of the will of the Father, the archetype, and
thus the freedom of God. Gregory, in his massive treatise *Against Eunomius
(Contra Eunomium)*, casts this in Trinitarian terms:

There is no difference at all between the will of the Son and of the
Father. For the Son is the image of the goodness [of God], according
to the beauty of the original. It's like when someone looks into a
mirror (it is perfectly allowable to explain this by means of material
illustrations): the image conforms in every detail to the original,
which is the cause of the image in the mirror. The mirror-image
cannot move unless the movement originates in the original.

When the original moves, the mirror-image of necessity, moves likewise.

Just so is it the case with the Lord, "the image of the invisible God" [Col. 1:15], who is immediately and inseparably united to the Father whose will he obeys in every movement of his own will. If the Father wills something, then the Son, who is in the Father, wills the same as the Father. Indeed, more precisely: He himself *is* the Father's will [emphasis mine]. For if in himself he possesses all that the Father possesses, then there is nothing of the Father's that he would not possess. Moreover, if he has in himself all that belongs to the Father, or shall we say, if he himself possesses the Father, then, along with the Father and everything that belongs to the Father, he of necessity also possesses the Father's will in toto.[36]

All that the Son is, wills, and does is a translation into the Son's own "indigenous" language as Word (*Logos*), that is, into his own mode of being, all that the Father is, wills, and does. This is Gregory's Trinitarianism (he speaks of the Holy Spirit in the subsequent paragraph). But, what Gregory's claim about Christ the Son, not simply in relationship to the other Trinitarian persons but in relationship to the full complement of human persons (*pleroma*), adds is this: we now see that the translation of the will or freedom of God that the eternal Son is as the Word (*Logos*) of God already contains within itself all of the possible words (*logoi*) of creation. In their creaturely modalities of freedom, all of the words of creation are needed to fully articulate or image the eternal Son, who is himself the Image of the will of the God the Father.

But notice what Gregory is saying. He is saying that the historical Jesus Christ—who while being one individuated human person among many is the eternal Son of the Trinity—is, in fact, in his historical concreteness and particularity at the same time the many of human existence. As the One–Many, he is the Image of God in its primacy. This is what Gregory means by designating Christ the prototype. He is the "whole lump of humanity" (*holon to phurama*) itself or the entire plenitude (*plêrôma*) of humankind, which all of humanity fills out as particular inflections or intonations of the prototype.[37] Thus, as David Bentley Hart says in his interpretation of Gregory:

The "essence" of the human is none other than the plenitude of all men and women, [and therefore] every essentialism is rendered empty: all persons express and unfold the human not as shadows of an undifferentiated idea, but in their concrete multiplicity and hence in all the intervals and transitions belonging to their differentiation; and so human "essence" can be only an "effect" of the whole. Every unlikeness, in the harmonious unity of the body of the Logos, expresses in an unrepeatable way the beauty of God's likeness. The

human "original," no longer a paradigm, is the gift and fruit of every peaceful difference and divergence; and only as this differentiating dynamism is the unit of the human "essence" imaginable at all, as the peaceful unity of all persons in the Spirit, who is bringing creation to pass and ushering in the Kingdom. And even in the Kingdom, that essence will not be available to us as a fixed *proprium*. According to Gregory, the final state of the saved will be one of endless motion forward, continuous growth into God's eternity, *epektasis*; salvation will not be an achieved repose, but an endless pilgrimage into God's infinity, a perpetual "stretching-out" into an identity always infinitely exceeding what has already been achieved; there will always be the eschatological within the eschaton, a continuous liberation of the creature.... The eschaton, thus conceived, brings nothing to a halt, returns nothing to its pure or innocent origin.... [It] is ... a perpetual venturing away from our world, our totality.[38]

It can thus be said that all particular persons, in the unique and often tragic histories that constitute them as persons, by virtue of their residence in the prototype—or stated differently, by virtue of their histories being embraced from beyond themselves through the incarnation—are of eternal and salvific significance. Christ as prototype frees creation in its fullness—from persons and their histories, to the ecological order, to the animal kingdom—to be a symphonic expression of the freedom of God, for in him the opposition between the universal and particular collapses inasmuch as he is the concrete universal (*concretum universale*), the One–Many, that sets all particularity free to exist beyond itself or "to be" in and for God. He is the tune—a jazz or blues tune of suffering divine things—that the symphony of creation, the many, plays.

As "lamb slain from the foundation of the world" (Rev. 13:8) and thus as suffering, killable flesh that culminates Israel's covenant with YHWH as a covenant with creation, Christ's Jewish, covenantal flesh is the harmonic or cadence of creaturely existence. Therefore, according to the theological terms Gregory sets out, human identity must be conceived as an identity constituted in the identity of the prototype himself, Jesus Christ. All particularity articulates the prototype and is an intonation or musical note sounding within the amphitheater of his flesh. As the horizon of all existence, Christ then frees or liberates all beings to, in fact, be and to exist toward the prototype, but within the inflection of creaturely existence.

To be set free in this way is, for Gregory, the very meaning of virtue, which is precisely what Christ restores to humankind. Here is where Gregory's vision of the person or identity of Christ in relationship to the identity of every human being connects to the work of Christ as an Easter work of abolition. He says:

"He made human nature participant in all good; for if the Deity is the fulness of good [*plêrôma agathôn*], and this is His image, then the image finds its resemblance to the Archetype in being filled with all good." Thus there is in us the principle of all excellence, all virtue and wisdom, and every higher thing that we conceive: but pre-eminent among all is the fact that we are free from necessity, and not in bondage to any natural power, but have decision in our own power as we please [*all' autexousion pros to dokoun echein*]; for virtue [*aretê*] is a voluntary thing [*chrêma . . . hekousion*], subject to no dominion [*adespoton*]: that which is the result of compulsion and force [*to katênagkasmenon kai bebiasmenon*] cannot be virtue [*aretê*].[39]

In several other places, Gregory reiterates this point about the incongruence between virtue, which turns out to be a way of talking about the image of God, and enslavement. In *On the Soul and the Resurrection (De Anima et Resurrectione)*, Gregory defines freedom in the following way:

Freedom is likeness [*exhomoiôsis*] to that which is self-determining [*adespoton*] and sovereign [*autokratês*]; it is what we were gifted with from the beginning but what has been tarnished . . . . Virtue [*aretê*] too is self-determining [*adespoton*] . . . . But God is the source of all virtue [*aretê*]. Hence, [to be free] is to be united with God so that, as the Apostle says, "God may be all in all."[40]

Or, in the *Catechetical Orations (Catechetica Oratio)*, he says the following:

He who made humans for participation [*metousia*] in his own [*idiôn*] good, and built into human nature the potentialities for every good thing, so that by them they might be impelled to the corresponding good, would never have deprived them of . . . the grace [*charitos*] of having no master [*adespoton*] and having one's authority in oneself [*autexousion*].[41]

There are several other passages that reflect the point of these passages or related points. On the basis of the understanding of Christ as the Image of God and of humans existing in the Image, Gregory has theological leverage against the social order at the level of how creation fills out the historical existence of the eternal Word as Jesus of Nazareth. He is able to discern the ways in which bondage to physical death, which has arisen as a result of sin, plays itself out in the sociopolitical order. Indeed, he can discern the ways in which societies structure themselves so as to write various forms of social death, from slavery and poverty (to name two of the big ones for Gregory) to the Holocaust, apartheid, and genocide (to name some atrocities of the twentieth and twenty-first centuries), into the very fabric of the social order. Gregory is clear that the sinful distinctions made between bodies—distinctions that call on some to rule

and others to be ruled; some to be killable flesh and others to do the killing—
are distinctions rooted in brute but arbitrary power:

> It is not nature but power that has divided humankind into servants
> and masters. For the Lord of the universe has ordained that only the
> irrational nature should serve man . . . . Therefore, he who is subject
> to you by custom and law is yet equal to you in dignity of nature. He
> is neither made by you, nor does he live through you, nor has he
> received from you these qualities of body and soul. Why, then, do you
> get so much worked up to anger against him if he has been lazy, or
> runs away, or perhaps shown you contempt to your face? You ought
> to look to yourself instead, how you have behaved to your Lord who
> has made you and caused you to be born, and has given you a share
> in the marvels of the world.[42]

What all of this means for Gregory is that God's soteriological action (i.e.,
Easter) is fundamentally a Christological action (i.e., the covenantal identity of
Christ as the Israel of God in relationship to the God of Israel). This soteriological action, its Christological interior, restores the image to its prototype, the
Image. I read each of the figures in part III of this book as engaged in a
struggle to reclaim this insight reclaims this insight but from the underside of
modernity and as turned toward the liberation of dark flesh. Like Gregory, they
see that Christ's life as it reaches its apex in Easter restores the image-status of
all persons, affirming and positioning all persons in the person of the eternal
Christ, the Son of the Trinity, so as to set them free. In so doing, they take up
the mandate of the theological ethics of Gregory's thought, but from the
vantage of those subject to the violent, racial conquest of modernity, the violence of (pseudo)theological whiteness. And this is the theological mandate:
exit the power structure of whiteness and of the blackness (and other modalities of race) that whiteness created, recognizing that all persons are unique
and irreplaceable inflections or articulations, not of the power/knowledge
nexus of race, but of Christ the covenantal Jew, who is the Image of God, the
prototype, and who as such is the fundamental articulation, through the Spirit
of God, of YHWH the God of Israel, the one whom Jesus called Father.

I mention the Jewishness of Jesus here because of its significance for
understanding the I/image of God. An understanding of Christ as the Image
of God and of all human persons existing in the Image, who is Christ, cannot
bypass or supersede YHWH's promises to Abraham and thus to Israel, for it is
from the history of this people's covenantal interactions with God and thus
from God's history that God takes up the history of the world. Moreover, they
are the people whose identity, in being a covenantal and thus a nonracial
identity, is always eschatologically in front of them. It always exceeds them.
After all, it is not until chapter 12 of Genesis and with the call of Abram that
Israel's identity is set in motion after he heeds YHWH's call to leave "Ur of the

Chaldees" (cf. Gen. 12:1–4). In leaving Ur, he leaves behind the identity that Ur assigned to him as Abram in order eventually to be renamed Abraham. This new name indexes his identity as an identity *in relationship*—to YHWH. And yet, it is still not until several chapters later that "Israel" is actually named (Gen. 32:27–29) and further still before they are a people. But what sets Israel's identity in motion is YHWH's call to Abram to leave "Ur of the Chaldees" in order to enter into his identity as Abraham, covenantal partner of YHWH.

To exist in Christ is to be drawn into such an understanding of identity, into the ecstatic and eschatological identity of Israel's covenantal promises.[43] But it is just such a mode of existence that yields freedom, just such a mode of existence that frees all beings to be unique articulations of Christ the Image, the prototype, so that together human beings across space and time might constitute a jazz ensemble that riffs upon and improvises within the eternal Word. Briton Hammon sees this as lifting off with the birth of Christ (chapter 6); Frederick Douglass, calling this a vision of the "pure and impartial Christianity of Christ," sees it as realized in the death of Christ (chapter 7); and Jarena Lee sees it as disseminated through time and space by the Spirit of Christ (chapter 8). Together they redirect race, providing a Christian account of New World black existence, an account that follows the itinerary of Christ's life from his birth through his death and resurrection to Pentecost. What they point to is a way of understanding New World Afro-Christian existence as more than a religious-cultural reflex to the Somewhat situation of the Americas in the face of the Somewhat of an opaque human consciousness. To argue this way is paradoxically to argue against freedom. Rather, what I seek to show is how these writers to varying degrees were pointing to a theological reality structuring the dawning moments of Afro-Christian existence in its wandering through the wilderness of modernity. Part III explores this theological-christological reality. I begin with Briton Hammon.

PART III

Redirecting Race

Outlines of a Theological Program

6

The Birth of Christ

A Theological Reading of Briton Hammon's
1760 Narrative

On Monday, 25th Day of December, 1747, with the leave of my
Master, I went from Marshfield, with an Intention to go on a Voyage
to Sea.
> —Briton Hammon, *A Narrative of the Uncommon*
> *Suffering, and Surprizing Deliverance of Briton*
> *Hammon, a Negro Man*

Without surrendering his divinity God was made our flesh .... By
means of my flesh I was drawing near to God, by means of my
faith I was called to a new birth. I was able to receive this new
birth from on high .... I was assured that I could not be reduced
to non-being.
> —Hilary of Poitiers, *On the Trinity*

Many [black] writers were quite aware that they were reshaping...the
Christian story...within the national crisis of slavery .... They
found a symbolic structure to give a measure of fixity in a life of
painful flux. In this sense, to recall one's history is to renew it.
> —John Sekora, "Red, White, and Black: Indian
> Captivities, Colonial Printers, and the
> Early African-American Narrative"

A number of antebellum texts by black writers employ Christian
theological ideas to envision black existence as free. Individually and
together, such texts as the 1760 *Narrative of the Uncommon Suffer-*
ings, and Surprizing Deliverance of Briton Hammon, a Negro Man,[1]

considered in this chapter; Frederick Douglass's 1845 *Narrative*, taken up in the next; and Jarena Lee's 1836 *Life and Religious Experience* and 1849 *Religious Experience and Journal*, taken up in the subsequent, and final chapter, suggest a critique of the pseudotheological foundations of modern racial reasoning, a critique that would reclaim Christology and, a fortiori, exegesis of the Bible from their deformed statuses. Through their imbedded theological moves, these texts respond in a most insightful way to the modern problem of race generally, and the theological problem of whiteness specifically, as outlined in part I of this book.

But also, the imbedded theological moves in these texts—moves that this and the next two chapters foreground—also suggest an alternative intellectual imagination from that which we saw particularly in the work of the later James Cone (chapter 4) and the work of Charles H. Long (chapter 5). Indeed, through my readings of Hammon, Douglass, and Lee, I attempt to move forward some of the insights of both the early Cone on the centrality of Israel for wrestling with and overcoming the modern problem of race and whiteness, and the insights of the later Albert Raboteau on the entry of all of creation into YHWH's relationship with the covenantal people of Israel through the mediation of Jesus of Nazareth. In this way, racial flesh is transformed into covenantal flesh. In short, I want to move forward Christologically Raboteau's curt but powerful phrase about "Praying the ABCs," a phrase employed to describe the posture of the children of former slaves as the inheritors of historical and intellectual fragmentation. I take up this phrase Christologically as an intellectual orientation on modernity and as arising, as the Latin American philosopher Enrique Dussel might say, from the underside of modernity.[2]

But why these antebellum texts and not others? I have selected these texts as part of making a broad claim about African American antebellum literary history. As a literary theorist or critic might select particular texts for their value in making a certain contemporary, theoretical claim, I have selected these texts for the assistance they lend me in my attempt to bring whiteness into theological visibility and to make a theologically compelling and intellectually serious response to this problem. Moreover, the texts of Hammon, Douglass, and Lee anticipate a number of the insights of later intellectuals in the struggle against racial reasoning generally and the hegemony of whiteness particularly, while avoiding American religious and cultural reflection; yet they avoid some of their most detrimental pitfalls. Through their imbedded claims, these texts help us see that success in destabilizing race as a founding and grounding category of existence is tied to how one imagines the person of Jesus Christ.

In autobiographically probing the meaning of human existence, these texts, some more successfully than others, point the way toward a theologically informed humanism. That is, they draw on a Christian self-understanding to unsettle racial self-understandings. In Christ, identity is instituted afresh in the covenantal humanity of God in Christ. Such a view of things entails

thinking of Jesus in his particularity as the *concretum universale*, the concrete universal, the one in whom all being is embraced. Conceiving Jesus of Nazareth in this way takes us beyond the Kantian moment and its conception of Jesus Christ as the abstract universal that religiously sanctions an oppressive conception of human existence and an oppressive vision of the sociopolitical order of things. In this chapter, I consider how the Hammon narrative captures and is captured by the nativity of Christ, and so antagonistically appropriates theological and, in particular, Christological ideas in the interests of destabilizing racial identity and beginning to theologically challenge the whiteness of modernity.

Theorizing Autobiography: Theorizing Hammon's *Narrative*

There are two principal difficulties facing a theological reading of Hammon's text. The first concerns the status of autobiography generally and the status of black writing within this genre particularly. The second concerns the specific status of Hammon's text (and, as the next chapters show, Douglass's and Lee's) in this genre of literature. Both concerns, which I address in this section of the chapter, center on the question of whether the black self can be adequately represented in autobiography at all, or if the black self always remains contained or captured by it, rather than liberated. Can a free story be told? And if so, under what conditions? These are the quite practical and yet quite theoretical questions that I offer as a preface to the reading of Hammon's 1760 *Narrative*.

Confessions: The Literary Status of Slave Autobiography

Geoffrey Galt Harpham, with a nod toward Paul de Man, Hans Georg Gadamer, and Augustine's *Confessions*, observes, "Autobiography... reflects and produces not self-understanding *per se*, but rather a particular kind of self-understanding, the kind we achieve 'in dialogue with texts.'"[3] This accords with the claims of a growing number of theorists of African American literature; namely, that, in the Bakhtinian sense, African American literature is "heteroglot," "double-voiced," and "polyphonous."[4] In double-voiced speech, one speech act determines the internal structure of another. The second, though hidden, affects the voice of the first by difference.

According to Henry Louis Gates Jr., African American literature is in this way internally "dialogical." That is, it is marked by "successive attempts to create a new narrative space for representation of the recurrent referent of Afro-American literature, the so-called black experience."[5] These attempts are "successive" in that the cross-pollinating and dialogical speech acts are not bounded by time in a purely linear way. In other words, the time of speech—and thus, the time of the self, which engages in speech acts and, I would say on

both philosophical and theological grounds, *is* a confluence of speech acts—is not restricted by *chronos* or chronology. This is why

> we read the relation of Sterling Brown's regionalism to Jean Too-
> mer's lyricism in this way, [Zora Neale] Hurston's lyricism to
> [Richard] Wright's naturalism in this way, and [Ralph] Ellison's
> modernism to Wright's naturalism in this way as well.... These
> relationships are reciprocal, because we are free to read in critical
> time machines, reading backwards, like Merlin moved through time.[6]

Gates goes on to state that the "critical time machines" in which reading takes place are time machines that are dialogical not just with respect to black writers. (This alone is an important point if for no other reason than that it states the obvious: black folks don't all think alike, and they don't all look at the world in the same way. This is precisely why something like dialogism must be the framework through which to understand black literature.) These "critical time machines" bespeak African Americans' literary engagements with other literary and intellectual traditions constitutive of modernity and of the West.

Herein lies, for my purposes, the importance of Gates's reference to lit-erary engagements with the Bible, as a central text of the religious traditions of the West, in "black sacred and secular myths discourse." Gates says:

> The direct relation most important to my own theory of reading is the
> solid black line that connects [Ishmael] Reed with Hurston. Reed
> and Hurston seem to relish the play of the [black writerly] tradi-
> tion.... Both Hurston and Reed write myths of Moses; both draw
> upon black sacred and secular myths discourse as metaphorical and
> metaphysical systems; both write self-reflexive texts which comment
> upon the nature of writing itself; both make use of the frame to
> bracket their narratives within narratives; and both are authors of
> fictions that I characterize as speakerly texts, texts that privilege the
> representation of the speaking black voice, of what the Formalists
> called skaz, and that Reed himself has defined as "an oral book, a
> talking book."[7]

Such is the polyphony of African American literature as a tradition of complex interactions with traditions. Shot through with multiple voices, it attempts to negotiate stratified white-over-black relations by envisioning and creating a new literary space. Harpham's work on autobiography insightfully deepens these remarks with an account of the autobiographer, one who would dare narrate the self and so create a new and liberated space for the self. Harpham's claim is most important in prefacing the analysis of Hammon's *Narrative*. The Ham-mon text is a kind of autobiography, and as such is a precursor to the nine-teenth-century slave narrative, which is also a kind of autobiographic writing.

Harpham says that *mimesis*, or imitation, is crucial to self-narration. "Successfully" narrating oneself implies a nonidentical repetition that, in fact, liberates the self by enlarging it to embrace, revitalize, and re-create reality. In autobiography, claims Harpham, the self is transfigured, which is to say liberated, from enclosure or hiddenness. To autobiographically tell the story of the self is to expand the self and so expand the world. In this way, the particularity of the self through writing comes out of its cloister, as it were, into visibility. The self becomes opaque for others and thus to itself. This is very much a "religious" experience, claims Harpham; he goes so far as to call it a "conversion." Autobiography as conversion configures reality as the dynamism of emancipatory relationality to and for another:

> When we say that autobiography is a discourse of conversion, we seem to have limited and defined autobiography. But when we study conversion itself, this limit expands rather than contracts, and we find ourselves looking at an enlarged category. The basis of autobiography now seems not to reside in a certain set of formal features or thematic concerns but rather in a way of reading in which the reading subject aligns himself in what de Man calls "mutual reflexive substitution" with the subject of a text—in which, in other words, a reader sees himself troped in a text. The writing of autobiography is an act of imitation in which the writer confirms and enacts his own conversion, away from a sense of the uniqueness of his or her being, and to an awareness of its tropological and imitative—and imitable—nature. Augustine is converted not when he simply reads the Pauline text, which he had already virtually memorized, but when he understands that it is a model for himself; and he understands himself when he grasps that he not only can imitate the example of [St.] Anthony and others, but that he has in fact been doing so all along. His ambition for his own text is that it takes its place in the chain of imitable texts, speaking to others as he had been spoken to. He hopes that his text will shatter his readers' self-sufficiency as his had been shattered. Just as conversion leads us to a larger view of autobiography, it also produces a larger and more inclusive view of the self.[8]

Harpham is at pains to show that the conversion language of autobiography is imitative, with a view to remaking and thereby freeing the self for others. Autobiography "translates the self out of selfhood," or self-enclosure, "and into discourse," or communion. Autobiographical writing is thus sociality par excellence. Such writing delivers the subject as an isolated and insulated entity beyond the horizons of an enclosed ego, an oppressive (because bounded on all sides) individuality. The writing of the expanded (racial) self, then, is not the writing of the contracted and confined (racial) subject.

I contend that this lack of identity, in terms of the enclosed ego, concerns, though not exclusively, the dialogical presence of the confessional tradition of spiritual writing in modern autobiography. The self of the discourse of Christian spirituality, to which early black writing in significant ways is related, is not the modern individualist subject. The self of confessional spirituality is an ecstatic and erotic self. Harpham's work on a most basic level is cognizant of this. In seeing the distinction between modern subjectivity and the self in Christian spiritual writing, his work accords with Charles Taylor's important work on the formation of the modern subject.[9] The writing of the self in patristic and medieval Christian spirituality is far from *auto*biographical insofar as "auto" signifies the structures of a modern, self-reflexive, and, in the end, enclosed subjectivity. According to Harpham, autobiography's language of conversion reveals the communality of writer and reader. They are in communion, a relationship of unity-in-difference that holds particularity intact while redemptively delivering the author to the particularity of an "other," namely, the reader. The relationship, however, is not unidirectional, for, interestingly, in autobiography, says Bakhtin, the reader becomes "author" through participation in the author's self, in the author's speech act.[10]

Confessions: The Theological Status of Writing Oneself

A certain shortsightedness does appear in Harpham's argument, however, especially because he consciously draws on Augustinian confessional writing, along with other modern philosophies of the self, as a way to understand the nature of autobiography. He does not make clear whether his linguistic and literary observations carry ontological weight—that is, whether they concern the structures of existence. Is "being" dialogical? Does "being-as-communion" mark reality?[11] And if so, what is the nature of communality? Yet, these are questions that go to the heart of Augustine's *theological* practice of autobiographical writing. Thus, Harpham's insufficient grappling with questions such as these and thus with their significance for the emancipation of the self delivered by autobiography calls for a supplementation of his otherwise insightful analysis.

For Augustine, from whom Harpham draws heavily, the self, along with the rest of creation, is a text that speaks the praise and glory of God. And so the self, like creation, is not a "closed" text ensconced within its own inarticulate invisibility; rather, the self, along with creation as a whole, is communal and in communion. Augustine's claim has a theological warrant: God relates to creation communally, not as another exterior to and at a distance from creatures, despite the fact of the ever-greater difference between Creator and creature. My point in following Augustine is simply to say that, in the strictest sense, God transcends the categories of interior–exterior. Augustine's most noted expression of this comes from the *Confessions* (3.6): "Tu autem, Domine, eras

interior intimo meo et superior summo meo [But Thou, O Lord, wast more within me than my inmost being, and higher than what is highest in me]."[12] Thus, the analogy between Creator and creature founds the analogy within creation as well, the full expression of which Augustine theologically claimed is Jesus Christ, the incarnate Logos. In Jesus of Nazareth there is the liberative communality of human beings and creation in their particularities and according to their *logical* cores—that is, according to who they are as creatures—in relation to the Creator, who ever exceeds them.

The chief difference among humans as the Scriptures portray it is one's status as a Jew or Gentile (Goyim) in relationship to YHWH. And thus difference functions covenantally. It is to be located inside of covenantal communion with YHWH. One can isolate four basic permutations of covenantal status:

1. One's status as a Jew: one in relationship with YHWH by means of YHWH's covenant with the people of Israel.
2. One's status as a Gentile: one not in relationship with YHWH by the direct or unmediated means of YHWH's covenant with the people of Israel.
3. One's status as a Jewish Christian: one in relationship with YHWH by the unmediated means of YHWH's covenant with the people of Israel with Jesus of Nazareth (Yeshua) as Messiah with YHWH's covenant.
4. One's status as a Gentile Christian: one in relationship with YHWH by means of YHWH's covenant with the people of Israel but only through the mediation of one from among this covenantal people, Jesus of Nazareth, the Messiah of Israel who as such is head of the Church.[13]

Given this taxonomy, the question of the meaning and status of whiteness as a Western, principally Gentile Christian, phenomenon can be theologically interrogated. If whiteness is understood nonessentially—if it is understood not as a given ("I'm just white; how I got to be so is, in the end, irrelevant," I can imagine someone saying) but as a feat or an accomplishment within the Western imagination, indeed as the history of an accomplishment—if whiteness is understood in these terms, the question then is, What did it and its history accomplish?

Its accomplishment was one in which Western, mainly Gentile, Christians no longer had to interpret their existence inside another story—Israel's. Rather, its accomplishment was to make Israel's story a moment within understanding the story of Western civilization as the story of white accomplishment. In this sense, Israel's story was made white: was made a moment within the mythical-poetic imagination of the West. Stated differently, whiteness is the accomplishment of interpreting the self simply by reference to oneself, and in this respect it is the uniquely "Christian" accomplishment of no longer having to

understand Christian identity as unfolding within another reality, the reality of Israel's covenantal story with YHWH. In other words, insofar as it is a distinctly "Christian" phenomenon, whiteness is the accomplishment of no longer having to leave behind a prior reality so as to enter into another one, although this is precisely what Abram, Hagar, Jacob, Ruth, and the Ethiopian Eunuch, to name just a few, had to do.

Ur of the Chaldees: *leaving* this place is Israel's story. As the very structure of the book of Genesis suggests, Israel is a people whose identity arrives later. It arrives only after being held in suspense for several chapters: Jacob is not renamed Israel until chapter 32. Israel is always catching up with itself. Its identity is deferred.[14] Nevertheless, the very deferral of Israel's identity is constitutive of its identity. Deferred identity is part of their story.[15] Indeed, even when Israel "arrives" at their identity, when they are named as a people, they can never fully seize it. Like Jacob–Israel, they must rely on the grace of the angel of YHWH to give them a name. Indeed, if the eminent Jewish scholar of the Hebrew Bible Jon Levenson is correct, even when one generation of the children of Israel arrives by grace at their identity, subsequent generations must nevertheless reappropriate and pursue afresh what it means to be Israel.[16] Each generation must re-receive the name of Israel from YHWH. This is the meaning of the covenant. The evangelical mission of Israel, by virtue of its form of life as the people of YHWH's covenant, is to witness to this covenantal story, which is the story of creation. This is their special election. But it is an election that is not to the exclusion of the world; rather, it is for the inclusion of all, to bring all into relationship with YHWH.[17]

By contrast, the accomplishment of "Christian" whiteness is the accomplishment of staidness and closure—indeed, of enclosure and thus bondage to race—as the new ground of identity. It is the accomplishment of no longer leaving where you were and going to a place, as YHWH says to Abram, "that I will show you" (Gen. 12:1–4). Whiteness fully accomplishes itself in the violent processes of extending its accomplishment of racial enclosure to nonwhite flesh, such that they become (inferior) racial accomplishments as well, the lesser mirrors that reflect the accomplishments of whiteness back to itself. With regard to populations internal to a given body politic, the violent processes of extending the accomplishments of whiteness to nonwhite flesh and to immigrant groups is called assimilation.[18] With regard to populations external to a given national body politic, an example of the extension of the accomplishments of whiteness to nonwhite flesh is evident in both the American slave trade and the wider problem of Western colonialism.

Augustine's performance of autobiography in his *Confessions* challenges this, inasmuch as it tells the story of the self as the story by which Augustine gave up or exited the story of accomplishment as closure and entered into a different history of accomplishment. Such is his politics of conversion. In this different history of accomplishment, the self realizes itself only as it enters

into God's accomplishment of creation—and this is the story of Israel— through the mediation of Jesus of Nazareth. Thus, for Augustine, autobiographical interiority, because it is mediated by Christ, becomes a "reciprocal interiority," an interiority with interhuman depth and that therefore witnesses to interhumanity.[19] It is this that a proto–slave narrative like Hammon's captivity narrative taps into insofar as one reads it, as I do with some assistance from Harpham, as "Augustinian."

However, the Christological ground of "Augustinian" autobiographical writing (the ground that grants it an interhuman and thus a nonessentialized depth) has an even deeper theological or Trinitarian warrant. As just indicated, in Jesus Christ there is the liberative and expansive communality of creation with its Creator, the ever-greater Other. For Augustine, the possibility of such communality lies in the Trinity. Though articulated in terms drawn from Plotinian Neoplatonism's understanding of emanation, Augustine's understanding of the communality of being undergoes baptism in Christian thought. Neoplatonism is transfigured by a doctrine of *creatio ex nihilo*. In itself the creature is nothing and from nothing; which is to say, in itself creation is invisible, enslaved to itself, and finally mute. Yet being's sublimity lies in its transcendence to itself evident in the dynamism of its unfolding that occurs ontologically in its becoming and empirically in history for the realization of its destiny of union with God.

Thus from the perspective of the dynamism of creation generally and of the human being specifically, who exists in the image of God, the creature is from God and the ground of its being ultimately is God. Thus the complementing theological claim of *creatio ex nihilo* is *creatio ex Deo*. God is the source of all being, the One from whom all creatures proceed, the possibility and ground of creaturely self-articulation in God's own nonsolipsistic utterance of Godself as Trinity. The creature exists within the "emanationist"—or, better, Trinitarian and sophianic—structure that is God. This procession, however, is not an emanation in continuity of essence, though it is related to God's essence. Rather, the "textual" continuity between Creator and creature is the continuity of God's self-determination to create through the eternal Word (*Logos*) and in the Holy Spirit. In this way, the Father remembers or autographs himself, as it were, in the eternal Word or Son of the Trinity, and thus in creation, which comes to be through the Son, the express image of the Father in the Holy Spirit.[20]

Augustine's *On the Trinity* gives a clue as to how his autobiographical *Confessions* as text participates in the Father's eternal writing—the text, as it were, that is the begetting of the Son, who is the image of God, through the Holy Spirit. The latter books of *On the Trinity* (books 9–15) probe the deeper recesses of human experience. Out of this probing emerge Augustine's famed psychological analyses of human being as image of God. Certainly, however, in the modern sense of psychology, the analyses are less than psychological

accounts of human existence. For Augustine's account of *mens* is intended to show how human existence necessarily opens up to and has the capacity for God. The psychic for him, then, is triadic: *mens–notitia–amor, memoria–intelligentia–voluntas*. The triadic structure of human being, however, is what it is because it is an image of the Triune God, a kind of emanation in the sense outlined above. Augustine's account of the triadic structure of the human *mens* attempts an account of how *vestigia Dei* structure being, the human being in particular.

Given this, Augustine's mapping of the human mind or soul through the vestiges of God upon it attempts an account of how being exists finally beyond itself, that is, "in" God, and so how creaturely being is ordered to God, but in such a way as not to occlude the ontological difference between created and uncreated natures: human being is fundamentally different from God. What relationship there is between God and God's creation is by way of creation being *in* the Image of God. And so, in itself, creation has no essence of self-possession. It is sheer gift, a gratuitous ecstasy, a beautiful of the Beautiful. Since the human being bears the image of God by being *in* the Image, and along with all created natures comes forth from God, human being is the parchment, as it were, on which God writes God's own self through and in another. Bringing the self to literary visibility in some sense participates in God's own self-announcement in another. When this participation fractures— that is, when the creature's self-articulation collapses into self-enclosure—the freedom and visibility of the creature becomes occluded. This Augustinian claim will prove crucial in understanding both what I want to do with the theological and scriptural claims embedded in the Hammon story and why I see the need to build on the implied theological claims of his narrative.

From what has been said, it is evident that Augustine's self-portraiture, as Harpham rightly observes, is of necessity a theological account of the self: indeed, of Augustine's own existence. It is an account that recognizes the autobiographical possibility of *Confessions* as text and of Augustine's own existence as textual, or narratological, residing in the radical nearness of God to the self, a nearness that, in fact, frees the self for confessional communicability. This communicability, as far as the *Confessions* goes, is a literary performance of the *imitatio Christi*, as well as an imitation of the saints insofar as they as saints—in the mode of existence that is particular and unique to each in his or her own specific *imitatio Christi*—reflect the *imago Christi*. Seen in this light, the performance of the *imitatio Christi* is an autobiographical remembrance of the Image of God, a remembrance that reshapes the world precisely in remembering the self. In fact, within the Augustinian schema, the world itself is an *imitatio Christi* made alive in the Holy Spirit in the mode of creaturely becoming, and it is the task of the human being to see the world as such (theological aesthetics) and to work for it to be such (theological ethics). Existing in the image of God, then, is a theological *datum* that also names a

theological task or a pragmatics. That task is this: the discovery of the mystery of the Trinity through bringing to fruition the image as likeness in the self and so in the world.

Augustine's *Confessions* is engaged in this task literarily through its narration of the self. It charts the path of Augustine's movement into likeness with God: it charts the journey of his conformity to the Image and, in so doing, offers a narrative of the world within which that transformation is intelligible.

It is precisely here, at the juncture of Christology, that my reading of Augustine to supplement Harpham must be refined. In *On the Trinity*, Augustine clarifies that to be conformed to the Image of God is to

> copy the example of this divine image, the Son, and not draw away
> from God. For we too are the image of God, though not the equal
> one like him; we are made by the Father through the Son, not born of
> the Father like that image; we are image because we are illuminated
> with light; that one is so because it is the light that illuminates,
> and therefore it provides a model for us without having a model itself.
> For it does not imitate another going before it to the Father, since
> it is never by the least hair's breadth separated from him, since it is
> the same thing as he is from whom it gets its being. But we by
> pressing on to imitate him who abides motionless; we follow him
> who stands still, and by walking in him we move toward him, be-
> cause for us he became a road or way in time by his humility, while
> being for us an eternal abode by his divinity.[21]

Augustine sees that it is possible for those who are the image of God to copy God, a task that he autobiographically performs in the *Confessions*, because in the most proper sense we are images of the Image of God, the eternal Son, who incarnate is Jesus of Nazareth. And so the task is to copy, or better, to exist within the eternal life of the Son incarnate.

This is what the Hammon text, perhaps unwittingly, attempts, as discussed below. For now, it is worth reiterating: the legislation or writing of the Father, the Father's own autobiographical text, is the Son of the Trinity, who is eternally with the Father. The yoke between autobiographer and autobiography, between author and text—in short, between eternal Father and eternal Son—is the Holy Spirit, who ever "qualifies" the writing of the Son and the Father's eternal understanding of himself, as it were, through the Son.[22] Given this general theological frame of reference, it must be the case, then, though Augustine here does not make it explicitly clear,[23] that in the Father's autobiography, who is the eternal Son in his eternal generation from the Father through the Holy Spirit, there is already the mysterious autobiographic articulation of creation; for the Father's self-articulation in the text of the Son is already filled with all difference—indeed, even the difference of creation itself. In the Father's eternal articulation of himself in the eternal Son, which occurs

as a (hypostatic) display of the divine essence, is the eternal speaking of himself as Creator as well. However, the latter occurs as a display of the divine will.

An Augustinian mode of Christian thought concludes from the fullness that is God, a fullness that is both at the level of the hypostasis and at the level of the divine essence, though of course the two cannot be neatly pulled apart, for in the divine life both features of divine coinhere. This fullness is that from which creation acquires being. In short, this relationship with the "outside" that is "beyond" the divine nature is determined by the Father in his dyadic relationship with the Son that in an eternal movement rests triadically in the Holy Spirit, according to Gregory of Nazianzus in his third theological oration, which is the first on the Son.[24] This is the theological structure of the auto-biographical within which is the possibility of the visibility of the creature. In the divine economy is the creature's existence, an existence that in speaking itself echoes God in whom, to speak apophatically, resides the supraessential fullness from which emerges all that can possibly be. This emergence of crea-tures, however, their *creatio ex nihilo*, is, in fact, a *creatio ex Deo*, because creation or being that is always becoming is a product of the will or energies, the un-fathomable expressivity, or beauty and wisdom, attending God's *esse*, or better, God's supra-*esse*. In biblical, rather than metaphysical, parlance, should there be creation, it will come to be through the Son: "All things were made through him."

This, the Augustinian heritage, is the context within which autobio-graphical writing as spiritual narration of the self finds final intelligibility. As book X of *On the Trinity* would seem to suggest in the context of this discus-sion, autobiographical writing as an act of self-remembering (*memoria sui*), self-understanding (*intelligentia sui*), and self-willing (*voluntas sui*) is, by the time one gets to book XIV, a trinity of remembering, understanding, and willing God. In the remembering, understanding, and willing of God, the world is reenvisioned through autobiography in a way that is consistent with a theo-logical self-understanding. Remembering, understanding, and willing God is the ever-greater context within which the remembering, understanding, and willing of the self is performed. The latter participates in the former as its united eschatological horizon and protological ground. And so there is the sense that for Augustine, the Trinitarian writing that is God calls forth from eternity, albeit in a temporal mode of that eternity (we call this time), the various temporal writings of the self in the genre of autobiography.

Confessions: The Question of the Status of Hammon's 1760 Narrative

From this one can begin to grasp how all writing and particularly autobio-graphical writing is a theological act. Of its nature, it is transgressive: the self can only be seen as a self and inscribed as such insofar as its intertextuality is reckoned with. Theorists such as Harpham and Gates thoroughly understand

this. My point is that the claim about the intertextual and polyphonous nature of the self has a deeper theological warrant, a warrant that when lost can lead to tyrannies of oppression. Modern racial reasoning is one such oppression.

Beyond the general question of the possibility of autobiographical writing, there is the more specific question of the possibility or impossibility of such writing as a way to tell a free story when engaged in by black folks as racial subjects. The problem is exacerbated, not diminished, precisely when theology is thrown into the mix. Is this not the point, in part at least, of work by such scholars as literary historian William L. Andrews and literary critic Bradley Scott Born?

Andrews identifies Hammon's 1760 Narrative as "the beginning [of] black autobiography."[25] This beginning, however, is not unproblematic, either literarily or theologically. Literarily, Hammon's tale, along with a number of other early writings by black authors, was dictated to, even cowritten with, whites. For this reason, his story raises the question as to whether "the black self can materialize in a white frame";[26] that is, it brings to the fore the phenomenon of "Black Message/White Envelope."[27] Theologically, Hammon's tale seems merely to lend further support to a racial ideology of white superiority buttressed by Christian discourse and ideas. His self-portraiture—a fourteen-page drama of fast-paced adventure, intrigue, and deliverance—was "cropped and framed according to the standards of an alienating culture." Hammon thus seems to celebrate "the acculturation of blacks into the established categories of the white social and literary order"[28] and, one may add, of the theological orders that reinforce the color line of white–black purism and white-over-black stratification.

In entering the fray of this discussion, I do not assume the mantle of literary historian or source critic in hope of clearly distinguishing the voice of Hammon from that of his editor. Rather, with assistance from recent work in early American literary scholarship, I approach Hammon's enthralling tale of deliverance with theological—more specifically, Christological—questions in view.[29] I am interested in how Hammon's literary gesture insinuates a decidedly theological response to the racial indexing of existence. In employing Christological categories and ideas within which to materialize the black self, the Hammon Narrative reclaims Christianity as salutary for Hammon's own, and thus for human, flourishing. His textual reclamation invests Christology with liberative possibilities that were yet to be realized at the time of his writing. Insofar as Hammon's text marks an emerging, certainly contested and ambivalent, moment of New World Afro-Christian faith, it signals the need for more complex interpretations of black religion. For as there can be resistance through the rejection of "the religion of the master," there can also be resistance through its appropriation. In the latter case, the resistance effects renewal.

The strategy of appropriation is not lost on John Sekora, an insightful commentator on early American literature. He notes that Hammon's tale in

many respects imitates that of a contemporaneously published captivity narrative, that of a young white male, one Thomas Brown. The Boston publisher Green and Russell released in a third edition the Brown captivity tale just a few months before releasing the story of Hammon's adventures. It is most likely not coincidental that in some places Hammon's *Narrative* repeats, virtually verbatim, passages from Brown's tale. Doubtless, the closeness between the tales in formal literary structure—that both "[use] essentially the same layout and typographical style . . . [and that] both undergo uncommon sufferings, [though] Brown's deliverance is 'remarkable' and Hammon's is 'surprising' "— is part of the mimicry to which I call attention. That closeness notwithstanding, Sekora still says:

> Outside [the] pages [of narrative], slavery was a wordless, nameless, timeless time. It was a time without history and time without immanence, the only duration slaveholders would permit. The slave narrative changed that forever. Many [black] writers were quite unaware that they were reshaping that forever. Many writers were quite aware that they were reshaping for their own lives the Christian story of the Crucifixion within the national crisis of slavery, and they were not daunted. They found a symbolic structure to give a measure of fixity in a life of painful flux. In this sense, to recall one's history is to renew it.[30]

To be sure, Sekora is looking forward from the captivity genre to the slave narrative, from Hammon to the likes of Harriet Jacobs (*Incidents in the Life a Slave Girl* [1861]), Frederick Douglass (the 1845 *Narrative*), and others. Yet what comes to fruition in slave narrative—namely, the effort to literarily overturn the silent nihilism of slavery as "a wordless, nameless, timeless time," the recovery of black being through speech that gave "a measure of fixity in a life of painful flux"—has its impulse, as Sekora suggests, in the captivity narrative.[31] This initial impulse happens through "Briton Hammon's presence as a subject for a captivity" tale. The introduction of Hammon as subject for such a tale, as already indicated, "for a time expands the scope of the captivity tale, but at the same time it creates the terms of possibility for the slave narrative . . . . The earlier tale of Indian captivity is easily turned to the later story of southern bondage. One escape teaches another."[32]

It is true that Hammon's presence as a black person, captured and surprisingly delivered, gives new depth and dimensionality both to the captivity genre and to the overall making of American literature.[33] However, Sekora's important observation also suggests that making a black person the subject of a captivity tale represents more than just literary broadening. It signifies theological expansion as well: "Many [black] writers . . . were reshaping . . . the Christian story . . . [drawing on its] symbolic structure . . . to recall . . . history [and] renew it." Hammon's tale of capture and deliverance engages the Chris-

tian story as "a symbolic structure within which to recall . . . history" and thus provocatively proposes a Christian theological framework, the divine economy, as that within which to materialize the black self.[34] In this, Hammon's tale suggests a theological reading of black existence, a reading that literarily calls it forth *ex nihilo* from the inarticulate *nihil* that was American slavery. The Hammon tale sees the Christian encounter, upon which theology in stammering speech meditates, as a source of the black self. It suggests that "deification" (*theôsis*), which refers in classical theology to one's being conformed to God through one's existence in Christ, is freedom. The *Narrative* portrays Hammon as "Christoform" and as materializing under the sign of the cross and within the mission of the Son. The self is claimed and narrated through an appropriation, rather than a mere dismantling, of Christianity and its heritage of theological ideas and experiences. If slave narrative writers such as Jacobs and Douglass, for instance, "were quite aware that they were reshaping . . . the Christian story," an important beginning of such a strategy is apparent in Hammon's tale of capture, deliverance, and entrancing intrigue.

That the editors of Hammon's story sought to employ Christian theological ideas to reaffirm, reinforce, and further establish "the color line," to employ an anachronism, is no small matter. In its literary pantomime, it parrots much of the logic of white slaveholding Christianity. In many respects, the story reinforces the codes of Enlightenment racial thought and the central place accorded to Christianity in founding and maintaining its discourse and social vision. The way *Narrative*, or perhaps more accurately, its amanuensis–editor, employs Christology as a frame within which to materialize the black author, albeit stripped of authority, affirms as much. It suggests, on one level, a Christology wedded to white racial supremacy and nonwhite subservience. In framing Hammon's return to his "good Master" after thirteen years in terms of a Christological movement of *exitus–reditus*, of kenotic departure and return—that is, as the movement from Christmas ("On Monday, 25th Day of December, 1747, with the leave of my Master" [3]) to Easter ("*My good Master was exceeding glad to see me, telling me that I was like one arose from the Dead, for he thought I had been Dead a great many Years, having heard nothing of me for almost Thirteen Years*" [13; italics original].)—*Narrative* invokes divine sanction on racial stratification in the social order. That is, it reads within the social order. Thus, it appears to affirm the notion that blackness has significance only as a parasite on whiteness. The possibility of autobiography seems to be denied, and so freedom becomes a dream deferred. On this reading, the Hammon tale reinforces a wholly untenable moral vision of the good—namely, that severed from whiteness, being is no-thing. Stated differently, severed from whiteness, black being is nonbeing.

Andrews's remarks bring attention to this problematic and readily apparent dimension of Hammon's *Narrative*. For Andrews, Hammon's message is clear: "Let the slave stray outside the known world of stratified white-over-black

relationships . . . and he will risk a life in limbo. He will become a type of the lost soul, disconnected from civilization's preserving institutions, sustained solely by the survival instinct." The black voice—if it is a "black" voice at all, given its mediation by an amanuensis–editor—speaks in affirmation of a racially stratified world of white superiority and black, if not all-out enslavement, certainly subservience. Andrews draws attention to the central role of theological language in facilitating white-over-black superiority in Hammon's self-portraiture. Indeed, such language virtually drives the narrative. Andrews observes, "Only 'Divine Goodness' is strong enough to restore the black man, 'like one arose from the Dead,' to his patron."[35] Andrews here singles out the social function of Easter rhetoric in Hammon's tale and points to the complicity of the language of the divine attributes—"Divine Goodness"—with racial oppression in the early American context. This complicity is continuous with the ontotheological bolstering of modern racial reasoning in Kant's discourse.

Bradley Scott Born's insightful work reaffirms Andrews's conclusions but in even more poignant terms. Born says, "Drawing upon the captivity narrative, the spiritual autobiography, and its related Christian typology of the sea, Hammon recounts the pilgrim's progress of a black man . . . . But this literary and religious acculturation proves [problematic], for despite Hammon's . . . Christian meditation . . . he remains very like a slave."[36] That is, Hammon's captivating tale leaves him in the end a captive, not to Native Americans but to colonial Americans, the institution of slavery, and the very structure of modern racial thinking. Born also points out that "the demands of the genre"[37] were as much religious and theological as they were literary, and as such they qualified and circumscribed Hammon's presence as a black person. Indeed, the genre was such that black being was allowed only so far as it was bleached, sanitized, and whitened. Hence, apart from the singular reference to Hammon as "Negro" on the title page, he racially does not exist. Yet by sleight of literary and theological hand, he does exist through attachment to his "good [white] Master," restoration to whom is his "surprizing deliverance": he once was lost, but now is found, "like one arose from the dead." Born thus rightly points out that Hammon remains captive to the conventions and intentions of early American captivity discourse, which it used as a pattern or symbolic structure through which all reality could pass for the construction of history. Early American captivity discourse thus invented a history—a cultural history—for a people who ostensibly lacked one. With the introduction of Hammon, a "Negro," into the genre, the reality of slavery and white-over-black relations was made to pass theologically through the template of Indian captivity. The result is that Hammon as black author remains captive to the social pieties espoused by the genre.

The place of Christianity in facilitating and maintaining Hammon's captivity within the captivity story, as Born sees it, is worth stating again. To the

extent that Christian language and its symbolism of water even allow for the materialization of a black autobiographical subject, to that same extent they "[delimit] the black mariner's identity" as well.[38] Hammon can be author only insofar as *Narrative* "[resurrects him back] into slavery,"[39] the institutional white church, and the stratified racial relations of colonial life.[40] He is allowed to be an author and to have public literary presence. This, to be sure, is novel. But he can do these things only as he affirms the social order. And this, to be sure, is not novel.

That Hammon's thirteen-year ordeal, 1747–1760, culminated in its publication as a captivity story is not without significance. Its publication comes at the height of the American provincial years, 1700–1755, when slavery among the English colonists was taking deep root. Winthrop D. Jordan observes, "[Slavery] ... forced the colonists to come to grips with novel problems which arose from the nature of the institution."[41] The confusion was mainly legal, revolving around the question of what colonial, and then American, slave society ought to be. Legal questions, however, were but an index of a broader sociocultural question: How ought white males relate to peoples of African descent so as to maintain control over a burgeoning black populace?

> While the colonial slave codes seem at first sight to have been in-
> tended to discipline Negroes, to deny them freedoms available to
> other Americans, a very slight shift in perspective shows the codes in
> a different light: they aimed, paradoxically, at disciplining white
> men. Principally, the law told the white male, not the Negro, what he
> must do ... to enforce slave-discipline.... This surely was a novel
> situation.[42]

The burgeoning presence of peoples of African descent and the rapidity and intensity with which slavery as an institution was establishing a foothold in North America—these were at once the boon and bane of the newly emerging republic. Again, Jordan observes:

> During the first quarter of the eighteenth century Negro slaves
> poured into the English colonies on the American continent in un-
> precedented numbers. This sudden enlargement of the slave popu-
> lation meant for white men a thoroughgoing commitment to slavery;
> the institution rapidly thrust its roots deeply into a maturing
> American society. For roughly the first sixty years of the eighteenth
> century slavery itself grew without appreciable opposition, ...
> gradually becoming barnacled with traditions, folkways, and a
> whole style of life."[43]

The captivity narrative as an indigenous colonial and folk literature suggested ways of navigating the social straits (as it would do during the Revolutionary War) in the face of such growth. Along with the gallows literature of

puritan New England, it offered a vision for a certain style of colonial life, one that reinforced white-over-black relations, justified through notions of racial purity, and sanctioned through a Christian religious mythology.[44] Hammon's presence in the genre, given the historical moment, is thus most important in reading the Narrative's ambivalent relationship to Christianity as a mode of existence, form of discourse, and skeletal structure within which to render visible black existence. Both Born and Andrews foreground how the Hammon Narrative, through Christian rhetoric, affirms slavery as a necessary institution for American social existence. They also highlight how Narrative was intended to assuage the white slaveholding conscience by suggesting the supposed black acceptance of a life of servitude. Indeed, Born's reading emphasizes how the Narrative communicates to a white readership that slavery as a form of life most suits the Negro, who accepts it under divine sanction. The message of Hammon's Narrative, then, according to Born, is that "the world beyond the shores of Massachusetts is a perilous one from which only reenslavement [can save]" Hammon and the burgeoning black populace of New World America. Hammon and his fellow blacks are "loose fish made fast again"[45] only in slavery, subservience to their "good Masters," and worship of the Christian God identified with the Christmas–Easter story of Jesus Christ.

But do not Andrews's and Born's respective readings of Hammon's Narrative, as important as they are, beg the possibility of a more "subtle war" being waged for the theological materialization of black existence?[46] Stated differently, the readings they offer seem, in my view, too one-dimensional. Born alludes to the possibility of Narrative's speaking on multiple levels; however, it would seem that racial critique waged within the very language that supposedly sanctions racial difference—namely, Christian theology—is not a possibility. Can there be a reading of Hammon's Narrative in which there is writing under a kind of erasure, a reading that restores Christianity as a liberating mode of existence and that restores Christianity's internal discourse of Christian theology as indeed a liberating rhetoric? If this is, in fact, a possibility, then there is a way in which the Hammon text can be understood to speak autobiographically within the voice of faith so as to lay claim to a freedom realized within faith.

Born observes that putting Hammon forward as a subject worthy of spiritual autobiography is a "strategy of the pen [that] proves to be a double-edged sword."[47] Drawing on Angelo Costanzo's study of eighteenth-century black autobiography, Born puts his finger on the double-edged moment in the development of American literature and its literary configuration of black being. He notes, "Adopting conventions of the spiritual autobiography enabled black narrators to cast themselves in the significant role of a Christian pilgrim whose life was connected with God's eternal plan."[48]

In the next part of this chapter, I follow Born's suggestion as applied to the literary economy of Hammon's Narrative. That is, I do what neither he nor

Andrews do for Hammon's *Narrative*: namely, offer a reading of it in which Hammon plays "the significant role of a Christian pilgrim whose life was connected with God's eternal plan" and in this role outlines an account of black existence that begins to overturn modernity's pseudotheology of racial reasoning. The genre of spiritual autobiography affords the Hammon story a way to reconceptualize black existence by joining it to the divine economy in Jesus of Nazareth. Here is where one encounters the sleight of pen in what Hammon's captivity saga unwittingly does: it locates the *logos*, or meaning, of black existence beyond the confining structures of race. The intertextual countervoice within Hammon's tale is to pull its readers into Hammon's struggle to leave "race"—to leave "Ur of the Chaldees"—and to convert, that is, to enter into another reality in which identity is reframed. This other reality is the story of Jesus of Nazareth as the leader of a movement *within* ancient Judaism.

The reading of the Hammon *Narrative* that I offer, then, is one in which the tale addresses the theological flaw that made possible the racial–metaphysical gaze, which Kant was theorizing for modernity at the very time *Narrative* was published. Kant, you will recall, drew on and altered Christology to accomplish this, severing Jesus from his Jewish roots and thus Christianity from Judaism. Hammon's *Narrative* does not jettison Christology as the solution to the modern racial problematic; rather, it returns to it in an effort to autobiographically renarrate and restore it and thus move toward a Christological account of freedom instead of bondage. This freedom, which is inaugurated in the birth narrative of Christ, comes literally to pass on the day of Hammon's textual birth, which the opening line of his tale indicates as December 25, 1747, the day he took leave of his "Master." To a closer consideration of his story we now turn.

A Theological Reading of Hammon's *Narrative* of Uncommon Sufferings

The reading of Hammon's tale of "uncommon sufferings" that follows does three things. Its first objective is to establish that Christian theological ideas frame the *Narrative*. More specifically, I show how the *Narrative* calls on Christology to represent self, nation, and world. Linked to key events in the narratives of the life of Jesus Christ as recorded in the Synoptic Gospels, the events making up the Hammon saga are held together by a messianic metanarrative. Indeed, messianism—of what sort, this, too, will need to be examined—is the urnarrative to Hammon's *Narrative* and thereby frames a vision of "scripturalized" and thus scripturally authorized national identity. That is, *Narrative* offers an enchanted vision, one established through Christological tropes, of nationhood and citizenship or national selfhood.

This anticipates my second objective for this part of the chapter: namely, isolating or being more specific about the nature of the messianism with which one is confronted in the Hammon saga. Clearly, the Hammon story encodes a form of messianism that articulates itself as American exceptionalism, an emergent American nationalism, and ultimately an American peoplehood. Hammon as a literary figure (or perhaps, better, "the Hammon persona"[49]) is the prop by which that exceptionalism, nationalism, and a conception of what it means to be an American people is represented. This, I think, goes some way in explaining the absence in the story of any real reference to Hammon as an enslaved black person or to his capacity to wield agency and authority in his own right. The reading I offer here suggests that though the Hammon persona may literarily be the protagonist of the tale, Hammon as black person is not its object as such. Its object is the subjectivity and consciousness of a nascent nation, a people in the process of transitioning from colonized outpost to sovereign nation-state.

Under the authority of an amanuensis–editor, Hammon's *Narrative* is conscripted into the construction and representation of an emerging sense of America and what it means to be a New England people, a people finally distinct from Old England. The Hammon text wants autobiographically to represent and work toward stabilizing the "I"-ness of this fledgling national self and to call on the symbols of theology and Scripture to assist in accomplishing this. What I want to establish under this second objective is that autobiography of what will soon be the "We" in the Declaration of Independence's "We the People" is being written as scriptural exegesis. The goal of this literary–exegetical enterprise is the Americanization of the modern racializing of Constantinianism, the establishment of American Christendom. In representing and constructing "the people" as American nation within this pseudotheological framework, the amanuensis–editor under the Hammon persona seeks to reorganize America's relationship to the European nations and their colonies.

My third objective in the reading offered here of Hammon's *Narrative* is to do what William L. Andrews has advised the critic to do when attending to narratives such as Hammon's: namely, to "pay special regard to seams or cuts [and creases] in these enclosed narratives," for these cuts and creases may prove "subversive to the text, when the presence of colorless white screens is deconstructed long enough for the absence to call attention to itself and demand a creative hearing for the silences in the text."[50] Thus, in this last gesture, I point to how a counterautobiographical construction of the meaning of nation and of black existence—one that would subvert the narrative of nation and its embedded narrative of whiteness that the Hammon persona seeks to tell—is struggling to emerge. Or stated differently, my task is to establish how against the grain of its dominant plotline the Hammon tale is also the record of a nascent Afro-Christian sensibility struggling to articulate itself both with and against modernity, indeed, from the underside of modernity.

My claim is that this counternarrative, rather than ceding the terrain of the Bible, occupies it counterexegetically, and in so doing issues a muted challenge to the dominant, pseudotheological vision of the modern construction of self, nation, and world and the codes of whiteness that are its interior analytic. The challenge occurs at the site of the psalmody that concludes the *Narrative* and reveals that the theological topos under critical interrogation is the same topos that was distorted in the modern production of whiteness and the blackness (and other racial inflections) that whiteness created. This topos is Christology in which Jesus Christ and Christianity came be to severed from their Jewish, covenantal roots. My last objective is to give a sense of how this Afro-Christian sensibility, and the Christological counterexegesis by which it functions, works, and to do this to set up how this Christian sensibility still struggles for articulation in Douglass's 1845 *Narrative* and in Lee's writings.

From the Birth of Christ to the Death of Christ: Hammon's Narrative and the Theological Performance of Whiteness

Telescoping the movement of his departure from and return to his master, the complete title of *Narrative* effectively summarizes the story. It reads:

> A Narrative of the Uncommon Sufferings, AND Surprizing Deliverance of Briton Hammon, A Negro Man,—Servant to General Winslow, of *Marshfield*, in New England: Who returned to *Boston*, after having been absent almost Thirteen Years, Containing an Account of the many Hardships he underwent from the Time he left his Master's House, in the Year 1747, to the Time of his return to *Boston*—How he was cast away in the Capes of *Florida*,—the horrid Cruelty and inhuman Barbarity of the Indians in murdering the whole Ship's crew:—the Manner of his being carry'd by them into Captivity. Also, An Account of his being Confined Four Years and Seven Months in a close Dungeon,—And the remarkable Manner in which he met with his *good old Master* in *London*; who returned to *New-England*, a Passenger, in the same Ship.
>
> BOSTON, Printed and sold by GREEN & RUSSELL, in Queen-Street, 1760. (2)

Hammon's story begins with his departure from his master, quite importantly, on Christmas day, the "25th day of December, 1747" (3), to go on a sea voyage. The reader is not told why Hammon departs from his "good old master." Is he on assignment; or, might he, in fact, be fleeing slavery in the New England colonies? An audible silence shrouds the *Narrative*'s opening words. Perhaps the silence signifies an editorial attempt to convert the story of a runaway into a tale of captivity. Speculating on this may have its benefits, but what is most important is the story as we have it, and as we have it Hammon's sea

departure does seem to deliver to him a modicum of "freedom" and "equality." On the sea, Hammon the "Negro" becomes Hammon the human being, and Hammon the New England servant becomes, at one point in the story, Hammon the full, British citizen. This is quite significant given that in 1760 when the *Narrative* was published, there was no independent, sovereign United States of America. Thus, in intimating that Hammon was a British citizen, the *Narrative* puts him on par with the other American colonists, who themselves were British citizens. Moreover, note the frequent use of the pronouns "I," "we," and "our" in the opening Christmas scenes: "I went from Marshfield . . . [and] . . . I immediately ship'd myself on board of a Sloop . . . bound to Jamaica" (3); "We sailed from Plymouth in a short time" (4); "We sailed for the Bay" (4); and "We loaded our Vessel" (4). Passages such as these indicate Hammon's humanity and agency, and in so doing they prompt the question of the significance of linking the opening moments of the *Narrative* with the biblical story of the birth of Christ. Such linkage seems to suggest that a Christian vision of reality, one that takes its bearing from the biblical birth narratives, is the basis of freedom. In becoming free on Christmas day, Hammon, it would seem, is represented as Christoform.

But such a reading is quickly called into question, for as Hammon gets further removed from North American shores, and thus from North American bondage, the very sea that granted him freedom places both him and his newly acquired freedom at risk. As the story has it, what makes this risk ultimately unbearable for Hammon is the fact that he is alone in the world. He is without a benevolent master to safeguard him from the malevolence he is to encounter on life's "restless billows," a malevolence, mind you, that Hammon would not have had to face had he not given in to seduction by the luscious fruit of freedom.[51]

An important purpose of the story it would seem, then, is not so much to construct and represent Hammon as an autonomous black agent as it is to accomplish two other closely tied objectives. The first of these objectives, it would seem, is to construct Hammon as fallen, as sinner. That is, the *Narrative* wants to represent Hammon's movement from a prelapsarian condition on American shores to his postlapsarian experiences with various, subsequent masters. Indeed, within the economy of the *Narrative* we discover that there are various kinds of masters—some kind, others less so. Thus, Hammon soon learns that not any master will do; only the master of his prelapsarian condition will suffice. In short, Hammon needs his American master, General Winslow, the master from whom he originally took flight.

With this, we discover perhaps the central purpose of the Hammon story: the construction and representation not of black agency and freedom per se but of what sets America apart as an emerging New World nation from the surrounding nations and peoples of the Old World, and especially what sets them apart from Britain, who in the colonial imagination is Old, rather than New,

England. On this reading, then, Christmas represents not so much the moment of Hammon's literary conformity to the image of Christ vis-à-vis his nativity or birth into freedom. Rather, it represents his fall, his having become a sinner and his subsequent passage through "baptismal waters"—literally on the sea—of purgation, renewal, and ultimate return to the homeland of his enslavement.

But here is where the *Narrative*'s second objective becomes clear. Christmas functions to represent America as prelapsarian and halcyon, as an edenic "Father"-land to those such as Hammon, who are in need of redemption. Though the *Narrative* foregrounds the former aspect of Christmas (i.e., the construction of Hammon as a fallen sinner on a salvific journey back to American enslavement), its deeper, less explicit interest, I think, is in subtly portraying the latter (i.e., the representation of America as a land on a redemptive and messianic mission).

Before saying more about how I see this messianism working itself out, allow me to justify some of the claims I have so far made by giving a reading of the *Narrative* beyond its opening, Christmas lines.

Not long after taking leave of his master, Hammon discovers that the sea is a dangerous place, a place where his humanity is held onto only tenuously. Quickly things turn for the worse: "We were cast away on Cape Florida," he says, "[and] . . . we knew not what to do or what course to take in this our sad condition" (4). The seafaring adventure comes to an abrupt halt as a band of Native Indians massacres the crew, takes Hammon captive, and, alas, sets the ship ablaze. In accordance with the conventions and intentions of the captivity genre, the *Narrative* demonizes Hammon's marauding assailants by attributing their raucous and vandalizing activity to barbarity and outright savagery. They are not human, so the *Narrative* suggests, and therefore ought not be expected to act in a civilized manner.

But here one wonders if this is Hammon speaking, or if it is an indication of editorial tampering? One wonders this because the *Narrative* seems immediately to compromise its own observations about the savage and demonic nature of the Native Indian captors when it notes that, for reasons unknown, they act mercifully (a divine attribute) toward Hammon. That is to say, they spare his life. For what reason? After all, they slaughter his shipmates, from the predominately white crewmen down even to "Moses Newmock, [a] Molatto" (6). With Hammon as the recipient of mercy at the hands of his captors, the *Narrative*, no doubt contrary to its intention as a piece of colonial captivity writing, acknowledges the Indians not as savages but as human beings.

After a number of weeks, Hammon eventually eludes his Indian captors and is rescued by Spaniards. This works to his detriment, however, for the Spanish, who had a colonial outpost in Cuba, in due course take him as their property. But from his plight with the Spanish, Hammon, we are told, was rescued by the governor of Havana, who "paid them ten dollars for [him]" (7).

Thus, the governor in effect purchased Hammon's freedom. Hammon was then allowed to stay in Havana and serve in the governor's employ and in this way avoid returning to either the Indians or the Spanish. But in the twelfth month of his employment to the governor of Havana, Hammon is again abducted, but this time, he says, by a "Press-Gang who immediately prested me... [to] go on board the [King of Spain's] Ship" (8). Upon refusing to board, he is imprisoned for four years and seven months. Through a series of events orchestrated by "kind Providence," the Havanan governor eventually gains knowledge of Hammon's "deplorable Condition," and "[delivers him] from the Dungeon" (8–9), returning him to the governor's service.

Events subsequent to his return to the governor's employ reveal that Hammon's service in the Havanan government was not a matter of political convenience as the *Narrative* intimates in the earlier scene of the purchase of Hammon's freedom by the governor. By the end of the present episode, on the other side of his second imprisonment by the Spanish, a crease emerges in the *Narrative* in which we learn that Hammon all along was held against his will by the Havanan governor, a condition from which he attempted to escape on numerous occasions. Indeed, says Hammon, "I endeavour'd Three times to make my Escape" (9). It was only in the third attempt that he succeeded. Thus, so far in the story, three groups are placed in an unfavorable light: the so-called savage Indians, the Spanish, and the Spanish governor of Cuba.[52] In the hands of each of these groups, Hammon's life and freedom are placed in jeopardy.

But there is a fourth group that is also represented unfavorably: namely, the British. How so? Well, as the story goes, Hammon succeeds in absconding from the Havanan governor by stowing away on an English warship. The ship's commander is one Captain Marsh, who is identified as "a true Englishman." His credentials as "a true Englishman" are confirmed by the fact that upon hearing the Spaniards' demands for Hammon's return, Captain Marsh "refus'd them" as he "could not answer [their request] to deliver up any Englishmen under English Colours" (11). It is at this point that the *Narrative* opens a fold in which Hammon's humanity is affirmed precisely through the affirmation that he is a British citizen and not common property. Hammon responds to this with loyalty as evinced by the fact that he joins the British navy and begins his commission as a sailor on Marsh's warship. All of this seems to suggest that the sea in general and the British in particular actually do deliver Hammon into a life of freedom, a life in which his humanity, agency, and will to self-determination are affirmed.

But as I have been cataloging, according to the *Narrative*, the sea is a place of danger, and this is no less the case now that Hammon has found a place of ostensive freedom among the British. For now with the English, Hammon finds himself once again upon the sea in numerous battles in various warships. Indeed, at one point, Hammon comes within inches of his life, "wounded in the Head by a small shot" (12) as a result of a battle in which seventy of his

shipmates were killed. And so, even with the British, Hammon remains in need of a deliverer.

The penultimate paragraph narrates the events leading to this deliverance, which entails his "miraculous" return to his original master and thus back into colonial- and state-sanctioned slavery. After serving on Captain Marsh's warship, Hammon found himself in England and commissioned to serve on another ship, which happened to be bound for New England. "Surprisingly," again the *Narrative* says, General Winslow, his long lost master, is aboard the ship. Hammon's "good old master," upon seeing him, is overjoyed: "My good Master was exceedingly glad to see me, telling me that I was *like one arose from the Dead*, for he thought I had been dead a great many Years, having heard nothing of me for almost Thirteen Years" (13; italics mine). The theological language that the master uses—that Hammon was like one resurrected from the dead—is critical here, for with these words the entire *Narrative* comes full circle, showing itself to be articulated between the bookends of the Christmas birth and Easter death and resurrection of Christianity's central character, Jesus Christ.

But who is "Jesus Christ" in the economy of the *Narrative* if not General Winslow himself, who like the Son of God departs from his halcyon abode to enter upon a messianic mission of redeeming sinners—like Hammon?—and restoring the "lost sheep" to the national fold (cf. Matt. 15:23–25; Luke 15:1–6)? Here "Jesus Christ" is a trope for General Winslow, who himself is a stand-in for the nation, the people of colonial America. He, too, enters the oppressive wild seas, reaching athwart the Atlantic to find Hammon after what may have been a thirteen-year search for a runaway. But as framed in the *Narrative*, General Winslow's intentions are benevolent in contrast to the Indians, the Spanish, the Cubans, and now the British. His intentions are a revelation of the goodness of an emerging American national character. What all of this means is that the slave owner General Winslow, insofar as he is a synecdochic figure for the nation, is the true object of the *Narrative*. But it also means that Hammon's sinful Christmas 1747 departure requires, according to the religious and pseudotheological economy of the *Narrative*, his resurrection or Easter return to slavery. Such a return affirms the messianic qualities of the nation and the people. Moreover, only in returning to the land of redemption can Hammon's "baptismal regeneration" on the rough and untamed seas of the world, in confrontation with savage and nonsavage masters alike, be efficacious.

Christology Redux: Hammon's Narrative and the Afro-Christian Struggle with and against Modernity

But does this state of affairs, the fact that a "black message" becomes sealed in an editorialized "white envelope," leave Hammon's *Narrative* as nothing but a text that ventriloquizes the messianic interests and vision of an emerging

nation? Are there seams, to use Andrews's terms, within the *Narrative* that, given a creative hearing, begin to articulate a countervision of self and nation? I contend that there are, particularly within the climactic paragraph of the *Narrative*. It is especially there that a scriptural, and indeed a theological, counternarrative of Hammon's existence and of the meaning of nation and peoplehood can be faintly heard against the pseudotheological master narrative. Indeed, it is there that we find the traces of an Afro-Christian sensibility struggling with and against modernity itself.

At the *Narrative*'s meridian point, Hammon is portrayed as sharing in his master's elation at having found him. He sings joyfully of the prospect of his "[return] to [his] own Native Land" (14). His exultation and sheer revelry at the prospect of returning to General Winslow are expressed in a biblical idiom. He says:

> And now, That in the Providence of that GOD, who delivered his Servant David out of the Paw of the Lion and out of the Paw of the Bear [cf. 1 Sam. 17:37], *I am freed from a* long *and* dreadful Captivity, among worse Savages than they; *And am return'd to my* own Native Land, to Shew how Great Things the Lord hoth done for Me; *I would call upon all Men, and Say,* O Magnifie the Lord with Me, and let us Exalt his Name together [Ps. 34:3]!—O that Men would Praise the Lord for His Goodness, and for his Wonderful Works to the Children of Men [Ps. 107:21, 31]! (14)

This passage is interesting because at the same time that it seems to affirm the story's representation of the early colonial political economy's goodness that is sanctified by Scripture, it also evinces creases that challenge that economy and its particular mode of scripturalizing the self and thereby the nation. It does this by leaving open a wide enough interpretative space in which the representation and indeed the meaning of the messiah and messianism is altered. On this counterreading, the messianic figure is no longer General Winslow. Instead, messianism attaches itself to Hammon. Importantly, the messianism that attaches to him, while Christological or linked to the person of Jesus Christ, is also Davidic and therefore linked to a theological conception of the ongoing significance of the nation and the people of Israel for Christian identity. Thus, the countermessianism that attaches to Hammon refuses the dominance of Christian supersessionism against Israel in the interests of forging the American nation and its own specific version of the Christendom of white-over-black relations and of the modern racial imagination.

The subtle and silent transformation of Hammon into a David–Christ figure begins with the reference to 1 Samuel 17:37: "David said moreover, The Lord that delivered me out of the paw of the lion, and out of the paw of the bear, he will deliver me out of the hand of this Philistine. And Saul said unto David, Go, and the Lord be with thee." Saul's prayer in this passage in effect unites

David to YHWH, the God of Israel. This, so the passage indicates, would be the reason for victory in battle should David triumph over Goliath. Within the crease of the theological counternarrative left open in this concluding paragraph of the saga, Hammon is subtly represented as a Davidic figure, who also resists the giant Goliath, albeit in the person of General Winslow, who stands in for colonial America. Hammon, like David of old, will be victorious only as the Lord, as Saul once said, is also with him. This passage is all the more intriguing, for on the reading I suggest, the *Narrative*'s hymn-like crescendo functions to subtly weaken the link between the supposed Christian deity of the colonial New Israel and the God of the biblical Israel. It does so by intimating a different orientation for the meaning of self and nation, one that appends itself to a different understanding of what it means to be a people. This different understanding takes its bearings from a different hermeneutic of Israel.

The other two scriptural references in the concluding paragraph are equally interesting. The Hammon persona, under editorial control, approvingly refers to Psalm 34:3 as the appropriate response to the events told in *Narrative* of his return to bondage: "O magnifie the Lord with me, and let us exalt his name together!" Once again, however, the surrounding verses of the psalm complicate a straightforward reading in which Hammon rejoices in his return to New England bondage. The surrounding verses on the one hand seem to affirm the amanuensis–editor's representation in which Hammon is safest when under the authority and protection of colonial America and General Winslow. After all, the surrounding verses speak of the psalmist's and so of Hammon's fears (v. 4), benightedness (v. 5), poverty, and need for deliverance (v. 6). His troubles came upon him ostensibly because he did not seek the Lord (v. 12)—where "Lord" here signifies General Winslow. Instead, Hammon sought to fulfill his own egocentric desire for freedom by taking flight from his master. In short, he was not righteous. However, upon returning to the Lord, that is, to General Winslow, Hammon is delivered, like the psalmist, from troubles, afflictions, oppression, and captivity (v. 19). No harm will come to those who return to God their master, though they may go through all manner of difficulties, even captivity, while away from their Master: "Many are the afflictions of the righteous." (v. 19).

All of this sounds like a neat scriptural summary of the events recorded in Hammon's *Narrative*. But if we read the Psalm 34 text inside the crease opened up through the 1 Samuel 17 passage, the psalm does additional, important work. It subtly moves the Davidic reading of the Hammon character that obtains from the 1 Samuel 17 passage in a more avowedly Christological direction. The Christological opening is most starkly apparent as we continue Psalm 34: "Many are the afflictions of the righteous; but the Lord delivers him out of them all; He guards all his bones; not one of them is broken .... The Lord redeems the soul of his servants" (vv. 19–20, 22).[53] The reference to not one of his bones being broken was commonly taken in Puritan exegesis and

more broadly in the Reformed and wider theological traditions as a reference to the crucified Christ of Good Friday and, more specifically, to the fact that Christ's legs were not broken as he hung on the cross. Christ endured such affliction for a just cause: namely, his refusal of and thus "departure from evil" in pursuit of peace (v. 14). It is precisely in departing or leaving evil (perhaps a veiled acknowledgement that Hammon was indeed a runaway and that he was attempting to scripturally justify his flight) that "the Lord redeems the life of his servants," "rescuing them from all of their troubles" (v. 17).

Read in this way, the reference to Psalm 34 reorients even the opening Christmas moment of the *Narrative*. That moment now becomes the moment of a new birth—a new, liberated way of being in the world that reaches its crescendo in the Easter event of the cross. This event begins on Good Friday and baptismally passes through the events of the sea as Holy Saturday. Only in passing through the sea of Holy Saturday can Hammon possibly appear as one raised from the dead. This circuit names the perfection of freedom in which there is the struggle against the powers that seek to rescind freedom. In other words, the Easter struggle is to culminate in Hammon's "redemption" (v. 22). But what is this redemption from the powers if not, as one raced to be black in modernity, resurrection into a new mode of identity, a new way of being in the world, one in which he is free? Hence, with this reference to Psalm 34:3 a seam emerges in the fabric of the *Narrative* in which Hammon comes to subtly reenact the life of Christ but in such a way that his life is positioned within a trajectory of freedom. A Christian sensibility, albeit articulated through the underside of modernity, struggles to bear witness to a theological conception of freedom and beyond a pseudotheological conception of bondage.

This counterexegetical reading of Psalm 34:3 already encodes a reinterpretation of the meaning of Hammon's experiences at sea. Those experiences, I have suggested, Christologically signify a different reading of Easter, especially of Good Friday and Holy Saturday. This different reading of Easter theologically reorients the opening scene and the meaning it imputes to Christmas. Now with this final reference to Psalm 107:21 and 31, the signification of Holy Saturday, the sea experience that took up the bulk of the *Narrative*, is itself expanded. How so?

I suggested earlier that the sea was a symbol of baptismal regeneration and as such was representative of those public rites that upheld a slave economy even as it indicated the righteousness of colonial America. With the Psalm 107 text, the sacramental or ritualized dimensions of the water symbolism are retained, but through the silences surrounding the psalm that symbolism is redirected. Water symbolism now signifies baptism as the public rite or liturgical act of freedom, a freedom that is consummated through the communicant's union—in this case, the union of Hammon—with Christ. Hence, the meaning of the scriptural economy of the self, and so the meaning of the nation, is again Christologically reoriented.

On the surface, vv. 21 and 31 seem to express Hammon's gratitude to God for God's goodness in returning him to servitude to General Winslow. But when one considers the surrounding verses, it is possible to hear another, more radical story. Against the background of the entirety of Psalm 107, Hammon's Christmas departure is his "going down to the sea in [a ship to] do business on great waters" (v. 23). While on the sea Hammon experiences "stormy winds . . . , waves" (v. 25), "troubles," and "distress" (v. 28). Such is his Holy Saturday experience of battling contemptuous "princes," rulers, and masters (v. 40). But out of the experience of being brought low through "oppression and sorrow" (v. 39), the one who is needy, namely Hammon himself, like Christ, is "brought up" or resurrected out of distress (v. 41). This silent reference to v. 41 of the psalm is crucial, for it redirects Winslow's statement as placed in the mouth of the Hammon persona, the statement that Hammon appeared to Winslow as one arisen from the dead. But resurrection understood in light of the counterreading I am suggesting of the psalm in relation to the Hammon story is one that would not deliver Hammon back to his master. That is, the Easter resurrection would not deliver Hammon back to Winslow. It would be the sign of his deliverance from Winslow, a deliverance rooted in the resurrection of Christ. Hammon's resurrection into freedom would be an articulation of Christ's resurrection—and vice versa. Resurrection would represent Hammon's triumph over "princes," rulers, and masters (v. 40). The three days of Easter would function to enact Hammon's freedom.

Such a suggestion, raises other questions. For one, it does not resolve the knotty issue of authorship: When, where, and to what extent in *Narrative* does Hammon himself speak rather than his amanuensis? Moreover, can Hammon's *Narrative* bear the full burden of success or failure in renarrating New World black existence Christologically? For after all, does not the Easter story, at least insofar as Hammon's voice and persona are under editorial control, deliver Hammon back into the white-over-black social relations of colonial life? Insofar as this is the case, Hammon's *Narrative* may be deemed an incomplete success. Jesus' nativity does deliver Hammon into the first-person pronominal situation of "I, we, and our," but even as it does this, *Narrative* delivers him into a situation in which his personhood is under constant literary threat.

However, what *Narrative* theologically suggests is far from a failure. It opens new possibilities for a rigorous theological critique of race and the exiting of whiteness. It points the way toward—and suggests a method appropriate to—what might be called a Christian theological vision of the concrete and of the particular. Persons are most fully who they are meant to be as they exit the nationalisms, cultural and otherwise, of "the far country," of "Ur of the Chaldees," so as to enter into God's election of creation as that election culminates in Jesus of Nazareth, the bearer of the story of Israel—the people of YHWH's covenant; not the people of race. One may judge that *Narrative* does not succeed, as scholars like Born and Andrews have done, as an isolated text.

But what would it mean to read the Hammon tale as part of a literary tradition that bears witness to an Afro-Christian struggle to theologically negotiate existence in the New World or in modernity? Read in this way, his tale can only be deemed a moment in a long history.

One must therefore extend the question of success or failure to subsequent literary moments that also suggest an Afro-Christian interrogation of and entry into the theological gestures of Hammon's narrative. In the following chapter, I show how Frederick Douglass's 1845 *Narrative* does this by reengaging the Easter moment that delivered Hammon back to his Boston master. I show how he attempts to narrate Easter and, in so doing, renarrate himself as free. Like Hammon's, Douglass's autobiography points to Christology as the theological site of contestation, the site at which to engage modern racial reasoning. Whether and to what extent he succeeds where Hammon's text at least partially falters and to what extent he erects his own set of problems, I now consider.

7

The Death of Christ

A Theological Reading of Frederick Douglass's 1845 Narrative

With captured
    friends
beneath the dull
    coolness
of a concrete sky
I sit and sweat
inwardly.

Drenched in
    bitterness
smelling of remorse,
we tug and strain
under laden
    backpacks
of unwanted time.

God, if only,
damn it if only
we could give it to
    the dead
we could all be
resurrected.

—Roger Jaco, "Easter"

I resolved to fight; and . . . I seized Covey hard by the throat; and as I did so, I rose . . . [and] it was a glorious resurrection.
    —Frederick Douglass, *Narrative of the Life of Frederick Douglass, an American Slave*

In chapter 6, I read Hammon's *Narrative* as engaged in a subtle effort to renarrate Christianity. The struggle was to narrate, against the grain of the dominant voice of the amanuensis–editor, a Christianity that did not function as the religious ground of national identity and that did not supply "cultural strength," to use Edward W. Said's term, to achieve American whiteness.[1] As I argue throughout this book, whiteness is not an essence. It names the conclusion of a history, the history of an achievement. The "strength" by which whiteness became a fait accompli is the strength by which Christianity was quite violently severed from its Jewish roots and subsequently redeployed, again quite violently, as the ground of Western civilization and white

cultural nationalism. In short, modern Western civilization is, in the strictest sense of the term, a racial accomplishment, the accomplishment of whiteness. But this accomplishment is a distinctively modern "Christian" accomplishment, an accomplishment rooted in the refusal to understand Christian identity inside Jewish covenantal life. (It follows from this, then, that contrary to the ways in which "Orientalism" has accustomed us to thinking, Jewishness cannot be understood in racial terms either.[2]) Alas, Christianity became the white man's religion.

With the declaration that he took leave of his master on the "25th Day of December, 1747," Hammon narrates an Afro-Christian struggle to exit the history of the accomplishment of race—the accomplishment of whiteness and of the vision of national identity that performs it. In struggling to subtly narrate his movement from bondage to freedom, not from the vantage of the "birth of a nation" but, rather, from that of the birth of Christ, Hammon race trades, though by the end of his tale whiteness exerts its religious strength again, pulling him back into the history of race and black subservience. What was important for my reading was not constructing an argument by which Hammon's story is a complete success, one in which Hammon lives "happily ever after," but to read Hammon's saga as the story of one struggling to live into Christianity in a different way—indeed, to occupy it in such a way as to depart from the history of racial achievement and enter into a different history of accomplishment, the yet-unfolding accomplishment of Israel's covenant with YHWH in Jesus of Nazareth.

In this chapter, I continue the investigation about an emerging Afro-Christian sensibility struggling with and against modernity by considering another text of American and African American letters, the 1845 *Narrative of the Life of Frederick Douglass, an American Slave, Written by Himself.*[3] Douglass's *Narrative* is important for my argument because it intertextually picks up where Hammon's tale leaves off: if, by virtue of the editorial control wielded over Hammon's *Narrative* by his amanuensis–editor, Easter delivers Hammon back into captivity, Douglass's 1845 *Narrative* struggles to undo this moment so that Easter will yield freedom rather than recapitulate him into bondage. For this reason, the 1845 *Narrative* aspires toward a resurrection in which Douglass is freed from bondage rather than returned to it, a resurrection in which Christian discourse functions differently in relationship to national identity and that, in some sense, undoes racial identity. As Douglass himself puts it in describing the Easter moment in which he realizes his freedom: "I rose" (64). It is my aim to assess theologically the strengths and limits of what Douglass does.

Douglass's central or explicit aim in the *Narrative* is to tell the story of his life in movement from bondage to freedom, from property to prophet, from chattel to abolitionist spokesman and public intellectual. In short, he wants to give a confession, in the tradition of St. Augustine, of how he remade himself

beyond the confines of how race defined his existence in America. A counter-narrative of identity, a saga told from the underside of modernity, one meant to give a different account of who he took himself to be and of his relationship to others: such is the story this celebrated text of American literature tells. Douglass engages in autobiographical jeremiad by engaging in a kind of "racialized writing," as historian Wilson Jeremiah Moses has said,[4] that had as its chief goal "throwing light on the American slave system" (102). Doing this required that he not only "re-present" himself in a different light, one that positioned him as, from the first, fully human, but that he re-present himself as one who had his humanity, indeed, his "true identity," stolen and then sold into America's political economy of slavery.[5] The result was that he and those like him were rendered inarticulate on slave plantations and before slave masters. The 1845 *Narrative* resists the ethics of this inarticulacy. In eleven suspenseful chapters, Douglass engages in a dramatic struggle of religious fortitude and imagination; he wages a veritable war of words, meant on the one hand to put forward a rhetorically compelling account of his humanity and on the other to make a case for his freedom in the context of the oppressive inhumanity of America's slavery system.

A central feature of Douglass's literary battle over the symbolic construction of racial and national identity is the critique of American religion ensconced within the *Narrative*. This critique and the contest over the symbolic construction of identity that it signifies does not operate simply at the level of the eleven chapters that make up the body of the text properly speaking. It is also at work in the literary battle being waged between the *Narrative*'s preface and the appendix. Famed northern abolitionist William Lloyd Garrison wrote the preface, which was meant, as literary scholar John Sekora has said, to authenticate the *Narrative* by sealing Douglass's "black" voice and "black" message inside a "white" envelope.[6] In the appendix, however, Douglass speaks in his own voice, offering a moving soliloquy, a poetic ode against the "slave-holding religion of this land" (97), or what he otherwise calls "the Christianity of America" (99), and for "the impartial Christianity of Christ" (97). It is this religious critique of how America defined who he was, along with how theology is enlisted into the critique, that I wish to foreground, and that for two reasons.

First, it will assist me in determining why an emancipatory politics of identity often embroils us in contradictions and why, insofar as this is the case, such a politics fails us. My reading of the *Narrative* shows that central to the problem at issue here is that such a politics often repeats the form of the self that needs overcoming. Second, taking a careful look at how identity works in Douglass's *Narrative* and the contradictions it ensnares him in—in his case, contradictions centering on gender or, more specifically, on the black feminine—will put me in a position to show how his approach to theology in relationship to what he takes religion to be actually aids and abets the problem

instead of providing a liberating alternative to the debilitating forms of self-identity it seeks to overcome. I want to consider why this is so, and in a final gesture, sketch a more theologically rigorous approach to how identity might be rethought and performed differently, given what Douglass puts on the table theologically.

To make my case I pay particular attention to two scenes in the *Narrative*—Douglass's account of the beating of Aunt Hester (called "Esther" in his subsequent autobiographies and in the remainder of this chapter) and the famed altercation with the slave-breaker Edward Covey in chapter 10 of the *Narrative*. How Douglass literarily represents these events captures the way in which he at once identifies the religious nature of how racial and national identity are construed in the modern world and the contradictions and failings attending that construal. For Douglass, remedying those failings requires a different vision of the ends of religion and a different deployment of theological discourse. Thus, the reading of the *Narrative* put forward here shows how, in literarily rescuing the dignity of black life and in putting forward a different vision of black identity, Douglass sought to reorient the American sacred mythos and its vision of American peoplehood.[7] Crucial to the *Narrative*'s strategy was, first, unmasking or critically interpreting how, as one sees at the end of Hammon's *Narrative*, the story of Christ's passion was made to do the sociopolitical work of grounding the political economy of slavery, and second, redeploying or reinterpreting that story in such a way as to make it comport to Douglass's flourishing as a black man—that is, as a black *male*—in America.

Hence, within the literary economy of the *Narrative*, a number of things struggle to emerge. Chief among them is a different way of understanding black identity. The overarching assumption of the *Narrative* is that a new understanding of black identity is possible only insofar as a different vision of national identity, of the meaning of human existence in America, is put forward. But this, as Douglass in the 1845 *Narrative* saw it, required that he reimagine the aims and ends of "American religion" itself, how religion is to function in the public sphere of politics, and how race ought to function in the American sacred mythos and in determining American peoplehood. Black religion—Douglass's take on it, that is, and the public work it is to do—is the ground of this new vision of racial and national identity. But what is "black religion"—to say nothing of "religion"?[8]

Setting aside for now my deep suspicion about how the category of "religion" works in modern religious thought,[9] it nevertheless is fair to say that in the 1845 *Narrative* black religion ultimately (but not uncomplicatedly) means the unique ways in which black folks have appropriated the religion of their masters, Christianity.[10] In addition to challenging the inner structure of American religion, the 1845 *Narrative* is also a subtle engagement with how Christianity has been appropriated by black folks. It challenges the fact that

they have assumed a religious posture whereby they acquiesce in their oppression. If Douglass is out to contest and redirect the religious-symbolic
construction of American national identity and the place of race in it, he is just
as interested in contesting and redirecting the religious-symbolic construction
of black identity and, crucially, how it is performed.

My aim is to catalog Douglass's complex and subtle endeavor to rechart the
territory of racial and national identity, which he carried out by autobiographically probing the intersection of the meaning of religion in general and of black
religion in particular as they bear on the question of race and nation. Through a
cultural reading of the cross of Christ and the atonement he effects, I expose the
constructive potential of what Douglass sought to accomplish in autobiographically recharting the terrain of black identity. But besides this, I question
just how new this supposedly new cartography of racial and national self-
understanding is and point out the limits of his approach to theology qua
cultural criticism. In short, I ask to what extent Douglass's endeavor succeeds,
and I show why in the end his effort to re-map black identity and agency in the
world tragically fails. It fails—its redeployment of the logic of the cross notwithstanding—because it repeats the very form of the self from which it seeks
liberation. But its failure is instructive, for it points to the tenacity of a culturalist
vision of the self within which Christianity, in being a "religion," gets closed.
Black liberation calls for Christian theological closure. In an effort to escape
modernity's racial gaze, modernity's original religious gesture is reproduced.

Because these two moments—the moment of constructive potential
and that of ultimate and contradictory failure—are so tightly interwoven in
Douglass's narrative portrayal of himself, they necessarily are tightly interwoven in my engagement with them. However, to avoid or at least minimize
potential confusion, it is important to keep these narratively unified moments
logically distinct; for on the one hand, there is Douglass's move to read the
dignity and the meaning of black life against the backdrop of Christ's passion,
a move that I argue is fraught with unrealized spiritual, intellectual, and sociopolitical potential that could provide a different way in which to engage in a
theology at the crossroads of culture. This is the moment of constructive potential in which the Christian imagination in modernity could be theologically
overhauled. And yet there is the problem, on the other hand, of *why* this
potential goes unrealized. The problem, I show, has everything to do with how
religion is conceived and how Christian faith and the theological enterprise are
framed in terms of the religious-aesthetic gaze.

Douglass's discourse succumbs, in the end, to the modernist discourse of
religion and the way in which religion performs the self nationally and culturally, which is to say, racially. Refusing to be open to how Christian faith
itself is even thought about, Douglass unwittingly circumscribes black identity within the form of the self he seeks to overcome. Douglass's construal of
religion as but a cultural artifact and reflex, and of theology as simply the

discursive voice of that artifactual reflex, proves integral to this circumscription. In fact, on this point, Douglass's approach to the intellectual life—to the way religion functions within and as a form of intellectuality—is a genealogical taproot of many of the problems criticized in part II of this book (chapters 3–5) insofar as they betray an inadequate grasp of how whiteness is funadamentally a *theological* problem, a problem that the modern discourse of "religion" aids and abets. Starkly put, Douglass's gesture puts on the table the fact that there is a way of *speaking* theologically while not *doing* theology, a way of reinscribing the problem that needs overcoming precisely at the moment of supposed hermeneutical exposure of the problem. I want to consider the tragic consequences of this, because, as cultural theorist Stuart Hall has said, "Identity is what is at stake."[11]

After giving the bulk of the chapter over to laying out this problem, I conclude by pursuing schematically what the way forward for theological reflection on identity—cultural and national—must entail for Christian thought. Here I step beyond Douglass—and much of the black intellectual tradition that inherits his mantle on how to think about religion and identity and much of contemporary theology as well in regard to these questions—in order to rethink the meaning of human existence and identity in light of Christ's passion, a path that Douglass indicates but never really enters upon. One might say that I want to read Douglass theologically against himself. Central to my proposal is drawing modern theology back into the pentecostal nature of Christ's passion. This allows me to reconceive identity under a different rubric, the rubric of human existence as "interhumanity." It will also become apparent that a theology of creation rooted in a Christian doctrine of Israel and, through Israel's election, a Christian doctrine of the nations, is crucial to the pneumatological reworking of identity that I propose.[12] From here I will be positioned to consider Jarena Lee's writings (in chapter 8), which are another moment in the elaboration of an Afro-Christian consciousness seeking to negotiate existence with and against modernity.

Easter and the Beating of Aunt Esther

I begin by turning to the *Narrative's* subtly complex scene of the beating of Aunt Esther, teasing out some of the ways in which the scene begins to unmask the fault line in how identity is often thought about and performed.[13] The scene is important because it brings together in one literary location the intertwined moments of constructive potential and ultimate failure that I mentioned above.

The scene takes place in the opening chapter, where the protagonist, "Mr. Plummer," the overseer who worked for Douglass's childhood master, Aaron Anthony, moves the scene's action. Yet as we will see, the real object of concern

in the scene is less Mr. Plummer than Aunt Esther. It is through Douglass's representation of Esther that he is able to cast the scene as one of indignity and as a metaphorical representation of the structure of black selflessness in slaveholding America. As a metonym of black indignity, Aunt Esther is the scene's primary subject, while Plummer is secondary. About the latter, Douglass says:

> He was a miserable drunkard, a profane swearer, and a savage
> monster. He always went armed with a cowskin and a heavy cudgel.
> I have known him to cut and slash the women's heads so horribly . . . .
> He was a cruel man, hardened by a long life of slaveholding. He
> would at times seem to take great pleasure in whipping a slave. (18)

And then, as if Plummer's function was to be but a literary prop (though he certainly is more than this: more on this anon), one whose function was simply to set up what is to follow, the scene's center of gravity decidedly shifts—to Aunt Esther. Douglass says:

> I have often been awakened at the dawn of day by the most heart-
> rending shrieks of an own [sic] aunt of mine, whom he used to tie up
> to a joist, and whip upon her naked back til she was literally covered
> with blood. No words, no tears, no prayers, from his gory victim,
> seemed to move his iron heart from its bloody purpose. The louder
> she screamed the harder he whipped; and where the blood ran fast-
> est, there he whipped longest. He would whip her to make her
> scream, and whip her to make her hush; and not until overcome by
> fatigue, would he cease to swing the blood-clotted cowskin. (18)

From this quotation—and from the scene's subsequent unfolding—Douglass shows how violence mediates white and black identity alike. Both, that is, are brokered through Plummer's "cowskin and a heavy cudgel" and sealed in fast-flowing blood. The result of Plummer's "bloody purpose" is to render white life articulate. Yet the articulacy of white existence is possible only by subjecting black life to a violent "hush" and distorting its speech into that of a harsh "scream." I have more to say momentarily about the nature of the violence portrayed in this scene. For now, however, it is enough to note an important implication of this scene as it bears on my present endeavor, which is to probe how identity is performed and often thought about. The implication is that violence is the deep structure, one might say, of the logic and practice of identity in America and in modernity.

But more must be said precisely on this point, for Douglass in this scene is not content simply to register the fact that violence mediates (in)dignity. Rather, the scene is out to show that the violence at issue is of a specifically religious and sacred nature, one that grounds the mythos of American exceptionalism and peoplehood and the vision of the aims and ends of humanity

nestled within it. The result is that the scene brings violence and the sacred into close proximity.[14] Brokering that nearness is, once again (as I show with respect to Hammon's *Narrative* in chapter 6), scriptural exegesis. That is, Old and New Testament Scripture is the contested ground of identity, the contested ground of who we take ourselves to be and how we orient ourselves in the world. The scene, therefore, grants insight into Douglass's broader strategy in the *Narrative*: namely, to do autobiography as exegesis—indeed, as a counterexegesis of the self—and exegesis as autobiography. Autobiography is thus done with a view to both challenge and struggle toward a different vision of the hermeneutical and theological basis of America's self-understanding and its vision of the human.

As a first step in establishing this claim, consider how the scene plays on Old Testament imagery. In speaking of Plummer's "bloody purpose," Douglass seems to align the overseer Plummer with the biblical figure Cain. His suggestion is that as Cain was bent on drawing his brother's blood (cf. Gen. 4, which employs the term "blood"), so white brutality, in the person of Plummer, does the same with regard to dark flesh. Plummer, too, is determined in his "bloody purpose." That purpose was not just to physically incarcerate the black "body in pain,"[15] but also to render it mute. In this way, the white man Plummer/Anthony, rather than the black (in the person of Douglass), is shown to be the savage, indeed, "a savage monster." This is the case because of the inarticulacy and illiteracy Plummer foists on Aunt Esther and even Douglass himself, who says that he had to labor through his own inarticulacy, as it were, to "commit to paper the feelings with which [he] beheld [the ghastly scene]" (18). Thus, the scene reveals that inarticulacy and illiteracy are the unique markers, the signs, of the loss of the self. By contrast, speech, articulacy, and literacy are the markers of dignity, freedom, and autonomous agency, markers that Douglass, as self-made man and abolitionist intellectual, represents himself as now embodying and so giving an account of how he got there.

The Old Testament dimensions of the scene receive further amplification when they are read to align Esther with the scriptural figure Abel. The crucial link is that for both Esther and Abel their inarticulacy and indignity is the condition for the articulacy and dignity of their antagonists. Both are articulate only in a nonconventional way: Abel, through his blood crying out from the ground; and Esther, through her "heart-rending shrieks," "screams," and the "hush"—all punctuated with the presence of fast-flowing blood. And then in both stories there is the third dramatis persona, God. In the fratricidal story of Scripture, God is the one to whom Abel's blood cries out, demanding in some sense that God justify himself by vindicating the slaughtered victim. In the scene of the whipping of Esther, it is again before God, the one who is seen as ostensibly underwriting the social arrangement of white dignity over black indignity in America, that prayerful tears are shed, crying out for the vindication of the victim Esther. The beating of Esther resonates against the back-

drop of Abel and Cain, and Douglass makes the claim that the "genesis" of black indignity and the coterminous loss of black agency lies in the moral and ethical failures of slaveholding Christianity. More starkly put, the scene, in fact, suggests that its genesis lies in God's failure, if not outright culpability, for the situation. God is culpable in that Esther's screams, which plead for a rectifying response, go unanswered. The situation thus appears analogous to that of Abel's cry to God—a cry, mind you, that is articulated not by Abel himself, who lacks agency, but by the Mosaic author—and the circumstances surrounding his cry (cf. Gen. 4:10).

This reading is only deepened once one takes into account how the dramatic persons in the scene of the whipping of Esther are further figured through New Testament allusions. Here Douglass, as is the case in much of the Christian tradition's reading of the Abel figure, subtly aligns Esther, an Abel figure herself, with Christ, though it is a weak Christ. In reading Esther Christologically, Douglass deepens his subtle attack on American religion's complicity in quelling black selfhood. Troped through Christ's Easter dereliction, Douglass's aunt, he says, could utter "no words, no tears, no prayers" that could effectively intervene in her plight. Thus, in one fell swoop, Douglass dramatizes how the black body is configured as the papyrus onto which religious letters are violently emblazoned to justify American peoplehood and the political economy of slavery. In linking the Old and the New Testament in this way, he suggests that black existence is forced into a quasi-scriptural economy that in fact ventriloquizes the political economy of slavery. This ventriloquism is at its most intense and most subtly masked in how the Easter story is made to function in the American sacred mythos. It is here that Douglass's religious critique of how identity functions in the national imaginary cuts deepest because, arguably, he wants to disclose the work the paschal story accomplishes sociopolitically in grounding both the American order of things and the meaning of human life for blacks and whites in that order.

In short, he intertextually explains, one might say, why Hammon's *Narrative* concludes with an Easter failure that resurrects Hammon back into bondage. Douglass represents this by framing the episode of the whipping of Esther in paschal terms and by representing Esther as a figure of the crucified Christ. In so doing, he takes his scriptural criticism and (counter)exegesis to its most trenchant level, the level of theology itself—the theology of the passion and of suffering. It is here as well that the promise of and problems with Douglass's strategy crystallize. The promise concerns the creative way in which Douglass uncovers how the Easter story is made to ground national identity by upholding the binary relationship of whiteness over blackness. The problems concern the way gender functions in his own redeployment of that story in the interests of providing a liberating account of black, racial identity.

To get at what I mean by this, I consider more closely how Douglass frames the beating of Esther through the Easter story. Subsequent to detailing

the "facts" surrounding Esther's beating, facts framed, as just argued, through allusions to Old and New Testament Scripture, Douglass immediately registers the psychic effects the beating had on him as a child:

> I remember the first time I ever witnessed this horrible exhibition.
> I was quite a child, but I well remember it. I never shall forget it
> whilst I remember any thing. It was the first of a long series of
> such outrages, of which I was doomed to be *a witness and a partici-*
> *pant*. It was the blood-stained gate, the entrance to the hell of slavery,
> through which I was about to pass. It was a most terrible spectacle.
> I wish I could commit to paper the feelings with which I beheld
> it. (18; italics mine)

Literary scholar Jenny Franchot has powerfully argued regarding this scene that Esther's suffering enables "[Douglass's] acquisition of 'manhood' " and, in this way, of autonomy.[16] She further observes, commenting on this scene as Douglass later tweaked it in *My Bondage and My Freedom* (his second autobiography), that "the whipping provokes [Douglass's] eventually emancipatory inquiry into the "nature and history of slavery."[17] The scene, in other words, allows Douglass to dramatize an ontology of slavery and the ethical structure of white articulacy and black inarticulacy. That ontology is one in which black identity has as its precondition a rupturing of the placid state of "childhood" innocence. The complementary aspect of this rupture is a recognition of one's state of inarticulacy and a concomitant desire to change that condition: that is, to bring articulacy out of inarticulacy. Such is the struggle for liberation.

In the concrete terms of this scene, the young Douglass, as "a witness and a participant" to the whipping of Esther, is "ontologized" into the cavernous and dark inner recesses of the indignity of slavery. He is brought into the *logos* or inner (ir)rationality of modern racial reasoning, and into the struggle for freedom, for a different mode of consciousness, that comes with having been so awakened. In Douglass's case, it is the black intellectual qua abolitionist orator and "representative man" who uniquely realizes this different, liberated mode of consciousness. What is distinctive about this new mode of consciousness and the kind of agency it makes available is its insight into the uses and meanings of religion for overcoming the indignity of inarticulacy and the loss of selfhood.

At the same time, the gender conventions at play in how Douglass has even represented the problem are disconcerting; for indignity or silenced agency, which amounts to no agency at all, and the feminine, particularly the black feminine, are made virtually equivalent for Douglass. Consequently, manhood, positioned as opposed to the feminine, is the place of redemption and therefore of "true" identity and agency. And again, how Douglass represents the Easter story is central to how these gender protocols work. Franchot has uncovered an important aspect of the problem about which I speak. It would, therefore, be worthwhile moving my argument forward by engaging

her important research. She has observed "that Douglass acquired his virile autonomy somewhat at [Esther's] expense":

> Receiving "some thirty or forty stripes" and suffering repeated whippings thereafter, Esther plays the sacrifice to his redemption.... Indeed, his success as abolitionist orator depends uneasily upon his recurrent invocation of the whipped woman.... [In short, Esther's] suffering provides him with his credentials as victim—critical to his self-authentication as fugitive slave-orator; her femininity enables him to transcend that very identification—a transcendence critical to his success as the "Representative Colored Man of the United States."[18]

Part of what is so insightful about Franchot's reading is her observation that the event had "the force of 'revelation'" for the child Douglass: that is, the event, through its "diabolic imitation of Christ's manifestation of the concealed divinity," disclosed for him "the hitherto disguised interior of slavery."[19] Franchot does not quite put it this way, but it is fair to say that that disguised interior is framed as at once metaphorically "Christological" but only by being at the same time somatically feminine. The religious problem, in other words, proves to be the Christological problem of the black feminine. Douglass, thus, brings the problematic of religion, race, and gender together. At their intersection, he registers both the meaning of his aunt's beating and the psychological effect it had on him.

This may be why "the awful force" of slavery "struck" him at that precise moment. Having been a voyeur of sorts to the beating, which is staged as a kind of rape in which he was made, as he says, "to participate," the child Douglass can no longer see the world as pure and virginal. Again, the epochal status of the beating reveals itself as it is the first of many beatings to which he will be privy. He realizes that the modern construction of race, which rationalizes black inhumanity, is a violent affair. But, as his language suggests, the world is now also complexly gendered in its violent configuring of race and disfiguring of persons. The beating inducts him into a vision of reality that, in short, is gendered and engendering. His employment of phallic imagery to portray the beating confirms as much, as he represents himself as about to pass through the hymenal veil, as it were, and so enter into "the blood-stained gate." Theological language, at this point, language by which Douglass deepens his imagistic use of New Testament Scripture, facilitates his portrayal of what he takes to be really going on behind the religious discourse that is America. For "the blood-stained gate" through which "[he] was about to pass" from innocence into (self-)consciousness was in fact his "entrance to the hell of slavery."

But what is this bloodstained gate, this descent into the "unholy" Saturday of slavery, the veritable sojourn through Hades, if not the brutal beating of Esther? And Douglass participates in this beating, he himself confesses, as a

witness. He participates by virtue of his identification with her insofar as he, too, was a slave. Her abuse, in other words, is vicariously his abuse; her inarticulacy is again vicariously his inarticulacy, an inarticulacy that he "wish[ed] [he] could commit to paper"; and the indignity of her femininity, which showed itself on her bruised body, is in fact his acquiescing to "femininity" in the face of the dignified masculinity, freedom, and articulacy of the brutal father-figure Plummer/Anthony. The important point in all of this is that the black female body made figural in his aunt's body becomes the *summum in nuce* of the indignity of chattel existence; woman or the feminine as acquiescent passivity effectively comes to represent what it means to be a slave, while the symbology of the Easter Pasch serves to facilitate that representation.

It follows from this that freedom, which entails the struggle for release from the condition of racial indignity, is for Douglass a struggle against the loss of masculinity. Hence, freedom as the movement toward liberated selfhood comes to be represented as resistance to the feminine, to enslaved unconsciousness. Resisting the feminine is part and parcel of the quest to seize the consciousness of manhood and thereby the self-consciousness of self-reliance, virile articulacy, and ultimately liberated identity. Douglass's aim, therefore, having entered into what historian Wilson Jeremiah Moses has called "the constrains of racialized writing,"[20] is to occupy the position as "master" of himself; that is, he seeks to occupy the position of self-reliant self-mastery as the mode of true agency and emancipated identity. Herein lies freedom—the freedom of manhood.

Easter and the Altercation with Covey

My reading of the beating of Esther shows how the symbology of the Easter Pasch facilitated Douglass's representation of the meaning of slavery and what it means to acquire liberated selfhood. That is, the Easter story was drawn into Douglass's dramatic portrayal of slavery's ontology through his alignment of Esther with Christ in his passion. In this gesture, it is important to see that Christ, too, is somatically feminized. By the time one gets to Douglass's account of his adolescent altercation with Covey in chapter 10 of the *Narrative*, however, there is a shift in how he deploys the image of Christ's passion. Christ is masculinized so that he is now the emblem of dignified manhood and, shall we say, strength over weakness: Christ overcomes the feminine and thus liberates the race. The Easter story, hence, becomes a "Gnostic" saga of the masculine self.

I now consider how the *Narrative*, having earlier "interpreted" the Easter story as one of feminine weakness, redeploys the passion narrative as a venture into the self-made strength of masculinity. It is worth stating again that central to my concern is how religion functions in all of this and why theology, when

operating within the confines of the modern analytic of religion and culture, abets rather than overcomes the problem.

The Religious Encounter with Covey

Chapter 10 of the *Narrative* unfolds as a series of "smaller" altercations. Douglass says that these altercations had as their goal beating him into submission and breaking his will for freedom. Eventually buckling under the weight of Edward Covey's brutality—for "[during] the first six months, of that year," he says, "scarce a week passed without his whipping me. I was seldom free from a sore back" (56)—Douglass records that his passion for freedom was eroding. And so, fairly quickly he is reduced to saying, "I was somewhat unmanageable when I first went there, but a few months of this discipline tamed me" and "Mr. Covey succeeded in breaking me. I was broken in body, soul, and spirit. My natural elasticity was crushed, my intellect languished, the disposition to read departed, the cheerful spark that lingered about my eye died; the dark night of slavery closed in upon me; and behold a man transformed into a brute!" (58).

In due course, Douglass reached his nadir in the great altercation of the chapter and of the *Narrative*. The account builds to this confrontation, the point where he reverses his "[transformation] into a brute," undoing "how a *man* became a slave" (italics mine). Thus, "manhood," as literary scholar Richard Yarborough has said about the *Narrative*, "is the crucial spiritual commodity that one must maintain in the face of oppression."[21] But how does Douglass represent this "spiritual commodity," and how does he "maintain [it] in the face of oppression"? On both scores, Douglass once again resorts to the Easter story, portraying it as the immaterial "superstructure," the "master-narrative," that structures his materially dramatic fight with Covey and hence his resistance to oppression.

Douglass one day takes ill with "extreme dizziness" to the point that "[he] trembled in every limb," and at "about three o'clock of that day [he] broke down; [his] strength failed [him] . . . [he] could stand no longer, [he] fell" (60). Covey nevertheless immediately demanded that Douglass return to work. "Exceedingly feeble," though, he does not comply. This merited Douglass a number of swift kicks and, finally, "a heavy blow upon the head, making"— like the crown of thorns forced upon Christ's brow—"a large wound." The result: "the blood ran freely" (61). Bleeding, Douglass remained on the ground, probably only semiconscious, and Covey, seeing him in this quasi-dead state, "left [him] to [his] fate."

With momentary relief, Douglass decides to abscond from Covey's plantation and to return to the town of St. Michael's for the intervention of Mr. Thomas, the master who sent him away to Covey, the "nigger-breaker," in the first place. En route, Douglass loses consciousness again from his wounds:

"I fell down, and lay for a considerable time .... For a time I thought I should bleed to death," he says (61). He lies there, as if dead; but with strength quickly found, he journeys on, arriving that night at Master Thomas's residence only to encounter his refusal to assist him and his subsequent insistence that Douglass return to Covey's plantation in the morning. As Douglass went out of his way to note the three o'clock hour of his beating the previous day, so now he goes out of his way to further establish the timeline: "I remained all night," he says, "and, according to [Master Thomas's] orders, I started off to Covey's in the morning, (Saturday morning,) wearied in body and broken in spirit" (62; parentheses in the original). This timing will prove most important for the symbolism of Douglass's account of his acquisition of dignified manhood. Seeing Covey coming toward him at about "nine o'clock" Saturday morning "with his cowskin to give me another whipping" (62), and therefore fearing for his life, Douglass, with success, retreats into a field to elude him. All of this occurred on Saturday, while on the previous day (Friday afternoon), Douglass was left as if dead, metaphorically crucified, with death symbolically descending upon him at the three o'clock hour (cf. Luke 23:44).

In all of this Douglass continues to wage the subtly antagonistic war against scriptural enslavement begun in chapter 1 of the *Narrative*. This scene continues his counterexegesis of Scripture and of the self by claiming Jesus' three o'clock hour of dereliction for himself. With this move, Douglass seeks to alter the very structure of Christian consciousness and slaveholding religion by carving out space for the dignity of black life and selfhood within Christianity. Stated differently, in bringing attention to the time of his own quasi-death at three o'clock, Douglass unites his death with the death of Jesus on Good Friday. The move makes the literary suggestion that God is manifest in black suffering and in the black struggle for dignity and selfhood.

But Douglass pushes the symbology further even as he complicates it. This can be seen in how he portrays his dealing with "an old advisor," a slave acquaintance, Sandy Jenkins, from whom he seeks "advice as to what course it was best for [him] to pursue." Sandy's counsel was for Douglass to

> go back to Covey; but that before I went, I must go with him into
> another part of the woods, where there was a certain *root*, which, if
> I would take some of it with me, carrying it *always on my right side*,
> would render it impossible for Mr. Covey, or any other white man, to
> whip me.... I at first rejected the idea, that the simple carrying of
> a root in my pocket would have any such effect as he had said,
> and was not disposed to take it; but Sandy impressed the necessity
> with much earnestness.... To please him, I at length took the root,
> and, according to his direction, carried it upon my right side. This
> was Sunday morning. (63; emphasis original)

This scene introduces ambiguity into Douglass's Easter portrayal of events, and as such it introduces ambiguity into his efforts to articulate a liberated and dignified self. The ambiguity has to do with the scene's questioning whether it is Christianity, even if a distinctively black Christianity, or the "root," which is emblematic of black folkways and customs, that will mediate his deliverance from Covey.

How Douglass literarily represents Sunday's and Monday's events—for Douglass's dealings with Sandy occur on Saturday—shows his dissatisfaction with both options. The first option would ground his dignity as a black man on the black feminine (and her supposedly acquiescent religiosity), while the second would ground it in black folklife and folkways. In the *Narrative*'s representation of things, however, these two ways of conceiving and rescuing black selfhood are not far apart and both are inadequate. Indeed, it would appear that the *Narrative*'s judgment against the black feminine entails as well a judgment against black folklife, which quite often was the carrier of Christianity among black common folk. Hence, both must be sublated—almost in Hegelian fashion (*Aufhebung*)—into his consciousness as free abolitionist intellectual. The scene's subsequent unfolding portrays just this.

Douglass, Folklife, and the Formation of the Black Intellectual

Before turning to the rest of the scene to see how this double judgment against the black feminine and black folklife as indices of weakness is worked out, I briefly consider a scene from chapter 2 of the *Narrative*, because it gives an important clue as to how Douglass understood "the folk" in whom was expressed a Christianity of (feminized?) weakness.[22] The scene is also important in that it is one of the first interpretations of the sorrow songs or the "Negro spirituals" as they are often called.[23] Crucial for my argument is the fact that Douglass frames his interpretation of the slave songs in language similar to what he used in describing the epochal status of the punishment of Esther only one chapter earlier in the *Narrative*. Coming to terms with the singing of the slave songs gave him "[his] first glimmering conception of the dehumanizing character of slavery." Those songs, he says, had the effect of "impress[ing] some minds with the horrible character of slavery, [more] than the reading of whole volumes of philosophy on the subject could do" (24).

Indeed, reminiscent of the sentiment Douglass expressed in recalling Esther's beating in which he said, "I remember the first time I ever witnessed this horrible exhibition. . . . I shall never forget it whilst I remember any thing. . . . It was a most terrible spectacle. I wish I could commit to paper the feelings with which I beheld it (18), Douglass expresses similar feelings here: "The mere recurrence to those songs, even now, afflicts me; and while I am writing these lines, an expression of feeling has already found its way down my cheek" (24). What we see in this similarity of feelings is that, for Douglass, the

black feminine and black folklife occupied two nodes of a continuum through which he sought to renegotiate the terms of black existence and the terms of his own existence as a black man. The more prominent node, I argue, was that of the black feminine. But, given Douglass's commentary on the songs, the significance of the second node is not to be underestimated.

Douglass observed that into these songs the slaves would, out of reverence, exultingly inject something about "the *Great House Farm*" (23; italics original) as they affectionately called the village-like plantation on which he lived as a child (22). Douglass then records that he really "did not...understand the deep meaning of those rude and apparently incoherent songs," with their references to "the Great House Farm," while he was a slave and existed—importantly, he adds—"within the circle" of slavery. While in slavery's circle, he continues, he "neither saw nor heard *as those without* might see and hear" (24; italics mine). But having stepped outside the circle, Douglass is able to claim access to the inner meaning and pathos of the songs. What it means for him to be an intellectual, one who has plumbed the depths of the slave songs and the inner caverns of common folklife, is defined precisely in this way: as intellectual, he can pull back the veil of consciousness and plumb the depths of the "true" meaning of religion and identity. This is possible because he himself has access to and is living out of a different mode of consciousness. In just this way, religious inquiry and theological analysis becomes cultural criticism—and nothing more.

Something like this, I want to argue, is evident in this scene. And there is a gendered dimension to it. Douglass's analysis of slave singing, the lifting of the veil, prefigures W. E. B. DuBois's peering into the souls of black folks. Upon lifting up the veil, what does Douglass see? According to literary scholar David Leverenz, he sees how "the slaves' anguish of deprivation and their rapturous hopes for deliverance joined in their vision of the Great House Farm, the symbol of oppression, glory...[and] repose."[24] He sees the cultural significance of the Great House Farm and the place it occupies in the trek toward liberated selfhood. The Great House Farm in the slave dirges symbolizes, on the one hand, the barrier to the realization of black dignity and selfhood. On the other hand, it symbolizes the place where black folks have gotten stuck in their movement toward freedom and full entry into modernity. The songs register this dissonance of consciousness wherein consciousness has not become self-consciousness and thus liberated to be itself. Instead, it remains suspended between rapturous hope and anguishing sorrow because the Great House Farm is the upper limit of an unhappy consciousness and the horizon of transcendence. Douglass notes how one song captures this dialectical sentiment:

> I am going away to the Great House Farm!
> O, yea! O, yea! O! (23)

Note how the last line of the stanza oscillates between an anguishing and suspenseful "O" and an exclamatory "yea." Significantly, it is the "O," rather

than the affirmatory "yea," that both opens and ends the line. Hence, Douglass concludes that at root songs such as this one "represent the sorrows of [the slave's] heart; and [the slave] is relieved by them only as an aching heart is relieved by its tears" (24). Douglass was able to grasp this because, as he says, he "neither saw nor heard *as those without* might see and hear." What he saw was the primacy of culture for decoding who we take ourselves to be and for interpreting the meaning of race, religion, and nation within culture's ultimacy.

For all of this, however, by incorporating the "the Great Farm House" into its music, the slave songs can only lyrically intone and thereby symbolize the barrier to the realization of black selfhood; they cannot overcome it. Thus, the songs at best signify an incomplete revolution in black consciousness; at worst, they signify no revolution at all. For precisely this reason, if black selfhood is ever to be attained, so the momentum of the *Narrative* suggests, this limitation in black folklife must be sublated, overcome. Along with the Christian life tied to it, it must be lodged within a different interpretive framework. The final part of the Douglass–Covey altercation does just this. In laying siege to the Christian Easter story, Douglass overcomes Covey; but he does so by overcoming Sandy's root (and black folk life tied to it) and the black feminine at the same time.

Overcoming the Feminine, Overcoming the Folk: The Fight with Covey

We are now in a position to return to the fight scene of chapter 10. With the root at his side, Douglass returns to Covey's plantation. Importantly, his return is made against the backdrop of the symbolism of the three holy days of Easter. Because he was not fully persuaded of the power of the root, Douglass actually expected a confrontation with Covey. There, however, was no fight. Rather, on "Easter" Sunday morning "out came Mr. Covey on his way to [church] meeting." Douglass continues by observing that "[Covey] spoke to me very kindly, bade me drive the pigs from a lot near by, and passed on towards the church. Now, this singular conduct of Mr. Covey really made me to begin to think that there was something in the *root* which Sandy had given me." And so Douglass became "half inclined to think the root to be something more than I at first had taken it to be" (63), that there actually might be something positive about black folk culture.

Douglass is quickly awakened from his slumbers: "All went well till Monday morning. On this morning, the virtue of the *root* was fully tested" (63–64). As it turned out, the root's virtue consisted only in delaying the inevitable, for on Monday morning Covey sets out to whip Douglass for the weekend's indiscretions. Douglass fully resists him, meeting violence with violence and, in the end, relies neither on black folk religion nor on American Christianity but, rather, on himself to bring about his own "resurrection." Identity begins and ends with the self. With this move, Douglass seizes manhood and thus

overcomes the black feminine even as he overcomes Sandy's root and the limitations of black folk culture in realizing his dignity.

To see more clearly how Douglass's victory over Covey is a masculine triumph of self-reliance, it is worth providing a few more important details of the altercation. "Long before daylight," Douglass says,

> I was called to go and rub, curry, and feed, the horses. I obeyed, and was glad to obey. But whilst thus engaged, whilst in the act of throwing down some blades from the loft, Mr. Covey entered the stable with a long rope; and just as I was half out of the loft, he caught hold of my legs, and was about tying me. As soon as I found what he was up to, I gave a sudden spring, and as I did so, he holding to my legs, I was brought sprawling on the stable floor. (64)

Covey's attempt to tie Douglass "with a long rope," as from a joist in the stable, invokes the beating of Esther, which he witnessed when just a child. Recall, Mr. Plummer, the cruel overseer, "used to tie [Esther] up to a joist, and whip upon her naked back" (18). Douglass, by eluding Covey's efforts to do the same to him, portrays himself as resisting Covey's efforts to feminize him through beating him. He seizes masculine dignity, and thus freedom, by refusing to submit: "Mr. Covey seemed now to think he had me, and could do what he pleased; but at this moment—from whence came the spirit I don't know—I resolved to fight; and suiting my action to the resolution, I seized Covey hard by the throat; and as I did so, I rose" (64).

Interestingly, Douglass's resolve to fight Covey and so deny white male dominance is a complicated Christian moment that is refracted through the Easter mystery and its language of the resurrection: "I rose." Douglass here claims New Testament authority to challenge scriptural enslavement. But what is also apparent here is Douglass's reversal of his negative portrayal of Christianity's Easter story as tending toward feminine docility and submissiveness. In laying claim to the Pasch for himself, his own freedom and dignity are now made coterminous with his being literally made Christoform or paschally shaped. The Easter story has now been recast as the story not of femininity but of the recuperation of masculinity. Rather than the accomplishment of whiteness, Douglass deploys Easter to culturally accomplish black masculinity as the overcoming of the black feminine. Such is his recovery—as he put it the *Narrative*'s important appendix—of "the impartial Christianity of Christ," a recovery that has embedded within it a problematic gendering of Christianity and of Christ.

To put the matter theologically, Douglass resists entering into a mode of existence in which, as is the case with Christ's mode of Triune existence, life or identity can only be received from another. More specifically, in the economy of creation–redemption, it can only be received from the feminine that is Mary–Israel.[25] In other words, there can be no *theotokos* (mother of God) in Douglass's

religious imagination, just as there cannot be one in the religious imagination of whiteness.[26] Insofar as this is the case, Douglass, in the inflection of blackness, simply mirrors the problem of whiteness back to itself. From this one sees in a most poignant way how Douglass has repeated the problematic oppositional logic that is at work in how race operates in the American myth of national identity.

The difference now, however, is that his problematic repetition of this logic and its religious infrastructure has brought to light the vexed relationship between race and gender (and indirectly, even class by virtue of his elevation out of the slave's status as one outside the circle and into the status of the [abolitionist] intellectual).[27] In other words, the problem of modern racial reasoning in Douglass's hands and in his effort to overcome it, metastasizes as it represents itself in the form of the problem of gender and the problem of class. This in no way means that gender and class are not problems in their own right. No. Rather, I am saying that Douglass's 1845 *Narrative* helps one understand that the problems of gender and class in modernity are prismatic moments of the problem of race. They function in relationship to the race problem, even as the race problem discloses itself in terms of gender and class consciousness.

Douglass's subsequent comments on his struggle with Covey make the gendered aspects of the fight strikingly apparent. Having encountered Douglass's resistance, Covey is "taken all aback" and "trembl[ing] like a leaf." At this Douglass was buoyed, "[holding] him uneasy, causing the blood to run where I touched him with the ends of my fingers" (64). Interestingly, here near the end of the altercation episode, the imagery of blood resurfaces—but with a difference. For now it is Covey who is bleeding, and it is Douglass who brandishes the symbolic lash, as his fingers become instruments of the very violence he once received and reviled. Having inverted the structures of power and authority, Douglass is now a Christ figure who can battle Covey for some two hours until Covey concedes defeat: that is, until Covey is made to acquiesce, as it were, to feminization. For, "the truth was," Douglass says, "he had not whipped me at all" (65), since at no point "had [Covey] drawn . . . blood from me, but I had from him." Now we see that the presence of blood has throughout the *Narrative* been the sign of the feminine. But finally, that this was all along not just a racial fight but also a gendered one, Douglass himself admits, for the altercation, he says, "revived within me a sense of my own manhood" (65).

What, in the end, are we to make of Douglass's newly acquired, virile dignity? To this point I have labored to show that the dignity Douglass seizes comes at the expense of the dignity of the black feminine and of the religiosity of black folklife in its on-the-ground forms. These forms entail both Sandy's root (or any non-Christian religious expression of black folklife) and the Christian expressions within black life about which Douglass commented as "one outside of the circle" in chapter 2 of *Narrative*. Insofar as it is the case that the dignity Douglass seizes comes at the expense of the dignity of black women

and the dignity of on-the-ground Christian realities in relation to which he is situated as intellectual, then Douglass enacts a vision of the self that tragically repeats the vision of the human under which he was held as a slave and against which he wielded his pen. The difference is that by positioning himself on the one hand as having overcome the black feminine and the on-the-ground expressions of black folklife, including its so-called feminine-like expressions of Christianity, and on the other hand as having overcome Covey's position of white, racial authority, Douglass can re-present himself as the masculine "master" of his own fate. Being master of himself means being the self-made religious-cultural critic qua black (abolitionist) intellectual. In short, Douglass becomes a proto-black theologian, a religious thinker of the emancipated self, and as such enters into modernity's promise and its pragmatics of democratic existence as self-determination.

Easter, Identity, and the Theology of Israel: A Postscript

This engagement with Douglass's *Narrative* sought to surface both the promise of and problems with the text's expression of a black Christian literary sensibility that tried to articulate itself both with and against modernity; and this engagement cries out for constructive response. Such a response could emerge from a number of possible vantages. A response could be pursued, for example, in the direction of a theology of gender (perhaps on the order of womanist and feminist theology[28]), or in the direction of a political philosophy that reconfigures the relationship between religious thought and political theory (perhaps on the order of Jeffrey Stout's recent and important statement on democratic pragmatism[29]). Or scholars might respond in the direction of a democratic philosophy of race, perhaps on the order of Cornel West's work toward a pragmatic philosophy of religion and a "tragicomic" conception of race or of Eddie J. Glaude Jr.'s recent attempts to develop an approach to black identity grounded in a pragmatic historicism that has been schooled in John Dewey's philosophy.[30]

Having critically engaged Douglass's *Narrative*, my intention as I conclude this chapter is not to take up any of these concerns—at least, not directly. Rather, it is to lay the groundwork for how a vision of identity might be developed beyond the intractable entanglements outlined above, one that builds on the theological promise of what Douglass does. When I mentioned in the introduction to this chapter that I wanted to sketch a more theologically rigorous approach to how identity might be rethought and performed differently, I meant, to use the language of Jeffrey Stout, to engage Christianity's "full-fledged truth-claims"[31] regarding the theology of Easter. For assistance in this I will reclaim and redirect moves made in patristic and medieval Christian thought.[32] In doing this, I want to imagine where Douglass's discourse might

go were one to build on the promise of his gesture to rethink identity from Easter not as a reflex of culture (and thus of race) but as a defining moment of YHWH's covenant with Israel and thus with the world.

From within the literary economy of the 1845 Narrative, Douglass helps us see that modern identity's contradictions and discontents are symptomatic of the failures of modern theology itself. That is, he helps us see that the modern theological imagination proves surreptitiously complicit in how the self comes to be forged in the kiln of sacrificial, "sacred" and therefore sanctifying, violence. As Michel Foucault so brilliantly drew out in his 1970s lectures at the Collège de France (addressed in chapter 1 of this book), war structures modern societies, and the biopolitics of racial identity are integral to the tactics of that warfare.[33] Douglass has already, in many ways, made Foucault's point. But he says more. His between-the-lines claim is that theology as a discourse has functioned to support this warfare of the self and "the hypocritical Christianity of this land" (97). He has autobiographically shown, perhaps more clearly than Foucault, and perhaps equally as powerfully as Italian philosopher Giorgio Agamben, how theology as a discourse buttresses the political economy, its social order, and the ongoing need for the figure homo sacer.[34]

It is precisely at this juncture that Douglass's religious indictment of the political economy of slavery is quite telling, even if it insufficiently extricates itself from or provides an alternative to the form of political life it criticizes. For my purposes, the importance of his indictment lies in the way it argues that behind the political economy of slavery lies a troublesome social performance of the Easter story. On his autobiographic reading of things, the Pasch proves to be not an alternative political and social arrangement but the cultural allegory, the sacred myth even, of the American political order.[35] Thus, the American political economy, as represented within the Narrative's textual horizon, is an economy of sacrifice, indeed, an economy that is calibrated through and, for this reason, requires sacrifice to maintain its totality, its social order.[36] The reading of the Narrative offered here shows that, within the terms of Douglass's cultural critique, the Easter story, laced as it is with modernity's logic of race, structures the American sacred mythos. This structure provides the terms and meaning of identity. My reading of the Narrative foregrounds the work that the Easter "mythos" does in the American political imaginary and also exposes how theology has often functioned to facilitate that imaginary.

As regards the social functioning of theological discourse, Douglass's indictment might be formulated as follows: Scripture and its theological significations have in actuality been made to function as the "immaterial" or "spiritual" superstructure that sanctions the "material" structures of power in the American social order and its political economy of slavery. Easter—to continue his indictment—does not represent an alternative mode of being in the world, for what the story, at least in its cultural performance, simultaneously covers over and enacts is the truth of power and its supposed ultimacy.

Hence—to unfold the final step in his indictment—there is and can be no actual recuperation of black selfhood apart from a prior narrative of self-sufficient power. For power *is* the truth of things; it *is* the story of being. It is this last move—seeing power as the metanarrative of existence and interpreting Christianity as a reflex, a cultural expression, of power—that leads Douglass to remain mired in this debilitating mode of the self, but now at the level of gender. Nevertheless, in showing how a narrative of power lies behind much of how we interpret who we take ourselves to be and how this narrative of power is at root religious and theological, Douglass does us a great intellectual service. For he unmasks, partially at least, the ideological ruse that lies at the heart of how racial and national identity are performed and thought about and how that understanding is mythically authorized through recourse to Christianity and Christian theology. In short, by miming their deepest intellectual procedures, Douglass has exposed to theologians the link between their intellectual reflections on and formulations of Christian doctrine (in this case Christology and atonement) and the forging of historical agents. He has exposed their position within this nexus and thus their role as mediator in the very production and reproduction of this nexus.

His unmasking of the ruse at the heart of how racial and national identity is thought about notwithstanding, what are we to make of the contradiction at work in *how* Douglass unmasks the problem? I suggest two ways of accounting for it. One important way is in terms of dogmatic theology. In reading the "spiritual" story of Easter as a story of (white, racial) power, which if modified can empower him to seize the "material" power of manly dignity, Douglass in fact reenacts the problem that must be overcome. He does this precisely in his foreclosing of an understanding of the story of the cross in which it is the telling of a different story of "material" power altogether. In this respect the inner logic of the theology of the passion is lost on him. He becomes blinded, in other words, to how the cross tells the true story of possession or power as a story of dispossessing the self that biopower creates and thus as a story of ascetic and aesthetic renunciation or, in short, as the story of Triune love. He cannot see that the cross of Christ is the revelation of power as the exchange of love wherein poverty and wealth, possession and dispossession, are not opposed to one another and racially stratified according to a logic of white supremacy. Unable to think other than within modernity's racialized discourse of whiteness (and the blackness that whiteness creates), Douglass cannot see how in the flesh of Christ crucified a wholly new social arrangement beyond the arrangement of whiteness is inaugurated, an arrangement in which poverty and wealth, possession and dispossession, articulate each other and thus are mutually constitutive.[37] This is the social arrangement of love that the passion enunciates.

Nor, for that matter, is Douglass able to see that this story of loving dispossession is a Trinitarian story of the repetition—a true repetition—of crea-

tion (Kierkegaard) and of the recapitulation (Paul, Irenaeus) of the many words of creation in the one, eternal Word of God (Maximus the Confessor). This truthful and thus positive repetition occurs through the Holy Spirit and abides in the womb of Mary–Israel. That is, this positive repetition occurs in the gift in whom all gifts, including the gift of dignity, are given. This gift is the Trinitarian gift of the Spirit. As the enactment of Israel's hope for a coming kingdom (with the appropriate signs marking its arrival; I return to this momentarily), this gift, which is sacramentally and liturgically received in the church and which structures creation and human life as themselves gifts, liberates all things into the possibility of not just being or existing, but into the possibility of flourishing, or what Maximus called "well-being," and through deification into the possibility of ecstatic, "super-well-being." In the dramatic movement from being to well-being to super-well-being, identity is preeminently conferred and the destiny of human existence realized. In foreclosing a more classically dogmatic approach to the theology of the passion, Douglass boxes himself into a fateful redeployment of the Easter story as a story of culturally illicit power.

This brings me to another equally if not more important way to account for the hiatus in Douglass's thought on this point. Douglass's error is that he has mimed the style of religious thought that he is actually trying to resist. Insofar as this is the case, he reflects the deficiencies of much of modern theology back to itself. He does this precisely by putting on display what happens when theological discourse functions as nothing more than the symbolic or religious superstructure of the materially or so-called real order of things. He also bears witness to the fact that this can be and quite often is done even when one makes "full-fledged," Christian "truth-claims."

When theology functions in this way, despite its rhetoric, it does not bear witness to salvation in any strong sense of the term. Rather, it witnesses to a purely human religious knowledge that is Gnostically accessed through some cultural calculus or discursive technique of power. On this basis, one can say that Douglass has tapped into a black religious Gnosis through his cultural rereading of the passion of Christ. But in doing this, he has only reflected back to modernity how modern theology has tended to function quite often to ground the political economy and order of things on the basis of a white religious Gnosis.[38] In this way, Christian thought has tended to ventriloquize the American social order rather than witness to an alternative form of sociopolitical existence. Theology's failure in this regard left Douglass (and many other black intellectuals besides him) with no live alternative by which to (re)imagine the world. (Though of course, there was the Christianity of those within the circle, the theological meaning of whose lives Douglass subjected to theological closure.) What was left was recourse only to a tragic inhabitation of the very vision of the self in need of overcoming. Thus, he, like many black intellectuals after him, could not help but be committed to a "radically democratic" vision of

the self with its grand religious or "eternal logic," as W. E. B. DuBois once said, of emancipation.[39]

Douglass's error, then, is only secondarily an error of not coming to terms with the theological depths of the paschal mystery, though it is this, but it lies primarily in how he unwittingly embraces the most pernicious aspects of modern religious thought's and modern theology's intellectual procedures and commitments. Much of modern theology has worked to obscure how the passion, in fact, sets personhood and peoplehood within a different moral and sociopolitical horizon because it sets them in a different theological horizon. Modern theology's fault, in other words, has often been in being a sounding brass and a clanging symbol with regard to how Christ relocates the world within God through his obedient love in the Spirit for the one he called Father. Such is to be the new ground of identity.

Herein, then, lies the instructiveness of Douglass's failure: it calls modern theology to reflect not only on the meaning of the human—and thus on the self—differently but on how it understands itself and its connection to life. It calls for it to reflect on what it means for it to be a "discourse," a mode of thought and practice of the self. On this point, French historian of philosophy Pierre Hadot's work on how ancient philosophy understood itself could prove quite useful. Hadot argues that in being a discourse, ancient philosophy was a way of life, a form of "non-Christian" ascetic spirituality.[40] What might it mean for modern theology to restore such a distinction by which Christian theology is a faithful "discourse" only to the extent that it witnesses to the form of life, the style of being, that is an aesthetics and ascetics of a Triune love that race trades? It was out of such an understanding that much of early Christianity maintained that it, too, was a philosophy, the true "discourse" of life and practice of the passion.[41]

Christian theology's distinctive contribution to how the self is thought about and practiced would be to understand the self as neither a static possession nor an entity aimlessly adrift in the world, nominalistically free to do as it pleases. Rather, it would be to conceive of the self in Christological terms: that is, in terms of how identity is forged anew in the Easter Pasch in which the love of the Father and the Son terminate on each other in the Spirit, even to the point of death. Easter so understood is a drama of "dispossession" rather than a dramatic display of possession or power as Douglass conceives of it following too closely modernity's religious mythos of race.[42] This, however, begs the question of what it means to have an Easter identity, what it means to exist "dispossessively" and not "powerfully." I contend, following a Trinitarian logic, it means living pentecostally or pneumatically. It means living in the Spirit.

A brief consideration of Acts 2, which represents this pneumatic way of existence, can help clarify what I mean here and so conclude the chapter. A

crucial sign of the coming of the Spirit, and therefore of conformity to the cross, is the ability both to understand and to speak languages that are not one's own. This sign indicates the reversal of the judgment that descends on humankind in Genesis 11 whereby God allows the various peoples of the world to remain trapped within their various self-enclosures of political and cultural national-isms. Such was the divine judgment against this way of being in the world. Pentecost indicates God's reversal of this judgment. Yet the reversal, it is critical to note, comes about only by way of God's faithfulness to God's own promise to Israel, the seed of Abraham. The promise was that Israel would be pivotal in how the nations and the peoples of the world would be delivered from their various national and cultural identity enclaves. The incommensurability of languages is emblematic of the problem of nationalism and so of the question of identity. The Christian claim is that Israel's pivotal position in the reversal of the judgment of Genesis 11 (a position that is never superseded) reaches its crescendo in Jesus of Nazareth, in the unity of his person and work.

How so? Christ's life, which culminates in "the hour" of his passion, is the pneumatological foil to Genesis 11, the foil that reverses creation's self-enclo-sure, first and ultimately, against God, and, second and no less important, within itself. Being instrumental in effecting this reversal is and remains the destiny of Israel. Its election, in this respect, is to mediate creation's re-creation. Through Christ, the seed of Abraham, the world in its entirety is conscripted into Israel's destiny, which turns out to be the world's destiny. From this it becomes clear that Israel's destiny is not solipsistic; its election is to be itself precisely by being more than itself: that is, by being for the world. It is to be a nonnationalistic nation, a different kind of people—the people of YHWH. This nonsolipsistic destiny is brought to fruition in Christ, who is at once child of Israel and Son of God/Son of man. He is most truly the former as he is the latter, and he accomplishes both in the Old Covenant/New Covenant economy insofar as he disrupts the linguistics of cultural and political nationalism, in-cluding the nationalism at work in how identity is conceived and performed. Having disrupted this faulty performance of language and therefore of identity, Christ reperforms it and, through the momentum of his life, draws creation into the grandiloquence of his reperformance. Such is the "pentecostalization" of the world, its being drawn into his incarnate or "passionate" way of existence into a new mode of speech and identity.

Christ's cry of dereliction anticipates the full pentecostalization of the world, and thus prefigures aspects of the miracle of languages in Acts 2. For purposes of my argument, it is important to note that the poverty or power-lessness of language signified in the cry of dereliction is the means by which Christ seizes anew the wealth of language and so rearticulates the meaning of identity, personhood, and peoplehood—redemptively. His life of linguistic dispossession, impoverishment, and powerlessness draws creation into the

kenosis of the "language" of the Logos. In this way he grants to creation a new, inflamed or Pentecostal tongue. Creation is given new, "spiritual" ears to now hear in Christ the language of the Triune God of love, but to hear it precisely in and as the various languages (*logoi*) of creation itself. It hears the divine language by being swept into the embracing overabundance of God's speech (the Logos), which both creates the world and then passionately releases itself into the world so that God might accompany the creature in its journey back to God and thereby into its self-realization. God's journey with the creature occurs in history—indeed, in the history and flesh of Israel, which culminates in Jesus of Nazareth. For he brings Israel's history, Christian thought affirms, to an ir-repeatably unique pitch, a pitch that in Christ is translated into the languages of the nations.

What emerges here is not only a reimagining of identity on the personal and cultural levels whereby the self is known in, through, and *as* another. What simultaneously becomes evident is a reimagining of identity on the level of national identity whereby the destiny of a given nation and its sense of peoplehood are bound to the destinies of other nations and their sense of peoplehood. But this internationalism—and merely modern cosmopolitanism—is theologically rooted in how Christ's existence unfolds in history as an eschatological movement toward the kingdom of God, which the church certainly haltingly but no less truly anticipates. To restate the point: what I gesture toward is a Christian theology of Israel and of the nations that un-asks and then re-asks the question of identity by situating the question within the horizon of creation's destiny, as is said in Orthodox Christianity, to be divinized. Such an understanding of identity, which has profound ethical consequences, leads to an understanding of nationhood and peoplehood that is not grounded in the politics of (political and cultural) nationalism. The condition of possibility for this lies in creation realizing itself by being ecstatically caught up into the divine language as sung in the revelation of God in Christ. Being thus enraptured, creation is restored to its proper theological identity. This is signified by its ability by the grace of the Spirit to speak a "foreign" or adopted language, the language of divine sonship, the language of God, as its own. Nationalism, or identity as construed in binary terms and therefore as self-enclosure, is broken.

This is signaled in Acts 2 through the double miracle of speech and audition, which is then followed in the rest of the book by the miracle of repetition. The miracle of speech is apparent in that certain of the Jerusalem Jews (cf. Acts 1) were granted the ability by the Spirit to speak the promises of the God of Israel, promises secured in the life of Christ, in languages not their own (2:1–4). The miracle of audition then follows: devout diaspora Jews were able to hear the promises of God translated, without diminution, into the dialects of the nations (2:5–6). The remainder of the book of Acts is a grand miracle of repetition, a new, different kind of repetition, by which the miraculous interplay of speech and audition reverberates into the amphitheatre of history.

Indeed, it (re-)creates history as an extension of Christ's Easter, as his passionate, pneumatological body.

This new history and body politic proceeds by way of the early Jews— or more accurately as Scripture tells it, by early Jewish-Christians—returning to the nations from which they had come and continuing to speak the truth of the God of Israel in the languages of their non-Jewish host nations. In the course of this new unfolding of history—the history of Christ's post-Easter body, which is his Easter body now made available to the world—a veritable revolution of language, and so of culture and identity itself, is effected. For each language, now having the language of Jesus as its destiny and so being released from its self-enclosures, is made open to other languages, the creaturely words of God sung in the Word of God. Identities become multilayered— "polyphonous" and marked by "heteroglossia," as Mikhail Bakhtin might say.[43] Such is the "interhumanity" of the peoples of the world.[44] The openness that marks Israel in its destiny to be for the world—an openness, mind you, that restores the openness of the nations—is part and parcel of the openness of creation to God, which Christ restores. Hence, as theologian Sarah Coakley has recently argued, the meaning of the human is to be firmly understood within the theological openness and vulnerability of creation before God.

Given this, it can be said that contemporary approaches to the self and to the question of identity often fail us because modern theology has in crucial ways failed us. It has failed us in that it has too often been nothing more than a cultural discourse, the discourse of "white" cultural-political nationalism that has had the privilege of not having to self-identify in this way. In this respect, it has been a "white" theology. It becomes apparent from this what it is that makes "white" theology "white." It is its "anti-Jewishness," its having been insufficiently paschal, "charismatic," "pentecostal," and spiritual. I do not mean by this that all "white" theology has actively and intentionally had a posture that is antagonistic toward Jews, though this has been true for far too much of it.[45]

What I mean is that what makes "white" theology "white" is that it does not do its work pentecostally; that is, it does not do it from within the distinctively Jewish-Christian horizon of the miracle of speech, the overturning of nationalism, the theological refounding of identity within the person of Jesus of Nazareth. It is unable to speak the truth of the God of Israel in a language— and therefore in a cultural and political orientation—that is not its own. It has been unable to fathom how another reality sacramentally and iconically bears God. This inability—the stammering of whiteness—infects its overall vision of the human person and leads to a repression of all other identities that it creates and then in binary fashion sets itself against. Douglass at some basic level grasps that the problem lies in this direction. He grasps that this inability bespeaks modern theology's ability to speak only the language and cultural ethos of whiteness whereby what is white is an end in itself and as such is

accomplished. He grasps that the cross in some way disrupts this nationalism and its problematic vision of the self. Yet, to the extent that he barricades himself within the citadel of the self-made, Emersonian–Franklinian man, Douglass remains trapped within the self-enclosure of the black masculine that the white masculine created.[46] Trapped in this way, he remained ensnared within and, indeed, repeated the contradictions of modern identity.

8

The Spirit of Christ

A Theological Reading of the Writings of Jarena Lee

Glory to God, for his glory stood over the doors of the Tabernacle.... Many added to the old Methodist Church...enquiring the way to Zion.

> —Jarena Lee, *The Life and Religious Experience of Jarena Lee, a Coloured Lady, Giving an Account of Her Call to Preach the Gospel, Written by Herself*

Ye are come unto mount Sion...the city of the living God, the heavenly Jerusalem...the church of the firstborn...to God the Judge of all...to Jesus the mediator of the new covenant.

> —Heb. 12:22–24

The Hammon and Douglass sagas, as I argue in chapters 6 and 7, chart an Afro-Christian sensibility struggling with and against a pseudotheological modernity. This modernity coincides with the accomplishment of race generally and with the accomplishment of whiteness specifically. Reading these texts in light of a set of contemporary theological questions, I argue that in both Hammon's 1760 *Narrative* and Douglass's 1845 *Narrative*, the black self is made visible within the history of Christ's enduring influence— indeed, within the history of freedom unleashed in his person and in his Jewish, covenantal flesh. As such, these texts witness to the fact that "a really adequate history of liberation is to be found where there is a humanly adequate response to the word of Jesus, in an unconditionally trusting discipleship of him."[1]

Within this discipleship, the racial protocols of modernity are destabilized; the self and indeed what is even meant by a "self" are redefined in response to the word of Jesus. Insofar as these texts frame an emerging Afro-Christian existence as a response that situates the self inside Israel's covenantal history, these texts point neither to a tragic nor to a tragicomic mode of existence. Rather, they point to a supratragic mode of existence, one that exceeds the horizon of modernity's racial gaze, which is predicated on the extirpation of Jewish consciousness insofar as it is oriental.[2]

This final chapter looks to Jarena Lee's autobiographical narratives—journals of a black woman's sojourn to "Zion"—as a correction and supplement to Hammon's and Douglass's efforts to give voice to an Afro-Christian consciousness articulating itself with and against modernity.[3] It explores how her writings seek to reshape the modern self at the crossroads of race and gender—Lee is clear that the two are inextricably bound together—precisely by bearing more deeply into Christology and into how Christianity might effect a truer liberation of the self. I read her spiritual autobiographical writings as entering into and probing more deeply the Christological- literary openings of Hammon's 1760 *Narrative* and Douglass's 1845 *Narrative*.

As the first step, I consider how Lee was "awakened" to Christianity and how the narration of her awakening raises questions about how moderns are born into the narrative of race. I am particularly interested in how her account of spiritual progress and her use of the genre of spiritual autobiography seek to resituate the self in a different economy of birth. I show that Lee's writings are a theological attempt to rewrite the self exegetically—that is, as an exegesis of Scripture. I then interrupt my direct engagement with Lee's spiritual narrative and the argument of my claim that she expounds the self as an exposition of Scripture so that I can reflect at a more theoretical level on how what I call the "exegetical imagination" functions in her discourse and, moreover, on how spirituality functions as a feature of the exegetical imagination. My reflections here are situated between an engagement with the work of Jewish thinker Michael Fishbane and the work of literary critics Carla Peterson and Katherine Clay Bassard. I then return to a close reading of Lee's narrative and her attempt to exegetically reshape the self, but a reading now informed by conclusions drawn from my theoretical reflections on spirituality as an exegetical practice. What must be borne in mind throughout this literary exercise is that insofar as Scripture for Lee is Christ's flesh, as it was for Origen of Alexandria, the exegesis of the self that she engages in entails an explication of the self inside the humanity and history of Jesus of Nazareth. The self, properly speaking, is Christological.

This last claim lies at the center of the overall objective of this chapter and thus is worth amplifying. I ultimately establish in this chapter the theological advance that Lee's account of the self makes over the representations of the self in the 1760 Hammon text and in Douglass's 1845 *Narrative*. Her contribution

is this: Lee grasps that in unfolding within the history of Jesus, the self unfolds inside YHWH's covenant with the people of Israel and thus inside Israel's ongoing election. Lee's way of signaling this is with her emphasis on Zion, a scriptural shorthand for the Davidic covenant.[4] According to Jon D. Levenson, what sets the covenant of Zion apart from the covenant of Sinai is that, with the former, because of the faithfulness of David in adhering to the stipulations of the covenant of Sinai, the Mosaic covenant, YHWH binds himself to uphold the covenantal relationship with Israel even if Israel at any point is unfaithful to the stipulations of the covenant. Thus, what the covenant of Zion represents is this: YHWH's relationship with Israel cannot be broken; the covenant is irrevocable inasmuch as YHWH himself swears to uphold it even if this entails YHWH's suffering through it.[5]

In moving in the literary direction of reimagining black life in relationship to Israel and Israel's covenant with YHWH, Lee in effect turns her gaze back to the heart of modern racial reasoning and to where the modern discourse of race went awry: namely, to the modern severing of Christianity from its Jewish roots. She understands, contra Kant et al., that Jesus is not to be understood as the highest expression of occidental wisdom, though expressed in oriental garb. Jesus is not the religio-moral exemplar of white accomplishment and of the supremacy and advance of Western civilization. He is the Jew who draws those who are not Israel into YHWH's promises with Israel. What she intuits is that YHWH's promises to Israel *are* God's promises to and with the world. Lee's spiritual writings reframe identity within this horizon, thus refusing to understand Christianity as the religious property or the cultural capital of the West.

This chapter, then, in large part translates the account of identity embedded in Lee's spiritual narrative—particularly around race and gender—into the idiom of theology. To this end, I pay particular attention to Lee's retrieval of the discourse of Israel's covenant of Zion for reshaping the self. More specifically, I attend to how her narrative of the self is suspended between the covenant of Zion and the event of Pentecost, the sending of the Holy Spirit after the ascension of Christ, fifty days after the Easter resurrection (Acts 1–2). Pentecost, therefore, is a Christological event. It is the capstone of Easter. In Lee's theological imagination, Zion and Pentecost are two sides of the same theological reality. Indeed, she holds the two together in such a way that the event of Pentecost, which brings the covenant of Zion to eschatological culmination, reshapes the self beyond the sociopolitical landscape of her own indentured servitude. Thus, Zion-Pentecost redemptively makes the self more than the self. The self is not a stable "I." Reconfigured in Christ, the self is itself in exiting the economies of racial-gender proscriptions, in leaving "Ur of the Chaldees," and in journeying into the economy of God as revealed in the flesh of Jesus of Nazareth, the economy of the covenant of Zion at Pentecost.

What Lee's writings, therefore, help us understand theologically is that Pentecost is an elucidation of the person and the work of Jesus of Nazareth in

relationship to YHWH's covenant with Israel and through this people with all peoples. By sending the Holy Spirit into the world, the sign of whose presence is the gift of speaking languages that are not one's own (*glossalalia*), those who are not of Israel and thus do not speak Israel's covenantal language can nevertheless through one from among this people—Jesus the Jew from Nazareth—be drawn into Israel's speech, the speech of YHWH's promises with this people. In other words, contrary to the claims of modern philosophy from a late-eighteenth-century thinker such as Johann Gottlieb Herder to the influential nineteenth-century philologist Ernest Renan and beyond, language within a covenantal horizon is not a hermetic enclosure tied to the essence of a people. Rather, language is open, and therefore Israel's speech, comprised of the syntactical elements and the vowel points of YHWH's promises to Israel, is not essentialized and therefore racialized speech. Hebrew, Yiddish, and Koine Greek, as the Jewish philosopher Jacob Taubes has said, have all been and are YHWH's language, the idioms of the promise.[6]

The insight of Lee's spiritual narrative that I explore in various way in this chapter is her understanding of Jesus as the semantic horizon within which she translates the self into YHWH's promises with Israel and "enquires the way to Zion." Mediating this process of translating and reshaping the self is an ecclesiology (an understanding of the church) whose substructure is mariological (or tied to a doctrine of Mary) of Israel as the *theotokos* or "mother of God."[7] In being tied to Mary, Lee's Christology links both self and church to YHWH's covenant with Israel and thus with the world. Thus, I will argue that the architecture of Lee's vision of the self opens the way for a theological undoing of modernity's pseudotheology of whiteness.

Toward a Theological Reading of Lee's Writings

The principle sources of what is presently known about Jarena Lee's life are her two autobiographical narratives: *The Life and Religious Experience of Jarena Lee, A Coloured Lady, Giving an Account of Her Call to Preach the Gospel* of 1836 (*Life*) and its significant expansion and republication thirteen years later as *Religious Experience and Journal of Mrs. Jarena Lee, Giving an Account of Her Call to Preach the Gospel* of 1849 (*Journal*), which carries the story of her life up to her fiftieth birthday. Lee's activities beyond those she records in her *Journal* of 1849 are unknown. She tells us that she was born free in Cape May, New Jersey, on February 11, 1783, but that her parents hired her out in 1790 to be a servant, no doubt due to her family's extreme impoverishment. At the time, she was but seven years old. That Lee had to be hired out—and at such a young age at that—witnesses to the tenuous and highly qualified status of northern black freedom.[8] Lee dwells briefly on her childhood so that she might move quickly

to narrate her conversion to Christianity and so enter into what obviously for her is the substance of her journals.

This brevity in dealing with her childhood, however, is not without significance. There are at least two ways of making sense of it. On the one hand, we can read Lee as wholly and utterly constrained by the conventions of the genre in which she writes, early American spiritual autobiography. The genre's protocols prescribed that the time lived under Christian influence, "Christian time" shall we say, is of paramount significance in bringing narrative coherence to one's life. Because Christian time filters memory, it receives the most narrative attention. Thus, because during her childhood she did not live under the banner of Christianity, Lee quickly passes it over. This is because non-Christian time is deemed empty time and vacant history. In short, it is meaningless. Thus, since her childhood was a non-Christian childhood, it receives short shrift.

The problem of the brevity of attention paid to her childhood is only heightened when one reads Lee's curt portrayal of her childhood as a metaphor of a general approach to black life in the New World. Metaphorically read, the four opening paragraphs Lee allots to telling the reader about her childhood reproduce a general ideology of Christian triumph over those existing in an infantile, uncivilized, and pre-Christian state of human nature. More specifically, the curtness of Lee's opening words, which narrate how she came to be a servant in a white household and how in that state of servanthood she was introduced into Christianity, mimes the general notion of the times: namely, that black existence can become visible only as it is inserted into the narrative of Euro-American civilization. That is, blackness is visible only to the extent that it functions as servant within the sociopolitical economy of whiteness, an economy not only bolstered by certain forms of Christianity but one that, in fact, came to be wholly identified with modern Christianity. The textual economy of Lee's spiritual narrative, it can therefore be said, reproduces the sociopolitical economy of Christian whiteness.

What other significance can there be, one might ask, to the opening four paragraphs, which in their brevity swiftly locate Lee within the social condition of servanthood? Moreover, Lee's servanthood is servanthood practiced in a Christian economy, a Christian domestic arrangement. To be sure, it is here, in this Christian home, that Lee is given access to the power of literacy. This suggests the possibility of a concealed moment of liberation while yet in the master's house. The possibility of literacy, as Lee narrates her childhood, is indelibly yoked to the Christianity she is introduced to in this domestic arrangement. Thus, writing emerges out of and exists, in some sense, within the confines of this home and its religio-economic order. This would suggest that the omega of Lee's spiritual narrative is already told on the alpha of the first page: the true domicile of black flesh and, even more, of black female flesh in

modernity is in the domestic sphere of Christian and patriarchal whiteness. Whatever legitimation there is will necessarily be constrained within this economy. It follows from this reading, then, that the expedient gait of the opening paragraphs of Lee's writings, which function in effect to erase her childhood and quickly thrust the reader into the arms of white Christianity, can be understood to reflect the broader experience of New World blackness. Indeed, Lee's experience becomes a metaphor of this experience, an experience in which the moment of origin—the past, history—is violently obliterated, so as to leave only the carcass or literary remains of four brief paragraphs.

Yet, such a reading, as important as it is, does not tell the whole story, for it also can be said that Lee employs the genre of the American spiritual autobiography to subversive effect. The question is not only *what* remains, but equally *what she does* with what remains—both the remains of her fragmented, four-paragraph childhood and the remains of the Christianity from which she reads or assigns meaning to that four-paragraph past. It is precisely here that Lee's literary subtlety, especially in its function of engaging the very white Christianity that sanctified her subservience within an economy of whiteness, must be reckoned with. I argue that Lee's *disremembering* of her childhood and, by metaphoric extension, the *disremembering* of a black past that is violently brought into the New World, is a peculiar *remembering* or reconstituting of it as well. In other words, the disremembering and remembering of her childhood is itself multivalent and, as Mikhail Bakhtin has suggested with respect to the genre and discourse of the novel, "heteroglot" and "double-voiced."[9]

The heteroglossia and double-voicedness of childhood in Lee's journals has to do with the way in which memory and time function in her autobiographical rescripting of the self. Melvin Dixon's theorizing about the use of memory and time by black writers speaks to the point I am making about the subversiveness embedded in Lee's account of her childhood. This subversiveness points to her efforts to subtly reconceive the drama of Christianity. It can be said, following Dixon, who draws on Robert Hayden's poem "Mystery Boy Look for Kin in Nashville," that Lee has "disremembered time" in order to remember it: that is, "to regain and reconstruct . . . [both] the past [and] history itself."[10] There is within Lee's disremembering of her childhood an active remembering of it so as to re-present herself in a distinctive way. For Lee, self-representation and cultural memory occur, as Bassard has recently argued, as and through the medium of Christian speech acts.[11] They occur, that is, in the mode of Lee's distinctive reception and experience of Christianity. Her reception and experience of Christianity is the context and ground of her narrative's intelligibility. Thus, while the lack of detail about her childhood and adolescence points to the broader obfuscation of black existence, it must also be recognized that she infuses her memory of this very obfuscation with a different kind of meaning. She infuses it with Christian meaning, a meaning that

in her experience of Christianity actually discloses the self. Therefore, memory, insofar as Lee uses it as a tool for the revelation of who she is, functions in a distinctively Christian way. Memory for Lee is Christian memory.

To clarify what I am after here, it is worth probing the details of how Lee narrates her initial encounter with Christianity. This encounter occurred during her tenure as a domestic and took place, according to Lee, in 1804 when she was twenty-one years old. There are two parts to the encounter. First, there is her initial religious "awakening"; following this is the deepening of her awakening into "conviction." Lee says she was awakened upon hearing the preaching of a Presbyterian minister. She probably heard the minister while worshipping with the family for whom she was a domestic. Race and gender, as Bassard has observed, code this formative experience to which Lee hurriedly introduces the reader after her terse four-paragraph introduction.[12] "At the reading of the Psalms," Lee recounts, "a ray of renewed conviction darted into my soul. These words, composing the first verse of the Psalms for the service: 'Lord, I am vile, conceived in sin,/ Born unholy and unclean./ Sprung from man, whose guilty fall/ Corrupts the race, and taints us all.'" Heart-piercing were those words for Lee, for through them, she says, I was "made to feel in some measure, the weight of my sins, and sinful nature" to the point that "I was driven of Satan, in the course of a few days, and tempted to destroy myself" (*Life*, 3–4).

The minister's words, which signified for Lee a practice of "scriptural enslavement,"[13] are an interpretation of Psalm 51, which has built into it an account of the Fall in Genesis. Verses 1–10 are particularly interesting for how they inform the Presbyterian minister's reading of Scripture and Lee's hearing of it. Here are the verses in full:

> Have mercy upon me, O God, according to thy lovingkindness: according unto the multitude of thy tender mercies blot out my transgressions./ Wash me thoroughly from mine iniquity, And cleanse me from my sin./ For I acknowledge my transgressions: and my sin is ever before me./ Against thee, thee only, have I sinned, and done this evil in thy sight: That thou mightest be justified when thou speakest, and be clear when thou judgest./ Behold, I was shapen in iniquity; and in sin did my mother conceive me./ Behold, thou desirest truth in the inward parts: and in the hidden part thou shalt make me to know wisdom./ Purge me with hyssop, and I shall be clean; wash me, and I shall be whiter than snow./ Make me to hear joy and gladness; that the bones which thou hast broken may rejoice./ Hide thy face from my sins, and blot out all mine iniquities./ Create in me a clean heart, O God; and renew a right spirit within me.

Bassard has a masterful reading of the enslavement at work in the minister's sermonic use of these verses and of Lee's hearing of them. She observes that

couched in the rhetoric of traditional Christian penitence, the racial
subtext of the verse is haunting: the sin (crime) for which Lee is
convicted (convicts herself) is that she was "born unholy and unclean" to a corrupt "race" that is tainted (by skin color) . . . . Thus a
biblical psalm about the universal condition of human sin is rewritten by Anglo-Christian precepts that exploit the social meaning of
blackness as a "taint" and "corruption." In addition, the versified
psalm performs a (re)gendering of the biblical text by insisting on the
paternity of fallen humanity, which erases the feminine "mother" in
Psalm 51. These levels of mediation have profound social consequences for the means by which Christianity was presented to and
adopted by African American women in the late eighteenth and early
nineteenth centuries in America.[14]

How does Lee's spiritual narrative, like Hammon's and Douglass's, attempt to
undo what Bassard is describing? How does she undo the minister's deployment of the biblical psalm as a text of scriptural enslavement, and how does she
frame her entry into Christianity, from the moments of "awakening" through
"sanctification," as undoing both the racialized pretext that overlays and controls the Presbyterian minister's reading of Scripture and the effects of that
pretext on Lee herself? How does Lee offer a different reading of this text
beyond the utter fragmentation of community it engenders?

Key to Lee's counterexegetical performance is the different "economy"—
the different discursive space of community and the different hermeneutical
horizon of meaning—in which she situates the psalm's dramatic action. That
different discursive space and hermeneutical horizon, as becomes clear from
her own preaching as an itinerate minister in the African Methodist Episcopal
(AME) church, is YHWH's covenantal relationship with Israel. Lee will come
to express this especially in the 1849 *Journal* in the shorthand scriptural term
"Zion." She will situate her understanding of the identity of Jesus and in
relationship to Jesus her own efforts to reconstitute or transfigure the body
(politic) within this covenantal space and hermeneutical horizon. In doing this,
Lee displays her skills as a deft theological interpreter of Scripture and refa-
shioner of the self. Indeed, my interest is in examining how Lee's spiritual
narrative functions, as Michael Fishbane says, as "poesis"—that is, as an exercise in theologically remaking the self and its world.[15]

Poesis: The Jewish-Christian Exegetical Imagination

Before exploring how Lee further explains her awakening and conviction and
how she moves her narrative from there to sanctification—all as a part of how
she reframes her life beyond white-over-black (female) race relations—it is

worth examining more closely what Fishbane means by "poesis" and thus what I, building on his insights, mean in saying that Lee's spiritual narration of the self is a poetic exercise in remaking self and world.

By poesis "I mean to emphasize," says Fishbane and I following him, "the fact that rabbinic exegesis is always 'made,' that every exegetical act is a conscious construction of meaning through the verbal conditions of Scripture. Indeed, for rabbinic culture, the sense of Scripture is never predetermined; rather, everything depends on creative readings of its inherent, God-given possibilities."[16] The "poetic" interpretation of Scripture, understood in the rabbinic-theological sense outlined by Fishbane, "creates a new heaven and a new earth for human inhabitation." Indeed, as "prolongation of scriptural speech through the exegetical imagination renews the world and gives it divine meaning. With this attitude Judaism elevates the creative act of interpretation to a type of *imitatio dei*."[17]

Fishbane's understanding of poesis and the exegetical imagination in Judaism is helpful in pressing forward my reading of Lee's literary practice of autobiography as scriptural exegesis in which she gives voice to a Christian consciousness struggling with and against modernity. As I understand it, Fishbane's approach to poesis is consistent with the account I give of Augustinian confessional practice in chapter 6 of this book. There I interpret Augustine's practice of confession as a practice of scriptural exegesis done as autobiography. I argue that, therefore, autobiography was for Augustine (and Hammon) a theological feat. Consistent with the point I press there, here I draw on Fishbane's sense of rabbinic exegesis to argue that Lee engages in an interpretive practice similar to the Jewish rabbis (and similar to Augustine). She is interested in crafting her narration of the self as "an exegetical act [that] is a conscious construction of meaning through the verbal conditions of Scripture."[18]

I contend that the verbal cue within which Lee's autobiographical discourse reimagines the world is the discourse of Jewish covenant and, more specifically, the notion of "Zion," a notion that I already said is struggling to emerge and control the portrayal of the self of the Hammon persona through his subtle engagement with the scriptural texts of 1 Samuel and the Psalms. It is through the notion of Zion, as Lee engages it, that she reads Scripture against the grain of an understanding of the self as accomplished, as is the case in modern racial discourse. For Lee the self is textually open insofar as it participates in the "prolongation of scriptural speech" that, despite the creature's rebellion against its Creator, seeks to "renew the world and give it [i.e., the self and the world the self inhabits] divine meaning." She, too, elevates "the creative acts of interpretation," in her case the autobiographical act, "to a type of *imitatio dei*," or more specifically, again in her case, to a type of *imitatio christi*.

Fishbane's invocation of the notion of *imitatio dei* in connection with the exegetical practice of both the rabbis (ancient and modern) and the medieval

Jewish mystics (and, building on him, my invocation of the notion of *imitatio christi*) is significant in two respects here. First, autobiography as scriptural exegesis, indeed as *imitatio dei* and as *imitatio christi*, entails a speculative theology that mandates what Fishbane calls "intertextual conversion" or what in the contemporary parlance of postliberal theology might be called "narrative" conversion. By intertextual conversion, Fishbane points to the "linkage(s) between all parts of the canon," linkages that constitute the canon as an internally coherent and fully contained story.[19] That is to say, it is a story whose meaning inheres in itself. Canonical meaning requires no external supplement. Because the canon is coherent and contained in this way, entry into the story at any one point brings one into the story as a whole, for any one part of the story is tied intertextually to every other part of the story.

According to such theologians as Hans Frei, George Lindbeck, and Robert W. Jenson and a host of other thinkers broadly influenced by them, the bane of modernity is the refusal to read Scripture as a contained narrative, the refusal to be converted into its story. From the eighteenth century into the nineteenth it came to pass that "what the biblical narratives [were understood to be] about [was deemed to be] something other than their character as cumulatively and accretively articulated stories whose themes emerge into full shape only through the narrative rendering and deployment itself."[20] The effort of postliberal theologians and biblical scholars has been to undo this antinarratival approach to scriptural texts and to give accounts of what it means to enter into the "realism," as Frei says, following Erich Auerbach in *Mimesis*, that inheres in the Scriptures in their own right.[21] Fishbane's notion of "intertextual conversion" as a feature of classical Jewish thought can also be read as pushing back against the modern problem that Frei terms "the eclipse of biblical narrative."[22]

What is interesting to me is how Jarena Lee's autobiographical practice points both toward the problem of the eclipse of biblical narrative and perhaps even more toward Fishbane's notion of intertextual conversion as a means of addressing the problem of the modern collapse in understanding biblical narrative as whole and complete in itself and as calling its readers into its wholeness. Lee grasps that it is precisely the eclipse of biblical narrative, an eclipse by which Scripture is caused to aid, abet, and articulate the narrative of modernity as a narrative of white accomplishment, that lies at the root of black scriptural enslavement. Indeed, Lee understands that the Presbyterian minister's reading of Psalm 51 is not a "narrative" reading of Scripture. It is a reading in which the Scriptures cease being read as YHWH's story of covenantal relationship with and fidelity to the people of Israel and how God's love for the world is displayed precisely in and through YHWH's election of Israel. Her approach to autobiography as scriptural exegesis moves to restore such a narrative approach to Scripture. "Zion" is the intertextual hook by which she enters the biblical world. From "Zion" she reads the Scriptures as an internally

coherent story and thus not simply as a moment within the telling of the story of the West, the story of Western civilization as white accomplishment.

Were Lee's discourse to stop here, it would simply be an antebellum precursor to theological postliberalism. I contend that it is much more. Lee's autobiographical discourse, like Fishbane's understanding of intertextuality, aims at "a higher conversion" than just an intertextual entry into an internally coherent, narrative framework of the Bible. The higher conversion at which both rabbinic intertextuality and Lee's autobiographical exegesis aspire is "the exegetical construction of reality and the transformation of the culture into the images produced by that exegesis." With the higher conversion of exegetical transformation, "the world of the text serves as the basis for the textualization of the world—and its meaning. Through exegesis new forms arise.... [But what] remains constant is the attempt to textualize existence by having the ideals of (interpreted) Scripture embodied in everyday life. The process of world-making is the ultimate *poesis* of the exegetical imagination."[23]

The important point here is that both Lee and Fishbane understand exegesis not merely as the process by which the interpreter enters the world of the Bible. This is not enough. Rather, it is the process by which the interpreter, in making exegetical entry into the world of the Bible, brings the body and the body politic; he or she brings the society in which the body is situated and encoded with meaning into the scriptural world with them, thereby transforming that world by (scripturally) textualizing it. Lee brings a body raced and gendered as the black feminine; she brings a body marked for labor as a domestic servant to whites—she brings all of this as exegete of the self into a scriptural world in which YHWH is declared master but performs mastery or Lordship differently. This is a world that, because YHWH is master, a wholly different logic of mastery and servanthood displays itself. In the person of Lee as interpreter and in the web of relationships constitutive of her bodily existence, the black body enters into the processes of the theopoetic remaking or retextualization of the world and redisplay of the meaning of the body. In short, Lee theologically rereads the world in rereading the self.

Thus, the exegetical entry of the self into the world of Scripture entails processes of reconstruction, the reconstruction of the very world that was exited in entering into the narrative world of Scripture. I use the word "exit" advisedly here, for the exited world, rather than being left behind, is actually recontextualized within or made subject to a new hermeneutic. The world is sociopolitically replotted within the scriptural narrative, a narrative whose center of gravity—and this is Jarena Lee's point—is YHWH's covenant with Israel or what in shorthand she calls "Zion."

Lee's Jewish and covenantal enactment of the exegetical imagination, thus, is an ethical performance of a newly "imagined community," as Benedict Anderson might say.[24] This is the community of YHWH's covenant with Israel as it culminates, as Lee sees it as a Christian, in Jesus of Nazareth. But the

community she imagines is one that resists the protocols of modern nationalism and the discourse of culture through which the violence of modern nationalism works itself out. Understood as a phenomenon of the modern Christian West, the violence of modernity is calibrated to overcome, in the interests of constituting "the People" as nation, the residual Jewishness within Christianity. To overcome this Jewishness, as I discuss in part I of this book, is to constitute modern freedom, "[the] gage and emblem of [which] is [sovereignty or] the sovereign state."[25] It is to constitute Christianity as property of the West.

At the ground of modern freedom is the formation of the modern self as citizen or as political subject, a self and subjectivity that is formed through a violent process of "subjection," as Foucault calls it. This process of subjection and thus of forming the modern self enacts a political technology by which moderns constitute themselves as individuals even as they are constituted as individuals.[26] As I observe in chapter 1 when considering Foucault's 1975–1976 Collège de France lectures, *Society Must Be Defended*, this violent process of subjection is a racializing process. In telling the story of the self in scriptural-exegetical terms centered in YHWH's covenant with Israel—that is, within the horizon of "Zion"—Lee seeks nothing less than the replotting of the body (politic) beyond the modern political technology of the racialized individual.

There is one last point regarding the exegetical imagination that must be addressed before returning to Lee's writings. It concerns the issue of spirituality, which Fishbane turns to in developing further the higher conversion embedded within intertextual conversion. I have already noted Fishbane's argument that the higher conversion embedded within intertextual conversion, the conversion in which the interpreter through midrashic exegesis enters into the world of Scripture, entails the exegetical construction, indeed, the reconstruction of reality, its veritable midrashic textualization. This reconstruction or reality entails "the transformation of the culture into the images produced by that exegesis."[27] The life world, in other words, is drawn into the scriptural text precisely through a form of exegesis that "activates the letters and words of scripture along a horizontal plane."[28] But Fishbane further suggests that the transformation of the life world, its midrashic textualization, is mediated through a spirituality, through practices of Jewish mysticism. Spirituality, so understood, is not something apart from exegesis. It is a moment within the exegetical imagination; it is "exegetical spirituality." Exegetical spirituality signals that that there is a vertical axis to exegesis, a "belief that the grammar of Scripture conceals traces of a hidden, supernal truth. The verbal dynamics of biblical sentences are thus expressions of esoteric processes deep within the Godhead. This being so, mystical exegesis rings true when this divine reality is revealed to consciousness."[29]

Thus, to employ the exegetical imagination midrashically is to study Scripture spiritually; indeed, it is to study it mystically, where mysticism here

means the transformation of the self beyond what it was at the beginning of the process of exegetical study and into the very mystery of the one being studied. "So viewed," Fishbane says, "scriptural study is an act that virtually transforms the practitioner into a symbolic configuration of the divine powers. The spiritual transformation of the exegete *through exegesis* is the profound truth repeatedly dramatized" in the Jewish exegetical imagination, which is the very performance of Jewish spirituality. "This is so principally because Scripture is a configuration of Divinity; accordingly, the interpreter is affected by the transcendental features which he penetrates in the course of study."[30] What Jewish spirituality as exegesis emphasizes, then, is the "interior process through which certain exegetical theologies are actualized and embodied."[31] It exemplifies "how, through exegesis, life imitates (and interiorizes) texts,"[32] and thus how the self in being opened up to YHWH in the configuration of Scripture—rather than being an identity that is hermetically sealed thus making interpretation of both text and self impossible—can be made to grow, change, and develop into more than itself. The self in this Jewish understanding, because of the one to whom it relates, is possessed of infinite depth. It is precisely this Jewish theological understanding of the self that Gregory of Nyssa taps into, building Paul's notions of *epektasis* (cf. Phil. 3:13) and *anakaphaleiosis* or recapitulation, which Irenaeus of Lyons was at pains to develop in combating anti-Jewish Valentinian Gnosticism and Marcionism.[33] For Paul, Gregory, and Irenaeus, the self is infinite because it is a mirror of the infinite, a mirror of YHWH.

Fishbane's interpretation of Jewish spirituality and mysticism in relationship to Jewish, midrashic exegesis goes far in explaining, as I will show, the spirituality and mysticism embedded in Lee's discourse. In her case, attending her performance of the exegetical imagination at the site of "Zion" is a Christian spirituality steeped also in a mysticism, a Jewish-Christian mysticism, of the infinite God and therefore of the self, being precisely in its finitude and in virtue of the relationship to YHWH a mirror of the infinite. The self being a non-essential reality is possessed of infinite depth, the depth of YHWH. At the center of Lee's mystical practice of the infinite is prayer. This mystical practice not only actualizes and embodies her exegetical theology of the self. It also embodies a mystical exegesis that transforms the self—this is Fishbane's "higher conversion" within the intertextual conversion or within narrative realism—by weakening the strong structures of race (and, within this, gender), on which modernity founds the self as a stable, rather than infinite, surface on which to enact white mastery, the mastery of the West. In Lee's discourse, the self as determined through protocols of race and gender is made to exceed these confines.

Before returning to a close reading of Lee's writings, but now against the backdrop of the theoretical approach to spirituality that I have just outlined, it is worth contrasting the theoretical approach to Lee's spirituality and exegesis

of the self suggested here to two other attempts to makes sense of the spirituality of Lee's *Life*, those of Carla Peterson and, again, Katherine Clay Bassard.

Peterson interprets Lee's discourse as the construction of a different economy of freedom, an economy of the "mystical" that stands against the slaveholding economy of antebellum nineteenth-century capitalism. Drawing on Luce Irigary, Peterson employs the notion of a "mystical economy" to capture Lee's literary resistance to the capitalist economy of antebellum, slaveholding life. In Lee's mystical economy, according to Peterson, "the individual self loses its boundaries to merge with the other congregants and with the Godhead." The mystical economy, thus, is an economy that is wholly other. Indeed, it is nonmaterial, existing "outside the labor market and its symbolic linguistic order and is characterized by the nonrational, the sensual, the oral, the carnivalesque."[34]

Bassard's understanding of Lee's discourse goes in a similar direction, though it takes a further step in that, on her reading of the phenomenon of spirituality in Lee's discourse, she locates the true moment of liberation in those moments of "pure revelation," those moments of encounter "between God's spirit and Lee's soul," where there are "no mediating structures like Bibles, hymnbooks, preachers, churches, or missionaries involved. Direct communication from God to her 'conscience,'" Bassard says, takes place "*outside* the narrative of conversion, [being] peripheral rather than central to the primary narrative frame."[35] It follows from this that the primary narrative frame, the frame of conversion, is, in the end, epiphenomenal to the primary phenomenon: direct or unmediated encounter between the soul and God. This, according to Bassard, is what lies at the heart of Lee's spirituality and at the center of her approach to identity, justice, and liberation. Therefore, such matters as the very production of Lee's narrative, the struggle to see her narrative through to publication against the protests of the male hierarchy of the AME church, the exegetical practice embedded in her narrative, and her search for a church home, for Zion—all of this is epiphenomenally subordinate at best to the primary "mystical" phenomenon of direct communication with God.[36]

But is all this not a form of Platonism in which Lee is interpreted as enacting a movement of "the alone to the Alone," to use the language of religious and philosophical idealisms from the ancient Platonism of Plotinus to the modern Platonism of the identity philosophy of German Idealism? A nonmaterialist, mystical return to the solitary self, to the true and authentic individual, a return that leaves material structures in place as one takes mystical flight from them is what one is left with on Peterson's and Bassard's readings of how spirituality functions in Lee's discourse. The mystically solitary self is what overcomes oppressive hierarchy and hegemony. However, Lee's spiritual exegesis of the self in the mode of autobiography, being closer to Fishbane's account of Jewish spirituality, is more subtle and complex than

this. Her discourse follows and in its own way displays the divine economy of God's incarnation. Far from being nonmaterialist, this economy is God taking up the structures of the world into God's own life and transfiguring those structures according to Jesus' cruciform existence. Put another way, Lee's discourse is "mystical" because it follows the mystery of the incarnation rather than the disembodiment of modern rationality and racial thinking.[37]

I have already started to consider how conviction functions in Lee's discourse. I now return to a close reading of her *Life* and further develop her understanding of spiritual progress in order to show how she engages in a literary performance of Christian spirituality that transfigures the self to become more than the self, more than what the modern discourses of race and gender determined for her.

Pentecost as Zion: Christian Spirituality and the Meaning of the Self

I indicated earlier that key to Lee's counterexegetical performance is the different "economy" within which she locates the dramatic action of the Presbyterian minister's words drawn from Psalm 51 in order to replot the body (politic). I claimed that Lee sought theopoetically to remake the self and the world, to extricate herself from an "imagined community" in which the social meaning of blackness is taint and corruption. In such a socially produced or "imagined community," the black woman is deemed particularly culpable because it is by means of her flesh that many are born into such sin and shaped in iniquity. Not only was this the assertion by virtue of the Presbyterian minister's use of Psalm 51, we saw it also to be a claim implicit to Douglass's 1845 *Narrative*, the religious quest to overcome the black feminine. Lee's spiritual narrative struggles against such a vision and against the ways in which Scripture is deployed in justification of this vision's "social imaginary."[38] Lee's literary objective is to reconstitute the social imagination and thereby reimagine what communal life together is and what it should look like.

Interestingly, Psalm 51 in its fuller context, especially vv. 18–19, with its invocation of Zion, points to the reimagined community toward which Lee's discourse strives. Indeed, a reading of Lee's fuller narrative account, her 1849 *Journal*, reveals that the discourse of Zion is at the center of her literary imagination and is a centerpiece of her preaching. The verses of Psalm 51:18–19 read:

> Do good in thy good pleasure unto Zion: Build thou the walls of Jerusalem. Then shalt thou be pleased with the sacrifices of righteousness, with burnt offering and whole burnt offering: Then shall they offer bullocks upon thine altar.

Lee's entire narrative is a search for this more expansive landscape, the land-scape of Zion, within which to relocate the Presbyterian minister's words. But her search is not simply for a better interpretation of the minister's *words*. It is a search for the very community that those words signify. Her search is for the enactment of the community of Zion.

It appears that, given her situation, Lee's turn to the discourse of Zion is meant to highlight two things. On the one hand, there is the labor around which Zion as a community is organized, a labor that contrasts with the labor required of Lee as a northern domestic. The labor of which the Psalm speaks is the labor of righteous sacrifice. This is the labor that founds a righteous community or just society. It is the labor on which the "walls of Jerusalem," the covenantal city of Zion, are to be built. Lee's exegetical suggestion, which makes its appearance within the first few paragraphs of her narrative, must be understood against the backdrop of her reference to Joel 2:28, which she quotes as the epigraph to her narrative. Her reference to this passage points toward the second thing she highlights about the discourse of Zion. If her implied reference to Zion from the later verses of Psalm 51 highlights the kind of labor—priestly, sacrificial labor—that makes for a just community, her reference to Joel highlights who these priestly, sacrificial laborers in the community of justice are. Joel 2:28 reads: "And it shall come to pass . . . that I will pour out my Spirit upon all flesh; and your sons, and your *daughters* shall prophesy" (italics original to Lee).

Lee aligns Psalm 51 and Joel 2:28 in such a way as to suggest that what distinguishes the community of Zion is not just the labor of righteous sacrifice. It is also that this righteous sacrifice employs all flesh, the flesh of both "your sons and your *daughters*," as priestly or ministerial workers. It is the Spirit's descent on all flesh, without discrimination, that makes this possible and so constitutes the community of Zion. Lee's autobiographical narrative is the story of her search for, her conversion into, and her journey in becoming a new kind of laborer, a minister, working to establish the just community. This community, as she sees it, is the Davidic community of Zion.

What I suggest so far, then, is this: Lee dislodges Psalm 51 from its po-sition as a text lodged in an antebellum economy of southern slaveholding and northern black indentured servitude by reading it within the economy of the covenant of Zion. She does this by expanding the exegetical scope of Psalm 51 to include verses 18–19, which explicitly speak of "Zion" and the "walls of Jerusalem" that YHWH builds through the sacrifices or labors of righteous-ness. But the scriptural text that ultimately warrants Lee's expansive reading of Psalm 51 is her epigraphical reference to Joel 2:28. This passage, which functions in effect as the preface or the opening bookend of her narrative, speaks of sending YHWH's Spirit on all flesh, the flesh of both "your sons and your *daughters*" to prophesy. Yet, in the wider context of this passage the

sending of the Spirit on all flesh witnesses to YHWH's faithfulness to the covenant of Zion, to construction of the walls of Jerusalem (the city of Zion), and to YHWH's presence to his people. Here is the Joel passage quoted in its wider context:

> And ye shall know that I am in the midst of Israel, and that I am the LORD your God, and none else: and my people shall never be ashamed.
>
> And it shall come to pass afterward, that I will pour out my spirit upon all flesh; and your sons and your daughters shall prophesy, your old men shall dream dreams, your young men shall see visions:
>
> And also upon the servants and upon the handmaids in those days will I pour out my spirit.
>
> And I will shew wonders in the heavens and in the earth, blood, and fire, and pillars of smoke.
>
> The sun shall be turned into darkness, and the moon into blood, before the great and terrible day of the LORD come.
>
> And it shall come to pass, that whosoever shall call on the name of the LORD shall be delivered: for in mount Zion and in Jerusalem shall be deliverance, as the LORD hath said, and in the remnant whom the LORD shall call. (Joel 2:27–32)

Lee's exegetical prowess does not stop here, however. Her description of her experience of sanctification (see below) makes clear that she reads the Joel text in light of the account of Pentecost, which records that Peter quoted Joel 2:28 to explain how it could be that YHWH's promises could be spoken in the languages of the nations. Moreover, Acts 2 is the Lucan record of how this event founds a new sociopolitical order, the order of the *ecclesia*, the church, as tied to the covenant of Zion.

The point I seek to make here is simply that from the moment of her awakening or conviction through to sanctification, Lee engages in the literary-theological act of taking Psalm 51 out of the mouth of the Presbyterian minister and recasting it so that it ceases being a text of scriptural enslavement. Lee situates it within the economy of Zion-Pentecost, which for her is the economy of Christ's flesh, the new economy into which her black female flesh is incorporated and made to signify differently, an economy within which black flesh is assigned new meaning. In framing her life as a spiritual progression from conviction or awakening, which I have discussed earlier, to conversion and then to sanctification—the steps of spiritual progression within the Methodist tradition from which she speaks—Lee maps her incorporation into the divine economy through a literary process in which the body is scripturally textualized or drawn into a new body politic.

From Conviction to Conversion: Replotting the Body

Since I have already addressed the first stage of spiritual progression in Lee's narrative, the stage of awakening and conviction, I will not cover that ground again. I will only say that in Lee's narration of the first stage in her journey of spiritual progression, one sees her retextualizing the discourse of birth and even reproduction, the discourse of *bios*, in modernity.[39] She does this by reinterpreting the meaning of Psalm 51, which in the mouth of the Presbyterian minister was deployed to signify the birth of blackness as taint or corruption and, by implication, the birth of whiteness as purity and holiness. For Lee, conviction overturns her status as a "convict" or incarcerated within this narrative of *bios* precisely by resituating existence within the theological economy of Zion as it culminates in Pentecost and in the founding of the pentecostal community of Zion, the *ecclesia* or church. Thus, it is at the level of conviction that Lee intertextually engages the discourse of birth, of reproduction, that the Hammon persona theologically struggled to escape by aligning his birth with the birth of Christ.

Following the account of her awakening or conviction, Lee then gives an account of her conversion. This second stage in her spiritual progression is distinct from the first in that in the stage of conviction or awakening Lee says that she lacked clarity about the identity of Jesus. Thus, "although at this time, when my conviction was so great, yet I knew not that Jesus Christ was the Son of God, the second person in the adorable trinity" (*Life* 32). Conviction for Lee was not simply a one-time event. Rather, it was a process that took place over months and years, culminating in conversion. The process of conviction entailed struggling against the modern narrative of reproduction and racial birth, as signified in the words of the Presbyterian minister, at the end of which was entry into the narrative of Jesus' birth or reproduction, his narrative of divine or Trinitarian "Sonship." Jesus' identity as the Son in relationship to the one he called Father signified for Lee the economy of a different mode of birth, (re)production, and ultimately community. It was this mode of divine generation—the eternal generation of the Son, as it is called in classical Christian theology—that Lee sought to claim as the ground of her identity and thus as the basis upon which she was brought into the family, the community of Zion as one of its covenantal daughters.

Therefore, conviction names the process by which Lee understood herself as led into the Trinitarian economy in which Jesus, as the Son of the Trinity, is eternally born of the Father and within whose eternal coming forth from the Father there also is the coming forth of creation. Entry into this divine mode of birth is what Lee calls conversion. Thus, conviction, the propaedeutic to conversion, is directional. It names the process, the task, and, indeed, the struggle that aims at reshaping the self Christologically: that is, out of the narration of

blood and birth into which one is conscripted on the basis of race and into the narrative of blood and birth signified in the divine Sonship of Jesus of Nazareth.

In the opening pages of her narrative, Lee attempts to capture something of the struggle that marked her conviction. She does this by retelling the events following her initial moments of awakening, after hearing the Presbyterian minister's words. Lee tells us that she was tempted on more than one occasion to commit suicide—"to destroy myself," which was her immediate response to hearing what the minister had to say (*Life*, 28) and again some four years or so later when "Satan's powers over me" were at their peak. On this second occasion, she "[concluded] that I had better be dead than alive. . . . I was again tempted to destroy my life" (30). Moreover, Lee tells us that between these bookend temptations to commit suicide she was afflicted with a number of physical ailments (28–30). But behind these afflictions and temptations to suicide was again a Christological problem. Lee tells us that she did "not [know] how to run immediately to the Lord for help." As a result, "I was driven by Satan" (28).

Lee's self-description as "naturally of a lively turn of disposition" (*Life*, 29) invites one to analyze the account of her satanic harassment in psychoanalytic terms. However, that is not what I want to do here, for it is what is theological about how she describes her trauma that is of particular interest. In analyzing her life, Lee is a shrewd reader of Scripture, because the description of her trauma is a retelling of the gospel accounts of the temptation of Jesus in the wilderness. According to the synoptic record, Christ was subjected to "satanic" harassment, culminating in his temptation to commit suicide by throwing himself down from an elevated plain (cf. Matt. 4:1–11; Mark 1:12–13; Luke 4:1–13). As Jesus was tempted to cast himself down, so, too, Lee entertains casting herself down by drowning on the occasion of her first temptation and by hanging on the occasion of her second. As Jesus was delivered through a feat of exegesis by which he countered Satan's exegesis of various texts of Scripture, so, too, does Lee, through the narration of her awakening and conversion, counter the "satanic" interpretation of her existence as a black woman marked by taint and corruption. Lee engages in this exercise of a counterautobiographical exegesis of the self by seeing her existence as an unfolding within or as a "recapitulation" (to use Irenaean language) of the life of Jesus. Herein lies her Christian theological response to the problem of modern racial reasoning. As Jesus is attended to by angels after his experience of the temptation to suicide, so, too, Lee says that "by some means, of which I can give no account, my thoughts were taken entirely from this purpose [of killing myself]. . . . It was the unseen arm of God which saved me from self murder" (28).

What is important in this is less the cosmogony in which Lee casts her struggle, a cosmogony populated with angels, demons, and Satan, than it is that the struggle she dramatizes takes place in her body—indeed, that it is a struggle over what gives the body meaning. Lee's answer is decidedly

theological: she connects her bodily temptation (to kill herself), and thus her body, with the struggle to remake the self. But she carries out the struggle to remake the self by relocating or replotting the body within the hermeneutical horizon of the gospel narratives of the life of Jesus. Christ's actual body is the hermeneutical horizon within which Lee situates her bodily existence. Thus, Lee's *Life*, in which she plots the journey of being a Christian spiritual progressive, proves to be a précis of the gospel narratives. Her body is Christoform; for just as each of the synoptics begins with an abbreviated introduction regarding the childhood and birth of its protagonist, Jesus of Nazareth, swiftly moving to Jesus' temptation as the preface to his public ministry of itinerate preaching and teaching, so, too, is this the case with Lee's narrative of the self. Her narration reenacts this basic structure of an abbreviated account of birth and childhood moving swiftly to temptation to suicide as the preface to an account of her itinerant preaching ministry.

The similarities in structure and plot, however, do not stop here: by linking her temptation to suicide to the temptation of Christ to do the same, Lee reveals her exegetical effort to portray how Christ's body in pain and temptation and her body in pain and temptation are concrete analogies of each other and thus are made to articulate each other.[40] Indeed, it is only when her scripturally exegetical representation of Christ and of herself as reenacting the life of Christ come to suffuse each other "without confusion" that Lee can literarily signal her transition out of the state of conviction and into the second state, the state of conversion.[41] It is only when her body is understood as a representation and articulation of Christ's body that she can say that "circumstances so transpired that I soon came to a knowledge of the being and character of the Son of God, of whom I knew nothing" (*Life*, 32). In other words, it is only then that Lee undergoes full ecclesiological and liturgical induction into the community of Zion, the church, through baptism: "I was baptized according to the direction of our Lord, who said, as he was about to ascend from the mount to his disciples, 'Go ye into all the world and preach my gospel to every creature, he that believeth and is baptized shall be saved (Mark 16:15–16)' " (32).

But notice what else Lee does in narrating her spiritual progression from awakening and conviction to conversion in this way. In a few pages, she reenacts the basic theological moves of the narratives of Hammon and Douglass. That is, she frames her life between the birth of Christ (see chapter 6 on Hammon) and the death of Christ (see chapter 7 on Douglass). However, she goes further than both Hammon's and Douglass's narratives in that she wants to literarily probe how the economy of Christ's historical life, from his birth to his Easter death, is not merely a cultural symbol, a modernist allegory of the self, an allegory expressive of modern accounts of *bios* or life.

Michel Foucault, Giorgio Agamben, and Étienne Balibar have each drawn attention to aspects of the pitfalls of such narrations of the self. But it was Foucault and even more so Balibar following him who have come closest to

showing how the narrative of modern *bios* is, in fact, a racial narrative. Yet, none of these theorists grasped how the racial narrative of modernity is a narrative of whiteness as a distorted Christian theological performance, though Foucault I think came closest. At a fundamental level, Lee grasped precisely this. Thus, the interest of her narrative is in literarily representing a theological response to the theological problem of whiteness as the problem of the constitution of modernity. Her spiritual autobiography seeks to capture how it is that responding to whiteness as a distorted theological performance requires that one leave the economies of modern *bios* (and the modes of capital accumulation tied to modern *bios*) and enter the nonracial economy of Christ's crucified, Jewish flesh.

Herein lies the significance of Lee's reference to Mark 16:15–16. This passage envisages neither the Christ of the annunciation as a symbol of racial birth nor the Christ of the resurrection as the one who symbolically legitimizes cultural strength. It envisages the Pentecostal Christ of the ascension, the one who at Pentecost will be present to his followers as the Spirit of Christ, as the one who constitutes a new history. In this history, the Spirit of Christ incorporates persons across time and space into the very form of Christ's crucified, bodily existence—crucified flesh.[42] What Lee, in short, has literarily done then is broaden the reach of Christ's historical, bodily existence so as to understand her own existential and historical moment as an articulation of Christ's own life and way of being in the world.[43] It is her understanding of Pentecost as part and parcel of the economy of Christ's bodily existence that allows her to accomplish this. Lee fills out this gesture in her account of sanctification.

Sanctification: The Pentecostal Reshaping of Black Existence

Lee's narrative moves fairly quickly to the final stage of the process of salvation, which she calls "sanctification." Here she embarks on the road leading to what she calls "full stature in Christ Jesus" for "the sanctification of the soul to God." In this final stage in Christian spiritual progress, one lives under the "increasing light of the Spirit" (*Life*, 33). In this life of continuing "baptisms of the Spirit" (40) such that "God [is] in the midst" of the soul for authority and "liberty among the people" (46), one observes how Lee's Trinitarian, Christological, and ecclesiological vision of identity comes into full view.

Sanctification, as the final stage of spiritual progression into a salvation in which God is in the midst of the soul, loops back to the initiating moment of awakening and conviction. To recall, in conviction, the Spirit of God directly encounters Lee in her soul or "conscience"; Lee then faces the deterring presence of the Evil One in a contest over the meaning of her body as socially inscribed through race and gender; finally, having been brought into the divine community through the encounter with God in the soul, Lee searches for a

"divine" community of "sanctified" people with whom her heart could unite. This search for a divine community in history, as it were, is a search coterminous with the so-called moment of the soul's mystical immediacy to God. In Lee's discourse, the movement from awakening and conviction to conversion unsettles any neat opposition between a state of the soul's immediacy to God and such mediating structures as the reading and interpretation of Scripture, and the church and its modes of governance. This is because, for Lee, the search for visibility (which happens in terms of an aesthetic and ascetic relation to God) and the search for community (for a people with whom she might also be related) are, in the end, one.

Lee recapitulates this movement in the account of her sanctification. However, it becomes clearer that the Holy Spirit, whether in conviction, conversion, or sanctification, propels the entire movement of salvation, but the Spirit does so through the concrete humanity of Jesus of Nazareth. I elucidate this point by considering Lee's prayer for sanctification, which opens the way for all else that follows in her narrative. Her prayer for sanctification becomes the locus of her understanding of the self as no longer fundamentally alone but, rather, of the self as communion. Moreover, I show how Lee through the moment of sanctification is about the task of making race and gender theologically resignify within the hermeneutical horizon of the flesh of Christ.

During her prayer for sanctification, the Spirit of God, as the episode goes, while moving directly on her soul, tells her to ask for sanctification. She therefore asks, "Lord *sanctify* my soul for Christ's sake" (*Life*, 34; italics original). Lee then records the following as taking place after making her prayerful petition:

> That very instant, as if lightning had darted through me, I sprang to my feet and cried, "The Lord has sanctified my soul!" There was none to hear this but the angels who stood around to witness my joy—and Satan, whose malice raged the more. That Satan was there I knew; for no sooner had I cried out, "The Lord has sanctified my soul," than there seemed another voice behind me, saying, "No, it is too great a work to be done." But another spirit said, "Bow down for the witness—I received it—*Thou are sanctified!*" The first I knew of myself after that I was standing in the yard with my hands spread out, and looking with my face toward heaven. I now ran into the house and told them what had happened to me, when as it were a new rush of the same ecstasy came upon me and caused me to feel as if I were in an ocean of light and bliss. (*Life*, 34; italics in original)

The marker "that very instant" indicates the rapid movement of Lee's discourse, and the rapidity of this movement reenacts the rapidity of the movement of the opening paragraphs of her narrative. Now again, at the stage of sanctification, there is rapid movement in the search for communion with

God. With "lightning" quickness, Lee is raptured into a supernal region in which once again she endures "satanic" harassment, as did Christ. In this supernal region of experience, Lee is cruciform and is immediately present to God, albeit in the form of Christ.

After she receives the immediate declaration from the Spirit of God that *"Thou are sanctified!"* and thus that she had become conformed to Christ's body, Lee inserts a temporal marker into her account of sanctification: "The first I knew of myself." With this marker, Lee quickly transports the reader back to the domain of mediation, the domain of time, space, and history. But the reader soon discovers that the domain of history in which sanctification presents itself within space and time is also Christoform. More specifically, it is cruciform. In other words, both the immediacy of spiritual encounter and the mediacy of historical existence are in Christ. Note how Lee represents the cruciform structure of her body in time, space, and history. She says, "The *first* I knew of myself after [the experience of prayer] I was standing in the yard with my hands spread out, and looking with my face toward heaven." With spread-out hands and a heavenward gaze, her body takes on—indeed, it becomes—the form of Christ crucified. Thus, Lee's discourse witnesses to what might be termed the analogical proximity of her body—its mode or *tropos* of existence as Maximus the Confessor says—to God. Her outstretched arms and raised head, in short, her body is theologically free in the form of the cross, the concrete form of the body of God incarnate.

It is worth noting that Lee imagines herself as liberated with the use of tropes and imagery that hark back interestingly to a patristic sensibility of Christian spirituality. For example, in the *Odes of Solomon*, the writer poetically declares,

1. I have stretched out my hands in offering to the Lord.
2. For the outstretched hands are a sign thereof,
3. Upright with hands stretched out, is the wood of the upright cross.
    Hallelujah! (Ode 27)[44]

Like the writer of the 27th Ode, Lee daringly through her prayer, which is guided she says by the Holy Spirit, imagines herself as a revelation of the economy of the flesh of God in Christ: free black existence, particularly her own existence as a black woman, as formed concretely on the cross of Christ. The crossbeams indicate God's crossing of her black body, God's bringing of the body into view as the body of Jesus. The body's grace, its aesthetic depth, is ascetically brought to view in the moment of sanctification. It shines forth from there, and thereby brings it to public view, its plenitudinous depth now shimmering forth. It is worth observing that the activity of the Spirit in Christian spirituality, which is the movement of God's Spirit in and upon the person, orients the person toward Jesus of Nazareth so as to draw her or him into the particularity of Christ's earthly life. The point of entry into his life is

the Easter event. Lee's discourse dramatizes this. That is, in her spiritual narrative, Christ and the believer come under pneumatic proscription. Pneumatically qualified, Lee as a black woman along with all of creation is united to God through God's embrace of the creature's condition in the humanity of Jesus.

That Lee's sanctifying prayer follows the contours of the economy of the Pasch is seen not just in the prayer's culminating moment in which her body visibly takes on the *Gestalt* of the cross; the entire structure of the episode follows the Easter *Triduum*. The temporal dynamics of her narration of sanctification, which suggests an eschatology of the self, as well as the very postures her body takes in the scene in which Lee describes her sanctification, are important in this respect. On this particular day, Lee begins to pray at about "four o'clock in the afternoon," seeking the blessing of sanctification (*Life*, 34). Reference to the four o'clock hour is literarily interesting in that there is but a one-hour difference between Jesus' Good Friday experience, which culminates at three o'clock, and Lee's blessing of sanctification. Moreover, Lee prays in a bent-over, kneeling posture. Like Christ who struggled to breathe on the cross, so, too, does Lee in this bent-over posture "[struggle] long and hard."

Yet, she does not find "the desire of her heart" (*Life*, 34). She does not find it because, she says, "Satan had hidden the very object from my mind." Unsuccessful, Lee employs resurrection language (as Douglass would do after her), saying, "I rose from my knees." However, before she stands fully erect, "as I yet stood in a leaning posture," she is told, presumably by the Spirit of God moving in her conscience, to "ask for sanctification." With this directive, Lee "again bowed in the same place." Upon receiving sanctification, having "bowed down for the witness," Lee says, "The first I knew . . . I was standing" (34). I have already shown how Lee figures her standing posture as cruciform. But one can also see that even the movement of postures figures her body as formed through the *triduum mortis*, and therefore as cruciform. The initial posture of bowing down "at about four o'clock" figures Lee entering into Good Friday and Holy Saturday. Her subsequent posture of standing to pray with outstretched arms and raised head signifies resurrection Sunday, which is the moment in which she employs the language "I rose."

In figuring the body as cruciform and as the site of God's labor to bring forth a different form of the self by means of a different form of birth or reproduction, I argue that Lee's discourse reclaims in performance a premodern approach to Christian spirituality but as specifically attuned to a modern problem: namely, the racializing of the body and the gender protocols inherent in this. Similarly, in figuring the body not just as cruciform but in its cruciformity as free to pursue a different posture or orientation in the world, Lee revives a premodern way of theologically conceiving the self but again as attuned to a modern problem. Consider the remarks of Basil of Caesarea, the fourth-century cleric and advocate of monastic spirituality, in his treatise

On the Holy Spirit. Here the significance of Lee's postures in prayer can be read in an important theological way:

> We make our prayer standing up on the first day of the week [Sunday] but not all of us know the reason: it is not only because, being risen with Christ and being bound to seek the things that are above, we are reminding ourselves, by standing upright on the day consecrated to the resurrection, of the grace that has been given to us, but it is also because this day is in some way an image of the age to come....
> This day is, in fact, also the eighth day and it symbolizes the fullness that will follow the present time, the day that never closes ... the age that will never come to an end.... It is therefore necessary that the Church should bring up her children to pray standing upright on this day, so that with a continual reminder of life without end we should not forget to make ready our food for the journey.... The upright posture ... makes our soul, so to speak, emigrate from the land of the present to that of the age to come. By contrast, every time we kneel and get up again we show by our actions that sin has cast us to the ground and the love of our Creator has called us back to heaven.[45]

One might also consider a comment of Diadochos, a fifth-century bishop of Photiki in northern Greece. In his *Visio*, he comments on Psalm 16:15, "I shall be refreshed with the vision of your glory." Lee in her prayer for sanctification suggests that she was privy to such a vision. After having assumed the form of the cross "with my hands spread out, and looking with my face toward heaven" while standing upright in the posture of the resurrection, Lee then says, "A rush of ... ecstasy came upon me, and caused me to feel *as if I were in an ocean of light and bliss*" (*Life*, 34).

Lee now suggests a proper experiencing of the world and seeing or understanding of herself precisely because her newly experienced seeing and engagement with the world is a living in the experience of the incarnate God in Christ. The light in which she sees the self and in which she reimagines the world is according to the "light" or aesthetics of Easter in which the quest to grasp or master the world and therefore enslave it are slain: thus, the similarity between Lee's discourse of spirituality and black visibility in the concrete humanity of Christ, which we have seen to be thoroughly Trinitarian, and Diadochus's highly Trinitarian and paschal sensibilities of spirituality. In commenting on Psalm 15:16 in his *Visio*, he says:

> The prophet speaks thus not because the divine nature itself has a definite face and form, but because in the form and in the glory of the Son the formless Father will reveal himself to us. For this is why it has pleased God to make his Logos enter the human form through the Incarnation—while he himself, to be sure—how could he not?—

remained in his all encompassing glory—so that man, beholding the condensed form of that glorified flesh—for form sees form—might be enabled, after his purification is completed, to see the beauty of the Resurrection as it manifests God.[46]

Diadochos's notion of "form seeing form" is crucial here, for it captures an important aspect of Lee's theological self-understanding and her approach to visibility and being public in the Crucified. The phrase points to a transfiguration of social, aesthetic, and even ontological prerogatives that would set genius over grotesquery, white over black, mastery over slavery, male over female, rich over poor, and public over private. The transfiguration is theological or, more precisely, Christological. For, portraying herself as free in the cross, passing as she does through the postures of the *triduum mortis*, Lee suggests what might be termed an analogy of glory and beauty by which Christ's flesh irradiates all flesh. The given form of Christ, a form imbued with an ever-abiding paschal content given in the body of God incarnate, Jesus of Nazareth, remains the definitive form of the truth and the salvation of being.

I have drawn on the language of ancient Christian spirituality to elucidate the significance of prayer, its postures, and its final cruciform shape for Lee's prayer for sanctification. It should be clear that her "mystical" economy does not easily fit within an opposition between the mediated and the unmediated or, in theological terms, in an opposition between eschatological and historical time, between apophaticism (the way of sheer negation or unknowing) and cataphaticism (the way of affirmation or knowing). The mediated and unmediated, the eschatological and the historical, and the apophatic and the cataphatic interpenetrate one another in the drama of the divine economy of the Jewish, which is to say, the covenantal flesh of Jesus of Nazareth, a drama set on the "stage" of the world and on which all the peoples of the world "act," as it were, "in Jesus Christ."[47]

This way of being in the world, the way of Christ's flesh, is also a new mode of sociality, of life together. It is life in God's covenant. If Douglass's discourse was unable to articulate this new form of life together to the detriment most negatively of black female flesh, then Lee's discourse is more successful. This is because her narrative of the self is embedded within a fuller Christology. According to this fuller vision of Christ, the flesh of Jesus is a social reality, a space into which one enters by the action of the Spirit. As the one who transfigures social reality by drawing creation into the space of Christ's flesh, the Spirit of Christ is the architect of a new mode of life together, that of the *ecclesia*, the church of Christ.

Lee does not give much working detail about her understanding of the Spirit of Christ as the one who transfigures social space by drawing creation into the space of Christ's flesh. Neither *Life* nor the longer *Journal* is a theological treatise. Yet, her account of her call to preach has embedded within it

important literary suggestions as to the theological direction such an account of the Spirit might take. What is interesting about Lee's narration of her call to preach is that she does not argue for her "right" to preach in terms of a liberal discourse of "rights." Instead, she makes a Christological case for her call as a woman to preach. Moreover, the case she makes is unusual, given the Protestantism out of which she speaks, for the argument she makes in justification of her call to preach proceeds from an understanding of the life of the church, an ecclesiology, that is rooted in a dual Marian reading of Mary of Nazareth as the *theotokos*, or "mother of God," and Mary Magdalene as the herald of the risen Christ. Lee interprets the Magadalene as recapitulating the Nazarene in such a way as to yield a Marian-ecclesiological account of her call "[to take] a text" or to preach. This account of her call to preach occurs immediately "after [the account of her] sanctification" (*Life*, 35) and in many respects is a continuation of the account of her sanctification. Thus, it, too, bears marks of the scriptural trope of the cross. But it is less the cruciform dimensions of the account of Lee's call to preach that I want briefly to consider; instead, my interest is her allusion to a doctrine of the two Marys to explain how persons are born into the economy of Christ's flesh by the Holy Spirit. The turn to Mary is central to Lee's further deployment of the exegetical imagination to complete the Christology at work in her literary attempt to reshape the self.

Toward a Mariology of the Self

The key passage in which Lee invokes both Marys in relationship to her call to preach is the following:

> For as unseemly as it may appear now-a-days for a woman to preach, it should be remembered that *nothing is impossible with God* [cf. Luke 1:36–38; italics mine]. And why should it be thought impossible, heterodox, or improper, for a woman to preach? seeing the Savior died for the woman as well as the man. If a man may preach, because the Saviour died for him, why not the woman? seeing he died for her also. Is he not a whole Saviour, instead of a half one? as those who hold it wrong for a woman to preach, would seem to make it appear. Did not Mary *first* preach the risen Saviour [cf. Matt. 28:1–10; Mark 16:9–10; Luke 24:10; John 20:18], and is not the doctrine of the resurrection the very climax of Christianity—hangs not all our hopes on this, as argued by St. Paul? Then did not Mary, a woman, preach the gospel? for she preached the resurrection of the crucified Son of God. (*Life*, 36)

What is most interesting for my purposes about Lee's argument is how it begins. Acknowledging the rarity of women preachers in the early to

mid-nineteenth century, Lee employs the exegetical imagination to resituate the "unseemliness" of her call to preach, grounding it in the saying "that nothing is impossible with God." This statement harks back to the Lucan account of the angelic announcement that the Holy Spirit would descend on Mary of Nazareth, already prefiguring the story of Pentecost (cf. Acts 2), impregnating her for the birth of Jesus (Luke 1:36). In response to Mary's question as to how this could be, the angel says, "For with God nothing shall be impossible" (Luke 1:37). Mary responds to this with her fiat: "Behold, the handmaid of the Lord; be it unto me according to thy word" (Luke 1:38).

Thus the story of the birth of Christ is the inner grammar by which Lee makes interpretive sense of her call to preach. In addition, at the same time that the story of the birth of Christ proves to be the grammar of her call to preach, it also returns her to the moment of her initial awakening at the beginning of her narrative, the moment in which she narrated her existence within a different economy of birth and reproduction: namely, the birth of Christ. It is now apparent that Lee's Christological account of the self relocates her not only with respect to modernity's economy and protocols of race but also with respect to how gender functions within and as an articulation of modernity's racial economy and protocols. To enter into Christ's flesh through the Holy Spirit's pentecostal overshadowing is to exit the gendered economy and protocols of modern racial reasoning.

Thus, Lee's Christological account of the self speaks back to the problem of gender as it intersects with the problem of race in modernity. That is, Lee's Christological account of the self addresses the matter of modernity's configuration of the black feminine as the deeper, structural dilemma of modern racial reasoning. One might say that, for her, the problem of black female flesh in modernity and thus the problem of modern racial reasoning are tied to the loss of a Christological doctrine of Mary as the one who in summing up, or recapitulating, Israel's history ties Jesus to that history. Indeed, it is precisely this theological move, by which Jesus is of Israel and is not a religious reflex of culture, that Douglass's discourse refuses, along with the wider discursive dimensions of whiteness and modern racial reasoning. By contrast, Lee's spiritual narrative imagines, through its retrieval in a Protestant context of the Christological doctrine of Mary as the *theotokos*, the utter centrality of female flesh as tied to the economy of Christ's flesh. Lee not only reclaims a classical Mariology to do the important modern theological work of unmasking and addressing modern racial reasoning, she also enters it, understanding it as a reimagining of the body and thus of social space.

And herein lies Lee's theological genius: in her literary disclosure of how black female flesh has come to be positioned in modernity as a problem that is pseudotheological in nature, she at the same time opens a new vantage from which to engage in the work of modern theology and so address whiteness as a theological problem. Indeed, by employing the Magdalene in the same pas-

sage, she opens a new vantage on Christian identity. In a literary act of courageous theological imagination, she refuses to hand Christian theology over
either to whiteness, to the blackness whiteness created, or to the racialized
gender conventions attending either of these. Instead, she receives herself
anew from Christ, understanding her body as articulating his body and his
body hers. This is what Lee's engagement with and reception of the ancient
doctrine of the *theotokos* affords her.

It is this Mariological understanding of Jesus that underlies Lee's rhetorical question: "Is [Jesus] not a whole Saviour, instead of a half one?" Such a
Christology provides the basis for Lee's interpretation of the fittingness of her
call to preach, which arises from Mary's fiat for the birth of Jesus, when she
accedes to being the body from which the Son of God is to have—and ever will
have—a body in which to dwell. Mary's body articulates Jesus' body at the same
time that his body, abiding in her, articulates Mary's. The fiat, then, as tied to
the body is a proclamation. It is a redemptive preaching of the body, inasmuch
as such preaching bears witness to a new sociopolitical reality, a new body
(politic). Moreover, the Marian gesture, her fiat, on Lee's reading, does not
cease with Mary the mother of Jesus. Mary Magdalene continues it insofar as
she carries within herself (as a recapitulation of Mary the mother of Jesus' act
of fiat) the postresurrection declarations to the disciples. In this respect, first in
the person of the mother of Jesus and then in the person of the Magdalene who
recapitulates the actions of the mother of Jesus, Mary was the first woman
preacher, the first to proclaim the advent of Zion in Christ's flesh. Thus, Mary–
Israel is the center point of a different mode of *bios*, a different order of things,
"for she preached the resurrection of the Crucified Son of God" (*Life*, 36).

Lee, therefore, sees—both in a nonsupersessionist doctrine of the *theotokos*
and in the ecclesiology apart from which this doctrine is unintelligible—the
basis for a new spirituality or "technology of the self," a new way of performing
existence, and thus a theological and exegetical reimagining of how to be in the
world. The new vantage from which Christian theology as a discourse on
Christian identity must operate in the modern world, then, is the Christological horizon of Mary–Israel. To be Christian is to enter into this horizon. But
where is this horizon concretely displayed, where is it made visible if not in
despised dark (and especially dark female) flesh? Is this not the flesh of homo
sacer, as Giorgio Agamben might say, the flesh that is impoverished, "despised
and rejected of men," flesh that in shame we "hide our faces from" (cf. Isa.
53:3)?[48]

But if this is the case, it follows that the poverty of dark flesh is where one
finds the wealthy God. This is where one must turn to find redemption, for it is
here that one finds a theological-social imaginary that fundamentally disrupts
the theological-social imaginary of whiteness.[49] To employ words Gregory of
Nyssa once uttered in his treatise *Against Eunomius*, one might say that it is
particularly in the poverty of dark, despised flesh that one finds the "new

creation in Christ" in whom there is "the sanctification of the whole lump of humanity by means of its first-fruits, [the fruits of Christ's own resurrected flesh]—the Christ who is both the form of God and the form of a slave."[50] In taking on the form of the slave, the form of despised dark (female) flesh there is the diclsoure of divinity, a disclosure that undoes the social arrangement of the colonial-racial tyranny (*tyrannos*), as the seventh-century theologian Maximus the Confessor called it, that is the darker side of modernity.

The theological performance of the self that I have narrated through engaging Hammon's 1760 *Narrative*, Douglass's 1845 *Narrative*, and Lee's 1836 text sits quite well, as I show in the postlude, with Maximus's theological narration of tyranny and with his effort to overcome such tyranny by imaging the world from the scriptural world of Jesus. I complete the argument of this book by considering his gesture more closely so as to have it throw further light on the profoundly theological Afro-Christian effort to exist beyond the protocols of whiteness and thus, like Maximus, reimagine the world from the scriptural world of Jesus and so overcome the racial tyranny of the darker side of modernity.

Postlude on Christology and Race

Maximus the Confessor as Anticolonialist Intellectual

Humankind has brought into being from itself the three greatest, primordial evils, and (to speak simply) the begetters of all vice: ignorance,... self-love and tyranny, each of which are interdependent and established one through another.... God [however]... healed [humanity] when it was sick...[by emptying] himself, taking the form of a slave (Phil. 2:7).... [Thus he fulfilled] the power of love,... in refashioning the human [being].

—Maximus the Confessor, *Ep.* 2
(*PG* 91.397A, C; *LMC*, 87–88)

Those who live...on the level of sense alone make the Word flesh in a way dangerous to themselves. They misuse God's creatures for the service of the passions and do not contemplate the reason of wisdom which is manifest in all things to know and glorify God from his works, as well as to perceive whence and what and why and where we are going from the things which are seen.

—Maximus the Confessor, *CTE* 2.41 (*PG*
90.1144B; *MCSW* 156)

The broad claim of chapters 6–8 is that a number of early Afro-Christians performed the self in such a way as to understand dark flesh as located beyond the pseudotheological and aesthetic gaze of whiteness. Moreover, I demonstrate that rather than abandoning theology to do this, they did it as a supremely theological act, an act one might perhaps say of countertheology in the face of the pseudotheology of modernity. Early Afro-Christians, in other words,

understood themselves as theological subjects, the meaning of whose bodies could only be understood in relationship to the economy of Jesus' Jewish body. With such a claim they redirected the discourse of race as it had come to inhere in their bodies precisely by redirecting Christian identity itself and thereby redirecting Christian theology as a discourse.

Intended to bolster this claim that early Afro-Christians understood their bodies as reinscribed in Christ's body and that this reinscription was the locus of a theologically secured freedom, the broad claim I now outline, in bringing the argument of this book to a close, is that Hammon's, Douglass's, and Lee's theological efforts—to say nothing of the efforts of many others that had space permitted I might have also examined—sit quite well, in fact, with the vision of another ancient theologian, one who carries forward what Irenaeus as anti-Gnostic intellectual (see the prelude) and Gregory of Nyssa as abolitionist intellectual (see the interlude) started.[1] This is the vision of the seventh-century monk-theologian Maximus the Confessor (580–662 CE), who in his own way anticipated the theological moves and especially the Christological vision at work in Afro-Christian faith in its New World emergence as outlined in part III of this book.

In what follows I provide what can here be only a sketch of the Confessor's theological anthropology and Christology, but done in such a way as to surface the fit between his theological vision and that embedded in the faith of those deemed, in the words of Frantz Fanon, "the wretched of the earth" and, in W. E. B. Du Bois's turn of phrase, those deemed "problem people."[2] My point in all of this is not to make the historically unsustainable claim that early Afro-Christians read Maximus the Confessor (or Nyssa or Irenaeus for that matter). Rather, it is to note the symmetry between their respective ways of understanding both the self and the task of theology in a world marked by tyranny, the tyranny structured in terms of some figured as obedient bodies and others as bodies to be obeyed. My claim is that a particular way of reading Scripture—reading against rather than within the grain of the social order—is the hinge holding together these two theological visions, the Maximian one formed before the advent of the modern/colonial world and the Afro-Christian one arising in its wake and as a response to it.

To surface what I take to be most important in Maximus's thought in developing this claim, I confine my analysis to a few texts in his corpus. It is especially through these texts that one can see how he anticipates Hammon's, Douglass's, and Lee's most crucial theological moves in their literary reimagining of the self and reinscription of the body as they carried this out from the underside of modernity.

The orienting text is *Epistle* (*Ep.*) 2, an early letter written to John the Cubicularius, a courtier in Constantinople, around 626 CE. The letter is often referred to simply as Maximus's letter "On Love." In this letter, Maximus

succinctly probes love, whose substance is the Triune God and which is the fundamental principle, or what he calls the *logos*, of creaturely existence. *Epistle* 2's encomium on love proceeds as a discourse on philosophical and theological ethics, as it might be called today. When human beings live in accordance with love, and thus in accordance with the Triune God who is love and from whose will creation arises, they live virtuously, he argues. That is, they participate in the divine life. Love, therefore, is a theological virtue; indeed, the supreme one. When human beings do not live in accordance with love, Maximus says, tyranny (*turannos*) is introduced and sets in motion a history of oppression tied to power, and expresses *phil-autia*, or self-love, rather than *phil-adelphia*, or love of humankind.

Thus, tyranny is self-love. As a distorted expression of love, it is the disposition that orders the world and the things of the world as the possession, as Kant might say, of the mature (as opposed to immature and hence childlike) self-constituting I or the *autos* and its "fortress mentality."[3] Such is the basic structure of colonialism, grounded in a will-to-possess and intellectually sustained by a will-to-forget.[4] In such a schema, *philautia* functions as a substitute for a doctrine of creation inasmuch as the self-constituting I creates a reality and draws all else into it by making it utility or assigning it a use value in the world of the I. In this false doctrine of creation, the world is both one and many before the Triune God as God's image gets distorted into a violent opposition between homogeneity and heterogeneity, unity and difference. Read in our twenty-first-century context, a context that is the offspring of the age of the Renaissance and the Enlightenment, *Ep.* 2, it can be said, unmasks whiteness as that *philautia* that assigns use value to all else according to an analytics of race that tyrannically divides creation. Moreover, Maximus already sees that such a utilitarian logic can and, in fact, often does articulate itself through theology inasmuch as it makes the Word flesh in a "dangerous way" (see the second epigraph to this postlude). In modernity, the enfleshing of Christ the Word has been in the interests of conquest or expansion and the forging of the Occident.[5]

On the one hand, *Ep.* 2 then becomes an interesting and unexpected resource for probing whiteness as a racial-colonialist way of ordering the world that, in fact, deploys the discourse of Christian theology to do its work. What is interesting about Maximus is that he foresaw how theology could be complicit in this fashion precisely through the rhetorics of orthodoxy. *Epistle* 2 constructs an alternative vision of theology, what can be called "difficult orthodoxy" or, as he himself might have no doubt preferred, ascetical (*askêsis*) or spiritual theology. The alternative vision he proposes turns on the link between Abram–Abraham and Jesus of Nazareth. Through this link, Maximus's Christology roots itself in the story of Israel. On the other hand, *Ep.* 2 and other texts in Maximus's corpus are interesting and unexpected resources for thinking about what it might mean to extricate Christian theology as a discourse from its

historic entanglements with the pseudotheological tyranny of whiteness and the Western conquest to own and order. That is, he enacts another modality of theological-intellectual production, and in this regard he can be viewed, to risk an anachronism, as an anticolonialist intellectual who is "against race."[6]

To *Ep.* 2 I link *Ambigua (Amb.)* 10's exegesis of the story of Christ's trans-figuration on Mt. Tabor (cf. Matt. 17:1–8 and parallels), through which Max-imus gives an account of the transfiguration of material reality rooted in a particular way of reading Scripture. Material reality is transfigured as it is drawn into the scriptural witness to Jesus and YHWH's covenant with Israel and thus out of tyranny. To be drawn into the scriptural witness to Jesus is to be drawn into the Torah and the words of the prophets, which he sees symbolized in the figures of Moses and Elijah who are on Mt. Tabor with Jesus. Thus, between *Ep.* 2 and *Amb.* 10, Christ becomes intelligible only in relationship to Abraham, Moses, and the prophets, or the people of Israel in their relationship to YHWH the Triune God. Therefore, what is Jewish about Jesus is essential to his divine identity as Son of God in the economy of redemption. His rela-tionship to Israel is not superseded. With this last move regarding Maximus's exegetical—and rabbinical?—practice in place, the arguments developed in parts I and II, and especially the constructive theological claims of part III, of this book will converge with the arguments of the prelude, interlude, and postlude in such a way as to reconceive the very task of theology for the twenty-first century, given its historically tyrannical performance inside of colonia-lizing whiteness.

A Sketch of Maximus's Theological Vision: The Mystery of Love

At the center of Maximus's theological vision is his understanding of love as both a theological virtue and a cosmic or ontological reality. These two aspects of love—the ethical and the ontological, but as held together within a theological-spiritual vision of reality—are evident in the opening of his *Centuries on Love*:

> Love is a holy disposition of the soul [i.e., the ethical as an orienta-tion], in accordance with which it values knowledge of God [i.e., the theological] above all created things [i.e., the ontological]. It is im-possible to reach the habit of this love if we have a possessive at-tachment to the things of this world [i.e., the spirituality of asceti-cism].
>   Love is begotten of detachment, detachment of hope in God, hope of patient endurance and longsuffering, these in turn are the product of complete self-control, which itself springs from fear of God. And fear of God is the result of faith in God. (*CL* 1.1–2; *PG* 90.961A–B; *MCSW* 36)

The initial step I take is to probe more precisely the link between the ethics and ontology of love within Maximus's theological-spiritual vision. I begin with his understanding of love as a theological virtue.

On the Theological Ethics of Love

Epistle 2 recounts how love achieves its final victory in a world marked by tyranny—that is, in a world that is now divided against itself because of its perversion of the love that grounds its being into numerous forms of self-love (*philautia*) that distort its being. Maximus enumerates five divisions within creation that have become distorted: humans against each other (with the accent on the division between the genders); the sentient against the non-sentient order; the terrestrial against the extraterrestrial order; the world of sense perception against the psychic order; and, finally, the creation as a whole in rebellion against the Creator.[7]

The last division, that between creature and Creator, is the highest of the divisions and is the one that is at the heart of all the others. It is the division by which the creature makes itself a competitor or rival to God. It is the division, Maximus says, by which the creature, out of the self-alienation of its sinful desire or distorted love, seeks to "be as god" (*PG* 91.877D). From this distortion of love in which desire on the part of the creature is no longer directed to the Creator, the entire order of creation falls under the spell of "the tyranny of evil," which divides created nature and set it against itself (*MCSW* 103). *Philautia* distorts the differences constitutive of creation into the tyranny of some aspects of the creaturely order lording over others.

Thus, for example, the fruitfulness of gender difference gets distorted through *philautia* into the tyranny of gender inequality. While Maximus does not put it this way, it can be said that patriarchy has it roots here and can be seen as a theological problem. Moreover—and this is immediately relevant to the argument developed in part III of this book—the tyranny of gender inequality plays itself out through reproduction, birth narratives or narratives of origins, and generation. The tyranny of gender inequality is the modality through which the tyranny of human inequality or the divisions within the order of human existence articulate themselves. All tyrannous divisions arise from here. Maximus sees the overcoming of the division between creature and Creator, and thus all of the other divisions within creation, as beginning with the division of gender inequality.

Crucial for him is the place of Mary of Nazareth, the *Theotokos*. Through her, a new narrative of origins is inaugurated, "another beginning of birth by nature" (*PG* 91.1052D; *LMC* 175). Taking flesh from her and divinity from God, Christ is "[conceived] without seed in a way beyond nature." Mary "[gives] birth to the Word beyond [the dictates of] being" (*PG* 91.1053A; *LMC* 175). In short, through Mary and in Christ, "nature is instituted afresh" by bringing together

what, in the ordering of the world through division, had once been opposed. In Mary's being both virgin and mother and in Christ's being both human and divine, a coincidence of opposites is realized, one that undoes the order of tyranny. For when Mary gives birth to Christ, God not only becomes incarnate in a human being, but, more specifically, God's life is staked or dependent on woman. Dependent on Mary of Nazareth's fiat, the second Adam's human condition and potential to enact human redemption rests on the second Eve. Such is the theological point of the dogma of the virgin birth of Christ.

I have made an argument similar to Maximus's particularly in part III of this book, albeit with the caveat that on this side of modernity the divisions within the human being as tied to the tyranny of gender inequality are now racially articulated. One can say that I have extended Maximus's argument regarding the virgin birth of Christ—instituting created human nature anew by inaugurating a new narrative of origins—by showing how the story of redemption in Christ is the story of exiting the narrative of origins that our modern world has sought to tell. The narrative of origins within the discourse of modernity is a narrative of how human beings came to be bearers of race and how within this narrative whiteness became theologically supreme as a modality of religious dominance and world commerce. Love, which is concretely embodied in Mary the second Eve and in Christ the second Adam, achieves its objective of overcoming the divisions within created nature by "reorient[ing] the passions"—that is, by redirecting both what and the way humans desire, extricating us from possessive self-love and ownership. In having the passions reoriented out of *philautia* and into the self-emptying of dispossessive love, the one who acts out of the virtue of love enters into "a perfect relation with God, with neighbor, and indeed with all creation."[8] This is Maximus's understanding of salvation in Christ, which is his understanding of divinization.

In setting the stage to explain how love accomplishes this, Maximus begins *Ep.* 2 with a consideration of the all-encompassing or cosmic nature of this virtue. All things, he insists, fall within its range and exist in relationship to love—either by living in accordance with it, and thus in an orientation of reception of the world and the things of the world, or in resistance to it, and thus in an orientation of self-love in which the self is the horizon within which all else is possessed and thereby rendered intelligible. In either case, all things still exist in relationship to love (in accordance with it or in perversion from it). In a Maximian vein, one might therefore say that love grants being to all that exists. It is the proton and eschaton of all things and as such is the ultimate principle of existence.

This general understanding of love is at work when Maximus says there is "nothing . . . more truly Godlike than divine love, nothing more mysterious, nothing more apt to raise up human beings to deification. . . . Everything is circumscribed by love," for every good, precisely to the extent that it is good, is

but a modulation of love (*PG* 91.393BC; *LMC* 85–86). "Love, which is said to be God himself" (*PG* 91.404C; *LMC* 91), consequently, "is the goal of everything" (*PG* 91.396B; *LMC* 86). It is the "final last desire" (*PG* 91.396C; *LMC* 86). Thus, love is divine in character, and because of its divinity, it divinizes or elevates to the level of divinity whatever orients itself in accordance with it. Because love is the very principle of what the ancient Greek theologians, including Maximus, called *theôsis* or divinization, its character is transformative or divinizing.

So central is such an understanding of love in Maximus's thought that not only is it the basis for his understanding of God, and therefore in the strict sense is it the touchstone of theology (*theologia*), it also is the basis of anthropology or his inquiry into the human, which he conceives as "theandric"—as that one for whom being oriented toward and united to God is fitting to it.[9] This fit is due to love. Indeed, love is what causes the reality of the Creator and that of creation to fruitfully converge—the dissimilarity between them at the level of nature notwithstanding. Rather than the creature–Creator distinction being the violent division of a purely extrinsic or parallel relationship, love, rendered concrete in Christ, enacts "the closest union" between the creature's and the Creator's modalities of existence (*PG* 91.1053B; *LMC* 175), causing these two modalities to thoroughly "interpenetrate" each other while in no way "annulling" the distinction between the natures that the modalities enact (ibid.). Indeed, the distinction between the divine and the human is precisely what love guarantees: the unity of God and creation realized through the unity between God and humankind "is achieved through the preservation [of the distinction], guaranteed by guaranteeing it. For the unification of the two poles comes to full realization to the exact degree that their mutual difference remains intact" (*PG* 91.69D–97A).[10] And it is through this unification that the "world is perfected as world, . . . that the world is given to itself, [that] each of us are given to ourselves, [precisely] when God gives himself to the world and to us in Christ: 'when he makes of [the world] a new mystery' [*PG* 91.1049A] and presents both it and us to himself."[11] Love as concretized in Christ, therefore, is the basis of creaturely identity and especially human identity, which is an identity that when theologically conceived can only be understood in relationship to God.

On the Theological Ontology of Love

But what kind of vision of human identity—to say nothing of divine identity—is at work here? For Maximus it is an ecstatic understanding of identity. That is, love names a twofold ecstasy (*ekstasis*) for him. On the one hand, it names the "ecstatic" relationship that God as the Creator has with creation. The "ecstasy" within God or the "ecstasy" constitutive of both the Triune relations and the divine nature, which the relations enact though they are not reducible to it, produces an ecstasy beyond the divine nature.[12] It produces, in other

words, the many; indeed, it produces that difference that has contained within it the possibility of all other differences. This secondary ecstasy that arises from the primary ecstasy that is God might be called the ecstasy of creation, the ecstasy of the many.[13]

But on the other hand, love in Christ also names the transcendent, ecstatic relationship that creation has in reciprocity toward its Creator. This second understanding of ecstasy images the first. Maximus argues that the unity of these two aspects of ecstasy—the "ecstasy" proper to God and that is generative of or images forth another ecstasy, the ecstasy of creation—occurs in Jesus of Nazareth, the incarnate Logos. Thus, ecstasy ultimately is another way of talking about how incarnation, as a phenomenon specific to Christ, is for just this reason a phenomenon indicative of creation as such. Incarnation tells us something about created human existence. It tells us of the destiny of humankind. As Maximus says in *Amb.* 7:

> By his gracious condescension God became man and is called man
> for the sake of man and by exchanging his condition for ours revealed
> the power that elevates man to God through his love for man. By this
> blessed inversion, man is made God by divinization and God [is]
> made man by hominization. For the Word of God and God wills
> always and in all things to accomplish the mystery of his embodi-
> ment. (*PG* 91.1084C–D; *CMJC* 60)

Incarnation is the centerpoint between divinity and humanity. It is the phenomenon by which these two realities touch even as it safeguards the distinction between what it means for God to be God and for humans to be human. Indeed, the difference between God and humanity is the very vehicle of both humankind's (and creation's) divinization on the one hand and God's hominization on the other.

Epistle 2 makes all of these theological moves, doing so by drawing on the Christological terms of the Council of Chalcedon of 451 regarding the *communicatio idiomatum,* or the exchange of properties between the divinity and humanity in Christ's flesh. According to this understanding of the person of Christ, developed most fully by Cyril of Alexandria (378–444 CE), the idioms of divinity and humanity refer to the single, unified person of Christ.[14] Maximus states it this way in *Ep.* 2:

> God is thus manifest in those who possess [this grace], taking shape
> according to the specific character of the virtue of each through love
> for humankind, and condescending to be named from humankind.
> For it is the most perfect work of love and the goal of its activity, to
> contrive through the mutual exchange of what is related that the
> names and properties of those that have been united through love
> should be fitting to each other. (*PG* 91.401A–B; *LMC* 89–90)

As this quotation makes clear, in the economy of redemption God only points to himself by pointing to humankind and the unity God has entered into with humankind due to love.

But there is another dimension to what Maximus says. The other, equally important theological point he makes about the communication of properties pertains not so much to the vertical exchange of properties between divinity and humanity in Christ as it does to the lateral, intrahuman exchange. This is the exchange that takes place on the horizontal plane of the immanent his-torical relations between human beings as they are reordered in his flesh or in human nature as he performs and embodies it. The basis of this lateral ex-change that heals created human nature and the relations constitutive of that nature is found in the vertical exchange of properties between divinity and humanity as they come together in the two-natured, or dyophysite, Christ.[15] That is, the vertical encounter of love in the philanthropic Christ is itself open and receptive. It reopens humanity to encounter divinity without humanity being swallowed up in the encounter. This is the point of the Chalcedonian insistence that the divine and human natures in Christ come together in his person (hypostasis) into the closest affinity or embrace (i.e., adiairetôs) but without confusion (i.e., asynchytôs).[16]

But more than this, Maximus conceives of human nature as being reo-pened in Christ, not simply to God but also to itself. Christ reopens humanity to embrace the many that is constitutive of created human nature and of creation itself. In this sense Christ reintegrates human nature, enacting it no longer within an order of tyrannical division but, rather, in an order of "peaceful difference," the one–many structure of creation.[17] He accomplishes this by drawing the rest of humankind into the specific modality or intonation of his existence, into the unique way in which he enacts being human, at the center of which is theandric love. I will have more to say about Maximus's conception of the specific content or the unique harmonics of Christ's theandric love, for this, too, is immediately relevant to the theological proposal I outline in this book in response to whiteness as a theological problem. For now, I want to be clear that Maximus is not engaged in a purely speculative or theoretical meditation. In fact, he is at every point engaged in the theological exegesis of Scripture. Indeed, he is engaged in an exegetical reflection on the Jewish Christ and the incorporation of creation and all of humankind into the specific modalities of Christ's wounded, suffering flesh.

Before considering this further, it is worth reiterating the fundamental point I have developed so far, and that point is this: in the hypostasis, or the specific modality by which he enacts or embodies what it means to be human, Christ restores the ecstatic exchange of properties between divinity and hu-manity. But importantly, this gesture contains within it the reopening of hu-man nature itself so that it is no longer hermetically sealed in upon itself within a "fortress mentality." For the insularity of human nature is the ground of

tyranny. It is that on the basis of which created human nature loses itself to itself or becomes alienated from itself. Christ enacts human nature in such a way, on the basis of the unity of creation in relationship to God, as to inaugurate what I have called (in an effort to interpret Maximus in the wake of the advent of modernity/coloniality) an intrahuman exchange of realities, an exchange of "properties" so to speak between human persons themselves. Maximus's proposal refuses anything like a logic of "separate but equal." It resists all political and cultural nationalisms, from the nationalism of a hegemonic whiteness to the various nonwhite nationalisms spawned in counterhegemonic resistance to whiteness. According to Maximus, both aspects of the exchange of properties—the interexchange between divinity and humanity in Christ, and the intraexchange within human nature—are necessary for the full articulation of what has occurred in the flesh of Christ. Both exchanges, which are united in Christ, are necessary in Maximus's theological humanism.

Consequently, when Maximus says that "through the mutual exchange of what is related ... the names and properties of those that have been united through love [are fitted] to each other," he is indicating that the same gesture of incarnation that fits divinity to humanity and humanity to divinity so that they can take on each other's names, also refits human beings to one another so that they, too, can be named from one another. The latter intrarenaming of the human (and the history it opens) occurs inside of the interrenaming of the human that has taken place in Christ and that Maximus speaks about with recourse to the *communicatio idiomatum* of Chalcedon. The violent history of conquest in modernity and the processes of racialization that function as the internal engine of this history have created a distorted, one-way expression of ecstatic identity as whiteness. The distortion lies in the fact that the pseudotheological identity of whiteness exports itself but never receives itself. In this sense it is nonreceptive because it is "philautically" rooted in humankind's alienation from itself through which it articulates its alienation from God. This is the structure of modern conquest anthropologically founded on white supremacy specifically and the modern invention of race more generally.

While Maximus knew neither the history of modern conquest nor its internal racial dimensions, nor that it would be Christian theologians who were most responsible for making arguments in justification of all of this, he did have insight into the root of the problem. Its root, as he sees it, lies in created nature's self-enclosure: the transformation of the one–many structure of creation into the tyranny of division through the agency of humans in their quest to be "gods" (in replacement of God the Creator) and thus to "create" their own reality. But this is the dynamic of whiteness, for precisely in this way, whiteness functions in modernity as a substitute for the doctrine of creation in its quest to create a reality into which all else must enter. Maximus saw in Christ the solution to the many violent and tyrannical divisions that could arise from a

vision of creation that functions in this way. In Christ, the gesture of ecstatic openness to God in human self-fulfillment, which is the gesture to receive oneself from God, is necessarily a gesture of openness to all created beings as revealing God. "To be" ecstatically is to receive oneself from other human beings precisely as the receiving of the self from God. Hence, being named from God entails being named from other human beings. In undoing whiteness as a theological problem, Christ leads human nature out of this disposition.

Thus, the *communicatio idiomatum* happens all the way down, as it were. It names the one event in Christ happening vertically on the one hand *between* the divine and human natures and also laterally on the other *within* the created human nature that is assumed in the incarnation. What the exchange of properties accomplishes on both levels is the inauguration of a mode of existence— or a *tropos*, as Maximus calls it—that can be called "being-in-another."[18] Vertically, the divine nature in the person (*hypostasis*) of Christ is itself only as it exists ecstatically "in" the created human nature he assumes. The same can be said of the reciprocal relation in which the created human nature in the person of Christ is fully itself as a human nature only as it exists ecstatically "in" the divine nature and thus is divinized. It can therefore be said that the different natures in the person of Christ exist in one another—and, importantly, only exist in this way.[19]

Similarly on the horizontal level, Christ inaugurates a revolution—but not of the Kantian sort!—within human nature itself. This is the revolution in which Christ performs or embodies a new way (*tropos*) of being human or of embodying and performing human existence. He performs human existence in such a way as to reintegrate the differences within created nature and thus heal the divisions within being. This healing entails causing the differences within created nature to subsist or ecstatically be in one another. At the level of the human, this means that human identity as Christ has instantiated it can be called an intrahuman identity. In such a theological understanding of human identity, human beings are most fully themselves only as they receive themselves from other human beings, for in receiving oneself from another—that is, in subsisting in another on the basis of shared humanity and thus on the basis of a shared, nonidolatrous status as creature in relationship to the Creator—one in fact receives God and thereby is most fully oneself. All human beings in this perspective become icons or bearers of God in their humanity.[20] Reimagining human existence in this way overcomes in Christ's flesh the divisive fragmentation within created nature and the possessive self-love grounding this fragmentation. It is precisely the disposition of possession or attachment, rather than dispossession or ascetic detachment, that lies behind the pseudotheological disposition of whiteness and the violent divisions that have come to mark human existence as the outworking of this disposition.

On the Scriptural Harmonics of Christ's Jewish Flesh

I argued earlier that Maximus's reflections on how Christ reintegrates created human nature beyond tyrannical division and into an arrangement of peaceful difference as the one and many was no purely speculative or theoretical meditation on his part, a fact that can easily be lost sight of given the density of his thought. But rather, not unlike Irenaeus of Lyons and Gregory of Nyssa before him, at every point he exercises the exegetical imagination. That is, he engages in the task of the theological interpretation of Scripture at the site of the flesh of the Jewish Christ, for in Christ's flesh both the world of Scripture and the natural world of the cosmos coinhere. Paul Blowers says that, for Maximus, "the Bible and the created world [are] mutually analogous—indeed interchangeable—economies of divine revelation."[21] It is necessary now to defend this claim and in so doing clarify what can be too easily overlooked about Maximus's theological vision; namely, that it locates all bodies inside the scriptural witness to Jesus of Nazareth and thus inside the covenantal story of Israel.

Even when Maximus resorts to what might seem to be the most esoteric of metaphysical speculations or the most austere reflections on the Christian life as a life of asceticism (*askêsis*), he is but unpacking what it means to be drawn into the scriptural witness to Jesus and thus into Israel's covenant with YHWH the Triune God. Far from being a closed identity, Israel's identity as YHWH's covenantal people, Maximus suggests, is not an identity of closure but one of openness to YHWH. In the transformation of his identity from Abram of Ur to Abraham follower of YHWH, Abram must leave Ur of the Chaldees and at YHWH's behest go into open, uncharted territory. His identity is not something he constructs. It always lies ahead of him. Indeed, he would only be named Israel through his progeny (Jacob) many generations in the future. The ground then of his identity is his openness to YHWH's call. It is this fundamental aspect of Israel's identity that Christ fulfills in such a way as to open even further Israel's openness. That is, Christ opens the path to YHWH the Triune God even to non-Jewish flesh and draws them into Israel's covenantal story. A new story of origins, or of birth, is in Christ's flesh given to all. Hence, it is from inside Israel's covenantal story, rather than from some general humanism or cosmopolitanism, that Christ in bringing Israel's story to crescendo reintegrates the differences of creation into their intended one–many structure. The distinctive harmonics of Christ's flesh therefore lies in Israel's covenantal story.

My claim is not that Maximus fully develops a Christian theology of Israel of the sort hinted at here. He does not. Rather, my claim is that he reads Scripture in such a way that something like this account of Israel is what he presupposes in formulating a Christology suited to the intellectual crises of

monothelitism and monenergism of his own historical moment. Moreover (and more important for my purposes), I claim that there is an affinity between Maximus's way of reading Scripture and the way early Afro-Christians such as those considered in part III of this book read Scripture, for both read against rather than within the social order. To be in Christ, both contend, is to be drawn out of tyrannical narratives of identity (and the social orders they uphold), such as modernity's narrative of racial identity generally and the pseudotheological narrative of whiteness particularly, and into the identity of Israel as performed in Christ's Jewish flesh. This gesture is most evident in two places in Maximus's oeuvre: *Epistle 2*, which I have already looked at but want to consider further, and *Ambigua 10*.

Epistle 2, Christ's Flesh, and the Story of Abraham

I have already considered the principle argument of *Ep. 2*'s encomium on love. In Christ, love reorients the passion in such a way as to draw humanity (and thereby creation) out of possessive self-love, or what Maximus calls *philautia*, and into the disposition of kenôsis (cf. Phil. 2:7), which is the disposition of dispossessive love. From the disposition of ascetical dispossession one enters into a perfect relation with God, neighbor, and all of creation. Indeed, from the disposition of dispossessive love, all of the divisions of creation are made to be peaceful differences inasmuch as the many of creation are ordered to God: "In this God is understood . . . [namely, that] in him [the *logos* of created things] are beheld together and they are bound together and raised to him, as the source and maker" (*PG* 91.400B; *LMC* 88–89).

I have yet to emphasize that the philosophical theology, which is also a theological ethics, of love that Maximus takes up in *Ep. 2* is an exercise in scriptural exegesis meant to disclose Christ who is love. But this can be pressed further, for Maximus's Christological exegesis takes its bearings from the scriptural narrative regarding Israel. The Christ he seeks to disclose and into whom one is to be drawn in the spiritual life is the Christ *of Israel*, beginning with Abraham. Thus immediately following the above quotation, Maximus says,

Perhaps it was this [i.e., being purified from the passions that rebel against love and that unleash tyranny in creation] that great Abraham achieved, restoring himself to nature's *logos* of being, or reason (*logos*) to himself, and through this being given back to God, and receiving God (I put it both ways, for both ways can be regarded as true). As man he was made worthy to see God, and to receive him, since he lived naturally in accordance with the perfect natural *logos* through love for humankind. He was led up [*anagô*] to this, having relinquished the individuality of what divides and is divided, no longer leading *agô*] another human being as if different from himself, but

rather knowing all as one and one as all. This is clearly not a matter of inclination, about which there is contention and division, while it remains irreconcilable with nature, but of nature itself. (*PG* 91.400C; *LMC* 89; translation slightly modified)

While Maximus does not here indicate the exact places in the scriptural witness regarding the story of Abraham to which he refers, it nevertheless seems clear enough that he presents John the Cubicularius with a condensed rendition of the scriptural account of Abram–Abraham's calling by YHWH (cf. Gen. 12).

In invoking Abraham, Maximus seeks to assure John that his encomium on the virtue of love is rooted in Scripture. His claim to him is that to be on the path of "ascetic struggle" is to be in the company of "Abraham and the other saints" in following YHWH's covenant of dispossessive love (*PG* 91.401B; *LMC* 90). Thus, Abraham's achievement must be taken with the utmost seriousness, for in heeding YHWH's call, he did not lose himself to YHWH, his identity being swallowed up in the very act of pursuing the call. Instead, in heeding YHWH's call he most fully "achieved" his identity as human, "restoring himself to nature's *logos* of being . . . [and restoring] reason [*logos*] to himself" (*PG* 91.400C; *LMC* 89). But it is as if Maximus immediately recognized the inadequacy of the language of "achievement" to capture what is going on in the scriptural narrative, for in "being given . . . to God" as Abram of Ur he "[receives] God" and so eventually receives himself as Abraham. Both ways of talking about what happens in the story of Abram–Abraham's calling are important. Indeed, Maximus goes out of his way to say that this double way of talking about Abraham must be regarded as true. Abram–Abraham's identity is simultaneously a leaving behind and an entering into. Through Abram's heeding YHWH's call, the division between Creator and creation or the interhuman relationship between God and creature is transformed into a peaceful distinction.

However, notice as well the link Maximus sees between the transformation of the transcendent interhuman relationship between Abram–Abraham and God and the transformation of the relationships within the immanent order of creation. He makes the tie in the sentence, "As man [Abraham] was made worthy to see God, and to receive him, since he lived naturally in accordance with the perfect natural *logos* through love for humankind." The first part of the sentence speaks of the healing of the Creator–creature division. Later, one learns that the healing of this division has a causal basis in Abraham's philanthropic disposition toward others. In living philanthropically, Abraham lived in accordance with reason (*logos*) and so through philanthropy, the love of humankind, was opened to see God and thus to live into the call to follow YHWH.

That the exegetical-theological imagination is also a social imagination here becomes clear when Maximus says that Abraham was engaged in the act

of "[relinquishing] the individuality of what divides and is divided." This distorted form of individuality is of the sort by which one relates to another as if
they were "different"—in a divisive way—"from [oneself]." Within the terms of
this divisive way of understanding the many, one human being relates to
another, he says, by "leading" (*agô*) them. It is worth observing that Maximus
employs two different words in this sentence for the one word that I have
translated with the English word "lead." God "leads" (*anagô*) Abram–Abraham
to love humankind, but Abram–Abraham used to lead (*agô*) others. Within its
varied lexical range, the latter word, *agô*, admits the sense of taking someone or
something with one as one might do a captive, a slave, or the booty of war. It
has the sense of leading someone or something forcibly away. This is how
Abram–Abraham ordered his relationships before encountering YHWH. He
related to others according to a distinction within humanity that placed him
above others. By contrast, YHWH leads (*anagô*) Abram–Abraham to love humankind in such a way that in so doing he "restores him" at the level of his
created human nature to his "original shape."[22] That is, he resurrects or re-
builds his humanity and so overcomes the alienation within creation. In this
sense, Abram–Abraham's old way of enacting his humanity and of envisioning
the human, Maximus suggests through his exegesis, is overcome. As a follower
of YHWH, he now perceives the unity of creation, "knowing all as one and one
as all." Thus, as a follower of YHWH, Abram-renamed-Abraham perceives the
one–many structure of creation in its orientation to God. His aesthetic is now
one that operates within creation's restoration to itself in being restored to
YHWH.

But finally, by the time one reaches the end of Maximus's exegetical reflections on the patriarch, it becomes clear that Abraham is for him an exemplar of
the incarnate Christ. To enter into Abraham's mode of existence is to enter into
Christ, for Abraham is a figure of Christ. "God [has taken] form in [him],
through his great love for humankind," he says (*PG* 91.401B; *LMC* 90). Moreover, Maximus says that in the very process by which in receiving God Abram
receives himself as Abraham something else crucially important happens: God
also receives himself through and in another. This is the *communicatio idiomatum*. Abraham's "ascetic struggle in accordance with virtue" is one "in
which and through which God receives his likeness to human beings" (*PG*
91.401B–C; *LMC* 90). This leads Maximus to the following conclusion, which
is thoroughly Christological and expresses a rigorous theological humanism:

> Love is therefore a great good, and of good the first and most excellent
> good, since through it God and man are drawn together in a single
> embrace, and the creator of humankind appears as human, through
> the undeviating likeness of the deified to God in the good so far as is
> possible to humankind. And the interpretation of love is: to love the
> Lord God with all the heart and soul and power, and the neighbor as

oneself. Which is, if I might express it in a definition, the inward universal relationship to the first good connected with the universal purpose of our natural kind. . . . This we know as love and so we call it, not divisively assigning one form of love to God and another to human beings, for it is one and the same and universal: owed to God and attaching human beings one to another. For the activity and clear proof of perfect love towards God is a genuine disposition of voluntary goodwill towards one's neighbor. . . . This is the way of truth, as the Word of God calls himself, that leads those who walk in it, pure of all passions, to God the Father. This is the door, through which the one who enters finds himself in the Holy of Holies, and is made worthy [like Abraham] to behold the unapproachable beauty of the holy and royal Trinity. (*PG* 91.401C–404A; *LMC* 90)

Here Maximus presents John the Cubicularius with an exemplification of what in another place he refers to as the Word's "[becoming] thick" or being made fat by undergoing a continual moral incarnation in the manners (*tropos*) or "practices of the virtues" (*vita practica*) of those who enter on Christ's way of love, which here means to identify with Abraham. In this way Christ in an ongoing way "becomes flesh" (*CTE* 37; *PG* 90.1141C; *MCSW* 156).

Much more could be said about what Maximus is doing here, but what is important for my purposes is this: the Christological vision of love in *Ep.* 2 is unintelligible apart from the story of Abraham and his covenant with YHWH. For to enter on the way of being that he inaugurates in giving himself to YHWH as Abram (whose identity was established in Ur of the Chaldees) and receiving himself from YHWH as Abraham (whose identity is in becoming Israel, and so lies in the eschatological future) is to enter on the way of Christ. Therefore, to enter into Abraham–Christ is to enter into Israel's covenantal story and to leave behind essentialist identities of tyranny. Afro-Christianity resuscitates this insight within a racialized modern/colonial world.

Ambigua 10, Christ's Jewish Flesh, and the Transfiguration

Maximus furthers this way of reading Scripture in *Amb.* 10 where he engages the story of Christ's transfiguration on Mt. Tabor (cf. Matt. 17:1–8; Mark 9:2–8; Luke 9:28–36). The principle theme of this *Ambigua* is the utter necessity of ascetic struggle (*praktikē*) to rightly comport oneself in the world and, indeed, to rightly see or aesthetically perceive the world as God's creation and not as a sphere of possession. Such comportment must be through the disposition of dispossessive love and not through the tyrannical disposition to own or be master. Through a "colonialist" posture, Maximus seems to say, one is assured of misperceiving the world and the things of the world as they reveal God and one's salvation.

Maximus wants to make the case to a group of Origenist monks, to whom *Amb.* 10 is addressed, of the centrality of engaging Scripture and the natural world in progressing toward union with God and its realization of the quest in Christ. Given the presumption of the Origenist monks of not only prioritizing the immaterial (or the spiritual) to the material (or the fleshy) but of seeing the latter as in need of being overcome, Maximus's goal was to make a positive case for the fleshly and the material as the vehicles to encounter God. The problem, as he seeks to clarify it, is not with matter or the flesh as such. It is with the will—the will-to-power as the will-to-possession—which distorts the meaning of embodiment so that material existence is made to signify problematically. Such is the damage done by the Fall. But it is just this point, though, that the Origenist monks have misunderstood. They have equated possessiveness toward the world with the world or material life being bad. *Ambigua* 10 seeks to correct the Origenist aesthetic by showing how in Christ material life, including bodies, is not done away with in the economy of redemption. Rather, it is transfigured. Bodies are placed within a new *ordo*, or social arrangement, the arrangement of Christ's flesh, and thus are made to signify so as to disclose God's glory.

Christ's "flesh" is the crucial category here, for his flesh transfigures all flesh. Adam G. Cooper recently captured how Maximus understands the significance of Christ's flesh:

> What is most striking about . . . [Christ's flesh] is that . . . [it] is ordered together with *invisible, intelligible* realities as an aspect of revelation, not [a] concealment [of God]. While the visible dimensions constitute indispensable elements in the economy [of salvation], Christ's transfigured flesh is seen already to take part in another order, . . . that is, the intelligible order. His flesh thus functions as the "bridge" between the intelligible and the sensible spheres. By virtue of the hypostatic union, it already transcends the normal sensible order; yet, by its location within the sensible order, it is the means by which we too may transcend the limited realm of the material and the finite.[23]

Cooper beautifully captures what is significant in a revelatory sense about Christ's flesh. In his flesh, creaturely flesh as such is healed from its fallen condition. That is, the link between flesh as a somatic and sensible reality and flesh as laden with an intelligible depth that was severed as a result of the Fall has been healed in Christ. By means of its intelligible, suprasensible depth, flesh has always been meant precisely through what it is as material reality to convey more than what its sensible contours alone could contain. When corporeality or the sensible and intelligible or the supersensible were severed in the Fall, the flesh became an enclosed sphere of power whose modus operandi became its passions, which were now no longer directed toward God. Maximus wants to outline how Christ's flesh reestablishes the bridge, as Cooper says, between

sensibility and intelligibility so that bodies, having been placed within a different order (*taxis*), can be made to signify divine realities but by means of corporeality.

But this is also where the conclusion Cooper draws from his analysis of Maximus's understanding of flesh must be restated, for as it stands it leaves the wrong impression. It is not so much that entering into Christ's flesh helps us "transcend the limited realm of the material and finite" as it is that flesh is the means through which the material and the finite, the fleshly and the corporeal, can be reconceived iconically as disclosing God. Maximus wants to restore materiality and corporeality to its rightful place, not transcend or merely overcome it, which is what the Origenist monks thought. Herein lies the importance of Maximus's reading of the story of the transfiguration in *Amb.* 10, for against the Origenists, he wants to make this point about the significance of corporeality—albeit, transfigured or as beheld in the Taboric light—in disclosing Christ.

Maximus makes this point by first turning to the metaphor of the "cloud" or the "veil" as a way of talking about "flesh." This language provides a segue to the biblical language of cloud, particularly, in the Old Testament. The cloud or flesh plays a positive role in leading the people of Israel under the direction of Moses through the desert after their liberation from Egypt (cf. Exod. 14:15–29). Maximus, however, is quick to observe that when the cloud is first mentioned in Scripture it is in connection with Israel's crossing the Red Sea to get to the Promised Land. This causes Maximus to link the notion of the cloud or the flesh with that of crossing over from one mode of being or aesthetic orientation (that connected with the realm of Egypt shall we say) into another (that connected with the Land of Promise). This analysis leads him to reflect on Christ's transfiguration in such a way as to bring together with Christ's incarnation the notions of the cloud and of crossing over. The story of the transfiguration brings these strands together to create something like what philosopher Jean-Luc Marion has called "the crossing of the visible."[24]

One sees what Andrew Louth has called "the mutually-encountering crossings-over—of God to humankind and of humankind to God," such that the transfiguration is both of Christ and the disciples.[25] They are thoroughly illuminated inasmuch as on the one hand Christ's face shines with unapproachable light and on the other hand in gazing on the irradiated Christ "the disciples [themselves] pass over 'from flesh to spirit.'"[26] But Maximus points out that because Christ's face was engulfed with the blinding light of Tabor, which was the light of his divinity, the disciples were unable to behold him directly:

> They were taught hiddenly that the all-blessed radiance that shone
> resplendently from [Christ's] face, as it overpowered the sight of the
> eyes, was a symbol of his divinity that transcends mind and sense and
> being and knowledge. He had neither form nor beauty, but they

knew him as the Word become flesh, and thus were led to regard him as fair with beauty beyond the sons of men, and to understand that He is the One who was in the beginning, and was with God and was God, and through theological denial [i.e., apophasis] that praises Him as being completed uncontained, they were led contemplatively to the glory as of the Only-begotten of the Father, full of grace and truth. (*PG* 91.1128A–B; *LMC* 109)

Unable to behold Christ directly because of his divinity, the disciples could only lay hold of him through the mediation of his radiant garments, which like the Exodus cloud would lead them on the path that YHWH–Christ designated. These garments have a twofold meaning, Maximus says:

The radiant garments [*leukanthenta himatia*] conveyed a symbol of the words of Holy Scripture, which in this case became shining and clear and limpid to them . . . . Or [the garments can be understood as symbols] of creation itself, which a base presumption regards in a limited way as delivered to the deceiving senses alone, but which can be understood, through the wise variety of the various forms that it contains, on the analogy of a garment, to be the worthy power of the generative Word who wears it. (*PG* 91.1128B–C; *LMC* 109)

Thus, the garments Christ wears to mediate his divinity are Scripture and creation itself, conceived together.

In elaborating on this point later in *Amb*. 10, Maximus is compelled to interpret the significance of the presence of Moses the scribe of Torah and Elijah the prophet at the event of the transfiguration. He concludes that the legal and the prophetic word of Israel—that is, Moses and Elijah—are the garments Christ wears and through which he communicates his divinity. They are Christ's flesh, and thus the disciples must grasp Moses and Elijah, who are the scriptural Old Testament witnesses, if they would "see" creation rightly and so be divinized. In other words, Israel as YHWH's covenantal people and creation as coming from YHWH are not two parallel tracks of revelation. Moses and Elijah as the jointly understood legal and prophetic word are the hermeneutic of creation, the revelatory key to the natural world in its openness, as said earlier, to be-in-another, that is, to be in Christ. Hence, to lay hold of Christ's garments is to lay hold of the meanings (*logoi*) of creation as they inhere in Christ, for Moses and Elijah disclose the meanings of creation in their being in Christ the Word (Logos) and thus in their being in their Creator.

To unfold this, Maximus goes into a series of interpretations of the figures of Moses and Elijah. Each one develops some facet of how they, and thus Scripture, are the garments or the flesh that Christ wears in disclosing who he is in his divinity. Together the interpretations are riffs on the claim that beholding Christ's divinity is possible only as one enters into the way of being

opened up by Torah and the prophets of Israel, who upheld the Torah when Israel was unfaithful to it. There can be no severance between Christ and Israel and so between Christianity and its Jewish roots. From *Ep.* 2 we learned that to behold Christ is to abide in Abraham, and now in *Amb.* 10 we learn that it means to lay claim to Torah and the prophets as they are set aglow in the light of Tabor as iron is set aglow in fire. Thus Maximus says in one of his interpretations of Moses and Elijah that the disciples "received illumination that the types of the mysteries exist in relation to and are referred to the Word, which is the Truth, and are brought into agreement with It, as the beginning and the culmination of the legal and prophetic work" (*PG* 91.1164A; *LMC* 130). In another of the interpretations, Maximus argues that Moses and Elijah are symbols of creation itself in both its sensible or materially visible and its nonsensible or immaterial dimensions:

> Anyone who says that the intelligible and sensible creation of the fashioner Word is understood through Moses and Elijah does not utterly stray from the truth. Of these Moses offers the meaning [*logos*] of the sensible, that it is subject to change and corruption, as his history of it clearly shows, declaring its origination and death. For the sensible creation is such as to have a beginning known in coming to be, and to look for an end determined by destruction. Elijah [offers the meaning] of the intelligible, neither declaring its coming to be in his account of it, as if it had been generated, nor defining it as looking for corruption through death, as if it were to die. For the intelligible creation is such as to have no beginning of its coming to be and commences and passes from non-being to being, it does not await an end of its existence defined by corruption. For it is naturally imperishable, having received this from God who willed to create it such. (*PG* 91.1164D–1165A; *LMC* 131)

The Mystagogia and the Pentecostal Space of Christ's Jewish Flesh

What Maximus ultimately describes is the unity of the natural law and the scriptural or written law, the world of creation and the narrative world of Scripture. But what must also be grasped is how this vision is itself a new social imaginary. While embryonically present in both *Ep.* 2 and *Amb.* 10, this theological, and as such social, imaginary becomes explicit in a powerful way in Maximus's meditation on *The Church's Mystagogy*, which can be read as a theological interpretation of Pentecost (cf. Acts 2). Because of the profundity of the passage, it is worth quoting in full:

> Being all in all, the God who transcends all in infinite measure will be seen only by those who are pure in understanding when the mind in contemplative recollection of the principles of beings will end up with

God as cause, principle, and end of all, the creation and beginning of all things and eternal ground of the circuit of things.

It is in this way that the holy Church of God will be shown to be working for us the same effects as God, in the same way as the image reflects its archetype. For numerous and of almost infinite number are the men, women, and children who are distinct from one another and vastly different by birth and appearance, by nationality and language, by customs and age, by opinions and skills, by manners and habits, by pursuits and studies, and still again by reputation, fortune, characteristics, and connections: all are born into the Church and through it are reborn and re-created in the Spirit. To all in equal measure it gives and bestows one divine form and designation, to be Christ's and to carry his name. In accordance with faith it gives to all a single, simple, whole and indivisible condition which does not allow us to bring to mind the existence of the myriads of differences among them, even if they do exist, through the universal relationship and union of all things with it. It is through it that absolutely no one at all is in himself separated from the community since everyone converges with all the rest and joins together with them by the one, simple and indivisible grace and power of faith. "For all," it is said, "had but one heart and one mind" [Acts 4:32]. Thus to be and to appear as one body formed of different members is really worthy of Christ himself, our true head, in whom says the divine Apostle, "there is neither male or female, neither Jew nor Greek, neither circumcision nor uncircumcision, neither foreigner nor Scythian, neither slave nor freeman, but Christ is everything in all of you" [Gal. 3:28; Col. 3:11]. It is he who encloses in himself all beings by the unique, simple, and infinitely wise power of his goodness. As the center of straight lines that radiate from him he does not allow by his unique, simple, and single cause and power that the principles of beings [tas archas tôn ontôn] become disjoined at the periphery but rather he circumscribes their extension in a circle and brings back to himself the distinctive elements of being which he himself brought into existence [tous tôn ontôn kai hup autou genomenôn diorismous]. The purpose of this is that the creations and products of the one God be in no way strangers and enemies to one another by having no reason or center for which they might show each other any friendly or peaceful sentiment or identity, and not run the risk of having their being separated from God to dissolve into nonbeing.

Thus, as has been said, the holy Church of God is an image of God insofar as [hôs] it effects [energousa] the same union of the faithful with God. As different as they are in such distinctives as language [diaphoroi tois idômasi] and from other distinctives as

regards where they are from [topôn] and manners and customs [tro-pôn], they are yet brought into a unity by the church through faith. God realizes this union among the natures of things without confusing them, but in lessening and bringing together their distinction, as was shown, in a relationship and union with himself as cause, principle, and end. (CM 1; PG 91.665B–668C; MCSW 186–88; translation modified)

The Greek that Maximus employs in this passage is somewhat elusive, but his sense is quite clear. He is saying that there is an analogy between the work that God does in making the many one with himself but without in the act of unifying them confusing what is distinctive about the many and the work that the church does. It does not a similar work but, rather, the same work as its archetype, albeit within the sphere of the faithful: "It effects the same union of the faithful with God" without a loss of what is distinctive regarding the many as to "language, places, and customs." Because the church does what God does, it is God's image. But its status as image is due to its being linked to, or its participation in, Christ's flesh so as to be his body. The church is the image of God because it participates in God's translation of himself on the plane of creaturely material life. This translation is Christ the covenantal Jew:

To be one and to appear as one body formed of different members is really worthy of Christ himself, our true head . . . who encloses in himself all beings by his unique, simple, and infinitely wise power of his goodness. . . . The purpose of this is so that the creations and products of the one God be in no way strangers and enemies to one another. (CM 1; PG 91.668A–B; MCSW 187)

Here Maximus is unpacking the dense claim he makes in *Amb.* 7 in correcting the cosmology of the Origenist monks:

We affirm that the one Logos is many *logoi* and the many *logoi* are One. Because the One goes forth out of goodness into individual being, creating and preserving them, the One is many. Moreover the many are directed toward the One and are providentially guided in that direction. It is as though they were drawn to an all-powerful center that had built into it the beginnings of the lines that go out from it and that gathers them all together. In this way the many are one. (PG 91.1081B–C; CMJC 57)

One way of making sense of what Maximus is doing in these passages is this: he is executing Christology at the intersection of two scriptural stories. The first is the story of the Tower of Babel (Gen. 11:1–9). The story preceding that of Abram–Abraham's call by YHWH (Gen. 12), the Babel story tells of the confusion of language and identity that results from the refusal to hear YHWH's

call and the resultant inability to speak rightly or in light of that call. The other story is that of the descent of the Holy Spirit (Acts 2) in which one reads of the Pentecostal reimagining and reordering of language and identity on the basis of a renewed auditory capacity.

The former story reflects an unredeemed way of imaging God's creation, and human being in particular, as both one and many, which is tied to the refusal to stand before and heed the word of the Holy. The result is the hardening of the divinely willed way in which creation is to be both one and many into a binary division of humanly willed homogeneity or diversity. Walter Brueggemann offers a similar interpretation of the Babel story of Genesis:

> The issue is not simply scattering [i.e., diversity or difference],
> for ... scattering may be either an act of punishment or the plan of
> salvation. Nor is the issue oneness [i.e., unity or identity], which may
> be the purpose of God or an act of human resistance. Either unity or
> scatteredness has the possibility of being either obedient or disobe-
> dient. The issue is whether the world shall be organized for God's
> purposes of joy, delight, freedom, doxology, and caring. Such a world
> must partake of the unity God wills and the scattering God envisions.
> Any one-dimensional understanding of scattering denies God's vi-
> sion for unity responsive to him. Any one-dimensional view of unity
> denies God's intent for the whole world as peopled by his many
> different peoples.[27]

Maximus affirms something similar to Brueggemann. He attempts to imagine how God has no stake in unredeemed ways of imagining homogeneity or diversity precisely because this opposition is ill framed. Rather, in Maximian perspective, the scriptural narrative reimagines both alternatives by calling creation into a different vision of itself as both one and many. Pentecost enacts this alternative vision. As he says commenting on Acts 4:32: "All [i.e., many] had but one heart and one mind [i.e., one]." At the root of this Pentecostal reversal of Babylon is the Christological performance of creation and the self, which is the insight at the heart of both early Afro-Christianity in its North Atlantic inflection and Maximus's thought. Both modulations of Christianity put a premium on Christ's Jewish flesh in their Christological–Pentecostal reimagining of the order of creation. Maximus, in particular, as it has been shown, develops this in relationship to the gospel accounts of the transfigu- ration. Christ with Moses and Elijah on Mt. Tabor, the joint witness to YHWH's singular covenant with Israel and creation, displays the one–many structure of existence.

The purpose here is not to give an exhaustive account of Maximus's thought. Rather, it is to note that, for him, the task of any interpretation of Scripture is to draw the reader into its witness to Jesus of Nazareth—indeed, to

draw the reader into the way in which Scripture repositions bodies inside the social space of Christ's Jewish flesh and how in being drawn into the socio-theological space of his body, one is drawn into a new body politic. Bodies signify differently in his body. Moreover, my purpose is to point out in light of the exigencies of modernity that such a Maximian interpretive strategy pre-supposes an understanding of Israel in which Jewish flesh does not function, to use Brueggemann's language, within a "fortress mentality."[28] It does not function like hermetically sealed, racial flesh.

Rather, it overturns the tyrannical logic of racialization with its covenantal logic of identity, for Jewish flesh is covenantal flesh tied to the calling and promise of YHWH, a calling and promise that Christ instantiates and through him the world enters.[29] To enter into Christ is to enter into YHWH's covenant, and this entry entails leaving behind through feats of ascetical struggle racia-lized identity. It is to exit whiteness and the identities that whiteness creates. Moreover, it is for theology to no longer function inside of whiteness and thus to no longer function tyrannically so as to make the Word flesh dangerously. Early Afro-Christians had a scriptural reading practice and theological sensi-bilities similar to Maximus's.

Tyranny and the Task of Theology: Toward the Epilogue

This engagement with Maximus the Confessor completes my attempt to begin a new kind of theological conversation, one that inaugurates a program for answering the following questions: What kind of discourse is Christian the-ology to be? Can it be more than an intellectual disease, kept around as the medical scientist might keep viruses around—to be studied only for purposes of producing antiviral solutions? Indeed, given its central place in constructing the world as we have come to know and inhabit it, how is theology as a discourse of meaning in a world of tyranny even possible?

The answer I have labored to develop is that the discourse of Christian theology is possible only if, as Karl Barth once put it, it begins from the beginning, only if it proceeds from a different intellectual posture.[30] Figures such as Maximus (and Irenaeus of Lyons and Gregory of Nyssa), understood in light of the Christian faith orientation of the many—like New World persons of African descent who were forced to inhabit the underside of modernity and exist on the far side of the Renaissance—offer insight into what this posture must be: indeed, into what the discourse of theology must become in the twenty-first century. This theme is addressed in the epilogue of this book.

But before turning to it, it is worth noting that Maximus gives an indi-cation as to what form the life of the mind generally and theology as a dis-cursive practice particularly must take if it would overcome rather than aid and abet tyranny, so much of which it has already participated in promulgating.

This indication also appears in the *Mystagogia*, near its end. After offering an interpretation of the various actions in the life of the church—the act of baptism, the giving of the holy kiss, the proclamation of the "One is holy," the chanting and singing, and so forth—as markers of how communicants are "transformed into [Christ] himself . . . through sensible symbols here below" [*metapoioûntos hêmâs pros heauton . . . dia tôn aisthêtôn symbolôn*] (CM 24; PG 91.705A; MCSW 208), Maximus then makes a case for how one can know that his talk about ecclesiology has real purchase in a world of tyranny, how it begins to undo tyranny and transform the world:

> The clear proof of this grace is the voluntary disposition of good
> will toward those akin to us whereby the man who needs our help in
> any way becomes as much as possible our friend as God is and we do
> not leave him abandoned and forsaken but rather that with fitting
> zeal we show him in action the disposition which is alive in us with
> respect to God and our neighbor. For a work of proof is a disposition.
> Now nothing is either so fitting for justification or so apt for divini-
> zation, if I can speak thus, and nearness to God as mercy offered
> with pleasure and joy from the soul to those who stand in need. For if
> the Word has shown that the one who is in need of having good
> done to him is God—for as long, he tells us, as you did it for one of
> these least ones, you did it for me [cf. Matt. 25:31–46]—on God's very
> word, then, he will much more show that the one who can do good
> and who does it is truly God by grace and participation because he
> has taken on in happy imitation the energy and characteristic of his
> own doing good. (CM 24; PG 91.713A–B; MCSW 211–12)

Maximus then establishes the theological warrant for the claim that caring for the poor is a sign of one's divinization, a marker that the one who acts charitably is "truly God by grace and participation."

The warrant, he says in effect, is God's hominization or entry into poverty; it is in poverty and with the poor that God announces his presence. This is not merely a "preferential option for the poor," as many theologians and religious scholars came to talk about these matters when liberation theology established itself as a discourse of modern academic theology in the 1960s and 1970s. It's more radical than even they spoke of, for in Maximian theological terms, the poor man *is* God. Maximus makes this claim with a full Trinitarian and Christological discursive apparatus upholding it, an apparatus embedded in a spiritual or what he called a mystical theology:

> And if the poor man is God [*Kai ei theos ho ptôchos*], it is because of
> God's condescension in becoming poor for us [*dia tên tou di' hêmâs
> ptôcheusantos theou sugkatabasiv*] and in taking into himself [*kai eis
> heauton*] by means of his own suffering along with us [*sumpathôs*] the

sufferings of each one [*pathê hekastou*] and "until the end of time," always suffering out of goodness and by virtue of the divine mystery [*aei di' agathotêta paschontos mustikôs*] in proportion to each one's suffering [*kata tên analogian tou en hekastô pathous*]. All the more reason, then, will that one be God or divinized who heals the hurts of those who suffer, doing so by his actions in loving men in imitation of God [*kata mimêsiv tou theou*]. In this, the one who is divinized and thus heals the hurts of those who suffer shows that in his disposition—and while safeguarding the difference between he and God [*kata analogian tês sôstikês pronoias*]—he nevertheless has the same power of saving Providence that God has. (*CM* 24; *PG* 91.713A–B; *MCSW* 212, but with periphrastic modifications to the translation)

This passage is striking for at least two reasons. First is the tangible work that the Christology of Chalcedon does for Maximus on the ground, as it were. Through the notion of the *communicatio idiomatum*, he argues that the point of intersection of the attributes of divinity and those of humanity is Christ's flesh.

Were Maximus to stop here, though, he would not be "orthodox," inasmuch as he would simply be affirming a partial aspect of orthodoxy. He adds, instead, that the flesh in which divinity and humanity are conjoined is Jesus' *poor* Jewish flesh. By entering into poverty—by having poverty articulate the wealth of divinity—the poverty–wealth binary and the class consciousness and racial sensibilities that function within this binary are broken down and re-ordered in Christ's flesh. Thus, the sign that a new social *ordo* has dawned with the advent of Christ is that those who are being divinized unite themselves to the poor since that is where Christ is. Add to this Maximus's comment that in healing the human condition, Christ emptied himself (*kenôsis*) to take the form of the slave, and one is led to conclude that the site of God's wealth is Jesus' *poor* and *enslaved* flesh. Having taken on the form of poverty and the form of the slave, God in Christ *is* the impoverished slave. As such, God enters into the hurts of those who suffer so that from inside those hurts, being fully identified with them to the point of communicating his divinity through them, he heals them. It is the poor slave, one might say, who is closest to God and so reveals God.

This leads to the second reason why this passage is interesting. It can be read as outlining the shape that the Christian intellectual life must take in a world of tyranny. Theology as a discourse, from systematic theology to biblical scholarship to pastoral studies, must think in relationship to and in *kenosis* toward, as Frantz Fanon so memorably put it, "the wretched of the earth"(see n. 2 above). With a Pentecostal ear to hear them in their languages speak the promises of YHWH and, having united itself to them, theology must rediscover itself as a suffering discourse and relinquish its identity as a discourse of possessive power through which class consciousness and racial sensibilities

still work. It must refuse what Pierre Bourdieu has called the "scholastic dis-position," which marks modern intellectual life.[31] Maximus captured some-thing of this in the passage quoted earlier from the *Mystagogia* in which he reimagines the one–many structure of creation. At the beginning of the pas-sage, he says that the mind must be trained to enter into this new imaginary and to think within it:

> Being all in all, the God who transcends all in infinite measure will be
> seen only by those who are pure in understanding when the mind
> [*nous*] in contemplative recollection [*theôrêtikôs analegomenos*] of the
> principles of beings [*tous logous*] will end up with God as cause,
> principle, and end of all, the creation and beginning of all things and
> eternal ground of the circuit of things. (*CM* 1; *PG* 91.665B–C; *MCSW*
> 186–87)

Here Maximus describes how thought itself must function ascetically: that is, how it must function in love and in resistance to *philautia* at the level of the life of the mind.

Thought must be self-emptying or kenotic. It must take the form of the slave and resist being an activity of mastery and thus of control. Theology and its allied disciplines must become a mode of "weak thought."[32] Maximus names this as the mind functioning "in contemplative recollection of the principles of beings" as revelatory of "God as cause, principle, and end of all . . . [the] eternal ground of the circuit of things." It is just this posture that Christian theologians refused, choosing instead theology in the mode of the "scholastic disposition," when they deployed theology to justify European ex-pansion and when they spearheaded the invention of discourses of race in relationship to theology to further justify Western expansionism. Racial dis-course within theology matured with Kant's theorizing of race inside the late eighteenth-century ideology of Enlightenment, which solidified the scholastic disposition as the disposition of the modern intellectual. It remains a question as to whether the discourse of theology in the twenty-first century can relin-quish the scholastic disposition and enter into one of ascetical poverty.

Epilogue

The Discourse of Theology in the Twenty-First Century

Because the present is continually changing, the theologian cannot be content with establishing and communicating the results obtained by some classical period; his reflection must be renewed constantly. For this reason, serious theological work is forced, again and again, to begin from the beginning.

—Karl Barth, *Protestant Theology in the Nineteenth Century*

[The challenge before us is] trying to determine [how the scholastic condition] affects the thought that it makes possible and, consequently, the very form and content of what we think.... [The] vision of the world associated with the scholastic condition is not a gratuitous exercise.... [It] is a systematic principle of error—in the realm of knowledge (or science), the realm of ethics (or law, and of politics) and in the realm of aesthetics.... The three forms of fallacy, being founded on the same principle...and thus linked by kinship, support and justify each other, and this makes them stronger and more resistant to critique.

—Pierre Bourdieu, *Pascalian Meditations*

Long before Marx and Gramsci would remind me, I understood that consciousness is shaped by the material realm, that learning takes place in a world of trouble.

—Michael Eric Dyson, *Between God and Gangsta Rap*

The perennial though increasingly invisible theological problem of our times is not race in general but whiteness in particular. The modern racializing of bodies in social space is unintelligible, apart from how Christian identity was reimagined during the Enlightenment and how both the content and the disposition animating Christian theology shifted. Christianity was severed from its Jewish roots, lopped off from the people of Israel to facilitate Western conquest. Thus it came to pass that Christianity became the cultural-religious reflex of Western existence. But what enabled this to occur? A shift in theological sensibility: Christianity's central figure, Jesus Christ, came to be racialized ultimately as a figure of the Occident, though as regards his bodily status he was deemed to be not of the West. As regards his flesh he was of the Orient, an oriental Jew. Reconceived as an occidental (rational) religion, Christianity was transformed into the cultural property of the West. Christian civilization became Western civilization, and vice versa. Thus, embedded within the social imaginary of the civilizations of the West is the theological problem of the *Rassenfrage*. I say theological because buried within it, indeed animating it, is the vexed theological, which is very much the political matter, as Baruch Spinoza put it, of the *Judenfrage*.[1] Modernity/coloniality *is* quintessentially the product of an ideological usage of Jesus.

I argue throughout this book that overcoming this problem will require the audacity of theological imagination. It must be audacious because it will require that theology (be it orthodox, radically orthodox, liberal, postliberal, or what have you) no longer do its work in Kantian fashion. It can no longer do its work as the enterprise of a *Bildungsbürgertum* or as an enterprise of the religious elite functioning in the interests of power. Theology can no longer be done out of what I would like to call the religious disposition. This disposition is similar to what the French sociologist of the intellectual life, Pierre Bourdieu, has called "the scholastic disposition":

> There is no doubt nothing more difficult to apprehend, for those who are immersed in universes in which it goes without saying, than the scholastic disposition demanded by those universes. There is nothing that "pure" thought finds harder to think than *skholè*, the first and most determinant of all the social conditions of possibility of "pure" thought, and also the scholastic disposition which inclines its possessors to suspend the demands of the situation, the constraints of economic and social necessity, and the urgencies it imposes or the ends it proposes .... [The scholastic disposition] is what incites people to enter into the play-world of theoretical conjecture and mental experimentation, to raise problems for the pleasure of solving them, and not because they arise in the world, under the pressure of urgency.... The scholastic situation (of which the academic world represents the institutionalized form) is a site and a moment of so-

cial weightlessness where, defying the common opposition between playing (*paizein*) and being serious (*spoudazein*), one can "play seriously" (*spoudaiôs paizein*), in the phrase Plato uses to characterize philosophical activity, take the stakes in games seriously, deal seriously with questions that "serious" people, occupied and preoccupied by the practical business of everyday life, ignore. And if the link between the scholastic mode of thought and the mode of existence which is the condition of its acquisition and implementation escapes attention, this is not only because those who might grasp it are like fish in water in the situation of which their dispositions are the product, but also because the essential part of what is transmitted in and by that situation is a hidden effect of the situation itself.[2]

While the entirety of this quotation is certainly important, I want to emphasize the last sentence, which is difficult to grasp because it is densely complex. There Bourdieu contends that a critique of scholastic reason (and so, of the religious mode of scholastic reason in theological and religious studies) entails rendering visible the invisible link "between the scholastic mode of thought"—the mode of thought of "*homo academicus*," Bourdieu says at another point in his critique—"and the mode of existence which is the condition of its acquisition and implementation." Bourdieu contends that the mode of thought of the scholar, the traces of which are left in his/her intellectual productions, and the mode of the scholar's existence *qua* scholar, that is, the scholar's way of being in the world, is precisely the "forgetting of being."

In this book I latch onto Bourdieu's insight, though in linking it to the issues of modern theology and the production of the modern/colonial world, I press Bourdieu's insight beyond what he was specifically addressing. I seek to identify the actual being that is forgotten in the "forgetting of being" that marks and indeed enables modernity. It is the forgetting or overcoming of the Jews as those whose very existence points to YHWH as God and Lord. In forgetting them, they are made to be the alien internal to the West, the figure through whom all dark people, as aliens external to the Western imaginary, are forgotten. What is it that is forgotten about them? It is the forgetting of the everyday practices of such people in their real worlds of pain, suffering, poverty, and death. This forgetting is the inner doxa out of which the theological work went forward to enact the modern world and to sustain it. And therefore there is a certain theological character to the entire process. Or better, the entire process is *pseudo*theological in character in that its condition of possibility is a distortion of Christian existence so as to restrict such existence to the West. Out of this, Christian existence and Western civilization are rendered equivalent. (Western) religious consciousness is born of this mutual inscription. Such is the intellectual-theological *habitus* of modernity.

This books calls for a new *habitus*, a new Christian theological-intellectual practice, one that arises from the everyday practices of the very people the forgetting of whom is the condition of the scholastic universes of "homo academicus." Their lives and the practices through which they negotiate their real worlds of pain and suffering and life and death must become the locus or the disposition out of which theology does its work. For as Maximus the Confessor has said, "the poor one"—the very one homo academicus forgets in the forgetting of being—"is God," and this is due to "God's condescension ... in taking upon himself by [Christ's] own sufferings the sufferings of each one. [Accomplishing this] "until the end of time" and out of the mystery of the divine life itself, [Christ wills] always to suffer in proportion to each one's suffering" (*CM* 24; *MCSW* 212, trans. modified). In connection with the poor one, at the various sites of the underside of modernity, and, in short, from the places of suffering—this is the locus from which theology must be renewed. To use Karl Barth's language, such places are the places of theology's new beginning, the beginning at which theology must begin again. It must begin with a new disposition, a new theological-intellectual *habitus*.[3]

Theology beyond (White) Scholastic Reason

In a revealing passage in an autobiographical essay he wrote for the *New York Times Book Review* in 1995 ("Shakespeare and Smokey Robinson") and that reappeared in 1996 in *Between God and Gangsta Rap: Bearing Witness to Black Culture*, Michael Eric Dyson tells a story that in part points to the disposition in which theology must reorient itself if it would transcend white scholastic reason: that style of intellection is at the heart of the theological problem of whiteness and of how theology today most often is done by white and nonwhite intellectuals alike.[4]

Dyson recounts how as a teenager living in a Detroit ghetto he developed a twofold intellectual passion. These passions were dialectically held together, one might say, by the conjunctive "and" of his 1995 *New York Times Book Review* essay and its book title in which the essay reappeared in 1996. On the one hand, under the tutorship of a woman of the neighborhood named Mrs. James, a woman whom he describes as "full-cheeked" and "honey-brown-skinned," an adolescent Dyson was guided through a "vast ocean of black intellectual and cultural life."[5] "We read," he says, "about the exploits of black cowboys ... [and] studied great inventors like Jan Matseliger, Garrett Morgan and Granville T. Woods.... She told us of the debates between W. E. B. Du Bois and Booker T. Washington."[6] Moreover, he tells us that Mrs. James instructed him in

> the poetry of importance of Paul Laurence Dunbar and Langston
> Hughes. In fact, I won my first contest of any sort when I received a

prized blue ribbon for reciting Dunbar's "Little Brown Baby." I still get pleasure from reading Dunbar's vernacular vision.... Mrs. James also taught us to read Margaret Alexander Walker. I can still remember the thrill of listening to a chorus of fifth-grade girls reciting, first in turn and then in unison, the verses to Walker's "For My People." ... The girls' rhetorical staccatos and crescendos, their clear articulation and emotional expressiveness, were taught and encouraged by Mrs. James.... She taught us the importance of Roland Hayes and Bessie Smith ... Marian Anderson and Mahalia Jackson ... Paul Robeson and Louis Armstrong.... We were taught to believe that the same musical genius that animated Scott Joplin lighted as well on Stevie Wonder. We saw no essential division between "I Know Why the Caged Bird Sings" and "I Can't Get Next to You." Thus the postmodern came crashing in on me before I gained sight of it in Derrida and Foucault.[7]

On the other hand, Dyson tells us that as a result of a gift of a collection of books, a veritable assemblage of "Harvard Classics," from the widow of "a staunch Republican who had recently died," who in contrast to the full-cheeked, honey-brown-skinned Mrs. James is left nameless in his account, he was introduced to and developed a profound and sustained love for some of the most treasured works of English letters. To name just a few of the ones he lists: Benjamin Franklin's *Autobiography*; the works of Marcus Aurelius and John Milton; Bunyan's *Pilgrim Progress*; the speeches of Lincoln; the works of the various metaphysical poets; Hobbes; Plutarch; the political philosophy of John Stuart Mill; and many others besides. The reading of these "Harvard Classics," Dyson says, "whetted my appetite for more learning and I was delighted to discover that it opened an exciting world to me, a world beyond the buzz of bullets and whiplash of urban violence." Understood in Bourdieuean terms, one might say that a scholastic universe was opened to Dyson. He, indeed, was being drawn into the scholastic disposition, the disposition in which learning is the escape from the worlds of pain, suffering, violence, and, if not actual death, then escape from that commuted death sentence that Orlando Patterson has called "social death."[8]

But then something quite arresting happens in Dyson's narrative. "One day," he says,

> [this] learning led me right to the den of danger. Inspired by reading the English translation of Sartre's autobiography "Les Mots" (*The Words*) I rushed to the corner store to buy a cigar thinking that its exotic odor would provide a whiff of the Parisian cafe life where the aging master had hammered out his existential creed on the left bank.... Just then, I felt a jolt in my back; it was the barrel of a sawed-off shotgun and its owner ordered me and the other customers

> to find the floor.... Long before Marx and Gramsci would remind
> me, I understood that consciousness is shaped by the material realm,
> that learning takes place in a world of trouble.[9]

Just as Dyson thought that there could be a somewhat easy replication of
Sartre's Parisian world, he was dangerously reminded that his engagement
with Sartre's work could not take place disengaged from the material reality in
which he found himself. Rather, his engagement with Sartre—or, to make a
substitution, with biblical texts and commentaries, or with historical, philso-
phical, and theological documents and ideas, or what have you—occurred
under the specific material conditions of the traumatic and arresting realities
of Detroit, Michigan.

There is as kind of "learning [that] takes place in a world of trouble," and
thus a kind of learning that itself is caught in the crosshairs of crisis. It is just
this crisis condition that Dyson frighteningly learned it was difficult to extract
himself from, for these are the conditions under which dark flesh exists and
labors. Indeed, crisis is the condition of the world, except for those places
where such conditions are suspended precisely as the precondition of work
itself. Bourdieu calls such places scholastic universes. What Dyson's story
conveys is that when scholastic universes collide with material realities, the
ideological separation of the two gets (potentially) unmasked for what it is.
With this separation unmasked for what it is, his story points to the need to
reconceive the very nature of intellectual work and discourses. On this latter
point, Dyson's story cannot help us, for it is unable to help us understand how
the Sartrean-Parisian world that evoked his aesthetic desire to thoroughly enter
a scholastic universe, on the one hand, and the dangerous world of a corner
store in a Detroit 'hood, a world of dark flesh, which is where his mimetic
desire sought to realize itself (vis-à-vis a cigar), on the other hand, were actually
a singular reality of crisis. It is unable to help us understand precisely how the
aesthetic imagination of the modern intellectual is conditioned on obfuscating
the real world of pain and cultural trauma as the condition of thought.

Nor for that matter does his story offer a way beyond the aesthetic and
cultural stranglehold that traps the nonwhite intellectual in that place of suspended animation and oscillation between scholastic universes (in Dyson's
example, the Sartrean world of the Parisian café) and on-the-ground, non-
scholastic material realities (again in Dyson's example, the world of "black
culture" as embodied in a corner store in a Detroit 'hood). But last, his story
does not help us grasp how the attempt on the part of nonwhite intellectuals to
escape the bind or the "crisis of the Negro intellectual" produced by scholastic
reason reproduces itself in a gendered inflection, or why it is that in the case of
Dyson's story the naming of the link between the Parisian café world and the
material reality of a Detroit corner store entails the fusion of these worlds in the
(phallic?) artifact of the cigar.

It is at precisely this point that we return to the problem I attempted to isolate around Douglass's 1845 *Narrative* and what importantly is *theological* about his conundrum. The theological question can no longer be deferred if the problem of modernity, in regard to which nonwhite flesh becomes a sort of miner's canary, is to be more deeply understood and reckoned with. But it is precisely in grasping what is theological about the modern condition generally and about the modern problem of whiteness in particular that one finds so little assistance in the work of so many that have taken on the modern problem of race. The tragedy is that whiteness continues to reign as the inner architecture of modern theology, and a fortiori theology continues to function as a discourse of death.

More positively, however, the value I want to take from Dyson's autobiographical story lies in how it illustrates the need for theology, insofar as it has functioned as a scholastic universe animated by the theological problem of whiteness, to reevaluate how it does its work, which from its modern founding has presupposed covering over its (violent) racial conditions of possibility. The analysis carried out in this book of how the racial imagination generally and the imagination of whiteness in particular theologically consolidated themselves (in part I) has in fact been a search (in parts II and III and the surrounding apparatus) for a new modality for Christian theology as an intellectual discourse, for at root this is the problem of modern theology. Theology must do its work no longer under the preconditions of the "forgetting of being." Rather, it must do its work in company with and out of the disposition of those facing death, those with the barrel of a shotgun to their backs, for this is the disposition of the crucified Christ, who is the revelation of the triune God. The question that must be addressed, then, is this: What does it mean to speak with theological imagination *from within* crises of life and death rather than in scholastic universes and out of the disposition of scholastic reason in the mode of the religious, the disposition whose condition of possibility turns from such painfully real worlds?

Dark Flesh and the Discourse of Theology in the Twenty-First Century

Doing theology from within crises of life and death requires that Christian theology reconceive itself as a discourse. Theological learning must be reconceived as a labor of life and death, a labor tied not simply to the resurrected Christ but to the Christ who was resurrected *from the dead* and in whose Jewish (nonracial) flesh, Christian thought claims, all of creation lives and moves and has being (cf. Acts 17:28). It is just such a vision that theology, functioning as racial discourse and in the intellectual modality of whiteness, has foreclosed. What I have started to do in this book is both name this problem and execute

such a reconceived practice of theology. Such a practice is not opposed to classically articulated theology, as my engagements in the prelude, interlude, and postlude with Irenaeus of Lyons, Gregory of Nyssa, and Maximus the Confessor, respectively, illustrate. Nor does it simply repeat them in fidelity to a "language game." What I show is that what matters is the disposition out of which they, and for that matter scripture itself, are read. Rather than read such figures according to the protocols of the scholastic disposition, which can yield both "orthodox" and "liberal" pronouncements, I attempt to engage them and Scripture in such a way as to begin to reimagine that locus of Christian theology called Christology. I do this by having such figures as Irenaeus, Gregory of Nyssa, and Maximus the Confessor speak in relationship to the conditions of a dark reality, by having them speak in relationship to the "Holy Saturday" conditions of dark flesh in modernity. For such conditions are in fact the conditions that Jesus, as the one whose life is a life of fidelity to Israel's covenant with YHWH, takes up.

Therefore, as a twenty-first-century discourse, Christian theology must take its bearings from the Christian theological languages and practices that arise from the lived Christian worlds of dark peoples in modernity and how such peoples reclaimed (and in their own ways salvaged) the language of Christianity, and thus Christian theology, from being a discourse of death— their death. This is the language and practices by which dark people, insofar as many of them comported themselves as Christian subjects in the world, have imagined and performed a way of being in the world beyond the pseu- dotheological containment of whiteness. To the extent that they have done this, they mark out a different trajectory for theology as a discourse. The language and practices, therefore, of dark people who have lived into a Christian imag- ination can no longer be deemed theologically irrelevant nor made invisible, which is what white intellectuals in the theological academy have tended to do. Neither for that matter, as is the claim of a growing number of black intellec- tuals, ought such language and practices be understood either as so many "g-d" narratives that when subjected to proper, critical scrutiny reveal themselves to be "significations" upon the inexhaustibility of either "black religion" (in its churchly and extrachurchly, its theological and nontheological expressions), nor ought they be understood in terms of an all-embracing "black humanism" as the taproot of "black culture."[10]

Instead, the languages and practices of dark people, most especially when they seek to comport themselves as Christians in the world, must be engaged precisely in their theological specificity: that is, as ways of narrating being beyond race, despite the surrounding world's persistence in holding them and itself hostage to the metaphysics of race and its ontology of forgetfulness. (One sees this persistence, for example, in how Western societies in both Europe and the Americas are presently negotiating the immigrant question, on the one hand, and the related question of global labor and capital, on the other.) The

solution I have started to theologically develop here picks up on those moments when Afro-Christians in modernity sought to execute a new way of being in the world beyond the racial imagination and yet not as a religious feat or a cultural reflex. Rather, I have called attention to what has been *theological* about their effort to overcome the problem. Their effort—sometimes successful, other times not; sometimes consciously speaking in a Christian idiom, other times not—is important insofar as it calls attention to the need to rend theology from the hands of whiteness rather than concede theology to whiteness. Indeed, it points to the need to reconceive theology beyond the racial imagination that has become its inner architecture. Such a reconception of theology entails, as Barth said, beginning from the beginning, that is, from the underside of modernity. The early Afro-Christian effort, an effort I have sought to theologically think within, is one that seeks to inhabit the world beyond racial and theological—the two are bound together—closure. It is the effort to inhabit the world beyond the theological problem of whiteness.

Notes

PROLOGUE

1. Recently Gil Anidjar has sought to do what Foucault was unable to fully pull off on just this point. See Gil Anidjar, *Semites: Race, Religion, Literature* (Stanford: Stanford University Press, 2007).

2. The geography I am mapping alludes to Paul Gilroy's notion of a "black Atlantic." Paul Gilroy, *The Black Atlantic: Modernity and Double Consciousness* (Cambridge, Mass.: Harvard University Press, 1993). I invoke this term here to signal that the argument being developed in this book has a geopolitical range that exceeds northern Europe and North America.

3. Walter Mignolo, *The Darker Side of the Renaissance: Literacy, Territoriality, and Colonization*, 2nd ed. (Ann Arbor: University of Michigan Press, 2003), and Enrique Dussel, *The Underside of Modernity: Apel, Ricoeur, Rorty, Taylor, and the Philosophy of Liberation*, trans. Eduardo Mendieta (Atlantic Highlands, N.J.: Humanities, 1996).

PRELUDE

1. I draw on two translations of *Adversus haeresus*: the older but complete translation in *AH*-A; and the newer but selective translation in *AH*-G. I use the abbreviation *AH* alone when I am not referring to a specific translation. *SC* refers to the critical edition of *AH*.

2. Denise Kimber Buell, *Why This New Race: Ethnic Reasoning in Early Christianity* (New York: Columbia University Press, 2005), 2.

3. Harold Bloom, "Lying Against Time: Gnosis, Poetry, Criticism" in Bentley Layton, ed., *The Rediscovery of Gnosticism: Proceedings of the International Conference on Gnosticism at Yale, New Haven, Connecticut, March 28–31, 1978*, vol. I:72.

4. The engagement with Irenaeus's account of the Valentinian-Ptolemaeic system of ancient Gnosis draws heavily on the following works: Robert M. Grant's fine introduction to his translation of portions of *AH* in *AH-G*, 1–53; Mary Ann Donovan, *One Right Reading? A Guide to Irenaeus* (Collegeville, Minn.: Liturgical, 1998); Cyril O'Regan, *Gnostic Return in Modernity* (Albany: SUNY Press, 2001); and Eric Osborn, *Irenaeus of Lyons* (Cambridge: Cambridge University Press, 2001).

5. The phrase "wayward reproduction" comes from Alys Eve Weinbaum, *Wayward Reproductions: Genealogies of Race and Nation in Transatlantic Modern Thought* (Durham, N.C.: Duke University Press, 2004). With it I am gesturing toward arguments I make in chapter 2.

6. The phrase "sublime waste" comes from Mark Larrimore, "Sublime Waste: Kant on the Destiny of the 'Races,'" in *Civilization and Oppression*, ed. Cheryl J. Misak (Calgary: University of Calgary Press, 1999), 99–125. Again, I am gesturing toward arguments I make in chapter 2.

7. This issue is taken up in detail in Elaine H. Pagels, *The Gnostic Paul: Gnostic Exegesis of the Pauline Letters* (Philadelphia: Fortress, 1975).

8. An interesting case has been made by Henry Green that ancient Gnosticism and its anthropological-religious categories were tied to class differentials. He documents well the social and economic conditions of the Jewish people, particularly of the upper classes, and argues that negative changes in these conditions were a catalyst for the Gnostic awakening. Henry A. Green, *The Economic and Social Origins of Gnosticism*, ed. William Baird (Atlanta: Scholars, 1985). While some of Green's thesis must certainly be questioned, his point can still be placed next to mine to support the claim that issues of racial construction and the realities of class formation are not mutually exclusive. Rather, race and class articulate each other. If Green's thesis has a glaring fault, it is this: he fails to account for how the Gnostics deployed their theological imagination in problematic ways to link a protoracial sensibility with class ideology.

But the larger point here is that Irenaeus helps us begin to grasp the analogy between (Gnostic) anthropological distinctions and modern racial ones. Following him, one is led to refuse the either/or between race and class that Walter Benn Michaels seems to box himself into. Walter Benn Michaels, *The Trouble with Diversity: How We Learned to Love Identity and Ignore Inequality* (New York: Metropolitan, 2006). Irenaeus sees through the smoke screen of what can be called ancient Gnostic, protoracial identity politics. He sees that it is a ruse for ideology. Hence, Irenaeus does not counter with his own crude version of a Christian "identity" politics—where identity is a prior fact or essence, regardless of whether that fact or essence is social or biological, that then must be represented in the world. He returns to Christian belief or what he calls "the Rule of Faith" as a response to the Gnostic ideological ruse, linking it to Christ's Jewish, covenantal body as that into which Christians enter and as that which determines Christian behavior. Christian identity is determined by Christ's flesh. His flesh does not merely represent who the Christian is. Rather, it determines or constitutes who they are.

In fairness to Michaels, I acknowledge the fascinating complexity of his position. Indeed, I find the argument he makes regarding the "mistake" of race in his essay "Autobiography of an Ex-White Man" most interesting and in the main persuasive.

Walter Benn Michaels, "Autobiography of an Ex-White Man: Why Race Is Not a Social Construction," *Transition* 73 (1997): 122–43. It is clear that Michaels's argument in *The Trouble with Diversity* is designed to fill out aspects of the earlier argument of "Autobiography of an Ex-White Man." It is just that, as of this writing, I am still thinking through whether or not it succeeds.

9. Donovan, *One Right Reading?*, 35–36.

10. Elaine Pagels develops a similar line of reasoning in "The Valentinian Claim to Esoteric Exegesis of Romans as Basis for Anthropological Theory," *Vigilae Christianae* 26 (1972): 241–58.

11. O'Regan, *Gnostic Return in Modernity*, 158.

12. John Behr, *The Way to Nicaea*, vol. 1 of *The Formation of Christian Theology* (Crestwood, N.Y.: St. Vladimir's Seminary Press, 2001), 123.

13. John Behr, ed., *St. Irenaeus of Lyons: On the Apostolic Preaching* (Crestwood, N.Y.: St. Vladimir's Seminary Press, 1997), 93.

14. For an overview of this problem and an example of how it is being dealt with in contemporary, post-Auschwitz Christian theology, see R. Kendall Soulen, *The God of Israel and Christian Theology* (Minneapolis: Fortress, 1996). While Soulen's overview of the problem of Christian supersessionism is helpful, it nevertheless is inadequate. Glaringly absent is any account, particularly in the modern setting, of how the general problem of modern racial discourse and the specific theological problem of whiteness on the one hand and the problem of Christian supersessionism on the other articulate each other. Moreover, Soulen does not address how this mutual articulation of problems bespeaks a deeper problem of how theological discourse comes to do new work in forging the modern world as we know it. In other words, what distinguishes Christian supersessionism in its modern and even post-Auschwitz inflections from earlier inflections goes unremarked. Especially in the arguments of part I of this book, I seek to clarify these connections.

15. Behr, *Way to Nicaea*, 1:124.

16. Ibid.

17. My reference to "imagined communities" is from Benedict Anderson, *Imagined Communities: Reflections on the Origin and Spread of Nationalism*, rev. ed. (London: Verso, 1991). On the centrality of *bios*, or the biological, in the process of inventing modern "man," see Michel Foucault, *The History of Sexuality*, trans. Robert Hurley, vol. 1: *An Introduction* (New York: Vintage, 1990); Michel Foucault, *"Society Must Be Defended": Lectures at the Collège De France, 1975–1976*, trans. David Macey (New York: Picador, 2003); Giorgio Agamben, *Homo Sacer: Sovereign Power and Bare Life*, trans. Daniel Heller-Roazen (Stanford: Stanford University Press, 1995); and Giorgio Agamben, *Means without Ends: Notes on Politics* (Minneapolis: University of Minneapolis Press, 2000).

18. Tzvetan Todorov, *The Conquest of America: The Question of the Other* (Norman: University of Oklahoma Press, 1999), 123.

19. Ibid., 30.

20. In particular, see Walter Mignolo, *The Darker Side of the Renaissance: Literacy, Territoriality, and Colonization*, 2nd ed. (Ann Arbor: University of Michigan Press, 2003) and *The Idea of Latin America* (Malden, Mass.: Blackwell, 2005). In the latter, Mignolo investigates the link between Spanish conquest, language, and racial discourse.

21. I am drawing here on the notion of the "limit" that Bonhoeffer develops in his lectures on creation, though I am extending it into Christology, as Bonhoeffer himself would certainly want. Dietrich Bonhoeffer, *Creation and Fall: Two Biblical Studies* (New York: Touchstone, 1997). Bonhoeffer unfolds his powerful Christology in *Christ the Center* (New York: Harper & Row, 1978).

22. I take this phrase from the title of a chapter in Dumitru Staniloae, *Theology and the Church*, trans. Robert Barringer (Crestwood, N.Y.: St. Vladimir's Seminary Press, 1980).

23. Walter Mignolo, *The Idea of Latin America* (New York: Routledge, 2005) and Imanuel Wallerstein, *The Modern World-System*, volumes 1–3 (New York: Academic Press, 1974–1989).

24. After developing the argument that is to follow, I was alerted to similarities between my claim and that of David Dawson, *Allegorical Readers and Cultural Revision in Ancient Alexandria* (Berkeley: University of California Press, 1992). There are points of contact between his talk of levels of meaning in Scripture and what I talk of here as the Irenaean notion of recapitulation having embedded in it a reading strategy in which concentric levels of meaning flow in and out of each other and how identity is constituted in this process. Dawson says:

> The contrast between allegory and typology grew out of an ancient discrimination of various '"levels" of meaning in scripture, a discrimination rooted in the difference between Hebrew scripture as "Old" Testament and early Christian literature as "New" Testament, a distinction produced in large part by christological exegesis of Hebrew scripture.... "Intratextual" readings of scripture draw on typology to create a single story line out of the diverse and often contradictory elements of scripture, allowing the Bible to be read as a unified narrative stretching from Genesis to Revelation.... [It can be said that such readings] ... create its own world, its own reality, into which believers are invited to enter. "Intratextual" readings of scripture thus become "readings" of culture and experience—efforts to absorb nonscriptural realities into the world of the Bible.... My approach ... endorses the intratextualist claim that texts can and do shape and reshape culture (they need not do so)." (15–16)

Dawson's framing of things bears the hallmarks of what is now typically called Yale school or narrative theology. While there are similarities between my method and style of theological argument, it would be a mistake to situate my arguments there. The rest of the argument of this book should start to clarify why.

25. While the theological claim regarding time in God and God as temporal sounds similar to the formulations of theologian Robert Jenson, it would be a mistake to assimilate my claim to his. See Robert Jenson, *Systematic Theology*, 2 vols. (New York: Oxford University Press, 1997–1999). Contra Jenson, God has time for creation and thus is temporal and historical because God transcends the line of purity and thus the opposition between temporality and atemporality. This is the meaning of transcendence as an attribute of divinity. That is to say, transcendence is what it means to speak of the eternity of God. It is therefore necessary to make a paradoxical affirmation;

to wit, the affirmation of God's *historical* transcendence, which is disclosed or rendered palpable in the life of the covenantal people Israel (and thus creation). Israel, and thereby creation, is God's partner in time. But this partnership does not entail God's leaving himself as eternal to be in this partnership. For the partnership is the covenant, and as such YHWH is on both sides of the arrangement holding it up within Godself. Therefore, God's relationship to time is never one in which God must in some way leave or otherwise transmogrify Godself so that God can be a genuine partner, a historical actor, in the covenantal relationship. Israel's coming-to-be is the theological reality of the covenant, which crescendos in the Israel of God, Jesus the Messiah.

CHAPTER 1

1. This term arises at critical junctures throughout this text, especially in this and the next chapter. I am obliged, therefore, to say something about how I am using it. I am borrowing the term "pseudotheological," and much of the sense in which it is used, from Michael Mack, *German Idealism and the Jew: The Inner Anti-Semitism of Philosophy and German Jewish Responses* (Chicago: University of Chicago Press, 2003). In this important work, Mack observes that "[by] *pseudotheology* I mean a secularized and politicized Christian theology" that terminates in an attitude and practice or, in short, a discourse of modern anti-Semitism (10). Having analyzed the nature of the modern pseudotheology of anti-Semitism, Mack then considers (principally philosophical) responses to it in Jewish thinkers as wide ranging as Moses Mendelssohn, Heinrich Heine, Raphael Hirsch, Abraham Geiger, Sigmund Freud, Walter Benjamin, Franz Rosenzweig, and Emmanuel Levinas, among others. What interests him about this group of thinkers is that they each offer a *counternarrative* of modernity, one that exhibits a "reversal of [modernity's] dominant *conceptual* narrative," its pseudotheology (12). These counternarratives open spaces for counterhistories that can reverse the dominant temporal or historical trajectory (in this case, the pseudotheological trajectory of modernity). In all of this, Mack is in careful conversation with such Jewish intellectuals as David Biale, Amos Funkenstein, Sander Gilman, and Paul Mendes-Flohr.

I am quite sympathetic to Mack's project and draw on it at critical junctures of my own argument, particularly in chapter 2. This said, the accent of my argument, and therefore my use of the term pseudotheology, differs in a quite important way from Mack's. I consider what Mack does not: namely, how the pseudotheological disposition that is modernity, the way in which it parodies theology, is itself a deformation of the Christian narrative grammar. I allude to this issue in the prelude's engagement with the second-century patristic theologian Irenaeus of Lyons. The important term for him in relationship to the ancient Gnostics was *metalêpsis* ("the use of one term for another" or "the transference or substitution of meaning" (Henry George Liddell and Robert Scott, eds., *Greek-English Lexicon (with Revised Supplement)* [Oxford: Clarendon, 1996], 1113.). With *metalêpsis*, Irenaeus was trying to describe how Gnostic theological-exegetical practice functioned, which is roughly equivalent to my own use of the term "pseudotheology." Irenaeus was interested in charting how ancient Gnosticism deformed and thereby parodied Christian theology by abstracting Christianity from its Jewish roots. He thus claimed that Gnosticism was metaleptic or

pseudotheological in character. Modern racial discourse is also a metaleptics, a pseudotheological discourse that, like ancient Gnosticism, abstracts Christianity from its Jewish roots. For a fuller unpacking of the Irenaean notion of *metalêpsis*, see Cyril O'Regan, *Gnostic Return in Modernity* (Albany: SUNY Press, 2001), 148–59.

2. Etienne Balibar employs this term in his essay "The Nation Form: History and Ideology," in Etienne Balibar and Immanuel Wallerstein, *Race, Nation, Class: Ambiguous Identities* (London: Verso, 1991), 86–106. "Nation," Balibar persuasively argues, names a particular construction of community or society, a specific way in which peoplehood is produced and then cohesively maintained or held together. According to Balibar, key to the process of "nationalization" is the "ethnicization" of the people in the very process of their production as a people, of their being called forth. As he has said more recently, "[The] ideal unity of the state and the people is also a way to designate the *nation*." Etienne Balibar, *We, the People of Europe? Reflections on Transnational Citizenship* (Princeton: Princeton University Press, 2004), 140–41. This unity of state and people as nation is brought to pass through a process of ethnicization. But ethnicization itself is also what I would like to term a "religionizing" process, a process that comes to rival and even take over the work once spoken of in theological terms. Thus, though Balibar does not put it this way, it nevertheless is accurate to say that there is a connection between the modern nation form and the modern construction of religion. The processes of religion are to be situated within the domain of the universality of the nation. Religionization, as part and parcel of the process of producing a people and thus the nation, is the process whereby "theological universality" gets absorbed into the universality of nationalism. Hence religious or, perhaps more accurately, theological identity in modernity, was made to function in relationship to the processes of nationalization. Religious identity became an outpost of the nation, of national identity. Herein lay the possibility of state or civil religions. They are central to the means by which the nation produces the people and thus speaks its will. In making these claims I draw on aspects of Balibar's characterization of the "nation form."

3. Michael Hardt and Kathi Weeks, eds., *The Jameson Reader* (Oxford: Blackwell, 2000), 33–36. By "political unconscious" Jameson means that "uninterrupted narrative," that unified or "single great collective story"—sometimes "hidden," sometimes "open"—which is, more often than not, the "repressed and buried reality" lying in some sense beneath the surface of all texts (35). To excavate this repressed and buried reality, the reality of the political unconscious, the interpreter must uncover how a particular text functions "as a vital [episode] in a single vast unfinished plot." But what is this vast unfinished plot? Quoting Marx and Engels in the *Communist Manifesto*, Jameson identifies it as "the history of class struggles: freeman and slave, patrician and plebian, lord and serf, guild-master and journeyman—in a word, oppressor and oppressed" (35). In chapters 1 and 2 of this book, from the vantage of an analysis of the emergence of modern racial discourse, I aim to uncover this unconscious horizon of the text of modernity. I should quickly say, however, that my affinity for the Jamesonian dictum that politics, even if repressed, is "the absolute horizon" of all texts and thus "of all reading and all interpretation" (33) is less inspired by the Marxist commitments that this dictum gives voice to than by its similarities on this point of hermeneutics with the theological orientation out of which my own analysis proceeds.

The nature of the similarities—and of the differences, for that matter—should become clearer as this study unfolds.

4. More often than not, recent work on race tends to accent the cultural as a way to intervene into the political. For example: Hazel V. Carby, *Race Men: The W. E. B. Du Bois Lectures* (Cambridge, Mass.: Harvard University Press, 1998); Paul Gilroy, *"There Ain't No Black in the Union Jack": The Cultural Politics of Race and Nation* (Chicago: University of Chicago Press, 1987); Paul Gilroy, *The Black Atlantic: Modernity and Double Consciousness* (Cambridge, Mass.: Harvard University Press, 1993); Paul Gilroy, *Small Acts: Thoughts on the Politics of Black Cultures* (London: Serpent's Tail, 1993); Paul Gilroy, *Against Race: Imagining Political Culture beyond the Color Line* (Cambridge, Mass.: Belknap, 2000); Stuart G. Hall, "Subjects in History: Making Diasporic Identities," in *The House That Race Built: Black Americans, U. S. Terrain*, ed. Wahneema Lubiano (New York: Pantheon, 1997); and Kamari Maxine Clarke and Deborah A. Thomas, eds., *Globalization and Race: Transformations in the Cultural Production of Blackness* (Durham, N.C.: Duke University Press, 2006). And then there is David Theo Goldberg's important work that probes race in its relationship to the establishment and practice of a discourse of the modern state: David Theo Goldberg, *Racist Culture: Philosophy and the Politics of Meaning* (Malden, Mass.: Blackwell, 1993); and David Theo Goldberg, *The Racial State* (Malden, Mass.: Blackwell, 2002). There is no work that I can think of that analyzes the problem of race, its arising and maintenance, as theological and religious in character, much less that shows the convergence of the religious-theological and cultural-political dimensions of the problem. This work is a small contribution to the task. One might say that the Black Theology project does precisely this work. Part of the task of part II of this book is to establish why, contrary to what one might think, this is not the case—Black Theology's important and ongoing effort to disclose what is religious about modern racial reasoning, notwithstanding.

5. In chapter 3, I unpack the claim that modernity—its politics; the processes by which it produces national peoples or a citizenry; and the rites, rituals, and modes of life it promotes for sustaining the people or citizens it produces—is pseudotheological or quasi-theological. For now, I will simply say that with the claim that modernity functions pseudotheologically or quasi-theologically, I mean that it functions by disassembling and then reassembling—and, in this way, appropriating for its own ends—the claims embedded in the Christian narrative about our social life together as creatures before a Creator. There are three important theoretical influences at work for me here. The first comes from social theorist Anthony Giddens's wide-ranging research into the nature of modernity and its structuration processes. Particularly important for me have been Anthony Giddens, *The Nation-State and Violence*, vol. 2 of *A Contemporary Critique of Historical Materialism* (Berkeley: University of California Press, 1987) and *The Consequences of Modernity* (Stanford: Stanford University Press, 1990). In the latter work, through his analysis of "trust" as a feature of modernity, Giddens shows that modernity itself calls for and requires a certain kind of faith (26–29). The research of Anthony Marx also confirms this. Anthony Marx, *Faith in Nation: Exclusionary Origins of Nationalism* (New York: Oxford University Press, 2003).

The second theoretical influence comes from the Germanist scholar of modern Judaica, Michael Mack, particularly, his *German Idealism and the Jew.*

The final important influence, one that I have developed an ambivalent, if not now distanced relationship to, is that of philosophical theologian John Milbank. The key text here is Milbank's *Theology and Social Theory: Beyond Secular Reason* (Oxford: Blackwell, 1992). While it is a significant shortcoming of Milbank's work that he has neither a theological account of race nor a narrative of his own formation as a British theologian who is heir to colonialist uses of both theological orthodoxy and liberalism, nor, finally a theological accounting of nineteenth-century and twentieth-century British imperialism as a religious, political, and cultural process (these are gaps that must be filled), his overall claim must still be reckoned with. That claim is that the secular, which social theory seeks to analyze and account for, feeds parasitically on Christianity's narrative of the meaning of the world by taking over and distorting it, and that Christian theology has been complicit in this. In this book, especially in part I, I draw out some of the consequences of Milbank's broader claim by showing that modern racial discourse flows from and is indelibly tied to the quasi-theological processes of modernity.

6. Witness Frederick the Great's authorship of several philosophical treatises, his intentional drawing on the works of Voltaire to guide and inspire his reign, his transformation of the Berlin Academy in 1744 into the cosmopolitan Academie des Sciences et Belles Lettres, and his installment of the French scientist and *philosophe* Pierre-Louis Moreau de Maupertuis as director of the Berlin Academy. For more on Frederick the Great, see T. C. W. Blanning, "Frederick the Great and Enlightened Absolutism," in *Enlightened Absolutism: Reform and Reformers in Later Eighteenth-Century Europe* (Ann Arbor: University of Michigan Press, 1990), 265–88. For more on the Berlin Academy, see Mary Terrall, *The Man Who Flattened the Earth: Maupertuis and the Sciences in the Enlightenment* (Chicago: University of Chicago Press, 2002).

7. My reading of this overall late-eighteenth-century situation is informed by several studies; the most influential on my reading of the situation are Reinhart Koselleck, *Critique and Crisis: Enlightenment and the Pathogenesis of Modern Society* (Cambridge, Mass.: MIT Press, 1988); Anthony J. La Vopa, *Grace, Talent, and Merit: Poor Student, Clerical Careers, and Professional Ideology in Eighteenth-Century Germany* (Cambridge: Cambridge University Press, 1988); Jürgen Habermas, *The Structural Transformation of the Public Sphere: An Inquiry into a Category of Bourgeois Society*, ed. Thomas McCarthy, trans. Thomas Burger (Cambridge, Mass.: MIT Press, 1989); Anthony J. La Vopa, "The Politics of Enlightenment: Friedrich Gedike and German Professional Ideology," *Journal of Modern History* 62, no. 1 (March 1990): 34–56; Anthony J. La Vopa, "Conceiving a Public: Ideas and Society in Eighteenth-Century Europe," *Journal of Modern History* 64, no. 1 (March 1992): 79–116; Steven Lestition, "Kant and the End of the Enlightenment in Prussia," *Journal of Modern History* 65, no. 1 (1993): 57–112; Jonathan M. Hess, *Reconstituting the Body Politic: Enlightenment, Public Culture and the Invention of Aesthetic Autonomy* (Detroit: Wayne State University Press, 1999).

8. For more on the claim that Kant bequeaths to modernity its first rigorously scientific and philosophically sophisticated theory of race, see the introduction by Robert Bernasconi and Tommy L. Lott, eds., *The Idea of Race* (Indianapolis: Hackett, 2000). They observe that "[one] finds in Kant not only a clear and consistent terminological distinction between race and species that was lacking in his predecessors but

also an insistence on the permanence of racial characteristics across the generations. Both features contribute to the claim that Kant, rather than, for example, Georges-Louis Leclerc de Buffon, was the first to develop a rigorous scientific concept of race" (viii). Much of Bernasconi's subsequent writings only amplify this claim. For example, Robert Bernasconi, "Who Invented the Concept of Race? Kant's Role in the Enlightenment Construction of Race," in *Race*, ed. Robert Bernasconi (Malden, Mass.: Blackwell, 2000); Robert Bernasconi, "Kant as an Unfamiliar Source of Racism," in *Philosophers on Race: Critical Essays*, ed. Julie K. Ward and Tommy L. Lott (Oxford: Blackwell, 2002); Robert Bernasconi, "Will the Real Kant Please Stand Up: The Challenge of Enlightenment Racism to the Study of the History of Philosophy," *Radical Philosophy* 117 (January/February 2003): 13–22.

9. Some Kant scholars question claims such as mine that there is a link between Kant's philosophy and his racial theory, which is also racist. For example, Thomas E. Hill Jr. and Bernard Boxill, "Kant and Race," in *Race and Racism*, ed. Bernard Boxill (Oxford: Oxford University Press, 2001); Robert B. Louden, *Kant's Impure Ethics: From Rational Beings to Human Beings* (New York: Oxford University Press, 2000). As yet, I remain unpersuaded by their arguments to the effect that Kant's critical philosophy (which includes his moral, political, and aesthetic outlooks) and his theory of race did not cross-pollinate. Part of my task is to take steps in showing that they did. That comes in chapter 2.

10. Cornel West, *Prophesy Deliverance! An Afro-American Revolutionary Christianity* (Philadelphia: Westminster Press, 1982).

11. Michel Foucault, *"Society Must Be Defended": Lectures at the College De France, 1975–1976*, trans. David Macey (New York: Picador, 2003).

12. For more on this, see Ann Laura Stoler, *Race and the Education of Desire: Foucault's History of Sexuality and the Colonial Order of Things* (Durham, N.C.: Duke University Press, 1995).

13. Michel Foucault, *The History of Sexuality* (New York: Vintage, 1980). The French title is *La Volonté de savoir*; a more accurate title for the English translation might have been "The Will to Know." This or something like it would have better captured the force of Foucault's study. It is worth noting that the lectures and *History of Sexuality* were in preparation at the same time. On more than one occasion, Foucault lamented that the part of the book in which he addressed the problem of race in its relationship to the problem of biopower and the biopolitical state received so little critical attention, for he took it to be quite important to his overall research agenda. Foucault's biographer James Miller calls attention to this in *The Passion of Michel Foucault* (Cambridge, Mass.: Harvard University Press, 1993), 241. In a conversation with several intellectuals that went under the title "Confession of the Flesh," Foucault responded in the following way when asked about the significance of the last chapter of *History of Sexuality*: "Yes, no one wants to talk about that last part [of the book]. Even though the book is a short one, but I suspect people never got as far as this last chapter. All the same it's the fundamental part of the book." Michel Foucault, *Power/Knowledge: Selected Interviews and Other Writings, 1972–1977* (New York: Pantheon, 1981), 222.

14. While there is certainly a distinction to be made between "race" and "ethnicity," that distinction need not cloud what I am going after here, which are the

conditions making possible the birth of "man" as the bearer of racial character. Ethnicity is a further conceptualization of the human that emerged out of the racial conceptualization. Homo ethnicus is a production within homo racialis. This further production had the purpose of doing work that the prior conceptualization of race alone could not do as the modern/colonial world-system matured. Immanuel Wallerstein puts it this way in his important essay "The Construction of Peoplehood: Racism, Nationalism, Ethnicity" in Etienne Balibar and Immanuel, Wallerstein *Race, Class, Nation: Ambiguous Identities* (London: Verso, 1991), 71–85: "A 'race' is supposed to be a genetic category, which has a visible physical form. There has been a great deal of scholarly debate over the past 150 years as to the names and characteristics of races. This debate is quite famous and, for much of it, infamous. A 'nation' is supposed to be a sociopolitical category, linked somehow to the actual or potential boundaries of a state. An 'ethnic group' is supposed to be a cultural category, of which there are said to be certain continuing behaviors that are passed on from generation to generation and that are *not* normally linked in theory to state boundaries." Wallerstein goes on in the remainder of the essay to show how each category fits within the overall unfolding of the modern capitalist world-system. Wallerstein deals with this issue also in *Historical Capitalism with Capitalist Civilization* (London: Verso, 1995). Recent philosophical engagements with conceptualizations of race as opposed to ethnicity or ethnicity as opposed to race or conceptualizing both together appear in Jorge J. E. Garcia, ed., *Race or Ethnicity?: On Black and Latino Identity* (Ithaca, NY: Cornel University Press, 2007).

15. Cornel West, *Prophesy Deliverance! An Afro-American Revolutionary Christianity* (Philadelphia: Westminister, 1982), 48–49.

16. Ibid., 47.

17. Ibid., 48.

18. Ibid., 49.

19. Richard Rorty, *Philosophy and the Mirror of Nature* (Princeton: Princeton University Press, 1979).

20. West, *Prophesy Deliverance*, 49.

21. Ibid., 49.

22. West has in mind the analysis of power in Michel Foucault, *Power/Knowledge: Selected Interviews and Other Writings, 1972–1977* (New York: Pantheon, 1981), 92–98. Mark David Wood has recently taken issue with West's use of Foucault's notion of power. Mark David Wood, *Cornel West and the Politics of Prophetic Pragmatism* (Urbana: University of Illinois Press, 2000), 109–45. Wood believes that Foucault's notion of power is "pantheological" and that, for just this reason, it explains nothing about how power actually works in the world. That is, for Wood, a Foucauldian notion of power does not have the "capacity to explain who uses power against whom and for what"; hence, according to Wood, West's use of Foucault's notion of power ultimately weakens "the contribution that prophetic pragmatism can make to the theoretical and practical task of waging a successful campaign against 'common capitalist foes' " (62).

23. Foucault, *History of Sexuality*, 92.

24. Ibid.

25. Ibid., 92–93.

26. Ibid., 93.

27. Ibid.

28. Ibid., 94.

29. Ibid., 93.

30. Ibid., 98.

31. Ibid., 96.

32. Ibid., 97.

33. Ibid., 99.

34. Ibid., 50.

35. Ibid.

36. Ibid., 51.

37. Ibid.

38. Ibid., 53.

39. Ibid., 55.

40. Ibid., 64.

41. Ibid., 65.

42. Ibid., 47.

43. Goldberg, *Racist Culture*, 46.

44. Ibid.

45. Ibid., 46–47.

46. Michael Hardt and Antonio Negri, *Empire* (Cambridge, Mass.: Harvard University Press, 2000), 93–113.

47. Goldberg, *Racist Culture*, 152. Goldberg devotes an entire monograph, *The Racial State*, to exploring more deeply the connections between the ideology of race and the modern state. It might quite naturally be asked why not engage Goldberg rather than Foucault next to West. Foucault is a more fitting figure given the argument I seek to make because, even more than Goldberg, Foucault sees that there is something "grammatically" and irreducibly mythological and religious about the discourses of the state and modern racism. On this point, Foucault grasps something that neither West nor Goldberg—nor, for that matter, any other critical race theorist that I know of—has grasped. My quarrel with Foucault is not with his recognizing what is mythical and religious about modern racial reasoning but with how he interprets this fact and in the process reinvents the problem. More on this anon.

48. It might be responded in West's defense that his call for and work toward a radicalization of democracy challenges my claim that there is an insufficient interrogation of the problem of modern statecraft. I do not think it does, however, for from *Prophesy Deliverance* (1982) through to *Democracy Matters* (2004), and thus from the early West through the later West, there is little to no analysis of how modern political forms, including democracy itself, are implicated in modern discourse generally and modern racial discourse specifically. Nor does West have anything to say about the central place of religion in this or of the signal alterations made to Christian theology in constituting modern discourse through the category of religion. This problem goes to the heart of my criticism of West's thought—and of much of intellectuals of black religion. The next section on Foucault intends to show that his genealogy of the modern state and the genealogy of race embedded in it bring us closer to understanding just these connections, though Foucault, too, finally remains

trapped within the history he is attempting to narrating himself and the rest of us moderns out of.

49. Michel Foucault, *"Society Must be Defended": Lectures at the Collège de France, 1975–1976*, trans. David Macey (New York: Picador, 2003).

50. Significant work remains to be done in just this respect. My own venture into the fray, as represented in this section, draws quite significantly on the following: Stuart Elden, "The War of Races and the Constitution of the State: Foucault's "*Il Faut Défendre La Société*" and the Poltics of Calculation," *boundary 2* 29, no. 1 (2002): 125–51; Ann Laura Stoler, *Carnal Knowledge and Imperial Power: Race and the Intimate in Colonial Rule* (Berkeley: University of California Press, 2002), especially chapter 6, "A Colonial Reading of Foucault: Bourgeois Bodies and Racial Selves"; Ladelle McWhorter, "Sex, Race, and Biopower: A Foucauldian Genealogy," *Hypatia* 19, no. 3 (2004): 38–62; Darrell Moore, "The Frame of Discourse: Sexuality, Power, and the Incitement to Race," *Philosophy Today* 42, no. 1 (1998): 95–107; and Hardt and Negri, *Empire*. Of these, the first two—Elden's and Stoler's work—have proven particularly important in helping me make my way through Foucault's genealogical account of modern racism.

51. I have been helped immensely by the explanation of Foucault on the disciplinary society in Miller, *Passion of Foucault*, 22–27. The following account of Foucault on biopower has benefited from Hardt and Negri's engagements with Foucault, inspired as they are by Gilles Deleuze's interpretations of Foucault's work, as well, though I have found much additional assistance and clarification from James Miller's biography of Foucault and Eric Paras. Eric Paras, *Foucault 2.0: Beyond Power and Knowledge* (New York: Other Press, 2006).

52. Adrian Hastings, *The Construction of Nationhood: Ethnicity, Religion and Nationalism* (Cambridge: Cambridge University Press, 1997). In chapter 2, I situate Kantian philosophy as intervening within late-eighteenth-century German cultural discussions that were negotiating a transition from an absolutist state form of governance to the nation form. The models of England and the United States were critical to those cultural negotiations. It was also in this context that modern racial discourse came into its own. That is, this is also the moment when modern racial discourse began to be formalized as "scientific" knowledge (*Wissenschaft*).

53. See especially lecture five, in which Foucault deals with the Normans and with the significance of William the Conqueror. Foucault, *"Society Must Be Defended,"* 87–111.

54. Hardt and Negri, *Empire*. Hastings has helped me concretize somewhat the theoretical work of Foucault, though Hastings's own arguments are independent of Foucault's. Hastings positions himself against such theorist and historians as Eric Hobsbawn (especially his 1985 *Nations and Nationalism since 1780*) and Benedict Anderson (see his 1983 *Imagined Communities*) to show "that England presents the prototype of both a nation and a nation-state in the fullest sense, that its national development, while not wholly uncomparable with that of other Atlantic coastal societies, does precede every other—both in the date at which it can fairly be detected and in the roundness that it achieved centuries before the eighteenth. It most clearly manifests, in the pre-Enlightenment era, almost every appropriate 'national' characteristic. Indeed it does more than 'manifest' the nature of a nation, it establishes it" (Hastings, *Construction of Nationhood*, 4–5).

For the last claim about the United States and the U.S. constitutional project, see Michael Donnelly, "On Foucault's Uses of the Notion of 'Biopower,'" in *Michel Foucault, Philosopher*, ed. Timothy J. Armstrong (New York: Routledge, 1991), 160–82.

55. It has been a thorn for other interpreters of Foucault as well, including no less a Foucault interpreter as Paul Rabinow, editor of *The Essential Works of Foucault, 1954–1984*, 3 vols. (New York: New Press, 1997–2000). Rabinow finds the notion somewhat incoherent. I, myself, would not go this far.

56. Michel Foucault, "'Omnes et Singulatim': Toward a Critique of Political Reason," in ibid., 3:316–17: "Briefly speaking, then: reason of state is not an art of government according to divine, natural, or human laws. It doesn't have to respect the general order of the world. It's government in accordance with the state's strength. It's government whose aim is to increase this strength within an extensive and competitive framework" (317).

57. Ibid., 3:320.

58. Ibid., 3:321.

59. Miller, *Passion of Foucault*, 300.

60. "Conversation with Foucault," *Threepenny Review* 1 (Winter–Spring 1980), 4–5, quoted in Miller, *Passion of Foucault*, 301. This interview, according to Miller, was first published in the fall of 1979 as a press release for the Tanner Lectures at Stanford.

61. Hardt and Negri, *Empire*, 23.

62. Ibid., 25.

63. Ibid., 24.

64. Foucault, *History of Sexuality*, 149. This is Foucault's way of referencing the nineteenth-century and twentieth-century phenomenon of racism. Such racism links itself to biology and is signally represented by the anti-Semitic racism of Nazi Germany.

65. Foucault, *Power/Knowledge*, 222.

66. Foucault, *History of Sexuality*, 148.

67. Foucault, *History of Sexuality*, 143.

68. For critical reflection on this point, the point about Kant's work offering a philosophical anthropology, see Frederick P. van de Pitte, *Kant as Philosophical Anthropologist* (The Hague: Martinus Nijhoff, 1971).

69. Michel Foucault, *The Order of Things: An Archeology of the Human Sciences* (New York: Pantheon, 1971; reprint, 1994).

70. Foucault, *History of Sexuality*, 149.

71. Elden, "War of Races and the Constitution of the State," 130.

72. Pasquale Pasquino, "Political Theory of War and Peace: Foucault and the History of Modern Political Theory," *Economy and Society* 22, no. 1 (1993): 79.

73. Stoler, *Race and the Education of Desire*, 62.

74. By this I simply mean that Foucault's argument will help me chart the way in which modern racial discourse contributes to the construction of religion as a category through which one gains knowledge of modern "man." As William T. Cavanaugh has put it, in modern terms, religion refers to the imagining of "a set of beliefs . . . [as arising more or less out of] personal conviction and which can exist

separately from one's public loyalty to the state." William T. Cavanaugh, *The Theopo-litical Imagination: Discovering the Liturgy as a Political Act in an Age of Global Con-sumerism* (London: T&T Clark, 2002), 31. Now while there are other serious li-mitations to Cavanaugh's analysis—particularly, that his analysis of the modern problem of religion takes no account of the modernity as a colonial reality and be-cause of this blind spot there is no account of how liturgy and sacramentality were themselves made to function within the religious constitution of the modern/colonial world—he is nevertheless right to see a deep connection between religion conceived of as personal conviction and the state's production of bodies or citizens. To this I would simply supplement Cavanaugh by observing that religion conceived of in terms of beliefs, the beliefs constitutive of a particular religious faith, get ordered accord-ing to a hierarchy of rationality that coincides with a hierarchy within the human species itself. This hierarchy within the species is the hierarchy of races. The most rational or reasonable religions are those that habituate the rational races toward loyalty to the state as its Ecclesia or what ensures humans' natural redemption or salvation and safety in a dangerous world. The irrational religions are those that do not so habituate the irrational races into citizens of the state.

In chapter 2, I am concerned with exploring in detail what is theological, or, better, quasi-theological and pseudotheological, about the problem of race. (For more on the terms "quasi-theological" and "pseudotheological," see n. 1 of this chapter.) For now in distinguishing what I mean by what is religious about the problem of race from what is theological about it—I mean to highlight the ways in which the doc-trinal terms of belief are deployed to sustain the intellectual conditions of modern racial discourse. I argue in chapter 2 that the chief doctrinal alterations occurred at the site of the humanity of Jesus of Nazareth and thus at the site of Christology and at the closely allied site of ecclesiology. More specifically, it occurred at the site of the nature of Christ's humanity as a Jew and as one who carries within himself the history and traditions of Israel as the modality of his carrying of the history of traditions of all humans. The shifts that occur in Christian theology that aid and abet the emer-gence of religion as a privatized category, on the one hand, and the rise of the state, on the other, have everything to do with the quest to strip Jesus of his Jewishness (and in this sense, to dehumanize him) and so to extirpate the Jew and, more specifically, what the Jew theopolitically signifies, from modernity. What is new in the modern moment is that this extirpation of the Jew is a racialized extirpation that functions in the service of created racialized subjects, which is also to say citizen subjects, for the state. It is this intellectual phenomenon that creates the conditions of modern racial discourse and practice.

75. Foucault, *"Society Must be Defended,"* 43. The first two lectures appeared previously in English in Foucault, *Power/Knowledge,* 78–108.

76. Foucault, *"Society Must Be Defended,"* 29.

77. Ibid., 45.

78. Ibid., 29.

79. Foucault, *History of Sexuality,* 92–93.

80. The classic text that explores the corporal nature of the king in medieval thought and life is Ernst H. Kantorowicz, *The King's Two Bodies: A Study in Mediaeval Political Theology* (Princeton: Princeton University Press, 1985).

81. Foucault, *"Society Must Be Defended,"* 35.

82. Foucault means to indicate with this term what he also means by the term "discipline." When sovereignty exercises itself by force and from the outside, as it were, power's display is often violent. Sovereignty has another way of functioning, however; namely, from the interior of subjects themselves. In a 1978 interview, Foucault explained himself on the matter of discipline and normalization this way: "In my book on the birth of the prison I tried to show precisely how the idea of a technology of individuals, a certain type of power, was exercised over individuals in order to tame them, shape them, and guide their conduct." Quoted in Miller, *Passion of Foucault*, 222. But this power comes to be exercised from within: "There is no need for arms, physical violence, material constraints. Just a gaze. An inspecting gaze, a gaze which each individual under its weight will end by interiorizing to the point that he is his own overseer, each individual thus exercising this surveillance over, and against, himself." Foucault, *Power/Knowledge*, 155.

83. Foucault, *"Society Must Be Defended,"* 48.

84. Ibid., 48–49.

85. Ibid., 46–47.

86. Ibid., 15.

87. Karl von Clausewitz, *Vom Kriege (On War)*, in *Hinterlassene Werke*, 3 vols. (Berlin: 1832), book 1, chapter 1, xxiv; quoted by the editors of Foucault, *"Society Must be Defended,"* 21 n. 9.

88. Foucault, *"Society Must Be Defended,"* 48.

89. For an interesting recent engagement with modernity read under the aspect of the state of exception, see Giorgio Agamben, *State of Exception*, trans. Kevin Attell (Chicago: University of Chicago Press, 2005). The chief foil for Agamben's argument is early-twentieth-century German political theorist Carl Schmitt.

90. Foucault, *"Society Must Be Defended,"* 49.

91. Ibid., 70.

92. Ibid., 59.

93. Ibid., 49.

94. Ibid., 66, 71.

95. Ibid., 71, 68.

96. Ibid., 69.

97. Ibid., 70.

98. Ibid., 69.

99. Ibid., 70.

100. Ibid., 69.

101. Ibid., 142.

102. Ibid., 51.

103. Cf. Goldberg, *The Racial State*.

104. Foucault, *"Society Must Be Defended,"* 59–60.

105. Ibid., 65.

106. Ibid.

107. Ibid., 37.

108. Ibid., 38.

109. Ibid., 81.

110. Ibid., 40.

111. Foucault, *History of Sexuality*, 148.

112. Ibid., 147.

113. Ibid.

114. Ibid., 148–49.

115. Ibid., 147.

116. Ibid., 149.

117. Ibid., 149–50.

118. Cf. Stoler, *Race and the Education of Desire*, 81.

119. Foucault, *Power/Knowledge*, 194.

120. Foucault develops this in an interview titled "The Ethics of the Concern for the Self as the Practice of Freedom," in *Essential Works of Foucault*, 1:280–301. This concern for a new, ascetic hermeneutic of the subject is also taken up in "Technologies of the Self" in ibid., 1:223–51 and in *The Hermeneutics of the Subject: Lectures at the Collège de France, 1981–1982* (New York: Palgrave Macmillan). Miller (*Passion of Foucault*) provocatively captures Foucault's interest in querying the practices of the freedom of the self. What appealed to Foucault about ancient ascetic practice, which takes a decisive turn with the rise of Christian asceticism, is the sacrificing of the self, the "submitting [of it] to a 'kind of martyrdom' " (323). Foucault did not have a palate for the self-mortification entailed in this approach to self-sacrifice as a technology of the self, Miller tells us. This was because that mortification oriented itself toward crafting a Christological and an eschatological subjectivity, a subjectivity that oriented the subject in the world not first and foremost from the subject's own will but, rather, from the will of God. As Christ of the synoptic Gospels is recorded as saying, "Not my will, but thine be done." Nevertheless, self-sacrifice harbored a certain appeal or "richness" for Foucault insofar as "the Christian arts of self-sacrifice" in effect declared that "no truth about the self is without the sacrifice of the self." This general sense of self-sacrifice, an approach to self-sacrifice that was immanent to the world and that no longer yoked itself to an illusion of transcendence, was a new "politics of our selves" (324–25). (Miller is making reference to the Howison lectures Foucault delivered at the University of California, Berkeley, on October 10, 1980. For more bibliographic information, see his notes.)

From this, one can see that Foucault's work, especially the work that emerges toward the end of his life, harbored religious and quasi-theological ambitions that had death, sacrificial death, as its arc. The goal of this quasi-theological quest was to search out "new forms of life." At the center of such forms of life would be a "homosexual ascesis" through which, as Miller says, quoting Foucault, we can "work on our selves" and perhaps even "invent—I don't mean discover—a way of being that is still improbable" (327). (Miller is making reference to Foucault's 1982 interview, "Sex, Power, and the Politics of Identity;" for additional bibliographical details, see 454–55 n.29.) All of this is to say that Foucault's thought in many ways sets itself up as a rival to Christian theology, especially to its claims that human willing is most human when such willing takes God as its proper object. According to both Augustine of the Christian West (for example, *City of God*) and Maximus the Confessor of the Christian East (for example, the important *Epistle 2* and *Ambiguum 7*), this Christological and ultimately Trinitarian order of willing is the ground both of worship and

of justice in the world. The question, then, that contemporary Christians must ask is how far down the Foucauldian road they can travel and yet remain Christian.

121. Foucault, *"Society Must be Defended,"* 71.

122. Foucault wants to distinguish his account of history from Hegel's philosophy of history, with which his proposal, he believes, might be erroneously confused. See *"Society Must be Defended,"* 58.

123. Foucault, "What is Enlightenment?" in Paul Rabinow, ed., *The Foucault Reader* (New York: Pantheon, 1984), 39.

124. Foucault, *"Society Must be Defended,"* 71.

125. Foucault, "What is Enlightenment?," 40–42.

126. Foucault, *"Society Must be Defended,"* 227.

127. Ibid., 87–111. The Levellers and Diggers (and a third group, the Ranters) were seventeenth-century "radical" Protestants with revolutionary ideas about the transformation of English society. A history of these groups can be found in Nigel Smith, *Perfection Proclaimed: Language and Literature in English Radical Religion, 1640–1660* (Oxford: Clarendon, 1989); the essays found in N. H. Keeble, ed., *The Cambridge Companion to Writing of the English Revolution* (Cambridge: Cambridge University Press, 2001); and in the essays collected in Andrew Sharp, ed., *The English Levellers* (Cambridge: Cambridge University Press, 1998). I am grateful to my colleague at Duke University in the English Department, Fiona Somerset, who was also a colleague of mine at the National Humanities Center during my time there, for giving me a crash course on the Levellers, Diggers, and Ranters and for referring me to the work of Nigel Smith and Christopher Hill to supplement my reading of Foucault.

128. Foucault, *"Society Must Be Defended,"* 227.

129. Ibid., 239.

130. Foucault's biographer, James Miller, makes just this point about Foucault's vehement opposition to antisemtism in observing that "[when] the six-day Arab-Israeli war erupted in 1967, a series of vehemently anti-Semitic student riots, orchestrated in part by the government, broke out in Tunis, leaving Foucault shaken and deeply saddened. As Daniel Defert puts it, 'Michel was profoundly philo-Semitic.' Throughout his life, he was haunted by the memory of Hitler's total war and the Nazi death camps: in his view the legitimacy of the Zionist state was simply not up for debate." Miller, *Passion of Michel Foucault,* 171.

131. Benedict Anderson, *Imagined Communities: Reflections on the Origin and Spread of Nationalism,* rev'd ed. (London: Verso, 1991).

132. Foucault, *"Society Must be Defended,"* 88.

133. Ibid., 88–89.

134. Jewish studies scholar and historian of German cultural, intellectual, and literary history Jonathan Hess is in agreement with me that one must look prior to the nineteenth century to locate the problem of race. He has observed that "the specific link between theological antagonism toward Judaism and a racially conceived, politically charged anti-Semitism . . . is not entirely a nineteenth-century innovation. This connection was forged as early as the 1780s, in the context of the initial discussions over Jewish emancipation and at a point at which modern concepts of race were in the process of being formulated" (Jonathan Hess, *Germans, Jews, and the Claims of Modernity* [New Haven: Yale University Press, 2002], 52).

135. I take this phrase from Bernard Yack, *The Longing for Total Revolution: Philosophic Sources of Social Discontent from Rousseau to Marx and Nietzsche* (Berkeley: University of California Press, 1992).

136. The issue of revolution and anti-Semitism is taken up by Paul Lawrence Rose, *German Question/Jewish Question: Revolutionary Antisemitism from Kant to Wagner* (Princeton: Princeton University Press, 1990).

137. This phrase is from Kant's *Conflict of the Faculties* in KRRT, 276; AA VI, 53.

CHAPTER 2

1. Etienne Balibar and Immanuel Wallerstein, *Race, Nation, Class: Ambiguous Identities* (London: Verso, 1991), 93. On the origins of the modern nation and modern national consciousness, see Benedict Anderson, *Imagined Communities: Reflections on the Origin and Spread of Nationalism*, rev. ed. (London: Verso, 1991), and Anthony Marx, *Faith in Nation* (New York: Oxford University Press, 2003). See also the essays collected in Geoff Eley and Ronald Grigor Suny, eds., *Becoming National: A Reader* (New York: Oxford University Press, 1996), and in Homi K. Bhabha, ed., *Nation and Narration* (London: Routledge, 1990). See especially the classical statement of nationalism by a scholar of the Bible and oriental languages, Ernest Renan, "What Is a Nation?" (1882), which is contained in both collections.

2. I am aware that Christian anti-Jewishness is not a phenomenon unique to modernity. Indeed, it predates modernity. Nevertheless, something quite new occurs with the advent of modern anti-Jewishness: anti-Jewishness is no longer simply an interfamily theological squabble between Jews and Christians. Rather, the theological infighting eventually comes to incorporate the Muslims (called "Saracens" in the Middle Ages) and in the late Middle Ages or the Renaissance threshold of the modern world gets linked to biology and to newly emerging theories of race, on the one hand, and to discourses of nation, on the other. It is this new shift—the racialization and nationalization of Christian anti-Judaism—that is of concern to me here, for it is this shift that we presently inhabit.

This way of casting the problem already sets my project—and the Christian theology of Israel that is embedded in it and that in subsequent work I will develop—apart from the theological project of John Howard Yoder, with which it might be easily confused. For, for all that one gleans from Yoder's project, it remains too one sided and, thus, conceptually and analytically limited and limiting. Yoder illuminates for us the link between a modern conception of Jews and how the modern state is imagined. Yet, he supplies no illumination on a certain aspect of this very problem: namely, how a discourse of race serves as the inner syntax mediating the relationship between a troublesome conception of Jews and Israel on the one hand and conceptions of modern statecraft on the other. It is my claim that modern theology's problems must be seen in triangulated fashion rather than in terms of a polarity. That is, they must be situated within the interconnections between the modern problem of race, the modern problem of Jewish existence, and the question of modern statecraft or the nation-state. That is, they must be situated in relationship to how medieval political theology transformed itself into modern political theology. At bottom, this shift from a medieval mode to a modern one is marked by Christianity's refusal to

envision its identity inside of YHWH's covenant with the people of Israel. And even in saying this, I must ever so quickly add that a Jewish theological covenantalism is not be confused with modern Zionism in the state of Israel. I speak of the former, not the latter. In its own way modern Zionism is deeply problematic, particularly in relationship to the Palestinians. I will resist going down that road, and stick to what concerns me here: the taproot of what I am pointing to is the Jewish question as a theological matter tied to Christianity's historical refusal to imagine itself as unintelligible, in an ongoing way, without dependence on the Jewish covenantal people. For a related claim, see Michael Mack, *German Idealism and the Jew: The Inner Anti-Semitism of Philosophy and German Jewish Responses* (Chicago: University of Chicago Press, 2003). The virtue of Mack's argument is its recognition of how theology is implicated in all of this. For another argument that is similar to mine—and Mack's for that matter—but that does not push the theological component of the problem as far as I do here and nevertheless recognizes the importance of shifts in theology to the problem of modern statecraft, see social theorist Mark Lilla's *The Reckless Mind: Intellectuals in Politics* (New York: New York Review of Books, 2001) and *The Stillborn God: Religion, Politics, and the Modern West* (New York: Knopf, 2007).

3. Kant puts it this way in the version of his lectures on logic edited by Gottlob Benjamin Jäsche in 1800:

> Philosophy . . . is in fact the science of the relation of all cognition and of all use of reason to the ultimate end of human reason, to which, as the highest, all other ends are subordinated, and in which they must all unite to for a unity.
>
> The field of philosophy in this *cosmopolitan sense* [emphasis added] can be brought down to the following questions:
>
> *What can I know?*
> *What ought I to do?*
> *What may I hope?*
> *What is man?*
>
> *Metaphysics* answers the first question, *morals* the second, *religion* the third, and *anthropology* the fourth. Fundamentally, however, we could reckon all of this as anthropology, because the first three questions relate to the last one. (*KJL*, 538; *AA* IX.24–25)

The significance of this series of questions for Kant's overall work as a philosopher is developed by Frederick P. van de Pitte, *Kant as Philosophical Anthropologist* (The Hague: Martinus Nijhoff, 1971).

4. *KRRT*, 276; *AA* VI, 53

5. The two theorists who have called attention to this are Emmanuel Eze and Robert Bernasconi. For example, Emmanuel Chukwudi Eze, "The Color of Reason: The Idea of 'Race' in Kant's Anthropology," in *Postcolonial African Philosophy*, ed. Emmanuel Chukwudi Eze (Cambridge, Mass.: Blackwell, 1997); Robert Bernasconi, "Who Invented the Concept of Race? Kant's Role in the Enlightenment Construction of Race," in *Race*, ed. Robert Bernasconi (Malden, Mass.: Blackwell, 2000); Robert Bernasconi, "Kant as an Unfamiliar Source of Racism," in *Philosophers on Race: Critical Essays*, ed. Julie

K. Ward and Tommy L. Lott (Oxford: Black, 2002); and Robert Bernasconi, "Will the Real Kant Please Stand Up: The Challenge of Enlightenment Racism to the Study of the History of Philosophy," *Radical Philosophy* 117 (January/February 2003): 13–22.

6. The essay "Von der verschiedenen Rassen der Menschen" ("Of the Different Human Races") was published in 1777. But its first life was an announcement for a new course Kant taught at the University of Königsberg in 1775. I have drawn on a recent English translation of the 1777 essay. I refer to it as *KDHR*. Because there is much verbatim overlap from the 1775 course announcement to the 1777 essay, in what follows I will often refer to them together simply as the 1775/1777 essay or sometimes simply as "Of the Different Human Races." However, when there are differences between the 1775 announcement and the 1777 essay that are germane to my argument, I will make a distinction between them.

7. I am grateful to conversations with political philosophy professor Susan Meld Shell for conversation about my work and, particularly, about Kant as a political thinker. I am quoting from an essay that she graciously allowed me to read and that as of this writing is unpublished. The paper is titled "Organizing the State: Transformations of the Body Politics in Rousseau, Kant, and Fichte." Some of these matters are broached in Susan Meld Shell, *The Embodiment of Reason: Kant on Spirit, Generation, and Community* (Chicago: University of Chicago Press, 1996).

8. Shell, "Organizing the State."

9. *AA* II.429. This opening paragraph appears only in the 1775 course announcement. It does not appear in the published, 1777 version of the document; translation mine.

10. For a biography of Kant that has a sense of this, see Manfred Kuehn, *Kant: A Biography* (Cambridge: Cambridge University Press, 2001).

11. *KDHR*, 12; *AA* II.432–33.

12. *KDHR*, 13; *AA* II.434.

13. *KDHR*, 14; *AA* II.435.

14. Ibid.

15. *KDHR*, 15; *AA* II.436.

16. *KDHR*, 21; *AA* II.442.

17. *KDHR*, 15; *AA* II.436; emphasis mine.

18. Mark Larrimore, "Sublime Waste: Kant on the Destiny of the 'Races,'" in *Civilization and Oppression*, ed. Cheryl J. Misak (Calgary: University of Calgary Press, 1999), 103. I have also benefited from conversations with Larrimore about this and other essays of his on Kant, race, and moral philosophy.

19. *KDHR*, 19; *AA* II.440.

20. I refer to Kant's *Mutmaßlicher Anfang der Menschengeschichte* of 1786, published in the Berlinische Monatsschrift. A translation appears in H. S. Reiss, ed., *Kant: Political Writings* (Cambridge: Cambridge University Press, 1970), 221–36, as "Conjectures on the Beginning of Human History." The point I am making here is significant in that the essay, understood against the backdrop of Kant's writings on race, reads the Jewish-Christian scriptural narrative as a symbol of the story of racial origins, of the emergence of the species from the lineal root genus that founds the empirical races. What is implied here, however, will become explicit in Kant's later writings on race. See the section of this chapter titled "Kant and the Great Drama of Religion."

21. *KDHR*, 19; *AA* II.440.

22. *AA* II.439; translation mine, but with assistance from an as yet unpublished revision of *KDHR* translation by Mark A. Mikkelsen.

23. *KDHR*, 19; *AA* II.440–41.

24. *KDHR*, 20; *AA* II.441.

25. "The Personified Idea of the Good Principle" is the title of a section from Kant, *Religion within the Boundaries of Mere Reason* (1793).

26. *KDHR*, 12; *AA* II.433.

27. Kant's *Reflexionen* 1520 can be found in *AA* XV, 875–884. The editors of the *Akademie* edition of Kant's *Gesammelte Schriften* have appended the *Menschenkunde* to their edition of his collected writings. They are collected in *AA* XXV.

28. Larrimore, "Sublime Waste," 113.

29. I am aware that some will attach different significance to the fact that Kant left these most extreme views out of print and even out of the classroom. It might be read as evidence that Kant was unsure about them and therefore held them tentatively at best. I, however, am more persuaded by Larrimore, who observes that while Kant did not air some of the claims of *Reflexionen* 1520, that does "not necessarily [mean] that he did not believe them—as self-reflective a pedagogue as Kant might well have censored himself." Larrimore, "Sublime Waste," 114. I am indebted to Larrimore's work for calling the importance of *Reflexionen* 1520 to my attention.

To what Larrimore has said I would add the insightful comment of the Italian political philosopher Domenico Losurdo regarding "censorship and self-censorship" to open his study of Hegel's political philosophy. The opening statement, interestingly, is made with regard to Kant:

> In 1766 Kant confessed in a letter: "Indeed I believe, with the firmest conviction and the utmost satisfaction, many things that I will never have the courage to say, but I will never say anything that I do not believe." At the time Kant's native Prussia was ruled by Friedrich II, an interlocutor and at times even a friend of the major representatives of the French Enlightenment, a king who flaunted his tolerance, at least with regard to religion and that which did not pose a threat to the governmental machine. Almost thirty years later, in 1794, the times are much more dramatic: Friedrich II has died, the restlessness caused by the French Revolution, even on this side of the Rhine has made Prussian censorship particularly severe, and the authorities have become intolerant even on religious matters. On this occasion, Kant writes another letter to express his feelings and thoughts: yes, authorities can forbid him from "fully revealing his principles," but that is—he declares—"what I have been doing thus far (and I do not regret it in the least)." (Domenico Losurdo, *Hegel and the Freedom of Moderns*, ed. Stanley Fish and Fredric Jameson, trans. Marella Morris and John Morris [Durham, N.C.: Duke University Press, 2004], 3)

Might it be that the conclusions Kant draws regarding the darker races and the vision he has of the destiny of whites be what he was hiding all along, only to be spectrally present in what he publically said?

30. In the *Reflexionen* 1520 version of the breakdown, Kant inserts a footnote here, that is, between (3) and (4). Giving no explanation, Kant simply says, "Chinese—Jews and Gypsies."

31. *AA* XXV.II.1187–88.

32. *AA* XV.878.

33. Larrimore, "Sublime Waste," 114.

34. I am indebted to Timothy McGee, one of my graduate students, for this formulation of what Kant is doing.

35. *AA* XV.879; my translation. My thanks to Christopher Browning, a scholar of Holocaust studies and fellow with me at the National Humanities Center during the 2006–2007 academic year, for helping me refine this translation.

36. Ibid.

37. I have borrowed this felicitious phrase from the deftly written and important work by Alys Eve Weinbaum, *Wayward Reproductions: Genealogies of Race and Nation in Transatlantic Modern Thought* (Durham, N.C.: Duke University Press, 2004).

38. I acknowledge that at the time Kant was writing on race during the decade from the mid-1770s to the mid-1780s, the people of the German-speaking lands had no colonial, commercial interests. Yet, as Suzanne Zantop, Susannah Heschel, and Jonathan Hess have each argued in response to Edward Said, this in no way prevented the Germans from engaging in "colonial fantasies." As Zantop has argued, a number of Aufklärer, including Kant, thought of reason in terms of the colonial conquest of untamed and savage lands. Susanne Zantop, *Colonial Fantasies: Conquest, Family, and Nation in Precolonial Germany, 1770–1870* (Durham, N.C.: Duke University Press, 1997); Susannah Heschel, *Abraham Geiger and the Jewish Jesus* (Chicago: University of Chicago Press, 1998); and Jonathan M. Hess, *Germans, Jews, and the Claims of Modernity* (New Haven: Yale University Press, 2002).

39. In a section titled "Appendix to the Transcendental Dialectic" (*KCPR*, 590–604; A642/B67–A668/B696), Kant explains what he means by the "ideas of reason" and the purpose of such ideas. The following quotation captures the core of his explanation:

> I assert: the transcendental ideas are never of constitutive use, so that the concepts of certain objects would thereby be given, and in case one so understands them, they are merely sophistical (dialectical) concepts.
> On the contrary, however, they have an excellent and indispensably necessary regulative use, namely that of directing the understanding to a certain goal respecting which the lines of direction of all its rules converge at one point, which, although it is only an idea (*focus imaginarius*)—i.e., a point from which the concepts of the understanding do not really proceed, since it lies entirely outside the bounds of possible experience—nonetheless still serves to obtain for these concepts the greatest unity alongside the greatest extension. (*KCPR*, 591; A644/B672)

40. *KCPR*, 591; A644/B672.

41. For an example of how this intra-European squabble played itself out in North and Central America in regard to the Amerindians, see David J. Weber, *Bárbaros: Spaniards and Their Savages in the Age of Enlightenment* (New Haven: Yale University

Press, 2005). Kant was clearly aware of this. He wanted to put an end to white folks killing each other. His German vantage point, he believed, gave a unique position on the problem. In fact, his claim seems to be that the German-speaking people had a unique perspective on the intra-European, white racial problem since, as of the time of his engagement with these matters in the final quarter of the eighteenth century, neither the Prussian nor any of the other German-speaking people had commercial interests in Europe's colonial enterprise. Aesthetically speaking, their interest was purely "disinterested." (This notion of aesthetic and moral "disinterestedness" will resurface in the religious writings [see the section below, "Kant and the Great Drama of Religion"].) As Kant viewed it, the non-European exterior and the bodies of the darker peoples associated with that exterior were, in the language of the third *Critique*, "sublime." The non-European sublimity of dark flesh triggered a certain kind of aesthetic activity within the white subject and within the European imagination. The sublime horror attending dark bodies and the non-European exterior was a horror that provided the occasion for the white imagination to reflect back on itself, on the perfect symmetry of the European interior. In other words, the nonwhite exterior instigated what might be termed a protonationalist reflection on the inner sanctum of whiteness itself, a reflection in which white racial consciousness equated itself with Western civilization come of age as "Christian" culture. From the vantage point of this enlightened cosmopolitanism, a cosmopolitanism that posited the teleological idea of a global civil society that would bring Europeans into harmony with one another in such a way as to solve their differences over colonizing the world without killing each other, Kant could then construct the idea of the kind of civil society needed to bring this vision to pass.

In this way, Kant reflects the kind of intellectual orientation one sees in such idealist and romantic thinkers of the late eighteenth and early nineteenth century as Goethe, Schiller, Fichte, and Schleiermacher on "the aesthetic state." Josef Chytry, *The Aesthetic State: A Quest in Modern German Thought* (Berkeley: University of California Press, 1989), and Marc Redfield, *The Politics of Aesthetics: Nationalism, Gender, Romanticism* (Stanford: Stanford University Press, 2003). In addition, Kant is an example of how "Christianity" gets reconstituted or mythologized inside of this—that is, inside the project of Western civilization now biopolitically racialized. Given this, Kant is a beachhead of the turn toward a search for German mythic origins among nineteenth-century intellectuals and the task of reimagining the nation. On this point, see George S. Williamson, *The Longing for Myth in Germany: Religion and Aesthetic Culture from Romanticism to Nietzsche* (Chicago: University of Chicago Press, 2005).

42. For a detailed account of Herz's thought and its significance for understanding the Prussian enlightenment as a wide-ranging social movement and social process, see Martin L. Davies, *Identity or History? Marcus Herz and the End of the Enlightenment* (Detroit: Wayne State University Press, 1995).

43. This basic summary of Platner draws on the work of Jonathan M. Hess in which he summarizes Platner's vision of anthropology as a science as follows:

> The knowledge [*Erkenntnis*] of the human being, it seems to me, should be
> divided up into three sciences. First, one can consider only the parts
> and operations of the machine without considering the restrictions which

these movements of the machine receive from the soul.... This is anatomy or physiology. Second, one can examine the forces and properties of this soul in the same manner, without ever taking the involvement
of the body into consideration; this would be psychology or, for that
matter, logic, aesthetics and a large part of moral philosophy. Finally,
one can regard the body and the soul together in their mutual relations,
restrictions and connections, and this is what I call anthropology. (Quoted
in Jonathan M. Hess, *Reconstituting the Body Politic: Enlightenment, Public
Culture and the Invention of Aesthetic Autonomy* [Detroit: Wayne State
University Press, 1999], 134)

My reading of Kant's *Anthropology* has been highly influenced by Hess's. Indeed, I
assume Hess's main lines of argumentation, supplementing it by drawing out how
Kant's vision of pragmatic anthropology or of anthropological utility is a utility or
practice, on the one hand, of white dominance that has as its flip side the policing, if
not the overcoming, of Jewish existence, on the other. Moreover, I seek to establish
what is quasi-theological about what Kant is doing.

44. *KC*, 141; *AA* X.138; translation modified.

45. *KA*, 3–4; *AA* VII.119; translation slightly modified.

46. Ibid.

47. For more on the relationship between *Kultur* and *Bildung* in late-eighteenth-
century and nineteenth-century German thought, see Raymond Guess, *Morality,
Culture, and History: Essays on German Philosophy* (Cambridge: Cambridge University
Press, 1999). For a monograph-length exploration of these matters, see Walter Horace
Bruford, *The German Tradition of Self-Cultivation: Bildung from Humboldt to Thomas
Mann* (Cambridge: Cambridge University Press, 1975). For more on it during the time
of Kant, see Walter Horace Bruford, *Culture and Society in Classical Weimar, 1775–1806*
(London: Cambridge University Press, 1962).

48. *KA*, 4; *AA* VII.120.

49. In the *Groundwork*, Kant says:

Autonomy of the will is the property that the will has of being a law to
itself (independently) of any property of the objects of volition). The
principle of autonomy is this: Always choose in such a way that in the
same volition the maxims of the choice are at the same time present as
universal law....

If the will seeks the law that is to determine it anywhere but in the
fitness of its maxims for its own legislation of universal laws, and if it thus
goes outside of itself and seeks this law in the character of any of its
objects, then heteronomy always results. The will in that case does not
give itself the law, but the object does so because of its relation to the will.
This relation, whether it rests on inclination or on representations of
reason, admits only of hypothetical imperatives: I ought to do something because I will something else. On the other hand, the moral, and
hence categorical, imperative says that I ought to act in this way or
that way, even though I did not will something else. (*KG*, 1043–44; *AA*
IV.440–41)

In the third *Critique*, Kant invokes the language of "disinterest" to describe the beautiful: "*Taste* is the ability to judge an object, or a way of presenting it, by means of a liking or disliking *devoid of all interest*. The object of such a liking is called *beautiful*" (*KCJ*, 53; *AA* V.211).

50. *KA*, 230; *AA* VII.325.

51. *KA*, 4; *AA* VII.120.

52. *KA*, 230; *AA* VII. 325.

53. *KA*, 238; *AA* VII.333.

54. *KA*, 124; *AA* VII.228.

55. Ibid.

56. *KA*, 124; *AA* VII.229.

57. Ibid.

58. Ibid. Kant is here referring to his own "An Answer to the Question: What Is Enlightenment?" in which he says,

> *Enlightenment is mankind's exit from its self-incurred immaturity. Immaturity* is the inability to make use of one's own understanding without the guidance of another. *Self-incurred* is this inability if its cause lies not in the lack of understanding but rather in the lack of resolution and the courage to use it without the guidance of another. *Sapere aude!* "Have the courage to use your *own* understanding!" is thus the motto of enlightenment. (*KE*, 58 [translation slightly modified]; *AA* VIII.35)

59. *KA*, 124; *AA* VII.229.

60. Kant takes up these matters as a part of unfolding book II of *Anthropology*, which concerns itself with "the way of cognizing the interior as well as the exterior of the human being" (*KA* 13; *AA* VII.125). In declaring that anthropology can provide examples—more negative than positive ones, he says—of the successful and unsuccessful enactment of the laws of reason, Kant articulates the logic that makes possible a transition from the first to the second part of *Anthropology*'s argument and to its culminating argument for the founding of a cosmopolitan society. Book II takes up what Kant calls "anthropological characterizations" in which he pursues a knowledge of "the interior of the human being from the exterior" (*KA* 183; *AA* VII/283). He divides his approach to cognizing the species' exterior so as to learn of its interior into an analysis that moves progressively from observations regarding the individual as such to observations about the species in aggregate. Thus, book II unfolds as follows: "1) the character of the person, 2) the character of the sexes, 3) the character of the peoples, and 4) the character of the species" (ibid.). This schematization obscures the fact that Kant splits the penultimate section on "the character of the peoples" into a section simply on the "peoples," which, despite my translation with a plural noun, in the German is actually singular ("*Der Charakter* des Volks"), and a section on the "races," which also is singular in the German ("*Der Charakter* der Rasse"). Kant's analysis of *der Volk* is wide ranging (nine pages in the *Akadamie* edition of Kant's works) compared with his account of *die Rasse*, which in *Anthropology* at least is noticeably thinner (less than one page).

There is a twofold explanation for this. On the one hand, the thinness of the section on race in the *Anthropology* reflects the fact that by 1775, three years after he

offered his first anthropology course, Kant started dealing with the issue of race and the races in a separate course run concurrently with the anthropology course. Thus, he need only give a summary of his views on race in the anthropology course. On the other hand, the terse comments Kant does make regarding race in *Anthropology* serve more than the purpose of giving a summary of his view of race. Rather, they provide a bridge between the prior subsection on the peoples, a section that explores the differences between nations, and the upcoming, final section on the species in the aggregate.

61. *KA* 222; *AA* VII.319.

62. Ibid.

63. *KA* 214; *AA* VII.311–12.

64. Ibid.

65. *KA* 215–16; *AA* VII.313.

66. *KA* 219; *AA* VII.317.

67. *KA* 220–21; *AA* VII.318. Is it not ironic that this should be spoken by one who never ventured beyond Königsberg or its immediate surroundings?

68. Zantop, *Colonial Fantasies.*

69. *KA*, 219–20; *AA* VII.317.

70. *KA*, 221; *AA* VII.318.

71. This is Klaus Epstein's interpretation of Kant. Klaus Epstein, *The Genesis of German Conservatism* (Princeton: Princeton University Press, 1966). But Frederick Beiser is correct to see a revolutionary impulse in what Kant was doing. Frederick C. Beiser, *Enlightenment, Revolution, and Romanticism* (Cambridge, Mass.: Harvard University Press, 1992). For a general overview of how Enlightenment thinkers related themselves to government and politics, see C. B. A. Behrens, *Society, Government and the Enlightenment: The Experiences of Eighteenth-Century France and Prussia* (New York: Harper and Row, 1985).

72. Mack, *German Idealism and the Jew*, 28.

73. Ibid.

74. Ibid., 28–29.

75. Ibid., 31.

76. Hess, *Reconstituting the Body Politic*, 196.

77. *KA*, 100; *AA* VII.205. Kant here betrays the degree to which his own discourse presupposed an early Orientalism, which, as we will see, his reinterpreted, rational Christianity expressed. For a now classic statement on Orientalism, see Edward W. Said, *Orientalism* (New York: Vintage, 1978).

78. This is perhaps the place to register what I take to be a significant lacuna in Said's otherwise insightful analyses of modern Orientalism: namely, its complete lack of an account of how the discourse of Orientalism arose as a counter-Jewish or anti-Jewish discourse. That is, Said has no account of Orientalism and the Jews. On one level, this is understandable, inasmuch as his focus of concern in *Orientalism* was Orientalist discourse as anti-Arab and anti-Muslim discourse. Yet, on another level, it seems to me that even an adequate account of this problem must reckon with the relationship between Jewish Orientalism as productive of non-Jewish Orientalisms, including Arab and Muslim Orientalism. Sadly, this problem is only at the beginning stages of being corrected in the scholarly literature. I note the following as

important scholarly interventions to correct this intellectual lacuna in scholarship on colonialism, postcolonialism, and Orientalism. Heschel, *Abraham Geiger and the Jewish Jesus*; James Pasto, "Islam's 'Strange Secret Sharer': Orientalism, Judaism, and the Jewish Question," *Comparative Studies of Society and History* 40 (1998): 437–74; Jonathan M. Hess, "Sugar Island Jews?," *Eighteenth-Century Studies* 32 (1998): 92–100; Hess, *Germans, Jews, and the Claims of Modernity*; Ivan Davidson Kalmar, "Moorish Style: Orientalism, the Jews and Synagogue Architecture," *Jewish Social Studies: History, Culture, and Society* 7, no. 3 (2001): 68–100; the essays collected in Hayim Lapin and Dale B. Martin, eds., *Jews, Antiquity, and the Nineteenth-Century Imagination* (Potomac: University Press of Maryland, 2003); Derek J. Penslar, "Zionism, Colonialism and Post-Colonialism," *Journal of Israeli History* 20, no. 2–3 (2001): 84–98; Ivan Davidson Kalmar and Derek Jonathan Penslar, eds., *Orientalism and the Jews* (Waltham, Mass.: Brandeis University Press and University Press of New England, 2005); and John V. Tolan, *Saracens: Islam in the Medieval European Imagination* (New York: Columbia University Press, 2002.

79. An anonymous writer in 1804, the year of Kant's death, explicitly states what Kant assumes and thus felt no need to state: namely, the deep, conceptual link between Jewish flesh and all other nonwhite flesh. As the following quote makes clear, the writer was well aware of late-eighteenth-century racial discourse, referencing the very same sources that Kant himself read. It stands to reason that, given Kant's notoriety, the writer probably knew of his work in anthropology and on race as well:

> Blumenbach has proven with certainty that the cause of degeneration among human beings is the receptivity toward stimuli affecting the external body and the activity of the animal mechanism in responding to these stimuli.... All anatomists are agreed that the color of human beings is caused by the color of the Malipighian layer of the skin, and Meckel found when dissecting a Negro that the brain itself was black. It is a universal assumption that the colors of human beings derive from bile and the liver affecting the blood. There is not a physician or natural scientist who will contradict these statements, and this is the ground on which I base my claim that the Jews are the sole cause of the human beings' degeneration from the beautiful Caucasian race, ... the sole cause of the dark color of all colored human beings.

While Kant is not this explicit, the logic that could lead this anonymous writer to make such a claim is subtly embedded in Kant's thought.

This statement comes from a tract entitled *Indisputable Proof That the World, Humanity, Christendom and All States Will Have to Perish unless Jewish Men Are Promptly Slaughtered and Jewish Women Sold into Slavery* (1804). Jonathan M. Hess alerted me to this passage in a paper he graciously allowed me to read in its unpublished form. The paper is entitled "Jewish Emancipation and the Politics of Race" and was originally delivered at the 2001 conference on the German Invention of Race at Harvard University. It has since been published in Sara Eigen and Mark J. Larrimore, eds., *The German Invention of Race* (Albany: SUNY Press, 2006).

80. *KA*, 100; *AA* VII.205.
81. *KA*, 100; *AA* VII.206.

82. *KA* 100; *AA* VII.205–6.

83. Steven Lestition, "Kant and the End of the Enlightenment in Prussia," *Journal of Modern History* 65, no. 1 (1993): 57–112.

84. See the chapter on Kant (chapter 6, "Kant and the Preservation of Metaphysics") in Ian Hunter, *Rival Enlightenments: Civil and Metaphysical Philosophy in Early Modern Germany* (New York: Cambridge University Press, 2001), which develops this point.

85. *KA*, 238; *AA* VII.332–33.

86. On the link between "bios" and the political, see especially the last chapter in Michel Foucault, *The History of Sexuality*, vol. 1: *An Introduction*, trans. Robert Hurley (New York: Vintage, 1990). See also the work of Italian philosopher Giorgio Agamben, who builds on Foucault's work: Giorgio Agamben, *Homo Sacer: Sovereign Power and Bare Life*, trans. Daniel Heller-Roazen (Stanford: Stanford University Press, 1995), and Giorgio Agamben, *Remnants of Auschwitz: The Witness and the Archive* (New York: Zone, 1999). If there is a serious lacuna in Agamben's work it is this: while he rightly sees the connection between homo sacer as the death-bound-subject and the killing of Jewish flesh, an insight already in Foucault and so, in itself, not new, to this point in his work he has no account of how a racial vision works in all of this, which Foucault did speak to.

87. Kant's essay on "Perpetual Peace" is in Reiss, *Kant: Political Writings*, 93–130.

88. *KRRT*, 130; *AA* VI.95.

89. For a fuller development of this claim, see Gordon E. Michalson Jr., *Kant and the Problem of God* (Oxford: Blackwell, 1999); Yirmiyahu Yovel, *Kant and the Philosophy of History* (Princeton: Princeton University Press, 1980); and Yirmiyahu Yovel, "The Interests of Reason: From Metaphysics to Moral History," in *Kant's Practical Philosophy Reconsidered: Papers Presented at the Seventh Jerusalem Philosophical Encounter, December 1986*, ed. Yirmiyahu Yovel (Dordrecht: Kluwer Academic, 1989).

90. *KRRT*, 129 30; *AA* VI.94.

91. Much of what follows is indebted to Mack's important analysis.

92. Mack, *German Idealism and the Jew*, 28.

93. Ibid.

94. Ibid.

95. *KG*, 1010 (translation slightly modified); *AA* IV.389. I was alerted to this passage by Mack, *German Idealism and the Jew*, 29.

96. *KMM*, 68 (translation slightly modified); *AA* VI.286. Referred to in Mack, *German Idealism and the Jew*, 31.

97. Mack, *German Idealism and the Jew*, 28.

98. I have followed Mack's translation rather than Gregor's at *KMM*, 105 (*AA* VI.331–32). See Mack's fuller rendering of the passage in *German Idealism and the Jew*, 37.

99. *KRRT*, 154–55; *AA* VI.125; translation slightly modified.

100. *KRRT*, 119; *AA* VI.80.

101. *KRRT*, 78; *AA* VI.30–31.

102. Recent scholarship increasingly affirms, on exegetical grounds, that Paul himself did not oppose spirit and law or charity and law as an opposition between the nonbodily and the bodily. Rather, Paul's notion of the spirit bespeaks the care of the body. Daniel Boyarin, *A Radical Jew: Paul and the Politics of Identity* (Berkeley: University of California Press, 1994), and Richard B. Hays, *Echoes of Scripture in the*

Letters of Paul (New Haven: Yale University Press, 1989). This emerging recognition of the nonopposition between spirit and letter and related distinctions in Paul's thinking is in keeping with the Jewish thought of the Old Testament.

But then again Steven B. Smith is surely correct when he observes (in comments he makes regarding Kant in the course of his illuminating study of Baruch Spinoza) that for Kant "[exegetico-]historical knowledge is not the point" anyway, for "the *Religion* distinguishes the art of scriptural interpretation from mere biblical scholarship (*Schriftgelehrsamkeit*). The interpreter is concerned with the moral meaning of scripture, the scholar in establishing the historical credibility of the text." And as far as the former is concerned, what is important is "the moral improvement of mankind." Therefore, the scriptural "text must be interpreted to meet the needs of morality." Steven B. Smith, *Spinoza, Liberalism, and the Question of Jewish Identity* (New Haven: Yale University Press, 1997), 183.

How is one to respond to Kant? Whatever answer one advances, it must refuse the hermeneutical dichotomy that is central to his outlook. It must refuse the division between interpretation (which theologians, philosophers, and the like are engaged in), on the one hand, and the strictly historical work of exegesis (which biblical scholars are engaged in), on the other. The nineteenth-century turn to hermeneutics and its solidification in the twentieth century has forever closed this gap: all exegesis presupposes interpretive, extra-exegetical judgments; all interpretations presuppose certain preinterpretive judgments. The question, then, concerns the merits of the unspoken judgments amd the work such preinterpretive judgments are meant interpretively to do. Recent work in the theological interpretation of Scripture by biblical scholars and the exegetical interpretation of Scripture by theologians reflects this shift in the intellectual state of affairs, and in my judgment this turn among certain biblical scholars is good. Yet, more than this is needed to overturn the Kantian problematic. Another naiveté—in my judgment, the more difficult one—must be overcome: that is, reflection on how Scripture seeks to disrupt the reality of the interpreter in the very act of interpretation, rather than leave that reality untouched in interpretation. This is the ultimate issue at stake in Kant's philosophical reading of Scripture and Paul, an issue that a simple advocation of the theological interpretation of Scripture still does not address but leaves intact.

I take up this matter later in the Interlude's consideration of Gregory of Nyssa as an abolitionist interpreter of scripture, and I expand upon it in my "Theology, Exegesis, and the Just Society: Gregory of Nyssa as Abolitionist Intellectual" *Ex Auditu* 22 (2006): 181–212. Moreover, in part III of this book, I include Briton Hammon (chapter 6), Frederick Douglass (chapter 7), and Jarena Lee (chapter 8) as scriptural readers who interpret in such a way as to overturn a world structured according to those who are slaves (or have the slave mentality [*Sklavensinn*]) and those who are free precisely through reconnecting Christianity to its Jewish roots at the Christological Archimedean point of Jesus of Nazareth. It is into his reality as a Jew and as the one who upholds the covenantal law of Israel for the sake of the salvation of Jews and Gentiles that they enter.

103. Michael Mack, "Law, Charity and Taboo or Kant's Reversal of St. Paul's Spirit-Letter Opposition and Its Theological Implications," *Modern Theology* 16, no. 4 (2000): 421–22.

104. Shawn Kelley has recently argued that it was the nineteenth-century biblical scholar Ferdinand Christian Baur whose Hegelian reading of the Bible and Christian history led him to argue that Paul was more Greek than Jewish and thus read Christianity as a Western religion. Kelly is surely correct in this. What I am pointing to here, however, is how Kant (and other mediating figures like the important Kantian biblical scholar and German theologian Wilhelm Martin Leberecht de Wette [1780–1849]) prepared the way for Baur, prefiguring his most fundamentals moves regarding Paul. Moreover, I seek to point to the root of how Paul came to be read in the formation of Pauline scholarship as a *theological* problem of white racial formation and its link to how Jewish identity came to be racially, rather than theologically, construed in light of Israel's covenant with YHWH. This point is absent from Kelley's otherwise fine and quite important study. Shawn Kelley, *Racializing Jesus: Race, Ideology and the Formation of Modern Biblical Scholarship* (London: Routledge, 2002).

105. *KRRT*, 104–5; *AA* VI.61–62.

106. *KRRT*, 104; *AA* VI.61.

107. *KRRT*, 105; *AA* VI.62.

108. Ibid.

109. *KRRT*, 118–19; *AA* VI.78–79.

110. *KRRT*, 119; *AA* VI.78–79.

111. *KRRT*, 119–20; *AA* VI.79–81.

112. *KRRT*, 154; *AA* VI.125.

113. Contained within this sentence is a Christian theology of creation, which I cannot unpack here, grounded in a Christian theology of Israel, which I do not fully develop here, either. The latter, particularly—a Christian theology of Israel—one that is situated against "Orientalism" and that thus is an intervention against theological whiteness, is the subject of continued research on my part. For now, I mention the following works as providing some assistance as I attempt to theologically rethink the question of Israel in relationship to the question of modernity, on the one hand, and the question of dark flesh, on the other: Jon D. Levenson, *Sinai and Zion: An Entry into the Jewish Bible* (New York: HarperCollins, 1985); Jon D. Levenson, *Creation and the Persistence of Evil: The Jewish Drama of Divine Omnipotence* (Princeton: Princeton University Press, 1994); N. T. Wright, *The New Testament and the People of God*, vol. 1 of *Christian Origins and the Question of God* (Minneapolis: Fortress, 1992); N. T. Wright, *Jesus and the Victory of God*, vol. 2 of *Christian Origins and the Question of God* (Minneapolis: Fortress, 1996); N. T. Wright, *The Resurrection of the Son of God*, vol. 3 of *Christian Origins and the Question of God* (Minneapolis: Fortress, 2003); John Goldingay, *Israel's Gospel*, vol. 1 of *Old Testament Theology* (Downers Grove, Ill.: InterVarsity, 2003); Richard King, *Orientalism and Religion: Postcolonial Theory, India and "the Mystic East"* (London: Routledge, 1999); Joel S. Kaminsky, "Did Election Imply the Mistreatment of Non-Israelites?," *Harvard Theological Review* 96, no. 4 (2003): 397–425; Joel S. Kaminsky, "Reclaiming a Theology of Election: Favoritism and the Joseph Story," *Perspectives in Religious Studies* 31, no. 2 (2004): 135–52; Kalmar and Penslar, *Orientalism and the Jews*; David N. Myers, *Re-Inventing the Jewish Past: European Jewish Intellectuals and the Zionist Return to History* (New York: Oxford University Press, 1995); and Bill V. Mullen, *Afro-Orientalism* (Minneapolis: University of Minnesota Press, 2004).

The idiom of music comes, on the one hand, from the medieval theologian St. Bonaventure, whose importance in my view is being overshadowed by the contemporary interest in the theology of St. Thomas Aquinas. This interest in Aquinas, also in my view, tells us just as much, if not more, about what Pierre Bourdieu calls the "scholastic disposition" evident in contemporary scholars' turn to Aquinas as it does about Aquinas himself. Bonaventure presents a Christology of poverty, indeed, a Christology in which there is a coincidence of opposites (*coincidentia oppositorum*) between divine wealth and poverty in the fleshly or bodily existence of Jesus Christ. It is precisely in this way that for Bonaventure Christ is God's *Ars Aeterna*, or the eternal art. See Bonaventure's *Commentary on the Sentences* (of Peter Lombard), his *Journey of the Mind into God*, and his *Breviloquium*. For secondary literature on Bonaventure's thought, one might begin with the following: Etienne Gilson, *The Philosophy of St. Bonaventure*, trans. Illytd Trethowan and Frank J. Sheed (Paterson, N.J.: St. Anthony Guild Press, 1965); Zachary Hayes, *The Hidden Center: Spirituality and Speculative Christology in St. Bonaventure* (St. Bonaventure, N.Y.: Fransciscan Institute, 1981); J. A. Wayne Hellmann, *Divine and Created Order in Bonaventure's Theology*, trans. J. M. Hammond (St. Bonaventure, N.Y.: Franciscan Institute, 2001); and Christopher M. Cullen, *Bonaventure* (Oxford: Oxford University Press, 2006). Now while it is true that, on a certain interpretation of Thomas Aquinas's account of being, the Bonaventurian outlook and the Thomistic one are not far apart, it can be argued that Aquinas posits in his metaphysics the conjunction of poverty and wealth as constitutive of being. In other words, being is full in its poverty.

Fair enough. But this vision of Aquinas is enclosed within what I would like to call a calculus of natural reason that positions all things within the order of being's poverty and thereby in relationship to God (any break between divine and creaturely being notwithstanding). The logic then of a chain of being is enclosed within a rational calculus. Alas, herein lies the fundamental problem, which no vision of sacramentality alone can overcome. Only YHWH's covenant, which has its own logic of communion entailed within it, can.

The other inspiration for my use of the idiom of music comes from my interest in thinking theologically about that quintessentially black musical expression, jazz, with its pathos-filled and yet deeply sonorous expressions and cadences. No such theological reflection—to be distinguished from a cultural-religious reflection—that I am aware of yet exists on this art form. Nevertheless, I point the interested reader to the following: Paul Berliner, *Thinking in Jazz: The Infinite Art of Improvisation* (Chicago: University of Chicago Press, 1994); Michael Alexander, *Jazz Age Jews* (Princeton: Princeton University Press, 2001); Bruce Ellis Benson, *The Improvisation of Musical Dialogue: A Phenomenology of Music* (Cambridge: Cambridge University Press, 2003); and of course that classical cultural-religious analysis of the related art form of the blues, James H. Cone, *The Spirituals and the Blues* (Maryknoll, NY: Orbis, 1972).

114. Kant's tacit celebration of the Greeks reflects a larger cultural sensibility taking hold of intellectuals at this time. This sensibility will only gain momentum in the nineteenth century. Williamson, *Longing for Myth in Germany*, and Stefan Arvidsson, *Aryan Idols: Indo-European Mythology as Ideology and Science*, trans. Sonia Wichmann (Chicago: University of Chicago Press, 2006).

115. KRRT, 274–75; AA VI.52.

116. *KRRT*, 275; *AA* VI.52.

117. Ibid.

118. *KRRT*, 275; *AA* VI.52–53.

119. *KRRT*, 275; *AA* VI.53.

120. Ibid.

121. *KRRT*, 275–76; *AA* VI.53.

122. *KRRT*, 276; *AA* VI.53.

123. *KRRT*, 121; *AA* VI.82; translation slightly modified.

124. Agamben, *Homo Sacer*.

125. The phrase "death-bound-subjectivity" comes from Abdul R. JanMohamed, *The Death-Bound-Subject: Richard Wright's Archaeology of Death* (Durham, N.C.: Duke University Press, 2005). JanMohamed is in critical dialogue, in part, with Agamben.

126. Besides his development of this theme in *Homo Sacer*, see Agamben, *Remnants of Auschwitz*.

127. Agamben's blind spot regarding the matter of race has been pointed out by the African philosopher Achille Mbembé. Achille Mbembé, "Necropolitics," *Public Culture* 15, no. 1 (2003): 11–40.

CHAPTER 3

1. Thomas J. Davis in a review for the *Library Journal*. Oxford University Press records the blurb on the back of the paperback edition of Albert J. Raboteau, *Slave Religion: The "Invisible Institution" in the Antebellum South* (New York: Oxford University Press, 1978).

2. Karl Löwith, *Meaning in History* (Chicago: University of Chicago Press, 1949).

3. This phrase comes from the fascinating work of Terry Eagleton, *Sweet Violence: The Idea of the Tragic* (Malden, Mass.: Blackwell, 2003). Yet what I intend in invoking it is well put by Löwith when he says, "The interpretation of history is, in the last analysis, an attempt to understand the meaning of history as the meaning of suffering by historical action." Löwith, *Meaning in History*, 3.

4. With the first of these questions I join many others in the critique of essentialism that has bedeviled interpretations of African American religious life. With the second, I am also signaling caution with interpretations of African American religious life, especially Afro-Christianity, in the pragmatist terms of John Dewey. This way of interpreting the religious life of African Americans has received perhaps its clearest expression in the quite important book by Eddie S. Glaude Jr., *In a Shade of Blue: Pragmatism and the Politics of Black America* (Chicago: University of Chicago Press, 2007).

5. These important lectures, at present, remain unpublished. I am grateful to Albert J. Raboteau for making a copy of them available to me and for conversing with me about them.

6. This theme is further developed in Albert J. Raboteau, *Canaan Land: A Religious History of African Americans* (New York: Oxford University Press, 1999).

7. For example, Anthony B. Pinn, *Varieties of African American Religious Experience* (Minneapolis: Fortress, 1998), 197–98.

8. Such an argument is made in Donald H. Matthews, *Honoring the Ancestors: An African Cultural Interpretation of Black Religion and Literature* (New York: Oxford

University Press, 1998). I engage aspects of Matthews's reading of *Slave Religion* throughout this chapter.

9. The debate is summarized in Raboteau, *Slave Religion*, 48–55. For the primary sources of the two sides of the debate, see E. Franklin Frazier, *The Negro Church in America* (New York: Schocken, 1974), and Melville J. Herskovits, *The Myth of the Negro Past* (Boston: Beacon, 1958). For an insightful analysis of the development of Herskovits that situates him in the field of American anthropology, see Walter Jackson, "Melville Herskovits and the Search for Afro-American Culture," in *Malinowski, Rivers, Benedict and Others: Essays on Culture and Personality*, ed. George W. Stocking Jr. (Madison: University of Wisconsin Press, 1986). Other important essays on the question of Africanisms and the Frazier-Herskovits debate are Joseph E. Holloway, "The Origins of African-American Culture," in *Africanisms in American Culture*, ed. Joseph E. Holloway (Bloomington: Indiana University Press, 1990), and Steve Vaughn, "Making Jesus Black: The Historiographical Debate on the Roots of African-American Christianity," *Journal of Negro History* 82, no. 1 (1997): 25–41. Vaughn places the discussion in the context of African American Christianity.

10. Lawrence W. Levine, *Black Culture and Black Consciousness: Afro-American Folk Thought from Slavery to Freedom* (New York: Oxford University Press, 1977), 19–30.

11. Raboteau, *Slave Religion*, 52.

12. Ibid., 54.

13. Ibid., 52–53.

14. See note 9.

15. Adam Kuper, *Culture: The Anthropologists' Account* (Cambridge, Mass.: Harvard University Press, 1999), 60–61. See also George Hutchinson, *The Harlem Renaissance in Black and White* (Cambridge, Mass.: Belknap Press, 1995), 76–77. The notion of cultural genius as a way to mark off group and racial distinctives is fundamentally Herderian. To be sure, Herder, as anthropological romantic, and Kant, who was the focus of attention in chapter 2 of this book, as anthropological idealist, differ. However, their differences notwithstanding, they both are out to identify the distinctive features of the races. Kant speaks primarily as if there is one ultimate race, the European, with the other nations as pale and inauthentic, racial shadows. The "realness" of the non-Europeans is in their approximation to the European. Aesthetics is the intellectual register in which the distinctions of racial groups emerge. Herder gives full historicity to all the races, refusing the notion of one race; he distinguishes many races and many cultures. In this view, the Berlin school of ethnography, and Boas as an important mediator of this approach to America, is fundamentally Herderian. Nevertheless, even the Herderian approach to culture and anthropology presumes the logic of the separateness of people groups without a way to speak of differential unity or the harmonics of difference. In this, the Herderian view remains Kantian and idealist.

16. Kathryn Tanner, *Theories of Culture: A New Agenda for Theology* (Minneapolis: Fortress, 1997), 23.

17. Jackson, "Melville Herskovits," 103.

18. Alain Locke, ed., *The New Negro: Voices of the Harlem Renaissance* (New York: Touchstone, 1992).

19. Hutchinson, *Harlem Renaissance in Black and White*, 31.

20. Kuper, *Culture*, 61.

21. Hutchinson, *Harlem Renaissance in Black and White*, 65–66.

22. Ibid.

23. Tanner, *Theories of Culture*, 23.

24. I am indebted to conversations with Eugene F. Rogers Jr. on the "low-flying" possibilities inherent in the language of *Volksgeist*.

25. Raboteau, *Slave Religion*, 48–52.

26. bid., 57.

27. Ibid., 58.

28. Vaughn, "Making Jesus Black," 26–27.

29. Raboteau, *Slave Religion*, 63, quoting Erika Bourguignon, "Ritual Dissociation and Possession Belief in Caribbean Negro Religion," in Norman E. Whitten and J ohn F. Szwed, eds., *Afro-American Anthropology: Contemporary Perspectives* (New York: Free Press, 1970), 88.

30. Raboteau, *Slave Religion*, 64–65.

31. Ibid., 72.

32. Ibid.

33. Ibid.

34. Ibid., 63. See also p. 58 where Raboteau observes that "the African devotee is possessed by the god who has replaced his personality and who impels him into the water, the god's own element."

35. Ibid., 64.

36. Matthews, *Honoring the Ancestors*, 13.

37. Ibid., 11.

38. Raboteau, *Slave Religion*, 4.

39. Ibid., 74.

40. Ibid., 5.

41. This is perhaps just as good a place as any to point out that Matthews is not the only one to read Raboteau in terms of a potentially stable African consciousness. Ethicist Peter Paris reads him this way; see Peter J. Paris, *The Spirituality of African Peoples: The Search for a Common Moral Discourse* (Minneapolis: Fortress, 1995). Matthews sees the ambiguous moment in Raboteau's intellectual apparatus, whereas Paris either does not or simply does not address it for what it is. He simply reads Raboteau through the African consciousness aspect of his historical analysis and does not deal with the uneasy fit this aspect of his analysis has with the way in which Raboteau at the same time wants to take seriously what was Christian in and about slave religion. What is important for my purposes is that Paris joins Matthews in reading Raboteau's historical analyses through blackness and the (in)stabilities of African consciousness.

Paris understands Raboteau's *Slave Religion* as positing a dialectical relationship between history and faith, between African spirituality and Christian existence. The dialectic, in Paris's reading, is finally resolved such that Africanity, though supposedly living and vibrant, is what is at work in New World black Christianity. Thus, Paris says:

> One of the most important marks of continuity between Africans on the continent and those in the diaspora is their common belief in a tran-

scendent divine power primordially related to them as the creator and preserver of all that is. Thus, when Raboteau concludes, "In the United States the gods of Africa died," he is referring to the demise of the specific content of African cosmological thought, namely, its sacred symbols, ritual practices, particular divinities and ancestral spirits. In spite of the loss of that specific substance, however, we claim that the "deep structures of African spirituality" survived throughout the African diaspora even though they assumed many different expressive forms.... Africans in the diaspora were able to preserve the structural dimension of their spirituality.... The preservation of their spirituality under the conditions of slavery was an astounding accomplishment, due principally to their creative genius in making Euro-American cultural forms and practices serve as vehicles for the transmission of African cultural elements. (Paris, *Spirituality of African Peoples*, 33, 35)

Paris's first quote ("In the United States the African gods died") comes from *Slave Religion*, p. 86. The second quote (the "deep structures of African spirituality" survived throughout the African diaspora) comes from Evan M. Zuesse, "Perseverence and Transmutation in African Traditional Religions," in *African Traditional Religions in Contemporary Society*, ed. Jacob K. Olupona (New York: Paragon House, 1991), 170. Paris employs Zuesse to clarify Raboteau. However, the clarification is in the direction of collapsing the distinction between African religions and New World Afro-Christian faith such that the "deep structures of African spirituality" remains constant, while presumably there can be no deep and abiding structure to Christian spirituality. This view thus has the effect of interpreting Raboteau's account of slave religion as the persistence of African consciousness as the final *animus* of Christianity, or any other religious expression for that matter, among the slaves.

What, then, is Christianity's ultimate status in relationship to African spirituality? Paris, following what he takes to be essentially Raboteau's position, declares that people of African descent merely "added Christianity to their cosmological framework" (Paris, *Spirituality of African Peoples*, 37). In fairness, it must be noted that Paris wants to affirm the reverse as well—namely, "the Christianization of African religions" (38). And to the extent that this is the case, Christianity, like Africanity, should be interpreted as a vibrant living tradition in its own right. It is a real historical phenomenon. Paris attempts to maintain his claims about the relationship between African religions and Christianity through what he understands as "syncretistic processes" that yield an "amalgamated whole" (38). But I argue that the double process, as Paris imagines it, fails, for, as it turns out, Africanization appears to have the final and total word. As he explains, Africanization had to do with "the internal life of the human spirit," while Christianization concerned the external and stylistic form under which an internal Africanization continues. Eventually internal Africanization envelops the external form as well. Indeed, this is "the peculiar propensity of Africans, especially in religion"—namely, "to retain inner values in spite of changes in their external conditions"; thus "African slaves turned many Euro-American cultural forms into receptors and conveyors of African religious and moral meanings." This was possible because "the African cultural past continued to be efficacious in the consciousness of

the slaves" (38–39). What one sees in all of this is how Paris's work inhabits the ambiguity of the early Raboteau.

42. Raboteau, *Slave Religion*, 72–73.

42. Ibid., 73–74.

44. Ibid., 74.

45. Robert Farris Thompson, *Flash of the Spirit: African and Afro-American Art and Philosophy* (New York: Random House, 1983).

46. Ibid., 18.

47. Ibid., 32.

48. Richard Price and Sally Price, *The Root of Roots; or, How Afro-American Anthropology Got Its Start* (Chicago: Prickly Paradigm, 2003), 2. See also Lee D. Baker, *From Savage to Negro: Anthropology and the Construction of Race, 1896–1954* (Berkeley: University of California Press, 1998).

49. Albert J. Raboteau, *A Fire in the Bones: Reflections on African-American Religious History* (Boston: Beacon, 1995), 2.

50. Ibid., 1–2.

51. Ibid., 2.

52. Ibid.

53. Ibid., 3.

54. Ibid.

55. Ibid., 2–3, 12–14.

56. Ibid., 3.

57. Ibid.

58. Ibid.

59. Ibid., 4–5.

60. Ibid., 5.

61. Ibid., 6.

62. Ibid., 13.

63. My reference to the "political unconscious" alludes to a notion promulgated by Marxist theorist Frederic Jameson, which refers to that "uninterrupted narrative" that is "the repressed or buried reality of [a] fundamental history" of which "the surface of a text," one might say, leaves traces." Michael Hardt and Kathi Weeks, eds., *The Jameson Reader* (Oxford: Blackwell, 2000), 35.

64. The following comments on Bourdieu draw heavily on engagements with Pierre Bourdieu, *Outline of a Theory of Practice*, trans. Richard Nice (Cambridge: Cambridge University Press, 1977); Pierre Bourdieu, *The State Nobility: Elite Schools in the Field of Power*, trans. Lauretta C. Clough (Stanford: Stanford University Press, 1996); and David Swartz, *Culture and Power: The Sociology of Pierre Bourdieu* (Chicago: University of Chicago Press, 1997). I am also indebted to conversations with my friend and fellow theologian Willie James Jennings, whose knowledge and understanding of Bourdieu's thought is staggering. Jennings's as yet unpublished paper "Making Visible the Invisible: On the Theological Problem of Whiteness" makes no small theological use of Bourdieuean ideas.

65. Raboteau, *Fire in the Bones*, 4.

66. Paul Gilroy, *The Black Atlantic: Modernity and Double Consciousness* (Cambridge, Mass.: Harvard University Press, 1993).

67. Raboteau, *Fire in the Bones*, 4.

68. Ibid.

69. Ibid., 33–34.

70. Earlier I indicated that the argument being developed here would be neither an essentialist nor Deweyan pragmatist interpretation of Afro-Christian life in its complexities. Nor, as will become evident in the next chapter, do I offer a strict recapitulation of the Black Theology project. Rather, I offer a theological imagination that seeks to think all reality from inside of YHWH's covenant and thereby echo YHWH's relationship with the world through the Jewish people as a covenantal group and not a race (or even a "Zionist") group. My claim is that it was from this vantage that such people as Henry Highland Garnet functioned as a Presbyterian minister within the scriptural imagination of Israel to disrupt the politics of America's nineteenth-century racial order of things. Such a theological approach contrasts with that offered by Eddie S. Glaude Jr. on the politics of early nineteenth-century black America (*Exodus! Religion, Race, and Nation in Early Nineteenth-Century Black America*). My claim is not that all African Americans of the nineteenth century functioned this way. Rather, it is that *some* did. Indeed, that it was an Afro-*Christian* imagination did not limit its public and political effectiveness on grounds that it was Christian. And thus, with Garnet, might it be that one sees not so much democratic piety as the theopolitical piety of an Afro-Christian spirituality?

71. I am grateful to Raboteau for allowing me to read these lectures, which are not yet published.

72. Raboteau, *Fire in the Bones*, 17.

73. Ibid., 22.

74. Albert J. Raboteau, "Afterword," in *An Unbroken Circle: Linking Ancient African Christianity to the African-American Experience*, ed. Fr. Paisius Altschul (St. Louis, Mo.: Brotherhood of St. Moses the Black, 1997), 162.

75. Ibid., 161–62.

76. V. Y. Mudimbe, *The Invention of Africa: Gnosis, Philosophy, and the Order of Knowledge* (Bloomington: Indiana University Press, 1988).

77. Raboteau, "Afterword," 162.

78. Raboteau, *Fire in the Bones*, 3.

79. Raboteau, "Afterword," 162. The suggestion of a deep connection between African religion and ancient Christianity is developed in the work of the Ghanaian theologian Kwame Bediako. Kwame Bediako, *Christianity in Africa: The Renewal of a Non-Western Religion* (Maryknoll, N.Y.: Orbis, 1995); Kwame Bediako, *Theology and Identity: The Impact of Culture upon Christian Thought in the Second Century and in Modern Africa* (Irvine, Calif.: Regnum, 1999); and Kwame Bediako, *Jesus and the Gospel in Africa: History and Experience* (Maryknoll, N.Y.: Orbis, 2004). In *Jesus and the Gospel in Africa*, see especially chapter 5, "Africa and the Fathers: The Relevance of Early Hellenistic Christian Theology for Modern Africa."

80. Richard Rorty, *Philosophy and the Mirror of Nature* (Princeton: Princeton University Press, 1979), 11.

81. Something of the complexity of the notion of vision in modern thought is taken up in Martin Jay, *Downcast Eyes: The Denigration of Vision in Twentieth-Century French Thought* (Berkeley: University of California Press, 1994). The few remarks to

follow on the philosophy of the icon come from such thinkers as Russian philoso-
pher, theologian, aesthetician, and physicist Pavel Florensky and theologian Sergeii
Bulgakov. Pavel Florensky, *Iconostasis*, trans. Donald Sheehan and Olga Andrejev
(Crestwood, N.Y.: St. Vladimir's Seminary Press, 1996); Pavel Florensky, *The
Pillar and Ground of the Truth: An Essay in Orthodox Theodicy in Twelve Letters*, trans.
Boris Jakim (Princeton: Princeton University Press, 1997); Sergei Bulgakov, *Bride
of the Lamb*, trans. Boris Jakim (Grand Rapids, Mich.: Eerdmans, 2002); Rowan
Williams, ed., *Sergii Bulgakov: Towards a Russian Political Theology* (Edinburgh: T&T
Clark, 1999).

82. Albert J. Raboteau, "The Legacy of a Suffering Church: The Holiness of
American Slaves," in *An Unbroken Circle: Linking Ancient African Christianity to the
African-American Experience*, ed. Fr. Paisius Altschul (St. Louis, Mo.: Brotherhood
of St. Moses the Black, 1997), 80.

83. Raboteau, *Fire in the Bones*, 9.

84. Raboteau, "Legacy of a Suffering Church," 80.

85. Raboteau, *Fire in the Bones*, 8.

86. Ibid., 10.

87. Ibid.

88. Ibid., 14.

89. Ibid., 56.

CHAPTER 4

1. Karl Barth, *Church Dogmatics*, trans. G. W. Bromiley et al., 4 vols. (Edinburgh:
T&T Clark, 1956–1975), 1:277. I will refer to this as CD.

2. Victor Anderson, *Beyond Ontological Blackness: An Essay on African American
Religious and Cultural Criticism* (New York: Continuum, 1995), 11–12.

3. Ibid., 11, 14.

4. Ibid., 13–15. One might respond by saying that Anderson's argument for a
"pragmatic theology" fulfills the need for a theological analysis of cultural idolatry.
This is partly correct, but it does not fulfill the need for a theological analysis of what
makes the culture of racial genius as the engine of modern racial reasoning itself, in
the weighty theological sense of the term, idolatrous. The argument for a pragmatic
theology is made in Victor Anderson, *Pragmatic Theology: Negotiating the Intersections of
an American Philosophy of Religion and Public Theology* (Albany: SUNY Press, 1998).

5. James Perkinson has recently sought to address the issue of "white theology."
However, he, too, misses what is distinctively theological about the problem of
whiteness in modernity. James W. Perkinson, *White Theology: Outing Supremacy in
Modernity* (New York: Palgrave Macmillan, 2004).

6. The documents here referred to are masterfully introduced and collected in
James H. Cone and Gayraud S. Wilmore, eds., *Black Theology: A Documentary History*,
2nd rev. ed., 2 vols. (Maryknoll, N.Y.: Orbis, 1993).

7. For information about the documentary, see the web page http://www.pbs.org/
thisfarbyfaith/ [last access date: May 24, 2006]. See as well the monograph by Juan
Williams and Quinton H. Dixie, *This Far by Faith: Stories from the African American
Religious Experience* (San Francisco: HarperCollins, 2003).

8. James H. Cone, "The Doctrine of Man in the Theology of Karl Barth," Ph.D. diss., Garrett Theological Seminary, Northwestern University, 1965.

9. Ibid., 11, 14.

10. Sadly, in my estimation, contemporary Barth scholarship has not attended enough to the significance of this for how one construes Barth's theology and what was at stake. Barth's thought represents the valiant effort on the part of one shaped by the intellectual sensibilities that produced Auschwitz, first, to reckon with those deep-seated sensibilities and, second, to do theology beyond them. But what were those sensibilities? They were the sensibilities by which German nationalism and folk consciousness seamlessly expressed itself as Christianity, at the ground of which was a posture of supersessionism against Israel but now rooted in racial consciousness. A significant part of Barth's response to this problem was to reclaim Israel for Christian self-understanding so as to break the stranglehold of German nationalism. As he put it, he sought to recover theology as rooted in "revelation" rather than in "the religion of revelation." Barth develops this distinction as part of his indictment of Christanity's functioning from the religious consciousness rather than from revelation in CD I/2:328ff. The theology of Auschwitz and the theology that produced Auschwitz—that is, the theology of his teachers—were the discourse of the religion of revelation. Barth summarized this problem in his important essay "Evangelical Theology in the 19ᵗʰ Century," which appeared in *The Humanity of* God (Louisville, KY: Westminster/John Knox, 1960), especially pp. 14–15. In response to this problem retrieved Israel as central to Christianity and its theological imagination.

While I myself do not think that Barth's retrieval effort was complete enough, Cone to his credit rightly picks up on what Barth was doing and what was at stake in what he was doing. A significant part of the argument in this chapter is to claim that, working within the confines of Cone's writings, Cone saw in Barth's fight against German nationalism a struggle against whiteness that Barth found difficult to in fact isolate and name in these terms. Operating from the European metropole Barth, one might say, was struggling to render the theological problem of whiteness theologically visible to itself. That is, Cone saw in Barth's deep wrestling with his nineteenth-century and early-twentieth-century teachers a fight against those white cultural sensibilities that take whiteness and Western civilization as the universal into which all parochial outlooks—let's call these outlooks, the outlook of the non-white colonies—must enter. In the modern Western imagination, the Jews have been figured as the apotheosis of the parachocial outlook. Thus they have functioned as the index against which all other nonwhite flesh is catalogued. For more on Barth's fight, intellectual and otherwise, against German nationalism, see Eberhard Busch, *Karl Barth: His Life from Letters and Autobiographical Texts* (Philadelphia: Fortress, 1976). What would contemporary Barth scholarship look like had Barth's significance been engaged in these terms, the very terms Cone and others (I am thinking here of theologian Frederick Herzog of blessed memory) attempted?

11. The text that addresses most fully Barth's approach to dialectic is Bruce L. McCormack, *Karl Barth's Critically Realistic Dialectical Theology: Its Genesis and Development 1909–1936* (Oxford: Clarendon, 1995).

12. James H. Cone, *Black Theology and Black Power: Twentieth Anniversary Edition* (San Francisco: Harper and Row, 1989), 34; emphasis mine.

13. Ibid., 34–35. This is a quotation from Wolfhart Pannenberg, *Jesus: God and Man*, 2nd ed. (Philadelphia: Westminster, 1977), 11.

14. Cone, *Black Theology and Black Power*, 35.

15. James H. Cone, *A Black Theology of Liberation: Twentieth Anniversary Edition* (Maryknoll, N.Y.: Orbis, 1990), 82.

16. Cone, *Black Theology and Black Power*, 37. The quotation in many respects captures the thrust of the Barth of *Die Römerbrief*. See especially the introduction to Karl Barth, *The Epistle to the Romans*, trans. Edwyn C. Hoskyns (London: Oxford University Press, 1968).

17. Cone, "Doctrine of Man in the Theology of Karl Barth," 161.

18. Cone, *Black Theology of Liberation*, 82.

19. Cone, "Doctrine of Man in the Theology of Karl Barth," 170.

20. Ibid., 9, 172.

21. Cone, *Black Theology and Black Power*, 35.

22. Cone, *Black Theology of Liberation*, 61.

23. Ibid., 60.

24. Within Protestantism, it is theologians of a more or less Barthian pedigree who have been at the forefront of contemporary discussions on the relationship between Israel and the church. I am here thinking of, to name but a few, Bertold Klappert, "Traktat für Israel (Römer 9–11): Die paulinische Verhältnisbestimmung von Israel und Kirche als Kriterium neutestamentlicher Sachaussagen über die Juden," in *Jüdische Existenz und die Erneuerung der christlichen Theologie*, ed. Martin Stöhr (Munich: Kaiser, 1981); R. Kendall Soulen, *The God of Israel and Christian Theology* (Minneapolis: Fortress, 1996); Eugene F. Rogers Jr., *Sexuality and the Christian Body: Their Way into the Triune God* (Malden, Mass.: Blackwell, 1999); Eugene F. Rogers, *After the Spirit: A Constructive Pneumatology from Resources outside the Modern West* (Grand Rapids, Mich.: Eerdmans, 2005); Robert W. Jenson, "Toward a Christian Theology of Israel," *Pro Ecclesia* 9, no. 1 (2000): 43–56; Scott Bader-Saye, *Church and Israel after Christendom: The Politics of Election* (Boulder: Westview, 1999); and George A. Lindbeck, "The Gospel's Uniqueness: Election and Untranslatability," *Modern Theology* 13, no. 4 (1990): 423–50.

25. On "mode of existence" (*tropos tês huparxeos*) in late patristic theologians, see Brian E. Daley, "Nature and 'Mode of Union': Late Patristic Models for the Personal Unity of Christ," in *The Incarnation: An Interdisciplinary Symposium on the Incarnation of the Son of God*, ed. Stephen T. Davis, Daniel Kendall, and Gerald O'Collins (Oxford: Oxford University Press, 2002). Entailed within this late patristic Christology is an ecclesiology in which the church, in being the social space that is humanity—a Jewish, covenantal humanity—of Jesus of Nazareth, must be conceived of inside of Israel's covenantal relationship with YHWH. Stated differently, ecclesiology is Israelology, but only by means of the mediation of Jesus of Nazareth, the Messiah of Israel who is the Head of the Church. Whiteness as modernity's quintessential theological problem has its basis in the equation between the church and Christ. Dogmatically this is absolutely correct—but only partially. For the problem is that the Christ in view in the typical forumation is one severed from Israel, which in terms of dogmatic Christology is deeply mistaken, with quite deleterious consequences.

Against this backdrop, George Lindbeck's recent call for an "Israel-like ecclesiology" as the centerpiece of a postliberal theological program, then, represents an important corrective for modern theology, given the direction early modern thought took in making whiteness and Western civilization coeval with Christianity. Lindbeck begins developing this position in "Confession and Community: An Israel-Like View of the Church," *Christian Century*, 9 May 1990: 492–96. But though Lindbeck's proposal points in a potentially fruitful direction, it still in my view does not go far enough. This is partly because his proposal, as the title of this essay suggests, positions the problem bedeviling modern theology on a community-individualism axis. An Israel-like view of the church overcomes an individualistic understanding of Christian redemption. But what this approach to the problem of modern theology cannot account for is how the community-individualism and the liberal-conservative options as we have them oscillate within whiteness itself. They are thus modulations within modern Christian supersessionism.

This leads to the second limit of postliberal, narrative theology. Because it has no account of whiteness as modernity's quintessential theological problem, it mutatis mutandis has no account of how its proposal for an Israel-like ecclesiology can itself avoid being a new plateau for a theological reiteration of whiteness, but now precisely at the site of Israel and precisely through its supposed theological non-supersessionism. An ecclesiology in which the church and Israel are "separate but equal" continues to perform (potentially at least, if not in actuality) racial thinking. What, therefore, does it mean to say that Israel is a covenantal people, not a race group, and what does it mean to talk about the church and Christians as abiding in the bosom of Abraham, in the womb of Mary, and thus inside of Israel and her covenant with YHWH, the Triune God?

I extend my claim that modern supersessionism is tied to racial performance and to a vision of Christian culture as Western civilization beyond the eighteenth century into the nineteenth in "The Bible, the Christian Life, and the Problem of Christian Supersessionism," a paper presented at the conference on Living, Preaching, and Teaching the Bible, sponsored by the Center for Catholic and Evangelical Theology, May 2006. I have expanded the argument of this paper into two articles that I am presently completing. The first is entitled "Oriental Jesus–Occidental Paul: Race, Myth, and the Conflicted Status of Jewish Flesh in Nineteenth-Century German Biblical Scholarship." The other is entitled "Israel, A Nation without Analogy: A Preface to Any Future Christology."

26. Karl Löwith, *Martin Heidegger and European Nihilism*, ed. Lawrence D. Kritzman, trans. Gary Steiner (New York: Columbia University Press, 1995), 70.

27. James H. Cone, *God of the Oppressed* (New York: HarperCollins, 1975), 115–20; in chapter 2, see the section, 'Who Is Jesus for Us Today?'"

28. Melito of Sardis, "A Homily on the Passover," in *The Christological Controversy*, ed. Richard A. Norris Jr. (Philadelphia: Fortress, 1980), 46–47. For a survey of Melito's theology, see Alloys Grillmeier, *Christ in Christian Tradition: From the Apostolic Age to Chalcedon (451)*, trans. John Bowden, 2nd rev. ed., vol. 1 (Atlanta: John Knox, 1975), 94–98. See also this book's prelude on Ireanaeus's recapitulatory Christology.

29. On the analogy of faith in Barth, note the following two quotations as examples:

Our reply to the roman Catholic doctrine of the *analogia entis* is not, then, a denial of the concept of analogy. We say rather that the analogy in question is not an *analogia entis* but according to Romans 12:6 the [analogy of faith], the likeness of the known in the knowing, of the object in thought, of the Word of God in the word that is thought and spoken by man, as this differentiates true prophecy in faith from all false prophecy. (CD I/1:243–44)

And:

The man who is capable of being a doer of the Word of this kind, i.e., a real hearer, is free in the New Testament sense of the term. The reference is not to any kind of freedom or any kind of ability. In accordance with the freedom of God Himself, His freedom to be Himself, what is at issue here is a man's freedom for God, for the "glorious liberty" of the children of God (Rom. 8:21), the *analogia fidei* of the divine freedom which alone really deserves to be called freedom. This, then, is a formal summary of the work of the Spirit in God's revelation. This work consists in freedom, freedom to have a Lord, this Lord, God, as Lord. (CD I/1:457)

I point out the following two important works in the secondary literature assessing Barth on *analogia entis*: McCormack, *Karl Barth's Dialectical Theology*, and Hans Urs von Balthasar, *The Theology of Karl Barth: An Exposition and Interpretation*, trans. Edward T. Oakes (San Francisco: Ignatius, 1992).

30. See particularly chapter 6, titled "Who Is Jesus Christ for Us Today?: Social Context, Scripture, and Tradition," in Cone, *God of the Oppressed*, 108–37. Here there is a development of claims made by Cone about the "the black Christ" in Cone, *Black Theology of Liberation*, 119.

31. Cone, *God of the Oppressed*, 64.

32. Ibid., 63.

33. Ibid., 70.

34. Ibid., 80.

35. Ibid.

36. Ibid., 80–81.

37. This problem is given theological consideration in Sheila Greeve Davaney, *Pragmatic Historicism: A Theology for the Twenty-First Century* (Albany: SUNY Press, 2000).

38. Cecil Wayne Cone, *The Identity Crisis in Black Theology* (Nashville, Tenn.: The African Methodist Episcopal Church and Henry Belin, 1975).

39. Cone, *Black Theology of Liberation*, 118.

40. Ibid., 119.

41. For critical assessments of Barth's "actualism principle," see George Hunsinger, *How to Read Karl Barth: The Shape of His Theology* (New York: Oxford University Press, 1991). Hunsinger summarizes the principle this way:

Actualism . . . is present whenever Barth speaks, as he constantly does, in the language of occurrence, happening, event, history, decisions, and act. At the most general level it means that he thinks primarily in terms of

events and relationships rather than monadic and self-contained substances. So pervasive is this motif that Barth's whole theology might well
be described as a theology of active relations. God and humanity are
both described in fundamentally actualistic terms. (30)

The issue of actualism is taken up in relationship to Barth's doctrine of election in
McCormack, *Karl Barth's Dialectical Theology*, 455–58.

42. It is Erich Przywara's doctrine of *analogia entis* that was exercising Barth. On
this, see, generally, Balthasar, *Theology of Karl Barth*. For a direct engagement with
Przywara himself on the matter of analogy and theology, see in English P. Erich
Przywara, *Polarity: A German Catholic's Interpretation of Religion*, trans. A. C. Bouquet
(London: Oxford University Press, 1935). For his exhaustive account, see Erich Przy-
wara, *Analogia Entis: Metaphysik: Ur-Struktur und All-Rhythmus*, rev. ed. (Einsiedeln:
Johannes-Verlag, 1962).

43. The vexing question of the *analogia entis* and its relationship to Barth's
alternative, the *analogia fidei*, is long overdue for a thorough monograph-length in-
vestigation in its own right. For an initial step in this direction, see Alan J. Torrance,
*Persons in Communion: Trinitarian Description and Human Participation, with Special
Reference to Volume One of Karl Barth's Church Dogmatics* (Edinburgh: T&T Clark,
1996), especially chapter 3, and McCormack, *Karl Barth's Dialectical Theology*, 383–91.
For more of a defense of Przywara in relationship to Barth, see Balthasar, *Karl
Barth*, 114–67.

44. CD I/1:40–41.

45. CD I/1:41–42.

46. CD II/2:19–20.

47. Karl Barth, "Der christliche Glaube und die Geschichte," *Schweizerische
Theologische Zeitschrift* 29 (1912): 6–7.

48. CD II/1:675.

49. Hunsinger, *Karl Barth*, 112–13. For more on Barth's actualism, see McCormack, *Karl Barth's Dialectical Theology*, 453–56, and Balthasar, *Karl Barth*, 99–100, 222.

50. Balthasar, *Karl Barth*, 241–42.

51. Ibid., 106.

52. On supersessionism of Barth's thought, see Soulen, *God of Israel and Christian
Theology*, and Rogers, *Sexuality and the Christian Body*.

53. I have used Balthasar's critique of Barth to illuminate where Cone found
Barth's thought wanting as he constructed his black liberation theology. My use of
Balthasar here, my fondness for his theology notwithstanding, must not be confused
with an uncritical endorsement of his theology, however, particularly on the question of Israel. Indeed, it is my view that his theology speaks with a forked tongue on the
matter of Israel. On the one hand, Balthasar affirms the absolute and ongoing centrality
of Israel and their covenant with YHWH for Christian theology and identity. Thus he
says, "for the eyes of faith, the 'riddle of Israel' does not exist, not even the riddle of
Israel's continued existence until the Last Judgment." Hans Urs von Balthasar, *The Glory
of the Lord: A Theological Aesthetics*, 7 vols. (San Francisco: Ignatius, 1982–1989), vol. 1:
Seeing the Form, 658. And yet, Balthasar can say the following in the epilogue to his
theological trilogy: "Israel is the people whom, throughout its history, God has dragged
along by the hair, forced to go where they would not go. And when, after all their failed

opportunities, they were placed for a final and irrevocable time before the choice of 'life and death' and rejected 'the life,' God, who 'never regrets or repents of his promises,' banished Israel once and for all out of fidelity to his promises." Hans Urs von Balthasar, *Epilogue* (San Francisco: Ignatius, 2004), 31. Or this, in *A Theology of History*: "The perfecting of God's covenant with Israel in Christ is at the same time the annulment of his special relation with Israel." Hans Urs von Balthasar, *A Theology of History* (San Francisco: Ignatius, 1963), 142. Or finally, this claim of the *Theo-Drama*: "The possibility of the Old Covenant no longer exists: it is transcended into the single possibility of the New Covenant." Hans Urs von Balthasar, *Theo-Drama: Theological Dramatic Theory*, 5 vols. (San Francisco: Ignatius, 1988–1998), vol. 5: *The Last Act*, 281. In this last quotation, a troubling cleavage is finally and irrevocably erected between Old Covenant and New Covenant, as if the latter is not the former in its ongoing integrity, and brought to crescendo. If one follows Balthasar's logic, one is perfectly warranted in saying—and were one to say it, it would be a deep theological problem—that the Mosaic covenant replaced the Abrahamic, or that the Davidic covenant replaced the Mosaic covenant, or that YHWH's covenant with Israel replaced the covenant of creation, and that these replace the communion of fidelity that marks YHWH's own life and out of which YHWH's relationship with Israel and thereby the world arose. Were one to think this way one would in fact not be thinking the covenant in a sufficiently theological way.

I mention this Balthasar-Israel problem because there is a link between this way of thinking and recent discussions by the current Roman Catholic pontiff (Pope Benedict XVI) to restore to the Good Friday Latin Mass a prayer for the "conversion" of the Jews.

But here again is where a theologically inflected jazz-musical imagination that sings YHWH's song (Psalm 137:4) can help us in thinking about the covenant in nonsupersessionist terms. It might be declared that a musical vision is at the heart of Balthasar's outlook. See *Truth Is Symphonic: Aspects of Christian Pluralism*, trans. Graham Harrison (San Francisco: Ignatius, 1987). There Balthasar offers his account of the Christological musicality, or the Christo-musicality, of Christian thought. But his theological vision of music is founded on a Christology of discontinuity with Israel so as to establish more of a cultural continuity, if not an identity, of Jesus Christ with the European West. The index of this cultural continuity, for Balthasar, is the classical music of a figure like Johann Sebastian Bach. In this Balthasar reveals his indebtedness to Barth, who took Mozart as the quintessential musical figure for theology, and who also was unable to hold to the end onto the positivity of Israel for Christian thought. The more recent movement in "radical orthodoxy" can be understood as an attempt to fix or overcome the Balthasarian musical problematic within a richer "catholic" outlook. This outlook, which emphasizes along with Balthasar the significance of Augustine for modern thought, stresses the Christo-musicality of being. Yet, radical orthodoxy also reflects the modern inability to emphasize that the song that Christ sings is the blues-inflected song of Israel's lamb, slain from the foundations of the world, the song of the poverty-stricken, suffering servant. For a "radically orthodox" account of music, see Catherine Pickstock, "The Musical Imperative," *Angelaki: Journal of the Theoretical Humanities* 3, no. 2 (August 1998): 7–30, and Catherine Pickstock, "Music: Soul, City, and Cosmos after Augustine," in *Radical Orthodoxy: A New Theology*, ed. John Milbank, Catherine Pickstock, and Graham Ward (New York: Routledge, 1999).

54. Anderson, *Beyond Ontological Blackness*.

55. Cone, *Black Theology of Liberation*, xi, xix.

56. Paul Tillich, *Biblical Religion and the Search for Ultimate Reality* (Chicago: University of Chicago Press, 1955), 13, 17.

57. Ibid., 13.

58. Paul Tillich, *Theology of Culture* (New York: Oxford University Press, 1959), 213 (emphasis in original).

59. Paul Tillich, *The Courage to Be* (New Haven: Yale University Press, 1980), 2–3.

60. Ibid., 15.

61. Ibid., 25.

62. Tillich, *Theology of Culture*, 24–25.

63. Tillich, *Courage to Be*, 27, 29–30.

64. Ibid., 29.

65. Tillich, *Theology of Culture*, 212.

66. Paul Tillich, "Religion and Secular Culture," in *Paul Tillich: Theologian of the Boundaries*, ed. Mark Kline Taylor (Minneapolis: Fortress, 1946), 121.

67. Tillich, *Theology of Culture*, 40–41.

68. Paul Tillich, *Systematic Theology*, 3 vols. (Chicago: University of Chicago Press, 1951–1963), 1:132; emphasis mine.

69. Ibid., 1:133.

70. Paul Tillich, "On the Idea of a Theology of Culture (1919)," in *Paul Tillich: Theologian of the Boundaries*, ed. Mark Kline Taylor (Minneapolis: Fortress, 1991), 42.

71. Ibid., 43.

72. Ibid. As Tillich makes clear in this essay, "substance" does not refer to a thing or the substance and totality of beings. He is striving here not to be an ontotheologian.

73. As Theunissen has shown in his important work on ontology and the sociality of existence, this is a problem bedeviling modern idealist philosophies. Michael Theunissen, *The Other: Studies in the Social Ontology of Husserl, Heidegger, Sartre, and Buber*, trans. Christopher Macann (Cambridge, Mass.: MIT Press, 1984).

74. The phrase "ugly broad ditch" was popularized by the eighteenth-century Enlightenment thinker, Gotthold Ephraïm Lessing (1729–81) in "On the Proof of the Spirit and Power," in H. Chadwick, ed., *Lessings Theological Writings* (Stanford: Stanford University Press, 1957).

CHAPTER 5

1. Charles H. Long, *Significations: Signs, Symbols, and Images in the Interpretation of Religion*, rev. ed. (Aurora, Colo.: Davies Group, 1995), 207.

2. See Robert Farris Thompson, *Flash of the Spirit* (New York: Vintage Books, 1984); Donald Matthews, *Honoring the Ancestors: An African Culural Interpretation of Black Religion and Literature* (New York: Oxford University Press, 1998); and Peter Paris, *The Spirituality of African Peoples: The Search for a Common Moral Discourse* (Minneapolis: Fortress Press, 1995).

3. I say "more or less" the order of the day because the other direction of note in the field is that of pragmatism in the Princeton University approach to religious studies. The key figures here are Cornel West, Eddie S. Glaude Jr., and Jeffrey Stout.

Cornel West, *The American Evasion of Philosophy: A Genealogy of Pragmatism* (Madison: University of Wisconsin Press, 1989); Eddie S. Glaude Jr., "Pragmatic Historicism and 'the Problem of History' in Black Theology," *American Journal of Theology and Philosophy* 19 (1998): 173–90; Eddie S. Glaude Jr., "Pragmatism and Black Identity: An Alternative Approach," *Nepantla: Views from South* 2, no. 2 (2001): 295–316; Eddie S. Glaude Jr., *Exodus! Religion, Race, and Nation in Early Nineteenth-Century Black America* (Chicago: University of Chicago Press, 2000); and Jeffrey Stout, *Democracy and Tradition: Religion, Ethics, and Public Philosophy* (Princeton: Princeton University Press, 2004). Engaging African American religious pragmatism is the subject of another project. For now, it is simply worth noting that the approach to religious studies that Long's work represents and the approach to religious represented in the Princeton school of religious pragmatism reinforce each other. This is most evident in the work of Victor Anderson and Anthony B. Pinn. Victor Anderson, *Beyond Ontological Blackness: An Essay on African American Religious and Cultural Criticism* (New York: Continuum, 1995); Victor Anderson, *Pragmatic Theology: Negotiating the Intersections of an American Philosophy of Religion and Public Theology* (Albany: SUNY Press, 1998); and Victor Anderson, "The Wrestle of Christ and Culture in Pragmatic Public Theology," *American Journal of Theology and Philosophy* 19, no. 2 (1998): 135–50. For more on Pinn's work, see the following note.

4. Anthony B. Pinn, *Why, Lord? Suffering and Evil in Black Theology* (New York: Continuum, 1995), 135.

5. Anthony B. Pinn, *Varieties of African American Religious Experience* (Minneapolis: Fortress, 1998), 4.

6. Ibid.

7. Ibid.

8. Ibid. This is actually a quote from Gordon D. Kaufman, *An Essay on Theological Method*, rev. ed. (Missoula, Mont.: Scholars Press, 1995), 8.

9. Ibid., quoting again from Kaufman, *Essay on Theological Method*, 8.

10. For other, more recent works in black religion that draw on Long's research, see as examples Theophus H. Smith, *Conjuring Culture: Biblical Formations of Black America* (New York: Oxford University Press, 1994), and Will Coleman, *Tribal Talk: Black Theology, Hermeneutics, and African/American Ways of "Telling the Story"* (University Park: Penn State University Press, 2000).

11. Long, *Significations*, 7

12. Charles H. Long, "The Meaning of Religion in the Contemporary Study of the History of Religions," *Criterion* 2, no. 2 (1963): 23.

13. Long, *Significations*, 17

14. Ibid., 22

15. Ibid.

16. Ibid., 23.

17. Martin Rumscheidt captures the meaning of *Kulturprotestantismus* in relation to Harnack's theological program. See the introductory essay to Martin Rumscheidt, ed., *Adolf Von Harnack: Liberal Theology at Its Height* (Minneapolis: Fortress, 1991). Rumscheidt says:

> This liberal theology [as advocated by Harnack] was not a theology of the Church but one of culture. For that reason, it is also known as *"Kultur-*

protestantismus," cultural Protestantism. The name was not the choice of liberal theology; it wanted to become the theology of the Church, a Church, however, which had also chosen to be a Church in relation to modernity. The primary addressee was the cultured individual of modern times who sought, in freedom from any strictures which associating with the institutional Church was believed to bring, to be religious and cultured, a person of reason *and* faith. And it found a strong, positive echo among that public for it held out the chance to provide successfully two much treasured values: the freedom of theology and the freedom of the individual to be, and remain, the final and authoritative arbiter. (41)

18. Long, *Significations*, 23

19. Ibid.

20. William F. Wertz, ed., *Toward a New Council of Florence: "On the Peace of Faith" and Other Works by Nicolaus of Cusa* (Washington, D.C.: Schiller Institute, 1993).

21. This, of course, points to the need for a fully dogmatic Christology that unpacks this, a task on which I am presently at work.

22. Long, *Significations*, 23.

23. Ibid., 23–24.

24. Long, "Meaning of Religion," 24.

25. Ibid., 25.

26. Ibid.

27. Long, *Significations*, 56.

28. Long, "Meaning of Religion," 23

29. Ibid., 25–26.

30. Indeed, Long approvingly notes the similarities between the history of religions and the Derridean deconstructionist program as propounded, for example, in Jacques Derrida, *Writing and Difference*, trans. Alan Bass (Chicago: Univeristy of Chicago Press, 1978), and Jacques Derrida, *Of Grammatology*, trans. Gayatri Chakrovorty Spivak, corrected ed. (Baltimore: Johns Hopkins University Press, 1997). For this, see Long, *Significations*, 81.

31. Long, *Significations*, 87.

32. Ibid.

33. Herein lay the significance of Bonaventure's theological defense of Franciscan vowels of poverty. For an exposition of this, see Zachary Hayes, *The Hidden Center: Spirituality and Speculative Christology in St. Bonaventure* (St. Bonaventure, N.Y.: Fransciscan Institute, 1981); Ilia Delio, "Bonaventure's Metaphysics of the Good," *Theological Studies* 60 (1999): 228–46; and J. A. Wayne Hellmann, *Divine and Created Order in Bonaventure's Theology*, trans. J. M. Hammond (St. Bonaventure, N.Y.: Franciscan Institute, 2001). Julian of Norwich's interpretation of her sickness—the mutual conjunction of her body in pain and Christ's body in pain—as a Trinitarian revelation and, indeed, as a revelation that re-reads the social order less in terms of the king's body but more in terms of Christ's body as a body politic, also makes my point about the poverty and wealth of being. On this, see Frederick Christian Bauerschmidt, *Julian of Norwich and the Mystical Body Politic of Christ* (Notre Dame: University of Notre Dame Press, 1999). But probably the modern thinker who more than any other theorizes the conjunction of the poverty and wealth of existence, over against the

stratification of the two such that the wealth of the few redounds to the poverty of the many, is the religious philosopher Ferdinand Ulrich. Ferdinand Ulrich, "Der eine Logos und die viele Sprachen: Religionsphilosophische Reflexionen über Gen 11, 1–9," *Salzburger Jahrbuch für Philosophie* 12/13 (1968/1969): 183–224; Ferdinand Ulrich, "Armut und Reichtum der Freiheit: Eine philosophische Meditation," *Evangelische Theologie* 46, no. 1 (1986): 46–73; and Ferdinand Ulrich, *Homo Abyssus: Das Wagnis der Seinsfrage* (Einsiedeln: Johannes Verlag, 1998).

34. Harriet A. Jacobs, *Incidents in the Life of a Slave Girl, written by herself* (Cambridge, Mass.: Harvard University Press, 1987 [Boston, 1861]). See also Jean Fagan Yellin, *Harriet Jacobs: A Life, The Remarkable Adventures of the Woman who Wrote* Incidents in the Life of a Slave Girl (New York: Basic Civitas Books, 2004). For a recent attempt to recover what is theological about Jacobs' life and *Incidents*, see J. Kameron Carter, "Race and the Experience of Death: Theologically Reappraising American Evangelicalism" in *The Cambridge Companion to Evangelical Theology*, ed. Timothy Larsen and Daniel J. Trier (Cambridge: Cambridge University Press, 2007).

35. Long, "Meaning of Religion," 26.

36. Long, *Significations*, 56.

37. Charles H. Long, "New Space, New Time: Disjunctions and Context for New World Religions," *Criterion* 24, no. 1 (1985): 7.

38. For more on cultural contact from the vantage of the conquering culture, see Long, *Significations*, especially chapter 7, "Conquest and Cultural Contact in the New World." For a consideration of the same from the vantage of the conquered, see chapter 8, "Cargo Cults as Cultural Historical Phenomena."

39. Long, "New Space, New Time," 4.

40. Ibid., 5–6.

41. Ibid., 6.

42. Ibid., 7.

43. Long, "Meaning of Religion," 26.

44. Ibid.

45. Ibid.

46. Charles H. Long, "A Look at the Chicago Tradition in the History of Religions: Retrospect and Future," in *The History of Religions: Retrospect and Prospect*, ed. Joseph M. Kitagawa (New York: Macmillan, 1985), 96.

47. Long, *Significations*, 125.

48. Ibid., 126; quoting Kenelm Burridge, *Mambu, A Melanesian Millennium* (Princeton: Princeton University Press, 1995), xv–xvi.

49. Long, *Significations*, 127.

50. Ibid., 128.

51. Ibid.

52. Ibid.

53. Ibid., 128–29.

54. Ibid., 128.

55. Ibid.

56. Ibid.

57. Ibid., 129.

58. Charles H. Long, "Civil Rights–Civil Religion: Visible People and Invisible Religion," in *American Civil Religion*, ed. Russel E. Richey and Donald G. Jones (New York: Harper and Row, 1974), 213.

59. Ibid., 211–13.

60. Ibid., 218.

61. Ibid.

62. Ibid., 219; italics in original.

63. Ibid., 214. The notion of a "second naïveté" invokes the work of Paul Ricoeur, who Charles Long draws on frequently. Strictly speaking, the second naïveté refers to Ricoeur's conviction that interpretation ought to lead us beyond a critical pre-occupation with a text—in Long's case, the "text" of the narrative of American civil religion—to a fresh encounter with the "sacred" reality being born witness to in the text. To remain preoccupied with a text is to remain stuck in a first naïveté, one might say. It is to remain blind and beholden to and perhaps even to perpetuate the "sacred" reality that lay behind a text, the reality to which the text bears witness. Understood in Ricoeurean terms, Long's history of religions project of opacity is a project of the second naïveté. For a critical engagement with Ricoeur, see Mark I. Wallace, *The Second Naiveté: Barth, Ricoeur, and the New Yale Theology* (Macon, Ga.: Mercer, 1990).

64. Long, "Civil Rights–Civil Religion," 215, 219. My reading of Long at this point could be positioned next to the "genealogy" of atheism given in Michael J. Buckley, *At the Origins of Modern Atheism* (New Haven: Yale University Press, 1987).

65. Long, "Civil Rights–Civil Religion," 214.

66. Ibid., 217.

67. Ibid., 216–17.

68. Ibid.

69. Ibid., 218.

70. Ibid.

71. Long, *Significations*, 207.

72. Vine Deloria, *God Is Red: A Native View of Religion*, 2nd ed. (Golden, Colo.: Fulcrum, 1994).

73. Long, *Significations*, 205, 209.

74. Ibid., 209.

75. Ibid., 212.

76. Ibid.

77. The notion of a "weak" ontology in preference to a "strong" one is explicated in Gianni Vattimo, *The End of Modernity: Nihilism and Hermeneutics in Postmodern Culture*, trans. Jon R. Synder (Baltimore: Johns Hopkins University Press, 1988). From Vattimo's account of "weak ontology," which is indebted to Heidegger's thought, one gets a sense of what a strong ontology is:

> The full implications of this cannot be understood unless placed within a more general interpretation of Heideggerian ontology as "weak on-tology." The result of rethinking the meaning of Being is in fact, for Heidegger, the taking leave of metaphysical Being and its strong traits, on the basis of which the devaluation of the ornamental aspects of the work of

art has always definitively been legitimated, even if through more extensive chains of mediating concepts. That which truly is (the *ontos on*) is
not the center which is opposed to the periphery, nor is it the essence
which is opposed to appearance, nor is it what endures as opposed to the
accidental and the mutable, nor is it the certainty of the *obiectum* given to
the subject as opposed to the vagueness and imprecision of the horizon
of the world. The occurrence of Being is rather, in Heideggerian weak
ontology, an unnoticed and marginal background event. (85–86)

78. Long, *Significations*, 211.

79. William R. Jones, *Is God a White Racist? A Preamble to Black Theology* (Boston:
Beacon, 1998).

80. Charles H. Long, "Assessment and New Departures for a Study of Black
Religion in the United States of America," in *African American Religious Studies:
An Interdisciplinary Anthology*, ed. Gayraud S. Wilmore (Durham, N.C.: Duke Uni-
versity Press, 1989), 36.

81. Ibid., 37.

82. Long, *Significations*, 7.

83. Ibid., 211.

84. Long, "Assessment and New Departures," 39.

85. Ibid., 38.

86. Long, *Significations*, 184.

87. Ibid., 52.

88. Ibid., 52–53. At another point, Long discusses the phenomenological *epoché* as
"a critique of a purely western semantic hegemony" (152).

89. Ibid., 193.

90. Ibid., 194.

91. Ibid., 193.

92. Ibid., 194.

93. Ibid., 193.

94. Ibid., 195. The extended citations that Long quotes are from Clifton H.
Johnson, ed., *God Struck Me Dead: Religious Conversion Experiences and Autobiographies
of Ex-Slaves* (Boston: Pilgrim, 1989), 62–63.

95. Long, *Significations*, 194.

96. Ibid.

97. Ibid., 195.

98. Charles Sanders Peirce, "Questions Concerning Certain Faculties Claimed
for Man (1868)," in *The Essential Peirce: Selected Philosophical Writings*, ed. Nathan
Houser and Christian Kloesel (Bloomington: Indiana University Press, 1992).

99. Nicholas of Cusa develops this notion in his 1462 tract *De non aliud*.
For a translation of this tract see *Nicholas of Cusa on God as Not-Other: A Translation
and an Appraisal of De Li Non Aliud*, trans. Jasper Hopkins (Minneapolis: Arthur J.
Banning Press, 1979).

100. The latter part of this sentence is a short expression of what I take to be at
the heart of Thomas Aquinas's metaphysics of being. Because Aquinas sought to be
first and foremost a theologian, his philosophy is scattered throughout his corpus,
invoked when needed to make a theological point. Nevertheless, an important place

where lines of his vision of existence, his ontology, are explained is the first question of *De Veritate* (I.1).

Though I have invoked Aquinas to assist me in making my own theological-philosophical point against Charles Long's religious philosophy of opacity, it is important that my use of Aquinas at this point be seen for what it is: strategic. That is, the argument I am developing here specifically and in this book more generally should not be read as simply a species of the current fascination with Aquinas that has gripped significant quarters of the modern theological guild, for I am acutely aware that any reading of Thomas Aquinas must be done in relationship to the history of Thomism, especially in relationship to the colonialist and racial side of this history. In this sense, Thomas and Thomism are not easily separated. The modern vision of the human being as the bearer of race or as marked with racial identity was made possible by fifteenth-century and sixteenth-century Portuguese and Spanish Thomist-Aristotelian intellectuals. Which is to say, modern colonialism and the world born of it arose within a Thomistic discursive space. This is undeniable, and it therefore raises questions that has been utterly evaded by modern theologians and philosophers who are turning—at least as far as this matter is concerned, in an uncritical and ahistorical way—back to Aquinas's thought; to wit, what was it about the Thomistic vision that made it susceptible to such racial-colonial usage? And when theology began to function in the fifteenth century in the discursive interests of European, global conquest, what was it about Thomism that lent itself to the justification of this new enterprise? Contemporary philosophers and theologians who turn to Aquinas can no longer evade these questions or let them go unasked in their work, for they are the elephant in the intellectual room. For those on the darker underside of the renaissance and modernity, Thomism particularly and theology generally is part of the problem, not necessarily the answer. And it is they who must be persuaded of the viability of theology as a discourse, given this history. This book is a step in the direction for theology's viability by taking up the colonial-racial problem, not evading it. My language of the darker underside of modernity comes from Walter Mignolo, *The Darker Side of the Renaissance: Literacy, Territoriality, and Colonization*, 2nd ed. (Ann Arbor: University of Michigan Press, 2003), and Enrique Dussel, *The Underside of Modernity: Apel, Ricouer, Rorty, Taylor, and the Philosophy of Liberation* (Atlantic Highlands, N.J.: Humanities, 1996).

101. I develop this allusion to Pentecost more fully at the end of the article. J. Kameron Carter, "Race, Religion, and the Contradictions of Identity: A Theological Engagement with Douglass's 1845 *Narrative*," *Modern Theology* 21, no. 1 (2005): 37–65.

INTERLUDE

1. John Howard Yoder, *The Priestly Kingdom: Social Ethics as Gospel* (Notre Dame: University of Notre Dame Press, 1984), 141–44.

2. Walter Mignolo, *The Darker Side of the Renaissance: Literacy, Territoriality, and Colonization*, 2nd ed. (Ann Arbor: University of Michigan Press, 2003). I am persuaded by Mignolo's claim and the mountain of evidence he presents showing that the "European 'discovery' of a 'New World' " is the constitutive feature of "the emergence of

modernity toward the end of the fifteenth century." Modernity, he shows, is inextricably bound to the processes of coloniality. These processes entail "constitution of the Spanish Empire, the expulsion of the Moors, and the success of trans-Atlantic expansion" (xi). Coloniality is the "darker side of the renaissance," the darker side of modernity. As he says, "coloniality is constitutive of modernity. There cannot be modernity, as has been conceived and implemented through the past five hundred years of history, without coloniality" (453). But Mignolo presses further, bolstering claims I make in part I of this book that the colonial difference that underwrites the modern world "has been based on racial classification," which itself is tied to religion (451).

Mignolo has his intellectual finger on the fact that coloniality as linked to raciality is tied to—indeed, is situated within—the theological imagination of Renaissance and subsequent modernist intellectuals, an imagination that, certainly for the Renaissance intellectuals, is tied to their Aristotelian and often Thomist/Roman Catholic sensibilities. For the subsequent intellectuals of the seventeenth through the nineteenth centuries, the religious optic through which coloniality and raciality will come to work (as the center of gravity shifts from the Catholicism of southern Europe in Spain and Portugal to France, England, and Germany in northern Europe) is principally Protestantism.

Mignolo's concern in *The Darker Side of the Renaissance* is not with the Protestant intellectuals of the seventeenth through the nineteenth centuries. His concern is with the Renaissance intellectuals mainly of the fifteenth and sixteenth centuries. His breakthrough, from my perspective as a theologian, is that he grasps that coloniality functions within and is a modulation of theology as a discourse. My qualm with Mignolo's account—and it is a significant one—is that he insufficiently narrates the nature of the shifts that took place within theology itself as a discourse that made colonial conquest amenable to discursive articulation inside of the discourse of theology in the first place. Speaking to this larger issue must await another day.

3. Mason Lowance, ed., *Against Slavery: An Abolitionist Reader* (New York: Penguin, 2000). Lowance says that it was not until late in the modern abolitionist movement (1830–1865) that "'gradualism' was replaced with an aggressive form of protest that led to the abolition of slavery with the Thirteenth Amendment to the [U.S.] Constitution in 1865" (87).

4. "Sin," Augustine says, "is the primary cause of servitude, in the sense of a social status in which one man is compelled to be subjected to another man. Nor does this befall a man, save by the decree of God, who is never unjust and who knows how to impose appropriate punishments on different sinners." *De civitate dei* 19.15.

5. "Such, with Christ who ever elevates my mind, is my best wealth: no tracts of fertile land, no fair groves, no herds of kine, no flocks of fat sheep. Nor yet devoted slaves, my own race who have been separated from me by an ancient tyranny. To people sprung from one land it gave the double name of free and slave. Nay, not from one land, from one God. And so came into being this sinful distinction." Gregory of Nazianzus, *De rebus suis* 80–82, PG 37.976A; quoted in *St. Gregory of Nazianzus: Three Poems*, trans. Denis Molaise Meehan (Washington, D.C.: Catholic University Press of America, 1987), 27.

6. Basil, *De spiritu sancto* 20.51, in *SC* 17.204; *NPNF*, 2.8.32.

7. Ibid.

8. Ibid.

9. Daniel F. Stramara Jr., whose fine essay alerted me to this passage in *On the Holy Spirit*, claims that Basil makes the theological move toward a theology of creation in which God is conceived of as Master because "his Christian conscience must have bothered him" in making the claim that some are necessarily slaves while others are necessarily free, and that this is a good thing. Daniel F. Stramara Jr., "Gregory of Nyssa: An Ardent Abolitionist?," *St. Vladimir's Theological Quarterly* 41, no. 1 (1997): 41. As a conjectural suggestion, this may be the case. However, I am unpersuaded. For it seems to me that Basil's theological claim does not arise from a pricked conscience. Rather, it reveals the theological-intellectual consistency of his conscience.

10. Michel Foucault, *The Order of Things: An Archeology of the Human Sciences* (New York: Pantheon, 1971; reprint, 1994).

11. In this regard, see Susannah Heschel, *Abraham Geiger and the Jewish Jesus* (Chicago: University of Chicago Press, 1998); Shawn Kelley, *Racializing Jesus: Race, Ideology and the Formation of Modern Biblical Scholarship* (London: Routledge, 2002); James Pasto, "W. M. L. De Wette and the Invention of Post-Exilic Judaism: Political Historiography and Christian Allegory in Nineteenth-Century German Biblical Scholarship," in *Jews, Antiquity, and the Nineteenth-Century Imagination*, ed. Hayim Lapin and Dale B. Martin (Potomac: University Press of Maryland, 2003); Jonathan Sheehan, *The Enlightenment Bible: Translation, Scholarship, Culture* (Princeton: Princeton University Press, 2005); and George S. Williamson, *The Longing for Myth in Germany: Religion and Aesthetic Culture from Romanticism to Nietzsche* (Chicago: University of Chicago Press, 2005).

12. This summary draws on the interpretations of Gregory of Nyssa offered by Jean Daniélou and John Behr, introduction to *From Glory to Glory: Texts from Gregory of Nyssa's Mystical Writings*, ed. Jean Daniélou and Herbert Musurillo (New York: Scribner's, 1961), and John Behr, *The Nicene Faith*, vol. 2 of *The Formation of Christian Theology* (Crestwood, N.Y.: St. Vladimir's Seminary Press, 2004), 458–73.

13. This phrase comes from Dumitru Staniloae, *Theology and the Church*, trans. Robert Barringer (Crestwood, N.Y.: St. Vladimir's Seminary Press, 1980).

14. This is what is taken up in David Bentley Hart, *The Beauty of the Infinite: The Aesthetics of Christian Truth* (Grand Rapids, Mich.: Eerdmans, 2003).

15. Paul J. Griffiths, *Religious Reading: The Place of Reading in the Practice of Religion* (New York: Oxford University Press, 1999), especially 40–41.

16. Bourdieu's notion of habitus does massive work in his theory of sociological knowledge and his understanding of practice, as guided by habitus, in structuring the social order. Key to what Bourdieu means when he speaks of habitus in relationship to practices is this: Practices are constitutive of structures as well as determined by them. Hence, structures are themselves socially constructed through the everyday practices of agents. Bourdieu's concept of habitus points to the integration of practices with structures and how those everyday practices (in this case the academic reading practices of an intellectual class) are both the product of a certain structural domain (i.e., the university) and the reproduction through those very practices of the structure along with the class-consciousness or dispositions of that structural domain. Thus at the core of Bourdieu's notion of habitus (and practice) is a theory, then, of intellectuals or *homo academicus*. Such a theory stresses the specific symbolic interests that shape the cultural production of an intellectual class. In the

case we address here, the cultural production at issue is that of scriptural exegesis. With recourse to the notion of habitus, I seek to call attention to the political economy of scriptural exegesis as a particular from of symbolic or cultural capital. Indeed, I seek to redirect that economy in the direction of exegetical contemplation, a contemplation structured by and then filling out the domain of Jewish covenantal life in relationship to YHWH. This "filling out" entails Gentile incorporation into the Jews' relationship to YHWH (cultural intimacy) through the mediation of one from among this people. This one is the Jew Jesus of Nazareth. This is the horizon where exegesis must function. In what follows I offer a reading of Gregory of Nyssa on these matters that supports this contention. Among other writings, Bourdieu explains his notion of habitus in *The Logic of Practice* (Stanford: Stanford University Press, 1990), 54. I have been greatly helped in my understanding of Bourdieu on practice, habitus, and his theory of intellectuals by David Swartz, *Culture and Power: The Sociology of Pierre Bourdieu* (Chicago: University of Chicago Press, 1997).

17. Maria Mercedès Bergadá, "La Condamnation de l'esclavage dans l'homélie IV," in *HE* 188.

18. I put "externally" and "internally" in quotation marks here to signal that from God's vantage there is no external or internal. This distinction arises from the vantage of the creature.

19. I am using "analogy" here in the theologically technical sense of the analogate actually participating in, but within a broader difference from, what it is analogous to. This is precisely what makes it an analogy and not a mere semblance. This is developed in P. Erich Przywara, *Polarity: A German Catholic's Interpretation of Religion*, trans. A. C. Bouquet (London: Oxford Univeristy Press, 1935), and more fully in Erich Przywara, *Analogia Entis: Metaphysik—Ur-Struktur und All-Rhythmus*, rev. ed. (Einsiedeln: Johannes-Verlag, 1962).

20. Michel Foucault, *Power/Knowledge: Selected Interviews and Other Writings, 1972–1977* (New York: Pantheon, 1981).

21. Jacques Derrida, *The Gift of Death*, trans. David Wills (Chicago: University of Chicago Press, 1995).

22. I borrow this phrase—the mirror of the infinite—from the brilliant essay by David Bentley Hart, "The Mirror of the Infinite: Gregory of Nyssa on the *Vestigia Trinitatis*," *Modern Theology* 18, no. 4 (2002): 542–56. For his argument questioning whether a gift can really be given, see Derrida, *The Gift of Death*. For a response to Derrida's argument, see John Milbank, "Can a Gift Be Given? Prolegomena to a Future Trinitiarian Metaphysic," *Modern Theology* 11 (1995): 119–61.

23. Stramara, "Gregory of Nyssa," 48.

24. An example of this kind of claim is R. Kendall Soulen, *The God of Israel and Christian Theology* (Minneapolis: Fortress, 1996). In fairness to Soulen, he has recently modulated such claims considerably. R. Kendall Soulen, "YHWH the Triune God," *Modern Theology* 15, no. 1 (January 1999): 25–54.

25. For clarity's sake, I use Image, with a capital "I," to refer to Christ as the primary Image of God, or as Gregory says, as the "Prototype." I use image, with a lower-case "i," to refer to human beings in their status, as the Genesis stories would have it, as being *in* the Image. For Gregory, human beings are images in the Image of God. This is amplified in the following discussion.

26. For more on chiasmus as a rhetorical device in the ancient world, see Stramara, "Gregory of Nyssa," 52 n. 50.

27. Nils Wilhelm Lund, *Chiasmus in the New Testament: A Study in Formgeschichte* (Chapel Hill: University of North Carolina Press, 1942), 40. Quoted in Stramara, "Gregory of Nyssa," 51–52.

28. Lund, *Chiasmus in the New Testament*, 41. Quoted in Stramara, "Gregory of Nyssa," 52 n. 50.

29. Stramara, "Gregory of Nyssa," 52.

30. Ibid.

31. With this notion of killable flesh, pointing to the theological significance of the insights of some recent critical theorists, see Giorgio Agamben, *Homo Sacer: Sovereign Power and Bare Life*, trans. Daniel Heller-Roazen (Stanford: Stanford University Press, 1995); Abdul R. JanMohamed, *The Death-Bound-Subject: Richard Wright's Archaeology of Death* (Durham, N.C.: Duke University Press, 2005); and Achille Mbembé, "Necropolitics," *Public Culture* 15, no. 1 (2003): 11–40. John Milbank also makes an effort to reckon with the theological significance of insights into "homo sacer" and killable flesh in John Milbank, *Being Reconciled: Ontology and Pardon* (New York: Routledge, 2003). There are lacunae in his argument, however. For more on all of this, see J. Kameron Carter, "Race and the Experience of Death: Theologically Dislocating and Relocating American Evangelicalism," in *Cambridge Companion to Evangelical Theology*, Timothy Larsen and Daniel Treier, eds. (New York: Cambridge University Press, 2007), 177–198.

32. Orlando Patterson, *Slavery and Social Death: A Comparative Study* (Cambridge, Mass.: Harvard University Press, 1982).

33. While alluding to Gregory's language of the "contract" that made the slave system of his day function and the implication that such a contract functions in stark contrast to YHWH's relationship with creation as rooted in an irrevocable covenant, I am also alluding to Abdul M. JanMohamed's recent theorizing (in *Death-Bound-Subject*) of the "death contract" as grounding the modern social order, a contract refracted through race. JanMohamed draws heavily on the work of philosophers Giorgio Agamben and Achille Mbembé.

34. *DHO* 22 (*PG* 44.204D; *NPNF* 5.411B); translation slightly altered.

35. *DHO* 16 (*PG* 44.181A; *NPNF* 5.405A); italics mine.

36. *CE* (*GNO* 2.215–16; *PG* 45.981D–984A; *NPNF* 5.272A); translation mine.

37. *CE* (*GNO* 2.70; *NPNF* 5.158B).

38. David B. Hart, "The 'Whole Humanity': Gregory of Nyssa's Critique of Slavery in Light of His Eschatology," *Scottish Journal of Theology* 54, no. 1 (2001): 64–65. What it means that "orthodox" Christian theologians employed theological discourse in justification of a racialized understanding of the modern world as we now know it goes completely unaddressed by Hart. This is a profound lacuna in his otherwise important meditation on Gregory.

39. *DHO* 16 (*PG* 44.184B–C; *NPNF* 5.405B).

40. *AR* (*PG* 46.101C–104A, *NPNF* 5.452A–B); translation mine.

41. *CO* 5 (*PG* 45.23C; *NPNF* 5.479B); translation mine.

42. *LP*, 81–82.

43. It should be clear from this understanding of Israel's identity that what I am suggesting is not assimilable to a modern "Zionist" understanding of Jewish

identity such as one finds in various currents within contemporary American evangelicalism. Such an understanding of Jewish identity in terms of modern Zionism is an articulation of modern racial reasoning, albeit geopolitically situated at the liminal frontier between the so-called Occident and Orient. Here Zionist Jewish identity (as an Occidental construction) needs its Orientalist-Palestinian other. What I am suggesting is just as much a critique of this view as it is of Christianity's severance of itself from its Jewish theological roots. Indeed, what must be grasped is the coherence between modern Zionism and Christianity's severance of itself from its Jewish theological roots. For what one sees with modern Zionism is what happens when Jewish covenantalism is forced onto the Procrustean bed of modern statecraft and nation-state formation, the inner logic of which is racial reasoning.

CHAPTER 6

1. *A Narrative of the Uncommon Suffering, and Surprizing Deliverance of Briton Hammon, a Negro Man, a Servant of General Winslow, of Marshfield, in New-England; Who Returned to Boston, after Having Been Absent Almost Thirteen Years* (Boston: Green and Russell, 1760). All references to Hammon's *Narrative* are made internally within parentheses.

2. Enrique Dussel, *The Underside of Modernity: Apel, Ricoeur, Rorty, Taylor, and the Philosophy of Liberation*, trans. Eduardo Mendieta (Atlantic Highlands, N.J.: Humanities, 1996).

3. Geoffrey Galt Harpham, "Conversion and the Language of Autobiography," in *Studies in Autobiography*, ed. James Olney (New York: Oxford University Press, 1988), 44.

4. For example, Henry Louis Gates Jr., *The Signifying Monkey: A Theory of African-American Literary Criticism* (New York: Oxford University Press, 1988); Henry Louis Gates Jr., *Figures in Black: Words, Signs, and The "Racial" Self* (New York: Oxford University Press, 1987); and Dale E. Peterson, *Up from Bondage: The Literatures of Russian and African American Soul* (Durham, N.C.: Duke University Press, 2000).

5. Gates, *Figures in Black*, 248.

6. Ibid., 248–49.

7. Ibid., 249.

8. Harpham, "Conversion and the Language of Autobiography," 45.

9. Charles Taylor, *Sources of the Self: The Making of the Modern Identity* (Cambridge, Mass.: Harvard University Press, 1989).

10. Bakhtin makes this point in a number of places. See the essay "Discourse in the Novel" in M. M. Bakhtin, *The Dialogic Imagination: Four Essays*, ed. Michael Holquist, trans. Caryl Emerson and Michael Holquist (Austin: University of Texas Press, 1981), 259–422. But see also Bakhtin's early work (though translated into English later) *Toward a Philosophy of the Act*, ed. Michael Holquist, trans. Vadim Liapunov (Austin: University of Texas Press, 1993).

11. For an explicitly theological, rather than literary, consideration of the question, see the following: John D. Zizioulas, *L'être Ecclésial*, vol. 3 of *Perspective Orthodoxe* (Paris: Editions Labor et Fides, 1981); John D. Zizioulas, *Being as Communion: Studies*

in Personhood and the Church (Crestwood, N.Y.: St. Vladimir's Seminary Press, 1985); and John D. Zizioulas, "Communion and Otherness," *Sobornost* 16 (1994): 7–19.

12. Augustine, *Confessions* in *Opera Omnia*, reprinted in volumes 32–47 of J. P. Migne, *Patrologiae Cursus Completus, Series Latina* (Paris 1844–64), 32:688; translation mine.

13. I have been aided in thinking through this by the following: Mark S. Kinzer, *Postmissionary Messianic Judaism: Redefining Christian Engagement with the Jewish People* (Grand Rapids, Mich.: Brazos, 2005); Karl Barth, *Church Dogmatics*, trans. G. W. Bromiley et al., 4 vols. (Edinburgh: T&T Clark, 1956–1975), II/2:94–194; Kimlyn J. Bender, *Karl Barth's Christological Ecclesiology* (Burlington, VT: Ashgate, 2005).

14. Some of these reflections, particularly about Israel's identity as an identity in deferral, build on conversations with and course papers of Amanda Beckenstein Mbuvi, a graduate student at Duke University completing the Ph.D. degree in Hebrew Bible/Old Testament.

15. Something close to this is Edward Said's point in his recently published lectures on Sigmund Freud. Edward W. Said, *Freud and the Non-European* (London: Verso, 2003).

16. Jon D. Levenson, *Sinai and Zion: An Entry into the Jewish Bible* (New York: HarperCollins, 1985), 81. Levenson says in interpreting Deut. 5:1–4:

> The goal of this speech, as of the covenant renewal ceremony in which it probably originated, is to induce Israel to step into the position of the generation of Sinai, in other words, to actualize the past so that this new generation will become the Israel of the classical covenant relationship (cf. Deut 30:19–20). Thus, life in covenant is not something merely granted, but something won anew, rekindled and reconsecrated in the heart of each Israelite in every generation. Covenant is not only imposed, but also accepted, it calls with both the stern voice of duty and the tender accents of the lover, with both stick (curse, death) and carrot (blessing, life) in hand. But it biases the choice in favor of life (Deut 30:19). (81)

17. See the following in which this point is made: Jon D. Levenson, "The Universal Horizon of Biblical Particularism," in *Ethnicity and the Bible*, ed. Mark G. Brett (Leiden: E. J. Brill, 1996), 143–69; Joel S. Kaminsky, "Did Election Imply the Mistreatment of Non-Israelites?," *Harvard Theological Review* 96, no. 4 (2003): 397–425; Joel S. Kaminsky, "Reclaiming a Theology of Election: Favoritism and the Joseph Story," *Perspectives in Religious Studies* 31, no. 2 (2004): 135–52; and Frank Anthony Spina, *The Faith of the Outsider: Exclusion and Inclusion in the Biblical Story* (Grand Rapids, Mich.: Eerdmans, 2005).

18. On the history of the American assimilation process as a history of racial alchemy—that is, as a process of making immigrants white—see the oeuvre of Matthew Frye Jacobson: *Whiteness of a Different Color: European Immigrants and the Alchemy of Race* (Cambridge, Mass.: Harvard University Press, 1998); *Barbarian Virtues: The United States Encounters Foreign Peoples at Home and Abroad, 1876–1917* (New York: Hill and Wang, 2000); and *Roots Too: White Ethnic Revival in Post–Civil Rights America* (Cambridge, Mass.: Harvard University Press, 2006). Something of the sheer violence involved in assimilation has been recently dramatized in a scene in the film *Gangs of*

New York (2002), directed by Martin Scorsese. The movie narrates the violent process by which an Irish family, having immigrated to the United States, became American. That the violence of assimilation remains the determining ground of identity for those formed by its logics, even when those performing its logic are not "white," has been brilliantly captured, though perhaps unwittingly so, in the more recent film production *Munich* (2005), directed by Steven Spielberg.

This line of reasoning on whiteness as an accomplishment that culminates in closure is indebted to an engaging and deftly illuminating conversation, again, with my friend and fellow theologian, Willie James Jennings. Over lunch, we discussed his and my research: the persisting and chameleon-like character of whiteness as a theological problem and the near impossibility of black intellectuals (and other non-white intellectuals, for that matter) to theorize in robust theological terms a vision of identity beyond the tight spaces on the underside of modernity into which dark flesh was sequestered.

19. This phrase was used by Romanian theologian Dumitru Staniloae to explain John Damascene's understanding of *perichoresis* in trinitarian theology. Dumitru Staniloae, *Theology and the Church*, trans. Robert Barringer (Crestwood, N.Y.: St. Vladimir's Seminary Press, 1980), 38.

20. While this argument is in many respects a précis of Augustinian trinitarianism, I have gone beyond Augustine by reading him in conversation with Eastern Orthodox theology.

21. John E. Rotelle, ed., *The Works of Saint Augustine: A Translation for the 21st Century*, vol. 5: *The Trinity*, trans. Edmund Hill (Brooklyn, N.Y.: New City Press, 1991), 223.

22. Here is not the place to fully develop this point as it is a compressed formulation of a Trinitarian theology, about which a book could easily be written in its own right. Nevertheless, to minimize possible confusion about my point, I will simply say that with the notion of the Holy Spirit as ever qualifying the relationship between Father and Son, I am drawing on claims developed by Romanian Orthodox theologian Dumitru Staniloae about the nature of divine subjectivity. He develops the claims in the brilliant essay, "The Holy Trinity: Structure of Supreme Love," which has been made a chapter in Staniloae, *Theology and the Church*, 73–108. He says:

> The divine subjectivity cannot be the subjectivity of a single "I." An "I" without another "I" and without an object, that is, a subject sunk within itself, is robbed of all reality. The content of the divine "I" must consist not in opposed subjects and objects, but in other subjects interior to itself in an internal intersubjectivity. Because they do not each individually possess natures, the divine "I's" can be perfectly interior to themselves. (77)

Staniloae develops this further, but now disclosing that this is but a meditation on the Trinitarian relations:

> [Where] there is relation, each sees the other directly, and only indirectly sees himself. The Father knows himself [directly] in the Son and [indirectly in] the Spirit, and here we see the supreme humility of supreme love.... The communion of two "I's" is necessary in order to experience the fullness of existence, but it is not sufficient. This fullness is experi-

enced totally only in the communion of three "I's." Communion between two does not open up an unlimited horizon; considered in itself it represents a certain act of limitation. The simple presence, or the awareness of the presence, of the third enlarges the dimensions of existence *to include in principle all that can exist*.... The Father gives himself wholly to the Son and the Son wholly to the Father. One who loves is not content with halves; he desires the other wholly and gives himself wholly. Hence the Son is the "only Son of the only Father." On the other hand, any idea of an egotism *à deux* is far removed from the love between Father and Son. Such an egotism limits the horizon, keeps everything else outside, holding it fast within an eternal nothingness, or at the most, treating it only on the level of object. Only when there is a Third does the love of the Two become generous and capable of extending and diffusing itself. It is only because there is a Third that the Two can become one not through the reciprocity of their love alone, but also through their self-forgetfulness in favour of the Third. Only the existence of a Third in God explains the creation of a world of many "I's," and the fact that these "I's" have been elevated to the level of partners with God in love. Only through the Spirit does the divine love radiate to the outside. (92–93; italics mine)

One might conclude from what I have quoted that Staniloae's way of imagining the Spirit in the divine life commits him to understanding creation, "the outside," as necessary to the divine life. This would be a mistaken conclusion, however; for Staniloae's broader point is that the "interiority" of the divine life is an "exteriority." It is not sealed within a binary closure between the Father and Son. But this "exteriority" of the divine life is precisely what makes an exteriority beyond the divine life, properly speaking, possible should God will this possibility into actuality. This exteriority beyond the divine life, properly speaking, is creation. And yet even here the language of "beyond the divine life" must be understood analogically, for, strictly speaking, there is no "beyond" to the divine nature. The "beyond" of the "beyond divine life" is a beyond that is, in fact, within the divine life by the will of the divine life and not the nature constitutive of it. In this Staniloae speaks out of a venerable theological heritage that includes Gregory of Nyssa, Maximus the Confessor, John of Damascus, and Gregory of Palamas, among others. But this approach to understanding the divine, Triune life is reconcilable, I contend, with Augustine's approach to autobiography or the writing of the self. Self-writing is a singular Christological-Pneumatological activity. It is Pentecostal, an act by which we speak in tongues.

23. The Victorines—particularly Richard of St. Victor—along with Bonaventure, who contemplates Christ as the Father's *Ars Aeterna*, deepen Augustine's insights on this point.

24. Gregory of Nazianzus puts it this way:

The three most ancient opinions concerning God are Anarchia, Polyarchia, and Monarchia. The first two are the sport of the children of Hellas, and may they continue to be so.... But monarchy is that which we hold in honor. It is, however, a monarchy that is not limited to one person, for it is possible for unity if at variance with itself to come into a condition of

plurality; but one that is made of an equality of nature, and a union of mind, and an identity of motion, and a convergence of its elements to unity—a thing which is impossible to the created nature—so that though numerically distinct there is no severance of essence. Therefore unity, having from all eternity arrived by motion at duality, found its rest in trinity. This is what we mean by Father and Son and Holy Ghost.

See the third of Gregory's theological orations in Edward R. Hardy, ed., *Christology of the Later Fathers* (Philadelphia: Westminster, 1954), 160–61.

25. William L. Andrews, *To Tell a Free Story: The First Century of Afro-American Autobiography, 1760–1865* (Urbana: University of Illinois Press, 1988), 39.

26. Rafia Zafar, *We Wear the Mask: African Americans Write American Literature, 1760–1870* (New York: Columbia University Press, 1997), 55.

27. John Sekora, "Black Message/White Envelope: Genre, Authenticity, and Authority in the Antebellum Slave Narrative," *Callaloo* 32 (1987): 482–515.

28. William L. Andrews, ed., *Sisters of the Spirit: Three Black Women's Autobiographies of the Nineteenth Century* (Bloomington: Indiana University Press, 1986), 38.

29. Cf. Katherine Clay Bassard, *Spiritual Interrogations: Culture, Gender, and Community in Early African American Women's Writing* (Princeton: Princeton University Press, 1999).

30. John Sekora, "Red, White, and Black: Indian Captivities, Colonial Printers, and the Early African-American Narrative," in *A Mixed Race: Ethnicity in Early America*, ed. Frank Shuffelton (New York: Oxford University Press, 1993), 103.

31. Arguably, it even precedes the captivity genre and harks back to the minimally investigated gallows literature of Puritan New England. Indeed, prelate Cotton Mather, a writer of captivity literature, also wrote, even more so, gallows literature. Andrews, *To Tell a Free Story*.

32. Sekora, "Red, White, and Black," 103.

33. For more on the significance of race in the development of American literature, see Eric J. Sundquist, *To Wake the Nations: Race in the Making of American Literature* (Cambridge, Mass.: Belknap, 1993).

34. Sekora, "Red, White, and Black," 103.

35. Andrews, *To Tell a Free Story*, 40.

36. Bradley Scott Born, "Writing on the 'Restless Billows': Black Mariners and Mutineers in Selected Works of Antebellum American Literature," Ph.D. diss., University of Kansas, 1993, 53.

37. Ibid., 55.

38. Ibid., 53.

39. Ibid., 64.

40. Ibid., 65–66.

41. Winthrop D. Jordan, *White over Black: American Attitudes toward the Negro, 1550–1812* (New York: Norton, 1977), 103–4.

42. Ibid., 108.

43. Ibid., 101.

44. Puritan New England gallows literature—sermons and confessions given just before a criminal's execution—and captivity narratives both introduced black sub-

jects into the genres in order to arouse social sentiment. However, by making blacks subjects, this literature not only guided social sentiment but also brought together law, race, and religion. This is starkly portrayed in gallows, or execution, homilies, where Christianity mediated law and race so as to make possible scriptural enslavement of people of color, women (in a few instances), and children (in one instance I have come across). Interestingly, the famed New England prelate Cotton Mather is a pivotal figure for both genres. Daniel A. Cohen, "In Defense of the Gallows: Justifications of Capital Punishment in New England Execution Sermons, 1674–1825," *American Quarterly* 40 (1988): 147–64; Daniel A. Cohen, *Pillars of Salt, Monuments of Grace: New England Crime Literature and the Origins of American Popular Culture, 1676–1860* (New York: Oxford University Press, 1993); Daniel E. Williams, "'Behold a Tragic Scene Strangely Changed into a Theater of Mercy": The Structure and Significance of Criminal Conversion Narratives in Early New England," *American Quarterly* 38 (1986): 827–47; Walter Lazenby, "Exhortation as Exorcism: Cotton Mather's Sermons to Murderers," *Quarterly Journal of Speech* 57 (1971): 50–56; Eli Faber, "Puritan Criminals: The Economic, Social, and Intellectual Background to Crime in Seventeenth-Century Massachusetts," *Perspectives in American History* 11 (1977–1978): 91–144; Ronald A. Bosco, "Lectures at the Pillory: The Early American Execution Sermon," *American Quarterly* 35 (1978): 156–76; and Wayne C. Minnick, "The New England Execution Sermon, 1639–1800," *Speech Monographs* 35 (1968): 77–89. The one sermon that I have come across in which a child is the criminal is by Henry Channing. It was preached in 1787. The sermon is interesting in that the child, whose execution occasioned Channing's sermon, is scripted as a Christ-killer. The child is a girl named "Hannah Ocuish, a Mulatto Girl, Aged 12 Years and 9 Months." In framing Hannah as a Christ-killer, Channing simultaneously makes her stand in for what must be domesticated from being wild and savage. That is, she becomes a trope signifying what must be purged from early American life, lest America, in accordance with early Puritan covenantal theology, be "discovenanted" as God's chosen people due to defilement. The sermon thus highlights the gender of the child (female) and her "darkness" and status as "Mulatto" servant or slave. Moreover, her racial and gender status is given theological meaning as they are implicitly positioned over and against the purity of America as the New Israel. Implied in this is a Christian, supersessionist outlook in relationship to Israel. Henry Channing, *God Admonishing His People of Their Duty, as Parents and Masters*, 2nd ed. (New London, Conn.: T. Green, 1787).

45. Born, "Writing on the 'Restless Billows,'" 64.

46. Sondra O'Neale's illuminating work, from which I have been profitably instructed, similarly wants to uncover Phillis Wheatley's "subtle war." O'Neale wants to question facile readings of Wheatley that see in her work an affirmation of the racial status quo. Wheatley wages a most "subtle war" of both literary and theological ideas against the early American social order of both white-over-black and gender relations. Sondra A. O'Neale, "A Slave's Subtle War: Phillis Wheatley's Use of Biblical Myth and Symbol," *Early American Literature* 21 (1986): 144–65. Also suggestive is Bassard, *Spiritual Interrogations*.

47. Born, "Writing on the 'Restless Billows,'" 54.

48. Ibid., 55.

49. I have already mentioned Andrews's important work and how he addresses the problem of editorial control in *To Tell a Free Story*. But see also Zafar, *We Wear the Mask*.

50. Andrews, *To Tell a Free Story*, 37.

51. I have taken the language "restless billows" from Born's dissertation, "Writing on the 'Restless Billows.'"

52. Another subtle undercurrent here is England's "Black Legend" against Spain. The Black Legend is the specific name that was given to Spain's *unique* colonial brutality in the Americas. England deployed the Legend in an effort to present itself as being a more benign, and therefore righteous, colonizer. The emergence of the Black Legend discourse must be understood in relationship to the shift in colonial power from the principally Catholic European South, which lead in colonial endeavors in the 15th and 16th centuries, to the principally Protestant European North from the seventeenth century forward, with England becoming the apogee of colonial power in Northern Europe. The Black Legend discourse was rhetoric of Northern European colonial legitimation for the displacement of Spain, the first European power to carve an empire out of the New World. For an overview of the Black Legend, see especially the introduction to Margaret R. Greer, Walter D. Mignolo, Maureen Quilligan, eds., *Rereading the Black Legend: The Discourses of Religious and Racial Difference in the Renaissance Empires* (Chicago: University of Chicago Press, 2007).

53. St. John, in his gospel, draws on Psalm 34 to bolster his interpretation of the death of Jesus:

> Because it was the eve of the Sabbath, the Jews were anxious that the bodies [of Jesus and the two other malefactors] should not remain on the crosses, since the sabbath was a day of great solemnity; so they requested Pilate to have the legs broken and the bodies taken down. The soldiers accordingly came to the men crucified with Jesus and broke the legs of each in turn, but when they came to Jesus and found he was already dead, they did not break his legs. But one of the soldiers thrust a lance into his side, and at once there was a flow of blood and water. This is vouched for by an eyewitness, whose evidence is to be trusted. He knows that he speaks the truth, so that you too may believe; for this happened in fulfillment of the text of scripture: "No bone of his shall be broken." And another text says, "They shall look on him whom they pierced." (John 19:31–37)

CHAPTER 7

1. Edward W. Said, *Orientalism* (New York: Vintage, 1978), 40. Roger Jaco's "Easter" appears in Bell Gale Chevigny, ed., *Doing Time: 25 Years of Prison Writing* (New York: Arcade, 1999). The poem is quoted in Houston A. Baker, Jr., *Turning South Again: Re-Thinking Modernism/Re-Reading Booker T.* (Durham, N.C.: Duke University Press, 2002), 11–12.

2. For more on the problem of Orientalism, see Said, *Orientalism*.

3. Douglass wrote two subsequent autobiographies over the course of his life: *My Bondage and My Freedom* (1855) and *The Life and Times of Frederick Douglass* (1881). All

three of these are included in Henry Louis Gates Jr., ed., *Autobiographies: Frederick Douglass*, vol. 68 (New York: Library of America, distributed by Penguin Books, 1994). For critical inquiry into the interrelationships between these autobiographies and his lifetime endeavor to write and rewrite himself, see Eric J. Sundquist, *To Wake the Nations: Race in the Making of American Literature* (Cambridge, Mass.: Belknap, 1993). I do not engage the autobiographies subsequent to the 1845 *Narrative* here as my aim is not do a literary history centered on Douglass and his autobiographical writings. Rather, my objective is to foreground the religious and deeply theological character of Douglass's approach to identity in the *Narrative* for its contemporary significance.

4. For more on this, see Wilson J. Moses, "Writing Freely? Frederick Douglass and the Constraints of Racialized Writing," in *Frederick Douglass: New Literary and Historical Essays*, ed. Eric J. Sundquist (Cambridge: Cambridge University Press, 1990). This article builds on Moses's observations to show that the constraints of racialized writing within which Douglass found himself had not only to do with his efforts to navigate the straits of race in America. It had just as much to with his efforts to redefine how race functioned in the determination of national and religious identity.

5. My use of the term "political economy" is informed by historian Jeffrey Sklansky's account of its use in late-eighteenth-century America and into the nineteenth century. Those uses were significantly shaped by Adam Smith's *Wealth of Nations* (1776):

> The name commonly given that synthetic science by Smith and his contemporaries was "political economy," by which they meant the study not solely of the production and distribution of wealth, the main focus of Smith's masterpiece. Political economy concerned as well the basis of social order broadly conceived to comprise psychology and ethics, law and politics.... In this inclusive sense as the science of human nature and society, political economy provided the foundation for late eighteenth-century Anglo-America political thought. (Jeffrey Sklansky, *The Soul's Economy: Market Society and Selfhood in American Thought, 1820–1920* [Chapel Hill: University of North Carolina Press, 2002], 14)

In speaking of the "political economy of slavery," then, I mean to indicate the way in which slavery regulated the sociopolitical order.

6. John Sekora, "Black Message/White Envelope: Genre, Authenticity, and Authority in the Antebellum Slave Narrative," *Callaloo* 32(1987): 482–515.

7. Religious studies scholar Craig R. Prentiss provides a useful working definition of myth for my purposes:

> [A myth is] a narrative that not only claims truth for itself but is also seen by a community as credible and authoritative. To hold that a narrative is credible means to understand it as being true, either literally, as is often the case, or in some sense, metaphorically. When the community sees a story as authoritative, the story is understood as setting a paradigm for human behavior. In other words, human beings point to the story to

authorize (give authority to) their preferences, to justify or re-create their social patterns, or to guide their decision making. So, . . . stories achieve the status of myth among a given people by the way they are *used*. (Craig R. Prentiss, ed., *Religion and the Creation of Race and Ethnicity: An Introduction* [New York: New York University Press, 2003], 5; italics original)

It is also informed by religious historian Eddie J. Glaude Jr.'s discussion of the ideological dimensions of myth in the same volume. Eddie S. Glaude Jr., "Myth and African American Self-Identity," in *Religion and the Creation of Race and Ethnicity: An Introduction*, ed. Craig R. Prentiss (New York: New York University Press, 2003), 29–31 and 40 n.7. For an argument for the philosophical and theological positivity of myth, an argument that I have started to become more suspicious of, see Ferdinand Ulrich, *Logo-Tokos: Der Mensch und das Wort* (Einsiedeln: Johannes Verlag, 2003), 165–349.

8. This question has been given renewed energy through the work of a number of scholars who have returned to the work of historian of religions Charles H. Long. For example: Anthony B. Pinn, *Why, Lord? Suffering and Evil in Black Theology* (New York: Continuum, 1995); Anthony B. Pinn, *Varieties of African American Religious Experience* (Minneapolis: Fortress, 1998); Anthony B. Pinn, *Terror and Triumph: The Nature of Black Religion* (Minneapolis: Fortress, 2003); and James W. Perkinson, "Reversing the Gaze: Constructing European Race Discourse as Modern Witchcraft Practice," *Journal of the American Academy of Religion* 72, no. 3 (2004): 603–29. Long's work has also been influential on the work of religious ethicist Victor Anderson. According to Long, "the religious" is the phenomenon that makes particular religious and theological discourses possible. Charles H. Long, *Significations: Signs, Symbols, and Images in the Interpretation of Religion*, rev. ed. (Aurora, Colo.: Davies Group, 1995).

9. Suspicion about how the category of "religion" functions in modern thought is raised in Talal Asad, *Genealogies of Religion: Discipline and Reasons of Power in Christianity and Islam* (Baltimore: Johns Hopkins University Press, 1993); Richard King, *Orientalism and Religion: Postcolonial Theory, India and "the Mystic East"* (London: Routledge, 1999). I broach the matter in chapter 5 of this book through my engagement with the work of historian of religions Charles H. Long.

10. Sharon Lynn Carson, "Ambiguous Tradition: Religious Language and Problems of Cultural Authority in Selected 19th-Century American Literature," Ph.D. diss., University of Washington, 1990; and Sharon Lynn Carson, "Shaking the Foundation: Liberation Theology in *Narrative of the Life of Frederick Douglass*," *Religion and Literature* 24 (1992): 19–34.

11. Stuart G. Hall, "Subjects in History: Making Diasporic Identities," in *The House That Race Built: Black Americans, U. S. Terrain*, ed. Wahneema Lubiano (New York: Pantheon, 1997), 291.

12. Behind this is an important theological assumption that I cannot fully develop here—namely, that the states of Christ's life, including Christ's Easter mode of existence, are ongoing and contemporaneous with each epoch and historical moment. This contemporaneity provides the basis for a theology of history and of culture(s), a theology in which each historical moment and cultural and political expression analogically participates in the divine economy of the Trinity as disclosed and historically

embodied in Jesus of Nazareth. The analogical participation of history in the Triune life must not be understood as placid and untrammeled. Rather, the way each epoch "exists" in Christ is riddled with tensions. This is because existence in Christ's economy is always an uneasy combination of sinful resistance to and embrace of the will of God that ethically expresses itself in how persons, groups, and nations relate to one another. I draw on several sources in how I am thinking about this. Among premodern and early modern theologians, I am drawing on Irenaeus of Lyons's *Adversus Haeresus*, the Christology of Maximus the Confessor, especially as articulated in *Ambigua* 7 and 41, and particularly the theology of seventeenth-century French theologian Pierre Bérulle. Among contemporary thinkers I draw on the work of W. E. B. Du Bois (what I find helpful and also seriously problematic with it), as well on the thought of African American religious historian Albert J. Raboteau; on the work of Hans Urs von Balthasar, as expressed in his theological trilogy on aesthetics, drama, and logic; the doctrine of analogy as put forward by the Thomist philosopher of religion Erich Przywara; and the thought of philosopher Ferdinand Ulrich on language, myth, and cultural folklore. As mentioned at various points in this book, my theological celebration of Balthasar and Ulrich have been been seriously tempered. W. E. B. Du Bois, *Writings: The Suppression of the African Slave-Trade, the Souls of Black Folks, Dusk of Dawn, Essays and Articles* (New York: Library of America, 1986); Albert J. Raboteau, *Slave Religion: The "Invisible Institution" in the Antebellum South* (New York: Oxford University Press, 1978); Albert J. Raboteau, *A Fire in the Bones: Reflections on African-American Religious History* (Boston: Beacon, 1995); Albert J. Raboteau, "The Legacy of a Suffering Church: The Holiness of American Slaves," in *An Unbroken Circle: Linking Ancient African Christianity to the African-American Experience*, ed. Fr. Paisius Altschul (St. Louis, Mo.: Brotherhood of St. Moses the Black, 1997); Hans Urs von Balthasar, *The Glory of the Lord: A Theological Aesthetics*, 7 vols. (San Francisco: Ignatius, 1982–1989); Hans Urs von Balthasar, *Theo-Drama: Theological Dramatic Theory*, 5 vols. (San Francisco: Ignatius, 1988–1998); Hans Urs von Balthasar, *Theo-Logic: Theological Logical Theory*, trans. Adrian J. Walker, 3 vols. (San Francisco: Ignatius, 2000–2005); P. Erich Przywara, *Polarity: A German Catholic's Interpretation of Religion*, trans. A. C. Bouquet (London: Oxford University Press, 1935); Ferdinand Ulrich, *Logo-Tokos*; Ferdinand Ulrich, *Homo Abyssus: Das Wagnis der Seinsfrage* (Einsiedeln: Johannes Verlag, 1998).

13. For a masterful engagement with this episode, which in a number of ways I draw on in what follows, see Jenny Franchot, "The Punishment of Esther: Frederick Douglass and the Construction of the Feminine," in *Frederick Douglass: New Literary and Historical Essays*, ed. Eric J. Sundquist (Cambridge: Cambridge University Press, 1990).

14. For a literary and philosophical engagement with this issue, see René Girard, *Violence and the Sacred* (Baltimore: Johns Hopkins University Press, 1977). This is a recurrent theme in his oeuvre.

15. Elaine Scarry, *The Body in Pain: The Making and Unmaking of the World* (New York: Oxford University Press, 1985).

16. Franchot, "Punishment of Esther," 143.

17. Ibid.

18. Ibid., 143–44.

19. Ibid., 141.

20. Moses, "Writing Freely? Frederick Douglass and the Constraints of Racialized Writing."

21. Richard Yarborough, "Race, Violence, and Manhood: The Masculine Ideal in Frederick Douglass's 'The Heroic Slave,'" in Frederick Douglass: New Literary and Historical Essays, ed. Eric J. Sundquist (Cambridge: Cambridge University Press, 1990), 167.

22. The interpretation to follow has been significantly influenced by David Leverenz, Manhood and the American Renaissance (Ithaca, N.Y.: Cornell University Press, 1989).

23. W. E. B. Du Bois's interpretation of the slave songs in The Souls of Black Folks (1903) takes its lead in many ways from Douglass's reflections on the songs. To my knowledge, a critical appraisal of the connections between their interpretations and its significance for the formation of a black intellectual imagination has not been done. The Douglass-Du Bois connection to slave singing itself is addressed in Jon Cruz, Culture on the Margins: The Black Spiritual and the Rise of Cultural Interpretation (Princeton: Princeton University Press, 1999). As for Du Bois's interpretation of the songs and its significance for his thought and beyond, see Paul Allen Anderson, Deep River: Music and Memory in Harlem Renaissance Thought (Durham, N.C.: Duke University Press, 2001); Ronald Radano, Lying up a Nation: Race and Black Music (Chicago: University of Chicago Press, 2003); Eric J. Sundquist, To Wake the Nations; and Shamoon Zamir, Dark Voices: W. E. B. Du Bois and American Thought, 1888–1903 (Chicago: University of Chicago Press, 1995).

24. Leverenz, Manhood and the American Renaissance, 125.

25. It follows from this that there must be a serious theological consideration of the meaning of the feminine. Such a consideration, at minimum, must refuse understandings of identity that begin with the self-constituted I—be it racial I of whiteness, blackness, or what have you; a masculinist, patriarchial I; or an I of a self-constituting feminine. These are all inflections of an "Ur of the Chaldees" that must be left behind as one diasporically makes one's way to another city, a city of YHWH's covenant. Among the work of feminist theologians that is struggling deeply with these matters, see Sarah Coakley, Powers and Submissions: Spirituality, Philosophy and Gender (Malden, Mass.: Blackwell, 2002).

26. The term theotokos was the subject of intense debate in the fifth century. The central persons of the debate were Cyril of Alexandria and Nestorius, the deposed Patriarch of Constantinople. At the heart of the controversy was whether "Mother of God" (theotokos) or "Mother of Christ" (Christotokos), and hence mother of an earthly man only, was the appropriate term of Christian confession. The Council of Ephesus (431 CE), sanctioning the position of Cyril, would affirm that theotokos is the term that affirms the incarnation of God in Christ and thus is the term appropriate to the Christian confession. For a historical engagment with the controversy, see Alloys Grillmeier, Christ in Christian Tradition, vol. 1: From the Apostolic Age to Chalcedon (451), trans. John Bowden, 2nd rev. ed. (Atlanta: John Knox Press, 1975), 447–87. For a collection of texts from Cyril and Nestorius documenting the controversy, see John McGuckin, ed., St. Cyril of Alexandria: The Christological Controversy—Its History, Theology, and Texts (Leiden: Brill, 1994).

My invocation of the doctrine of the *theotokos* in the context of a theological reading of Douglass's 1845 *Narrative* and in the context of analysis of and response to whiteness as a theological problem is to point to the significance of this doctrine for how identity has come to be thought about and inflected through race and how it can be rethought. This doctrine says that to rest in Christ is to receive one's identity from him but through the covenantal mediation of Israel–Mary. This means that Christian identity cannot be made to comfortably rest on the Procrustean bed of the racial outlook that is the inner architecture of modernity without, on a fundamental level, rendering unintelligible, if not nonsensical, the possibility of the Gentiles declaring through their existence in Christ that the God of Israel is God for the Gentiles too (*Christos kurios*). Indeed, Christian identity within the horizon of the Christological doctrine of the *theotokos* cuts against the grain of our modern social imaginary, for, read against the backdrop of modern racial reasoning, Christian identity is necessarily a "contaminated," "impure" identity, for modernity's racial logic functions from an analytics of purity. ("To be black," to reason in modern racial terms, "is not to be white," and so forth). Insofar as this is the case, Christian identity cannot be the identity of whiteness. It is closer or analogous to the "impurity" of interracial or Mulatto identity. It is in just this sense that the confession of Mary the mother of Jesus as *theotokos* or mother of God points toward the disruption of modern racial logics, indeed, the disruption of any self-constituting identity formation. Indeed, interpreted within the horizon of modern racial reasoning, Christ's existence, being both divine and human, is mulattic or "interracial." And therefore, to exist in him is to exist "interracially." One need only look to Nazi Germany, to apartheid South Africa, and to nineteenth-century and twentieth-century U.S. miscegenation laws, with their insistence on maintaining the purity of racial blood, to see what a scandal Christianity so understood entails. Such an understanding of Christianity means entering into "interracial" proximity with Jesus the Galilean-covenantal Jew. This very act—the act of being Christian—would be an apocalyptic act, an act of judgment on the racial construction of identity and of Christianity's central role from the fifteenth century in constituting raciality as central to the modern world. But also, such an act would be an eschatological act. Indeed, it would be a sign of the "coming body" of redemption, as Gregory of Nyssa says in his *Antirrheticus against Appolinarus*.

What I am suggesting here also has a basis in the Hebrew Scriptures of the Old Testament in which Abram called by YHWH to leave Ur of the Chaldees and thereby to enter into the identity of Abraham is miscegenistic (cf. Gen. 12). This is because the coming to be of the people of Israel is grounded in Abram's obedience to YHWH's calling. With YHWH's calling Abram's life was disrupted, "contaminated" one might say, and inter-sected. The people of Israel are the product of YHWH's inter-section with Abram-to-become-Abraham-to-later-become-Israel. They are not prior to the calling. Rather, the calling and Abram's obedience and relationship to YHWH, the one who is to be the God of Israel, is what produces the people. Thus, Abram's "interracial" relationship—and here I speak analogically, but it is a real analogy—with YHWH produces the "interracial" people of Israel. In short, the Jewish covenant is inter-communal. From the first, it defies every logic of purity, for it presupposes the coming together of YHWH as Creator and Israel as index of creation. Indeed, the "inter-raciality" of YHWH's covenant with Israel and thereby with the world is born witness

to in the genealogies recorded in the gospels of Matthew (1:1–17) and Luke (3:21–38) in which non-Jews like Tamar and Ruth are included in Jesus' Jewish genealogy and thus reckoned as Jews. Insofar as the doctrine of the *theotokos* is meant to highlight the humanity of Jesus, it also highlights the *Jewish-covenantal* humanity of Jesus and points to overcoming, from the vantage point of the covenant of the tyranny of logics of purity, the quintessential modern expression of which is whiteness and the racial outlooks it produces to maintain itself.

27. I suggest here but do not develop the link between race and class. It is a connection that reappears in my consideration of Jarena Lee in chapter 8. Indeed, I point to the race-class connection in chapter 2, in the analysis of modern racial reasoning as cosmopolitical reasoning. There I show how cosmopolitics is both a political posture and a class orientation, the orientation of a *Bildungsbürgertum*. This scene in Douglass's *Narrative* points to how race articulates itself through class protocols and in the process masks the ways in which race drives class in the (re)production of the body (politic). This phenomenon is subjected to analysis in several of the essays in Kamari Maxine Clarke and Deborah A. Thomas, eds., *Globalization and Race: Transformations in the Cultural Production of Blackness* (Durham, N.C.: Duke University Press, 2006), and is the subject of the brilliant study by Rey Chow, *The Protestant Ethnic and the Spirit of Capitalism* (New York: Columbia University Press, 2002). See also Antonia Darder and Rodolfo D. Torres, *After Race: Racism after Multiculturalism* (New York: New York University Press, 2004).

28. For a classical expression of womanist theology, see Delores S. Williams, *Sisters in the Wilderness: The Challenge of Womanist God-Talk* (Maryknoll, N.Y.: Orbis, 1993). See also the essays collected in part IV, "Womanist Theology," and part V, "Black Theology and Black Women," in James H. Cone and Gayraud S. Wilmore, eds., *Black Theology: A Documentary History.*, 2nd rev. ed., 2 vols. (Maryknoll, N.Y.: Orbis, 1993).

29. Jeffrey Stout, *Democracy and Tradition: Religion, Ethics, and Public Philosophy* (Princeton: Princeton University Press, 2004).

30. Cornel West, *The American Evasion of Philosophy: A Genealogy of Pragmatism* (Madison: University of Wisconsin Press, 1989); Eddie S. Glaude Jr., "Pragmatic Historicism and 'the Problem of History' in Black Theology," *American Journal of Theology and Philosophy* 19 (1998): 173–90; Eddie S. Glaude Jr., *Exodus! Religion, Race, and Nation in Early Nineteenth-Century Black America* (Chicago: University of Chicago Press, 2000); Eddie S. Glaude Jr., "Pragmatism and Black Identity: An Alternative Approach," *Nepantla: Views from South* 2, no. 2 (2001): 295–316; Glaude, "Myth and African American Self-Identity"; and Eddie S. Glaude Jr., "Tragedy and Moral Experience: John Dewey and Toni Morrison's *Beloved*," in *Pragmatism and the Problem of Race*, ed. Bill E. Lawson and Donald F. Koch (Bloomington: Indiana University Press, 2004).

31. Stout, *Democracy and Tradition*, 14.

32. A good summation of the patristic traditions on these matters is Grillmeier, *Christ in Christian Tradition*. On medieval thought and the theology of Easter and the atonement, see Jaroslav Pelikan's fine work, *The Christian Tradition: A History of the Development of Doctrine*, vol. 3: *The Growth of Medieval Theology (600–1300)* (Chicago: University of Chicago Press, 1978).

33. Michel Foucault, *"Society Must Be Defended": Lectures at the College De France, 1975–1976*, trans. David Macey (New York: Picador, 2003).

34. Jeremy R. Carrette, *Foucault and Religion: Spiritual Corporality and Political Spirituality* (London: Routledge, 2000), and Giorgio Agamben, *Homo Sacer: Sovereign Power and Bare Life*, trans. Daniel Heller-Roazen (Stanford: Stanford University Press, 1995).

35. For more on this, see Paul Harvey, "'A Servant of Servants Shall He Be': The Construction of Race in American Religious Mythologies," in *Religion and the Creation of Race and Ethnicity: An Introduction*, ed. Craig R. Prentiss (New York: New York University Press, 2003).

36. John Milbank, *Theology and Social Theory: Beyond Secular Reason* (Oxford: Blackwell, 1992).

37. This claim is developed by two modern thinkers—one a theologian, the other a religious philosopher—in quite interesting ways: Hans Urs von Balthasar and Ferdinand Ulrich. See the former's treatise on finite and infinite freedom in Balthasar, *Theo-Drama*, 2:189–334. See the latter's Thomistically inspired ontology, which is marked by what he calls the poverty and wealth (*Armut und Reichtum*) of being, in Ulrich, *Homo Abyssus*. A concise expression of the latter's fundamental doctrine appears in Ferdinand Ulrich, "Armut und Reichtum der Freiheit: Eine philosophische Meditation," *Evangelische Theologie* 46, no. 1 (1986): 46–73.

38. See the prelude's engagement with Irenaeus and his struggle against Ptolemaeic Valentianism.

39. See Du Bois's 1933 address, titled "The Field and Function of the Negro College," in W. E. B. Du Bois, *The Education of Black People: Ten Critiques, 1906–1960* (New York: Monthly Review, 2001), 116.

40. Pierre Hadot, *Philosophy as a Way of Life*, trans. Michael Chase (Malden, Mass.: Blackwell, 1995), 264–76.

41. Ibid., 126–44.

42. In many respects, this is precisely what theologian Sarah Coakley has attempted to do in her recent work on theology, gender, and feminist theory, *Powers and Submissions*. A central feature of her agenda is to reengage the question of what it means to be a creature before God (55–68) as the basis for grappling with the question of female identity. Her approach has led her to criticize, on Christological grounds, what she calls "the repression of 'vulnerability'" in feminist theology (3–39). Though in the main I am deeply sympathetic with and have learned a lot from Coakley's endeavors for my own work in theology, philosophy, and race, I do nevertheless have some reservations. For it does in the end appear that she wants to hold out some "space" that is in an a priori sense "feminine," a space that, to use her phrase, comes dangerously close to repressing vulnerability. This can be seen, I think, in her attraction to an understanding of *kenosis* that would interpret the Christological "self-emptying" of Phil. 2:11 as "choosing *never to have* certain false and worldly forms of power" (11; italics hers). The implication is that Christ could have chosen them, but simply didn't. What is risky in this interpretation is that it presupposes what Maximus the Confessor denied of Christ: namely, a gnomic will. For Maximus, a gnomic will arises out of the creature's false self-understanding of itself, an understanding whereby the world and even God is imagined as a binary and thus rival power in relationship to

the self. The creature in this circumstance must deliberate as to how it will relate itself to this rival power or potential enemy so as to preserve its identity. On the level of choice and action, this "gnomic" posture expresses itself by vacillating before and having to calculate its relationship to the good. For Maximus, Christ *cannot* will or act in such a way because he is always already oriented toward the good or the will of God not as his rival. He is always already positively vulnerable toward the good. Such is his disposition of obedience before God and in the face of what is good. In this respect, there is no vacillation, for his will is fixed on the good. For more on this, see Maximus's important "Opusculum 3," which appears in Andrew Louth, ed., *Maximus the Confessor* (New York: Routledge, 1996), 192–98. Louth's introduction also takes a careful look into the matter of Christ's "gnomic" will.

All said, Coakley's attempt to theologically reimagine the meaning of the feminine has implications well beyond feminist inquiry. It has the potential to reconfigure how any number of sites of identity—from race, to gender, to sexuality, to politics— might be theologically rethought. Proof of this is Coakley's recent turn to consider- ations of racial identity in America as part and parcel of her work in dogmatic theology.

43. It has been argued that there is a deep Christological undercurrent to Bakh- tin's thought, especially as regards the notions "heteroglossia," "polyphony," and "dialogism." M. M. Bakhtin, *Toward a Philosophy of the Act*, ed. Michael Holquist, trans. Vadim Liapunov (Austin: University of Texas Press, 1993); M. M. Bakhtin, *Art and Answerability: Early Philosophical Essays*, ed. Michael Holquist, trans. Vadim Lia- punov, suppl. trans. Kenneth Brostrom (Austin: University of Texas Press, 1990). For critical reflection on this aspect of Bakhtin's thought, see Alexandar Mikhailovic, *Corporeal Words: Mikhail Bakhtin's Theology of Discourse* (Evanston, Ill.: Northwestern University Press, 1997).

44. My use of the notion of "interhumanity" is informed by Ferdinand Ulrich, "Der eine Logos und die viele Sprachen: Religionsphilosophische Reflexionen über Gen 11, 1–9," *Salzburger Jahrbuch für Philosophie* 12/13 (1968/1969): 183–224. What I term "interhumanity," Ülrich speaks of under the rubric "Mitmensch."

45. On this general problem, the problem of Christian supersessionism, in Christian thought, see R. Kendall Soulen, *The God of Israel and Christian Theology* (Minneapolis: Fortress, 1996).

46. Douglass's indebtedness to the individualism of Benjamin Franklin and Ralph Waldo Emerson is critically reflected by Rafia Zafar, "Franklinian Douglass: The Afro-American as Representative Man," in *Frederick Douglass: New Literary and His- torical Essays*, ed. Eric J. Sundquist (Cambridge: Cambridge University Press, 1990). Douglass's Emersonianism is expressed perhaps most poignantly in his address before the students of the Indian Industrial School at Carlisle, Pennsylvania, titled "Self-Made Man," which can be found in John Blassinghame and John McKivigan, eds., *The Frederick Douglass Papers*, Series One, vol. 5. (New Haven: Yale University Press, 1992), 545–75.

CHAPTER 8

1. Hans Urs von Balthasar, *Theo-Drama: Theological Dramatic Theory*, 5 vols. (San Francisco: Ignatius, 1988–1998), 3:28–29.

2. In speaking of the "supratragic," I am alluding to modern configurations of the tragic, comic, and tragicomic. For example, Raymond Williams, *Modern Tragedy* (Stanford: Stanford University Press, 1966); Cornel West, *Prophetic Fragments: Illuminations of the Crisis in American Religion and Culture* (Grand Rapids, Mich.: Eerdmans, 1993), 164–65; and Terry Eagleton, *Sweet Violence: The Idea of the Tragic* (Malden, Mass.: Blackwell, 2003). On the Jew as oriental other within the modern Occident, see Ivan Davidson Kalmar and Derek Jonathan Penslar, eds., *Orientalism and the Jews* (Waltham, Mass.: Brandeis University Press and University Press of New England, 2005).

3. Jarena Lee, "Religious Experience and Journal of Mrs. Jarena Lee, Giving an Account of Her Call to Preach the Gospel, Revised and Corrected from the Original Manuscript, Written by Herself," in *Spiritual Narratives*, ed. Susan Houchins (New York: Oxford University Press, 1988). "Religious Experience" (1849) is an expansion of Lee's 1836 spiritual autobiography. For the 1836 text, see Jarena Lee, *The Life and Religious Experience of Jarena Lee, a Coloured Lady, Giving an Account of Her Call to Preach the Gospel: Revised and Corrected from the Original Manuscript, Written by Herself*, in *Sisters of the Spirit: Three Black Women's Autobiographies of the Nineteenth Century*, ed. William L. Andrews (Bloomington: Indiana University Press, 1986). This chapter engages only the latter, referencing it as *Life*, followed by the page number.

4. A clear distinction must be drawn between Lee's exegetical invocation of the language of Zion as the language of Jewish covenant and the Zionism of the modern state of Israel. The latter is a species of modern nationalism and traffics in modern discourses of racial and cultural difference, as well as in discourses of Orientalism. It thus bears the marks of the contradictions and problems of modern identity formation. Zionism reflects, one might say following Foucault, the modern nationalist quest to police national borders by policing *bios* itself. The significance of this is that in Zionism Jewish identity comes to be understood as an ambiguous and even conflicted racial identity, an identity both white and nonwhite, of both the Occident and the Orient. Jewish identity is no longer understood principally as a theological identity tied to an understanding of covenant and election. Within this framework, Israel's election is for the sake of YHWH's love of all. Theologically understood, then, Israel is a nation without analogy; they are a nonnationalistic (particularly in the modern sense of the term) nation. I am developing these themes further in a manuscript on a theology of Israel. On the making of modern Jewish identity into a racial identity, see Karen Brodkin, *How Jews Became White Folks and What That Says about Race in America* (New Brunswick, N.J.: Rutgers University Press, 1998), and Eric L. Goldstein, *The Price of Whiteness: Jews, Race, and American Identity* (Princeton: Princeton University Press, 2006). On modern Zionism, see Yoram Hazony, *The Jewish State: The Struggle for Israel's Soul* (New York: Basic, 2000). On Orientalism, see the now classical work by Edward W. Said, *Orientalism* (New York: Vintage, 1978). But Said's work must now be understood in relationship to Kalmar and Penslar, *Orientalism and the Jews*.

5. Jon D. Levenson, *Sinai and Zion: An Entry into the Jewish Bible* (New York: HarperCollins, 1985).

6. Jacob Taubes, *The Political Theology of Paul*, trans. Dana Hollander (Stanford: Stanford University Press, 2004), 3–4.

7. The language of *theotokos* was at the center of the fourth-century Christological controversy between Nestorius and Cyril of Alexandria. For more on this, see chapter 7, n. 26.

8. For more on the tenuous status of freedom in the antebellum North, see Eddie S. Glaude Jr., *Exodus! Religion, Race, and Nation in Early Nineteenth-Century Black America* (Chicago: University of Chicago Press, 2000).

9. M. M. Bakhtin, *The Dialogic Imagination: Four Essays*, ed. Michael Holquist, trans. Caryl Emerson and Michael Holquist (Austin: University of Texas Press, 1981), esp. the essay "Discourse in the Novel," 259–422.

10. Melvin Dixon, "The Black Writer's Use of Memory," in *History and Memory in African-American Culture*, ed. Geneviève Fabre and Robert O'Meally (New York: Oxford Univeristy Press, 1994), 19, 21.

11. Katherine Clay Bassard, *Spiritual Interrogations: Culture, Gender, and Community in Early African American Women's Writing* (Princeton: Princeton University Press, 1999).

12. Ibid., 87–107.

13. Frederick Douglass, "Narrative of the Life of Frederick Douglass, an American Slave," in *Autobiographies: Frederick Douglass*, ed. Henry Louis Gates Jr. (New York: Penguin, 1994), 17. See chapter 6 in this volume, as well.

14. Bassard, *Spiritual Interrogations*, 96.

15. Michael A. Fishbane, *The Exegetical Imagination: On Jewish Thought and Theology* (Cambridge, Mass.: Harvard University Press, 1998), 2.

16. Ibid.

17. Ibid.

18. Ibid.

19. Ibid., 3.

20. Hans W. Frei, *The Eclipse of Biblical Narrative: A Study in Eighteeth and Nineteenth Century Hermeneutics* (New Haven: Yale University Press, 1974), 150.

21. Erich Auerbach, *Mimesis: Representation of Reality in Western Literature* (Princeton: Princeton University Press, 2003).

22. Frei, *Eclipse of Biblical Narrative*.

23. Fishbane, *Exegetical Imagination*, 3–4.

24. Benedict Anderson, *Imagined Communities: Reflections on the Origin and Spread of Nationalism*, rev. ed. (London: Verso, 1991).

25. Anderson, *Imagined Communities*, 7.

26. Foucault's comment in his essay "The Political Technologies of Individuals," in which he summarizes what his work in its various phases has been about, is helpful in more fully specifying the political technology of the individual that Lee's spiritual narrative fights against:

> Let's say very briefly that through studying madness and psychiatry, crime and punishment, I have tried to show how we have indirectly constituted ourselves through the exclusion of some others: criminals, mad people, and so on. And now my present work deals with the question: How did we directly constitute our identity through some ethical techniques of the self which developed through antiquity down to now? That was what we were studying in the seminar.

There now is another field of questions that I would like to study: the way by which, through some political technology of individuals, we have been led to recognize ourselves as a society, as a part of a social entity, as a part of a nation or of a state. I would like now to give you an *aperçu*, not of the technologies of the self but of the political technology of individuals. (Quoted in Luther H. Martin, Huck Gutman, and Patrick H. Hutton, eds., *Technologies of the Self: A Seminar with Michel Foucault* [Amherst: University of Massachusetts Press, 1988], 146)

27. Fishbane, *Exegetical Imagination*, 4.
28. Ibid., 106.
29. Ibid., 106–7.
30. Ibid., 110–11.
31. Ibid., 7.
32. Ibid., 8.
33. Gregory develops his notion of the soul as possessed of infinite depth and thus as on a journey of infinite duration into God, who is infinite, in his *Life of Moses* and his *Commentary on the Song of Songs*. In his Songs commentary, Gregory says:

The great Apostle told the Corinthians of the wonderful visions he enjoyed during his time of mystical initiation in Paradise... and he testifies: *I do not count myself to have apprehended. But forgetting the things that are behind, I stretch myself forth to those that are before* [Phil. 3:13]. And clearly this is meant to include even the *third heaven* which Paul alone saw; for Moses told us nothing of it in his cosmogony. Yet even after listening in secret to the mysteries of heaven, Paul does not let the graces he has obtained become the limit of his desire, but he continues to go on and on, never ceasing his ascent. Thus he teaches us, I think, that in our constant participation in the blessed nature of the good, the graces that we receive at every point are indeed great, but the path that lies beyond our immediate grasp is infinite. This will constantly happen to those who thus share in the divine Goodness, and they will always enjoy a greater and greater participation in grace throughout all eternity. (Quoted in Jean Daniélou and Herbert Musurillo, eds., *From Glory to Glory: Texts from Gregory of Nyssa's Mystical Writings* [New York: Scribner's, 1961], 211–12)

34. Carla L. Peterson, *"Doers of the Word": African-American Women Speakers and Writers in the North (1830–1880)* (New Brunswick, N.J.: Rutgers University Press, 1995), 76.
35. Bassard, *Spiritual Interrogations*, 95.
36. Ibid., and Peterson, *"Doers of the Word,"* 77.
37. Paul Gilroy, *Against Race: Imagining Political Culture beyond the Color Line* (Cambridge, Mass.: Belknap, 2000); and David Theo Goldberg, *Racist Culture: Philosophy and the Politics of Meaning* (Malden, Mass.: Blackwell, 1993). What Gilroy refers to as the "raciology" of rationality, Goldberg calls "racialized discourse." What is important in Gilroy's and Goldberg's respective understandings of "raciological rationality" and "racialized discourse" is that whiteness functions by abstracting nonwhite

flesh into its reality. This is the logic of mastery. By contrast, in Christ, YHWH as creator enters into a reality that "naturally" is not YHWH's own. In this respect, in Christ, YHWH takes the form of the servant.

38. I take the term "social imaginary" from Charles Taylor, *Modern Social Imaginaries* (Durham, N.C.: Duke University Press, 2004):

> By social imaginary, I mean something much broader and deeper than the intellectual schemes people may entertain when they think about social reality in a disengaged mode. I am thinking, rather, of the ways people imagine their social existence, how they fit together with others, how things go on between them and their fellows, the expectations that are normally met, and the deeper normative notions and images that underlie these expectations. (23)

39. Alys Eve Weinbaum, *Wayward Reproductions: Genealogies of Race and Nation in Transatlantic Modern Thought* (Durham, N.C.: Duke University Press, 2004).

40. My use of the phrase "body in pain" comes from Elaine Scarry, *The Body in Pain: The Making and Unmaking of the World* (New York: Oxford University Press, 1985). Lee, through her representation of her body in pain and agony, is attempting to "unmake the world." However, as I have said, this unmaking is theological in a way not taken up in Scarry's text. Lee's attempt to unmake the world by replotting the meaning of her body in pain, agony, and temptation is quite similar to Julian of Norwich's attempt to do the same: both replot the meaning of their bodies as bodies in pain and agony as articulations of Christ's body in pain and agony. Moreover, both understand the rearticulations of the meaning of their bodies as disclosing the Trinity or God's presence in our pain, or, more properly, God's taking up of our pain into the pain of his suffering love for the world. Norwich records this in her *Divine Showings*. For an important secondary account of what Norwich is doing, see Frederick Christian Bauerschmidt, *Julian of Norwich and the Mystical Body Politic of Christ* (Notre Dame: University of Notre Dame Press, 1999).

41. The phrase "without confusion" refers to the principal language of the Council of Chalcedon in which Christ was declared to be of a divine and a human nature, but that those natures did not meld into a third something, a *tertium quid*. Rather, they were in a relationship of the closest and deepest intimacy even as what was proper to the respective natures remained intact. They were related to each other "without confusion." The text that perhaps more than any other has determined our modern approach to Chalcedon is Adolph von Harnack's late-nineteenth-century text, *Lehrbuch der Dogmengeschichte/History of Dogma*. More recently, see Jaroslav Pelikan, *The Christian Tradition: A History of the Development of Doctrine*, vol. 1: *The Emergence of the Catholic Tradition (100–600)*, 5 vols. (Chicago: University of Chicago Press, 1971–); and Alloys Grillmeier, *Christ in Christian Tradition*, vol. 1: *From the Apostolic Age to Chalcedon (451)*, trans. John Bowden, 2nd rev. ed. (Atlanta: John Knox, 1975).

42. My use of the language of "form" has been influenced by the work of theologian Hans Urs von Balthasar (*Seeing the Form*, vol. 1 of *The Glory of the Lord: A Theological Aesthetics* [San Francisco: Ignatius Press, 1983]).

43. An aspect of the theology of Pierre Bérulle (1575–1629), a theologian of the French Oratory, captures in a powerful way precisely what I am claiming that Lee's

autobiographical discourse of Christian spirituality does. In "On the Perpetuity of the Mysteries of Jesus Christ," Bérulle argues that there are things both past and present or perpetual in the mystery of the incarnation. Indeed, there are things "over as regards their execution, but present as regards their power." In this sense, for Bérulle, the incarnation is not merely a past happening. In his technical sense of the term, it is a "state" (*état*). Indeed, as he says in his "Discourse on the State and Grandeurs of Jesus," "Jesus is a world, a splendid world"—his flesh is an inhabitable social terrain, a vast intellectual, geopolitical, and spatiotemporal field, we might say—"according to authentic theology, and this is true for many more reasons than philosophy ever knew when referring to the human person as a world in miniature." William M. Thompson, ed., *Bérulle and the French School: Selected Writings* (Mahwah, N.J.: Paulist, 1989), 112. In the social field and state (*état*) or way of being that is the Jewish man Jesus of Nazareth, Christ's humanity, indeed, his existence, is perpetual, articulating itself in the existences of those drawn into his state or way of being in the world. Thompson captures this aspect of Bérulle's thought wonderfully:

> If you will, there is a power of deification perpetually at work in the events of the incarnation. In this sense, the "states" of Jesus are archetypes of "states" in the Christian: "For the incarnation of the Word is the basis and foundation . . . of the deification of all the states and mysteries sharing in the life and earthly voyage of the Son of God upon earth . . . . Jesus . . . wishes that we have a unique share in these various states, according to the diversity of his will for us and our piety toward him" [quotation from *Oeuvres de piété* 17, col. 940]. (Quoted in introduction to Thompson, *Bérulle and the French School*, 37)

A "state" in the Bérullian sense, then, refers to the permanent conditions and aspects of the life and mysteries of Jesus, whose actual historical actions were transitory but whose inner dispositions or existential orientation as they append to and can never be decoupled from those historical actions are permanent and, as such, can be adored and entered into. Inasmuch, then, as the states of Christ are the basis of communion, it is intelligible why Bérulle says that "Jesus is a world" or, as I would like to say, that he is a biosocial field and an intellectual terrain. It is in just this Bérullian sense of "state," I contend, that Lee understands her own existence as carrying Christological weight. Her existence is an articulation of the existence of Jesus of Nazareth. Her body articulates his (and his hers: this is the basis of the former) because her dispositions or existential orientation is tied to Christ's human actions, albeit under the conditions or historical moment of New World black existence, the moment in which whiteness is the pseudotheological problem out of which Lee's own existence as a woman raced as black is filled with toil and despair.

What I am suggesting here, because of the language of being united through "existential orientation," is not to be confused with the critique leveled against Cone's theology in chapter 4 of this book. The big difference, I suggest, between the reading I am advancing here of Lee (drawing on Pierre Bérulle) and Cone's taking up of the Heideggerian-Tillichian approach to the "existentialle" is that Lee's and Bérulle's approach to these matters lodges the existential inseparably in the historical and therefore in the particularity of Christ's flesh. Thus, the existential for them points to

how Christ's historical particularly is the basis of freedom as communion. Moreover, for Lee (and again for Bérulle) all of this is but an extension of the distinct way of being of the Triune God of Israel. I say "Triune God of Israel" when neither of them employed this terminology because both do understand that it is only by means of the concrete body, flesh, and history of Jesus that the "state" of the Triune God is made available to us. Thus, the state of the Trinity is mediated to us in the state or world of Jesus. And insofar as the state or world of Jesus is not severable from the state or world of Israel in relationship to YHWH the God of Israel, it can be said that Jesus mediates the state of YHWH as Triune God of Israel to us.

44. This translation, with some modifications, is from James H. Charlesworth, ed., *The Odes of Solomon* (Oxford: Oxford University Press, 1973). For critical commentary on the *Odes*, see James H. Charlesworth, *Critical Reflections on the Odes of Solomon* (Sheffield: Sheffield Academic Press, 1998).

45. David Anderson, ed., *Basil: On the Holy Spirit* (Crestwood, N.Y.: St. Vladimir's Seminary Press, 1980), 100–101; translation modified.

46. Quoted in Edouard des Places, ed., *Diadoque de Photicé: Oeuvres Spirituelles* (Paris: Editions du Cerf, 1955), 175; translation mine from the Greek.

47. World as "stage" and the peoples of the world as "actors" in a drama oriented toward and moving in Jesus Christ raises the question of Christology to a pitch that is not explicitly considered in this volume, though the prelude, interlude, and postlude can be taken together as a propaedeutic to a Christology that considers such questions. For now, it can only be said that the world as stage is not an empty space, nor are the persons and peoples of the world merely actors wearing dramatic masks, nor is it to be understood that freedom is squelched in all of this. Rather, following Hans Urs von Balthasar:

> The world is the stage which has been set up for the encounter of the whole God with the whole man—"stage" not as an empty space, but as the sphere of collaboration of the two-sided form which unites in the encounter.... The Christological form as such is, absolutely, the form of the encounter between God and man. This encounter bears the form of the Incarnation, already in the Old Testament and still in the Resurrection. For this reason...this encounter also has the form of a totally human encounter with the God who has become man." (Hans Urs von Balthasar, *The Glory of the Lord: A Theological Aesthetics*, 7 vols. [San Francisco: Ignatius, 1982–1989], 1:303–4)

48. On homo sacer, see Giorgio Agamben, *Homo Sacer: Sovereign Power and Bare Life*, trans. Daniel Heller-Roazen (Stanford: Stanford University Press, 1995).

49. I develop the Christian theological point of the need to receive the Jewish Savior at the site of despised dark flesh and thereby enter into the body politic of his wounded, nontriumphalist flesh in J. Kameron Carter, "Race and Experience of Death: Theologically Dislocating and Relocating American Evangelicalism," in *Cambridge Companion to Evangelical Theology*, Timothy Larsen and Daniel Treier, eds. (New York: Cambridge University Press, 2007), 177–198.

50. Gregory of Nyssa, GNO II.70.13–24, NPNF 2nd series V.158B.

POSTLUDE

1. It is precisely this point—that is, what is so obviously theological about how many Afro-Christians engaged their early-nineteenth-century and later moments—that goes unaddressed in much of the literature on the various aspects of the lives of people of African descent. Eddie S. Glaude Jr. comes close to remedying this—but only close. Eddie S. Glaude Jr., *Exodus! Religion, Race, and Nation in Early Nineteenth-Century Black America* (Chicago: University of Chicago Press, 2000). The problem with his analysis is that it reduces nineteenth-century Afro-Christian existence to a Deweyan pragmatic calculus. Take his engagement with David Walker's *Appeal to the Coloured Citizens of the World* (1830), a text central to the "Exodus History" around which the first part of *Exodus* is organized. On Glaude's reading, Walker's *Appeal* is indicative of an incipient "pragmatic historicism." Such a historicism aimed to re-narrate the historical existence of people of African descent on the basis of what Glaude calls "critical intelligence: an intelligence that was the sum of impulses, habits, emotions, and discoveries that indicated what was desirable and undesirable in future possibilities and that worked ingeniously on behalf of an imagined good for people of African descent" (35). Glaude does not address the explicitly theological discourse that foregrounds Walker's jeremiad and that gives voice to his arguments. Walker frames his *Appeal* in this way: "These positions I shall endeavor, by the help of the Lord, in the course of this *Appeal*, to the satisfaction of the most incredulous mind—and may God Almighty who is the Father of our Lord Jesus Christ, open your hearts to understand and believe the truth." Peter P. Hinks, ed., *David Walker's Appeal: To the Coloured Citizens of the World* (University Park: Penn State University Press, 2000), 3–4.

Or take Henry Highland Garnet, a figure central to the "Exodus Politics" around which the second part of *Exodus* revolves. Garnet's willingness to "force the End" or to engage in violent resistance in the face of racial terror, on Glaude's reading, "was based on a pragmatic view of race shaped by an ironic view of moral reform that took seriously the cycle of existential pain and unrest that penetrated deeply the lives of African Americans, slave or free" (146). In the end, Garnet's Christianity gets interpreted in instrumentalist terms, as a pragmatic response to the existential trauma of racial existence in America. It is this existential trauma of an endless cycle of pain and unrest, death and rebirths, in slavery that makes sense of Garnet's Christianity. The problem is not that Glaude does not acknowledge that Garnet drew on his Christianity to negotiate the trauma. After all, he rightly acknowledges that "Garnet's [1843] address is best understood in Christian terms, not as an example of African religious sentiments put to political use. His appeal to Christian piety and devotion...grounded his call to slave insurrection" (156). Rather, the problem is that, for Glaude, Garnet's use of Christianity is pragmatic, utilitarian, and instrumentalist and thus intelligible in terms beyond those Garnet himself employs, which are theological. Thus, Garnet, Glaude tells us, rejects the Exodus story because as a story it could not be drawn on to violently force the End. This rejection is not a theological rejection but is based in pragmatism.

What this misses, however, is that, rather than rejecting the Exodus story, Garnet is interpreting it Christologically and thus in his own way embracing it. In

other words, he lodges Exodus in the death of Christ. This is important because it can now be seen that Garnet, as I said in regard to Jarena Lee in chapter 8, is showing how Christ's existential condition, caught at the crossroads of life and death, articulates the existential condition of those raced as black in modernity at the same time that it is the calculus of the Old Testament story of the Exodus. Or as Maximus the Confessor might say, the *logos* of those raced as black in modernity is lodged within and indeed articulates the existential, material, and bodily conditions of Christ, the eternal *Logos*, in such a way as to free every *logoi* of all existing things in their existential, material, and bodily conditions from tyranny. Christ the Logos secures this freedom because he has already forced the End, thus making any subsequent enforcements of the End, on this side of the Eschaton, possible. Christ is the Exodus and so to embrace him is to enter into the End he has forced, the eschatological End. Maximus develops this vision of Christ with profound rigor in *Ambiguum 7*, a translation of which can be found in *CMJC*. Thus, Garnet's call to enforce the End is a supremely theological—indeed, a radically Christological—moment. It is a moment that seeks not to move beyond the Exodus (or Israel) but to enter into its existential depth, a depth which Christ articulates and that articulates the existential condition of those raced black in modernity.

2. Frantz Fanon, *The Wretched of the Earth* (New York: Grove, 2004; original, 1963) and W. E. B. Du Bois, *The Souls of Black Folk* (New York: Penguin, 1989; original, 1903). Du Bois declares in the opening lines of chapter 1 of his book, "Between me and the other world there is ever an unasked question:... How does it feel to be a problem?" (3)

3. Walter Brueggemann, *Genesis: A Bible Commentary for Teaching and Preaching* (Atlanta: John Knox, 1982), 100.

4. The theoretical literature on colonialism, which in part is the subject matter of the field of postcolonial studies, is now vast. And hence, my few references to it throughout this book, and in this postlude, do not begin to capture its complexity. Given the emphasis of this book, it was necessary to bring it up even if only to skirt its edges. For more on the problematic of colonialism and postcolonial theoretical responses to it, see Edward W. Said, *Orientalism* (New York: Vintage, 1978); Homi K. Bhabha, *The Location of Culture* (New York: Routledge, 1994); Patrick Williams and Laura Chrisman, eds., *Colonial Discourse and Post-Colonial Theory: A Reader* (New York: Columbia University Press, 1994); Leela Gandhi, *Postcolonial Theory: A Critical Introduction* (New York: Columbia University Press, 1998); and Gayatri Chakravorty Spivak, *A Critique of Postcolonial Reason: Toward a History of the Vanishing Present* (Cambridge, Mass.: Harvard University Press, 1999).

5. See particularly chapter 1 ("The Americas, Christian Expansion, and Racism") of Walter Mignolo, *The Idea of Latin America* (Malden, Mass.: Blackwell, 2005).

6. I borrow this phrase from Paul Gilroy, *Against Race: Imagining Political Culture beyond the Color Line* (Cambridge, Mass.: Belknap, 2000). Maximus offers a vision of intellectual production that is also "against race" but is against it without recourse, as is Gilroy, to a Kantian-inspired vision of the cosmopolitan. I show in chapter 2 of this book why cosmpolitanism does not escape the problem of race but culminates it. For another turn toward the cosmopolitan, see Anthony Appiah, *Cosmopolitanism: Ethics in a World of Strangers* (New York: Norton, 2006).

7. Maximus addresses these divisions in *Amb.* 41 (*PG* 91.1305C–1308C; *LMC* 157–58).

8. Blowers's and Wilken's introduction to *CMJC*, 43. A succinct entry point into Maximus view of the passions (i.e., desire, pleasure, fear, grief, and the like) is in *Ad Thal.* 1, in which he considers their origins. The passions (*ta pathê*), he says, "were not originally created together with human nature.... But following what the eminent Gregory of Nyssa taught, I say that on account of humanity's fall from perfection, the passions were introduced and attached themselves to the more irrational part of human nature" (*CCSG* 7.47; *CMJC*, 97). To grasp what is at stake in this, one must add to this statement the claims of *Ad Thal.* 21 in which Maximus distinguishes between humankind's "natural passibility" (*phusin pathous; CCSG* 7.129; *CMJC*, 111) or its capacity by means of its natural volition to move toward its final end in God, and what might be called its fallen passiblity and what Maximus himself calls the "corruption of unnatural passions" (*phthoran tôn para phusin pathôn; CCSG* 7.127–28; *CMJC*, 110).

In the latter fallen state, humankind's will functions deliberatively. That is, it no longer functions in a natural movement toward the final end of the Good that is God. Instead, volition functions in a vacillating, deliberative manner. It wavers between taking God as its final good and therefore receiving all things as a revelation of God or receiving things as ends *for me* and thus as having their end in the created order as such. In the latter perspective, things do not bear God. They become objects for possession, objects whose meaning inhere, to revert to a Kantian language, in the apperceiving subject. This, Maximus declares, is the "fantasy" or fiction that "natural passion" engages in when not guided by God as its good end.

We are now can return to the claims of *Ad Thal.* 1. What is "not originally created together with human nature" is the "corruption of unnatural passions." What was originally created with human nature was natural passibility or the potential of the will to move toward its final end in God. It is precisely humankind's natural passiblity, operative now under the constraints of the liability to passions, that Christ assumes, reorients, and thus heals. Moreover, according to Maximus, this reorientation or healing takes place precisely through his entry into the covenantal story of Israel through his Marian conception and birth, thus inaugurating a new birth narrative, a new story of origins, a liberating account of (re)production. It is just this theological insight that I have claimed to be at work particularly in Hammon's and Lee's liter-ary efforts within the horizon of Christian identity to theologically move beyond a tyrannizing narrative of the coming to be or the birthing of nonwhite in relationship to white flesh in modernity. It is worth bearing this brief account of the passions in mind when below I explicate Maximus's vision of the restoration of the one-many structure of creation, for the restoration of the passions as ordered to God.

9. For an expansive consideration of Maximus's theological anthropology, see Lars Thunberg, *Microcosm and Mediator: The Theological Anthropology of Maximus the Confessor* (Chicago: Open Court, 1995).

10. Quoted in Hans Urs von Balthasar, *Cosmic Liturgy: The Universe According to Maximus the Confessor*, trans. Brian E. Daley (San Francisco: Ignatius, 2003), 257; translation slightly modified.

11. Ibid., 257–58.

12. "Ecstasy" appears here in quotation marks to indicate that the ecstasy proper to the human person in their union with God is not the same in the divine life. The Triune God need not "exit" himself in order to be genuinely ecstatic to himself. To fully explicate Maximus on this point would require a full inquiry into his Trinitarian theology, which is beyond my immediate purposes here.

What is immediately relevant about his Trinitarianism to this study and thus is worth mentioning here is Maximus's belief that the Triune God is the movement of perfection. Indeed, the perfection of God's nature as God is expressed in God's movement toward multiplicity in the mode of his existence. To say that God is movement presupposes that there is something like distance and even distinction and otherness in God. There are several places where he develops this. The three that come to mind are *Amb.* 10, *Amb.* 1, and the *Commentary on the Our Father*. From *Amb.* 10 we learn that the notions of monad, dyad, and triad as they relate to God must not be thought of in terms of matter, for here "each dyad is established by number and so is each monad, as a part completing it, so that together the monads take away uncircumscribability" (*LMC*, 142). The monad and dyad would simply be a group of monads, two "separate but equal" points between oscillating extremes in which the movement from one point in the dyad to the other entails loss. Such an understanding of the monad and the dyad is inadequate to contemplating the Triune God, for the infinite God's movement is one in which God need not lose himself in order to find himself. The otherness or dyadic distinction constitutive of the difference between Father and Son is not one in which a gulf separates them. The so-called gulf is always already traversed or moved beyond in the triad of the Holy Spirit. God is "Pentecostal."

But there are two important payoffs to Maximus's seemingly arcane reflection. With such an understanding of God as monad-triad in place, he can claim that this infinite movement by which God is understood as Trinity entails within it both the possibility of material reality should God choose to create it and God's interactions with this reality in salvation history. But also, this understanding of God as simultaneously monad in essence and triad in mode of existence means that each of the persons of the triad bears within themselves the other persons. They exist in each other. That is, there is a communication of idioms at the level of the *hypostases* or the distinct persons themselves. In other words, the persons of the triad only display themselves by disclosing another. They bear each other within themselves and thus are incommunicable without each other. Indeed, what, or rather who, they communicate is each other precisely in communicating themselves. The triune identity is therefore ecstatic. But Maximus goes further. By inserting the incarnation into this, he draws creation generally and the human being in particular into the ecstasy of the triune identity, conceiving of the human being, through the incarnation, as an image of the ecstatic, Triune God. Here is the passage in the *Commentary on the Our Father* that captures this:

> In becoming incarnate, the Word of God teaches us the mystery of knowledge of God because he shows us in himself the Father and the Holy Spirit. For the full Father and the full Holy Spirit are essentially and completely in the full Son, even the incarnate Son, without being themselves incarnate. Rather, the Father gives approval and the Spirit cooperates in the incarnation with the Son who effected it,

since the Word remained in possession of his own mind and life, contained in essence by no other than the Father and the Spirit, whole hy-
postatically realizing out of love for man the union with the flesh.
(*MCSW,* 103)

Maximus goes on from this quotation to argue for how this act of divine philanthropy sutures the division in creation by which created nature has become fragmented
with each part tyrannically sealed off from the other parts in possessive self-love.

13. See the analysis of multiple senses of ecstasy in Maximus's thought in
Thunberg, *Microcosm and Mediator,* 422–25.

14. Alloys Grillmeier, *Christ in Christian Tradition,* vol. 1: *From the Apostolic Age to
Chalcedon (451),* trans. John Bowden, 2nd rev. ed. (Atlanta: John Knox, 1975), 480–83.
John McGuckin captures beautifully what was at issue in the ancient debates, most
prominently carried out between Cyril of Alexandria and Nestorius, surrounding the
communicatio idiomatum, which the Council of Chalcedon in 451 upheld:

The exchange of properties meant linguistically associating both sets of
attributes (e.g., divine attributes such as raising the dead and human
attributes such as being weary, or weeping) indiscriminately as a result
of the incarnation whereby they were concretely associated in the life of
Christ. For Cyril, and for later theology after Chalcedon, this was per-
missible on the basis that both sets of differing characteristics could be
radically associated on the basis of the single personality who stood as the
active subject of them both. The viability of the entire method, however,
stood or fell on this matter of single subjectivity. At the time of the present
controversy that was the very issue that was being fought over. Cyril
propounds the method of the single subject, but as far as Nestorius was
concerned the linguistic method only served to confuse the issue of the
distinctness of the different natures (physeis) visible in the incarnation.
(John McGuckin, ed., *St. Cyril of Alexandria: The Christological Controversy—Its History, Theology, and Texts* (Leiden: Brill, 1994), 153 n.45)

15. What I am raising here is a larger dogmatic, theological matter that would
require a fuller account of the difference between the exchange of idioms between the
divinity and humanity that is "internal" (for lack of a better word) to Christ on the one
hand and the "exchange" that takes place among the many that fill out the unified
human nature on the other, which the Son of God takes up as the modality of his
human existence as Jesus of Nazareth. I am pointing to the link between Christology
on the one hand and a theological anthropology informed by Christology and Trinitarianism, on the other. One way to fill it out might be in terms of Hans Urs von
Balthasar's notion of the Trinitarian inversion for understanding the Christology.
Hans Urs von Balthasar, *Theo-Drama: Theological Dramatic Theory,* 5 vols. (San Francisco: Ignatius, 1988–1998), 3:183–91.

My point is not to invert the priority of the divine in relationship to Christ's human
nature as Christological dogma calls for. Indeed, here is precisely where the language of
inversion becomes inadequate on the plane of Christology. Rather than call it Christological inversion, I prefer calling what I want to do a Christological extension or embrace;
what happens in Jesus' humanity is extended to embrace the history of creation, in-

cluding humanity, across time and space. Thus, creation and humanity are recapitulated into the positivity of covenantal communion by being situated in Christ's Jewish humanity. Creation and humanity are thereby rearticulated beyond every violent division. A version of this was presented in the prelude's account of Irenaeus, who conceived of Christ as recapitulating the nations and even the narrative of what it means to be a nation or a people in himself. It stood as the basis of Gregory of Nyssa's Christologically grounded abolitionist theology of Easter. Maximus theorized the Christological framework with the resources of Chalcedon in such a way that the Irenaean and Gregorian theological claims are rendered even more intelligible. The theological warrant for their theological ethics becomes crystalline.

16. For more on the formula of Chalcedon, see Grillmeier, *Apostolic Age to Chalcedon*, 551–54.

17. The language of "peaceful difference" risks sounding a lot like John Milbank's "ontology of peace." John Milbank, *Theology and Social Theory: Beyond Secular Reason* (Oxford: Blackwell, 1992), 380–434. While there may be some affinities between our languages, it would be a mistake to interpret my proposal in strictly Milbankian terms, for, in fact, the theological program I am initiating here calls Milbank's program into question precisely to the extent that it still, in my view, intellectually enacts a strong, colonialist Christianity. In contrast to what I propose here, Milbankian "radical orthodoxy," like aspects of Yale school narrative theology and aspects of "ressourcement" theology among Roman Catholics, has yet to reckon with the ways they perform theology in continuity with Catholic and Protestant theology's racial-colonialist past. That past articulated itself in terms of theological orthodoxy and presented itself in terms of a sacramental and liturgical imagination.

But let me quickly add that one would be equally mistaken to reduce the program of intellectual reflection being initiated here to a species of theological liberalism, particularly as it came into its own in nineteenth-century theology and matured from the twentieth century forward. The history of such theological liberalism, in the American context at least, is being brilliantly written at present by Gary Dorrien in his multivolume *The Making of American Liberal Theology*. What must be grasped is the racial-colonial theological continuity between modern orthodoxy beginning in the fifteenth century (this is when Europe began its campaign of global conquest) and theological liberalism from the nineteenth century to the present. Stated differently, what must be grasped is how theological liberalism is not an aberrancy but, rather, the culmination of modern theological orthodoxy as the discursive space within which the modern world as we have come to know it was forged. Thus, what I am trying to develop here proceeds from the supposition that the pole of theological orthodoxy in its modernist inflection and that of theological liberalism, in fact, form a single reality that must be thought beyond. They are the poles between which whiteness as a theological problem oscillates and within which Christian identity remains tyrannically and grotesquely distorted.

18. I have taken this phrase from Hans Urs von Balthasar, who employs it in his groundbreaking monograph, *Cosmic Liturgy*, on the Confessor. My use of the phrase goes beyond Balthasar's, however; he employs it only in relationship to the divine and human natures in Christ as being fitted to one another, and I am seizing on the Confessor's claim that the fit between divinity and humanity in Christ, in fact, refits

in his flesh the many of creation toward one another. It is through this secondary refitting within the orders of creaturely existence, beginning with the order of human existence, that the *Logos*, Maximus says, becomes "becomes thick" or undergoes a kind of continued moral incarnation in the manners (*tropos*) or "practice[s] of the virtues" (*vita practica*). In this way, the Word never ceases to "become flesh" (*MCSW*, 156; *PG* 90.1141C). In other words, as human existence becomes open to itself, the Word is revealed.

This insight is crucially important, given the racial-colonial constitution of modernity, in which through analytics of race the non-European world was conceived or invented as "nonwhite" and non-Christian and thus subject to the "violent evangelism" of colonialism. It was this theologically sanctioned colonialism that brought people of African descent forcibly into the New World of Europe and especially the Americas. It was also this theologically sanctioned colonialism that made the humanity of Amerindians a point of vigorous debate with Bartolomé de Las Casas on one side and the entire theological guild of his day against him on the other. Luis N. Rivera, *A Violent Evangelism: The Political and Religious Conquest of the Americas* (Louisville, Ky.: Westminster/John Knox, 1992). The theology of the conquerors, who were all "orthodox" theological thinkers mostly in the tradition of Thomas Aquinas, was one that maintained the vertical dimension of the exchange of properties of which Maximus spoke, for this had established itself as a staple of Christian tradition. What went unheeded was Maximus's Christological insight into the horizon dimension of "being-in-another." They refused that aspect of orthodoxy that called on humans to receive themselves from other humans precisely in receiving themselves from God. It is the seriousness with which Maximus took these two dimensions of Chalcedonianism that makes him an anticolonialist intellectual.

19. Here would be the place again were there the space to engage the exceedingly technical post-Chalcedonian discussion regarding how the natures exist together in Christ. A host of neologisms were coined in an attempt to capture this dynamic, all centering on the notion of *hypostasis*. The term that that won pride of place as best articulating the way in which the natures come in the *hypostasis* of Christ is *en-hypostasis*. Eventually this term would become a way of affirming that natures subsist in a *hypostasis* and not without one and that therefore in Christ humanity is appropriated by and thus subsists in the Son of the Trinity. Maximus would become a central figure in clarifying this. On the history of the term's use leading up to Maximus, see Alloys Grillmeier, *Christ in Christian Tradition*, vol. 2: *From the Council of Chalcedon (451) to Gregory the Great (590–604)—(Part II) The Church of Constantinople in the Sixth Century*, trans. John Cawte and Pauline Allen (Atlanta: John Knox, 1995), 186–99 and 282–312. On Maximus's further development and clarification of the term, see Balthasar, *Cosmic Liturgy*, 222–33.

20. Christoph Schönborn, *God's Human Face: The Christ-Icon*, trans. Lothar Krauth (San Francisco: Ignatius, 1994).

21. Paul M. Blowers, "The World in the Mirror of Holy Scripture: Maximus the Confessor's Short Hermeneutical Treatise in *Ambiguum ad Joannem* 37," in *In Dominico Eloquio—in Lordly Eloquence: Essays on Patristic Exegesis in Honor of Robert Louis Wilken*, ed. Paul M. Blowers, Angela Russell Christman, David G. Hunter, and Robin Darling Young (Grand Rapids, Mich.: Eerdmans, 2002), 409.

22. This brief lexical analysis draws on the entries for *agô* and *anagô* in Henry George Liddell and Robert Scott, eds., *Greek-English Lexicon (with Revised Supplement)* (Oxford: Clarendon, 1996), 17–18, 102.

23. Adam G. Cooper, *The Body in St. Maximus the Confessor: Holy Flesh, Wholly Deified* (Oxford: Oxford University Press, 2005), 38–39.

24. Jean-Luc Marion, *The Crossing of the Visible*, trans. James K. A. Smith (Stanford: Stanford University Press, 2004). Chapters 3 and 4 of this text, "The Blind at Shiloh" and "The Prototype and the Image," respectively, are particularly important for my argument. Also important for my argument is Marie-José Mondzain, *Image, Icon, Economy: The Byzantine Origins of the Contemporary Imaginary*, trans. Rico Franses (Stanford: Stanford University Press, 2005). According to Mondzain, the icon is an economy all its own, an economy that redeems our sinful aesthetic economies of perception. Mondzain helpfully says:

> Consideration of the image is still a sacred cause today only because the fate of thought and liberty are at stake in it. The visible world, the one that is given to us to see: is it liberty or enslavement? In order to be able to envisage a world radically founded on visibility, and starting from the conviction that whatever constitutes its essence and meaning is itself invisible, it proved essential to establish a system of thought that set the visible and invisible in relation to each other. This relation was based on the distinction between image and icon. The image is invisible, the icon is visible. The economy was the concept of their *living* linkage. The image is a mystery. The icon is enigma. The economy was the concept of their *relation* and their *intimacy*. The image [i.e., Christ the Son of God] is eternal similitude, the icon [i.e., creation] is temporal resemblance. The economy was the theory of the *transfiguration of history*. (3)

I am using the phrase, "the crossing of the visible" (taken from Marion) within Mondzain's terms, for Mondzain rightly sees that the transfiguration is about the transfiguration of history itself, suturing the gap that has arisen because of the sinful Fall of humankind between the visible, material, and corporeal and the invisible, nonsensible (or what Maximus calls the intelligible), and incorporeal. With the Fall and the economy of the sin it inaugurates, what is meant to be an icon in relationship to the divine image becomes idol, a surface on which gazes can be frozen in plays of power. The divine economy of the transfiguration is meant to transfigure the economy of the Fall and thereby open up a new history. This new divine history or economy is not held hostage to history but, rather, is one that "exceeds all historical circumstances in order to reveal the meaning of history itself" (48).

25. Andrew Louth, ed., *Maximus the Confessor* (New York: Routledge, 1996), 70.

26. Ibid.

27. Brueggemann, *Genesis*, 100–101. Willie James Jennings alerted me to the importance of Brueggemann's commentary for the argument I am making in relationship to Maximus's thought.

28. Ibid., 100.

29. While I am in the main celebratory of the post-Auschwitz interest on the part of a number of Christian theologians and other religious scholars in having a non-

supersessionist understanding of Israel, I do nevertheless have grave concerns precisely with how Jewish flesh and identity are being conceived in this post-Auschwitz historical and theological moment. For many of these intellectuals, Jewish flesh still functions as racial flesh. Indeed, it functions in many of their outlooks like a species of whiteness, even if it is "off-white" in its whiteness. To the extent that this is the case, post-Auschwitz theologians and religious scholars still operate in an Auschwitz intellectual framework. For more on the whiteness in relationship to the forging of Jewish identities in modernity, see Eric L. Goldstein, *The Price of Whiteness: Jews, Race, and American Identity* (Princeton: Princeton University Press, 2006).

As an aside, it would also be interesting to interrogate the so-called New York intellectuals—people like Lionel Trilling, Sidney Hook, Eliot Cohen, Irving Howe, and Irving Kristol; and even some of their wide-ranging heirs in the nontheological world from Philip Roth to William Kristol, as well as those in the theological world—with these issues in mind. Is Jewish identity, in the end, a racial identity? In chapter 2 of this book, I argue that modernity conceived it as such. I am constructively arguing, however, for its theological reconception as covenantal, which is how early Afro-Christians engaged it in their attempts to perform Christian identity differently than their masters.

30. Karl Barth, *Protestant Theology in the Nineteenth Century: Its Background History* (Grand Rapids, Mich.: William B. Eerdmans Publishing Co., 2002).

31. Pierre Bourdieu, *Pascalian Meditations* (Stanford: Stanford University Press, 2000). 32. The phrase "weak thought" is a play on Gianni Vattimo's notion of "weak ontology." Gianni Vattimo, *The End of Modernity: Nihilism and Hermeneutics in Postmodern Culture*, trans. Jon R. Synder (Baltimore: Johns Hopkins University Press, 1988). Vattimo is building on Heidegger's thought in the collapse of Western metaphysics:

> The result of rethinking the meaning of Being is in fact, for Heidegger, the taking leave of metaphysical Being and its strong traits, on the basis of which the devaluation of the ornamental aspects of the work of art has always definitively been legitimated, even it through more extensive chains of mediating concepts. That which truly is . . . is not the centre which is opposed to the periphery, nor is it the essence which is opposed to appearance, nor is it what endures as opposed to the accidental and the mutable, nor is it the certainty of the *obiectum* given to the subject as opposed to the vagueness and imprecision of the horizon of the world. The occurrence of Being is rather, in Heideggerian weak ontology, an unnoticed and marginal background event. (85–86)

The problem, in my view, with Vattimo's attempt to appropriate Heidegger's weak ontology is this: there is nothing weak about it, for his ontology on the one hand exemplifies the scholastic disposition as strong thought and on the other is what allowed Heidegger with intellectual integrity to support Nazism. Pierre Bourdieu, *The Political Ontology of Martin Heidegger* (Oxford: Polity, 1991); Mark Lilla, *The Reckless Mind: Intellectuals in Politics* (New York: New York Review of Books, 2001); Richard Wolin, *The Politics of Being: The Political Thought of Martin Heidegger* (New York: Columbia University Press, 1990); and Richard Wolin, *Heidegger's Children: Hannah*

Arendt, Karl Löwith, Hans Jonas, and Herbert Marcuse (Princeton: Princeton University Press, 2001).

EPILOGUE

1. The theological *as* the political and the political *as* the theological and both in relationship to the forging of the modern world—this is subject of the recent study by Mark Lilla, *The Stillborn God: Religion, Politics, and the Modern West* (New York: Knopf, 2007).

2. Pierre Bourdieu, *Pascalian Meditations* (Stanford: Stanford University Press, 2000), 12–14.

3. Karl Barth, *Protestant Theology in the Nineteenth Century: Its Background and History* (Grand Rapids, Mich.: William B. Eerdmans Publishing Co., 2001), 2–3.

4. Michael Eric Dyson, *Between God and Gangsta Rap: Bearing Witness to Black Culture* (New York: Oxford University Press, 1996). I was reminded of this story, which I first encountered some years ago, in reading Karla K. C. Holloway's provocative and recent engagement with it from her perspective as a literary theorist. Karla F. C. Holloway, *Bookmarks: Reading in Black and White* (New Brunswick, N.J.: Rutgers University Press, 2006), 155–63. This reading of Dyson builds on her analysis.

5. Dyson, *Between God and Gangsta Rap*, 126.

6. Ibid., 127–28.

7. Ibid., 126–28.

8. Orlando Patterson, *Slavery and Social Death: A Comparative Study* (Cambridge, Mass.: Harvard University Press, 1982).

9. Dyson, *Between God and Gangsta Rap*, 130–31.

10. An example among black intellectuals in which black religion represents so many "g-d narratives" that signify out of the opaque inexhaustibility of the religious can be found in Victor Anderson, " 'We See through a Glass Darkly': Black Narrative Theology and the Opacity of African American Religious Thought," in *The Ties That Bind: African American and Hispanic American/Latino/a Theology in Dialogue*, ed. Anthony B. Pinn and Benjamin Valentin (New York: Continuum, 2001). More recently, one finds this kind of intellectual vision at work in James Lorand Matory, *Black Atlantic Religion: Tradition, Transnationalism, and Matriarchy in the Afro-Brazilian Candomblé* (Princeton: Princeton University Press, 2005). The problem of Matory's vision is not with a claim that "survivals" in African "religion" or that religion be understood as an inert residue of a pristine and hermetically sealed past. This old-style understand of African survivals is overcome in Matory's discourse. Matory does, however, keep the deeper moment within which the old-survivalist vision of religion functioned: namely, that religion is a manipulable and constitutive feature of identity. The difference is that in his vision we manipulate it rather than be manipulated by it. That is, dark people are active agents (for their own purposes) in the manipulation process. At root through this basic outlook on religion as manipulable and a constitutive feature of identity is the inheritance of how whiteness in its fifteenth-century genesis and sixteenth-century intellectual consolidation came to theologically constitute itself in bringing about the modern world that we now know and inhabit. While I cannot fully defend this claim here, I will only point to the oeuvre of Christopher Columbus to make my point,

especially his 15 February and 4 March 1493 letters to Isabella of Castille and Ferdinand of Aragon, the monarchs of Spain. These documents, which summarized Columbus's first voyage, are early witnesses to this peculiar use of "religion," which is part and parcel of the enactment of a racial-aesthetic imagination that set out to justify the conquest of the Americas through an emerging vision of whiteness. These documents are found, respectively, in J. M. Cohen, ed., *The Four Voyages of Christopher Columbus: Being His Own Log-Book, Letters and Dispatches with Connecting Narrative Drawn from the Life of the Admiral by His Son Hernando Colon and Other Contemporary Historians* (London: Penguin, 1988), 115–23, and Margarita Zamora, *Reading Columbus* (Berkeley: University of California Press, 1993), 190–97.

What Matory and other contemporary intellectuals have done is make a virtue of the category of religion without an adequate understanding of its vice. Its vice is that this category is tied to the theological operations of whiteness in modernity. That is, "religion" as an anthropological category of modernity was born of theology and the new way it came to function in giving birth to and then sustaining the modern world. The result of not reckoning with this problem is that such discourses on religion as one finds in Matory, discourses that take up this category for its potential to make sense of how lived religions function on the ground for those on the underside of modernity, unwittingly replicate the intellectual structures of whiteness at the very site of "black religion." Moreover, unwittingly such "new" deployments of religion prove not to escape theology and the problems it has historically unleashed. Rather, they prove to be bad theology—theology yet suffused with the pseudotheological, which is to say, the racial vision of modernity. Hence paradoxically, religion so deployed continues to sustain the discursive phenomenon of whiteness and the world it has created for itself.

Index

Printed in the USA/Agawam, MA
March 18, 2024

Race